THE STERN STEWART ROUNDTABLES

DISCUSSING

THE

REVOLUTION

IN

CORPORATE

FINANCE

Edited by Donald H. Chew, Jr.

BLACKWELL
Business

DISCUSSING THE REVOLUTION IN CORPORATE FINANCE

© Blackwell Publishers, 1998 for this collection.
© Stern Stewart Management Services for all individual
articles.

Blackwell Publishers Inc.
350 Main Street
Malden, MA 02148

Blackwell Publishers Ltd.
108 Cowley Road
Oxford OX4 IJF, UK

British Library Cataloguing in Publication Data

A CIP catalogue record for this book is available from the
British Library

HBISBN   0-6312-0990-5
PBISBN   0-6312-0822-4

Printed in the USA

Table of Contents

Introduction

Since its founding in 1982, Stern Stewart & Co., the New York corporate finance advisory firm, has done much to "translate" the modern theory of corporate finance into a set of prescriptions that practicing executives can use to increase the value of their companies. Stern Stewart is best known as the formulator and popularizer of Economic Value Added, or "EVA," a measure of periodic corporate performance based on economists' concept of residual income. Described by *Fortune* magazine as "today's hottest financial idea," EVA has supplanted earnings per share as the primary internal performance measure (and basis for incentive compensation) at a large and growing number of U.S. corporations. Notable among such companies are Coca-Cola, Monsanto, Eli Lilly, and Briggs & Stratton. Moreover, the movement has also begun to spread to non-profits and overseas companies. The U.S. Postal Service is a client of several years' standing, and the German giant Siemens was featured in a recent issue of the *Economist* as a new adopter of the EVA financial management system.

But EVA is not all that Stern Stewart is known for. Given its aim of providing advice to corporations grounded in the most current academic thinking in corporate finance, it was natural that Stern Stewart should start its own finance publication. In the fall of 1981, while working at the Chase Manhattan Bank, Joel Stern and I (with the help of Joseph Willett, now Chief Financial Officer of Merrill Lynch) founded a publication called the *Chase Financial Quarterly* to complement our corporate finance advisory work for the bank. Its purpose, more broadly, was to help bridge what we saw as a "gulf" between modern finance theory and much corporate practice by translating current research into practical recommendations for corporate policy. Four issues later, in November 1982, we and other members of Chase Financial Policy left the bank to form Stern Stewart & Co. We also renewed our publishing efforts by starting the *Midland*

Corporate Finance Journal. The purpose of the *MCFJ*, like that of its predecessor, was to bring to the attention of senior management the practical import of theoretical developments in finance for a wide range of corporate decisions: capital budgeting, dividend policy, capital structure, risk management, international financial management, and performance measurement and incentive compensation.

Then, in 1988, with the sponsorship of the Continental Bank, Stern Stewart launched a new publication called the *Journal of Applied Corporate Finance.* Although sponsorship has since passed from Continental to Bank of America (as a consequence of their merger in 1994), the journal is about to complete its tenth year of publication.

One of the most popular features of the *JACF* has been the series of roundtable discussions that have appeared over the years. Unlike the articles, which are written mainly by academics, the roundtables are an attempt to create a dialogue between theorist and practitioner by representing the views of senior executives and investment bankers alongside those of prominent academics. Besides editing all these roundtables (and arranging many of them), Stern Stewart's other main role in these discussions has been to furnish the moderator. In 10 of the 17 roundtables collected in this volume, either Joel Stern or Bennett Stewart (and, in several cases, both) serve as the discussion leaders and agents provocateur.

The roundtables are organized into six categories. Like *The Revolution in Corporate Finance*—for which this book is intended as a companion volume—this book begins by focusing on the subjects of stock market valuation and efficiency. Next are two widely ranging discussions of "Corporate Strategy," one featuring well-known strategy consultant C.K. Prahalad and the other prominent business historian Alfred Chandler. From valuation and strategy, the book moves to the corporate financing decision and leveraged restructuring.

In this third set of discussions, the dominant figure is Harvard Business School's Michael Jensen, whose "free cash flow" theory of takeovers and LBOs becomes the central hypothesis for exploration. Take the Bank of America Roundtable on "The Link Between Capital Structure and Shareholder Value" with which that section begins. In response to Jensen's initial exposition of his argument, top financial executives from an oil company, a printing company, and a commercial bank furnish suggestive evidence that "the agency costs of free cash flow are alive and well" in corporate America today. For public companies in mature industries with significant overcapacity, Jensen argues that an LBO-like structure combining high leverage with concentrated equity ownership can add value by encouraging the payout of excess capital and reduction of capacity.

But this solution begs the question: What about companies with significant growth opportunities and limited debt capacity? In the same Bank of America roundtable, Jensen holds out another solution: an "EVA-based" internal performance measurement and incentive compensation system. This EVA financial management system is the subject of the fourth, and longest, section in this book. What does EVA have in common with an LBO? Where LBOs make the cost of capital "both explicit and contractually binding" by converting most of the old equity into debt, an EVA financial management system simulates the conditions of an LBO by charging operating managers for their use of all investor capital, equity as well as debt. And, although such simulated incentives may be less powerful than the real ones, EVA has one advantage over the LBO that will often prove decisive: it provides the "feel" of ownership without imposing the costs of high leverage.

The fifth and final section contains three discussions concerning two topics of increasing interest to corporate treasurers: derivatives and risk management, and capital budgeting for direct foreign investment in emerging markets. In these discussions, as throughout the book, the practitioners' views can differ sharply from academic theory. But, in spite of such differences, there is often an interesting cross-fertilization between theory and practice that makes the exchange both entertaining and instructive.

Donald H. Chew
New York City
September 29, 1997

HOW THE STOCK MARKET VALUES COMPANIES

RELATIONSHIP INVESTING
AND
SHAREHOLDER COMMUNICATION

JOEL STERN: Good morning, and welcome to this discussion of relationship investing and shareholder communication. The general purpose of the Roundtable will be to consider the recent rise of institutional investor activism and the opportunities it holds for corporate management to increase their share values by cultivating relationships with "longer-term" investors.

Some finance and legal scholars have proposed that companies give institutional investors greater voice in corporate strategic decisions, perhaps by inviting them into the boardroom. But another possibility—probably somewhat less troubling to management—is to improve the quality of their communication to investors by providing information that goes beyond what is provided by conventional accounting statements. Thus, one of the major themes in the discussion will be the limitations of current financial reporting. We would like to consider ways to improve the quality of corporate shareholder communications by devising new financial measures, or perhaps non-financial measures, that would give a more realistic picture of long-run corporate profitability.

■ In fact, there are no fewer than five major issues that we would like to address this morning. **First** is the longstanding controversy about the relationship between market efficiency and accounting disclosures. As most of you are aware, Chicago-school financial economists tend to think that by the time the information is released by the auditors, investors have already found alternative sources for that information. According to this view, most accounting information is already reflected in stock prices when disclosed, and thus there's not much point in improving accounting if nobody pays much attention to it. So we want to start by exploring what role, if any, more realistic accounting could play in improving the efficiency of capital markets.

■ The **second** major subject is a very intriguing one called "relationship investing." Stated in brief, the underlying proposition is that publicly traded companies can increase their share values by targeting a particular group of "patient" (or, as I prefer to call them, "value-based") investors. We at Stern Stewart have long argued that there are "lead steers" who effectively dominate the pricing process on Wall Street. Some obvious names that come to mind are Warren Buffett and Peter Lynch, but there are many others. And it may well be worth a considerable corporate effort to enlist such investors among the firm's major shareholders.

■ The **third** issue is whether and how we can improve existing financial measures of performance. The current search for relationship investors may reflect in large part the inadequacy of the accounting information that is regularly disclosed by companies to sellside analysts—the largely meaningless quarterly compilation and reporting of earnings per share. To the extent this is so, better financial measures could help stimulate relationship investing. Such measures could become a new language, in effect, for communicating with and thus attracting sophisticated investors.

■ **Fourth**, corporate IR efforts may also want to make use of *non-financial* performance measures—of things like product quality, and customer and employee satisfaction—that could help investors better evaluate future corporate performance. Ned Regan, who has been kind enough to join us this morning, is leading a research effort in that direction, and I'm confident he will tell us about the promise these kinds of measures hold out for improving the dialogue between management and shareholders.

■ **Fifth** and last is the broader issue of corporate governance and board supervision, and how it interacts will all these other issues I've just mentioned.

To discuss these timely and provocative matters, we have assembled a very distinguished group of participants, and I will mention them now in alphabetical order:

BASIL ANDERSON is the Chief Financial Officer of Scott Paper Co. Basil has just succeeded in instituting at Scott a major change in the financial measures that guide the company's investment planning, periodic performance evaluation, and executive compensation decisions.

CAROLYN BRANCATO is executive director of the Columbia Institutional Investor Project at Columbia Law School. Carolyn, who runs her own economic consulting firm called Riverside Economic Research, also recently completed work as staff director of the Competitiveness Policy Council's study of corporate governance and financial markets.

GEOFFREY COLVIN is Assistant Managing Editor of *Fortune*, and a member of the magazine's Board of Editors.

JUDITH DOBRZYNSKI is a senior writer at *Business Week*. Judy wrote the magazine's recent cover story on "Relationship Investing" and, some time before that, the cover story on "Corporate Governance."

ALEX LEHMANN was formerly Vice President of investor relations at Whitman Corporation, and now is a consultant specializing in valuation issues. While at Whitman, Alex developed a very proactive approach to corporate IR—one that I think you'll find quite interesting.

NELL MINOW is one of the principals (another is Robert Monks) of the Lens Fund, a highly-publicized active investor that takes large positions in underperforming companies. Their role in spurring the break-up of Sears is probably their major accomplishment to date, but they are also hard at work at American Express, Kodak, and Westinghouse.

KRISHNA PALEPU is Professor of Accounting and Finance at the Harvard Business School. Krishna, along with Harvard colleague Robert Kaplan, is in the process of putting together a symposium on non-financial measures of corporate performance.

EDWARD REGAN has been New York State Controller for the past 14 years—and a remarkably effective one, judging from the performance of the State's pension fund over that period. Starting midnight tomorrow, however, Ned will cease to be a politician and will become President of the Jerome Levy Institute, an economics thinktank at Bard College. There he will lead a research project on corporate governance.

JOSEPH SHENTON is President of OLC Corporation, a corporate investor relations consulting firm that studies the behavior of institutional investors and now has close to 150 corporate clients. Joe is in the business of trying to help corporations choose the appropriate investor clienteles and then help ensure that such clienteles are heavily represented in the shareholder base.

DEREK SMITH is Executive Vice President of Equifax Inc. in charge of insurance information services. Besides adopting a new internal financial measurement system, Equifax recently announced a leveraged Dutch auction share repurchase that was widely applauded by Wall Street. It should be interesting to hear the thinking behind that *financial* strategy—and the message Derek thinks it has sent to the company's investors.

EUGENE VESELL is Senior Vice President of Oppenheimer Capital. Gene and his colleagues, who have about $25 billion under management, have been practicing relationship investing long before anyone thought to give it a name. They have $18 billion invested in the equities of some 65 companies, giving Oppenheimer Capital an average position of about $250 million, and a 10% or greater ownership stake in about half their portfolio companies.

JEROLD ZIMMERMAN is Professor of Accounting at the University of Rochester's Simon School of Business. He is also the founding co-editor of the *Journal of Accounting and Economics*, a distinguished publication produced at the University of Rochester. Jerry has been among the four or five superstars in accounting research over the last 15 to 20 years. Last but not least are my Stern Stewart colleagues, **BENNETT STEWART**, who will serve as my co-moderator in this discussion, and **DON CHEW**, a founding partner of Stern Stewart and Editor of the Continental Bank *Journal of Applied Corporate Finance*. With that introduction, let me turn the floor over to Bennett Stewart.

What Accounting Was Never Meant to Be

STEWART: Thanks, Joel. Well, as you can see, we've been remarkably successful in narrowing the focus of this discussion.

Let's begin with this issue of the accounting framework that seems to underlie a lot of the concern expressed about the "short termism" of corporate America. Accounting conventions require corporations to expense much of their long-term investment, their R&D, their outlays for employee training, software investments, and so forth. The concern expressed by corporate managers is that investors focus myopically on near-term accounting results, thus placing an excessive discount on payoffs expected from promising long-run investment. Such allegedly systematic undervaluation of corporate investment then forces corporate managers to underinvest in the corporate future, or at least to invest in the wrong projects.

Let me begin by asking Professor Jerry Zimmerman to give us an academic perspective on these issues. Jerry, how is it that we have ended up with the current accounting system? And has it accomplished what it was really intended to do, or is it failing us in some important sense?

ZIMMERMAN: In the interest of full disclosure, let me preface my remarks with a disclaimer. The view I am about to offer is not widely held among my accounting colleagues, many of whom would likely argue that my views are speculative—that is, not sufficiently backed up by the existing body of accounting research. But, in fact, there is quite a bit of evidence that supports what I'm about to say.

Bennett Stewart has written an article called "Market Myths" in the *Journal of Applied Corporate Finance* that

does a wonderful job of summarizing the ways in which accounting conventions fail to measure economic reality. I agree with almost everything Bennett has to say in that article, but I think he's left out probably the most important market myth of them all—namely, the notion that accounting numbers were ever demanded, or *intended* for use, by shareholders for the purpose of valuing companies. Although accounting numbers do provide some information to investors, they are not a primary source of information for our capital markets. And, as long as institutions like the SEC and FASB continue to regulate disclosure, I suspect reported accounting numbers will never be very useful for investors in setting stock values.

The accounting systems that we have today—the historical-cost-based numbers that we all love to hate—have developed over hundreds of years. They can be traced back to the first "joint stock" or publicly owned companies of the 14th Century and even earlier. The problem that the accounting and auditing systems were originally designed to solve was the very basic problem of stewardship. Take the case of the East India Trading Company, which was an early joint stock company. Let's say they had a manager 4000 miles away running a trading post, and they shipped that person a boatload of goods. The purpose of accounting was to ensure that the manager used those goods to serve the company's interests and not just his own.

Another important function of accounting—one that developed somewhat later with the rise of public debt markets—was to control conflicts of interest between a company's bondholders and its shareholders. The problem was this: How could managers, as representatives of the shareholders, make credible promises to the bondholders that they would not pay out excessively high dividends

or invest in excessively risky projects? To reduce these conflicts, companies contracted privately with their bondholders to hire reputable, third-party accounting firms to gather and report certain kinds of information that would be useful in monitoring management's compliance with debt covenants. This was all done privately; there was no SEC, no public regulatory body, to demand that this information be provided. And the system worked.

STEWART: At this point, though, Jerry, the companies were closely held, right? The owners were not widely dispersed as they are today?

ZIMMERMAN: No, these joint stock companies had lots of owners. The East India Company had hundreds of shareholders.

Today, of course, the SEC would have us believe—and this is another part of that same market myth your article fails to mention—that the 1929 stock market crash was caused by inadequate financial disclosure and that the existence of the SEC now somehow protects us from further stock market crashes. But, having recently experienced the Crash of 1987, we now know that the SEC and mandated financial disclosure do not prevent stock market declines.

So, the *primary* function of the financial accounting system was never—and nor is it today—to provide information for valuation decisions. It was designed to provide *internal* measures of performance to serve as guides in running companies, and to protect outside investors from opportunistic managers. It's basically an auditing function: Count the cash and make sure the inventories are what they're supposed to be. It's a basic control system. It is not *primarily* a system for shareholder valuation of companies as going concerns.

Of course, many people still believe the primary function of these systems is to provide information for valuation, but this expectation has created an enormous problem for the public accounting profession. Those who bought into this accounting myth 50 years ago are now in a Catch 22: The partners of what used to be the Big Eight firms (it's now down to the Big Six, of course) are saying to themselves today: "Yes, we can provide this information for valuation. But every time the stock market crashes, we get sued for poor financial disclosure. We are being litigated out of existence."

Today, the legal costs of Big Six firms are running at about 10 to 15% of their total revenue. Because they can't get insurance any more, they're self-insuring. If we have a few more big lawsuits, we will no longer have a Big Six audit industry. In that event, the SEC may eventually end up requiring American corporations to be audited by a government body like the GAO.

Although accounting numbers do provide some information to investors, they are not a primary source of information for our capital markets. And, as long as institutions like the SEC and FASB continue to regulate disclosure, I suspect reported accounting numbers will never be very useful for outside investors in setting stock values.

—Jerold Zimmerman

STERN: Jerry, you mentioned that one objective of accounting statements was to provide information for lenders to the company. If this information helps lenders make better judgments about credit risk, why wouldn't that kind of information also be useful to shareholders?

ZIMMERMAN: For one thing, lenders are really insiders in a way that, at least in the U.S., outside shareholders can never be. As part of their credit evaluation, lenders routinely ask corporate borrowers to provide extensive financial disclosures that they then keep privately. That kind of confidential exchange of private information is not permissible between management and shareholders in the U.S. This private exchange of information can be valuable because there is often important strategic information that companies don't want to disclose to their competitors, but only to certain investors.

Another important difference between lenders and shareholders is that lenders care primarily only about downside risk. Lenders are much less interested than shareholders in going concern values, and much more concerned about liquidation values. They want to know what the assets will be worth if the company can't meet its interest payments.

STEWART: But, Jerry, isn't it possible that a perception could become a reality? You're saying that the accounting system was never *intended* to be a system for measuring value by the stock market. But isn't it conceivable that, through the efforts of the SEC, it could have become one. After all, the research you have published in your own *Journal of Accounting and Economics* has shown that stock prices respond in fairly predictable ways to earnings "surprises." Doesn't that partly contradict your position?

ZIMMERMAN: No. Going back to the seminal research of Ray Ball and Phil Brown in 1968, the stock market anticipates *most* of the news in accounting earnings by the time the numbers are released. The market has more timely sources of information than accounting numbers, including voluntary management disclosures and financial analysts' reports. Joel described the importance of "lead steers" in the pricing process. I doubt these people use accounting earnings as their primary source of information about companies' future cash flows.

Keeping Three Sets of Books:
The Case of Scott Paper

STEWART: Let me turn now to Basil Anderson. Basil, as CFO of Scott Paper, would you say that Jerry's view of the "irrelevance" of accounting to the stock market valuation process is one that is shared by your senior manage-

ment colleagues at Scott? And what do you find when you talk to your investors? Are they greatly interested in your quarterly financial results?

ANDERSON: One of the big challenges for us as a company is trying to reconcile the internal management information we need to run our business with the kind of information we *think* is required by investors on the outside. Of course, what we think investors want is to some extent dictated by SEC disclosure requirements. But, if we can believe people like Joel Stern and Bennett Stewart, there may well be kinds of information required by investors that are different from what is required by the SEC. To the extent this is true, companies could end up seeing a need to keep three different sets of books. And keeping three sets of books is not only costly and time-consuming, it can create lots of internal confusion about what the company is trying to achieve.

At Scott, we have developed an information system and financial performance measures that we feel are appropriate across a range of corporate decisions: capital budgeting, evaluation of divisional performance, management compensation awards, and so forth. And the financial measures we use to guide those decisions are quite different from what we're required to report to the SEC.

Communicating with investors, however, continues to pose the greatest challenge for us. Although the securities analysts and other representatives of the investment community I interact with tend to ask questions very much consistent with what the SEC and the accounting profession requires, these numbers have very little to do with how we manage and evaluate our own performance internally. Without any definite sense of the kind of information investors want from us, we simply try to do the best we can to respond.

STEWART: Basil, let's suppose you are rolling out a major new product line in Europe, and the costs associated with that investment will be expensed for two or three years before any benefits begin to show up in your financial statements. According to accounting conventions, much of that investment must be treated as an expense that reduces reported earnings. Yet, viewed from the perspective of a business person or an owner, it really represents an investment in the future.

How do you reconcile those two perspectives? How do you prevent yourself from underinvesting?

ANDERSON: Our own history of investment and capital spending would show that the perceived short-term focus of Wall Street has not prevented us from embarking on big expansion projects with longer-term payoffs. We do the best we can to inform Wall Street about the expected payoffs from our investment. But, as I said earlier, the disparity between how public accountants treat this investment and how we regard it internally creates a challenge for us in communicating with investors.

ALEX LEHMANN: Communicating effectively with investors is indeed a challenge. But it also represents a continuous opportunity to provide the kinds of information investors need to value a company. Basil referred to the expected payoffs from Scott's capital projects. Clearly that is what investor relations is all about: helping investors get a feel for the expected payoffs from both existing and new investment, and creating realistic expectations about the level of future cash flow and the investment necessary to provide that growth.

The Case for Accounting Reform

STEWART: Let me turn now to Krishna Palepu of the Harvard Business School. Krishna, you have a perspective on this issue that is somewhat different from Jerry Zimmerman's.

PALEPU: I would say my view of the world complements more than it contradicts Jerry's view, but I strongly disagree with part of his opening statement. The original intent of the accounting system may well have been the internal control and monitoring functions that Jerry described, but the limitation of this kind of historical analysis is that it may obscure important evolutionary change. In 1993, it may not be all that useful to be looking at the East India Company. The world economy has changed significantly over the past 300 years, and it's not implausible to me that the basic function of the accounting system could have evolved along with it. Part of the job of academic accountants like Jerry and me is of course to *describe* the past, and to explain why the existing accounting system looks the way it does. But another role for us academics is to suggest the possibility for change, to take a role in *prescribing* changes in the accounting system that would make accounting information more useful to investors.

For this reason, I welcome the SEC's challenge to the accounting profession to provide better measures of performance, non-financial as well as financial. Such measures ought to be designed to help investors monitor the value of their investments and keep track of how well management is using the capital they have committed. In fact, I believe the FASB has explicitly adopted this aim as their top priority in their ongoing redesign of the accounting system.

But despite the FASB's professed aim of facilitating communications between managers and investors—and here I'm about to agree with Jerry—the great majority of the FASB's actual rulings are really done with the mentality of a traffic cop: They just want the road to be clear; they don't seem to care as much whether any-

Even if the market is pretty good in valuing companies in the aggregate, individual companies may well be either overvalued or undervalued because of "information asymmetries" between managers and outside shareholders. If I were the CFO of an undervalued company, one of my principal responsibilities would be to figure out a way to get my story out. And one way to accomplish that would be to devise useful leading indicators and then make them the centerpiece in the voluntary or non-SEC part of my investor communications program.

—Krishna Palepu

body drives on it or not. For this reason, the FASB basically doesn't want to play an active role in addressing a problem like the one Bennett is talking about—that is, the treatment of long-term investment and R&D. If you look at the items on the FASB agenda at any point in time, there will always be a lot more items that relate to either expenses or liabilities, and a lot fewer to revenues and assets.

So there's a definite bias in terms of what the FASB is trying to do. As Jerry suggested, the accounting standards are designed more to protect the interests of creditors than to shed light on the going-concern value that accrues largely to shareholders. Creditors are interested primarily in the downside, but shareholders are interested in the upside as well. Shareholders are interested in assets as well as liabilities, future revenues as well as current expenses. So I think we need to move toward an account-

ing system that aims to tell more of the complete story—while still keeping in mind, of course, who is telling the story and their incentives to get the story right.

STEWART: But, it seems to me that accounting still has one necessary and inescapable limitation. It is based upon historical results, it is a recording of past events. Since investors are by their nature forward looking, I don't see how we can expect any accounting-based system to play a major role in the dialogue that needs to take place between management and investors.

PALEPU: I disagree. In many cases, a company's recent history may well be the most reliable guide to the future and, hence, to its going concern value. At the same time, you could supplement these historical disclosures with some leading indicators that might actually tell investors where the company is going.

STEWART: Would you give us some examples of what you mean by leading indicators?

PALEPU: Well, suppose a company is making an investment in the design and marketing of a new product. When evaluating the progress of that investment for internal purposes, management will generally have a set of intermediate goals or milestones they use to assess whether they are on track. Companies could disclose some of these internal goals to the investment community without giving away the store.

Now, it's true some managers are worried that disclosure of strategic information could undermine their firms' competitive position. But while such concerns are valid, they are probably overstated—because competitors typically cannot replicate a really innovative strategy just by reading about it. For example, take the case of Walmart. Its strategy has become a matter of public knowledge, but very few competitors have been able to replicate it.

Indeed, I would argue that if a company's strategy can be readily replicated by another company, then it is not a source of sustainable competitive advantage. Much of the value of corporate strategy, I suspect, comes not from strategy *per se*, but rather from how effectively the strategy is implemented.

STEWART: Krishna, that reminds me of the message of your Harvard colleague Amar Bhide, who wrote a great *Harvard Business Review* article called "Hustle as Strategy." Amar's argument is that strategic brilliance is becoming less important to corporate success than execution and efficiency.

For example, I recently read in *Business Week* that whereas it took Chrysler two and a half years and $1.7 billion to come up with a new compact model, it took General Motors five or six years and some $3 billion

to develop its own compact, the Saturn. It's not hard to see from these two numbers why GM is having such problems. But what really struck me about this story is that I was learning about these time-to-market and investment cost measures—things that are really critical to evaluating the operating efficiency of auto manufacturers—*not* from the company's annual or quarterly reports, but from reading *Business Week*. This is precisely the kind of information investors need to know to gain a competitive edge.

So, it's no wonder investors don't expect to learn much from reading a company's annual report. Even if companies did disclose such information in their quarterly or annual reports—which they typically don't, unless it puts them in a consistently favorable light—it's already stale information by the time it comes out.

PALEPU: But there are many ways of communicating with shareholders that can be far more effective than the annual report. The annual report is simply the culmination of the financial reporting process; it's often more a ceremonial event than a source of information. Some companies use quarterly reports to provide management discussions of capital spending and progress toward meeting stated corporate goals. For example, if your internal corporate objectives include an increase in customer service and a decrease in new product cycle times, then it makes a lot of sense for management to tell the investment community about these goals, and about its progress in meeting them. It makes sense to give investors a roadmap, if you will, and then promise that you will faithfully chart your progress in bad times as well as good.

Credibility is, of course, a very important part of this whole disclosure process. To the extent you succeed in establishing credibility with

the investment community, a corporate IR program may have far more ability to supplement its financial disclosures with information about some of the nonfinancial leading indicators I mentioned earlier.

STERN: Krishna, let me present an alternative hypothesis, perhaps in a somewhat extreme form. Let's assume that all this accounting information is of absolutely no value to investors at all; it plays no role in determining the price of a company's shares. Assume further that you know the management of a poorly performing company was about to be replaced by a management team with a reputation for delivering results. Would that alone be sufficient basis for committing investment funds to such a company?

PALEPU: Management reputation certainly plays a major role. But if I were putting $100 million into a company, I would also like to know something about the new management's plan for reforming the business, for creating new growth, and for funding that growth. For example, if I were going to invest in IBM, I would need to know more than just that Lou Gerstner was coming in to run IBM and that he had a lot of stock options.

STERN: I would argue that top management's reputation represents a very important part of this market valuation process. Take the case of Eastman Kodak reported in today's *Wall Street Journal*. The article announced that Chris Steffen, the CFO hired a few months ago to push forward the restructuring of the company, is now leaving. There was a 15% drop in the price of Kodak's shares as soon as the announcement was made. When it was first announced he was coming on board, there was an almost identically large *increase* in the price of the shares.

I would argue that Steffen's reputation for doing what needs to be done significantly altered investors' expectations of future performance at Kodak. No accounting system that measured historical performance would have helped investors make the decision to buy when Steffen came on or to sell when he left. All you needed to know was whether he was coming or going.

NED REGAN: I think the shares would have dropped even if Steffen hadn't resigned. Yesterday's *Wall Street Journal* showed clearly that two people were trying to run the same company. I read that story and said to myself: "Goodbye Kay or goodbye Steffen."

Old-Fashioned Relationship Investing: The Case of Oppenheimer Capital

STERN: Well, I suspect we will come back to Kodak later in this discussion. But now let me turn to Eugene Vesell of Oppenheimer Capital. As I said earlier, Gene started practicing a kind of relationship investing long before anybody thought to give it a name.

Gene, would you tell us about Oppenheimer Capital and how it works? For example, do you use accounting-based information in evaluating investment candidates, or do you place more emphasis on other non-financial, perhaps more forward-looking, indicators?

VESELL: Joel, before I answer your last question, let me respond to the point you just made about reputation. You suggested that all you need to know about a company is management's reputation. Well, I essentially agree with that statement, but I would add that there's one other important consideration: the extent to which management's compensation is tied to shareholder value.

We at Oppenheimer have about $26 billion in assets under management. Our total equity investments are in the $17-$18 billion range. So we're fairly large, but not one of the

We like companies that are run as if they were private; maximization of cash flow and minimization of taxable reported earnings are the goals we want management to pursue. The fact that the company is run to maximize cash flow, not earnings, sends a very powerful signal to us that they are managing like owners. Our own firm, Oppenheimer Capital, is owner-managed; we're a publicly traded MLP with significant management ownership. And we look for other companies that are owner-managed...We want managers to be owners with us.

—Eugene Vesell-

giants. And, unlike the giants, we tend to take very concentrated positions. As you mentioned earlier, we have about 65 positions (though a typical account will own only 35-40 stocks). Hence, an average position is about $250 million. However, we do have a dozen holdings over $400 million.

STEWART: What percentage of the stock does that typically represent?

VESELL: We often own 10% or more of a company's shares. In our larger companies, that obviously tends to be a little smaller; for example, we own only about 5-6% of Sprint. But, in our smaller companies, our stakes are quite large. We own 20% of Dole, over 15% of Sundstrand, 14% of Transamerica, and over 15% of Freeport McMoran.

STEWART: Let me stop you with Freeport McMoran. That's a very difficult company to analyze from the outside because of the depletion allowances and the diverse kinds of

assets. How do you evaluate a company like that? Their accounting statements are virtually meaningless.

VESELL: I couldn't agree more. Well, as Joel was suggesting, it's the reputation and the incentive compensation of the top management that were perhaps the most important factors driving our investment decision. The quality of the board of directors was also important.

With respect to the assets themselves, the best we could do was to assess their value using very imprecise, essentially qualitative judgments—although we did have some hard numbers on "proven reserves." The company's principal asset is a copper and gold mine in New Guinea, and we used those estimates of reserves to make a present value calculation of the value of those assets. And after making some back-of-the-envelope adjustments for their other assets and liabilities, we said to ourselves:

"Gee, what you can touch here is worth 50% to 75% above the current stock price."

But, once more, what we were really banking on was the reputation and incentives of management. In the case of Freeport McMoran, management had a record for both finding new assets and then, once they found them, of managing those assets very efficiently.

STEWART: But how would you know they were managing assets efficiently if you couldn't make sense of the financial statements?

VESELL: Well, as you say, historical accounting numbers were not much of a guide. The company has dual incorporation in Indonesia and Delaware, which even complicates the accounting more, because Indonesian tax laws allow you to write off a fair amount of the capital spending. And let me stop here and point out that we *want* our companies to write off their investment as quickly as possible. We like companies that are run as if they were private; maximization of cash flow and minimization of *taxable* reported earnings are the goals we want management to pursue.

So, in this case, we were able to look through the accounting statements to find the cash flows generated by the mining operations. And the fact that the company is run to maximize cash flow, not earnings, sends a very powerful signal to us that they are managing like owners. We also used the very solid stock price performance following the merger of McMoran Oil and Freeport Sulphur as another useful indicator of their ability to manage assets.

STEWART: I understand that, although the company is very adept at finding mineral reserves, they don't insist on taking them out of the ground.

VESELL: That's right. Unlike many natural resource companies, they have specialized in doing only what they do best. If they find new mineral reserves, they're not committed to developing them. They will sell the reserves if they can find a buyer willing to pay a high price for those reserves, presumably because the buyer brings more value added to the mining process. As managers, their aim is not to maximize assets under control, as so many American companies have done, but rather to maximize rates of return on capital and thus shareholder value. They really know how to manage investor capital.

And, as I mentioned earlier, we invest in companies where there's clearly a strong bond of common interest between management and the shareholders. Our own firm, Oppenheimer Capital, is owner-managed; we're a publicly traded MLP with significant management ownership. And we look for other companies that are owner-managed, either directly or through incentive compensation schemes like Stern Stewart's leveraged stock purchase plan. We want managers to be owners with us.

STERN: Gene, would it also make a difference if boards of directors had significant stock ownership?

VESELL: It may make a difference in some cases, but I'm not as convinced. Because of our large positions, I'm often asked the question, "Do you like inside or outside boards?" My answer is always, "A plague on both their houses." I know a lot of CEOs who serve as directors on other companies' boards. When I have asked them about their role on these other boards, they tell me quite candidly: "We don't have the information and the time to be very useful."

STERN: But, perhaps the reason they don't have time is that they don't have much of a personal stake in the outcome. They simply receives the fees and the reputational enhancement of sitting on another company's board.

But what if you could get board members to invest their annual directors' fees in, say, slightly out-of-the-money options that are taxless to them until exercise, and on the same basis as the managers? Would that make you feel better about their level of commitment to shareholders?

VESELL: It would, but I'm not sure it's practical from a time point of view. I'm on the board of a private company, and I've got 30,000 options. We had a board meeting in which we were contemplating an acquisition, and the material we were asked to review in preparation for the meeting was several inches think. I just don't have time to do this. So I agree with Jack Welch's position at GE; he sits on no boards other than GE's.

But I agree with you 100% in principle. If you could get people who would serve as full-time, professional directors—people who really have something to offer—then your board incentive system could become very important.

STEWART: So, Gene, what you seem to be saying is that the corporate governance issue we've heard so much about is a phoney.

VESELL: Totally. The real issue is getting the managers inside the company to run the company in the interests of shareholders. You've got to provide *management* with the right incentives to add value.

GEOFF COLVIN: I couldn't agree more that the key is to provide management with the right incentives. But who is going to provide those incentives? Only one body: the board. And since these incentives almost always increase the risk of management's pay package, imposing them may be a disagreeable task. I would argue that, for obvious reasons, outside directors have a somewhat better shot at doing this than insiders—and for this reason, the outsiders versus insiders debate is important.

Back to Accounting

STERN: Jerry, what's your response to the suggestion that we can improve our accounting system?

ZIMMERMAN: In the enthusiasm to improve financial disclosures, there's something important that's being left out of this discussion. We have a set of institutions in place in this country that have a good deal of control over these disclosures. We can sit around this table and dream up the world's best financial disclosures, but the critical question is: "What will the SEC do? What will the FASB do? And what will the plaintiff bar do?"

In Bennett's article called "Market Myths," he shows quite clearly that accounting numbers do not reflect economic reality, and that sophisticated investors—the people who dominate the price-setting process at the margin—quite sensibly pay little attention to accounting numbers. At the very least, our capital markets are quite capable of correcting the distortions built into our accounting framework.

In place of conventional accounting numbers, Bennett proposes making several modifications of accounting conventions to arrive at a financial measure he calls "economic value added," or EVA. Now, how does he do it?

STEWART: Actually, Jerry, in fairness to Joel, I should confess here that most of these ideas were originally his.

ZIMMERMAN: Okay, how do *they* do it? Well, they capitalize corporate R&D instead of expensing it all immediately; they use the full-cost accounting method rather than the successful efforts method; and they add back non-cash expenses like deferred taxes and amortized goodwill to the income statement.

But what are they really doing in the process? Where did these num-bers originally come from? They came from the SEC and FASB. It is these same institutions, and the incentives of the people running them, that are at the heart of the problem. They are not really interested in becoming part of the solution. So why do we think that, if Krishna and his colleagues derive better accounting numbers, the SEC and FASB will sanction them? It's these very same institutions that for 60 years now have been mandating accounting disclosures that Joel Stern and Bennett Stewart then have to undo.

STEWART: I too have little hope for acceptance of these measures by the SEC and the FASB. In fact, an endorsement by the SEC would almost necessarily limit their usefulness to the most sophisticated investors—the kind most companies ought to be attempting to reach. In my experience, the most effective shareholder communications are those that focus on performance measures that companies have devised for their own *internal* purposes and to fit their own special circumstances. And when management volunteers to tell the market about those customized measures—especially when such a communication strategy is combined with significant management stock ownership—then I can see investors responding very strongly to such disclosures. But, again, I don't think it's either necessary for, or realistic to expect, the SEC to endorse these more customized kinds of performance measures.

PALEPU: Well, I think the SEC and the FASB can play a positive role in this process. I recently attended a conference on "Financial Reporting in the 21st Century" that had as its declared goal a fundamental rethinking of the U.S. financial reporting system. That conference, I would also point out, was sponsored by one of the Big Six accounting firms and had the blessing of the FASB.

ZIMMERMAN: That may be so, Krish. But I think the overriding concern of professional accountants today is to change the financial reporting system in ways that will reduce their exposure to lawsuits. That's the main thing public accountants are thinking about right now, not improved numbers for valuation purposes.

PALEPU: Well, I agree that we also need to revise auditors' legal liabilities and the excessive litigation our system invites. But that doesn't preclude the possibility of changing accounting measures for the better. We could solve the legal problem in part by restricting private rights of action to only the most minimal set of disclosures. And, by so doing, we could then provide corporate managers with much more freedom to customize their disclosures in a way that sheds light on the value added by their own activities.

Now, of course, you could still object that there's little need for better accounting if the market is already efficient. But I disagree. My view of market efficiency is that, on average, the value of the market portfolio consisting of all companies is probably priced correctly. But even if the market is pretty good in valuing companies in the aggregate, individual companies may well be either overvalued or undervalued for long periods of time because of what academics refer to as "information asymmetries" between managers and outside shareholders. So although a *portfolio* might be correctly valued, many of the individual stocks that make up their value could be significantly undervalued. Because managers could know more about their firm's prospects than outsiders, the market will automatically discount the value of those shares to reflect their informational disadvantage.

So, if I were the CFO of an undervalued company, I think one of my principal responsibilities would be to figure out a way to get my story out. And one way to accomplish that, as I suggested earlier, would be to devise useful leading indicators and then make them the centerpiece in the voluntary or non-SEC part of my investor communications program.

DON CHEW: Krishna, Joel was suggesting earlier that the most effective shareholder communication is the kind targeted for a small, highly sophisticated group of investors—the lead steers, if you will. But there are major regulatory barriers to sharing information privately with only certain investors. Have you thought of a way of getting around these SEC barriers to talking privately to a small group of investors? Or should companies instead design all-purpose communications that seek to reach all investors at their own levels of sophistication?

PALEPU: Well, I agree there are legal barriers, not to mention competitive risks, to sharing certain kinds of information with outside investors. But I think such risks have been greatly exaggerated. Even within the current institutional framework, there is much that could be done. In fact, I have done a number of case studies describing innovative disclosures some American companies have recently devised. For example, Home Depot, a retailer with an innovative strategy, discloses in its annual report a lot of data about the way its stores are managed. And Comdisco, the world's largest computer leasing company, provides detailed information on how it assesses and manages the residual values of its leased computer equipment. In both these cases, the information disclosed is critical for investors in assessing management performance and estimating share values.

STEWART: I too think the competitive risks of sharing strategic information have been overstated. As you said earlier, Krishna, strategy itself has been devalued by technological advances in information and the increasing pace of change; and, as a consequence, execution and flexibility are becoming the keys to success.

What really matters to investors today is not corporate strategy, but the management *process* and the incentives that go along with them. For this reason, I think companies could benefit greatly just by focusing their disclosures on how they manage, what their goals are, how they monitor their progress in meeting those goals, and what their incentives are to bring it all off. So, it's not the specifics of strategy that are important—indeed, in some sense, a company's strategy is changing everyday—but rather the corporate process that would give investors a sense of management's alertness and incentives to respond to continuous change.

Abolish the SEC?

VESELL: As a long-time value-based investor, I was delighted to hear Professor Zimmerman's view about the irrelevance of accounting for stock market investors. I don't mean to suggest that accounting is completely useless. Accounting is sort of the language that you have to learn to get started. But then, as an outsider, you have to learn to translate those numbers in a way that allows you to get a sense of what's going on inside the company.

ZIMMERMAN: That's right. We know that investors are always looking for profits in undervalued or overvalued stocks. And we also know that accounting numbers do have some information content. When they're announced, whether it's in Jakarta or elsewhere, the stock market reacts. But that isn't what accounting numbers were designed to do.

The fundamental difference between Krishna and me is that he has a lot more faith in the SEC than I do. My view is that if I've gone to the same witch doctor for the last 60 years and he's killed off every one of my relatives, I think it's time to shoot the witch doctor. If you want to have improved financial disclosures in this country, the best way is to abolish these blocking institutions and let the companies innovate and invent disclosures that make sense.

STEWART: You think we should abolish the SEC...entirely?

VESELL: I would agree with that.

STEWART: So what you're advocating is essentially a free-market, voluntary, unregulated system of disclosure?

ZIMMERMAN: That's right. And I would also eliminate the insider trading laws. You really can't communicate effectively with the lead steers under the existing insider trading laws. Even if Basil at Scott Paper has the world's best story, he can't whisper it to somebody like Gene Vesell.

STERN: Ned, as New York State Controller until midnight tomorrow, what do you think about these outrageous statements from Professor Zimmerman that we don't need any regulation of disclosure at all?

REGAN: Well, it's less outrageous than having Congress appoint the GAO to audit Scott Paper. But that's about all I can say for the proposal. I can't go along with the idea of an unregulated, completely voluntary market in corporate disclosure. It seems obvious to me we need regulation of disclosure.

ZIMMERMAN: Capital markets worked fine before 1933. Stocks were bought and sold...

REGAN: And a lot of little people were left with worthless paper.

ZIMMERMAN: A lot of people were left with significantly less valuable paper in 1987, too. Stock markets go up and down, despite the best intentions and efforts of auditors and regulators.

Prior to the founding of the SEC in 1933, most NYSE companies issued audited financial statements. Firms have an incentive to do that without the SEC. But look at what the SEC and the FASB have done to our accounting systems. It's because the accounting numbers do not reflect economic reality that people like Joel Stern and Bennett Stewart can make a living advising companies how to undo the harmful effects that come from using those numbers to make decisions.

REGAN: But the SEC doesn't prevent a company from disclosing its strategy, from disclosing its level of customer satisfaction, and the quality of its goods and services relative to that of its peers. They could do all that today, but they don't. The CEO of Scott talks about all these things with his division chiefs, but he doesn't talk about them with his board and with his shareholders. There's nothing in the world to prevent all of this from being discussed in the boardroom and communicated to investors in language they can understand.

So, you can still have your regulatory framework to provide a minimum amount and type of disclosure. But management can exceed that minimum whenever they wish. If they don't, at some point, some Scott shareholders are going to file a resolution to demand to see how the company judges the quality of its product as compared to its competitors. Shareholders know that that issue is discussed everyday on the shop floor at Scott Paper and they would like to know that information.

The Promise of Nonfinancial Measures

STERN: Ned, you are directing a taskforce of sorts to develop nonfinancial performance measures. Would you share with us some of your findings and recommendations?

The SEC doesn't prevent companies from disclosing their strategies, from disclosing their levels of customer satisfaction, and the quality of their goods and services relative to that of their peers. They could do all that today, but they don't. There's nothing in the world to prevent all of this from being discussed in the boardroom and communicated to investors in language they can understand.

—Edward Regan

REGAN: There is a lot of work going on today on nonfinancial measures of corporate performance. There is a study being conducted by an AICPA group headed by Ed Jenkins, the Chicago partner of Arthur Anderson. Another is a group led by Bob Eccles and Jim McGee in Cambridge that is being sponsored by Ernst and Young and the FEI, the Financial Executives Institute. A third study is being done in Toronto by a group of former business people and scholars to assess how these nonfinancial factors— including, interestingly, the corporation's social reputation—correlate with financial results and stock market performance. And Bob Reich at the Labor Department has started a fourth study that will attempt to measure employee satisfaction and involvement and correlate those measures with stock price. So that's at least four groups, and there are probably others doing it.

The AICPA study, like the FEI study, is looking to develop nonfinancial measures such as the ones I've just mentioned—quality of goods and services, employee satisfaction, and customer satisfaction; there are at least a dozen items on the agenda at the moment. Essentially what they are trying to do is to develop industry standards and norms for, say, the paper industry. (And, Basil, I'm making things up here a little bit, but I'm still a politician until midnight.) For example, there might be a measurable standard for customer satisfaction in the paper products industry that could be compiled and reported to investors like the New York State pension system.

And I think it's important to note that this study is being sponsored by the official institution of CPAs and undertaken by some of its members. Some of these CPAs have declared, at least in private to me, that their primary motive for conducting the study is their level of dissatisfaction with existing financial measures as indicators of future performance and value. They have told me that the current financial reporting system doesn't work—and that's, of course, exactly what we're hearing now from people around the table who are far better versed than I on this subject.

Now, I'm not saying this dissatisfaction with current accounting measures is the *prevailing* view among CPAs. Ed Jenkins doesn't necessarily have smooth sailing among his colleagues in conducting this study.

STEWART: So we all agree, then, that quarterly reports don't mean very much to investors?

REGAN: That's right. And, frankly, few people in the public pension system industry are even capable of understanding such reports. You're wrong if you think politicians who run public pension funds are capable of understanding this stuff.

STEWART: Well, why couldn't public pension funds retain investment advisers like Institutional Shareholders Services to do the research for them?

REGAN: They can't pay what somebody would pay a Morgan Stanley or Oppenheimer Capital to do due diligence on a company. And that's one reason I think this research on nonfinancial measures is important. These measures could be especially valuable to public institutional investors, to institutions like us that can't afford to have financial experts on their payroll and who don't relate well—and I put myself at the head of this list—to narrowly focused financial information. This is private-sector-oriented information, but public pension funds arc run by public-sector, civil-service-oriented individuals. And it seems to me that a promising way to enhance the ability of what I refer to as the "new" or "reawakened" public-sector shareholder is to give the

people that run those institutions a corporate performance report on something to which they can relate.

Marty Lipton recently proposed the idea of an internal business audit; it's really a revival of something Peter Drucker has been proposing for years. It would not be a financial audit, but a business audit. My guess is that, if the companies themselves began to experiment with the disclosure of these kinds of nonfinancial performance measures, such disclosures would be widely accepted and encouraged by the investment community.

More on Non-Financial Measures

STERN: Let me turn to Carolyn Brancato, who is staff director of this project with Ned Regan. Carolyn, would you summarize the major findings and proposals of this work to date?

BRANCATO: I want to add a couple of observations to Ned's comments.

One of the key nonfinancial measures of performance whose development we hope to encourage is some method of assessing how much, and how effectively, companies are spending to reposition themselves strategically to compete in world markets. As in the Scott Paper example mentioned earlier, I'm thinking of capital expenditures with longer-term payoffs, not something that will show up immediately in the bottom-line EPS.

Why do I think there's a need or demand for such measures? Let me explain by offering a brief recent history of Wall Street. I started my career in 1967 as a securities analyst. In those days we used slide rules, we read Graham & Dodd, and we were fundamentalists. In the late '60s, the institutional investors as we now know them—the pension funds, the mutual funds, and so on—accounted for only about 28% of the equity holdings in the country. (They now

account for upwards of 55%.) Most of the money that was managed came through large investment banking and brokerage houses, and it was managed for large individual accounts. Even the retail money was sort of herded together, and so there was a group of houses that engaged in quite a lot of fundamental analysis.

Brokerage commissions at that time were fixed, not negotiated as they are today. The move to floating commissions in the early 1970s led to a major change in the way Wall Street did business. Many of the big research houses phased out much of their fundamental research activities.

But, as fundamental analysts in the late '60s, we routinely attempted to look through accounting statements to get at normalized, cash-flow-based measures of corporate performance. We never simply took the income statement and the balance sheet at face value. We started with reported accounting numbers, then examined the footnotes, and ended up adding our own layers of information—some of which we got from talking directly to company CFOs. There was also, of course, a whole cadre of technical analysts—the "head and shoulders" people, if you will—but we sort of looked down our noses at them and said, "No, we're fundamentalists and we really know the company."

But today things are different on Wall Street. Consider the consequences of the tremendous flows of money into institutional investors. The large pension funds simply don't have the ability to make these fundamental decisions; in fact, their portfolios are indexed as often as not. In short, the money has moved away from these fundamental-oriented houses that were dominant in the late '60s.

So, largely as a result of these changes, we are now looking to groups like Oppenheimer Capital and the Lens Fund to reinvigorate the old-fashioned

kind of fundamental analysis we once practiced. At the same time, as Ned just mentioned, we're also looking for new, particularly nonfinancial, measures of corporate performance. Such measures will help those kinds of investors who can't do the sophisticated financial analysis themselves. For example, we're looking for new ways to reflect R&D, and worker training and education— and for proxies for employee and customer satisfaction—that tend to correlate strongly with current and future corporate performance.

STERN: Are you arguing, then, that the shift from fixed to floating commissions and the increasing flow of funds to institutional investors was a bad thing?

BRANCATO: The consequences have been mixed, good and bad. On the one hand, the growth of pension funds means that our economy has become more effective in distributing wealth throughout the system. On the other hand, there are many companies that feel very constrained by having their shares in the hands of large institutions. They don't know quite how to deal with some of these large pension funds that are sitting on huge piles of money, but whom they believe lack the financial sophistication to understand their financial reporting. Twenty-five years ago, companies felt they could sit down with a relatively small group of analysts and tell their story to a receptive, fundamentally-oriented audience. That's no longer true today.

LEHMANN: I would like to add a different perspective here. On the domestic equity side, only about 10% of all tax-exempt funds managed are indexed. In my experience as a director of corporate IR, index managers typically do not have the need to talk to corporate IR people. But I have found many more fundamental managers who are quite receptive to direct contact with the corporations

they invest in. I would also point out that the active buyside manager is way ahead of all but a handful of sellside analysts when it comes to valuing businesses. And corporate IR practices have adapted to this reality by seeking much more direct contact with the buyside than when I entered the field ten years ago.

In Search of The Lead Steers

STERN: Let's turn now to Joe Shenton, who is an adviser to corporations on targeting investor clienteles. Joe, what do you think about what Carolyn just told us about Wall Street?

SHENTON: We have studied the effects of changing the commission structure on Wall Street, and our basic conclusion is that the market was much more efficient with respect to information flows in 1967 than it is today—and precisely for the reason Carolyn just mentioned: without fixed commissions, many brokerage

houses lost their financial incentive to do fundamental research. In 1967 brokers earned 35 to 50 cent commissions for moving a share of stock. Today they earn only four to six cents a share.

For this reason, the quality of sellside research has fallen off dramatically over the past 25 years; indeed, the sellside has become essentially irrelevant to the major lead steer investors—to people like Gene Vesell, for example.

VESELL: I was one of those brokers in the 1970s. And there was a very good economic reason for allowing the brokerage commissions to float. In the old days, investors were being forced by regulation to subsidize the research activities of my brokerage firm and others. I think we're far better off with market-based commissions. This way, investors who are willing to pay their broker for fundamental research can volunteer to pay them directly, without having it built into the commission schedule.

SHENTON: I don't dispute that floating commissions are a better deal for investors. But it has affected corporate disclosure and investor relations in some sense for the worse. If I were a company in the late '60s or early '70s and I wanted to communicate effectively to the investment community, I would visit the ten to twelve sellside analysts that covered my industry, tell them my story, and they in turn would spread the word for me. They had every incentive to do so in those days.

Take Otis Bradley, who was a very well-known and widely-followed analyst of computer stocks in the '60s. When Otis announced a buy recommendation, that company's stock would go flying off the charts. Bradley was the epitome of a lead steer investor—and he was a sellside analyst! When an Otis Bradley research report came out, the information would be all over Wall Street and reflected in the stock price within minutes.

Today, by contrast, the best research is clearly being done by people far removed from the sellside. I was very interested in hearing Gene Vesell's account of how he gets his information. As Gene just told us, it has almost nothing to with the quarterly reports required by the SEC. The issue here is not who's mandating the information, it's who's smart enough to supplement the publicly available information with other, more reliable and useful kinds of information. In my experience, the smartest investors tend to find alternative, often nonfinancial, kinds of information— and they use that information to earn higher rates of return.

STERN: Where do they get the information from?

SHENTON: They dig it. And they get some of it from management.

STERN: If that is so, then why are you maintaining that markets are less efficient today than they were in 1967?

SHENTON:Because the best research is not shared, it is not spread around Wall Street the way it once was.

STERN: Why would that make any difference? I thought stock prices were set at the margin.

CHEW: In fact, a recent study—by Jeremy Stein of MIT and Ken Froot and Andrei Shleifer of Harvard— shows that stock prices now respond far more quickly to corporate news than they did in the '60s and '70s. And, given the advances in information technology, it would be very surprising to find that markets were less efficient today than 25 years ago.

SHENTON: Well, I agree with you both that the information is reflected quickly in the price of the stock. But I'm not talking about prices here, but about information flows. The information flows between companies and the investment community are not nearly as direct as they once were. As I said, a corporate IR director can no longer send his message to ten or twelve sellside analysts and be confident that the market is getting the word. And, deprived of these customary channels, many companies today just choose not to make the effort to tell their story. Instead, they fall back on the SEC safe harbor and disclose just the bare minimum.

But let me also say this. Before I started my consulting firm, I worked in corporate investor relations for 17 years; and, in spite of what you may be reading in the press, there's nothing new about relationship investing. John Neff was giving me heartaches in 1973, when I was director of IR at Northwest Industries. He was the most active investor I have ever seen. Relationship investing has been around in the same way venture capital has been around. It's the same model of corporate governance that is also used in LBOs, which of course came out of the venture capital industry. It's simply the model of highly sophisticated investors buying large stakes in companies and then having very good channels of communication (often including board seats) and very strong incentives to get information.

STEWART: So, even if the brokerage firms no longer have a strong interest in doing fundamental research today, the high rates of return promised by relationship investing have provided a new incentive for gathering fundamental information.

SHENTON: I agree. But, as I said earlier, there's nothing new about relationship investing; it's been there all the time. The brightest investors have always found ways to get information that give them a real competitive edge.

And for those companies worried about legal liability from providing unorthodox types of disclosure, I have another message: You don't need written disclosures to communicate with lead steer investors. There are lots of other ways to do so that don't violate the securities laws.

But, to reach lead steers, the first thing you have to do is to find out who they are. As Joel suggested earlier, there may be 50 investors who really determine the stock price of Scott Paper at the margin. These are the people who buy or sell in large quantities when the price falls too low or rises too high. All the other 5,000 investors may increase your trading volume, but they don't have any material effect on the stock price.

STEWART: But doesn't this sort of contradict Ned's point about the importance of this passively managed money sitting in public pension funds?

SHENTON: Yes, it does. I'm saying that the corporate IR strategy ought to aim for the highest common denominator. If you aim your financial communications for the most sophisticated investors, they will take care of the share price. Don't worry about the mass of investors. Instead seek out the 50 investors that are going to make a difference to your stock and communicate with them.

STEWART: That's part of the reason why I am very uncomfortable about *mandating* the use of nonfinancial information. I'm not saying that nonfinancial information is unimportant. It's clearly very important for *internal* management purposes.

Three years ago I was doing some work with Whirlpool on performance measurement, and they had put together a very sophisticated system for measuring customer satisfaction, product quality, employee commitment, degree of innovation—and it was all summarized on a single page. It was spontaneously developed by the company for their internal purposes. That makes all the sense in the world; and it may even make sense to share some of this information with outside investors. But to standardize these measures across all companies and then *mandate* their disclosure to investors seems pointless.

BRANCATO: Our commission has never suggested that such disclosures be mandated. We recommended that they be developed to close this information gap between the small groups of very sophisticated investors doing fundamental analysis and the large pension funds indexing huge blocks of money. As Ned said, these funds simply don't have the resources to do sophisticated financial analysis. And the nonfinancial measures we're now experimenting with—even if the most sophisticated investors do not need them to value the shares—could provide useful information to guide the investment decisions of the less sophisticated investors.

STEWART: But that's precisely my point. If investors are unwilling to pay for the information in the form of a higher stock price, then why do it? I just don't see how disclosure of these *standardized* nonfinancial measures

can help companies increase their stock prices—which, to me, is the true test of effective disclosure.

BRANCATO: My point is this: These nonfinancial measures of performance, by closing the information gap between the fundamentalist lead steers and more passive indexed investors, can serve to extend this informational basis for relationship investing in a way that involves a much broader base of investors.

VESELL: I should point out, however, that we at Oppenheimer manage a lot of public pension money, including some of New York State's. We're talking about $5 or $6 billion of public money that we're delighted to manage. So this information gap may not be as large as we are making it out to be.

STERN: So, even though commissions have disappeared, it would seem from Gene's comment that we have evolved into a system where 50 to 100 lead steers now do the work that some 1,000 security analysts were doing 25 years ago. And this system seems to work quite well—so much so that Oppenheimer Capital is winning over the business of public pension funds because of its ability to generate superior returns.

A Corporate IR Perspective

ALEX LEHMANN: There is another kind of information gap that divides even the fundamentalists. As I said earlier, there is a tremendous divergence between most brokerage or sellside research—which is based on the accounting model and geared toward predicting next quarter's EPS—and the approach of sophisticated buyside institutional investors, as represented by somebody like Gene Vesell.

I represented Whitman Corporation for about eight years starting in 1983. It's a fairly complex company, a

conglomerate. At that time, the company was comprised of six independent, freestanding businesses. My job was first and foremost to communicate one on one with the buyside. I set myself the task of identifying our 50 largest shareholders, getting to know them, and maintaining an ongoing dialogue with them. We discussed the company's goals and strategies—typically in terms of cash flows rather than conventional EPS. And, in the course of many discussions, it was always my aim to clarify any corporate actions or decisions that might have led to misunderstanding or uncertainty.

Put a little differently, our purpose was to create an appropriate or realistic set of investor expectations. The key was to establish and then maintain credibility and, by so doing, to try to make a complex company as simple as possible for investors to understand. As I said, most of our communications effort was directed at the buyside investment community, the people who owned our stock. The sellside analysts came in later in the process and proved very useful in leveraging our buyside efforts.

I discovered a few things along the way. First, to communicate effectively, you have to value the company's businesses regularly; such regular exercises in valuation give you the ammunition for productive discussions with investors. Then you have to be timely and consistent. Maintaining a sense of continuity is key, for example, when there is a change at the top. I served three CEOs during my eight years and, as you would expect, they each had different views about what the company should be or become. Also, maintaining reasonable expectations is difficult when management deviates from a carefully explained strategy or when it makes overly optimistic earnings predictions. The result is a credibility gap.

The active buyside manager is way ahead of all but a handful of sellside analysts when it comes to valuing businesses. Corporate IR practices have adapted to this reality by seeking much more direct contact with the buyside than when I entered the field ten years ago.

My job was first and foremost to communicate one on one with the buyside. I set myself the task of identifying our 50 largest shareholders, getting to know them, and maintaining an ongoing dialogue with them. The sellside analysts came in later in the process and proved very useful in leveraging our buyside efforts.

—Alex Lehmann

When you look at the portfolio turnover of different institutional investors, you will find that there are many who are interested in little more than higher EPS next quarter. Knowing my lead-steer investors, I had to decide how much time I wanted to spend with each of them. Most important, though, 35 of the 50 largest holders in 1983 were still with us when I left the company in 1991. Investors like nothing better than holding on, provided management performs and creates value.

STERN: Judy, from your vantage point at *Business Week*, what do you make of Alex Lehmann's approach to corporate investor relations at the Whitman Corporation? Is it something that many other companies might be able to borrow?

DOBRZYNSKI: I find the approach very interesting. In my experience, companies pay far too much attention to the sellside analysts. And I think it's the companies themselves that are inviting the investment community to focus on the quarterly numbers. If companies want the analysts to focus on longer-term performance measures, they ought to start talking to the buyside people—and perhaps they could even attempt to educate the sellside in the process. Maybe the sellside isn't as limited as we're all making it out to be.

So, in an important sense, then, companies are really getting the kinds of investors they deserve. If you appeal to the lowest common denominator, that's what you'll wind up getting—at least that's the message that Alex and Joe Shenton seem to be giving us.

The Case of Equifax

STEWART: Derek, as the former CFO of Equifax, and now an Executive Vice President running one of its major business lines, you have faced this kind of issue of being evaluated periodically on an EPS basis. Your company now seems to be undergoing a transformation of sorts, a significant change in both its internal management process and in its disclosures to the investment community. Could you tell us a little about what prompted these changes?

SMITH: Let me start by saying that much of U.S. accounting and regulatory process is counterproductive and archaic. As a consequence, it is reducing the competitiveness of U.S. companies in the global marketplace. Many poor management decisions are made in order to make public companies look good in terms of improved financial results. Fortunately, some companies such as Scott and Equifax are trying to manage *value* by creating new performance measures, a "second set of books." But I contend that too many important business decisions of U.S. companies continue to be driven by short-term accounting results—by management's belief that the investment community forces them to maximize reported earnings—and by executive compensation systems that reward management according to EPS instead of long-term value.

The issue I've heard everyone discuss is how we ought to *measure* value. But, frankly, I'm not as interested in measuring value as I am in how we're going to *create* value. It's this focus on creating value, and our level of dissatisfaction with the effectiveness of conventional measurement systems in driving value, that prompted Equifax to implement a new financial framework. We wanted to redirect our overall process toward the pursuit of value—or, more precisely, to minimize any temptation provided by our accounting system to interfere with rather than encourage the creation of value.

VESELL: Could you say a little more about the difference between creating value and measuring value?

SMITH: The accounting system reflects historical performance. But, given the pace of change today and the power of on-line information technologies, these accounting *statistics* have minimal value as real-time decision tools. As CFO, I couldn't wait for reported financial results. By the time those numbers were calculated and consolidated, new market developments, competitive events, and changing conditions usually had made them obsolete.

Management at Equifax has determined that there are two critical success factors in creating value—possibly the two most important—that traditional reporting methods ignore. The first is people. We must have superior people focused on the right issues, and we must be able to monitor their performance in meeting our most critical goals. The second is the business, or management, processes Bennett mentioned earlier.

This second critical factor made us face the realities of the problems created by the accounting systems. There are simply too many ways to produce better accounting results by making business decisions that fail to add value or, even worse, reduce value. Our old system was not encouraging the kind of value-creating behavior in our operating executives that we wanted.

But, try as we might to free ourselves from the traditional system and decision rules, traditional methods and habits of behavior die hard. For every relationship investor that really will give you a long enough time horizon, there are a whole slew of conventional EPS investors who, even if they don't ultimately set your price, can certainly divert your attention.

**Accounting for Marketing:
The Case of CUC International**

STEWART: Well, let me give you an example I came across recently where this kind of conflict between ac-

counting and economics comes into play. Take the case of a cellular phone business that pays Radio Shack $500 for each new cellular subscriber it signs up. The $500 amounts to a finder's fee, a marketing outlay that will take the company about two years to recoup.

Now, because of this heavy initial outlay, which the accounting system forces you to expense entirely in the year incurred, fourth-quarter earnings would be significantly reduced by a sharp growth in new sign-ups in that quarter. And what tends to happen, I'm told, is that in the fourth quarter of every year, sales come to a standstill because people are beginning to look at the year-end earnings figures that drive their bonuses. So here's an example where an accounting policy and incentives tied to the earnings are clearly having a material adverse impact on the business.

PALEPU: But, in fact, Bennett, companies can and do capitalize some of their marketing expenditures. Paul Healy at MIT and I just finished writing a case about a company with an accounting problem very similar to the one you just described. The company, which is called CUC International, is also in an annual subscription kind of business. It's also the kind of business where you spend a lot of money signing up somebody; and then if they stay with you, you make a lot of money because the service itself doesn't cost much to deliver.

Therefore, to the extent you can retain your subscribers, you have what amounts to an annuity for a significant period of time. The problem faced by CUC's management was finding a way to communicate to the market that its marketing outlays had a promising payoff down the road.

The way CUC initially chose to communicate its prospects was to capitalize a significant portion of their

marketing outlays. But when they did so, a number of highly vocal sellside analysts criticized the accounting practice as too aggressive. So the company was faced with the choice of flouting the accounting norms endorsed by the analysts or finding some alternative method of convincing the investment community it was really creating value through these marketing outlays.

STEWART: But if they're using more conservative accounting methods, and everybody knows that, then shouldn't the higher "quality" of earnings be acknowledged by the market in the form of a higher P/E ratio? Isn't that what the theory says should happen?

PALEPU: Well, there are two reasons why that might not happen in this case. For one thing, CUC is a somewhat smaller company; and, at the time it was facing this problem, it had a relatively limited institutional following. And I happen to believe that such companies still operate in what I would call "pockets" of market inefficiency—in less efficient segments of the market.

My second point is that the problem is not just one caused by accounting distortions. There is a real economic uncertainty surrounding the payoff from these marketing outlays. That is, when you sign up new subscribers, there is no guarantee they are going to stay with you beyond a quarter or two. CUC's managers have a better handle on this than outsiders, but it is difficult to communicate this kind of information effectively.

So, to overcome this communication problem, CUC went back to conservative accounting and then undertook a very bold change in the *financial* structure of the company. They went out and borrowed a lot of money to pay a special dividend and repurchase their shares in the open market. And although this dramatic recapitalization did not lead to an immediate increase in its share value—

We used a major change in financial structure, including a significant repurchase of our stock, to accomplish two important value creation initiatives internally and to communicate that information to investors.

One, we were reducing our cost of capital through increased financial leverage. Two, we were indicating our internal commitment to increasing the capital efficiency of our ongoing businesses.

—Derek Smith

this took place over the next year or so—it did achieve one very notable change: It led to a very sharp increase in institutional ownership of CUC's shares, from 5% to 88%. And, interestingly, more active and sophisticated institutions like Tiger Management and Fidelity began reporting purchases of very large stakes.

So I would describe this as using financial change to "signal" management's confidence in the firm's prospects. And, over the two years following the recap, the value of the shares—including the large cash distribution—rose by some 96%.

BRANCATO: That story illustrates perfectly the existence of the information gap between sophisticated, fundamentals-driven investors and more passive institutions. If CUC had been able to devise an effective measure of its subscribers' satisfaction, it might not have had to resort to such a financial solution—and it might have retained its less sophisticated investor clientele in the process.

The Equifax Recap: Signalling Through Capital Structure

STERN: Derek, while you were still CFO at Equifax, the company did a somewhat similar financial recapitalization—a Dutch auction share repurchase—that was very well received by the market. What were you thinking when you did that, and what message did that send to your shareholders?

SMITH: That decision was part of a comprehensive change in the financial philosophy and measurement systems that guide our corporate decision processes at Equifax. We needed to find a way to communicate the value implications of these changes, and so our new financial structure was intended to be a powerful signal of these changes in the operating approach of the company. In effect, we used a major change in financial structure, including a significant repurchase of our stock, to accomplish two important value cre-

ation initiatives internally and to communicate that information to investors.

One, we were reducing our cost of capital through increased financial leverage. Two, we were indicating our internal commitment to increasing the capital efficiency of our ongoing businesses.

The *internal* message sent by our leveraged recapitalization was probably even more important than the external one. I was more concerned about signalling to our own management team the importance of making management decisions consistent with increasing value for our shareholders. I believe that if we do the right things internally, the market will figure out what we're doing, even it does take some time to get the point across.

STERN: Well, it didn't take much time for the market to react. My understanding is that your shares went up by some 20% within a month or two of the announcement.

VESELL: How did you decide on your capital structure? Were you driven by the rating agencies or by the economics of the business?

SMITH: We wanted to maintain a prudently leveraged capital structure—one that would enable us to command an investment-grade rating. The second part of your question is more difficult to answer. I hesitate to say that our leverage ratio was dictated entirely by the economics of the business because the rating agency decisions are driven only partly by pure economics or cash flows. As you know, there are some rating agency criteria that don't seem completely consistent with the economics of an information technology business.

To illustrate my point, a lot of Equifax's market assets are not on our books. We're in the financial and insurance information reporting business. The value of these businesses is not driven by hard assets, but by databases and information gateways that don't show up on the balance sheet. If you were using only the traditional financial ratios to assess our credit risk, none of our important assets would show up in the analysis.

STERN: If you can't kick it, how can you borrow against it?

SMITH: That's certainly the old formula. So, to keep our rating consistent with our true risk profile, we had to communicate to the agencies the unique nature of Equifax. We proved to be successful in telling our story, in part because there is a somewhat new appreciation of the ability of certain intangible assets to generate cash flow to service debt over the long term. To make your case with the rating agencies, you really have to take the initiative to educate them. But, if you take the time and do the job well, they are an intelligent and responsive audience.

VESELL: I'm frankly surprised you've succeeded in doing that; the rating agencies have a strong conservative bias.

SMITH: It wasn't easy, but we achieved a mutual understanding.

STERN: Well, Derek, if you were as persuasive with the rating agencies as you were in making the case in your most recent annual report, I can see why you were able to succeed. Equifax's new annual report provides very effective discussions of the company's new financing policy and financial measurement system.

Clientele Effects

STEWART: Joe, how would you expect the market to react to that kind of fundamental change communicated by Equifax? Would the investor base change? And what has your research shown about how different kinds of investment clienteles affect share prices?

SHENTON: Let me start by responding to the last question first. As you know,

There may be 50 investors who really determine the stock price of Scott Paper at the margin. These are the people who buy or sell in large quantities when the price falls too low or rises too high. Corporate IR strategy ought to aim for those 50 investors. If you aim your financial communications for the most sophisticated investors, they will take care of the share price.

—Joseph Shenton

Bennett, we at OLC have done some research demonstrating not only the existence of very different investor clienteles, but also that different kinds of investors tend to seek out different kinds of companies to invest in.

We started by taking ten of the most popular investment approaches and then assigned each of some 5,000 institutional investors to one of those ten categories. At one end of the spectrum is the Miller and Modigliani discounted cash flow approach that Stern Stewart has transformed into its EVA corporate performance measure—the kind that LBO investors were presumably using throughout the '80s. At the other extreme are technical analysis, indexation, and other purely computer-driven methods of trading. Between these extremes, and ranging from active to passive, are strategies like earnings momentum models, sector rotation models, and a variety of others.

Our next step was then to attempt to determine whether these different investor clienteles were attracted to different kinds of companies. For example, we used your Stern Stewart performance 1,000 rankings to come up with the following insight: As companies move up in your ranking system—thus becoming more profitable and more valuable in the view of the stock market—the more active, value-based investors increase their percentage holdings. And when companies move down in your MVA ranking system, the value-based investors bail out and the passive investors come in and take their place. (And, incidentally, I should point out that when we tried to find these clientele effects using other ranking systems like *Fortune*'s or *Business Week*'s—ranking systems that essentially measure size rather than profitability or value added, the clientele effects disappeared.)

Now, what are these clientele effects I'm talking about? Well, think about the story Derek just told us about Equifax. That story, quite frankly, wouldn't mean much to the average sellside analyst. Of course, you can talk to sellside analysts and try to educate them that the company is moving to manage for long-term economic value, but you won't get much of a response. The sellside has a vested interest in stimulating a lot of short-term trading, not in encouraging long-term investing. Consequently, their principal interest is in forecasting next quarter's EPS. To make an effect on sellside people, you really have to talk in standard EPS terms.

Early in the process of contemplating this fundamental change in its financial measurement system, Equifax decided that they were going to appeal to a fairly small group of investors—say, the 50 most sophisticated institutions out of a potential 5,000. They targeted their presentations to that group of 50, and half of those investors eventually became investors in Equifax. And this was certainly not a serendipitous event; these were the lead steer investors.

Now, what did Equifax accomplish by this? Well, what they really did was to shorten the time it took the market to place the proper value on the firm's shares. Without such a targeted IR program, it probably would have happened naturally anyway. But it would have taken much more time, and there likely would have been a lot more volatility in getting there.

The fact of the matter is, the market's ability to value shares properly depends greatly on the quality of the information management is providing. If you do a poor job of communicating with investors, you're much more likely to be undervalued at any given time. But if you instead design your communication to appeal to the people who are going to set the price—and you can figure out who they are—then you can influence the valuation of your shares.

STERN: But what about the other investors? Do you make any attempt to court them?

SHENTON: I have nothing against passive investors, but they're just not equipped to respond to fundamental issues. And it's far more cost-effective to devote a company's IR budget to influencing the views of the most sophisticated, value-based investors—most of whom, in my experience, tend to be long-term investors. In fact, such investors make their money by taking advantage of some of the short-term "noise" trading, by profiting from the fluctuations caused by less sophisticated investors' trading on the last quarter's earnings.

So, when Equifax set about communicating its story, it chose 50 investors from the active investor categories. In helping companies choose their investors, we look for investors that have taken similar risks, but without a large concentration in the given industry. For example, I would examine Gene's portfolio at Oppenheimer to evaluate whether Equifax represents a good fit. And if there were few other information services companies in the portfolio, and Oppenheimer had showed a willingness to take on companies with a moderate degree of financial risk—or, more pointedly, it had shown itself to be attracted to companies volunteering to increase their financial leverage—then we might have a nice fit.

STEWART: Joe, are you saying that relationship investors by and large fall into this top category of value-based, sophisticated, fundamentals-oriented investors?

SHENTON: Absolutely. Gene Vesell is clearly a value-based, fundamental investor. So is Warren Buffett. When I was at Northwest Industries in the '70s, Buffett was a 5% holder and that was relationship investing.

And let me make one very critical point about shareholder communications. Disclosure is not a one-way communication; it's really about establishing a two-way channel. Effective corporate IR means seeking out and listening to influential investors. This can help management design the performance measures that investors find useful. It's this kind of two-way communication and beneficial exchange that is the ultimate goal of relationship investing.

STEWART: If a company finds that it has an inordinately high proportion of passive investors, does that tell you anything?

SHENTON: If you have mostly passive or short-term investors—and a lot of companies do—it's either because your company is reasonably well run and has taken the attitude the market will take care of itself, or it is poorly run and value-based investors have bailed out. One thing our research has disclosed is that a "passive neglect" approach to corporate IR—as reflected by an increasing proportion of passive, short-term investors—is associated with an *increase* in a company's beta. That's very clear from our data. On the other hand, having lots of value investors can be bad news as well as good. A sharp increase in value investors could mean they sense a change of management control in the offing.

But, in general, it's good to have value-based investors. For example, look at what is happening in healthcare today. The most sophisticated investors are seizing profit opportunities created by the general devastation of healthcare stocks. These investors were not short-term earnings momentum or sector types; they were long-term investors taking advantage of the opportunities created by such short-term trading strategies.

STEWART: Does having more active, sophisticated investors typically lead to a better dialogue with management, and thus to better corporate governance?

SHENTON: Well, that's likely to be true if management's primary objective is to maximize the value of the company's shares. If your interests as a manager are identical with those of investors, then you clearly want to communicate regularly and clearly with investors. They should be viewed as your partners in the enterprise.

But if management is not completely committed to maximizing value, then they're not likely to want to get too close to investors. In such cases, the long-term, sophisticated investors are not likely to hold your shares. And the short-term, passive types that will hold your shares will effectively keep the firm on a very tight tether, responding to every blip in quarterly earnings.

Superactive Investors: The Case of the Lens Fund

STEWART: Let's now turn to Nell Minow, who, together with Bob Monks, recently launched the Lens Fund. Nell, how would you characterize the Lens Fund? Are you just an ordinary active investor, or does your style take you off the charts?

MINOW: We're very much off the charts. Normally, when you talk about active versus passive investors, you're really just talking about whether they're buying or selling. We are in the business of active management of the ownership rights conferred by common stock. Most money managers buy stock that they hope will go up. We buy stock and then we try to make it go up ourselves by exercising the rights that come with share ownership.

Our first case study was at Sears, where we used our initial purchase of

Relationship investing is not something new; it's been with us since the days of the joint stock companies and Adam Smith. Whether we're talking about venture capital for start-ups, LBOs for mature companies, or the management of large public companies, the essence of relationship investing is the same: it's having large-stake investors, and supplying them with information about and some measure of influence over corporate strategic decisions.

—Nell Minow

100 shares to initiate a process that led eventually to the break-up of a company that had become too large and lost its focus. By the time that break-up took place, we had accumulated enough shares to make up all of our costs (including a full page ad in *The Wall Street Journal* that called the board of directors a "nonperforming asset") and then some.

I would like to comment on a couple of the things that have been said. I was especially interested in Professor Zimmerman's opening point that the fundamental purpose of accounting was to monitor the stewardship function of corporate management. It seems to me that the real issue underlying this discussion is that of stewardship: Are managers doing the best possible job for the shareholders whom they supposedly represent, or are there signficant agency costs arising from conflicts of interest between management and shareholders?

Now, in order to answer this question, investors need good information. When I'm looking for information, I want the kind of information that will best help me to evaluate what the CEO and directors are doing. I don't need to hear everything that they hear in the boardroom; my agenda as a shareholder is limited, which is one consequence of my limited liability. But, as Bob Monks and I said in our book *Power and Accountability*, there is a reason accounting principles are called "generally accepted" and not "certifiably accurate." The best you can say is that they provide some consistency. You may be comparing apples and apples, but that does not answer your question about tomatoes. For this reason, Bennett, I think you are wrong to dismiss the relevance of nonfinancial measures for shareholders—I think that Carolyn Brancato and Ned Regan are on to something potentially quite valuable.

I also have another major objection to something I heard earlier. In communicating with investors, companies should not underestimate the importance of index investors. Information is not just about buying and selling, gentlemen. Information is about how you behave as an owner. And index investors can become very active as owners. Certainly that's been true of CALPERS, Wells Fargo, and a number of institutions I've worked with. And let me tell you that these institutions, even the indexers, want all the information they can get. If institutional investors didn't want information and influence, Bob Monks and I would not have started the Lens Fund.

What kinds of information do they want? Well, one thing they clearly value is all the information they can get about executive compensation plans. One piece of information that is not currently required, but one I find immensely useful, is the dilution impact of stock option plans. And my old firm, Institutional Shareholder Services, helps a lot of institutional investors by providing them with this information.

Now, I agree with Joe Shenton that relationship investing is not something new; it's been with us since the days of the joint stock companies and Adam Smith. Relationship investing has in fact been crucial to economic development (if it had not taken hold, we would be living in a socialist society today). As an entrepreneur myself, when I go to seek venture capital, the first thing the venture capitalist asks me is, how many seats can he have on the board? And this is the essence of relationship investing, whether we're talking about venture capital for start-ups, LBOs for mature companies, or the management of large public companies. It's having large-stake investors, and supplying them with information about and

some measure of influence over corporate strategic decisions.

In the case of Eastman Kodak, we intend to stay with Kodak to see through some major changes. We put our money where our mouth is. And if you get our money, you're going to get our mouth. And Joe Shenton is quite right, by the way, in saying that the best corporate executives will want to listen to what we have to say.

STERN: How long have you been in Kodak?

MINOW: Since the fund began—that is, about a year ago.

STERN: Why did you get into Kodak in the first place? Or, more generally, how do you choose to make your investments?

MINOW: We have invested in four companies to date. It's our intention to be substantial investors in no more than four companies at any given time, so that we can pay very careful attention to each of them.

One of our investment criteria is significantly substandard rates of return over several time horizons: one-year, three-year, and five-year periods. We work with Batterymarch, which provides all kinds of numbers for us on strategic momentum. We want to know if they're drifting downward or if they've already started to go back up.

We also do things like NEXIS searches on management to see whether we can isolate management as the variable that is depressing the stock. We're looking for companies where there's the largest possible gap between the value that could be there and the value that the market is showing. And it has to be a gap that we can influence. If it's a company that has industry-wide problems, if it's in a heavily regulated industry, or if management has a substantial number of shares, then we're not going to get into it. It has to be something where we can affect the outcome by

acting as shareholders, within the authority and by using the rights that accompany stock ownership.

STERN: How do you decide when it's time to get out? Kodak, for example, recently took a very positive step by encouraging its managers to buy stock in the company.

MINOW: Yes, we were thrilled about it.

STERN: And the stock price has since gone up by more than 25%. What else do you think they might do to enhance its value?

MINOW: We continue to believe that Kodak is highly susceptible to change if pushed. The imaging technology in their business is changing very dramatically and they have invested heavily in it. But their efforts to diversify have been disastrous, and we think that there's money to be made by reversing the process.

STEWART: I think there's two major changes Kodak can make. One, as you suggest, they can unwind the diversification. They have a very large chemical company, they have imaging, they have photography, and they have the pharmaceuticals company. Simply splitting the company into pieces—whether as independent companies through spin-offs to shareholders or by selling some of the businesses to other companies—should create considerable value.

The second thing you could do would be to stop using the huge gross profit margins on film to subsidize other businesses. As in so many conglomerates I've observed, the cash flows from the profitable businesses end up being wasted on organizational inefficiencies; they never make it down to the bottom line. Kodak has a huge management infrastructure that is crying out to be rationalized by going through the kind of core process redesign that has been laying off middle managers across America. Either Kodak's top management just can't make the hard decisions, or they've lost sight of the fact that it's execution that matters. It's not grandiose strategic thinking, but process redesign that makes the difference these days.

MINOW: That's right. And results are what the compensation scheme has to be designed to promote. And that's what the board has to be designed to promote.

STERN: Nell, are there certain kinds of nonfinancial measures you have asked Kodak to provide?

MINOW: We wrote Kodak a 22-page letter filled with questions about options we wanted them to consider. All but one page described strategic and financial initiatives; one page related to governance issues, focusing on the relationship between shareholders and directors. We did not say we wanted them to make those changes immediately. Rather, we said we were intelligent people with a significant financial investment at stake. And that, given the limits of *publicly available information*, we had certain questions that we wanted to explore with management. We met with Whitmore and Steffen several times, and we continue to be in close contact with the company.

PALEPU: Would you make public the brief that you wrote Kodak?

MINOW: It's not public at the moment, and won't be unless our communication with management breaks down.

PALEPU: But, if you're convinced your analysis is correct, why not make the document public and rally the support of other investors? This may give you even more leverage with management than you have now.

MINOW: True, but until we feel that leverage is needed, our approach is less confrontational. First we go to the CEO. If that works, fine; then we don't need to go farther. If that doesn't work, then we go to the board of

directors. And if that doesn't work, and only then, do we go to the shareholders, and the press.

VESELL: What is your exit strategy?

MINOW: We have an exit price in mind when we go in—although that is subject to continuous revision. In fact, we have already taken some gains in Kodak because the price run-up made it more than 25% of our portfolio. We are designed to be an enhancement to an indexed portfolio. At the moment, it's all our own money, but we hope to change that fairly soon.

VESELL: How do you determine the price at which you're going to sell?

MINOW: Based on a sort of a traditional investment-banker, break-up-value analysis. This is not going to continue to be our strategy forever, but all the companies in our portfolio at the moment are there because they are conglomerates. That's one thing shareholders really have the information and the power to change in underperforming companies; they get to decide whether this should really be one big, diversifed company or three separate companies. That's where there's the biggest opportunity to add value.

STEWART: Nell, what you are saying is that the '80s ended too soon. The deconglomeration wave reached as far as R.J. Reynolds; but, when it receded, we still had companies like Procter & Gamble and Sears and GM that needed to be restructured back into their basic parts. So, what you and Bob Monks are really now doing is the unfinished work of the restructuring of the '80s.

MINOW: Well, I think of what we're doing as a refinement of the takeover era. The takeover era brought some very important corrections, but it did so in a brutal and scattershot way. I think that we can do it in a more humane and, ultimately, more efficient way.

STERN: Four at a time? It may take forever at that rate. I would hope that just the threat of the Lens Fund owning stock would prompt many underperforming companies to reform from within—even if you never arrive. That would be a true sign of your effectiveness.

MINOW: I agree. In fact, I think the most telling measure of our success will be when the announcement of our investment becomes itself a buy signal to the general market. And I think that will happen. When Steffen's departure was announced yesterday, we got about a dozen phone calls from institutional investors with substantial stakes in Kodak asking us what we were going to do and if we wanted their help.

VESELL: What have been the results of your approach to date?

MINOW: As we near the end of the first year, we have substantially outperformed the S&P index with a 20.5% return. It would be about twice that if Westinghouse hadn't continued to be so recalcitrant. But keep your eyes on Westinghouse.

Incentive Compensation as a Substitute for Takeovers

STEWART: In 1985, CEOs or CFOs would likely have been concerned about their stock prices in large part because of the threat of hostile takeover. That threat seems to have all but disappeared. Basil, are you still concerned about Scott Paper's stock price? And are you more or less concerned than, say, back in the mid-1980s?

ANDERSON: In fact, I would argue that, because of fairly recent changes in our incentive compensation plan, the management and employees of Scott Paper are probably *more* concerned about our stock price today than they were five or ten years ago. In the past, our company's compensation philosophy was to pay higher-than-average salaries and modest bonuses. Today, our salaries are set at roughly the median level for large companies, but there is lots more incentive-based pay and stock options. So my own personal compensation, as well as that of most of our top executives, now depends significantly on how the stock performs.

STEWART: Nell, do you find now that the new SEC disclosures on management compensation are helpful to you as an investor? Do you think that's a productive change?

MINOW: Yes, I'm absolutely delighted about it. In fact, I think the disclosures provided by the compensation committee are the most important ones of all for investors. I want to know what companies are trying to achieve with the compensation plan. It's not how much the CEO gets paid, but the goals the company is setting for him. Are they trying to maximize earnings per share or long-term economic value? I like to see these goals spelled out clearly. But if I instead see just a lot of boilerplate in the compensation report, then I become very suspicious.

STEWART: Then you would agree with Michael Jensen that it's not how much we pay our CEOs that really matters, but rather how they are paid?

MINOW: Very much so. I want to see that the interests of the shareholders and the managers are closely aligned. If that's the case, then I'm delighted if the CEO makes a bundle.

But, at the same time, let me repeat a recent remark by Bud Crystal that really struck me. He said that if you go short on every company that gives restrictive stock grants to the CEO, you're going to make out like crazy. Why? Because that company is effectively saying, "We don't think the stock's going to go up, but we want the CEO to get something anyway." It reminds me of Sears' grant to Mr. Martinez of yet another "guaranteed bonus." A guaranteed bonus—which,

incidentally, is my favorite oxymoron—really tells you something about whether the man is willing to bet on himself or not.

CHEW: The same thing seems to hold for relationship investors. There's a study that demonstrates that when Warren Buffett and other relationship investors buy common stock, then that's a buy signal for the other stockholders—the stock will outperform market averages over the next few years. But if Buffett takes a convertible preferred instead of the common, then that's a sell signal. The signal, as you suggest, Nell, is in the structure of the contract.

MINOW: Yes, and that's the reason that the compensation committee report is going to be tremendously important.

As for other potentially valuable nonfinancial disclosures, I was very much influenced by Dick Crawford's book about human capital. I'd like to know from companies how much money they're spending on training and their employee turnover rate. I also look at the quality of the products and the extent to which there is a commitment to total quality management. If somebody gets the Baldridge Award, I think that's very useful information.

I also love to see disclosures about the governance component of the company. I want to make sure that they have a governance system that encourages listening. This includes having a majority of independent directors, an independent nominating committee, and, perhaps most important, regular private meetings of the independent directors without the CEO or other company employees. And I look to see the level of activism in the company. If I bought every company that CALPERs targeted, I would be making terrific returns. Last year, on an investment of $500,000, CALPERS made $137 mil-

lion in extraordinary returns in their shareholder initiative program. And I would defy anybody in the room to find another investment that made that kind of return.

Investing for the Long Run

STEWART: Gene, how do you contrast your approach in investing with that of the Lens Fund? It seems there's some similarities in that you both take major stakes—but you're not quite as provocative.

VESELL: Well, I'd say we're not quite as *vocal*. We may in fact be equally provocative.

STEWART: Do you make recommendations to companies that they make certain changes?

VESELL: We certainly do. We are not at all hesitant to talk about things that we think we know something about. Such things would generally be financial rather than operational, often involving management compensation.

But incentive compensation is by no means a panacea. We've found, to paraphrase Buffett, that if you have good assets but you're not in bed with good people, the people will win out. It's very hard to make money if you've got a really bad management. Most of the scars I have acquired during my years in this business have come from situations where we attempted to combine good assets and bad people.

STEWART: But you don't have an investment in Kodak or Sears. Why is that?

VESELL: It's not our cup of java. We try, in general, to invest in good businesses; and, in some instances, the businesses are better than the accounting results would suggest. We know Chris Steffen very well because we own about 10% of Honeywell, and we're very familiar with what he did there. We're just not knowledgeable enough about Kodak. We don't swing at every pitch.

DOBRZYNSKI: Do you have a predetermined exit point? How and when do you decide to get out and take a gain?

VESELL: When we go into a company, we establish what we think is the rational economic value of the enterprise; and we buy if that value is significantly higher than the current stock price. But once we buy a company, our time horizon—as Buffett said when he bought his stake in Coca Cola—is forever. We don't want to sell.

In fact what we want to achieve is the continuous value creation, if you will, that can be achieved by a management intent on maximizing cash flow over the long haul. If the assets are managed correctly, and if the free cash is either reinvested in projects above the cost of capital or returned to shareholders (if there are no promising projects), then management can achieve continuous value creation. And's that the process we try to foster at Oppenheimer-owned companies. But, when we live with our investments for a long time, we constantly monitor the price/value relationships of our companies very carefully.

STEWART: Gene, you heard Derek Smith talk about share repurchase earlier, and you just mentioned it now. How do you look at dividends, which are just another way of distributing cash to investors? Does dividend yield or dividend payout enter into your valuation method?

VESELL: No, not really. Dividends are just one of several ways you can return your excess capital to investors—and we prefer stock repurchase.

STEWART: Do you typically tender your shares into repurchase offers?

VESELL: Only if the offer is made at a large premium over the stock price. Otherwise, and provided we feel it's a company in which want to increase our investment, we almost always choose to increase our proportional ownership instead of tendering our shares.

STERN: Gene, are there big risks to you from having to pay a huge premium to take a large equity position to get in, or from having to take a huge discount to get out?

VESELL: Not if we're correct in our buying or selling decisions. Because we're typically buying things that are out of favor and other people are selling, it's surprisingly easy to buy them. And if the company does well, then it should be relatively easy to get out.

Let me give you an example. At one time we owned as much as 25% of Fruit of the Loom. We started buying it at $12 or $13, and then it went down to six or seven. So we had no trouble buying all we wanted. We own somewhere between 5% and 10% of the company now. We started selling it in the high 30s and then sold more in the high 40s. There was no problem selling it at that point in time.

So if you're right, there's no problem. And even if you're wrong—we have owned a lot of American Express and haven't done very well with it—there can still be plenty of liquidity.

Indexed Activists: The Case of New York State

STERN: Let me turn back to Ned Regan, who, as I mentioned earlier, is now serving out his next to last day as a public servant. Ned, Joe Shenton has sort of suggested that it may not be worth companies' spending much time with indexers like your New York State fund. Yet you've defied his expectations in a way by becoming an active investor in a number of cases. Would you tell us why you've chosen this unusual blend of activeness and passivity?

REGAN: Well, it's not just New York State. There are other pension funds getting involved in corporate governance on a selective basis. This involves hundreds of billions of dollars of assets, and it's growing.

Our own system for investing is quite different from what we've heard described today. We don't look at compensation and most other governance issues. I don't care about inside boards or outside boards. In fact, there are just two important considerations for us—and what I'm about to say is probably true of many of the large public pension funds. First, we are virtually permanent owners; we don't sell—and so we are concerned only about the long-term performance *prospects* of corporations. Second, we try to identify chronic underperformers. Having done so, we then attempt to determine if and how their strategy, their culture, and ultimately their performance can be improved—and, most important, whether the board understands this. After we identify these companies, we don't play the chase-the-headlines-and-gang-up-on-them game, provided they understand what needs to be done.

STEWART: Is that because you're convinced that these more forceful actions would not work?

REGAN: It's because we are permanent owners and have a fiduciary duty to do something constructive about the egregious underperformers in the portfolio.

STERN: Isn't it true, though, Ned, that your forebearance could partly reflect something else? It may be dictated in part by the fact that your own personal net worth is not affected by the potential increases in the value of the portfolio if you became even more active? You don't get paid based on the performance of the portfolio.

REGAN: Of course not. But I do get elected based on it. The taxpayers contribute next to nothing to our pension fund, and they like that. I could get re-elected on that alone.

STERN: Well, let me put it this way. Let's say you knew that if the value of the New York State portfolio went up by 20% during your tenure, you would have a very strong assurance of being re-elected. Now, the question I'm asking is this: What if you could double that amount to 40% by becoming even more activist than you are now? Would you consider doing it? Or would you acquire a reputation as a trouble maker among your political colleagues?

REGAN: Well, these are not matters that I really think about much. Again, our approach is very simple: We're permanent owners (and, as I said, there are hundreds of billions managed by funds like ours). And we have a fiduciary duty to do something about the clearly identified underperformers in the permanent portfolio.

We have developed our own system for picking the underperformers. And, on the basis of that system, we recently identified National Medical Enterprises and A&P. In the case of National Medical Enterprises, we had become quite involved with the company well before its problems made the headlines. And we're now in the midst of discussions with A&P as to whether we will solicit votes against their board. We also came across A&P before *Forbes* or anyone else ran stories on them.

Of course, two swallows a spring don't make, but we think we're on the right track. And, from my vantage point, it appears that some of the large public pension funds are headed in a very similar direction—and for the very simple reason I just mentioned: If you're not going to sell that underperforming stock, what are you going to do about it?

STERN: Why don't you sell it?

REGAN: Because we're indexed, we're permanent owners. There are probably no more than 200 people in

the country who understand the biggest investment movement in the country—and thousands of well-informed people who don't. I am continually amazed by the level of ignorance about the large public institutional investors in this country. We've been indexed, permanent owners for twelve years, it's no secret. Ten or eleven years ago we were the largest indexer in the country. We had more assets indexed than all the rest combined. But all that's changed. Now there's some $300 or $400 billion being indexed in this way.

But, to come back to your original question, Joel, we don't sell stocks because we are civil-servant oriented; we're a long way from being professional stock pickers. And, as you know, over the long run, indexed funds outperform 75 or 80% of all professional money managers.

I would also tell you that, when running an indexed fund, it is very important to maintain the discipline of the index—in our case, we index against the S&P 500 and 400 and the Russell 2000. By selling just one stock, I would be undermining the discipline of the index. In fact I once discovered that, when I turned my back, my staff at the other end of the hall just couldn't resist doing the same thing—deviating from the index. They wanted to create their own "enhanced" S&P 500 in the worst way, but I quickly stopped that.

So we rode IBM down but we rode everything else up. And, as most of you probably know, New York State has been very well served by just matching billions of dollars against the S&P 500. We pay about $20,000 a year to manage the $20 billion we have in indexed equities—and we have simply ridden the market up over the past 12 years. If we hadn't been indexing, our asset management fees would have run $30-40 million per year.

So, we don't deviate from the index. Adhering to the discipline is essential. And I think my staff's the best in the country.

STERN: But what does that mean when you say they're the best in the country? They're the best at earning the market rate of return?

REGAN: We have the lowest transaction costs of any of the pension funds. The annual costs of running our $60 billion fund are well below a million dollars. As a consequence, New York taxpayers have gotten what amounts to a free ride on the stock market boom of the last 12 years.

STEWART: Ned, could you tell us more how you would go about energizing poorly performing companies?

REGAN: It's a fairly deliberate process. In the case of National Medical Enterprises, we filed a resolution with the company just last week—but this was after lengthy analysis that revealed to us that the company is in trouble. Similarly, in the case of A&P, we started to analyze their problems at least six months ago.

STEWART: So, although you can't pick stocks that are undervalued in the classic Graham and Dodd fundamental sense, you can pick stocks that have underperformed. And then you can use the voting power that comes with your shares, together with the voting power of the other funds, to bring management to the table. Like Nell Minow, you serve as catalyst investors to bring about dramatic change in those companies.

REGAN: But many large public investors do this, although we don't make a lot of noise about it. In fact, we deliberately avoid publicity when doing this. When I told the *Wall Street Journal* and the *New York Times* about A&P, they ran awful stories saying that I was waging a "proxy war." As a consequence, I didn't say a word to them about National Medical Enterprises.

VESELL: I know something about A&P. We used to own 10% of the shares. A German family owns 51% of it.

REGAN: That's right. We think that family has one idea in mind, and it is not the minority shareholders. So, we are planning to mount a solicitation of the 50 largest minority shareholders to withhold the vote from the board of directors.

STEWART: Is this Joe Grundfest's "just vote no" approach?

REGAN: That's right. We've done some very elaborate analysis of the company, which we have shared with the company and will share with the other shareholders. And we'll probably do something similar with National Medical Enterprises when their shareholder's meeting comes around, which is not for another six months or so.

So what is our motivation here for doing all this? I get satisfaction—and there are dozens of public pension fund trustees like myself—just from my sense of doing my job correctly. It has nothing to do with money. When we saw the problem at National Medical Enterprises, we acted to uphold our fiduciary duty to our beneficiaries to maximize the return to the fund. And you're going to see a lot more public pension funds doing the same thing in the next few years. I don't know what name you people will give that kind of investing, but that's what's coming.

STEWART: Ned, it seems to me that your two levers to promote change are the vote and the publicity that comes with public office.

REGAN: But I have never sought public attention for this activity; in fact, I've discouraged it.

STEWART: But, without some kind of a threat, aren't you just a paper tiger?

BRANCATO: I don't see how you could view somebody with $60 billion under management as a paper tiger.

REGAN: Our approach is to influence companies through relatively private dialogue, at least initially. What we are doing is to file resolutions with individual companies asking for changes in the corporate by-laws that would require the proxy to be opened to long-term shareholders to put in a couple of hundred words analyzing the performance of the company. The independent directors would then have the right to counter with their own couple of hundred words. By putting this dialogue in the corporate proxy, we could limit the excesses of the media that I prefer to avoid. Of course, we need some media exposure, but this would enable us to contain the excesses that come with a telephone call or a press release.

STEWART: Forgive me for pressing this point, but I just don't see how such indirect means can force really recalcitrant managements to move.

REGAN: Well, let me put it this way. We do a report showing chronic underperformance, and then we share that with management and the board. If they don't respond, then we send this report to other fiduciaries with a cover letter that says: "We have determined that you hold this stock in your portfolio. Here's a 20-page study that shows that this company is underperforming and, most important, has no interest in reforming. You, as a fiduciary, should withhold your vote from this board. If you don't, you are breaching your duty because the value of your portfolio is going to remain unnecessarily low unless you help us initiate change." So hopefully they vote with us and we end up with, say, a 35% vote against the board.

STEWART: Fantastic. That's just what I wanted to hear you say.

STERN: Well, this is a most fortunate ending to this discussion—because I really wanted to give Ned Regan the last word before going off to his new assignment. It also gives us the opportunity to salute him for a job well done.

REGAN: Joel, you may take this as my last word as a public official.

"LEAD STEER" ROUNDTABLE
New York City, May 9, 1989

JOEL STERN: On behalf of both the Continental Bank's *Journal of Applied Corporate Finance* and the National Investor Relations Institute's (NIRI) Education Foundation, I would like to welcome you all this morning to our roundtable discussion. I would also like to thank the management of NYNEX for allowing us the use of their boardroom for this session.

For the past 25 years or so, I have been trying to spread some ideas about what academic research has told us is supposed to account for the market values of securities. What we want to accomplish here today is to ask people who are significant players in the money management business "lead steers" I like to call them-what they think are the principal determinants of market value. In the process, we would also like to find out whether there are indeed such people as the "lead steers." Are there just a handful of dominant sophisticated investors that effectively set market prices for individual stocks, or does the small investor also play an important role in the pricing process?

The reason I think such issues important is that over the years I've had the opportunity of speaking at board meetings and management committee meetings at well over a thousand companies. In the overwhelming majority of cases, I have encountered responses that range from the politic (something like "well, you may be right, but I have trouble squaring that with my own experience") to the somewhat less civil ("you can't be serious, the market certainly doesn't behave like that").

I do have a store of fond memories, however. And one of my favorites took place on a day when Binkley Shorts and I appeared on *Wall Street Week.* On that day, Capital Cities Communications announced it was acquiring ABC; and unlike many of the acquisitions that have been announced in recent years, the stock price of the acquiring company went up, and substantially. Capital Cities' shares increased upon the announcement from $165 to almost $175. But, what is more remarkable, on the very next day it was announced that Warren Buffet's Berkshire Hathaway was going to acquire a very large equity stake in this transaction at approximately $185 a share. Upon that announcement, the shares of Capital Cities rose from $175 to over $200 in very short order.

Events like this one persuade me that there is some very important expectational role played by people like Warren Buffet and perhaps like some of the people who are in this room. And we would like to find out from them today whether the things that academics feel are important in the valuation process are the same factors that make professional money managers and security analysts feel that shares are under- or over-valued in analyzing securities and in managing portfolios.

I'd like to begin by raising the issue of valuation within a very narrow context-that is, what is the engine that drives the value of a firm? Later on this morning, we'll devote time to the restructuring questions that have become important in the last few year-such as the impact on value of LBOs and other large recapitalizations, and the resulting changes in management incentives. We want to find out not only why those things seem to matter, but why they seem to matter now and didn't seem to be so important 15 or 20 years ago.

■

Before I start, let me introduce our distinguished group of panelists. They divide fairly neatly into two groups, practitioners and academics. I will start with our practitioners:

CHUCK BRUNIE is chairman of the NYSE listed Oppenheimer Capital, an investment counseling firm he started two decades ago. It currently manages about $17 billion.

CARL FERENBACH is one of the partners of Berkshire Partners, which has done over 30 leveraged buy-outs. Carl used to run M&A for Merrill Lynch.

DICK FREDERICKS is a General Partner and the senior bank analyst for Montgomery Securities (and a very good one I might add).

JOSEPH GRUNDFEST is Commissioner of the SEC and has been a leader in bringing economic-based analysis to bear on regulatory issues.

JOHN LAFFERTY is an Executive Vice President of Stein Roe & Farnham, and Director of Quantitative Research. Stein Roe has $18 billion under management.

BINKLEY SHORTS is a Senior Vice President of Wellington Management Company, which manages $38 billion.

BENNETT STEWART is my colleague at Stern Stewart.

Our representatives from the academic world are:

31

YAKOV AMIHUD, who is a visiting Professor of Finance at New York University, but whose permanent position is at Tel Aviv University.

BARUCH LEV is the Niemela Professor of Accounting at the University of California at Berkeley as well as a trustee of NIRI's Education Foundation.

RICHARD ZECKHAUSER is Ramsey Professor of Political Economy at Harvard University's Kennedy School of Government.

■

PART I: THE VALUATION OF STOCKS

I would like to start by asking a question of Binkley Shorts. Binkley, I once heard you say on *Wall Street Week* that you don't think dividends are very important in the valuation process. What did you mean by that?

BINKLEY SHORTS: As a small cap manager, I'm looking for companies that will appreciate dramatically over a long period of time. For such companies, the dividend policy is an "inverse" reflection, if you will, of the firm's ability to profitably reinvest their capital in their business. A high dividend carries with it the implication that the company has few good investment opportunities in its own business. So, although dividends may give you current income, they can also be a sign that future growth is limited.

STERN: But there are highly capital-intensive industries that need huge sums of money for investment every year, and yet they too pay fairly sizable dividends as a percentage of their earnings and their cash flow. How do you account for their behavior? I'm not just referring to public utilities now, but to companies in forest products, steel, aluminum, and cement. All of these industries have historically paid fairly high dividends relative to their earnings, and all the while they have essentially been paying it out with one hand and recapturing it with the other either through borrowings or through new equity offerings. Why shouldn't firms that you follow do the same thing if they want to sell at a higher price?

SHORTS: A company that reaches a given level of maturity typically tries to repackage itself for a different kind of investment group than my own. In order to do that, they may be trying to offer different investment characteristics and they may have expectations that that's what their share-

■

IN CASES WHERE THE Q RATIO IS GREATER THAN ONE, THE STOCK MARKET DOES NOT RESPOND POSITIVELY TO ANNOUNCEMENTS OF DIVIDEND INCREASES. IN THESE CASES, THE MARKET APPEARS CONTENT TO HAVE THE FIRM REINVEST THE EARNINGS PRESUMABLY BECAUSE IT FEELS THE FIRM'S INTERNAL REINVESTMENT OPPORTUNITIES ARE GOOD.

—YAKOV AMIHUD—

holder base wants. A small growth company, by contrast, would attempt to offer its investors a very different set of characteristics.

YAKOV AMIHUD: Some recent research supports Binkley's viewpoint in the following way. It shows that the market's reaction to dividend increases differs across two different kinds of companies. The study begins by splitting the sample of dividend-increasing companies into two groups: those whose "Q ratio" (the market value divided by the replacement value of the assets) is higher than one and those with Q ratios less than one. Those firms announcing increases in the dividend with Q ratios below one see a significant increase in share price. The low Q ratios can be interpreted as a sign that the market thinks the firm has been "overinvesting, " in which case investors would rather have the money outside of the firm and in their own hands. In cases where the Q ratio is greater than one, however, the stock market does not respond positively to announcements of dividend increases. In these cases, the market appears content to have the firm reinvest the earnings presumably because it feels the firm's internal reinvestment opportunities are good.

STERN: But this brings me back to my earlier question: How do you account

for the behavior of those types of firms that are essentially turning right back to the market to raise new equity to recapture the dividends they have just paid out? An example, incidentally, would be the commercial banks. If you add up the dividends of the 10 money center banks over the last 6 or 7 years, you find that almost 100% of the dividends paid were recaptured by those banks by raising new equity. Imagine paying out all that capital with the one hand, only to ask for it back with the other.

CHUCK BRUNIE: But, Joel, the banks don't really need capital. There hasn't been a bank failure in this century when that bank did not have a capital ratio above the legal requirement; the bankruptcies resulted from liquidity shortages. The industry has excess capital because Congress insists on it.

STERN: Yes, but I still don't understand how banks are better served by going through the process of paying out the dividends when they will then have to go right back out to raise new equity to meet their capital requirements.

Dick, why don't we ask you that question? You're the senior banking specialist we have here. Why do the major banks seem to continue to pay out dividends as if the problems of the last 10 years have no bearing at all?

DICK FREDERICKS: The first thing I would note is that banking is a mature business; so the prospects for growth and price appreciation are limited. And while your characterization of the 10 money center banks is correct, there is another side to this issue. Those banks can have a growing dividend, or just maintain a flat dividend, and still provide some return to investors even when their stock prices are not appreciating much. If you look at S & P returns over a long period of time, you will see that dividends are a significant part of investor returns.

STERN: I guess the question I really should have asked is this: Do you believe that the total rate of return that would be earned by an investor would in any way be altered by the dividend policy? That is, if you get dividends in one hand, don't you lose the same amount of capital appreciation potential on the other-and generally on the day the stock goes ex-dividend? So, if there are no free lunches here, and what you gain in dividends you must lose in capital gains, then why is there such a fetish for paying cash dividends?

JOHN LAFFERTY: I can give you one answer that goes back to the Tax Reform Act of 1986. Because of tax reduction, the "keep rate" on dividend income since Reagan took office has gone from 30 cents on the dollar to 72 cents. The keep rate on capital gains, by contrast, has fallen from 80 cents to 72 cents. And if you then factor in inflation, there has been a significant shift in tax policies that once favored capital gains over ordinary income. Based on tax factors alone, market preferences have recently been in a multi-year shift away from capital gains and toward dividend income. This shift may well have run its course, but we think the "demand" for dividends has been significantly increased by the fact that Congress has reduced the rate of taxation on them relative to capital gains.

STERN: I have a problem with that. You say that the capital gains tax today is higher than it was recently and that the dividend income tax has come down considerably with the decline in the personal income tax rate. But the fact is, the capital gains tax rate is zero unless you volunteer to sell off some shares. There are alternative ways for you to recover capital from the firm without voluntarily paying a tax. The tax can be avoided, for example, simply by borrowing modest amounts of money against the value of the portfolio.

LAFFERTY: Certainly true. But, I've always had difficulty with the argu-

■

THE DIVIDEND PAYOUT RATIO IS SYSTEMATICALLY LOWER, ON AVERAGE, IN FIRMS WHERE MANAGEMENT IS A LARGE SHAREHOLDER. IN THESE CASES, I'M CONFIDENT THAT MANAGEMENT KNOWS WHAT'S GOOD FOR THE STOCKHOLDERS BECAUSE THEY ARE THEMSELVES MAJOR STOCKHOLDERS.

—YAKOV AMIHUD—

ment that individuals can leverage up unleveraged firms by a phone call to their banker. It certainly can be done. But, this doesn't change the fact that the capital gains tax rate is factored into the price people are willing to pay for a company in the stock market. Someone will ultimately pay the tax. Because that tax is levied on inflation as well as real gains, and given the current level of inflation, we may now be looking at an effective 60% rate of taxation on capital gains.

AMIHUD: One problem with this discussion so far, I think, is that we are implicitly assuming that management acts on behalf of the shareholders. At the same time, however, I would point out that there is a systematic difference in dividend policy between firms in which management holds a substantial proportion of the shares and firms which are not closely held. In fact, we observe that the dividend payout ratio is systematically lower, on average, in firms where management is a large shareholder. In these cases, I'm confident that management knows what's good for the stockholders because they are themselves major stockholders.

So, from this observation alone, I would be tempted to argue that it may not be in the best interest of shareholders, on average, for companies to make large dividend payments. On the other hand, dividend payments may play an important role in

the large, widely held public corporation in dealing with the problem of the separation of ownership from control that exists in such companies. In particular, it may be useful in conveying information to outside investors and in returning excess "free cash flow" to investors.

STERN: Joe, to follow up on Yakov's comment, do you think it would be a good idea, from a public policy standpoint, to encourage managements of firms to have larger equity stakes in the firms they manage? This might strengthen their incentive to act in the interest of their shareholders.

JOSEPH GRUNDFEST: I think it would be a terrific idea to relate the compensation of managements more closely to criteria that measure economic performance. In many large public companies today, the position of CEO is a sinecure in which the CEO starts receiving his pension while he is still running the corporation. If you have a look at the research in this area, you will come across some very interesting findings. For example, the data suggest that it may be easier to be indicted as a member of Congress than it is to be fired as CEO of a large corporation. That says something about the lack of the disciplining effect that emanates from the board. Not many boards are willing to actually step in and say to a CEO, "Look, you're not doing a good job, and we can't afford to let you serve to the age of 65 and retire gracefully. You're out today and we're going to get somebody in here who really knows what he's doing."

That's the stick, but a board also has to provide a carrot. Some research indicates that there's a lot of "post hockery" in compensation decisions. If a company has a good year, it's all because the CEO is a genius. If the company has a bad year, the results are attributed to "macro effects" that the CEO can't possibly control. As a result, salaries tend to rocket upward; and if they ever go down, they tend not to go down by very much. When they go up, however, they tend to go up by more significant amounts. In general, my argument would not be that management is systematically overpaid or underpaid, but rather that it is systematically mis-paid. If we were smarter about how we paid our managements, our managements would make smarter decisions.

One way of reforming current compensation practices is to make sure that management has a significant portion of its own wealth tied up in the performance of the firm. There are lots of ways to achieve that result besides stock ownership. Indeed, I think it would be a mistake to try to dictate by government policy how that result is to be achieved. But I think it's a result that makes a heck of a lot of sense because, as things stand now, when you get to be a CEO, you arc no longer 'incentivized' to perform-you are in the clear.

More on Dividends

STERN: We're going to come back to the issue of incentive ompensation in the second half of this discussion. But, for now, I just want to try to focus on the supposedly important variables in the process of valuation.

If I understand you correctly, Binkley. you're saying that as long as firms have superior rates of return on their operations, your feeling is that it would be in the interest of shareholders to discourage a large dividend payout and thus encourage large reinvestment. This way they would not have to pay it out with one hand only to recapture it with the other. Is that your view, Binkley?
SHORTS: Yes, I agree with that.
STERN: John, would you say that the people at Stein Roe & Farnham feel the same way? Would you be discouraged,

■

for example, from buying shares in firms like Digital Equipment and Berkshire Hathaway that pay dividends, have never paid a dividend, and have essentially indicated that, as long as they've got good prospects, they never intend to pay dividends?
LAFFERTY: We have basically two kinds of clients: tax-paying individuals and tax-free institutions. I would be inclined to argue that the real "lead steer" investor—the marginal investor, if you will—is the tax-paying individual, who still directly owns two-thirds of all equity capital in this country. For this reason, we would argue that tax law changes have to be given significant consideration as a determinant of asset prices. If you significantly change the percentage of income from an asset that a taxable investor is allowed to keep, you're going to change investor preferences and you're going to change asset prices. "Dividend" stocks have outperformed "capital gains" stocks since the point in 1986 when the capital gains rate rose and the dividend rate was reduced.
STERN: Chuck, could you explain where you think we are at the moment?
BRUNIE: I have two thoughts. First, I think that different investors buy stocks for many different reasons. Some buy on the basis of cash flow. some buy growth stocks that usually reinvest most of their earnings without double-taxation, some buy stocks for dividend income and so forth.

Second, some years ago, Stan Schwartz at Oppenheimer did some research that I found quite interesting.

He ran 80 tests of various combinations of 12 different variables to determine which had the strongest correlation with future stock price in-crease. (One-half assumed perfect foresight and one-half were based on known data.) He found that three of the top four predictors included recent or future dividend growth, while four of the worst six included yield. In fact, the only two that beat the universe every year were: (a) greatest growth in dividends in the past 12 months (eight percentage points better per year); and (b) greatest growth in dividends in the next 12 months (16 points better).

So, although dividend yield doesn't seem so important, the growth of dividends seems to be.
STERN: Yes, but what if we were to say that the growth of dividends depends on another more fundamental variable: namely. the profitability of the firm's operations. In that case, wouldn't you really be saying that dividend growth is a proxy for something else? It's not really the growth in the dividend that's driving the stock price, but rather the change in operating profitability which in turn allows management to increase the dividend.
RICHARD ZECKHAUSER: Joel, I think you're trying to describe the world as if all investors in it were Joel Sterns. And that is quite different, I think, from the world we live in. People have studied what happens to stock prices when you increase dividend payouts, and they tend to go up-just as if the world didn't understand what Joel Stern says.

Now, if we were sitting around the corporate boardroom, the consensus would probably be as follows: "Most of our investors expect that when we have moved to a higher plateau in earnings, we will pay them more dividends. We've done 58 surveys, and their expectation is that we will increase the dividend. Given these expectations, we could do one of two things: (1) we could do what many people want us to do—increase our dividends, which will increase our stock price and probably make our shareholders happier; or (2) we could cut the dividend and send shareholders a number of academic articles explaining how they can take their stock (probably now depreciated after the announcement of the cut) and go to the bank and borrow some money against it. We would also include a note saying, 'Please read these articles and be happy that we just cut your dividend for you.'"

STERN: Coming from the academic community, Richard, I'm surprised that you can still go back to Cambridge after this meeting is over.

As you well know, the deeper question here is not about simply living up to investor expectations, but about something more fundamental in the valuation process. The theory suggests that if people receive dividends on one hand, they will end up receiving that much less in capital appreciation. Companies that do pay dividends do not thereby increase their stockholders' total rate of return simply by paying dividends. And to the extent there is a tax penalty for dividend-paying firms, total stock returns may actually be reduced by paying dividends.

ZECKHAUSER: But, Joel, there are more complex issues that have to be dealt with in setting dividend policy than total long-term returns. There are different types of firms, and some firms clearly should be paying out a higher proportion of their earnings than others.

Boone Pickens, for example, saw that many oil companies were wasting capital through reinvestment in wells that, given the level of oil prices, were clearly not going to yield accept-

able returns. Pickens saw that such companies could significantly increase their values simply by getting the money out of the ■ firms through dividends. (He actually used royalty trusts, which are essentially just tax-advantaged ways of paying dividends.) In this sense, higher dividends helped to curb management's natural tendency to keep building the oil empire by drilling ever more wells. And the experience of the oil industry in the early 1980s clearly supports Yakov's story about the market responding positively to dividend increases only by firms with low "Q" values which is clearly what oil companies were when Boone started to become active. At that time, you will recall, virtually all Wall Street oil analysts agreed that you could buy oil "cheaper on Wall Street" than by drilling for it.

There is a second problem your analysis ignores, Joel. The market values companies on the basis of the information it receives about the future. And the information about what companies will do in the future is very poor. It's very hard even for management to know what's going to happen. Nevertheless, investors are always trying, in very subtle ways, to interpret management's actions.

Now, given the scarcity of reliable information about the future, you have to ask yourself the following question: If investors typically respond positively to announcements of dividend increases, does that mean that the stock market is systematically making a mistake? My answer would be no. The stock market knows that, on average, the company is in a better position than it was a year ago. Occasionally companies raise their dividends and the stock price falls. In those cases, I would argue, investors rationally dismissed the dividend as an unreliable signal about future growth prospects—or perhaps even viewed higher payouts as a sign of diminished opportunities for reinvestment. In such cases, I would also argue that management underestimated the market's ability to see through the *form* of the dividend signal to the underlying *content*—namely, the information about future cash flows.

I do agree with you, though, Joel, in the following sense: If I were starting a company today, I would announce immediately that we are never going to pay dividends. Maybe we'll have to reverse that policy 25 years from now—if we have no attractive investment opportunities and share buy-backs have been eliminated. But, for now, we will establish an explicit policy of no dividends, so that nobody will be disappointed by our failure too pay them. But, my policy would be very different if I were a well-established company that for 186 years had sent its stockholders a letter with its annual report saying, "Stern Industries has paid dividends every year. We've never had a dividend decrease. My grandfather did it, and his grandfather before that." If you suddenly tried to reverse that policy, and said, "Well, we've got a new theory, and we're going to cut your dividend," then investors would clearly suspect your motives and your stock price would go down.

STERN: Ah, but there would be a way to accomplish the dividend cut, even in that case. In order to convince the market that the prospects of Stern Industries have not deteriorated, we would announce that we are not going to cut the dividend right away, but rather 18 months or 2 years from now. Then people will have plenty of time to recognize that the cut is not a sign of hard times,

LAFFERTY: Your stock's going down right away.

ZECKHAUSER: It depends on what you say is the reason for it. You have to make clear to investors why you are cutting the dividend because they will always suspect the worst.

STERN: Yes, but that's because so many companies have announced dividend cuts because, they claimed, they had good prospects in sight, and then found themselves lucky to still he in business after the next quarter.

I continue to believe that all you have to do is to separate the announcement from the event by a sufficient amount of time so that investors will have time to study the case and determine whether or not the company's prospects are really going downhill.

ZECKHAUSER: Joel, once again, I think you assume that the market is filled with people like yourself. As you said, if I cut my dividend today, I would get mixed in with all the people who are cutting the dividend because things are looking pretty bleak.

But let's assume that we're sitting around the boardroom again and we say, "Well, we can't cut the dividend today because they'll surely interpret that as bad news. So let's announce a Stern dividend cut—one that takes place 18 months in the future—and struggle through for the next 18 months. Now, Joel, if that strategy proved effective, it would soon be adopted by all

■

OCCASIONALLY COMPANIES RAISE THEIR DIVIDENDS AND THE STOCK PRICE FALLS... IN SUCH CASES, I WOULD ALSO ARGUE THAT MANAGEMENT UNDERESTIMATED THE MARKET'S ABILITY TO SEE THROUGH THE *FORM* OF THE DIVIDEND SIGNAL TO THE UNDERLYING *CONTENT—*

—RICHARD ZECKHAUSER—

those companies with lousy prospects, and then the market would come to regard that strategy in the same way it now regards immediate dividend cuts. So I'm just saying it's not as simple as you suggest. If you cut your dividend because you have good reinvestment prospects, it will be difficult to distinguish your company from others that have done so out of distress.

AMIHUD: The important issue raised by dividends, as Richard suggests, is about information. How do we get information out of management about what is going on inside? If we know that management has a consistent policy of raising dividends when it expects cash flows to go up in the future, then dividend increases should be a good predictor of higher future earnings. In fact, recent research shows that stock analysts update their predictions on earnings after dividend announcements, and also that "unexpected" earnings in the quarters following dividend announcements are significantly correlated with the dividend changes.

But, raising the dividend is, I think, a very costly way to convey information to outsiders. If there were a less costly way of communicating with investors, I suspect we should see a much less positive reaction to dividend announcements, and far less reliance on dividends by public companies.

BRUNIE: Alcoa was a very interesting case. They announced that they would

pay out as a dividend one third of anything they earned over $6 a share.

STERN: Was that because they were going to "share the wealth" with their shareholders?

BRUNIE: Exactly.

STERN: But what does that mean? It means the shareholders now have the cash amount of the dividend plus shares worth that much less by the amount of the cash that was just paid out. And many of them have to pay taxes on the money they have just received. I don't understand how they are better served.

BRUNIE: Well, instead of paying it out they might have used that dividend for low-return projects...

STERN: Therefore, the reason for distributing the cash was not to "share the wealth" with the shareholders, but ...

BRUNIE: ...to prove to the shareholders that they're not going to keep it for perks or larger bonuses for themselves.

STERN: . . .or squander it on investment opportunities that might not have any rate of return. I think all of us around the table would share that point of view. ALL I've tried to do here is to cut through the conventional rhetoric about the role of dividends and then to ask the question, Do you honestly believe that a firm that has never paid a cash dividend will sell on a yield basis, as they sometime say, if they pay a cash dividend? And will paying a dividend somehow over time provide higher returns to shareholders than in the absence of paying dividends at all?

BARUCH LEV: There is some evidence on this question, Joel. There was a recent paper on dividend initiation, which demonstrated that there was a very significant increase in the stock prices of firms that had never paid dividends and began to do so for the first time. And the opposite happens, of course, when firms that have established a dividend pattern stop or decrease it. There are really very few phenomena in economics for which the evidence on investor reaction tells such a consistent story. If you increase dividends, you generally get a positive price reaction; if you decrease dividends, you almost always get a negative price reaction.

Apparently there are some practices which we don't fully understand—and dividends is one of them. As economists, we just don't understand the great preoccupation with dividends. All we can say, at this stage, is that some people like dividends and that's why firms pay them.

BENNETT STEWART: I'm troubled, Baruch, when you present the results of the research that way-because there is an obvious selection bias at work in the case of dividends. The companies that cut them were ones that found themselves unable to maintain the payment at historic levels. So the cut in the dividends was a sign that bad times were coming. It wasn't the divided cut per se, but very probably the indication that the company's prospects were deteriorating that made it sensible to conserve cash. On the other hand, companies that announce an increase in dividends, or initiate a dividend for the first time, most likely did so because they had fallen prey to the common myth that increasing dividends would help the stock price. Because they expected to earn high rates of return, they could confidently increase the dividend.

So, to return to this earlier point, the correlation between dividends and stock prices is not a causal relationship. Investors are simply responding in knee-jerk fashion to dividend increases because they have been conditioned to do so by the behavior of management.

LEV: But do you really believe that firms are falling prey to a "myth"? Can a myth persist year after year, decade after decade?

■

RAISING THE DIVIDEND IS, I THINK, A VERY COSTLY WAY TO CONVEY INFORMATION TO OUTSIDERS. IF THERE WERE A LESS COSTLY WAY OF COMMUNICATING WITH INVESTORS, I SUSPECT WE SHOULD SEE A MUCH LESS POSITIVE REACTION TO DIVIDEND ANNOUNCEMENTS, AND FAR LESS RELIANCE ON DIVIDENDS BY PUBLIC COMPANIES.

—YAKOV AMIHUD—

STERN: Well, I would argue that the restructuring of the 1980s, which has generally brought about a strengthening of managerial incentives to increase stock prices, is also changing the role of corporate dividend policy. In a leveraged recapitalization or an LBO (as Carl Ferenbach will no doubt tell us in the second part of this program), the first thing that goes is the dividend. And yet, from the time the firm is recapitalized until it eventually goes public again, the value of the company often increases dramatically—all without benefit of any dividend distributions at all.

FREDERICKS: Joel, there is another interesting alternative to dividends for a company that is generating more cash than it can effectively reinvest in its business. Rather than paying the excess cash as a dividend, it can initiate a stock repurchase program. A stock repurchase program has the additional virtue of providing a strong statement from management to investors that we as the management want to increase our stake in the company by buying (generally at some premium over market) from people who are willing to sell. It's a very effective way to sharpen management's focus on the core business and thereby increase the value of the shares.

STERN: Let me ask you this question, Dick. Aren't you bothered that boards

of directors seem to treat dividends as a fixed cost, so that once they raise the dividend, only a calamity can get them to cut it? This discussion brings to mind the case of a company—I'd rather not mention its name or industry—but this company paid out 65% of their earnings in cash dividends because they found they really didn't need the money in the business. Then the technology of the industry changed and a huge amount of capital expenditure was needed for that company to remain competitive with what became the leading player in the industry. The leading player in the industry went public for the very first time and paid no dividends and announced that their policy would be to pay no dividends unless they ran out of superior projects.

The chairman of the company paying out 65% of its earnings turned to me and said, "What are we going to do about our dividend? We need the money in the business." And I said, "Why don't you just discontinue the dividend?" And he said, "Yes, but if I do that, my share price will go straight down toward zero." (Actually, it only fell from $31 to $6.) And I said to him, "Why did you have a dividend policy that was 'sticky' on the downside? Because even if there is only a distant possibility that you will need to retain the cash for new investment, aren't your shareholders better served by having a policy that involves periodic share repurchases when its clear that we don't have the projects—that is, lumps of distribution rather than a continual, quarterly dividend payment that the board of directors will be loathe to change?

FREDERICKS: I agree with you.

LEV: But, Joel, you spoke earlier about dividends as a signal. The very fact that it takes a calamity to make management cut the dividend is what makes dividends a credible signal to investors of management's beliefs about future earnings. Investors would not respond to the dividend signal unless they felt that managements were very reluctant to reduce the dividend. Similarly, investors believe that by increasing the dividend, management commits itself to a higher payment in the future, which is only possible if future earnings are higher. The "stickiness" of dividends is what makes them a credible signal to investors.

AMIHUD: There is also another story—one which has a different lesson. This one is about a good corporation in a stable industry. When they found themselves with profitable opportunities and the need too step up their investment, management announced a cut in the dividend along with the new investment opportunities-and the stock price went up. That was the case of Gould Inc. in 1983.

In this case, management somehow succeeded in conveying the signal in a credible manner to the market despite the cut in the dividend. The interesting question is, how can the firm signal favorable prospects while at the same time cutting the dividend?

GRUNDFEST: I would agree that signals are by their very nature "noisy," and that there's a real cost to developing credibility and a reputation associated with corporate signals. But, in the case of dividends, you can tell a credible story in which a dividend increase means either a stock price increase or decrease. You can tell an equally credible story that will cause a dividend decline to lead to either a stock price increase or decrease, depending on surrounding industry factors and the credibility of the management sending the signal.

This leads to an important observation about the role of dividends in public corporations. There are other forms of organization in which sig-

■

A STOCK REPURCHASE PROGRAM HAS THE VIRTUE OF PROVIDING A STRONG STATEMENT FROM MANAGEMENT TO INVESTORS THAT WE AS THE MANAGEMENT WANT TO INCREASE OUR STAKE IN THE COMPANY BY BUYING (GENERALLY AT SOME PREMIUM OVER MARKET) FROM PEOPLE WHO ARE WILLING TO SELL. IT'S A VERY EFFECTIVE WAY TO SHARPEN MANAGEMENT'S FOCUS ON THE CORE BUSINESS...

—DICK FREDERICKS—

naling costs are lower, in which there is far less "static" on the line, and in which management and owners can communicate much more freely. I am thinking specifically of the LBO, which is where I think much of this discussion (not to mention Corporate America) is heading. A private company is a situation in which none of the conversation about dividends we've been having here really has to occur because, if you need to signal to your equity owners, they're right there in the board room and don't have to read any tea leaves.

Earnings Per Share

STERN: I'd like to move on now to a different subject. Until about the mid 1950s, the predominant view was that if you didn't pay dividends, you weren't going to sell at fair value. What was interesting then was that the firm whose market capitalization increased the most in value was a company that did not pay any cash dividends at all. It was IBM.

So people did a "rethink" and then came to the conclusion that it's not current dividends that matter, but rather the ability of the firm to pay those dividends out of earnings. So the focus shifted to earnings, earnings per share, and the bottom line. The

concern that I have had over the years is that the calculation of earnings and earnings per share is so much affected by accounting conventions that these numbers often have little to do with economic reality. Entries like amortization of good will, deferred income taxes, and LIFO affected reported earnings without reflecting any change in operating cash.

Now, the question I would like to put before the panel is this: Setting the issue of dividends aside, is earnings or earnings per share the engine that drives value? Or is it really the underlying cash flow that such earnings are meant, but often fail, to represent? Dick, would you comment on that one?

FREDERICKS: My own industry is a relatively mature one. I believe the most important thing about earnings for investors, as with dividends, is the "second derivative"—that is, the momentum or the rate of change. I find that the best correlation to stock price movements in banking is with the change in the rate of growth in earnings per share. If the growth rate is accelerating from 4 percent to 9 percent to 14 percent in successive years, then that's a reasonably reliable signal that value is increasing. It's the incremental changes that are important.

STERN: But, is it earnings that are important or the cash flow underlying those earnings?

FREDERICKS: There are an awful lot of accounting problems with the financial industry. And trying to define cash flow for a bank is fairly difficult, much more difficult than in an industrial company. I do like the notion of cash flow and cash-flow multiples. But I have not been very successful in my efforts to convert earnings statements into cash-flow equivalents.

STEWART: Dick, let me see if I can pose the question in this way. I believe you are saying that what is important about earnings are the surprises, the unexpected component of earnings. But there are times when a company has to choose between two accounting methods which have different consequences for earnings and cash flow. That is, one method will increase reported earnings, but, by so doing, it will also increase corporate taxes paid and thereby reduce corporate cash flow.

To make this dilemma more concrete, an acquisition takes place and it is a purchase acquisition—one where it's possible to assign some part of the purchase price to assets that can be expensed against both book and tax earnings to reduce the tax Liability of the firm. The alternative would be to put the premium into goodwill, which will be amortized against earnings over a much longer period of time. In so doing, you will increase reported earnings, but also increase the tax liability and thus reduce corporate cash flow.

Thus, it becomes a question that senior management wrestles with. Is it really earnings that matters to the market, or is it cash flow? Which one would you choose?

FREDERICKS: Cash flow.

LAFFERTY: I agree, it's cash flow that matters in this kind of case. But, for most companies, *changes* in earnings and cash flow tend to track each other fairly closely.

STERN: Well, I think it's important to focus on this issue because so many firms refused to switch to LIFO inventory accounting during the high inflation period not long ago. They refused to do so because it would have reduced their reported earnings, even while conserving tremendous amounts of cash.

A finance scholar from Carnegie-Mellon named Shyam Sunder wrote his doctoral dissertation on the effects of LIFO on share prices. He dis-

IN TODAY'S WORLD, MANAGEMENTS PAY A PRICE FOR PERSISTING IN THOSE POLICIES. TODAY, IF YOU TRY TO MAXIMIZE EARNINGS PER SHARE AT THE EXPENSE OF CASH FLOW, YOU ARE INVITING SOME OTHER COMPANY THAT DOES LOOK AT CASH FLOW TO COME ALONG AND TAKE YOU OUT. BECAUSE THEY ARE LOOKING AT THE UNDERLYING ECONOMICS.

—CARL FERENBACH—

covered that all these firms had to do was simply to announce their intention to switch to LIFO and their stock prices went up-all they had to do was threaten to save money on taxes. Yet you couldn't get companies to switch because they felt that bottom-line EPS was the thing that mattered to the market (or, perhaps more important, their bonuses were tied to EPS).

CARL FERENBACH: But, Joel, in today's world, managements pay a price for persisting in those policies. Today, if you try to maximize earnings per share at the expense of cash flow, you are inviting some other company that does look at cash flow to come along and take you out. Because they are looking at the underlying economics.

BRUNIE: Yes, that's true.

STERN: You're both suggesting, then, that the fact there are corporate raiders out there who are clearly focused on cash flow should be forcing management to concentrate more on generating cash than manipulating earnings. You see, Carl, I'm just trying to help anybody who might be reading this roundtable and trying to figure out what they can do to avoid buy-out people like you.

LEV: I've just had the opportunity to survey twenty years of research on the relationship between earnings,

cash flow, and stock price. And I was astounded by the results. Changes in quarterly and annual earnings, or in unexpected earnings, tend to explain about only 3 to 4 percent of changes in stock prices around the earnings announcements. This suggests that stock prices and earnings changes are very weakly correlated. Cash flows and returns on equity don't do much better than earnings per share. All these measures are highly correlated with one another, and all of them as a group explain very little of stock price changes.

What explains a lot of the stock price (or return) variation, however, are long-term changes in earnings and cash flows. I ran a cross-sectional regression analysis of five-year stock rates of return on five-year changes in earnings and found that these long-run earnings changes explained about 40 percent of the differences in stock rates of return.

STEWART: Baruch, that seems to be making a very strong statement that the market is not short-sighted, as so many people claim, but instead appears to be accounting for the long-term payoff from good business decisions. So, for example, if a company were to step up its research and development in a way that would reduce its short-term earnings but generate large benefits down the road, then the market appears to recognize and reward the trade-off. And, in fact, there is good academic evidence that the market responds positively, on average, to announcements of increased capital investment and R&D—at least in industries with good growth prospects.

LEV: That is one possible reading of my findings. You might be right. But another possibility is, of course, that short-term earnings or related measures are very noisy because of the many unrealistic accounting conventions, and because of the manipulation of these conventions. Quite a few managers are playing games with earnings, at least on a year-to-year basis.

GRUNDFEST: Well, I suspect that doesn't come as much of a surprise to anybody at this table.

STEWART: I interpret your results differently, Baruch. I interpret them as saying that the market is attempting to determine the present value of cash flows over the entire life of the business. If this is so, we really shouldn't expect to see near-term earnings or cash flow relate closely to stock price movements unless those earnings changes are providing a highly credible signal about the long-term prospects of the company.

LEV: Yes, that is what most academics believe. I tend to believe that unexpected earnings function as a signal to capital markets. But it appears that they are really not a very informative signal.

BRUNIE: But how, then, do you explain the success of the Value Line rankings? Their top picks have a good long-term record in outperforming the market. And Eisenstat's model includes earnings surprises as one of his few variables.

LAFFERTY: Cash flow is really the most fundamental variable. But a lot of the world talks about earnings per share. And the reason that this can go on is that the changes in the two measures are typically not all that different. In the short run, changes in earnings are the most changeable element of cash flow; and it is these changes that convey new information about the prospects for future profitability.

The non-earnings elements of cash flow-depreciation, deferred taxes, and the like-tend to track assets and changes in them tend to lag changes in earnings. So that, in the short run, the focus on earnings, I would argue,

■

CASH FLOW IS REALLY THE MOST FUNDAMENTAL VARIABLE. BUT A LOT OF THE WORLD TALKS ABOUT EARNINGS PER SHARE. AND THE REASON THAT THIS CAN GO ON IS THAT THE CHANGES IN THE TWO MEASURES ARE TYPICALLY NOT ALL THAT DIFFERENT... I WILL SAY THAT I HAVE SEEN CASES WHERE MANAGEMENTS HAVE TRIED TO IMPROVE EARNINGS SIMPLY THROUGH ACCOUNTING CHANGES—BUT THEY WERE NOT VERY SUCCESSFUL.

—JOHN LAFFERTY—

is really a focus on the changeable part of cash flow.

Now there are some Mickey Mouse differences when companies make changes in accounting policies that change reported earnings without affecting cash flow; but the market usually ignores these effects.

STERN: The reason why we care about this issue is to address the concerns of people that sit in the boardroom. They may have to make the decision about switching to LIFO inventory accounting. And if they believe that you focus on earnings and earnings per share rather than underlying cash flow, then they are not going to switch to LIFO.

LAFFERTY: Well, I will say that I have seen cases where managements have tried to improve earnings simply through accounting changes—and they were not very successful. For example, several years ago Westinghouse lengthened the depreciable life of its assets relative to GE's; and although its reported earnings improved, the stock market didn't buy it.

But, again, I think the market is looking to surprises in earnings to provide a signal. I would call this the "Value-Line effect," where all of a sudden the company's margins are four

points higher than people expected. That tells me something about future profitability.

STERN: Well, then, let me just ask you about this very quick laundry list. Amortization of goodwill in acquisitions—do you think that matters? It reduces earnings but has no effect on cash whatsoever. Coke of Los Angeles was bought by Northwest Industries for what somebody told me was a "very high price." I said, "What do you mean by such a high price?" He said, "Well, the book value is only $35 million. The market value of the stock was something like $65 million before the offer, and they paid $195 million. They're going to have to amortize well over $100 million in goodwill. Think of what that's going to do to EPS."

STEWART: I can show you another more recent example of that, Joel. When Don Kelly was attempting to sell some businesses to clean up his LBO, it was widely cited in the press that potential purchasers were reluctant to pay the prices the company was asking—merely, it seemed, because they would have to record and then amortize large amounts of goodwill against their earnings.

STERN: Now, John, would you say that amortization of goodwill is something corporate planners ought to worry about?

LAFFERTY: No, not unless it changes corporate tax payments. If it doesn't affect cash flow or cash taxes, I would argue that it shouldn't affect the stock price.

PART II: THE MARKET'S VIEW OF CORPORATE RESTRUCTURING

STERN: The first part of our discussion was devoted to the fundamental factors that allegedly account for share prices and changes in share prices. In this next part, I want to explore how boards of directors and senior management can act on behalf of the shareholders to enhance value by focusing on restructuring the firm, recapitalizing the firm, and strengthening management incentives. To begin this process, I want to ask Carl Ferenbach what he thinks of the general changes that take place in companies as the result of restructuring and recapitalization.

FERENBACH: I can't speak for the community at large (although I would suspect that other people probably look at things much the same way we do), but our starting point is the individual transaction itself and the underlying economic fundamentals that drive it. First, we attempt to determine whether a given business is an appropriate business for this kind of recapitalization. It must have sufficient cash flow stability and tangible assets to enable it to carry the debt load-which means you have to be able to pay both interest and principal on that debt. And, of course, it has to earn an acceptably high rate of return on investment to compensate the equity holders at the bottom of the capital structure.

Now, when evaluating an LBO candidate, we typically attempt to project operating cash flows over a 5-year period, while all the time recognizing that no business we've ever owned (and we have owned over 30 of them) has ever made a 5-year projection. The analysis also typically assumes that we will sell the investment at the end of the fifth year at the same multiple for which we bought it. Given this kind of analysis, we will only participate in deals that promise to yield a rate of return of 35 to 40 percent on our initial equity investment.

STERN: Per year?

FERENBACH: Yes, per year. One has to have a great deal of confidence in management in order to be willing to take those risks. For this reason, one

▪

IN PUTTING TOGETHER AN LBO, ONE HAS TO ENSURE THAT MANAGEMENT'S FINANCIAL INTERESTS ARE PRECISELY PARALLEL WITH THOSE OF THE OTHER INVESTORS. IF THOSE INTERESTS ARE NOT PARALLEL, THEN YOU'VE ADDED A RISK BEYOND THE FINANCIAL RISK OF THE TRANSACTION WHICH CAN DOOM THE PROJECT.

—CARL FERENBACH—

also has to ensure that management's financial interests are precisely parallel with those of the other investors. If those interests are not parallel, then you've added a risk beyond the financial risk of the transaction which can doom the project.

STERN: When you talk about a rate of return on the equity portion of 35 to 40 percent, that reflects the very high ratio of debt to equity on the transaction. If you were to restate the leverage down to a more normal level—say, one that would warrant an A or BAA rating—then what kind of operating return on net assets would that be the equivalent of?

FERENBACH: In today's market, the weighted average cost of capital for a low-risk business capitalized with 40% debt and 60% equity is about 16 percent. That's the rate of return you need on net assets-that is, on the total purchase price for the acquisition, total debt plus equity. Now, if you capitalize that same business with 60% senior debt, 30% subordinated debt, and 10% equity—which is a typical structure— then your pre-tax cost of capital falls to under 12%. So, in answer to your question, I guess you could say that we expect our LBO companies to earn at the margin more than 12 percent pretax on the total debt and equity investment.

STERN: So, given that you typically pay a large premium over market to

acquire these companies—often 50 percent or greater—you're clearly saying you expect to make significant improvements in the operating performance of the business. My next question is, given that very often the management in an LBO is exactly the same group of people you had before, what is expected to bring about these improvements in operations? What is energizing management to perform so differently?

FERENBACH: First and foremost is their equity ownership. In our model, they have to buy some stock. It means they use their own resources in order to acquire an equity stake in the business. Over and above that stake, they are also given the opportunity to participate in an option interest—an earn-out arrangement, in effect—which provides management an even larger ownership stake if performance exceeds certain targets. Under these circumstances, we and our other investors are delighted to see them end up with a bigger equity stake.

But the short answer to your question, Joel, is that management-owned equity is the principal tool by which we manage our businesses.

STERN: John, do you think the firms in which you have equity investment would do much better for the shareholders if the management had similar equity stakes that they paid for? And why do you think companies don't do it now?

LAFFERTY: Well, my answer to your first question is, perhaps, but not necessarily. You could certainly provide management with much stronger incentives than they now have to increase shareholder values, but that alone would not necessarily produce the desired result. If management does not understand what drives stock prices—if they are focusing their attention on the wrong "value drivers"—they may not do the right things. They have to be given incentives that will direct them to achieve returns that exceed the cost of capital in their business. If you could provide those kind of incentives, then we could clearly be in favor of that. But just providing management with an equity stake may not be sufficient.

FERENBACH: Joel, I think there is an important difference between an LBO and the way a public company is run. In an LBO, the board is comprised only of people who have invested in the business. And when they invested in the business, that investment was based on a business plan that was worked out with the management prior to making that investment. So there is a set goal, one that is clearly established in everybody's mind. The fundamental direction is there. In contrast to a public company, our focus is solely on operating cash flow—that is, earnings before interest, taxes, and depreciation. And all this reported earnings business below is basically numbers that we ignore. They're not relevant to us.

STERN: You're saying that you're looking only at the operating cash flow?

FERENBACH: Right. But, having said this, it is also important to point out that the allocation of any excess resources to future capital investment is critical to our plan. Our ability to make a profit is not simply a matter of "arbitraging" assets in a business by shutting down all reinvestment and by liquidating the firm. You cannot make a profit in one of these business just by paying down debt. The business has to grow if it is going to be sold or taken public again. And given the kind of debt load in LBOs, you have to plan very carefully to ensure that you can make the additional investment necessary to grow the business. Of course, all on-going capital projects will have to be subjected to

■

THE ALLOCATION OF ANY EXCESS RESOURCES TO FUTURE CAPITAL INVESTMENT IS CRITICAL TO OUR PLAN. OUR ABILITY TO MAKE A PROFIT IS NOT SIMPLY A MATTER OF "ARBITRAGING" ASSETS IN A BUSINESS BY SHUTTING DOWN ALL REINVESTMENT AND BY LIQUIDATING THE FIRM. YOU CANNOT MAKE A PROFIT IN ONE OF THESE BUSINESS JUST BY PAYING DOWN DEBT. THE BUSINESS HAS TO GROW IF IT IS GOING TO BE SOLD OR TAKEN PUBLIC AGAIN.

—CARL FERENBACH—

thorough scrutiny; and unprofitable investments will have to be scrapped. But you still have to invest in those capital projects that will provide the future growth So, there is a very tight monitoring process in setting the capital budget.

STERN: You generally do friendly transactions?

FERENBACH: Only friendly.

STERN: Would you suggest to management worried about unfriendly takeover attempts that they ought to invest their own cash to acquire a significant equity stake in their business? And not only management, but would you also suggest that board members also be required to have purchased large equity stakes as well?

FERENBACH: I think it would meaningfully change the point of view' of both management and the board if they were substantial owners of the company. It would also greatly reduce their conflict of interest when responding to unfriendly takeover bids thereby benefiting their stockholders.

STERN: John, do you think that if both management and the hoards of directors were to have major equity stakes, the values of those firms would be higher?

LAFFERTY: Necessary but not sufficient. As I said before, what you need in addition too the incentives is to keep people focused on operating decisions that matter rather than, say, just trying to increase earnings per share. Just because the management owns a loot of stock doesn't mean that they will focus on the teal variables.

Now, what are the fundamental variables that determine share values? We have three elements in our model: (1) real return on investment (measured in cash flow terms); (2) the long-term real growth rate in assets employed; and (3) a real discount rate, or cost of capital, that reflects risk, taxes, and the pure rate of interest. If management is focused on those three variables-and, especially, on the spread between real ROI and the real cost of capital-then, yes, I would agree that the more stock they own, the better for their public stockholders.

STERN: But if they have a large equity stake, wouldn't that encourage them to behave in exactly the way you are suggesting?

LAFFERTY: I would hope it would But, there area lot of people who track insider transactions and it's my understanding of that literature that insider transactions don't do a good job in predicting share price movements.

STEWART: I think there is a big difference between individual managers buying and selling stocks, and the signal sent to the market when management and investors make a statement in a specific transaction that they are banding together. I'm not surprised that we don't see a very good correlation between insider transactions and share prices. But, when management and investors unite their interests by means of an LBO, or even a major recap, then that sends a very positive signal to the market.

FERENBACH: Another important difference between a public company and an LBO is that managers and investors in an LBO must also sell their holdings together as a group. Otherwise they can't sell at all. Thus, management investors, and the board are all locked into the deal.

STERN: Carl, it's my understanding that, in most public companies, if management has a significant equity stake, it is typically in the form of stock options rather than a cash investment in equity. Is that right?

FERENBACH: That's correct. They don't have their cash invested.

STERN: How would you feel about the idea of having management buy in-the-money options on their own company's stock and paying cash for just the in-the-money portion? For example, if the stock were trading at, say. $20 and they were given options with an exercise price of $18, then they would be asked to pay the $2 dollar difference. On top of that, I would also suggest that the exercise price on those options be increased at, say, 8 or 10 percent a year over the time frame they were to be exercised. Would starting a program like that encourage you to place a higher value on the company?

LAFFERTY: Well, I agree that management options should certainly be more oriented toward cash payments.

STERN: Yes, because this way if they don't exercise, they lose their own money. And not only that, if you build in this exercise price, then they've got to beat that compound rate of return or else they're not going to exercise-in which case they're going to lose their full investment.

STEWART: What Joel is talking about was actually put into practice, at least in substance, by the Henley Group of San Diego. The company was a spin-off of essentially unwanted companies from Allied Signal that were called "Dingman's Dogs" after its chairman, Michael Dingman. Dingman had acquired a reputation over

■

WHEN THIS "LEVERAGED EQUITY
PURCHASE PLAN WAS FIRST
ANNOUNCED, THE MARKET VALUE OF
THE HENLEY STOCK WENT
UP ABOUT 10 PERCENT.

—BENNETT STEWART—

the years for establishing large incentives for his operating managers; and this policy has proved very effective in producing operating improvements and creating wealth that has been shared among shareholders, management, and employees alike.

In the case of the Henley Group, Dingman introduced a plan whereby the senior management of the company was invited to purchase freshly issued shares of the company, representing 5 percent of the stock of the company, at a slight premium over the current stock price. The company agreed to lend management 90 percent of the purchase price through nor-recourse notes with the 10 percent differential to be contributed by the management people themselves. The total purchase price for the stock was about $110 million; and management thus contributed about $11 million.

What did this accomplish? On the upside, if the stock appreciated, management had a levered stake that would appreciate at 10 times the rate of an unlevered stockholder's interest, thus giving management a very powerful incentive to perform well. But, if the stock failed to perform, the management-owned shares would be returned to the company, the notes would be canceled, and management would lose its $11 million investment. When this plan, which was called a "leveraged equity purchase plan was first announced, the market value of the Henley stock

went up about 10 percent. The announcement also gave rise to two lawsuits, by the way but they were both dismissed as being without merit.

STERN: Joe, what do you think about the idea of in-the-money options with a rising exercise price as a way to motivate management?

GRUNDFEST: It's one of a hundred possible strategies. If ore wanted to start by criticizing it, one could say, "Well, what about net-of-market risk? You are forcing management to bear market risk; and thus their compensation will be determined by important factors cover which they have no control." Now, your proposal may be an appropriate arrangement in some cases, but there could be other situations where it makes sense for all of the important compensation variables to be within management's control.

For example, suppose a company has four divisions. Why should one manager's compensation depend very much on the performance of another manager's division? Maybe each manager's compensation should be tied directly to the performance of his division by looking at variables that the manager can directly control, such as cash flow generated by his division. At that point, a manager can be compensated with cash bonuses based on divisional performance.

STERN: Are you referring to the idea of partial spin-offs of divisions-those cases in which the parent corporation issues stock in ore of its subsidiaries to the public and then gives operating management direct ownership of some of the new stock?

GRUNDFEST: No, that's a separate development. These spin-offs and partial IPOs you're talking about are driven more by the market's negative reaction to conglomerate structures. It's become fairly clear from the restructuring movement of the 1980s that the conglomerate form of corporate organization has become obsolete. Many conglomerates that exist today are left over from the "conglomerate era" of the 1960s, when the market at least appeared to be encouraging companies to diversify through acquisition. That experiment in corporate structure has power to be a failure. In a large number of situations, it would make sense to break these structures apart. But there are some structural rigidities, to put it politely, that are preventing the marketplace from completely dismantling these inefficient conglomerates.

Your basic point, however, makes sense. The specific implementation of the concept that you just described might work very well for one company, but it might be inappropriate for another It might work well for some individuals in a company and be inappropriate for others. This is a situation where I think it's very hard to buy a policy off the rack. The same comment applies, by the way, to the prescription that corporations consider the use of much larger debt ratios. These prescriptions must be applied very carefully and selectively.

STEWART: Carl, can I ask you how LBOs resolve this issue? Isn't it true that management bears market risk in an LBO? So how does an LBO address the, problems that Joe was raising, which I think are important?

FERENBACH: The easy answer is that 90 percent of LBOs involve single-line businesses, and compensating the managers of such operations is a relatively straightforward task. But setting up compensation plans for the large conglomerates that you are talking about is an extraordinarily complicated job. Trying to determine the contribution to total value of each of the business units and then pushing management equity down into them is a major undertaking.

More on LBOs

LEV: I would like to interject a note of skepticism about LBOs. I recently came across two studies that look at the performance of LBO companies both before and after the buyout. Although operating cash flow seems to increase, on average, over the short post-LBO period examined, it's very difficult to tell if those increases are coming from real increases in operating efficiencies or from short-term tax savings or from "running down assets." Both studies, for example, suggest that some of these large gains from LBOs are coming from decreases in R&D and in capital expenditures. If that is the case, then the future of some of these LBO firms may have been sacrificed to achieve what are really very temporary and unsustainable returns.

GRUNDFEST: I have to take issue with your reading of the evidence. The SEC has looked at this R&D issue. We found, first of all, that the vast majority of LBOs and other acquisitions take place in sectors of the economy that are not R&D-intensive. So there is not much room to make cuts to begin with. To make the point with a specific example, Macy's didn't do a lot of R&D before its LBO, and it isn't doing a lot today.

LEV: True. But for those companies that are not R&D-intensive, there tends to be a decrease in another measure of long-term investment—capital expenditures.

GRUNDFEST: I'll get to that issue in a moment. My second point is this: SEC evidence demonstrates that the companies that become targets are the ones that do less R&D, on average, than other companies in the same industry. That is, in R&D-intensive industries, it is the companies that *lag* their industry in R&D that are taken over. R&D leaders tend not to he takeover targets.

My third and final point is that you have to look at the quality of the R&D that gets done in any of these situations. Not all R&D is economic. Much of what is called R&D by corporations is, for want of another word, stupid R&D! Demonstrably *stupid* R&D! And taking that sick old horse out and shooting it row is the best thing you could do for the corporation, for consumers, and for your shareholders.

LEV: Does that mean that all the R&D done by LBO companies is clever R&D?

GRUNDFEST: No. no, no, no. But let me give you an example of what I mean. Take a company like Unocal, which has spent hundreds of millions of dollars on an oil shale conversion project. You can argue about the price at which oil shale conversion becomes an economic means of producing energy. But, whatever the answer to that question. I believe the conversion project was a stupid investment because there are competing technologies that would become rational at far lower prices of oil. Therefore, I don't think there was ever a significant chance that Unocal would earn an acceptable rate of return on the money it invested in that technology.

I would also point out that if a company gets taken over and if it has a good, viable research project, the acquiror is not going to just bury that research effort if it can get the value for it someplace else in the economy. You don't take your colts out and shoot them.

LEV: Well, I'm talking specifically about management buy-outs, not takeovers in general—and about all long-term capital investments, not just R&D.

GRUNDFEST: As for R&D, it works the same in either case. But, as for capital expenditures. Michael Jensen's 'free cash flow" argument does a creditable job of explaining why capital investment might be expected to fall in the average LBO—because many LBO candidates were probably reinvesting too much cash in the first place rather than paying it out to stockholders, who could then reinvest that cash in new growth opportunities.

FERENBACH: My experience with divisional buyouts is precisely the opposite suggested by Professor Lev's studies. When we have bought subsidiaries or divisions of parent companies, we typically find that the parent companies have been "upstreaming" the cash rather than reinvesting in the business. As a result, we often find ourselves increasing the level of capital spending. I don't know how you would get the data to track that particular kind of phenomenon hut I think that's true of a big chunk of the LBO market.

STERN: You're talking about privately held divisions of publicly traded companies?

FERENBACH: Right. Now, in the case of LBOs of entire public companies-which are typically companies that generate excess cash-in such cases it's not uncommon to find that they've had difficulties finding economic projects for reinvestment. So it's not surprising to me that the data would suggest that in fact there is a reduction in new capital invested in those kinds of buyouts.

GRUNDFEST: I think Carl's point is exactly right. In our own studies of LBOs, we found several examples of divisions of companies that were spun off that had previously been starved by senior management.

■

SEC EVIDENCE DEMONSTRATES THAT THE COMPANIES THAT BECOME TARGETS ARE THE ONES THAT DO LESS R&D, ON AVERAGE, THAN OTHER COMPANIES IN THE SAME INDUSTRY. THAT IS, IN R&D-INTENSIVE INDUSTRIES, IT IS THE COMPANIES THAT LAG THEIR INDUSTRY IN R&D THAT ARE TAKEN OVER..

—JOE GRUNDFEST—

These were cases where the LBO group would come in, increase the amount of capital investment, and the businesses improved dramatically.

It is also possible to find examples of LBOs, and acquisitions generally, that have then spun off perfectly good research projects or sold them to other companies. A recent example is the case of Sarnoff Laboratories and its treatment after GE's acquisition of RCA. Rather than shutting it down, GE spun off Sarnoff Labs into a free-standing R&D operation. Sure, Sarnoff has changed, and we can debate whether the change is for the better or the worse. But Sarnoff continues to do some terrific work and that resource has not beer lost to the economy. Moreover, I suspect that something like this typically happens to valuable R&D operations during takeovers.

More on Changing Management Incentives

STERN: Dick, may I ask you why the banks don't restructure and get all of these value-enhancement benefits? The banks are involved in lending money to finance so many of these restructurings. How could it have escaped the attention of the managements and boards of the banks that there are opportunities to add value—not necessarily by going private, but at least by changing management incentive compensa-

tion in a meaningful way? Why haven't the barks done it?

FREDERICKS: There clearly has beer some restructuring that has gone on in the industry. But I wish they would do a lot more. I've done studies and written reports that have shown, year after year, that there is no correlation between pay and performance in banking. The only correlation with executive pay is asset size. It is what I call the "brother-in-law" syndrome. One bank executive looks at another and says, "That guy makes that much! My bank is as big as his. I've got to have it, too But there's absolutely no correlation with performance and shareholder value.

STERN: Do you think it is the regulatory structure that prevents the restructuring from taking place?

FREDERICKS: Yes, that's an important factor in fact I have gone to at least one bank and suggested that they go private. The problem with restructuring banks is that you can't pile leverage on leverage. So it's harder for the unaffiliated buyers—some call them raiders—to leverage their equity capital in buying out a bank.

Now, about this issue of management's equity ownership, I've got to tell you that I go crazy when I don't see management ownership. And I would much rather see a big cash ownership—perhaps bought at a discount—but I like to see a big ownership of stock paid for with cash. And I like to see it deep down into the organization, as far down as I can see.

AMIHUD: I have two questions here. One is, Why do you have to take a firm private to bring about these improvements in performance? Can't you leave it public and still make all the same operating improvements? After all, in LBOs equity investors sacrifice the liquidity of their claims, and my research suggests that this liquidity is quite valuable.

Second, Why don't the large blockholders get together and bring a resolution to the board meeting to institute a compensation plan for management which ties their pay more directly to performance?

FERENBACH: I can answer your first question, and maybe Binkley can answer your second. There are in fact LBOs that continue to have public stock outstanding. R.J. Reynolds is only one example, and there are a growing number of large recapitalizations, also known as "public LBOs," in which management borrows to pay out a large distribution to shareholders. So there isn't any reason why you can't recapitalize a public firm and leave a portion of it in the hands of the existing shareholders, who can then participate in the upside.

But, while there are many examples of companies that have successfully recapitalized without changing the board, I would also say that intuitively (and thus without any statistical basis whatsoever) it is likely to have a greater potential for success if you had instead a new investor group that was putting a meaningful amount of money into the business and that was determining how much management was going to put into the business, how much they were going to own, and how they were going to get it out-an investor group that, after hammering out this agreement, would then represent all of the shareholders. I just think you have a higher probability of success under this kind of arrangement than if you just take the existing board, existing management, and then try to go out and buy all but 20 percent of the common stock.

STERN: Instead of referring to it that way, is it not possible that a "public LBO" could take place through a large dividend? Management could borrow a huge amount of money and then

distribute it to the shareholders. And if management-owned shares and board-owned shares do not participate in the dividend but get extra shares instead, then management and the board will effectively have increased their proportional ownership.

FERENBACH: That has been done in a number of cases. Public stockholders will sometimes receive a piece of paper, a subordinated note, in exchange for a good percentage of their shares. This means that these investors are going to get their return in the form of interest rather than dividends. And they're thus going to get it by contract rather than relying on management discretion.

SHORTS: There's one aspect of these recapitalizations that we regularly look for, because we think it's such a good deal. That is when a company dividends out a substantial dollar amount and offers an option to shareholders to either take a subordinated note for the extra shares, or to hold onto their shares in the recapitalized company. Whenever we see one of these deals, we choose to hold the shares.

STERN: Why?

SHORTS: Because it works. It's everything you had suggested would happen. Management owns 80 percent instead of 15 percent of the company and you are participating in a very interesting phenomenon.

STERN: There are, it seems to me, two distinct kinds of public LBOs. One is merely a change in the capital structure of the firm; a cash dividend is distributed equally to all shareholders and there is no proportional change in share ownership. The second kind is the one in which management does not participate in the dividend, but instead chooses to increase its share ownership. So, Binkley, would I be correct in assuming that you would instinctively place a significantly higher value on the shares of the second alternative?

SHORTS: Yes. Another of the screening techniques that we have found useful is the percentage of equity ownership by management: the higher, the better It's a clear signal to me as an investor.

STERN: Carl, why would a firm like Coca-Cola not borrow, say, $15 billion dollars and do a leveraged recapitalization, and then have its stub value go absolutely haywire? Why are we talking about companies that are only a fraction of the size of Coke? Why doesn't IBM do it? Why doesn't Johnson & Johnson or Merck go through a recapitalization? These companies have practically no debt. Why wouldn't it make sense for them to use the same principles you use in order to create value?

FERENBACH: Well, let's start with the idea that the largest deal ever done was the $25 billion RJR-Nabisco buyout. Now, the size of these companies you're talking about, Joel, would require buy-out prices on the order of $50 billion or more. I haven't studied any of these companies, but given the price you would have to pay, and the amount of leverage needed to support that price, I would start by assuming that either these companies can't reliably service the debt or can't earn a high enough rate of return on the equity to justify the financial risks.

STEWART: Take the case of Merck. The market value of its equity is $25.6 billion, and the assets on the books are around $6 billion. What you are saying, Carl, is that if you attach a takeover or LBO premium on top of $25.6 billion, and then leverage the buyout to 80 or 90 percent of total capital, then any forecast of current earnings will not be able to cover the interest payments—because the current stock price multiple of 20 or higher is predicated upon continued aggressive investments and growth.

So, from this exercise, I would conclude that the best defense against a takeover—and, indeed, the only reliable defense—is ultimately a higher stock price, a higher multiple.

STERN: I'm not talking necessarily about an unfriendly takeover Look at the case of Coca-Cola. They are a company with over 90 years of history. And they have always prided themselves on not borrowing money. Now, what puzzles me is this: Why is it that other people who are sizable owners of Coca-Cola—say, Peter Lynch-why aren't they going to those companies and saying, "I don't think you ought to borrow $15 billion— because Bennett says maybe you can't service it-but how about, say, $8 billion? And then pay your big dividend, increase management's percentage ownership, and let's get on with creating more value than we have." Why don't these passive "lead steers" make the effort of going to the board and the management and say, "Let's get that value up"?

FREDERICKS: I think there's a difference between what happens when you take a company private and what happens in most large public companies. In private companies I'll bet you have only a handful of directors at most. These big public companies, on the other hand, have 20 and 30 directors, many of whom have no direct interest in the company. So,

before you can begin to make significant changes in large public companies, you have to start by cutting the number of board members and by substituting really active guys (preferably with a large financial interest in the company) for your typical outside directors.

A More Active Role for Institutional Investors?

STERN: There seem to be two types of investors in capital markets today. One could be described as active. People like, say, Irwin Jacobs and Carl Icahn will go in and actually take control of companies. Then there is the second type of investor—some of whom are sitting at this table—who are more passive investors, like yourself, Chuck, and like Binkley. I'm kind of interested to know why it is that, with your large equity stakes, you don't go to the firms you have large investments in and say to them, "I think you ought do the following three or four things to get the equity value up significantly." And, essentially, the things you would be recommending are some of the same policy changes that have been introduced by LBO people like Carl Ferenbach. Why don't you do it?

SHORTS: Well, for one thing, Joel, it is a very labor-intensive activity. We've done it on a couple of occasions and it has gotten to the point where we've had to hire added legal staff. My company today has a three-and-a-half person legal staff involved in these kinds of activities. The small cap area

consumes a disproportionate share of their time. Going any farther toward an activist role becomes very expensive and time-consuming.

But we've found an easier solution; and it is something we do all the time. We write what amounts to a form letter to the boards of directors of many of our companies, telling them that their incentive program for management is inadequate and that they ought to reconsider their management incentive package, particularly the stock option plan.

STEWART: Let me make an even less ambitious proposal. I'm a bit confused as to what happened, for example, when U.S. Steel bid to acquire Marathon Oil. When the bid was announced, the stock price of U.S. Steel took it on the chin. But, when the proposal was submitted to a shareholder vote, the shareholders of U.S. Steel approved the acquisition. And I have seen this happen many times. Can you tell me why that happens?

GRUNDFEST: A former colleague of mine at the SEC, Bernard Black (who is now at Columbia Law School), has done some interesting research that bears or this issue. Bernie has a hypothesis that builds upon Michael Jensen's "free cash flow" theory of takeovers, and it goes as follows: Some firms over the years develop a reputation for not investing very wisely and not being able to generate good returns in their basic businesses. The shares of these companies are already marked down by the market to reflect investors' expectations that the firm will throw good money after bad. (This would explain, by the way, why oil companies were selling at Q ratios below .5 during the early 1980s, when the claim was that it was far cheaper to buy oil on Wall Street than get it out of the ground.)

Well, as Bernie's theory goes on to explain, there is more than one way to burn money. The first, of course, is too continue too reinvest excess cash in businesses that fail to earn competitive returns. But the second most popular method for dealing with excess capacity in declining industries is the way that U.S. Steel chose-that is, you can make overpriced diversifying acquisitions, you can overpay foot a company like Marathon Oil.

Now, the point that the SEC study makes is that, from an investors' perspective, these two strategies are equally destructive; they yield the same substandard return or corporate capital. It is for this reason, Bernie argues, that when U.S. Steel announced its clearly overpriced and counterproductive acquisition of Marathon Oil, the stock price of U . Steel was only slightly affected. It went down a bit, but very little relative to the amount of the alleged overpayment, because the market had already expected management to waste the money. And the market was right. In effect, the management of U.S. Steel announced to their stockholders, "You expected us to burn the money but we're going to surprise you. We're going to burr it by over-paying for Marathon as opposed to doing all those foolish things that we have traditionally done in steel."

So, if a company has signaled to the marketplace that it fully intends to waste its free cash flow, and if it then just changes the way it wastes its free cash flow, then you're rot going to improve the situation or make it that much different. That's one possibility why the buyer's stock price often doesn't fall when announcing diversifying acquisitions.

STEWART: So, rather than reinvesting in steel or diversifying into oil, it would have been far better if they had simply bought back their stock and paid the capital out to their stock-holders.

GRUNDFEST: That's right.

STERN: Well, Joe, I would argue that if the market is convinced that investing additional dollars in your existing industry is a certain way of destroying shareholder value, there's always the chance that making the acquisition, ever at a price that appears too be terribly high, might turn out to be successful. And maybe that's why the buyer's stock price doesn't go down more.

GRUNDFEST: Of course, you can come up with an equilibrium in which overpaying for an acquisition doesn't move the acquirer's stock price at all. But it all depends on investors' expectations before the deal is announced. Take the situation where Kodak acquired Sterling. There Kodak overpaid by an amount that caused a huge loss to the stockholders in Kodak. In effect, I would argue that Kodak surprised the market; the market thought Kodak was smarter than that. Instead of following the strategy the market expected, Kodak announced they were acquiring a drug company—and for a very high price.

More on the Role of Institutional Investors

AMIHUD: What I am hearing in this discussion is that there are ways to make important improvements in large public companies, but that most investors don't really want to do all the work necessary to make the changes.

They don't want to do all the work so that all the other passive investors benefit at their expense. It's the classic "free-rider" problem. Foot example, if I sue the company on behalf of the shareholders, I may not get adequately compensated for my efforts unless I have a very large equity stake. So, maybe what is needed is some kind of regulation to overcome this problem, and thus give investors the incentive to become more active in monitoring management and boards.

STERN: I would be very careful about prescribing more regulation.

AMIHUD: Well, Joel, in the case of the "free-rider" problem. the market solution breaks down; and we may need a regulatory solution to this problem. For example, why don't we have an equivalent to the class action suit for shareholders? This way, shareholders who know' how to get more value out of the company but would otherwise be deterred by the free-rider problem—could benefit from their activism.

Another possibility would be to create an entity that would act like a trustee on behalf of stockholders, inform them about the consequences of management decisions, and advise them on how' to vote. In effect, they would monitor management. And unlike the individual board members, the stockholders' trustee should be a separate firm that has a strong interest in developing and maintaining a reputation as an independent arbiter of values. In effect, such a firm would become an independent "auditor" of shareholder value a function which conventional auditors, needless to say, are not currently paid to perform.

STEWART: Well, essentially that result is achieved in a takeover—when somebody like Carl Icahn or Coniston Partners or Irwin Jacobs acquires a stake in companies.

AMIHUD: Yes, but unless you have enough resources to take stakes in the companies and then risk changing the policies, you won't get compensated for your efforts. If you conduct a proxy fight against management and you win, you alone bear the costs while all shareholders benefit. And this reduces your incentive to monitor management and try to change its policies.

GRUNDFEST: There are two levels of answers to this "free-rider" problem. First, I would say there is one strategy other than a takeover that can avoid the problem. A group of lead steer investors could sit down together and say, "Look, among us we own 40 percent. That's large enough a stake to make it worthwhile to deal with this free-rider issue collectively. Why don't we all agree to chip in so much and we'll do this together as a group? Here's the kitty in the ratio of our equity positions as of this date; if you wind up buying mote equity, you've got to chip in more." This kind of arrangement would be one way that the free market could deal with the free-rider problem among investors.

It's not as if there is some secret list of anonymous investors that have significant equity positions in a company's stock. Have a look at the Spectrum books. They describe institutional investor holdings in large corporations. You're all listed in there; and you all know who your friends are in those companies. If everyone in this group agrees that there is a company out there that can really achieve a lot by "incentivizing" its management, and if you figure that the cost of dealing with it aggressively is, say, $50,000, perhaps it doesn't make sense for any one of you to bear that expense alone. But, for five of you working together, it may be the most rational thing in the world. You pick up the phone and call each other and talk.

BRUNIE: What's the rule on these kinds of discussions among investors?

I thought they were prohibited. We tried to do a takeover of ABC years ago. We called on them at 4:00 P.M. As I recall, at 8:30 the next morning we had a surprise audit by the IRS and the SEC. If you area mutual fund, isn't there a different set of regulations you must comply with?

GRUNDFEST: Well, you do have to be careful. For example. you have to be cautious about the number of investors you contact and the nature of your contacts so as to avoid a charge that you have engaged in an illegal proxy solicitation. You have to be careful, but it can be done. In addition, pension funds have to be cautious because they are subject to an additional set of requirements.

Indeed, this is an example of yet another problem we have brought upon ourselves We have created these vast pools of capital and then, through a variety of regulations designed "to protect the beneficiaries," we have tied investors hands behind their backs. Your lawyers will tell you, and they will be right, that the most prudent thing for you to do as an individual find manager is to be passive. That way you don't take any risks. you don't expose yourself to fiduciary duty problems and the like. Once you start becoming active, you may be increasing your potential returns, but you are also dramatically increasing your individual risks.

Thus, we have agency problems not only in the management of public corporations, in terms of getting managers to do what's in investors' best interest. but we also have an agency problem or the investor side of the equation. The problem is, how do you get fund managers—whether it's mutual funds, pension funds or what have you—to do what's in the best interest of the beneficiaries, giver the legal regime in which they operate?

FERENBACH: What was the experience of Texaco, where after Icahn had stirred the pot, the funds seemed to become actively involved?

GRUNDFEST: The funds did become more actively involved. They were led, to a large measure, by some of the public pension finds that are subject to a much easier set of restrictions. They are not as constrained by ERISA and a wide variety of other concerns. That's also one of the reasons why we're likely to see the public pension funds—California State. New' York City, etc.—out front on these challenges to management. Legally, it's easier for them to do it. Also, politically, it fits in with much of their agenda. You often have political types run-ring these organizations and when they identify a social issue they can jump on while running the pension fund, that's heaven on earth.

IN CLOSING

STERN: Before we close. we have time to take a question or two from the press people who are with us. Let's start with Floyd Norris of the *New York Times*.

FLOYD NORRIS: For companies where investors in fact have a very difficult time knowing what is going on inside them, what other signals are available and more trustworthy than the dividend policy to ensure that companies trade at their fair values?

ZECKHAUSER: The key, I think, to having good communication with the investment community is to have large shareholders. About a third of the firms that are listed in Value Line have large shareholders who own 15 percent or more of the firm's shares. To go back to the case of LBOs, the task of communication between management and shareholders' is much easier when you have people like Berkshire Partners owning large shares of companies, sitting on the board, and overseeing operating management. Presumably lots of people looked at these companies before Berkshire came in and bought them. But Berkshire was the ore that said, "I think we can do something with it." They were able to pay a higher price, I would argue, in large part because their presence would close this communication gap that otherwise reduces the value of large public companies with a broadly dispersed shareholder base.

Two of the principal benefits of large shareholders are that they free managements (1) to focus on the future, not attempting to build current earnings at the expense of those years to come, and (2) to avoid costly forms of signaling, such as paying dividends. This implies that with other factors equal, firms with large shareholders should have lower present earnings, higher future earnings, and thus more attractive price/earnings multiples. In recent research, John Pound and I have found that across a broad sampling of industries, the presence of a large shareholder boosts price/earnings multiples by roughly 10 percent.

Unfortunately, many managements tend to worry that large share holders, will end up being hostile shareholders. But there is a symbiosis, a dependency, between the monitor and the monitored, shareholders and professional management. And I think the best arrangement is one that turns this symbiosis to advantage. For this

■

IN RECENT RESEARCH, JOHN POUND AND I HAVE FOUND THAT ACROSS A BROAD SAMPLING OF INDUSTRIES, THE PRESENCE OF A LARGE SHAREHOLDER BOOSTS PRICE/EARNINGS MULTIPLES BY ROUGHLY 10 PERCENT...

—RICHARD ZECKHAUSER—

reason it's good for companies to have large shareholders. And, the very fact that there are large shareholders out there, presumably monitoring the interests of all the owners, should he reassuring to small shareholders. This closer relationship between monitor and monitored should end up increasing the value of the firm.

SHORTS: But, for the typical large public corporation with a broadly dispersed stockholder base, the problem they face in communication is this: What can a large public company provide in the way of an inside signal to their shareholders to tell them what's really going on—a signal that the shareholders will believe?

There is a lot that could he done by corporate investor relations people to educate shareholders about what's going on inside the company. For one thing, they ought to be telling the shareholders what criteria they should he looking at in order to measure management's performance. And having clearly set forth those criteria, the IR effort should periodically report back to the shareholder on management's progress in measuring up against that plan. That's what I would consider a high-quality investor relations program.

LAFFERTY: I would advise investors to seek out companies whose managements' clearly communicate their intentions to maintain return on capital at acceptable levels or who have credible programs for improv-

ing return to theselevels over time. At the same time, some managements are now beginning to seek out investors they deem desirable because they approach investment from the same general perspective as the management does. Clearly, if both sides are using the same vocabulary—that is, the same value drivers"—then the chances for successful two-way communication and "fair value" are improved.

SHORTS: So far, we are talking as if management *wanted* to communicate its expectations and its performance more clearly to shareholders. But I think that a very high percentage of corporate managements are trying to obfuscate rather than clarify what's going on behind the scenes. And because the market demands a premium return for bearing additional uncertainty, that process of deliberate obfuscation makes stock prices lower than what they might otherwise be.

STERN: How can that be in management's interest? Wouldn't that increase the probability of an unfriendly tender offer—because it could be done at a lower price than otherwise?

SHORTS: Well, yes, I think you're right The takeover threat is a 1980s phenomenon stimulated by more relaxed government oversight and the introduction of junk bond financing as a takeover and restructuring tool. One of the great accomplishments of Michael Milken has been to put management or notice that complacency and unresponsiveness to shareholders is not acceptable. This is a lesson that managements are still learning. ■

JOSEPH WHITE: Good morning, I am Joe White, Dean of the University of Michigan's Business School. Let me welcome all of you—students, faculty, guests, and friends—to the First Annual Symposium on Global Financial Markets presented by the Mitsui Life Financial Research Center. We have an extraordinarily distinguished panel to whom you'll be introduced in just a few minutes. But first, it's my great pleasure to introduce Mr. Koshiro Sakata, President of the Mitsui Mutual Life Insurance Company of Tokyo. Mr. Sakata has journeyed here from Tokyo for the sole purpose of speaking to us at this first symposium, and we are deeply honored to have him here to open these proceedings.

KOSHIRO SAKATA: It is a great pleasure for me to convene this first symposium of the Mitsui Life Financial Research Center. I would like to thank the co-directors of the Center, Professors Han Kim of the University of Michigan and Tak Wakasugi of the University of Tokyo, and everyone who has contributed to the making of this event. Also I am honored by the presence of a distinguished group of panelists—a group that includes two Nobel laureates.

About a year has passed since the opening ceremony for the Center last fall. Since that time the Center has been very active. It has sponsored two speakers in the distinguished lecture series: Professor Merton Miller of the University of Chicago (who is also a panelist here today) and Mr. Toyoo

VOLATILITY IN U.S. AND JAPANESE STOCK MARKETS

*Selections from the
First Annual Symposium on
Global Financial Markets*

*Sponsored by the
Mitsui Life Financial Research Center
University of Michigan*

Ann Arbor, October 3-4, 1991

KOSHIRO SAKATA

Gyohten, formerly Vice-Minister of the Japanese Ministry of Finance and now an adviser to the Bank of Tokyo. I was extremely pleased to learn that only a week after his lecture Professor Miller was awarded the Nobel Prize in Economics.

In addition to the Distinguished Lecture Series, the Mitsui Life Financial Research Center has begun publication of working papers and reprints of previously published research. Thus far, 44 working papers and 13 reprinted articles have been made available to over 1,000 academics and research organizations. Thanks to the efforts of Professors Kim and Wakasugi, and to the support of the University of Michigan Business School, I am convinced that the Center will continue to accumulate new insights into the operations of global financial markets, and to disseminate this valuable knowledge around the world.

We have witnessed an astonishing transformation of the Cold-War political and economic systems of the past 40 years into a new economic order with an uncertain future. Paralleling these developments, Japanese financial markets have also experienced a significant increase in uncertainty and volatility in recent years. Today's symposium, which is devoted to the subject of "Volatility in U.S. and Japanese Financial Markets," is thus a very timely topic. I have great expectations for this event, and hope that you will also enjoy and benefit from it. Thank you very much.

WHITE: President Sakata, on behalf of the entire Michigan Business School community, let me thank Mitsui Life for your commitment to and support of the Center. And let me also thank you for gracing us with your personal presence today.

The Mitsui Center, as President Sakata mentioned, is co-directed by two people: Professor Takaaki Wakasugi, from Tokyo University, and Professor E. Han Kim, the Fred M. Taylor Professor of Finance at the Michigan Business School. I will now turn the floor over to Professor Kim, who will serve as moderator of the first part of this program.

PART I:
STOCK MARKET VOLATILITY AND ITS CONSEQUENCES

HAN KIM: Let me begin by joining President Sakata and Dean White in welcoming all of you to the First Annual Symposium sponsored by the Mitsui Life Financial Research Center.

The U.S. and Japanese financial markets are the world's largest. Together they represent two-thirds of the world stock market capitalization. Both countries have experienced substantial volatility in financial and real estate markets, with sometimes disturbing implications for the global financial system and financial institutions throughout the world.

The U.S. public became more sensitive to the negative aspects of market volatility after the stock market crash in October 1987 and the bout of market turbulence in October 1989. The Japanese public also experienced the negative side of market volatility during the summer of 1990. The Nikkei average reached its peak of 39,000 in December 1989. But by the end of August 1990, it had fallen by some 40% to its current level of about 24,000.[1]

These events have led financial economists to write numerous scientific papers on market volatility and stock market mechanisms. In addition, various regulatory agencies and exchanges have commissioned reports to investigate the crash of '87. Although these studies have provided new insights into the workings of the stock market, there is still considerable controversy about the causes and consequences of market volatility and the merits of proposed regulations. There is even disagreement,

as you will hear, about whether market volatility has indeed increased significantly in recent times.

Today we are privileged to have with us five distinguished panelists representing the viewpoints of investors, regulators, the financial industry, and academics. I will now briefly introduce each of them in the order in which they will be speaking.

JAMES TOBIN was the 1981 Nobel laureate in Economics and is Sterling Professor Emeritus of Economics at Yale University. Professor Tobin won the Nobel Prize for his pioneering work in macroeconomics, monetary theory, and fiscal policy. He has also made seminal contributions to modern portfolio theory and our understanding of financial markets.

WENDY GRAMM was reappointed last year to her second term as the Chairperson of the Commodities Futures Trading Commission (CFTC). As such, she is the top federal regulator of futures markets. Her position places her at the center of the controversy over the impact of index arbitrage on market volatility.

MITSUO SATO is Deputy President of the Tokyo Stock Exchange. Prior to joining the Exchange in 1986, Mr. Sato had a distinguished career in the Japanese Ministry of Finance.

STEPHEN TIMBERS is Senior Executive Vice President and Chief Investment Officer of Kemper Financial Services. Mr. Timbers has responsibility for managing a portfolio worth more than $63 billion. In addition, he served as a member of the New York Stock Exchange Blue Ribbon Panel on Market Volatility and Investor Confidence.

MERTON MILLER is the Robert R. McCormick Distinguished Service Professor of Finance at the University of Chicago's Graduate School of Business. Professor Miller, who won a Nobel Prize in 1990, is widely regarded as the "founding father" of modern financial theory. Professor Miller also served on the Blue Ribbon Panel on Market Volatility and Investor Confidence.

We will now hear from Professor Tobin.

JAMES TOBIN

TOBIN: Thank you, Mr. Kim, President Sakata, Dean White. I am honored to be the first person to speak at what is to become, I gather, an annual symposium.

---

1. Editor's Note: As of the date of this writing (May 6, 1992), the Nikkei had fallen about another 15% to below 18,000.

The last time I participated in a conference on market volatility was in October of 1989. The conference was held at the Federal Reserve Bank of New York. The President of the New York Fed, Gerald Corrigan, was presiding at this conference of economists; and every few minutes he would get another message from outside telling him how far the stock market had fallen in the previous hour. I only hope that history does not repeat itself at this symposium.

I want to begin with some preliminary observations with full knowledge that anything I say that is wrong will be corrected several times— and ultimately, of course, by Merton Miller. I'm really a macroeconomist and, as far as I'm able to tell, the field of macroeconomics is held in about as much esteem by finance departments as the study of astrology.

In thinking about this problem, I began by asking myself when and why is volatility in stock markets a problem. Economists don't really have much of a theory about volatility, and so there is no reliable conceptual guide to an optimal level of volatility. Indeed, we don't even have general agreement about what represents the best time period for measuring volatility. Should we measure it minute by minute, month by month, or over periods of years? Which of these measures of periodic volatility matters most to professional portfolio managers, to corporations, and to individual savers managing their own portfolios?

> **A one-day drop of 20% makes us wonder whether the market is doing a good job in performing its social role as an allocator of resources. It makes us question the usefulness of the "signals" the market is sending to savers and businesses about where to invest their capital....**
>
> **Not only could the market give off wrong signals at different times, but also its volatility could be exaggerating the risk of corporate investment. That is, if there is significantly more volatility in corporate stock prices than in the fundamental corporate earnings streams, stock price volatility could increase risks to market investors out of all proportion to the economic risks of corporate investment. And this in turn could cause equity prices to be lower than they should be, and so reduce corporate real investment.**
>
> **—James Tobin—**

The answer to such questions would probably depend largely on how often portfolio managers trade or how often individuals need to withdraw money from their portfolios. Personally, it wouldn't matter much to me whether stocks fell 20% in one day or instead gradually dropped 20% over several months. My welfare would be just as badly damaged by a gradual decline as by an abrupt fall.

For this reason, I think the current concern about volatility is not mainly about volatility *per se*. It arises rather from our suspicion that volatility is a symptom of more fundamental problems with the market. A one-day drop of 20% makes us wonder whether the market is doing a good job in performing its social role as an allocator of resources. It makes us question the usefulness of the "signals" the market is sending to savers and businesses about where to invest their capital. In other words, I don't think we would mind so much if, as perhaps many people still believe, we were convinced that the volatility of the stock market reflected fundamental economic variations, or changes in fundamental economic values. But it's the evidence that market values can change by 20% without any perceptible, plausible economic cause that casts serious doubt on the efficiency of the entire stock market pricing mechanism—a mechanism that, after all, is supposed to direct the flow of savings among competing enterprises and industries.

Another point I want to make at the outset is this: According to portfolio theory, the volatility that matters to portfolio managers would not be the simple variances of market averages, or of the prices of any particular stocks. It would rather be the covariance of stock returns with their entire portfolio of assets. And it's that "co-volatility," if you will, that seems to me a more important economic concern. For individual savers, a large portion of wealth really represents "human capital," the current and future earnings power arising from their own set of skills and experience. Investments whose returns are *negatively* correlated with changes in the value of human capital are, from a social standpoint, the most desirable kinds of investment. And, for this reason, I'm not sure that volatility *per se* deserves attention apart from covariance.

Let me also say that I become a little alarmed when I see that the first thing many people recommend to the Soviet Union and other former Communist countries is that they establish a stock market. A stock market is said to be the central institution of capitalism, and in a sense I guess that is true. But perhaps you don't start with the central institution when you're creating a capitalist system from scratch.

Let me return to the function of our own financial markets. The basic function of these securities markets, the stock and bond markets, is to connect savers with the corporations that invest in real assets. The corporate securities markets are supposed to repackage the risks of real corporate investment for financial investors in an optimal manner. The stock market, as I mentioned before, is also supposed to produce valuations of corporate securities that guide portfolio managers and other savers, and provide reliable signals to guide the officers of corporations in making their real investment decisions. That is the classical theory of the stock market as the allocator of resources from savers to businesses. That is its justification for being.

If the market is giving off bad signals, it's not doing its job. Not only could the market give off wrong signals at different times, but also its volatility could be exaggerating the risk of corporate investment. That is, if there is significantly more volatility in corporate stock prices than in the fundamental earnings streams being produced by those corporations being valued, then stock price volatility may be increasing risks to market investors out of all proportion to the economic risks of corporate investment. And this in turn could cause equity prices to be lower

than they should be, and thereby reduce corporate real investment.

It's true that corporations don't raise most of their capital by issuing new shares. They raise most of their capital by issuing debt and retaining earnings. Nevertheless, we have a classical theory of corporations—or we used to have one, at any rate, before the rise of "agency cost" theory—that said professional managers act for the most part on behalf of their shareholders. That theory also said that managers intent on maximizing shareholder value should and do use signals from the stock market as guides in their decisions whether to retain and reinvest corporate earnings, or to return capital to the stockholders through dividends or stock repurchases. So this makes stock prices important for corporate managers even if they never intend to raise new equity.

The theory that managers act to maximize shareholder value was challenged, of course, by Adolph Berle and Gardiner Means back in the 1920s. And though most classical economists until recently dismissed or ignored their assertions of the negative consequences of the separation of ownership from control, the original notions of Berle and Means have been revived—and with all the mathematical elegance necessary nowadays—in the form of "agency" theory. As formulated by Michael Jensen and William Meckling while at the University of Rochester, the theory purports to demonstrate how conflicts of interest between management and shareholders reduce the value of large public corporations with widely dispersed ownership. But, for all its fancy mathematics and theoretical reasoning, modern agency theory is simply a more palatable version of the old Berle and Means idea.

So, given the possibility of major agency costs, we can't even be sure that if the stock market were giving managers the right signals, managers would be responding properly to them. But if we assume most managers *do* attempt to do the right thing by their shareholders, then there is legitimate concern that stock market volatility may be imposing a short-term mentality on American managers and corporations. This is the argument that has come not only from American observers and American managers themselves, but also from Japanese officials and managers. Japanese companies are regularly said to have longer-term planning horizons, which enable them to make large investments with the expectation that several years of losses will be justified by eventual gains in market share and access to export markets.

If the stock market were always giving the right signals, the fact that the CEO of an American corporation is forced to consider the latest quotation of his shares at 4:30 every afternoon would not be a problem—even if his likely tenure as CEO is shorter than the duration of the real assets in which the corporation has invested. That disparity wouldn't matter, because in theory current stock price movements are supposed to reflect investors' collective judgment about the long-run value of the company. And if current prices do indeed reflect the present value of all future expected cash flows, as the theory says, then there is no irreconcilable conflict between a manager's incentive to maximize short-term market value and to maximize the long-run value of his or her company. That is, if managers invest effectively for the long term today, then the future value of that investment strategy should be reflected in today's stock prices.

But if American managers are correct in their belief that current prices fail to reflect long-run values, then they may rationally adopt short-term horizons that could reduce the value of their corporations over the long term. American managers may be voting no confidence in the signals they're getting from the stock market itself when they doubt the market's ability or willingness to value long-term commitments.

The alternative to relying on market signals is to have people making corporate investment decisions who are charged institutionally to have a long-term horizon. For example, the responsibility of the trustees of Yale University is to manage its endowment as guardians of the University's future. They do in fact guard the future. They in effect say, "Even though we have a large endowment and major needs right now, we can't spend the principal because if we do it won't be there 100 years from now." (And Yale University, as I'm sure we all agree, is the very model of an immortal institution—at least it's been around longer than the United States of America.)

I have the impression that the managers of Japanese corporations take a view of their companies that is much more akin to that of Yale's trustees. They don't take their signals from the market. On the other hand—and this is pure speculation on my part—the Japanese stock market may also be far more divorced from economic fundamentals, and thus a far less reliable predictor of future values, than

the U.S. market. And so, if the Japanese market is indeed much more of a casino, much more liable to a 40% decline, then it still may not matter that much to the people running Japanese corporations. They will simply carry on as before, using their own judgments to guide corporate investment decisions. In the U.S., however, the consequences for corporate managers of ignoring the stock market are much greater—or at least they were much greater until the takeover market ceased to operate after 1989.

But let me return to my earlier question about whether the U.S. market is providing reliable signals to corporate managers. My colleague at Yale, Bob Shiller (who will be speaking here tomorrow), dropped a bomb on efficient markets theory when he demonstrated that the variance of stock prices was several times what it should have been if stock prices were simply reflecting the variance of future dividends. And the fact that there is now a large literature devoted to trying to refute Bob's work is probably the best indication of its importance. My judgment of that literature, by the way, is that it is what Britishers call "too clever by half." It is full of contrived models that attempt to justify the actual volatility of U.S. stock prices by envisioning a range of expectations of future dividends and earnings that greatly exceeds the range of past data. So my sympathies in this empirical controversy are clearly with my colleague.

Let me conclude with one final point. One feature of a stock market crash and its aftermath is that investor expectations tend to be extrapolative. Bob Shiller conducted a survey of stock market investors after the crash of 1987. He found that the principal reason people reported for selling after the crash was that they feared the market was going to continue to decline. Their decisions to sell reportedly had nothing to do with the economic events of the previous week, nothing to do with macro policy changes featured in the press. A large number of people were simply afraid the market was going down further.

The pure theory of financial markets assumes that market reactions to economic events take place in "instantaneous" jumps, whether up or down. The adjustments to the "equilibrium" price are supposed to be immediate; there are supposed to be no predictable trends following major moves. But if it is true, as Shiller's survey suggests, that investors collectively expect trends to persist, then there's really no such thing as a "new equilibrium," there's no price stability. Stability in markets depends on investors having differences of opinion. You have to have people who are willing to buy as well as sell at any given time. But if investors consistently move in herds to buy or sell, then prices will consistently "overshoot" and thus fall above or below their true values. And if that is the case, then portfolio managers and corporate managers are right to be troubled by stock market volatility.

And I'll just leave it at that. Thank you.

KIM: Thank you very much, Professor Tobin. Now we will hear from Dr. Wendy Gramm, Chairperson of the CFTC.

WENDY GRAMM

GRAMM: Thank you very much. As a former academic economist myself, I'm really delighted to be on a panel with two Nobel laureates—even if I am here only to play the role of designated regulator.

In discussions of volatility, it seems taken as a tenet of faith that the mere presence of volatility is *prima facie* evidence of a market problem. But, in my remarks, I will try to persuade you that volatility may not be such a cause for concern as conventional wisdom would have it.

It's true that prices are now more responsive to market developments around the globe. But such price movements, it's important to recognize, are simply the consequence of markets that are today better able to reflect ongoing changes in fundamental factors affecting supply and demand. This improved price responsiveness has been brought about by greater institutional participation, increased capital mobility, the expansion of screen-based trading systems—and also by increases in the capacity of the systems and institutions themselves to handle more trading.

Along with improved price responsiveness there has also been a significant increase in trading volume and liquidity—not only in corporate equities and debt instruments, but also in derivative instruments such as futures and options. So, given this apparent robustness of the financial marketplace, it's hard to argue that these markets are now suffering under a burden imposed by "excessive" volatility.

In addition, studies have reported that the volatility of the 1980s, the period when stock index futures and options trading got underway, was not particularly high compared to that of prior decades.

In fact, volatility in the '80s was considerably lower than in the depression years of the 1930s and '40s. And this leads me to suspect that those people who claim that volatility has risen do not share economists' understanding of what constitutes volatility. Dispelling popular misconceptions about volatility is important because our understanding of volatility and the changes that are taking place in the global economy will influence the direction of regulatory policy in the future.

As always, regulatory policy should seek to ensure that high standards of business conduct and fair competition are maintained. This is crucial if financial markets are to continue to serve their social purpose of allocating risks and resources in this changing global environment. On the other hand, determining what is a fair price, an optimal level of participation and volume, or an optimal number of tradable financial assets are clearly not decisions that should be undertaken by regulators or politicians. Not only do regulators not have a magic formula for knowing what equilibrium prices or quantity should be, they also, for all their good intentions, do not operate under the same incentives that ensure the efficiency of competitive markets. Rest assured, the public will not tolerate a market in which prices do not reflect true value.

Regulatory determination of how much should be traded and at what price will be futile at best, since enterprising individuals will find a way to circumvent the regulation—for example, by trading in other markets. At worst, regulatory policy of this nature could do serious harm to the viability of the market, causing the business to move offshore or overseas.

Let me now turn to the subject of volatility and price discovery.

A primary way for information to be incorporated into financial asset prices is by means of trading. As more sources of information become available and the methods for processing information improve, trading will almost certainly rise. If prices change in response to more frequent revision of investor valuations, then more trading will likely result in greater reported *intra-day* volatility. But even if such short-term volatility goes up, longer-term volatility may be unaffected. And, to the extent increased volatility is simply a reflection of the more frequent arrival and processing of new information, it is fully consistent with market efficiency.

To those who think that derivative markets play a special role in contributing to volatility, I would respond in two ways. First, derivative markets have been developed primarily to help investors and corporations cope with volatility by acting as a mechanism for the transfer of price risk. For example, by selling stock index futures, an equity portfolio manager can substantially reduce the risks associated with price volatility. Futures markets thus provide a solution for those who own financial assets, yet feel that current price volatility is unacceptable.

Much of the confusion surrounding the issue of futures markets and volatility has to do with the fact that hedging demand for futures typically increases in response to increases in volatility. Thus, the volume of futures trading and volatility may be *correlated*, but this does not mean futures *cause* the change in volatility. An increase in futures volume is simply a response to, not the cause of, increased volatility. The popular association of futures with volatility is analogous to the reasoning that since there is an increase in firemen at the scene of a fire, firemen must therefore be the cause of the fire. In fact, just as firemen are there to put out fires, futures markets are there to contend with volatility.

Besides facilitating hedging, the existence of futures markets enhances efficient price discovery. Unfortunately, this contribution has also become a basis for charges that futures trading is responsible for market volatility. When information affecting

> **Much of the confusion surrounding the issue of futures markets and volatility has to do with the fact that hedging demand for futures typically increases in response to increases in volatility. Thus, the volume of futures trading and volatility may be *correlated*, but this does not mean futures *cause* the change in volatility. An increase in futures volume is simply a response to, not the cause of, increased volatility. In this sense, the suggestion that futures trading results in excess volatility in the cash market amounts to shooting the messenger.**
>
> **—Wendy Gramm—**

asset value arrives, careful investors will choose to trade on the information in either of the two markets, the cash or the futures, depending on which best suits their investment strategy, liquidity preferences, and cost considerations. So, when the futures market is the more cost-effective way to trade on some information, the price effects of that information will first show up in the futures market.

Once again, the subsequent price adjustment in the cash market does *not* mean the futures market *caused* the price change in the cash market. The futures market is not the cause of volatility; the volatility is caused by fundamental changes in supply and demand. The futures market is simply the *vehicle* through which changes in information, expectations, and risk preferences are first made. The suggestion that futures trading results in excess volatility in the cash market is off the mark; it amounts to shooting the messenger.

The claim that there is "excess volatility" and that regulators should do something is thus ambiguous. Before we intervene in the markets to eliminate excess volatility, we need an understanding of what volatility is and what the costs are which it imposes on markets and society. When one states that there is excess volatility, we must ask what constitutes the right amount of volatility? And how would this level be defined?

We at the Commission have learned that, depending on one's perspective, definitions of volatility vary greatly. For example, some people hold that only a large downward price movement constitutes volatility, while an upward price movement is simply a "recovery." What this distinction ignores is that liquid markets need people on both sides of the market, buyers and sellers. And while price volatility can be measured in a number of ways, such as the price range or variance of price changes, both upward and downward movement must be considered with equal weight.

As mentioned earlier, empirical studies that have measured the actual level of stock market volatility, and not the perception of volatility, do not support the conclusion of increased volatility. For example, William Schwert's historical survey of stock market volatility shows that, except during the Depression, the level of volatility has been relatively stable since the mid-nineteenth century. Professor Schwert's study also shows the episodes of October 1987 and October 1989 to have been very short-lived aberrations.

One final point about volatility: it's not clear that lower price volatility is always more desirable for the economy. Suppose you could legislate that a market have *no* volatility. Would this be a good thing? To eliminate volatility is to fix prices. No volatility means that prices are unable to adjust to changes in information regarding supply and demand. Command economies have certainly demonstrated to the world the chronic inefficiencies associated with attempts to fix prices. The consequences of price fixing—as should now be clear if it wasn't before—are shortages, long queues, and grossly distorted resource allocation.

Much of the confusion about the role of the futures markets in contributing to stock market volatility stems from a failure to understand the relationship between the cash markets and the markets for derivative securities. Perhaps the most popular misconception is that there should exist a balance between the stock and derivative markets, the premise being that volatility results from excessive volume in the derivative markets. In the U.S., pundits frequently cite statistics showing that the so-called "dollar volume" of trade in index futures is consistently greater than that of equity trading on the NYSE. But let me say that there is absolutely no reason, theoretical or empirical, to suggest that volume in one market should match or not exceed that of another. It simply does not make sense to compare the two.

First, it is difficult to convert futures contract volume into dollars. While a futures contract represents a contingent claim on the asset underlying the contract, the true value of most futures contracts at any given time is close to zero. This follows from the fact that futures positions are marked-to-market at the close of each trading day. As a result, conversion of contract-based futures volume by reference to the current value of the asset underlying the contract—that is, multiplying the current futures price times the contract size—greatly overestimates the true value of futures contracts traded.

Second, volume in the derivative instrument could be less than or greater than the volume of the underlying assets, depending on many factors. To begin with, there are differing motivations for trading in the cash and derivative markets. While cash markets facilitate the exchange of ownership rights, derivative markets facilitate the transfer of risk. For example, as mentioned earlier, stock index futures provide portfolio managers with an inexpensive means to adjust their risk exposure without having to sell assets. Take the case of a portfolio manager managing a wide variety of stocks who turned temporarily bearish on the market. He could choose to sell all his stocks at their current prices, with the intent of later reacquiring the same positions. Or he could instead sell stock index futures and lock in the current price. Because the use of stock index futures involves a fraction of the transactions costs, he would likely choose this strategy. And for this reason alone, one would expect futures volume to be greater than volume in the cash market.

Furthermore, as investors and portfolio managers seek to monitor and rebalance their futures positions more actively in response to changing market conditions, volume increases can occur even as the extent of hedged positions remain unchanged. In the process of making adjustments to their hedge positions—for example, by rolling over contracts as they approach maturity—hedgers are likely to generate a considerable amount of volume.

Another dimension lost sight of in public discussions of volatility is the positive economic role played by speculators. For futures markets to perform their important functions of risk shifting and price discovery, there must be adequate liquidity to meet the demands of business and hedging interests. The presence of speculators in the market helps ensure that hedgers can lay off risk when they want to, and at a price that is an accurate reflection of market conditions. Speculators thus fill liquidity gaps by their willingness to assume risk. Yet, despite the well-documented importance of speculators to maintaining liquidity and price efficiency, we continue to hear calls for regulatory measures to curb speculation.

In sum, the claim that there is too much futures volume or excess speculation and that regulators should do something to curb it does not rest on very firm ground. Those who wish to use a regulatory approach to limit trading of a particular type, or in a particular market, should keep in mind that our principal goal as regulators is to maintain active and liquid markets.

So, what, then, is the appropriate regulatory response to volatility?

In my few remaining minutes, I will briefly examine the case for what is probably the most popular regulatory proposal—circuit breakers. Regulatory responses to volatility have included placing additional restrictions on trading such as trading halts, price limits, and up-tick rules like NYSE Rule 80A, which applies to index arbitrage.

So let's think about what such circuit breakers are supposed to accomplish. On the one hand, circuit breakers are thought to be useful for addressing systemic problems. For example, a trading halt is said to provide a period in which amounts can be tallied, margin calls made, and funds collected, thus ensuring the financial integrity of markets. We can imagine a football game, where a time-out allows the coach to review strategy with key players, send in a new play, and allows us, the viewers, the chance to make a run on the refrigerator.

Quite apart from systemic considerations, proponents also argue that circuit breakers are useful in controlling excess volatility as well as unwarranted price movements. For example, it is suggested that by slowing down trading, including strategies such as index arbitrage, volatility can be lowered. However, the use of trading halts to allay regulatory concern over excess volatility may be self-defeating. In a close game, we typically see more hustle and desperation plays after the two-minute warning. Similarly, traders may alter their trading strategies as prices approach their limits. Fears of illiquidity or being locked into a position may trigger additional trading and create order imbalances, which in turn may actually *increase* volatility. Indeed, there is persuasive academic evidence that indicates that volatility increases both before and after periods

when it is difficult to trade, such as when markets go through transition periods like the open and close. Circuit breakers, by making it difficult to trade, may well have similar effects.

Simply because market participants cannot trade during halts does not mean that they stop revising the prices they are willing to settle for as new information arrives. Stopping trading does not stop the flow of information. As Stephen Ross has pointed out, trading that is suppressed in some periods will simply reappear in another period; and the same seems true of volatility. This suggests that trading halts simply result in the transfer of volatility over time or across markets, rather than eliminating it. When one market is closed down, trade will move to other markets, and so, it appears, will volatility.

Since prices themselves convey information, measures to stabilize prices may have the unintended effect of cutting off the flow of the information embedded in prices. Circuit breakers may thus impede the price discovery process. While circuit breakers and trading halts are designed to stabilize prices or to dampen price moves, there is no evidence that indicates that they curb subsequent price changes. For example, as Richard Roll will likely tell you tomorrow, his recent study of the equity markets of 24 countries during the 1987 market crash found that, after controlling for differences in price volatilities, price limits had no differential effect on the subsequent rate of decline in prices.

A recent study we performed at the CFTC examined the relationship on two volatile trading days—October 13 and 16, 1989—between the triggering of circuit breakers in stock index futures and changes in the volatility of stock prices and stock index futures prices. And our study found strong evidence in support of the above predictions.

First, circuit breakers do not appear to have moderated intra-day market volatility, particularly on October 13, 1989. In the instances following the triggering of circuit breakers in the S&P 500 futures market on the 13th and the 16th, there is no evidence that price volatility in the stock market decreased. Also, on October 13th, volatility in both futures and the stock market increased markedly in the trading period immediately *after* the circuit breakers were removed.

Second, we found evidence of volume migration on October 13th. When the S&P 500 index futures market and options market were closed due to the circuit breaker, volume migrated to the Chicago Board of Trade's Major Market Index (the "MMI"). In addition, several traders reported that uncoordinated market closings and limits on the 13th led traders to shift to the markets that remained open for trading or were unconstrained by limits.

Third, we found evidence indicating that a binding circuit breaker in one market leads to increased volatility in unconstrained markets. The volatility of both the MMI futures contract and MMI stocks increased during the nine-minute period on October 13 when the S&P 500 futures market was constrained by limits while the MMI was not. For example, it was reported that when the Chicago Board Options Exchange (CBOE) was closed, CBOE traders who had written options were driven to futures and equities markets.

In short, the effectiveness and purpose of circuit breakers needs more careful examination. Do circuit breakers serve any purpose? If so, is it for systemic considerations only? What kind of rules might be invoked to reduce uncertainties associated with the initiation and duration of the trading halts? And how should the use of circuit breakers be coordinated globally?

Now let me turn, in closing, to regulatory issues of the future. Most important, what should regulators do to preserve market integrity while contributing to economic growth?

Perhaps the most important lesson for regulators is that individual countries cannot isolate their markets if they wish to be a player in the global arena. They cannot have it both ways. They cannot enjoy the benefits of an expanded free marketplace and be protectionist at the same time. And policymakers cannot endorse a regulatory policy that constrains prices or volatility, or that only permits the upward movement of prices. There are people on both sides of the market—producers and consumers, investors and savers, buyers and sellers. To suggest that one is more important than the other is to disadvantage the other.

Also, since a well-functioning financial market often contains solutions to its own problems, regulators should be wary of proposing regulatory solutions. Markets that are free to reach efficient solutions will provide useful economic signals that guide decision makers. Equally important, experience has taught us that sometimes regulatory responses may go beyond their original intentions and produce new problems. A regulatory agency has a responsibility to ensure that financial markets are fair, open, competitive, and innovative enough to meet the changing needs of market participants.

Thank you.

KIM: Thank you, Dr. Gramm. Our next speaker is Mr. Mitsuo Sato, Deputy President of the Tokyo Stock Exchange.

MITSUO SATO

SATO: Thank you very much, Professor Kim. First of all, let me say that I feel honored to share the panel with these distinguished scholars and high-ranking officials. I also greatly appreciate the effort by the Mitsui Life Financial Research Center to arrange this joint U.S.-Japanese symposium—an especially important undertaking, I believe, in view of the increasing financial interdependence between the two countries.

Volatility in financial markets is clearly of major concern to us all. Everyone agrees that excessive volatility will interfere with the functioning of an equity market in the national economy, increasing risk premiums and raising the corporate cost of capital. In light of this widespread concern about volatility, I will discuss the recent behavior of the Tokyo market from the perspective of market regulators—a perspective, I hasten to add, that does not pretend to be rigorously analytical or scientific.

As is well known, Japan experienced a two-stage stock decline in 1990, first in the spring and then later in the fall. Taken together, these two periods saw a 40% decline in the value of the Japanese market, representing more than than 230 trillion yen, or $1.7 trillion, in losses. The recent "paybacks" scandal, moreover, has further depressed the market.

The first phase of the market decline, which took place in the spring of 1990, was essentially a market correction, reflecting changes in Japan's economic fundamentals. The second phase, however, at least in my view, was more a reflection of political than economic developments.

The market drop in the spring, which was peculiar to Japan, took place against the background of rapidly rising interest rates. During the period from 1986 to mid-1989, Japan conducted a loose monetary policy intended to stimulate domestic demand and reduce external surpluses while at the same time helping to sustain the value of the U.S.

dollar. The general feeling of Japanese policymakers then was that a stronger yen, while helping to right external imbalances, might have endangered the financing of the U.S. deficits.

But this situation, which was quite favorable to the equity market, did not last for long. In response to diminishing external surpluses and growing direct investment abroad, the value of the yen weakened in the last half of 1989. This depreciation, combined with rapid growth in the money supply, robust economic expansion at home, and higher interest rates abroad, strengthened the concerns of monetary authorities about future inflation. Reflecting this concern about inflation, the official discount rate was doubled in less than one year, rising from 3.25% in September 1989 to 6% in August 1990.

Japanese monetary authorities also were anxious to curb the so-called "asset inflation," a legacy of the easy monetary policy, because of its adverse effects on the distribution of income and wealth. As a result, long-term interest rates jumped from 5% to 7% around the turn of the year. And this in turn led to a 28% decline in the stock market in the spring of 1990. The overvaluation of stock prices in late 1989 also undoubtedly contributed to the steepness of the correction.

The event that seemed to trigger the large market decline in the fall of 1990 was the sudden invasion in the Persian Gulf. Like other major stock

> **Who or what, then, was the real villain in the crash of '87? My best guess is that it was just the lack of sufficient adaptation by the entire financial system to the development of derivative markets and new trading strategies. The separation between the cash and derivative markets in the U.S. allowed the two markets to become disconnected at a critical time. The New York Stock Exchange halted the use of the DOT system, which led to a free-fall of the futures in Chicago because index arbitragers could no longer step in to buy futures and sell stocks. And this situation fueled investor panic by keeping the futures abnormally discounted, thus causing investors to anticipate a further selling rush. Had the cash market instead been allowed to function, the situation would have been much less traumatic.**
>
> **—Mitsuo Sato—**

markets at this time, Japan's stock market was greatly affected by the resulting uncertainty about oil prices, which in turn increased uncertainty about future inflation and interest rates. Aside from these political developments, however, there were no significant changes in Japan's economic fundamentals during the period. And this second, more puzzling, decline in stock prices led many observers to ask the following question: Could recent financial innovations, particularly the rise of stock index futures and options, have contributed significantly to this 40% drop in the value of Japanese stocks?

But before addressing this issue, let me comment briefly on the controversy over futures and program trading that arose after the U.S. market crash of October '87. Critics of the futures market argued that the very existence of portfolio insurance and the futures market led to investor overconfidence and hence overvaluation of the stock market. They did so by promising to provide investors with a relatively costless means of getting out of the market. But, as it turned out, of course, portfolio insurance using futures did not work as expected during the crash. And, in this sense, the "illusion of liquidity" created by futures may have set the market up for a great fall.

Another widely heard criticism was that the actions of index arbitragers in buying and selling between the futures and the cash markets had the effect of destabilizing the cash market. In effect, this argument goes, a sell-off in the futures markets was transmitted through "inter-market vibration" to the cash market, setting off an avalanche of selling. Others argued that the futures market, by facilitating "mechanical trading" of large blocks, was discouraging conventional, fundamentals-based investors.

None of the above arguments against futures is very persuasive. One can counter the first objection simply by noting that stock prices plunged not only in the United States, but also in other countries where derivative markets did not exist at all, or were not widely used. As for the second, it seems contradictory to put the blame on index arbitragers. In fact, as I will suggest later, the arbitrage link between the two markets was severed during the crash. Had it remained intact, the situation may have been better than it actually was, as I will discuss later.

It is not as easy to dismiss the third objection— that "mechanical trading" could disrupt more conventional trading activity based on fundamentals. Nevertheless, it seems likely that conventional traders ought to be able to adjust over time for the "noise" that such strategies may introduce into prices. At any rate, it seems clear that, given the important hedging uses of the futures and other derivatives markets—a role that Dr. Gramm just described so well—our only choice is to accommodate "mechanical trading" within the system.

Who or what, then, was the real villain in the crash of '87? My best guess is that it was just the lack of sufficient adaptation by the entire financial system to the development of derivative markets and new trading strategies. The separation between the cash and derivative markets in the U.S. allowed the two markets to become disconnected at a critical time. The New York Stock Exchange halted the use of the DOT system, which led to a free-fall of the futures in Chicago because index arbitragers could no longer step in to buy futures and sell stocks. And this situation fueled investor panic by keeping the futures abnormally discounted, thus causing investors to anticipate a further selling rush. Had the cash market instead been allowed to function, the situation would have been much less traumatic.

But one thing is clear from this experience: this dynamic relationship between the futures and cash markets has changed the financial system, and we have now accumulated considerable experience in managing this interaction. We have learned important lessons.

Now, what about the Japanese situation? Based on our understanding of the U.S. experience in 1987, we have chosen to integrate the cash and derivative markets in Japan. But even this greater integration has not made us immune to the problem of excess volatility.

First, with the introduction of index futures to Japan in 1988, index arbitragers became active. And such activity resulted in heightened stock price volatility on the day the futures contracts expired, essentially because of the concentration of large orders involved in closing out the arbitrage positions. This problem was addressed by following the U.S. precedent—that is, by adopting in September 1989 the so-called "special quotation" that permits such orders to be absorbed by much greater liquidity at the opening of the following day.

Coping with the stock market plunge in the spring of 1990 was more difficult. In that case, what was probably an inevitable market correction was made worse by coinciding with an unwinding of index arbitrage positions. A substantial volume of index arbitrage positions initiated in December 1989 ended up being liquidated in a very weak cash market. For this reason, index arbitrage sales were assigned blame for the stock market decline by people whose principle concern is with the cash market.

The same experience with index arbitrage was repeated during the second decline in the fall of 1990. And, in response to those two experiences, we have taken several steps to deal with this situation, including the disclosure of index arbitrage transactions and raising margins on futures and options.

Thus, the Japanese experience with, and concerns about, derivative markets are remarkably similar to those in the U.S. But there are also important differences as well. For example, there are virtually no portfolio insurance strategies in Japan. But perhaps the most important difference has been what we suspect to have been a major shift of equity trading away from the cash to the futures market in Japan. Since its inception in 1988, the index futures on the Nikkei 225 that are traded on the Osaka Stock Exchange have grown very rapidly, with the size of the market having more than doubled in the past three years. Given the decline in the size of the cash market, the futures market is now more than five times as large as the underlying cash market. This differs from the U.S. situation, where the volume of futures on the S&P 500 is roughly equivalent to that of the underlying market in New York—and U.S. stock index futures have been around considerably longer than their Japanese counterparts.

Furthermore, the entire Japanese equity market—that is, cash plus futures—has grown rather steadily at an annual rate of 10% over the period in question. So, if we assume that the *total* demand for equity in the Japanese economy has grown at a stable rate, it's conceivable that investors have collectively changed their preferences away from the cash to the derivative instruments. Also, declines in stock trading volume have differed significantly among those stocks comprising the Nikkei 225 and those that do not. Trading volume in the former has declined by more than 70% during the period, while the volume in the latter has fallen by only 40%. And the volume of stocks traded over the counter, none of which is part of the Nikkei 225, has in fact doubled during the same period. All of which suggests investors have substituted futures trading for some stock investments. Further, the futures market expanded sharply in 1990, suggesting perhaps that investors were seeking the higher leverage built into futures to cope with the tighter monetary conditions.

Several factors may account for this apparent shift from the cash markets to derivatives. First, as discussed by Dr. Gramm, futures trading is more attractive to investors because of lower trading costs, higher leverage, and easier diversification. Also, the futures market permits investors to sell short quickly and efficiently. In the cash market, short-selling is severely restricted, chiefly because of an undeveloped stock lending market in Japan. Further, a very thin cash market since 1990 may have made it difficult for large investors to trade in blocks, forcing them to resort to the futures market to execute their trades. Also, investors' education about futures trading has advanced of late, so that many more large investors have now acquired the skill and experience necessary to trade futures actively. Last, Japanese investors may have become more capital-gains minded in the presence of the higher prices and hence lower cash yields on equities, at least in the years leading up to 1990. And this in turn could have blurred the distinction between those instruments yielding dividends and those not.

Now, this shift, to the extent it has indeed occurred, has important implications. For one thing, it implies a weaker stock market as compared to the derivative markets. Derivatives are beneficial to the economy only insofar as they contribute to a stronger cash market by providing hedging opportunities that would not otherwise exist. No one, of course, can raise funds in the derivative markets as such, however large such markets have become. In this sense, we should avoid having the tail wag the dog.

Also, as Professor Wakasugi will discuss tomorrow morning, the effect of index arbitrage on stock price volatility may well depend on the relative proportion of arbitrage transactions. A booming futures market could generate a greater volume of index arbitrage, thereby increasing the volatility of, and thus weakening, the underlying market. A weaker cash market could drive still more investors to the futures market, thus further eroding confidence in the entire equity market. And, in view of these possibilities, we are at the moment seriously addressing this imbalance between the two markets.

Let me close by repeating a point made by both Professor Tobin and Dr. Gramm. It is important to distinguish between two kinds of market volatility, avoidable and unavoidable. I believe it would have been impossible for the Japanese stock market to have avoided most of the volatility we experienced during those two periods in 1990. The first, as mentioned, reflected changes in economic fundamentals in Japan, and the other was caused by uncertainty arising from a major political event. Nevertheless, the derivative markets may be introducing an element of artificial volatility into our equity markets. And if this is so, then we must attempt to control that effect through better regulation of these markets. In the final analysis, of course, any valuable financial innovation will cause some temporary disruptions. Our role is to ensure that the necessary market adjustments take place so as to maximize the social and economic benefits while minimizing the costs.

Thank you very much.

KIM: Thank you very much, Mr. Sato. Our next speaker is Stephen Timbers, Chief Investment Officer of Kemper Financial Services.

STEPHEN TIMBERS

TIMBERS: Thank you, Professor Kim, Mr. Sakata, and Dean White.

I am going to talk about stock market volatility from the point of view of a practitioner—that is, one who invests in the stock market every day. This was a *very* hot topic in late 1987, and for most of '88, '89, and early '90 as well. In fact, I was once on a panel in Los Angeles with a managing director of Salomon Brothers and the publisher of *Investors Daily*; and the two of them had to be restrained from coming to blows. They obviously had a lot of themselves invested in this issue.

Let me also start by saying that, from my point of view, it's not really a question of *average* volatility. The real issue here is rather something that has been labelled *episodic* excess volatility—that is, episodes of abnormal price changes. Now, everyone has his or her own definition of "abnormal," but I take the view that a two percent change up or down in the market in one day is abnormal. And I'll explain to you why I think that's abnormal.

If you examined stock price data stretching back to the beginning of this century, you would note a couple of things. First, you would see that the early 1930s were far and away the most volatile period in our market history. And,

> [With Rule 80A] the New York Stock Exchange has effectively said that, when the market moves two percent, it's time to curtail certain types of trading strategies—or at least to make them more difficult or more costly.
>
> The 80A rule is being given a one-year trial by the SEC. The NYSE reviewed the rule after it had been in effect for five months—and that period included, by the way, a major market decline in the third quarter of 1990. Based on that five-month review, the NYSE concluded that the rule resulted in a decline in index arbitrage activity. It also concluded that both the cash and futures markets functioned well, that they remained linked throughout the period, and that this linkage helped guard against a freefall in markets. The NYSE has accordingly recommended that Rule 80A be made permanent.
>
> —Stephen Timbers—

the first half of this year, by contrast, there have only been four days, or 3 percent of total trading days, in which the market moved up or down two percent. And, as I will discuss later, I think much of that decline in volatility since 1989 reflects some of the new regulatory measures that have been put in place.

Why are these big market movements cause for concern? Well, let's consider how they might affect a couple of different constituencies. First of all, for fundamentally-oriented money managers, volatility makes it very hard to execute orders. Many times during the '80s we put in orders to sell a stock at, let's say, $43; and five minutes later it was executed at $41. There was nothing that happened with regard to the fundamentals of that particular company at the time. The only thing our traders reported back to us was that the "programs" came in and moved the market in general; and because our stock is part of that market, it was carried down with it. And the result

although not comparable to volatility in the '30s, we also experienced a significant increase in volatility during the period of 1987-1989. If not comparable to the '30s, the stock market volatility experienced in that period was certainly unlike anything most of us had experienced in our own lifetimes.

Now, things have died down a lot since then. For example, over the period 1982 to 1988, daily price movements up or down exceeded two percent in about 8 to 9 percent of the total trading days. In

was that we got a poor execution for our clients. Such abrupt price movements, to the extent they drag down all companies together, also tend to undermine the value of research in individual companies.

Likewise, if you're a corporate executive, you're not too happy if your stock is moving as if it's just another commodity, and thus failing to reflect the fundamentals of your company. For instance, in October of '89, Proctor & Gamble fell 7% in price in about an hour-and-a-half. Not much had happened at Proctor & Gamble, but a tremendous amount of its market capitalization simply evaporated during that 90 minutes. If I were the President of Proctor & Gamble, I would really be wondering about the markets. And, of course, if you were unfortunate enough to happen to be planning to sell an equity issue into the market at that time, this kind of price volatility could be especially painful.

And consider the effect of volatility on stock brokers. The average broker has no way really to explain these episodes of excessive volatility to his clients, thus complicating his life. Ultimately, of course, such volatility could undermine the confidence of the general public. If investors see that their wealth can drop by 23% in one day in October 1987—and by 7% in an hour-and-a-half in October 1989—then volatility could become a public policy issue. People remember these kind of events and their behavior is influenced by these memories.

Now what about those studies of market volatility that are supposed to reassure us? Most of these studies have been done in a mathematical-oriented way by academicians. Unfortunately, I have yet to see one by a crowd psychologist or a sociologist; I think it's this kind of study that could really shed light on how big market declines affect the behavior of individuals. My concern is not that the market goes up or down. My concern is that it happens too fast or too dramatically. Contrast the third quarter of last year, when the market dropped 17% in a rather orderly fashion, with the decline in October of 1987, when it all happened in one day.

So, if we could agree that episodic excessive volatility exists, and that it has little or no social value, the important questions become: Why does it happen, and what can we do about it?

Now, why does it happen? Most explanations have focused on certain structural changes that took place in the market in the 1970s and 1980s. The biggest one was probably the institutionalization of the market, where you concentrated buying and selling power in fewer and fewer hands. Also important was the rise of index funds or passive managers—those who run their portfolios to mimic the performance of an index and thus avoid all fundamental decisions. We also had during this period advances in technology that enabled the market to react more quickly to information. And then, of course, we had all the new instruments, particularly derivatives, that create the possibility for new types of strategies like portfolio insurance and index arbitrage.

We also saw during this period a tremendous increase in proprietary trading activities by broker-dealers. In the old days, we thought of broker-dealers as mainly agents acting for clients. Increasingly, however, they trade their own portfolios in addition to acting as agents. And finally, I should mention the linkage among global markets as a relatively new source of volatility.

Such changes have introduced, I think, a whole new set of issues to investors: Do markets move faster than they once did? Do some players really benefit from lower costs at the expense of others? And do some investors have preferred positions in the market that were created for other purposes, but now can be used in this new environment in a different way? Such possibilities and concerns have given this question of the market's fairness to individual investors a new prominence, because these market changes and new instruments have the potential to give rise to new forms of potential market manipulation, different forms of front-running, and the like.

Of course, some people respond by saying, "Well, if we can isolate a cause or culprit, then we can solve the problem. If there's one entity, or one practice, that's standing between us and fair and continuous and safe markets, then we can eliminate this episodic excessive volatility." But I think it's a futile exercise to look for a *single* cause of increased volatility in the stock market. Many factors obviously influence investors' decisions at any given moment, and it's really the confluence of certain factors and practices that are associated with the big moves.

Having said that, though, I think we should pay attention to a particular form of trading strategy, index arbitrage. Now I doubt very much anyone's ever going to prove that it *causes* market breaks. And if you're trying to come up with some solutions, you don't want to interfere with those parts of the system that work reasonably well. If the market is working well 95% of the time, and you have a problem with it maybe 5% of the time, you don't want to undermine the effective behavior of the market by making major regulatory changes designed to eliminate the possibility of a handful of relatively minor mishaps. The concern with index arbitrage is that, while it may be difficult to prove it *causes* episodic excess volatility, it has clearly been *associated* with each major episode over the past five years.

Now that I've suggested that there is too much volatility, and why it may be occurring, let me turn to the solutions. The solutions that have been proposed to address the problem of excess volatility can be grouped into five different categories.

The first one, circuit breakers, are intended to stop or slow down the market when things get out of hand.

The second has to do with greater coordination of rules and regulations among markets and different regulatory authorities. Among the proposals falling into this category are uptick rules, increased margin requirements and restrictions on short sales.

The third category of proposals is designed to improve detection procedures and capabilities and to raise common reporting standards. This is something on which there's hardly any disagreement. We don't have all the data we need to monitor the markets, and a lot has been done in this area.

The fourth category is education. We clearly need to educate the public about the uses and workings of the new instruments and strategies so that they don't react with so much fear of them.

And fifth and last are proposals relating to the issue of access—access to a certain type of vehicle like Superdot on the New York Stock Exchange.

What regulatory action, if any, has been taken in response to these proposals? And what have been the consequences of such regulatory changes?

I think a number of things have happened since this period. First of all, there has been a voluntary cutback in certain trading strategies by many brokers. There are far fewer brokers doing index arbitrage today than there were in the '87-'89 period. Second, some circuit breakers have been put in place (and I'm going to talk about one in a second). Third, there was the Stock Market Reform Act of 1990, which empowered the SEC to adopt rules to prevent price manipulation and to protect investors when the stock market comes under stress. Now, so far this law has really acted more as a threat than anything else, but I think there has been increased surveillance by the GAO, the SEC, and the CFTC of all market actions.

And, finally, there is Rule 80A. Rule 80A, also known as the index arbitrage tick test, is a rule of the New York Stock Exchange that restricts execution of index arbitrage orders when the Dow advances or falls 50 points from its previous day's close. Specifically, when the market has moved 50 points, 80A establishes an uptick or downtick restriction if you're trying to sell or buy an S&P 500 stock. And it remains in effect until either the market retreats back to 25 points from the prior close or until the end of the day.

Now, I want you to note that that 50 points is approximately the two percent I began by using as my definition of excess volatility. The New York Stock Exchange has effectively said that, when the market moves two percent, it's time to curtail certain types of trading strategies—or at least to make them more difficult or more costly.

The 80A rule, moreover, is a provisional one; it is being given a one-year trial by the SEC. The NYSE reviewed the rule after it had been in effect for five months—and that period included, by the way, a major market decline in the third quarter of 1990. Based on that five-month review, the NYSE concluded that the rule resulted in a decline in index arbitrage activity. It also concluded that both the cash and futures markets functioned well, that they remained linked throughout the period, and that this linkage helped guard against a freefall in markets. The NYSE has accordingly recommended that Rule 80A be made permanent. The rule will be reviewed in an open session of the SEC on November 1st.

So, I believe that the rule has been a success, and that we have experienced fewer episodes of excessive volatility recently as a result of it.

In closing, let me just say that, on this issue of market volatility, I think there has been far too much effort either to blame the problem on a *single* cause, or to prove that *no* problem exists. At the same time, there's been too little effort spent in trying to create confidence in the stock market for all potential investors, and that's where I hope we will concentrate our attention in the future. Thank you.

KIM: Thank you, Mr. Timbers. Our last panelist is Professor Merton Miller, who needs no further introduction.

MERTON MILLER

MILLER: Thank you, Han.

In the last five years, you've read over and over again in our newspapers (and those in Japan) that the introduction of stock index futures in 1982 has led to a surge in the volatility of the U.S. stock market. Today, in the words of a former Mayor of Chicago, I am going to "deny those allegations and defy the allegators." But don't just take my word for it. I will show you the evidence and let you judge for yourselves.

But, why should you care about volatility? Because the volatility of a price series is one indicator of the riskiness of the asset it represents. Common stocks, for example, are more volatile and, hence, much riskier capital assets than Treasury bills. And what the critics of index futures are charging is that the index futures markets, which have been traded since 1982, have made common stocks much riskier than they had been in the past. This has frightened away investors, has made common stocks less attractive as investments, and has raised the cost of capital to U.S. firms. The same charges, I might add, are now being heard in Japan.

Well, have the risks of common stock in the U.S. really increased? Let's look at the record and see. Let me first give you a quick glimpse of the full record in complete detail. Figure A shows the volatility of monthly returns on the value-weighted S&P 500 index based on daily returns during the month. (All this data, incidentally, comes from the ongoing research on historical stock market volatility by Bill Schwert of the University of Rochester that Wendy Gramm mentioned earlier.)

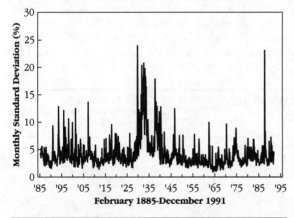

FIGURE A   VOLATILITY OF MONTHLY RETURNS TO A MARKET INDEX OF NYSE STOCKS BASED ON *DAILY* RETURNS WITHIN THE *MONTH*

February 1885-December 1991

As you can see, it's a very jagged series—there's a lot going on. There's so much going on, that it may be easier to first get a broad overview of volatility by turning to Figure B, which is a statistically smoothed version of Figure A. It's a moving average, a familiar form of statistical smoothing. And thanks to the smoothing technique used, the series can be extended back even further than the one in Figure A,

because daily data are only available since 1885. But, Figure B goes all the way back to 1834.

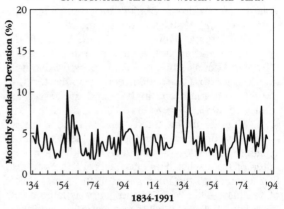

FIGURE B   VOLATILITY OF MONTHLY RETURNS TO A MARKET INDEX OF NYSE STOCKS BASED ON *MONTHLY* RETURNS WITHIN THE *YEAR*

1834-1991

Note, first of all, that volatility itself is volatile— it goes up and down. The upward bulges typically occur after market crashes. There was a big bulge in the 1850s, and an even bigger one following in 1929. And, of course, towards the end of the series, we see the crash of 1987. Volatility always tends to go up after a crash. That's one of the few things we really know about the volatility of stock prices. And that's understandable because a crash raises the risk of stocks, or at least makes people more aware of the risk.

Milton Friedman once said that the crash of 1987 was a blessing in disguise because it taught some people that stock prices go down as well as up. Stocks are risky securities and being caught in a crash is one of the risks you take. If you can't live with that, don't buy stocks. Buy treasury bills.

Although the volatility goes up after all crashes, it goes up higher and, as you can see, it stays up longer after some crashes than others. The severity seems to depend on the extent to which the stock market crash was accompanied by financial distress and financial panic in the economy, especially bank failures. The 1930s, for that reason, were extremely volatile—by far the most volatile period in U.S. history. The 1987 crash, by contrast, had much less effect on the economy because it did not trigger any major financial distress in the economy. Our recent banking problems are minor compared to those of

1930, when the Federal Reserve let the money supply collapse by 30%. No banking system can survive that kind of mismanagement; ours didn't, and it dragged our economy down with it.

I think you'll agree that for the 150-year period as a whole, there's no clear evidence of any trend in volatility, up or down. But let's turn the microscope up a notch and get back to the unsmoothed version based on average daily data in Figure A. Again, the '30s are far and away the most prominent feature; they stand out as a highly volatile period. Also note the double dip, to use a currently popular term, in the 30s—the main one in 1929 and the secondary tremor in 1937.

Using the unsmoothed daily data the '87 crash now shows up as a very big spike. But notice that the volatility dies down relatively quickly. It's very different from what happened after 1929. Note also that, contrary to the impressions in the press, spikes of volatility—little "mini-crashes," not as large as '87 to be sure, but nevertheless very easily discernible—are really quite common. One or more such spikes of that kind can be found in every decade. There were a couple in the 1970s that were related to oil shocks and there were a couple even in the supposedly placid '50s and '60s. The critics who blame volatility on futures just have very short memories.

So much, then, for the broad historical sweep of stock market volatility over the last 100 years or more. Let's now turn the microscope up another notch to Figure C and see what's happened to volatility since futures trading was instituted.

Figure C shows the volatility both of the underlying stock index and the index futures market since 1982. You'll notice that volatility started up towards the end of 1982; that was a recession year in the United States and the market was not doing well. But the economy recovered and volatility stayed low, as it generally does in boom times. The period of 1983 to June 1987 was, indeed, a strong boom period in the American economy. Again, one can see the big spike of October 1987, but note also how rapidly the volatility subsided after that. Notice there was no long-term up-swing in volatility prior to the crash that might have signalled to the regulators that a crash was on the way. And note, finally, the blip at the end. That is the so-called mini-crash of October 13, 1989 (which I will return to later).

The failure to see any clear evidence of a rising trend in volatility on a monthly or daily basis has led critics, in desperation, to call for turning up the microscope still another notch. They've even invented a new term, "episodic volatility." The argument that they make is this: "Okay, average volatility hasn't gone up. But a person can drown in a river even though its average depth is only two inches of water!" To make that point they concoct a variety of special purpose statistics designed to show that short-term volatility so measured has increased.

But has it? Figure D shows volatility based upon 15-minute returns within the day. Do you see any trend of rising volatility here? Not really. The only striking feature of the data remains the huge, but very temporary, spike of October 19-20, 1987.

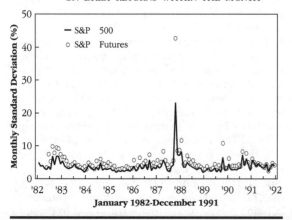

FIGURE C VOLATILITY OF MONTHLY RETURNS TO A MARKET INDEX OF NYSE STOCKS BASED ON *DAILY* RETURNS WITHIN THE *MONTH*

January 1982-December 1991

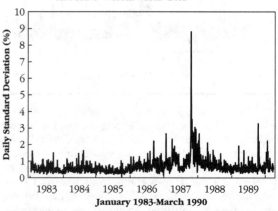

FIGURE D VOLATILITY OF DAILY RETURNS TO THE S&P INDEX BASED ON *15-MINUTE* RETURNS WITHIN THE *DAY*

January 1983-March 1990

What I conclude from this (and of course you're free to draw your own conclusions) is that there is no evidence that the day-to-day volatility of the stock market in the U.S. has exploded upward in recent years—and certainly none that could be traced clearly to index futures. Volatility now is pretty much what it always has been.

Why, then, all this agitation about futures and volatility if there's no basis for the charge in fact? I think there are at least three reasons why these charges persist.

First, many of the critics do not really understand index futures and how they work. And that's not entirely surprising. These are new instruments after all. They've been around less than ten years all told. And they're more complicated than our old ways of doing things because they can involve two markets at the same time and not just one.

Take index arbitrage and program trading. How many times have you read in the *New York Times* or the news columns of the *Wall Street Journal* that the market fell today because of index arbitrage and program trading?

But that simply can't happen! Index arbitrage by definition involves two simultaneous *equal and opposite* transactions—one down and one up. They offset each other and can't have any net effect on the level. If the level changes, it has to be for some other reason—though that reason may not jump out at you from the news accounts.

> The intensity of the criticism of stock index futures can be attributed in no small part to the efforts of people selling products and services that compete with the futures exchanges. Index futures have been so successful because they are so cheap and efficient a way for institutional investors to adjust their portfolio proportions. As compared to adjusting the proportions by buying or selling the stocks one by one and buying and buying or selling T-bills, it is cheaper to use futures by a factor of 10. That's tough competition and you almost can't blame some of the old-line investment houses for throwing up charges of "volatility" as a smokescreen behind which to demand government protection from their competitors.
>
> —Merton Miller—

Which brings me to my second reason for the continued criticism on volatility—namely that when the market goes down suddenly (or up for that matter), there doesn't always have to be a smoking gun. And because there is no obvious smoking gun, many people, including some in the current administration like Nicholas Brady, our Secretary of the Treasury, assume that the market must be malfunctioning. But big market moves can be caused by seemingly very small events because these events, small in themselves, may be signalling a possible change in the economic climate.

We have a saying in Chicago that when a cloud appears in the sky over LaSalle Street in August, soybean prices fall by 12 cents a bushel. Why? It's just a cloud, not rain. But it may just be the first sign that the rains are on the way and that the crop may be a big one. Of course, it may not become a big crop. But if you are long soybeans, you can't afford to take that chance.

And the same is true with stocks. The value of stocks depends not on their current and recent past earnings, but on their expected future earnings. And those prospective earnings are very much a matter of the economic climate. It doesn't take much to put a chill on those future prospects. And when there's even a little chill, the non-linearity of the underlying valuation process can produce a big swing.

For example, suppose you have a stock paying a dividend of $1 per share currently. And suppose you expect that dividend to grow by 7% a year. And suppose further that your risk-adjusted discount rate for dividends on this stock is 10%. Then, by the familiar growth formula calculations, the stock will sell for $33 ($1/(.10-.07). And its dividend yield will thus be 3 percent.

Now suppose that the chill comes along and the public becomes just slightly less optimistic about future dividend growth. Say 6-1/2% a year, rather than 7%. And because of feelings of increased risk, suppose the public raises its risk-adjusted discount rate to 10-1/2% instead of 10%. Then, these two seemingly tiny adjustments will imply a price for the share of $25, not $33.

That's a 25% drop in just the blink of any eyelid! That's unfortunate perhaps, but that's the way it is with long-lived assets like stocks or long-term bonds. Fixed-income investors are fully aware of the volatility that goes with long-duration bonds. Well, stocks are just about the longest-duration asset there is, except for real estate. And long-duration assets can fluctuate dramatically, even where there is no immediately obvious precipitating cause.

But, of course, sometimes there is a smoking gun. And that brings me to the so-called "mini-crash" of October 13, 1989. Our Secretary of the Treasury, Nicholas Brady, had been complaining about futures ever since the crash of 1987. So when the mini-crash of October 13, 1989 occurred, he was ready to pounce. "That's it," he said. "We've had it with these wild, futures-caused gyrations. Let's transfer jurisdiction over stock index futures to the SEC. The SEC will smother them with affection (or at least they'll smother them)."

But in the case of the mini-crash of October 13, 1989, there actually was a smoking gun. The leveraged buyout of United Airlines collapsed. And with it, so did the prospects for many other leveraged buyouts. Futures had absolutely nothing whatever to do with Brady's Crash. It wasn't even much of a crash as crashes go; it was not even in the top 30. But, as the old saying goes, any stick will do to beat a dog.

It is probably true, as Steve Timbers just suggested, that far fewer firms are doing index arbitrage these days. But it's not likely for the reason Timbers stated—Rule 80A. The real reason is that these markets today are so efficient that there's no money in it anymore for the marginal players. And some of the brokerage houses have chosen to time their announcements of their decisions to exit the index arbitrage activity—decisions motivated at bottom by

economics—in order to appear to accommodate regulators and investors. It has become "politically correct," to use a popular phrase, for investment banking houses to bash the futures markets.

Which brings me to my final point about current criticism of futures markets. The intensity of the criticism of stock index futures can be attributed in no small part to the efforts of people selling products and services that compete with the futures exchanges. Index futures have been so successful because they are so cheap and efficient a way for institutional investors to adjust their portfolio proportions. As compared to adjusting the proportions by buying or selling the stocks one by one and buying and buying or selling T-bills, it is cheaper to use futures by a factor of 10. That's tough competition and you almost can't blame some of the old-line investment houses for throwing up charges of "volatility" as a smokescreen behind which to demand government protection from their competitors.

Those of us who believe that the markets should make these judgments, not the government, can at least help to blow these smokescreens away by presenting the evidence and that is what I have tried to do today. Thank you.

KIM: Thank you very much, Mert. When I was a visiting professor at the University of Chicago about 14 years ago, they had then—and still have as far as I know—a system in which students are made to bid for the right to take MBA courses. Merton Miller's courses always commanded the highest prices and were the first to be sold out. And I think, judging from this presentation, you can probably understand why.

Today's panel has certainly raised a number of interesting issues. Tomorrow morning we have scheduled several academic presentations that will provide more in-depth analysis of the issues discussed. I hope you will be able to join us, and I thank you all for your attendance and participation today.

PART II:
VOLATILITY AND
MARKET EFFICIENCY

MICHAEL BRADLEY: Welcome to the second part of the Mitsui Life program. This morning I have the sincere pleasure of introducing two giants in the economics profession. Each is an eminent scholar in his own right, and each has had a profound effect on the development of the field of financial economics.

I will now introduce them both, but in the reverse order in which they will be speaking.

Our second speaker today will be **RICHARD ROLL**, who is the Allstate Professor of Finance at the John E. Anderson School of Business Administration at the University of California at Los Angeles. Dick received his Ph.D. from the University of Chicago in 1968. This time and place has a special meaning for all academics in finance. Much of the work that was done at the University of Chicago in the late 1960s defined what we know today as the field of financial economics. It was the pioneering work of these scholars that literally created the field. The most visible public acknowledgment of the importance of this work was the action taken by last year's Nobel Prize committee, when they formally recognized financial economics as a *bona fide* social science by awarding the Nobel Price in Economics to William Sharpe, Harry Markowitz, and, of course, Merton Miller. In a very real sense, this prize should also be shared by some of Professor Miller's colleagues at Chicago around the late '60s: Richard Roll, Eugene Fama, Michael Jensen, Myron Scholes, and Fischer Black.

And if Dick Roll also deserves to be considered one of the founding fathers of financial economics, his accomplishments since the late '60s have been no less impressive. There is no major field in financial economics to which Dick hasn't contributed an important paper. His work spans the entire spectrum of our profession. He has written about market efficiency, the relevance of the capital asset pricing model, time-varying expectations, and mergers and acquisitions. His most recent research efforts, which he will describe today, are an attempt to explain the relationship among international financial markets.

Our first speaker today will be **ROBERT SHILLER**, who is the Stanley B. Resor Professor of Economics at Yale University. It has been said that the measure of a man can often be judged by the quality of his enemies. On this score at least, Robert Shiller is a giant in the field of financial economics.

I first became aware of Bob's work when I was a student at Chicago, and then an Assistant Professor at the University of Rochester (I find it difficult to distinguish these two periods in my life). In those days, an alarm was sounded throughout the profession that a professor from Yale—an economics professor no less—had the temerity to suggest that the emperor had no clothes. Contrary to the basic postulate of efficient market theory, Shiller claimed to produce evidence showing that the volatility of stock prices could not be explained by the volatility of "fundamentals" such as corporate dividends and earnings. This was nothing short of heresy to those of us in south Chicago.

Professor Shiller's argument was simple and powerful. It was something akin to the Grossman and Stiglitz paradox that markets cannot possibly be as efficient as financial economists suggest; because if current prices truly incorporated all available information, and everyone believed this to be so, then no one would have an incentive to produce information. And if no one produced information, then how could markets be kept efficient?

Well, Professor Shiller posed a similar conundrum. He said that if stock prices reflect the discounted value of all expected future dividends—a proposition we all teach our students—then why are stock prices so much more volatile than dividends? Surely the possibility of changes in the interest rate and the growth rates, the only missing variables in his equation, could not account for the volatility we observe in stock prices.

Professor Shiller concluded that the excess volatility in security prices is not due to differing expectations in the flow of dividends, but rather to investors' propensity to trade on fads and fashions, thus giving rise to speculative bubbles. This, needless to say, represented the antithesis of the "rational" investors posited by efficient markets theorists.

In response to the calls to rid the profession of this meddlesome priest, there was a flurry of Ph.D. dissertations coming out of Chicago, each intended as a response to Shiller's conclusion. It took no less than two professors at MIT, Bob's alma mater, to produce what was known as the "Shiller Killer"— and it was proudly advertised as such by the authors.

Now, I don't mean to get into the specifics of this debate, but just to emphasize the enormous intellectual activity stimulated by Shiller's work. And, in terms of the ongoing debate over market efficiency, I think the tide may have turned somewhat in Professor Shiller's favor in recent years. His provocative and path-breaking research has spawned a renewed awareness of the limitations of the efficient market hypothesis. Work in the area of time-varying expectations and market microstructure is a direct response to the provocative questions posed by Shiller and others.

So, with that as a backdrop, let's now begin with Bob Shiller.

ROBERT SHILLER

SHILLER: Thanks, Michael. I sometimes think the difference between my position and that of mainstream financial economists is exaggerated. I am in fact quite sympathetic to some of the claims of efficient markets theory. For example, I always like to repeat the statement Fischer Black made in his paper called "Noise." He said—and I'm paraphrasing here—that he's very confident that stock prices lie most of the time between half of and twice their fundamental values. I think I agree with that.

What I want to talk about this morning are some ideas discussed in the beginning of a paper I wrote at the request of the Twentieth Century Fund, a research foundation engaged in economic, political, and social policy studies. They got the idea that one of the sources of the economic problems in this country is a tendency toward short-termism—a tendency caused by institutional investors trading very rapidly, losing sight of fundamental values, and influencing corporate business decisions in a bad way.

And there are many others, of course, who share this idea. In 1989 Senator Nancy Kassebaum introduced a bill called the "Excessive Churning and Speculation Act of 1989," which proposed to tax the short-term capital gains of pension funds as a way of discouraging them from trading so much. Although this bill is now dead, other people who have taken up this call include George Bush, Nicholas Brady, and others convinced that the nation's short-term, speculative mentality is cause for concern.

The Twentieth Century Fund people probably found that there was a relatively short list of academic people who would take these issues seriously. But they called the right person, because I tend to believe that businessmen, practitioners as opposed to academics, are generally right when they say there's a problem. On closer inspection, it usually turns out there are intangible reasons why they might be right—reasons that economists don't want to consider. But, as a somewhat unorthodox economist, I'm always eager to try to get the broadest possible perspective on these issues.

Fortunately, however, I don't have to come up with policy recommendations on this matter on volatility. Quite frankly, I don't have any clear answers to this question, What should we do about volatility in financial markets? My sole intent here is to suggest that maybe there is indeed a problem, and

that businessmen and regulators worried about such issues are not just conjuring up phantoms.

Let me start by reviewing the evidence on the speculative nature of stock price movements. Let's go back to October 19, 1987. Between 1:15 and 4:00 that afternoon, the Dow Jones Average fell 16 1/2%. As far as I know, nobody has produced a plausible economic or fundamentals-based explanation for this price movement. The only real news was the stock market crash itself; there doesn't seem to have been anything else going on.

It's true that some people have cited the tax law changes, proposed on the 14th of October, that would have discouraged takeovers. And it's a plausible enough theory that if a tax law discourages takeovers, it could significantly reduce values. In fact, there's a rather convincing paper by Mark Mitchell and Jeff Netter that produced evidence of an impact of these tax announcements on stock prices. But that impact occurred *five days before the crash*! My understanding of efficient markets theory is that the market responds *immediately* to economic news; it doesn't wait five days. Even if there are decision lags, even if people need some time to think over what this news from the House Ways and Means Committee really means, there's still no plausible reason why all investors should later reach a decision all at the same time.

The mini-crash of October 13, 1989 was different. In that case, it's very clear that the triggering event was the news of the collapse of the UAL deal—news that came just minutes before the stock market began to plunge. But, my problem with this case is that the market reaction seems disproportionate to the new information; the news just doesn't seem to be of any consequence. After all, it was news about a collapsed deal for a company whose value represents less than 1/2% of the whole market.

But let's get back to October 1987. Merton Miller earlier argued that, with securities of long duration like common stocks, even modest changes in expected dividend growth and discount rates could lead to significant changes in value. He was using the Gordon dividend discount model, which says that stock price (V) equals the current dividend (D) divided by the discount rate (r) minus the dividend growth rate (g). In equation form, $V = D/(r-g)$. In his numerical example, Professor Miller showed that just by raising r and lowering g by half a percent each, you could reduce investors' estimate of the value of the firm by 25%.

Well, there's no evidence that there was any adjustment of either "r" or "g" at the time of the stock market crash of '87. In fact, there were surveys which asked about both of those variables (although maybe not in just the right terms). In September of 1987, Richard Hoey of Drexel asked his sample of institutional investors to project their expected real bond yield; and they gave him an average number of 4%. When he asked them again two months later— that is, shortly after the crash—that expected yield had fallen to to 3.7%. So there's no evidence of an increase of discount rates before and after the crash.

Moreover, Blue Chip Economic Indicators had done a survey of their 51 respondents for the first three days of October 1987, asking them to predict pre-tax profits in current dollars. In the beginning of October of 1987, these people predicted a 7.1% growth rate over the period 1988 to 1992, and 7.3% growth from 1993 to 1997. In the next survey of the same group in March of 1988, the respondents predicted a 7.0% growth rate from 1990 to 1994, and 7.5% growth from 1995 to 1999.

So there's no evidence of any change in those expectations. And it thus seems pretty clear that, during the Crash of '87, investors were responding primarily to developments in the market itself—that is, to the sharp decline in prices. It was a sort of vicious circle, with people watching prices go down deciding to sell their shares before prices dropped

Based on the kind of evidence I've just cited about financial markets, I'm inclined to take a Pigouvian view of business cycles.... In answer to the question, "What are the causes of the business cycle?" Pigou wrote a book that set forth two major categories: "real" and "psychological"... But, after hundreds of pages describing the real factors, he then concluded that as much as half of the business cycle could be attributed to psychological causes.

In my opinion, no economist since that time has come up with a better estimate of the economic importance of psychological or behavioral factors. Harkening back to Fischer Black's statement that stock prices typically lie between half and twice their true value, I like to cite Pigou's assessment of 50% as the best estimate that is currently available of the psychological component of business cycle fluctuations.

—Robert Shiller—

any further. And if that was indeed the case, then I question how we can still cling to the basic notion that markets are basically efficient.

One reaction of economists has been to dismiss the crash as an aberration. It's just one observation, one data point; and if there are such aberrations, they are rare. But I find this argument unconvincing. I think the crash is symptomatic of a larger problem, because I think that most price movements of any size are unrelated to news about fundamentals. The only reason we single out some event like the crash of '87 is that it serves as a kind of event study. For those of us skeptical about the efficiency of markets, we demand to see some plausible explanation why prices could fall by over 20% in one day.

Now, an alternative approach to explaining the crash is to argue that price movements themselves revealed important information about the market itself. For example, some studies by economists—notably, those by Bulow and Kemperer, Gennotte and Leland, and Jacelyn, Kleidon and Pfleiderer—have suggested that the sudden price declines showed that there was much less liquidity in the market than investors had supposed. And viewed in this way, investors could have sharply and suddenly raised their required rates of return, thus causing prices to plummet. So, even though there was no news about fundamentals, investors learned from the abrupt decline in prices that they had overestimated the liquidity of the market—that is, the ability of investors to sell without lowering the price. And this may in turn have been the result of excessive, and mistaken, reliance by investors on various forms of "portfolio insurance," which were supposed to protect them from precipitous declines.

At any rate, I think these kinds of explanation are they way you have to go to come up with a satisfactory explanation of the crash that is consistent with market efficiency. Unfortunately, however, there's no evidence that supports that theory, or at least none that I'm aware of. There's no evidence that liquidity became abruptly lower in 1987.

The most straightforward explanation, then I think, is one that is *inconsistent* with market efficiency—namely, a speculative bubble. People were selling, in short, simply because they thought other people were going to sell.

As far as I am able to determine, I am the only person anywhere who did a questionnaire survey after the crash of '87 asking people what was on their minds. Now, this may be an unreliable surveying technique, but I simply asked people what was on their mind. During the week of the '87 crash, I sent out questionnaires to 2,000 individual investors and 1,000 institutional investors, and got back a total of about 1,000 responses.

Besides asking a number of specific questions, I also asked the investors to write down their own theory of the crash. And although their interpretations were not very impressive or coherent, their response to a follow-up question was interesting. That is, when I asked them whether their own theory was "more about fundamentals, such as profits or interest rates, or more about market psychology," two-thirds of the U.S. respondents picked market psychology, and only one third chose fundamentals.

I later attempted the same experiment in Japan—with the help of Fumiko Kon-Ya of the Japan Securities Research Institute and Yoshiro Tsutsui of Osaka University. We sent out questionaires to Japanese institutional investors asking for their views about the causes of the U.S. crash of '87. Three quarters of them thought the crash was due to market psychology, and only one quarter due to fundamentals such as profits or interest rates.

In exploring investor views of the mini-crash of October 13, 1989, I did things a bit differently. Rather than mail questionnaires, in order to get to respondents while their memories were still fresh, William Feltus and I did a survey by phone. (Unfortunately,

the event came on a Friday, so we had to wait until Monday to make the calls.) And we asked investors the following question: "Which of the following statements better represents the view you held last Friday: (1) the news of the collapse of the UAL deal, because of its implications for future takeovers, is a sensible reason for the drop in stock prices; or (2) the UAL news of Friday afternoon should be viewed as a focal point, or attention-grabber, which in turn prompted investors to express their doubts about the stock market." In response, 62% picked the latter explanation, while only 38% described the UAL news as a sensible reason.

We also asked this follow-up question: "Did you hear about the UAL news before you heard about the market drop on Friday afternoon? Or did you hear about the UAL news later, as an explanation for the drop?" And 40% responded that they heard it before the drop, 60% said after. The fact that as many as 60% of these market professionals heard about the UAL deal only after the drop suggests that it's difficult to infer causality from the UAL news alone.

Now, let's turn to Japan and the stock market drop in the Nikkei.

Critics of our surveys about the U.S. crashes objected to the fact that we hadn't done any pre-crash surveys. So, anticipating the possibility of a crash in Tokyo, Tsutsui, Kon-Ya and I started doing surveys at six-month intervals beginning around June of 1989. We asked both Japanese and U.S. investors for their expectations over various horizons for both the Nikkei and the Dow. We asked both groups to predict both indexes. And there was a very striking difference—in fact, an incredible spread—between Japanese and U.S. investors in their predictions for the Nikkei over a one-year horizon. For example, if Japanese investors said they expected the Nikkei to go up by up 10% in the next year, U.S investors typically said they expected it to go down by 10%—and roughly this 20% differential was present throughout the entire series of surveys leading up to the decline of the Nikkei in 1990.

Unfortunately, the drop in the Tokyo stock exchange was not a one-day event as it proved to be in the U.S. And though I don't claim to understand what happened, let me give you one result from our surveys that suggests an important role for investor speculation. We asked Japanese investors whether they thought they were in the market for the short term or the long haul. In fact, we worded the question as follows: "Although I expect a substantial drop in stock prices in Japan ultimately, I advise being relatively heavily invested in stocks for the time being, because I think that prices are likely to rise for a while." I think we can all agree that, to the extent investors endorse that statement, they are speculating.

Well, according to our first surveys conducted in mid-'89, 40% of Japanese investors said yes to that question. At the beginning of '91, after the market had fallen some 40% from its high, only 10% of Japanese investors still agreed with that same statement. So this suggests to me that there was a major speculative component underlying the large fall in the Nikkei. And I don't think it serves any purpose to try to ignore it.

But having said that, let me now talk a little bit about what policy lessons we might draw from these observations. And let me say right from the start that I'm not going to come up with specific policy recommendations. I will say, however, that such speculative behavior is kind of a depressing lesson for economists. It's very difficult for us to model these things; it suggests we may have learned the wrong research skills. The strong suggestion from this evidence is that much that occurs in financial markets doesn't make sense in terms of fundamentals.

I also suspect that what we have recently learned about financial markets probably extends to macroeconomic issues as well—that is, to matters like the business cycle. For example, there's a recent fashion in the macroeconomics literature called "real" business cycle models. Such models try to make sense out of macroeconomic fluctuations entirely in terms of optimal responses to new information about fundamentals. In fact, the only thing that drives most of these models is technological change. That is, the ups and downs of the business cycle are being caused predominantly by technological progress, which uproots some industries while giving rise to others.

But based on the kind of evidence I've just cited about financial markets, I'm inclined to take what I refer to as the Pigouvian view of business cycles. A. C. Pigou, an economist who engaged in a famous dispute with Keynes in the '20s and '30s, wrote a book in 1929 that attempted to identify the sources of what he called "Industrial Fluctuations." Now, although his methods were bad by present standards—they involved a lot of intuitive judgments based on his extensive reading of history—I nevertheless tend to credit his judgment in this matter.

In answer to the question, "What are the causes of the business cycle?" Pigou set forth two major categories: "real" causes and "psychological" causes. Under real causes of the business cycle, he listed all the factors coming from outside the system: harvest variations, inventions, industrial disputes, changes in fashions, and wars. But, after hundreds of pages of historical analysis describing these real factors, he then concluded that as much as half of the business cycle could be attributed to psychological causes.

In my opinion, no economist since that time has come up with a better estimate of the economic importance of psychological or behavioral factors. It's just too intangible to document such factors using the standard conventional research techniques, and it certainly can't be attempted in the current research environment. But, harkening back to Fischer Black's statement that stock prices typically lie between half and twice their true value, I like to cite Pigou's assessment of 50% as the best estimate that is currently available of the psychological component of business cycle fluctuations.

So the question is now, How do we deal with these psychological causes? It's very hard to know what to do, and there's very little research in this area to guide us. But that doesn't mean that policymakers in Washington should utterly ignore the situation. They have to do something, if only because no policy amounts to a policy of sorts. For example, a policy not to tax financial markets is inherently a policy to tax something else.

My colleague, Jim Tobin, has come out rather strongly in favor of transactions taxes, and this seems to be one of the most popular measures people are now proposing to curb speculative behavior. (This, incidentally, was the policy measure advocated by Keynes in 1936.) And a number of others have proposed other taxes on capital gains.

The problem with such proposals is that it's awfully hard to know if such taxes are going to make prices better reflections of fundamentals. If you could identify the speculators and tax only them, maybe you could push prices back to their right levels. But what is effectively being proposed, of course, is to tax everybody who trades in the market. So it's pretty uncertain whether these taxes will have any beneficial effect, or any real effect at all.

I say this, in part, because of what I have learned about real estate markets. Based on my research in that area, I am equally confident that there are speculative booms and busts in real estate. And when you consider that transactions costs in real estate are just enormously higher than those in the stock market—realtors' commissions for selling residential homes are about 7%, on average—it seems highly unlikely that raising transactions costs in financial markets will eliminate speculation and reduce volatility.

So the small policy changes proposed thus far, including things like the circuit breakers proposed by the Brady Report, don't seem to me to have much promise. But there may be one aspect of this problem that we can do something about. And that's this issue of "short termism" I mentioned earlier. Here again, though, I'm not going to offer any specific policy proposals; I'm just going to tell you what I think the problems are.

The charge of "short-termism" and its association with speculators is actually a fairly old and familiar one. Graham and Dodd made this argument in the 1930s. But it seems to me that, starting in the 1980s, there was major revival of concern, expressed by business leaders in both the U.S. and the U.K., about a short-term bias in corporate behavior being driven largely by pressures from financial markets. For example, corporate managers worried about takeovers—or perhaps having their bonuses tied to near-term earnings—could face strong incentives to boost short-term performance by cutting back on valuable R & D and other long-term investments. And many corporate executives have complained about such pressures and their consequences.

Although most economists are inclined to dismiss such claims as expressions of self-interest, I tend to take such claims seriously. It's a critical issue for corporate managers: namely, do you try to promote the long-term interest of your company, even if the market will lower your stock price as a result, or do you just try to mollify the market by keeping up short-term earnings and deferring valuable investment? This is potentially a very serious problem.

Japanese investors and managers, by contrast, are supposed to be more patient. Japanese managers are said to be willing, for example, to lose money on some business proposition for many years if they think that in the long term this will be good for their business. They will allegedly fund research and development or marketing expenditures to penetrate markets that American managers will not. American managers are said to believe that the U.S. stock market doesn't reflect the expected future value of such investment in their stock prices.

Now, there is a "rational expectations" interpretation of this set of managerial incentives and their consequences that has been set forth by Jeremy Stein and a group of other economists. And their story goes something like this: To the extent the market fails to reflect the value of long-term investment in current stock prices—or fails to penalize those companies that do not invest for the future—managers may have incentives to boost current earnings while hiding cutbacks in long-term investment from stockholders that will ultimately reduce earnings. Such managers are effectively stealing from the future to create the appearance of higher profits today.

Now, this is another kind of classic agency problem—one that could exist even under rational or efficient markets. However, I think these kind of agency problems would be greatly intensified by the tendency of markets to be speculative.

So it's really an issue of whether our managers somehow find themselves under incentives to "play the game" and just pretend. If many managers, just to keep up the appearance of profitability, are not doing what they really believe is in the long-run best interests of their stockholders, then that is a major national problem. It's a smaller version of the problem we see in the Soviet Union today where the people "pretend" to work and their employers "pretend" to pay them. That is the real enemy of productivity and I think it's a matter of national concern. Somehow it seems to me that some policy regulating financial markets might help improve things—though in ways that are very hard to quantify and prove.

BRADLEY: Thanks, Bob. Now, I suspect we'll hear a somewhat different side of the story from Richard Roll.

RICHARD ROLL

ROLL: Well, let me begin my response to Bob by saying that anybody who's been married can appreciate the value of the argument that there are psychological factors affecting human behavior. I would be the last person to deny the importance of these things.

In fact, because I'm not just an academic but also a businessman, and therefore probably subject to short-termism (although I wouldn't say that was really the case), let me add that I really wish Bob were right about markets being inefficient. Because if they were, and we could detect when the market were overvalued or undervalued, we could sure do a heck of a lot better for our clients in the money management business than we've been doing. I have personally tried to invest money, my client's money and my own, in every single anomaly and predictive device that academics have dreamed up. That includes the strategy of DeBondt and Thaler (that is, sell short individual stocks immediately after one-day increases of more than 5%), the reverse of DeBondt and Thaler, which is Jegadeesh and Titman (buy individual stocks after they have decreased by 5%), etc. I have attempted to exploit the so-called year-end anomalies and a whole variety of strategies supposedly documented by academic research. *And I have yet to make a nickel on any of these supposed market inefficiencies.* So, when Bob Shiller says that our markets are subject to short-termism and speculative swings, I would be very glad if Bob would tell me when we're in the midst of one, so I would then be able to profit from it.

I do agree with Bob, however, that financial economists don't understand volatility in markets. There's considerable evidence that much of the volatility in stock prices cannot be explained by what happens to fundamentals. I don't have the slightest quarrel with that observation. In fact I have contributed to the literature on so-called "excess" volatility. I did a paper a few years ago on orange juice prices.

When investors see large price changes, they become more or less fearful; and they suddenly increase or decrease their required rates of returns on risky assets, thus leading to immediate, and sometimes fairly significant, changes in prices. If I could tell when investors were going to raise or lower their discount rates above or below some long-run norm, I could exploit their behavior to make money. In that case, Bob Shiller would be justified in saying that markets were not efficient. But if there's nothing investors can exploit in a systematic way, time in and time out, it's very hard to say information is not being properly incorporated into stock prices....

There isn't much we can do to change the volatility of markets. In fact, most of the current proposals for curing high volatility (or short-termism) will amount to shooting ourselves in the collective foot.

—Richard Roll—

I picked orange juice specifically because it's a commodity whose price should be determined almost entirely by the weather in a particular region of Florida—at least in those days before Brazilian imports became important. And though I found that orange juice prices did indeed predict the weather in central Florida, the volatility in orange juice prices was overwhelmingly greater than anything that could be explained by possible changes in the weather. (And if there's anything that's an exogenous variable, it's the weather. It's the one thing we really don't control.)

From that evidence, I concluded that psychological factors affect prices. In fact, in my own money management business, one of the sources of risk we consider is "investor confidence." If there's anything more psychological than that, I don't know what it is. When investors see large price changes, they become more or less fearful; and they suddenly increase or decrease their discount rates, their required rates of returns on risky assets. That's a purely psychological reaction that leads to immediate, and sometimes fairly significant, changes in prices.

As I suggested earlier, if I could tell when investors were going to raise or lower their discount rates above or below some long-run norm, I could systematically exploit their behavior to make money. In that case, Bob Shiller would be justified in saying that markets were not efficient. To me, market inefficiency means that astute investors can consistently take advantage of some systematic defect in market prices that enables them to know when prices were going to move up or down.

As Bob suggests, the market may have a price that is very different from "fundamentals." But I would also insist that fundamentals really are in the minds of investors. Merton Miller mentioned yesterday that stocks are assets with very long—in fact, theoretically infinite—durations. And, as some research has shown, over half of the present value of the Dow Jones 30 industrials reflects the market's expectation of earnings beyond a five-year horizon. So, if you're talking (as Steve Timbers did yesterday) about the current price of Procter & Gamble, there's nothing really definite or certain today about what's going to happen to the company's dividends and earnings over the next 10 or 20 years. Investor estimates of such fundamentals are themselves greatly influenced by market psychology.

So, I agree with Bob that investor psychology plays an important role. But, I have to keep coming back to my original point that a true market *inefficiency* ought to be an exploitable opportunity. If there's nothing investors can exploit in a systematic way, time in and time out, then it's very hard to say that information is not being properly incorporated into stock prices. In fact, information is being incorporated into the price through the filters of the millions of people evaluating that information.

Perhaps we could somehow get people to evaluate information more accurately, or more consistently, so as to eliminate some of the price volatility. But until we dream up some method—and I am very skeptical about any existing proposals to interfere with markets—there isn't much we can do to change the volatility of markets. In fact, far from fixing the problem, most of the current proposals for curing high volatility (or short-termism) will amount to shooting ourselves in the collective foot. If anything, these proposals will reduce market efficiency and make things worse rather than better; they may well even end up *increasing* volatility.

Regulatory intervention in markets will certainly divert resources away from the private sector to the public sector. This is the best argument for Jim Tobin's proposed transactions tax. Whether it's small or not, it's a tax. If you like taxes—and Jim Tobin likes taxes—then you're for any tax. If you're like me, you're against taxes. I'd rather have the government be smaller than larger, and transaction tax is one

more source of government growth. There is absolutely no assurance that a transaction tax would reduce volatility.

This brings me to the subject of my talk: a comparison of volatility across global markets. In the past few years, I've written a series of papers that attempt to examine the effect on market volatility of policy measures like transactions taxes, circuit breakers, and margin requirements. More pointedly, I was attempting to see if these policy measures reduced the severity of market crashes. My conclusion, stated briefly, is that there is no evidence from my studies—or anyone else's, for that matter—that any such institutional arrangement dampens volatility.

In one study, for example, I looked at the experience of 24 countries during the crash of '87 to estimate whether the extent of the crash in individual countries was influenced by such things as portfolio insurance, program trading, specialists, transactions taxes, and so on. I looked at about ten different variables. And the only thing I could find that affected the extent of the crash was the typical "beta" relationship between that particular national market and a world market shock. I also found very little evidence linking these betas to any institutional characteristics of the markets involved.

Now that's not an explanation for the crash. It so happens that the crash of '87 occurred in every major market around the world to a greater or lesser extent. Why that happened, I don't know. I think it was "psychological" in the sense that people suddenly changed their estimates of required discount rates, probably in response to market movements in the preceding days. If you look at the timing of the crash, you'll see that in the preceding week there was a tremendous market movement in the U.S. (on the Friday preceding the Monday of the crash). There were also significantly negative market movements in many other countries, although most were not as large as that in the U.S.

The subsequent U.S. crash, however, was by no means the largest one in world markets. In fact, roughly half of the 24 countries saw larger percentage declines in the value of their stock markets. But whatever the cause of the crash, whatever the triggering variable that caused investor psychology to change around the world, it didn't seem to be affected by the particular regulations and institutional arrangements in different countries. Therefore, I don't think that by changing one of those institutional characteristics we would have altered the price drop that occurred in October of 1987 in any important respect. Nor do I think we would likely change the volatility we experience in a normal period.

In fact, this lack of any correlation between such institutional characteristics and market volatility is what led me to do the current paper you have before you. Quite frankly, I was puzzled by the results of my own studies. Before undertaking these studies, I had expected to find some connection between things like margin requirements, transactions taxes and volatility; and I didn't find any.

What I did discover, however, was that there are large and persistent differences—systematic differences—in stock market volatility across different countries. And in undertaking the study I will now describe, I began with the supposition that some fundamental differences across national markets must be causing these striking differences in volatility. I also felt that by examining the behavior of these international markets, we could perhaps learn something more about the underlying causes of U.S. market volatility. So, in my remaining few minutes, I'd like to present a partial explanation why national stock markets have differing levels of volatility.

There is considerable variation in the level of volatility across national stock markets. For example, the annual standard deviation of South Africa's stock market is about 30%, whereas that of the Canadian market is less than 10%. Countries like Mexico and Hong Kong also have comparatively high levels of price volatility, around 25%. By comparison, the average volatility of the U.S. market, at 14%, is actually fairly low. Japan's also used to be quite low, but its volatility has increased substantially in the last year or so to about 24%.

Now, since these figures are based on stock market *indexes*, the first thing that occurred to me was the possibility that the differences in volatility were spurious—that is, they were simply the result of the numbers of stocks included in the different national indexes. Some countries have a lot of stocks in their index, some countries have just a few. Whereas Mexico has about 13 stocks in its index, the U.S. has 500. And it occurred to me that the high standard deviation of the Mexican market may simply reflect the fact that the index of 13 stocks is not a well-diversified portfolio.

Sure enough, I found that if you adjusted these comparative volatilities for the number of stocks in the national index, then part of the cross-country

differences volatility disappeared. But it was only a relatively small part. In fact, I would have loved to have discovered that the *entire* reason for differences of across country volatility was that they had different numbers of stock in their indexes. If that were the case, then we might have uncovered some universal law, in effect, about what constitutes a natural level of volatility. But, unfortunately, that did not turn out to be the case. Construction of the indexes doesn't account for most of the differences in volatility that we observe across countries.

So, I was led to look for other explanations. And, always trying the simplest way first, I then thought of the possibility that such differences in volatility were caused by differences in the composition of the industries in the different national stock indexes. Some countries specialize in manufacturing, some in mining, and some countries are broadly diversified across many different industries. Was it possible, I asked myself, that the primary reason for differences in volatility was simply that countries specialize in different industries?

To answer this question, I began by developing a set of industry indexes for global shocks. From Goldman Sachs I obtained an industry code for each stock in each national market index. The 97 different industries in the original data were combined into seven broad industry groupings: finance, energy, utilities, transportation, consumer goods, capital goods, and basic industries. Using a straightforward econometric procedure, I constructed global industry indexes reflecting all the stocks in a particular industry sector regardless of country. The final step was to determine whether and to what extent these global industry factors explained the overall volatility of each national stock market.

I found roughly half of the cross-country differences in stock price volatility can be explained by differences in industrial composition. Roughly 50% of the volatility in a given national market's return *on a daily basis* can be explained by what happens in other national markets with similar industrial groupings on the same day. For some countries, the amount explained is much higher than 50%.

I was very surprised by the empirical strength of this explanation. I didn't think one would be able to explain much of the volatility in one country by what was happening to sector composition returns in other countries. These results are striking confirmation of the extent to which the integration of global markets has really been accomplished.

Finally, I want to mention some findings about the international pattern of return correlations. Is it possible that not only the volatility that we observe across countries, but also the correlation of returns between pairs of countries, can be explained by industrial composition? For example, to what extent is the correlation between Japanese and U.S. stock returns a function of the similarities or differences in their industrial structures?

To examine this proposition, I constructed two covariance matrixes: one using just the raw index returns for each country, and a second constructed by weighting the global industry factors by the weights of those industries as they apply to each national market. After looking at the pattern of correlations in each of those two matrixes, I believe it is justified to conclude that similarities or differences in underlying industrial structure determine a significant part of the international patterns. It's really the underlying industries that are being correlated when you look at correlations between two national markets.

Now, to get back to the topic with which I started: does all this mean that there's no role for psychological factors in national market returns and levels of volatility? I don't think so. It may very well be that psychology affects the energy sector in Australia. But even if it does, my results suggest that the energy sector in the Netherlands is also going to respond to those same psychological factors. In that sense, there appears to be a lot more coherence in what happens across countries than you might have inferred from listening to people who say psychological factors are the main driving force. Psychological factors may be underlying much of these developments; but whatever the underlying trigger, such behavioral influences seem to be having similar effects on stocks across countries.

And I will just quit here. Thank you.

A Brief Dialogue on Market Efficiency

BRADLEY: Thanks, Dick. We still have time to take a question or two from the floor.

In fact, let me start this off by asking Dick Roll to give us his assessment of the current validity of the efficient market hypothesis. Michael Brennan, a past President of the American Finance Association, recently stated that he no longer believed that markets were efficient, and that market efficiency should thus no longer be the primary paradigm in finance. And he cited two studies in particular that had confirmed his skepticism about the efficient markets. One paper he cited was by our own Vic Bernard and Jacob Thomas showing an anomalous relationship between earnings and stock price movements. The other work he mentioned was that of Bob Shiller, Dick Thaler, and Werner DeBondt—work that suggests the market systematically over-reacts to new information.

Dick, what do you make of all these new studies?

ROLL: Well, I'm a little puzzled by them. I'm very familiar with the work on unexpected earnings predictions, and with research on a lot of the other so-called anomalies. And, as I said before, as a professional money manager I would be the most delighted person in the world if some of these strategies really worked—because my clients could make a tremendous amount of money if they did.

I've tried to make money by exploiting these so-called inefficiencies, with real dollars—both my own and others'. And I haven't made any money. Why is this? Real money investment strategies don't produce the results that academic papers say they should.

JOHN McCONNELL: My experience is the same as yours, Dick, except with a lot fewer dollars.

SHILLER: I would like to step out of character for a moment and say something on behalf of the efficient markets hypothesis. When I was at the American Finance Association meetings a few years ago, my friends in finance departments were then very excited about the "January effect"—that is, the idea that you could make money by buying at year end those stocks that had gone down the most in December and then selling them in January. These friends of mine were even proposing that I invest money in a scheme to exploit that effect. But I didn't; I told them about the efficient markets hypothesis.

But let me also say that I interpret it a little bit differently from most financial academics. This is my version of it. I said that I had read about the January effect in the *Wall Street Journal* and *Barron's*. And if everyone that reads those publications already knows about this effect, then the trading strategy is not going to work. It can only work if there is a lapse of attention, if you will. The January effect was hardly noticed for 50 years. But now that everybody's talking about it, you can't expect it to work. And I think markets are efficient in that narrow sense.

And, by the way, Dick, I thought you were making money.

ROLL: We do make money in investment management, but we make it by trying to get a more mean-variance efficient portfolio. We beat the indexes, which is the name of the game in money management. But the issue we're raising here is this: Can you make *more* money by exploiting an earnings prediction rule or the January effect. My experience has been that these so-called anomalies disappear when you actually try to exploit them.

I'll give you an example. I too once tried to make money on the January effect—on this alleged tendency of those stocks that go down the most at year end to rise sharply in January. It's not true, incidentally, that for 50 years this January effect was there and nobody noticed it. *Stock Traders Almanac* has been mentioning the January effect for years. And lots of people on Wall Street have known about it.

SHILLER: But it wasn't a fad yet.

ROLL: But everybody on Wall Street knew about it.

Anyway, I read all this literature on the January effect, even wrote a paper on it, and then I tried to make money from it. On December 27th, 1988, I bought the 25 stocks that went down the most in the preceding 18 months, and I held those stocks for the next six months. In the first six months of the next year, 14 of the 25 stocks went bankrupt. But the rest of them made money. My suspicion, of course, is that academic studies may have somehow failed to account for those companies that went bankrupt or were delisted for other reasons.

Now, that's just one experiment. But I've tried a lot of these things, and I don't find they're very useful. And, again, I'm puzzled. The empirical results are persuasive, but then when you go out to exploit the rule, they don't seem to work.

BRADLEY: Professor Kaul?

GAUTAM KAUL: Dick, you mentioned that, like Bob Shiller, you felt that investor psychology is an important part of the stock market. In fact, I would argue that one of the primary functions of the stock market is to reflect what investors collectively feel is the economic future of our corporations and the general economy. But what, if anything, does this have to say about investor "rationality?" Are there any good reasons for attempting to control or manage investor psychology through policy measures?

ROLL: In one sense, I believe that psychology is the *only* thing in the market. It's the psychological attitudes that people have about the future that determine prices. But there is an important difference between what I'm suggesting and what Bob is saying. Bob is saying that most people get carried away, either in one direction or the other. Sometimes the market is way overvalued, sometimes it's way undervalued.

Now, in one sense, that's probably true. You have to remember that prices are forward looking. They are attempts to estimate future cash flows. And compared to what those cash flows eventually turn out to be, the current values are almost certain to have been too high or too low. The real question here is this: If you were "more rational" than the typical investor, could you consistently identify those moments when the market is overvalued or undervalued?

So I don't have the slightest doubt that sometimes the market is too high and sometimes it's too low. I just wish Bob would promise to tell me which it was on a timely basis, so that we could both profit from his foreknowledge.

SHILLER: The market is significantly undervalued about once every ten years. But that's the problem. You can't get rich quick. It's not like closed-end mutual funds, where you can arbitrage the discount. Well, you can't do that in the stock market. You just have to wait a long time for the market to come back to the proper level. For this reason, I think there are lots of apparent profit opportunities in assets that are not exploited.

KAUL: My question is not so much about how to exploit investor psychology, but rather how to regulate markets so as to prevent them from getting too high or too low.

ROLL: Well, we could follow Larry Summers' suggestion and prohibit dentists and retired persons from trading because they tend to be worse traders than institutions. But, seriously, there may be some policy measures that would lower volatility. Some people still think increased margin requirements would reduce volatility. I don't happen to be one of those people, because there have been empirical studies which indicate that changing margin requirements has no effect.

BRADLEY: Bob, neither you nor Dick offered any definite policy prescriptions. But what about this managerial short-termism you mentioned at the end of your talk. If managers are consistently sacrificing the long-term value of their companies for short-term profit, whether because stock prices fail to reflect the value of long-term investment or because their bonuses are tied to near-term EPS, then what can regulators do to overcome this myopia?

SHILLER: The situation I described was this. Corporate managers sometimes have the opportunity to increase earnings by cutting back on valuable investment. I am sure this goes on at many companies, especially when bonuses are tied to quarterly or year-end accounting numbers. And if this problem becomes widespread enough, as I said earlier, it could become a national concern.

BRADLEY: Then you would agree, Bob, that it is a good thing for the stock market to monitor managers more carefully. Perhaps, then, more active or more vigilant investors represent a solution to this short termism.

SHILLER: Well, I agree that having active investors is certainly better than having no stock market oversight. The most chronic case of short-termism was the situation in the Soviet Union, where the manager of a firm had no interest in the price of the firm.

ROLL: Well, let's suppose that managers regularly exploit these opportunities for their own benefits, which a good number of them probably do. It's not clear to me what policy the government could use to combat these agency conflicts between managers and their shareholders. Some people have argued that new SEC disclosure laws could be used to correct this problem, but I remain skeptical. Even though we know this agency problem exists, it's hard to think of a policy change that would mitigate it.

One of the most recent acts of government intervention has been to shut down the takeover markets. Although some observers have said that the threat of takeovers was a primary cause of corporate myopia, I remain unconvinced. In many cases, I suspect that we can correct the agency problem of myopic managers only by having *more* takeovers, or at least greater shareholder involvement in corporate governance.

BRADLEY: Well, on that note, let me bring this symposium to a close. Thank you all for helping to make this program a success.

CORPORATE STRATEGY

GLOBAL COMPETITION IN THE '90s

BENNETT STEWART: Yesterday, we were privileged to hear C.K. Prahalad, one of the foremost corporate strategists in the country, present his vision of global competition in the 1990s. As C.K. began by noting, we have seen a remarkable power shift over the past 20 years. Once mighty industrial giants such as General Motors, RCA, Pan Am, and CBS have been humbled by upstarts like Toyota, Sony, British Airways, and CNN.

What C.K. has attempted, both in his talk yesterday and in a series of articles (with co-author Gary Hamel) published in the *Harvard Business Review* over the past few years, is to develop nothing less than a general unified theory, if you will, of corporate competitiveness. As C.K. has written in the latest issue of the *HBR*, the aim of his work is to provide answers to the following questions:

> *Why do some companies continually create new forms of competitive advantage, while others watch and follow? Why do some companies redefine the industries in which they compete, while others take the existing industry structure as a given?*

Central to C.K.'s thinking is the concept of "core competence." I will not attempt to define it here—I suspect this will be an important part of our discussion this morning. I will instead simply restate C.K.'s prescription that companies should identify their core competencies as precisely as possible, invest in the capabilities necessary to build and maintain their core competencies, and then seek to extend or "leverage" these competencies across multiple businesses.

This morning, the Continental Bank has brought together a distinguished panel of senior corporate executives who have volunteered to explore these notions of corporate strategy with C.K. They will undoubtedly reinforce many aspects of his thinking, while perhaps challenging others. I myself have a few reservations or biases—which will likely become clear later—about how these strategic concepts actually work out in practice. But, for now, let me briefly introduce all our panelists.

■ **CHARLES CLOUGH**

is the Chairman of Wyle Laboratories, a distributor of semiconductors and other computer components with approximately $530 million in sales.

■ **DENNIS ECK**

is President and Chief Operating Officer of The Vons Companies, the leading grocery retailer in Southern California, with $5 billion in sales through some 350 stores.

■ **FRANK PERNA**

is President and Chief Executive Officer of MagneTek, Inc., a $1.3 billion manufacturer of electrical equipment. The company produces such items as fluorescent lighting ballasts, transformers, motors, and controls.

■ **ROBERT PERRY**

is Chief Financial Officer of Dames & Moore, Inc., a $350 million worldwide environmental and engineering consulting services firm—and perhaps the largest of its kind.

■ **C.K. PRAHALAD**

whom I've already mentioned several times, is the Harvey Fruehauf Professor of Business Administration at the University of Michigan. Described in a recent *Washington Post* article as "the hottest strategy consultant around," C.K. has done extensive consulting for companies such as Eastman Kodak, Phillips, Motorola, and Honeywell.

■ **ED THOMPSON**

is Chief Financial Officer of the Amdahl Corporation, a company that has traditionally designed and manufactured mainframe computers, but that has also begun offering software and open systems. Amdahl is 44% owned by Fujitsu, and I look forward to hearing from Ed what it *really* is like to work with a Japanese company.

■ **LEN WILLIAMS**

is President and Chief Executive Officer of MacFrugal's, which bids well to become the McDonald's of the bargain close-out store business. They have well over 200 stores with about $550 million in sales. I note that Southeastern Asset Management owns 15% of the stock of the company. This means that my good friend Mason Hawkins, a well-known value-based investor, has confidence in Len. We'll soon see if that's justified.

Core Competence and Corporate Renewal

STEWART: I'd like to begin this discussion by asking C.K. to expand on an argument that he made yesterday—one that I endorse wholeheartedly. He said that there really is no such thing as a mature business. There are only, let's say, prematurely aged companies or aged managements. Some of our corporate clients tell me, "Bennett, this is a tough business. It's just very difficult to build value in this business. You can't expect us to thrive and grow as you would, say, in the biotechnology business."

So, C.K., do you accept the premise that there are inherently mature businesses? Or is this just an excuse for poorly motivated or unimaginative managements?

PRAHALAD: Maturity is in the way you provide a certain functionality to customers. Industrial history is full of examples. Steinway thought pianos was a mature business—and the way they serviced their customers it was indeed a very mature business. But Yamaha didn't see it the same way. True, they still make grand pianos, but they have also extracted the functionality called digital sound, and they have been able to grow that part of the business by 30% to 40% a year.

Now, there are obviously some products that become obsolete, such as the buggy-whip. But by thinking about the functionality underlying a given product or a service, and looking beyond the particular product itself, companies often discover new sources of growth and renewal.

STEWART: Well, let's take grocery retailing, which is Dennis's business at the Vons Companies. That's a fairly mature business, right? There's only so much stuff people can cram into their stomachs. How do you make a growth business out of food, Dennis?

ECK: Our industry is widely perceived to be mature. That perception is at best a half-truth. What is true is that parts of our business are intensively competitive. We respond by discovering new areas from which to grow and profit. Those areas, needless to say, are receiving most of our focus and investment.

Let me be more specific. We have what we call cross-over categories. These are products nearly all retailers now sell. Things like detergents, paper, beverages—all of these are easily available to all other retailers and discount chains to sell. We have inevitably lost market share in these categories. First, by availability and because pricing has emerged that has been very difficult for us to match with our cost structure.

What we have done in response to shrinking margins and sales in cross-overs is to think about our customer more carefully. We ask ourselves: What kinds of products can we develop that will be difficult for our competitors to duplicate? So far, we've been very successful in adding floral, bakeries, and health care. We emphasize service and services. We have tried to make ourselves the best one-stop shopping point for people who want to get efficiently through the week. This reduces our need to compete on price.

Vons' business is not mature—although if we had simply stayed with our old products, we might have been in trouble today. Vons is hoping to do $250 million in floral by the end of 1994. This is a business that in 1990 did $17 million. The great thing about floral is that it operates at times up to 70% gross margin. This also helps us to be priced more competitively in the cross-over categories.

STEWART: Let me turn now to Frank Perna at MagneTek. Frank, as in Dennis's case, I would guess you too were operating in a mature market.

The electrical equipment business—things like transformers and motors and controls—does not appear to be a growth industry. Have you been able to find a way to create growth in what appears to be mature businesses?

PERNA: Many of our product lines come from businesses that we have acquired from other companies. In most cases, the sellers thought they were mature. But we bought these product lines with the idea that, no matter what happens, people still require certain types of electrical equipment. The opportunity we saw in these businesses was to build up more efficient distribution channels. And, once having established those channels for our base products, we could then use them to distribute new generations of more energy-efficient equipment. As one example, new technologies have enabled us to provide the same level of fluorescent lighting with 25% to 30% less energy.

So what we've really done is to use a distribution platform for supposedly mature products to launch new technologies and thereby generate some very exciting growth.

STEWART: Would it be fair to say that your distribution channels are the "core competence" of MagneTek?

PERNA: Yes, I think the core competence of our company is really its distribution channels—far more so than its products.

STEWART: C.K., can distribution channels be a core competence, in your scheme of things?

PRAHALAD: It can. But let me make a distinction here between what I call infrastructure and what I mean by a core competence. In many if not most cases, a distribution system is simply part of the infrastructure a company has built. It's what you do with the distribution system that has the power to turn it into a core competence.

Core competencies can, over time, become capabilities. What I mean by "capabilities" are the minimal skills that allow a company to compete. Strategy consultants these days like to talk about capability-based competition as if it were something unusual. But all competition is based on capabilities. You cannot compete if you don't have capabilities. Providing just-in-time inventory is a capability that is required today if you even want to be considered as a supplier. Capabilities are things that companies need just to play in the game.

A third distinction I want to make is between core competencies and intangible assets such as brandnames. In my articles, I define core competence as a set of multiple, harmonizable technologies and skills. My writings tend to focus on technology-based core competencies, but you can have marketing-based core competencies just as well. Things like global distribution and global brand management can also be core competencies.

For something to be a core competence, it should pass the following three tests: One, does it uniquely differentiate this company from other companies. Two, can it be leveraged to take advantage of trends in multiple businesses? And, three, is it difficult for competitors to imitate?

So, to return my earlier statement about Frank's company, distribution capabilities can become a core competence. But it all depends on what the company does with the channels.

One more comment in this context: Bennett, you asked whether the ballast business is mature or not. Just think about what would happen if people in China and India and Indonesia began buying as many bulbs per capita as we have in the U.S. This would become one of the fastest growing businesses in the world; and, as I was arguing yesterday, that is a good reason for companies like Frank's to develop a global reach. Is that a fair comment, Frank?

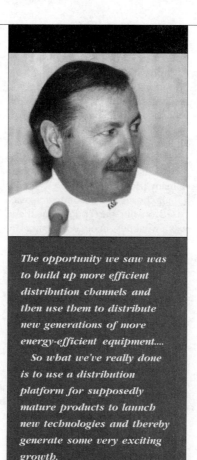

The opportunity we saw was to build up more efficient distribution channels and then use them to distribute new generations of more energy-efficient equipment....

So what we've really done is to use a distribution platform for supposedly mature products to launch new technologies and thereby generate some very exciting growth.

—Frank Perna—

PERNA: Yes, that's true. That's one of the reasons we have begun thinking about expanding into overseas markets in the last couple of years. A third of all the electricity consumed in the world is consumed in North America, and another third is consumed in Europe. Most of the world's population, however, is outside these two continents. As countries in Asia and elsewhere become more technically advanced, they will certainly use more electrical equipment—and the first thing is lighting. So, we expect global markets to extend the life of our products quite significantly, even those products we are currently phasing out in North America.

STEWART: C.K., to explore your concept of core competence a little further, you said companies should attempt to extend or "leverage" their core competencies across multiple businesses. But think about a company like Toyota, which has been extremely successful by focusing on just one business: automotive manufacturing. Or think about the success of Intel in microprocessors, or Dell Computer in distributing computers through mail-order catalogues. Why is it necessary for companies to have multiple businesses? Why can't they be content to dominate their customary businesses?

PRAHALAD: To describe Toyota as being only in the automotive business is inaccurate, because they're in other businesses as well. Even within the automotive business, there are many different products and markets. The markets for Cadillacs and pick-up trucks are quite different. Toyota has also moved into small earth-moving equipment, and made plans for aircraft manufacturing as well. In fact, I would argue that the long-term competition for Boeing is not only going to be Airbus, but Japanese companies like Toyota. So the critical question for management is: Can we extend our core competencies to other businesses?

Or take the case of Dell Computers, since you mentioned it. Dell has created a whole new capability in distribution—one that effectively bypasses the store-fronts controlled by companies like Compaq and IBM. It is management's job, I would argue, to look for related products that can be distributed through the same channels they've established for computers. This is what I mean by "leveraging" a core competence. For example, Dell has the necessary customer knowledge and infrastructure to become a powerhouse in software distribution. This way, software consumers would no longer have to read all the magazines to find out what software is available. Dell could effectively provide this service to its existing customer base. This would be a natural extension of its core competence—one that would transcend individual businesses.

STEWART: Okay, so you're saying that Dell's distribution expertise, its core competence, was not built up initially with the intention of selling software. But, having created that competence, management today—somewhat serendipitously—has been put in the position to expand into other products.

PRAHALAD: That's right. Companies never start out with the intention of extending a core competence across multiple products. You have to start by building a business. It's on the back of the business you build core competencies and, in so doing, you end up providing the platform for further growth.

The Benefits of Sharpening Focus: The Case of Wyle Labs

STEWART: Charlie, how would describe the core competencies of Wyle Laboratories?

CLOUGH: Well, the core competence of our business was created out of an intensely competitive situation that our company found itself in about 12 years ago. At that time, the three largest companies in the electronics distribution business controlled about 80% of the market; and there were five or six smaller firms like ours that had the rest. And these three dominant companies were large and financially strong. So, given our own modest size and limited financial resources, we decided to abandon our strategy of being a broad-line distributor of electronics and to specialize in one prod-

uct: semiconductors. In so doing, we made a real break with the history of electronics distribution. We felt our best opportunity lay in concentrating our resources to build a core strength in semiconductors. We would then use this core capability to compete more effectively against all the other broad-based distributors—those companies for which semiconductors was only one of many products.

Our choice of semiconductors was based on our perception that there was a weakness in our competitors in this area that we could exploit. That weakness was lack of technical capability. The success of these large companies had been built primarily on their merchandising capabilities; indeed, their approach to electronics distribution was not much different from the approach of mass food distributors. Their strategy was to achieve scale economies by using their merchandising expertise to distribute a wide variety of products. They would inventory all the products locally, and provide very good service and low pricing. The companies were also managed by financial kinds of people with no real grasp of the technical side of the business.

In deciding to concentrate only on semiconductor products, we also chose to build a very strong technical capability by training electrical engineers to become our salesmen. And this too was a radical break with industry practice. We also used our technical salesforce to provide value-adding services that the big companies could not. For example, we used our engineering capabilities to help our corporate customers design cost-reducing semiconductor systems.

But now, a decade later, we face a new challenge. The barriers to competition we built up with our engineering expertise have been eroding as other companies have improved their technical marketing skills too.

Although we probably still maintain an edge over our competitors, they have begun to go global—they have moved into Europe. And we're now pondering our strategy as to how we can supply unique services to enable us to compete and win.

STEWART: What companies do you consider to be your competitors?

CLOUGH: Arrow Electronics is one, Avnet is another.

STEWART: Have those companies maintained a broad line of electrical products, or have they chosen, like your company, to narrow their focus to semiconductors?

CLOUGH: They have maintained a broad-line national and now a global product strategy. By contrast, we have remained almost completely focused on semiconductors and have limited our marketing activity to major U.S. markets. Also, we sell only the products of U.S. semiconductor manufacturers—no Japanese or Korean lines.

STEWART: Why is that?

CLOUGH: Patriotism is part of it...

STEWART: You and Sam Walton.

CLOUGH: ...but there was also some sound business logic behind that decision. I had the conviction—even five or six years ago—that the American position in this industry was fundamentally stronger than the Japanese position, in spite of what people were saying in the popular business press and in places like the *Harvard Business Review*. The Japanese had built their capability in semiconductors around a very strong manufacturing capability that produced commodity kinds of products. But, I saw the profitable part of the semiconductor business moving away from commodities, which the Japanese companies dominated with their manufacturing skills, and toward products like microprocessors, where two American companies were emerging as the leaders. As I saw it, the microprocessor was going to become the driver of the semiconductor industry, not commodities like memory. Two companies, Motorola and Intel, would become world-wide leaders in microprocessors. And so we decided to ally ourselves very closely with those two American companies; and these alliances have proved to be very productive for us.

So our conviction proved to be right. Today, it's the microprocessor that drives electronics. The microprocessor sank IBM and revolutionized the electronics industry. What had built great companies like IBM, Unisys, and other giant computer companies was engineering, research and development, and a highly technical marketing knowledge of computer systems. Well, that all went by the board with the 386, the 486, and now the Pentium. Today, because of the microprocessor, a small company can build and sell the same system as IBM a hell of a lot cheaper and move it faster to market.

So, again, our core competence is in semiconductors. But we're now struggling with the question of whether to broaden our focus by adding other adjacent product lines around this technical capability, or by competing with our two principal competitors on a global basis. We haven't made a decision yet.

STEWART: C.K., would you be willing to offer Charlie some free consulting advice? What would you do if you were in Charlie's shoes?

PRAHALAD: If you're a reasonable consultant, the first thing you learn is *never* to give free advice.

But I will say this. What Charlie just described is an interesting way of starting to think about how companies build core competencies. There are two things he said that I think are especially important. The first is that management realized they had to think of an alternative way to compete rather than just imitating their

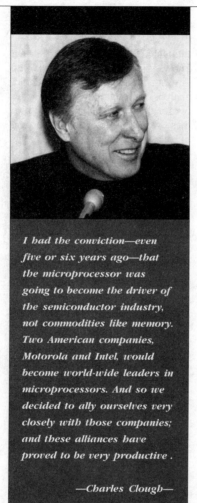

I had the conviction—even five or six years ago—that the microprocessor was going to become the driver of the semiconductor industry, not commodities like memory. Two American companies, Motorola and Intel, would become world-wide leaders in microprocessors. And so we decided to ally ourselves very closely with those companies; and these alliances have proved to be very productive .

—Charles Clough—

competitors. To me, that is a very critical part of the nature of competition in the '90s. That realization leads to what I like to call "competitive innovation." It is not providing different products, but rather changing the *ways* in which companies compete.

My second point is this: Although Charlie stressed the narrowing of his corporate focus, the company's core competence in semiconductor engineering has likely already provided the company with a significant new source of revenues that was not expected when the company first de-

cided to focus only on semiconductors. Given that you now specialize in selling semiconductors, I would bet that, as a result of your technical skills, your company also does a lot of application engineering for the companies that buy your semiconductors.

CLOUGH: That's exactly right.

PRAHALAD: That application engineering represents an extension of your core competence in distributing semiconductors. As a consequence of building technical capability into your sales force, the company has now become a technical adviser of sorts, a systems developer. You are no longer just taking Product A to Location B. You have acquired a much deeper understanding of the needs of your customers. And I would argue that your ability to assist them in designing applications of the products you sell is not something other companies can easily duplicate.

Eventually, of course, other companies will. And that raises what to me is the more interesting question, the real challenge, of corporate strategy: How do you keep upgrading your competencies?

Acquire, or Build from Within? The Case of Dames & Moore

Let me turn now to Bob Perry. Bob, could you just give us a thumbnail sketch of your company? Clearly, as an environmental consulting service, it would seem that you would have promising growth opportunities, both at home and abroad. How do you plan to grow the company?

PERRY: We started out about 54 years ago as a consulting firm specializing in "geo-technical" engineering. That's a fancy word for studying the ground on which people build refineries and power plants. We started out with one office in California, and today we have 117 offices around the world and over 3,000 employees. Roughly a third of our offices are outside the United States.

Besides expanding geographically, we have also moved into other types of engineering and environmental consulting. We have added geology, hydrology, meteorology, ecology, toxicology, and many other "ologies." We've sort of captured the market on ologies in the entire environmental framework, and we're one of the largest engineering and environmental consultants in the world today. About the same time we were expanding into the various ologies, we also initiated our move to global operations. We expanded our office network around the world to be closer to our clientele, which includes the overseas operations of most of the major American corporations as well as some foreign governments.

Our company went public about a year ago, and the issue we're facing today is how to find other avenues of growth. One possibility is to lengthen the amount of time we spend on a particular project. In other words, instead of acting just as a consultant, we're now looking to get more involved in the actual design and construction of projects of an environmental nature. We have a certain amount of that capability in-house, but the question that we face now as we try to grow is this: Should we grow slowly and patiently by just expanding in an in-house way with our own people? Or should we look more towards larger acquisitions— we have already made a number of smaller ones—to expand into design and construction in a very quick, major way?

STEWART: Bob, it strikes me that both you and Charlie seem to be struggling to define not so much a core competence, but what C.K. might call a "strategic intent"—that is, the broader mission that's going to guide your company's growth over the

longer term. Would you agree with that, C.K.?

PRAHALAD: Well, without any detailed knowledge of either of the companies, I'm uncomfortable offering any kind of analysis or prescriptions. But there are two or three issues that stand out in these two cases—and in the earlier case of ballasts and electrical equipment as well.

First, it seems clear that all these industries are going through a period of change and evolution. So the question is, How can companies create for themselves a roadmap that will help them anticipate and respond to the course this evolution eventually takes? One cannot predict exactly what the products will be even just three years down the road, much less five or ten years. But one can predict with some confidence the fundamental capabilities that will be necessary for companies in a given industry to exploit those specific commercial opportunities that actually materialize.

For example, with respect to Frank's ballast business, it seems virtually certain that miniaturization will be one of the major challenges, and thus opportunities. And so all the enabling technologies that will help the company acquire the capability to miniaturize should be explored. Do you agree, Frank?

PERNA: Yes, I do.

PRAHALAD: So, technology is not really much of a surprise at all. We can more or less say what will happen in many of the technical parameters over the next five or ten years. What is uncertain, and what is critical for businesses, is the intersection of technology and customer functionalities. The purpose of creating the roadmap—the broad strategic architecture, if you will—is to galvanize companies into preparing for the future, to set the energies of people in the right direction. This way, when the change does occur, and a new set of

consumer requirements becomes clear, companies will have built the capabilities that will enable them to respond quickly.

STEWART: What factors would you consider in choosing among different ways of achieving necessary capabilities or technology? For example, how would you choose among the alternatives of acquiring a company, licensing vendors, forming an alliance, or building capabilities from within?

PRAHALAD: First, you want to be as clear as possible about your strategic intent, and about the capabilities that will be essential to realize it. Having determined the desired capabilities, the question then becomes this: What is the lowest-cost, lowest-risk approach to getting that particular skill or capability?

Now, with regard to this second matter, I'm willing to make two broad propositions. The first is that companies that cannot grow from within will not necessarily be able to exploit collaborative arrangements. Time and again I have seen companies entering into alliances or joint ventures or undertaking acquisitions because they do not have faith in their own organizations to build a capability internally. They think that some other company's skills will substitute for their lack of ability. And such companies generally wind up being disappointed.

You may still acquire a company, it's true, but often without realizing any strategic or synergistic benefits from the acquisition. That is, acquisitions may add something to your balance sheet and P & L, but the capabilities may never be successfully developed or integrated into your own organization. Learning capabilities from an acquired company, and thus assimilating that acquisition, is quite a different task from buying the company.

So, I would argue that the ability of a company to leverage all kinds of collaborative arrangements depends heavily on its existing capacity for internal growth. In the case of hi-tech companies, moreover, acquisition is the very last thing I would consider. I'd much rather start with internal growth and, if that won't work, then consider licensing arrangements and possibly alliances. Acquisitions have a lot of toxic side-effects, especially in high-technology industries. Every hi-tech small company has a culture of its own. That is why they are hi-tech—they are all prima donnas. It's difficult to acquire such companies and make it work because you can't really *own* these kind of people.

STEWART: IBM certainly made a mess of its forays into telecommunications.
PRAHALAD: It was not only IBM. Look at GE's acquisitions of Intersil and Calma. The history of hi-tech acquisitions is littered with sad stories like these. Such acquisitions can cause problems for the acquirers, too. Acquisition-oriented companies are saying something to their own employees. How would you feel if you were a top scientist in a hi-tech company, and your management repeatedly went out and acquired another company instead of investing inside the firm?

Global Partnership: The Case of Amdahl

STEWART: How about *partial* acquisitions? For example, Fujitsu owns 44% of Amdahl. In fact, let me now ask Ed Thompson to tell us about Amdahl. Yesterday, C.K. talked of the need for companies to achieve economies of scope by extending the corporate reach into new areas. Does Amdahl serve to extend the reach of Fujitsu? What does each party bring to the table and how does the relationship work?
THOMPSON: Well, the origins of our relationship with Fujitsu go back to 1970, when we went out and tried to

The greatest benefit we get from our relationship with Fujitsu is in technology, in the "R" part of R & D. They're awfully good in basic research in areas like semiconductor technology, optical fiber, communications, even artificial intelligence.
We, conversely, are awfully good in the "D" part of R & D, in developing commercial applications for their research.

—Ed Thompson—

raise venture capital in the domestic capital markets and failed. We just didn't have the ability then to raise $50 million of five-year money to develop a large-scale processor to compete against IBM.

We did find one or two venture capitalists in the U.S., as well as a German company, willing to put up a little money. But most of the venture capital ended up coming from Fujitsu. Their investment was based on the promise of our technology and the way it could potentially complement their manufacturing op-

erations. If our technology proved to be successful, they could become a supplier of sub-assemblies and complements to us.

So Fujitsu looked at their investment in Amdahl in a way very different from that of a traditional venture capitalist. They were not looking for an immediate return on investment. In fact, to this day they've never sold a share of our stock. They viewed us as a company that had the potential to keep their factories loaded as well as a valuable source in a mutually beneficial exchange of technology. And our relationship with Fujitsu is now over 20 years old.
STEWART: So they manufacture for you?
THOMPSON: They manufacture some sub-assemblies and components. For example, they developed the bipolar ECL technology that is the chip technology in our large-scale processor. The architecture is ours. The design is ours—the micro code, the macro code, and what have you. But we selected their chip technology.
STEWART: You say you *chose* their chip technology. You really had complete freedom to make that choice?
THOMPSON: Yes, we did, at least in that particular case. And then at a point in time, we had to make some commitments on certain volumes to Fujitsu after exhausting our domestic supplier's ability to produce a high-performance bi-polar ECL chip at a competitive cost.

But let me return to the point Charlie Clough made earlier about the importance of the microprocessor, because it's also having a profound effect on our business as well. About five years ago, we too recognized the dramatically reduced cost structure inherent in that technology, and so we knew where the marketplace was going. In fact, I would say that our distinctive core competence is our knowledge of what's going on in large corporations with the largest computer installations in the world. Based on the changes we were seeing in the market, we selected Sun Microsystems and its SPARC chip for our future RISC-based processor in developing a platform using microprocessor technology. This will enable us to deliver a very attractive cost/performance processor for the large-scale open-systems marketplace. And that development is underway right now.

STEWART: But how do you benefit from being associated with Fujitsu in this way?

THOMPSON: Generalizations are always risky, but let me attempt a big one. The greatest benefit we get from our relationship with Fujitsu is in technology, in R & D. They're damned good in the "R" part of R & D. The stereotypical view of Japanese suppliers is that they are good copiers, but not good inventors. You know, they take existing technology, reverse- engineer it, and come up with a high-quality product that they then mass distribute and sell very cheaply.

But, the reality is quite the opposite in our relationship with Fujitsu. They're awfully good in basic research, in areas like semiconductor technology, optical fiber, communications, even artificial intelligence. We, conversely, are awfully good in the "D" part of R & D, in developing commercial applications for their research. And our ability in this area stems, as I said before, from our experience with and knowledge of customers that we've built up over many years. We are sometimes able to know our customers' requirements even before the customers are aware of them—although anticipating customer demands in this way can be a risky proposition.

STEWART: How does the technology transfer between the two companies actually take place? Is there a lot of interchange between your research efforts and Fujitsu's?

THOMPSON: Yes, there is a good deal of interchange. We actually make each other insiders with regard to ongoing developments in our technology. Our mutual knowledge helps both of us make better investment decisions, decisions about where they're putting in a lot of money and where we're putting in a lot of money. And, together, we do spend a lot of money on R & D. For example, Fujitsu is a $25 billion company that is spending about 11% of sales on R & D. We are a $2.5 billion company spending about 15% of our sales on R & D. So, we view our R & D as in some sense a joint effort. Both companies figure out together what it makes sense for us to develop in common, and what to develop separately.

**Hi-Powered Lo-tech:
The Case of MacFrugal's**

STEWART: We have one more company yet to hear from. So let me turn to Len Williams, President of MacFrugal's. Len, your company is a bargain-basement, close-out firm. It seems to be at almost the opposite end of the spectrum from some of the large Japanese, hi-tech companies C.K. was describing yesterday. Do these principles of strategy really apply to a company like yours? Or is it all fairly high-falutin' stuff?

WILLIAMS: I think the same principles apply in our case. In fact, I think C.K. might find our story quite interesting. Our core competence amounts to just one thing: We believe we are the best high-gross-profit-margin buyers in the country. That is the basis of our business. And we've worked hard to maintain this core competence. We continue to be the best buyers of the kind of merchandise that we sell.

Now, it's true that, over time, we have reduced our percentage margins somewhat because of increased competition. If we had insisted on our old margins, we would have been excluded from trading in some of the best merchandise. So we've shifted one piece of our equation to become more competitive, to maintain our original core competence, if you will.

STEWART: But how does your company actually operate? How do you buy this merchandise?

WILLIAMS: We have about 20 people who buy merchandise 100% of the time, and they have lots of support staff. We buy in the U.S. and in a dozen other countries. We buy regular close-outs, we buy overproduction, we buy in virtually any situation where waste occurs in manufacturing and distributing goods. We also buy down-time in equipment.

STEWART: You buy down-time in equipment?

WILLIAMS: If we find a plastics company that has too much resin and machines aren't working, we'll bang out four or five products by the truckload. If we find a company that prints children's books and needs to flatten out their production schedule, we help them out. We buy goods any way we can. We're like old-time merchants. We buy onshore and offshore, and we're very, very flexible.

Our principal assets are money and space. We have a lot of distribution center space and lots of cash, and we can do lots of deals. One of our competitors at the moment has a cash problem, and they're going to sink like the Titanic; it's not even that big a problem, they just can't pay fast enough.

We also operate very differently from the normal retailing practice of low margins and high turnover. We don't care an awful lot about turn. What we care about is, do we have the product? We are, in fact, our own suppliers. We don't rely on suppliers to give us merchandise. We rely on ourselves to have the merchandise. For this reason, we earn high gross margins.

STEWART: How does a company like this get started?

WILLIAMS: It all started about 40 years ago with a wild entrepreneur—a man whom I've since met, talked to, and tried to understand. He began by selling some unusual products out of his station wagon. He found so much product he eventually opened a store. And now we are well on our way to having 300 stores, and the founder lives with his money in Fresno.

But I'll tell you what kind of guy he is. After I was in this business a year, and understood what I thought I could from being there, I went to see him—to see what he could teach me. And when we finished our conversation for the day, he said to me: "Do you have a strong back? Reach in my car." So I pulled out this huge African statue made out of wood. He said: "I found 400 of them. I got them all for eight bucks each."

So then I paid him $11, and later sold them for $30. It's that kind of business. So we have a different deal every day, a different way, different needs. We have a very lean management. And, as I said, we're very flexible.

STEWART: It strikes me that retailing is an industry that tends to have a geographic focus. In other words, you'll find a company like Walmart focusing largely on American markets, as opposed to going overseas. Is that because consumer tastes and customs vary so much across countries that it becomes a quantum leap to sell abroad?

WILLIAMS: I worked for an American company in Europe for four years. And we had businesses in three countries. And I've watched other American retailing businesses operating in other countries. The margins in retailing are narrow. And I've observed that the connection between success-

Our core competence amounts to just one thing: We believe we are the best high-gross-profit-margin buyers in the country. We buy regular close-outs, we buy overproduction, we buy in virtually any situation where waste occurs in manufacturing and distributing goods. We buy goods any way we can. We're like old-time merchants. We buy onshore and offshore, and we're very, very flexible.

—Len Williams—

ful retailers and their customer is often visceral; and this implies the need for geographic, local, ethnic specialization. To translate a merchandising format from country to country is very, very difficult. Marks & Spencer couldn't make it in North America. J.C. Penney, for which I once worked, couldn't make it in Europe. Sears couldn't make it in Europe. A few companies have done it, like Bennetton. But it's a very tough thing to do.

But, having said all that, I'm going to Mexico City next weekend to try to

start to learn what it takes for us to be in Mexico with free trade. Canada is easy, it's like America. I'm Canadian. You don't have to go there to figure it out. But Mexico is very different. And we're going to see if, with free trade, we can find opportunity. The population density in the cities makes it potentially attractive. And we already feel we understand Hispanic people, because they represent about 35% or 40% of our action in Southern California and the Southwest.

STEWART: Would the same thing be true of Vons, Dennis?

ECK: Pretty much. We've sent our people around the world to look for ideas and different ways of doing things. In one case, a man came back to me and said, "Dennis, you have to go to Veracy, Italy. It has the finest deli in the world." So when I next went to Europe, I rented a car and went to Veracy, Italy. And it *was* maybe the finest deli in the world.

When I returned from Europe, the man asked me, "Well, are we going to build one like that?" And I said, "No, we're not. But we're going to steal a few of his fixturing ideas, because they show product much more effectively." As I explained to him, in Veracy, Italy, you're surrounded 100% by Italians. In that setting, the product assortment, mixture, and the goods can be uniquely tailored. Therefore, the assortments can be dominant. The problem for us is we would need Italians to buy the products, and there aren't that many in a cluster in Los Angeles. (The fixtures, though, work beautifully with our Southern California assortment.)

I have a view that says when we go to borrow things from other companies, we often look at the wrong thing. We look at the superficial—in our case, at the products on display. What we should be looking for are the things that are truly transportable across markets. In this case, it was the display techniques, not the products.

STEWART: Do you carry that principle of ethnic specialization, if you will, down to the individual store, so that each store has the autonomy to merchandise and focus on its particular market, its particular neighborhood? Or do you try to get some economies of scale by standardizing things across the board?

ECK: We do both at the same time. We run three distinct formats. We have Pavilions stores, which we refer to as our "republican" format. It's a high-touch, high-feel store with expansions of product that you won't find in most supermarkets. It's meant to attract people who are really interested in food. Interestingly, there hasn't been a recession in our sales in Pavilions.

STEWART: The Clinton tax plan hasn't kicked in yet.

ECK: Well, it's what you have left over that counts.

At the other end of the spectrum, we have a group of stores we call Tianguis. They are designed for first- and second-generation Hispanic people who have immigrated to Los Angeles. In Tianguis, we try to recreate not only the products and services, but the actual "feel" of shopping they experienced in Mexico. These stores have also turned out to be very good for Asian people. They also put great emphasis on same-day freshness.

Then we have Vons, our middle group of stores. We give the managers of these stores flexibility in tailoring their product assortment and styles of service.

All three groups of stores are supplied by the same distribution channels. They are supervised by the same management and utilize all the same support systems. So, though we have three distinct operating styles, we achieve scale economies with a single support and coordination system.

STEWART: Len, tell me more about why you are looking south of the border to expand your business.

WILLIAMS: Well, you'd have to be crazy not to, because there are so many people there. As I said earlier, we feel we understand Mexican tastes because we're already dealing with Mexicans in Los Angeles and the Southwest. I would also say that some of the early alliances of American with Mexican companies have turned out quite well. Walmart, for example, went in and formed a valuable alliance.

STEWART: Dennis, it would seem to me that a company like Walmart represents a formidable competitive threat, even to innovative grocery retailers like Vons? There have long been rumors of their intent to penetrate the grocery side of the business, and there have been some false starts. But still, the company is not to be taken lightly. How do you respond to that type of threat?

ECK: Our method of responding is to continue what we're attempting to do now. We will seek out and specialize in those products and services that ordinary supermarkets cannot provide. As I mentioned earlier, we've been moving our focus away from cross-overs toward high-margin specialties like floral, delis, and bakeries. I don't believe Walmart will want to follow us there. Our current strategy is to move as far away from direct competition with Walmart as we can. This, while recognizing that we still rely on cross-over categories now at less margin. We have moved our business to a heavy emphasis on service, variety, execution, and freshness. That's the weakness of general merchandise.

But having said that, it has yet to be proved that a general merchandiser can succeed in the food business. It is rare for a food company to succeed in general merchandise. As we've

already mentioned, there has not been much success by either of these industries in expanding overseas.

PRAHALAD: I think the importance of this notion of distinct national and ethnic tastes has been greatly exaggerated. As a consequence, there is more global opportunity than is commonly believed for businesses that appear very much bound to local tastes and based on one-on-one contact with consumers. For example, if you take both the merchandising and grocery retailing businesses, a significant portion of the buying already takes place overseas. So one part of the business, the supply part of the chain, has already become global.

But what about the customer interface? Are there general principles that you can transport across cultures and countries? To me the reason why large food retailers and merchandisers have not been very successful in Europe and in Asia is the domination, until quite recently, of small mom-and-pop stores. This has been embodied in the tradition of people going out and buying bread every morning at 11:00 o'clock when a fresh batch comes out. All that behavior, I would submit, is based on a certain lifestyle. It has nothing to do with an immutable national character, as people like to claim.

For example, if you went to France ten years ago and asked a Frenchman, "Would you eat frozen foods?", he would say, "Absolutely not." But, as things have turned out, a penchant for frozen foods has little to do with being French or American. It has much to do with lifestyles. If both husband and wife are working, frozen foods become an eminently respectable thing to serve. And, if you go to Paris today, I assure you you *will* find frozen foods. It's remarkable how simply increasing the number of dual income households can change what has been held to be the national character. But changes in wealth and lifestyle clearly affect consumer tastes, and in fairly predictable ways.

I would also argue that Asia—at least the large, metropolitan areas—will prove a better market for American-style food retailing than Europe. Why? Because—and you may be surprised to know this—more women work in Asia, and at better jobs, than those in the United States. And the same thing is happening within the large Indian community in London. Today, you can buy all kinds of packaged Indian food. People always tell me that Asians have this desire for freshness—and that may be true, especially if only one of the couple is working. But if both of them are working, they behave no differently from us.

ECK: Well, we actually sell to Asia. We charge a fee for busloads of Asian businessmen to tour our Pavilions stores—twenty-eight hundred bucks a bus. There is an enormous interest among Asian businessmen in our style of merchandising.

Corporate Structure:
Centralized vs. Decentralized

STEWART: Let me ask a broader question. Yesterday C.K. was talking about the need for corporations to transcend their business unit mentality and encourage co-operation among different functions and businesses to exploit new growth opportunities more effectively. What are some of the remedies the companies at this table have devised to break down those organizational barriers to co-operation? How do design your measurement and reward system to encourage teamwork among different operating units?

PERRY: A few years ago, our overseas operations felt that our MIS system wasn't giving them the information they wanted quickly enough and tai-

We have about 35 foreign offices in 19 different countries and we have spent millions integrating our overseas operations into the U.S. system. As a result, we now have one common worldwide accounting system that enables us to share resources and people among different offices in a way that better serves our clients and leads to the greater good of the whole company.

—Robert Perry—

lored to their specific needs. So we spent several million dollars implementing a separate MIS system for our overseas operations. But it has turned out to be a failure. So, in the last couple of years, we have spent millions more integrating our overseas operations *back* into the U.S. system. As a result, we now have one common worldwide accounting system.

What this means, for example, is that an engineer from our Paris office could spend five hours working on a project in Tokyo on a Friday afternoon, and the Tokyo project manager

would have that time recorded in his overall job costing summary on the following Monday. So our supervising managers know the time spent on their projects by all their engineers around the world, almost instantaneously. And that, of course, gives us great cost control of the projects that we perform.

We have about 35 foreign offices in 19 different countries. And there is a lot of mixing of our people working on projects. In other words, if we have a major project in France, we might bring in people from Germany and the U.K. and Italy to work on it. So our organization allows us to share resources and people among different offices—to move them to where they are most valuable—in a way that better serves our clients and leads to the greater good of the whole company.

STEWART: Bob, your company was for most of its life a partnership, and then you went public and became a C corporation. How, if at all, has this change in organizational form affected the sense of teamwork within the company?

PERRY: We were a partnership for 53 years until we went public just about a year ago. We went public for several reasons, one of which was we felt it was getting a bit unwieldy to run such a large operation as a partnership.

In the tradition of our partnership, the profits were distributed according to the profit of the *entire* firm, not the particular profitability of, say, the German or French or Australian office. All the profits were pooled and then distributed according to overall capital interests.

STEWART: And did that practice motivate people to work together more effectively?

PERRY: Yes, it did. It eliminated a great deal of provincialism.

CLOUGH: I was manager of one of Texas Instruments' European semiconductor operations for several years.

The units were organized geographically; for example, there was a TI-Deutschland, a TI-France, and a TI-Italia that all operated independently. And the conflicts, the barriers to cooperation, created by that system were difficult. The problem began with the time-honored international rivalries: the Italians didn't trust the French, the French with cause feared the Germans, the Germans looked down on the Italians. This problem was compounded by the corporate practice of driving profit measurement down to the lowest common denominator within a complex organization. Within each of these countries, we had what were called "product customer centers." These centers had the responsibility to design, manufacture, and market their product—and they were each measured individually on their profit contribution, or lack thereof. So not only did we have little incentive to coordinate our design or production activities with those of other units, but we had a duplication of functions that could have been performed in one place for all Europe.

Since then, Texas Instruments—along with many other companies, I suspect—has done away with this fragmentation of the company into hundreds of individual profit centers. All these different units have now been consolidated into six or seven operating divisions. TI has also stopped organizing according to geographical boundaries. Today, for example, they have one person who's responsible for their entire MIS capability on a worldwide basis. And the primary measure of success within the company is the profitability of the worldwide organization.

THOMPSON: Several years ago, we went to cross-functional process reengineering teams—teams made up of engineers from the different countries, people from the different strategic business units and field business units, and some corporate people as well. Prior to forming these teams, we had operations in some 30 countries all designing, marketing, and installing systems in ways that may have been optimal from the perspective of the individual unit, but which failed to optimize the value of the entire enterprise. We found that bringing all these people together ended up providing us with a better understanding of the needs of the total corporation.

In one case, interestingly enough, our direct experience in serving clients caused us to make a change in how we were organized internally. This happened in Europe, when we were installing general ledgers and trying to figure out the optimal distribution of those systems. As a result of what we learned from that experience, we reorganized the company to reflect the new systems implementation we came up with. So, our corporate structure was changed to fit the requirements of our customers, instead of just allowing our internal structure to dictate the kind of systems we installed.

STEWART: Ed, given that the world seems to be moving away from the mainframe and toward more distributed systems, how have you addressed the need to redirect your resources and, perhaps, cannibalize your basic business? Have you made that transition? And how are you addressing that organizationally?

THOMPSON: Let me first say that we are *not* cannibalizing the mainframe business. That business is alive and well, although we have changed the name: It's now called "centralized processing." It's always going to be there.

But I agree the business is changing, and it's changing pretty dramatically. To reflect that change, we have changed the compensation plan for our sales organization to encourage them to concentrate more heavily on what we see as our growth opportunities—software and professional services, and the open systems we now offer. But, having said that, the big bucks are still in our central-processing operation.

STEWART: The big bucks in what respect—sales or gross profits?

THOMPSON: Both, although the margins are beginning to shrink, and will continue to do so over time.

STEWART: Well, what about the returns? I ask because I understand the mainframe business is being hurt by substitution in the form of distributed processing. So there must be excess capacity in mainframes relative to what was anticipated. And thus there needs to be a major withdrawal of resources, or at least a slowdown in the commitment of resources, to the mainframe business.

THOMPSON: That's certainly true, at least relative to what was anticipated. Five years ago, the large-scale processor business capacity was growing at 40% to 50% per annum. The forecasts for the next five years are only half that, about 25% per annum. And with the price competition and the commodity feature of the business, prices are going down at about that same rate.

So, the large-scale compatible processor business is a zero-growth business in terms of total industry revenues. Fortunately, though, we are in a position where we're increasing our market share. Today, we have a worldwide share that's probably in the high teens, and we expect to move rapidly into the low or mid-20s. Thus, the revenue and volume parts of it still look pretty good for us. But the margins are under a lot of pressure, and that is starting at the top and it's collapsing all the way down on the minicomputer business. In fact, the margins on all parts of the hardware side of the business are collapsing.

So, as I said, we are in the midst of a substantial transition that will move us partly into the professional services and software business, and into the open-systems licensing business over time. We will still be in the hardware business as well, but using architectures and technologies that have been optimized for cost and performance.

Changing the Management Scorecard

PRAHALAD: I would like to return to this issue of why business units don't collaborate, because I think it has a lot to do with the problems at our largest companies—the IBMs, the ITTs, the General Motors of the world. To me, the really basic issue is this: What is the scorecard for top management? What is their primary goal? Most top managements simply side-step the question by aggregating the financial numbers of all their business units and coming up with a single financial measure for the corporation. But, as Charlie was arguing in the case of TI, this kind of divisionalized, decentralized structure forces people to think and act in very narrow ways. It breeds turf wars.

If you think about the dimensions of corporate strength in a large diversified company, it's not just a matter of expanding markets by selling in multiple countries. More fundamentally, it's a matter of leveraging commonalities among business units, or what I like to call the "white spaces" between business units. Most of the new opportunities for corporations do not exist within the box called the business unit; they tend to span those boxes, or to exist in these white spaces, if you will. People focusing only on their business units will inevitably fail to seize such opportunities.

So, given this limitation, why do managers use financial performance as their scorecard? And why do they continue to use decentralized corporate structures? Two reasons, I think:

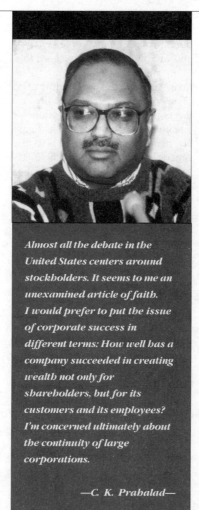

Almost all the debate in the United States centers around stockholders. It seems to me an unexamined article of faith. I would prefer to put the issue of corporate success in different terms: How well has a company succeeded in creating wealth not only for shareholders, but for its customers and its employees? I'm concerned ultimately about the continuity of large corporations.

—*C. K. Prahalad*—

One, it makes top management's job extremely easy. What do you do if one of your business units is not performing? You change the manager. This way, you've pretended to address the problem, and you're essentially off the hook. The second reason, which I won't go into now, has to do with restrictions our governance system places on communications between management and investors—restrictions that make it difficult for companies to communicate in ways other than the language of quarterly earnings.

Now, there is no value added in that kind of relationship between top management and corporate divisions. Top managers in this decentralized system are functioning at bottom no differently than portfolio managers who trade in and out of stocks. But, if you believe you're running an operating company, then top management must take some responsibility for creating synergies, for making the value of the total corporation worth more than simply the sum of its divisions. Of course, management must continue to make sure that divisional managers have strong incentives to be market-focused and entrepreneurial. At the same, though, they must continually ask themselves: How do I use corporate oversight and corporate functions to leverage the different divisions, to identify and take advantage of growth opportunities that could be pursued more effectively by people from different parts of the organization acting in concert?

You cannot produce co-operative behavior unless you take a broader view of corporate performance than that provided by financial measures. You certainly will never achieve a sharing of the agenda. And that, in my opinion, is why so many of the recent corporate success stories feature Japanese instead of American companies. It's not because Japanese top managers are smarter than American managers. They have simply tried much harder to provide people throughout their organizations with a broad understanding of the corporate mission, with a vision of the corporate future. At the same time, they have continued to encourage individual entrepreneurship and accountability at the business unit level.

So we need to ask the question: To what extent can you decentralize and multiply profit centers without destroying incentives for co-operative planning and action? At what level of senior management do you begin to hold people accountable not for business unit performance, but for the success of the organization as a whole? If you look at the three levels of management below the top that characterize most American companies, each of them is typically evaluated according to the same set of numbers. The business unit managers are looking at monthly or quarterly performance, and so are the group managers and the sector managers. If all of them are marching to the same drummer, then where is the value added by the upper layers? They don't bring a different perspective to operations.

In Defense of Decentralization and Corporate Focus

STEWART: That's true enough, C.K. But let me play devil's advocate and ask the following question: What's to prevent the organization-wide pursuit of this grand co-operative vision from degenerating into an unchecked quest for growth and market share? It seems to me that this is one of the big problems faced by many Japanese companies today. In this quest for growth and continuous renewal, they have diversified well beyond their capabilities and ignored profitability altogether. So where's the accountability necessary to rein in the impulse toward excessive growth?

As you said yesterday, C.K., the best corporate system is one that achieves an ideal tension between the short term and the long term. You have to pay attention to both simultaneously; and it seems, to me at least, that too many Japanese companies have sacrificed profitability for market share. Much of this increased market share, I'm willing to bet, will never translate into profit or shareholder gains. As one observer recently put it, the Japanese economy is now "choking on an orgy of overinvestment."

One of the things I was struck with during your presentation yesterday—and in your articles as well—is this: There is not a single reference to the financial or stock market performance of any of the companies you hold up for emulation. How successful, for example, has NEC been in its financial performance relative to GTE, the American counterpart you cited? Has it earned extraordinary returns for its stockholders over this long period of time? What has been the result of NEC's being among the top five companies in market share in each of the three main areas of the computers and communications business? And isn't it in some sense misleading to compare NEC with large, diversified American companies, when the traditional format in America is not to have companies that are broad in scope, but rather to have industries made up of smaller, more focused companies?

Take the computer industry. Andrew Grove, the CEO of Intel, has stated that the American computer industry is going from being vertically integrated to "horizontal." It is moving away from dominance by companies like IBM with integrated proprietary systems that are all things to all people. IBM effectively said to its customers, "You have to take my whole product line if you want any of it." Today, of course, we have the open architecture driven by the central processing unit, and the result is that the industry has fragmented into classes of specialists—everything from Intel to Microsoft to Dell to Compaq to Apple.

So, C.K., it seems to me we should not be comparing NEC against a GTE, as you do. Rather, we should be comparing an NEC to the combination—or the sum, if you will—of an AT&T, an Intel, an Apple, a Hewlett-Packard, and a Microsoft. You see, you have to ask yourself the question: Would AT&T or GTE be more

valuable and productive companies if they were all of sudden to acquire Apple and Intel and Microsoft? I very much doubt it.

THOMPSON: They couldn't afford it.

STEWART: Right, and that only goes to reinforce my point. These companies are far more valuable and efficient operating alone. I'm very skeptical about the ability of individual companies like GTE and AT&T to achieve the economies of scope you identify in NEC. Your argument seems perilously close to the fallacy that NEC is a better company than AT&T simply *because* it has a broader scope, simply because it participates in all of the C & C industries of the future? But I'm very skeptical that this is a prescription for building shareholder value, and by that I mean long-term value as well as short-term value.

CLOUGH: Bennett, let me add something to what you're saying. The same arguments apply to the electronic industry. The electronic industry isn't merely in the process of change, it is going through a revolution. We have killed our kings and queens, and now we're assassinating our presidents. The very large, historically successful companies in this industry have created enormous problems for themselves—many of which stem from sheer size—and they are now under tremendous pressure to shrink and change.

The embryonic companies of today that are going to be successful in the next ten years are companies that don't want to do it the way IBM did. For example, if you have a uniquely valuable idea for creating and marketing teleconferencing electronic equipment, you want to focus just on design and marketing. You don't want to invest in large manufacturing entities. You don't want to go out and buy the land and build on it, because you don't bring anything to the manufacturing ballgame. Your manufacturing skills are not as good as those of people who have been honing their manufacturing skills for 20 years. And, in many cases, you may not want to market it either. Your brilliance resides in the fact that you can create this unique and better electronic equipment.

People today don't want to make investments in areas beyond their expertise. This is the new American model of enterprise—smaller companies with limited funding and resources relying on outsourcing and other forms of networking or partnerships. It's adherence to the principle of comparative advantage, focusing only on what you do best and getting other people to do the other stuff they do better. And that's really a departure from the way electronic companies operated from the late 1950s until just the last few years.

STEWART: C.K., in one of your articles, you criticized Motorola for skipping the round of 256K Dynamic Random Access Memories, or DRAMS. You argued that doing so made it very difficult for Motorola to participate in the 1-Meg stage. But, with hindsight, this seems to have been the right decision for Motorola. As Charlie said earlier, memories today are commodities. And, as a consequence, it seems clear to us now that the Japanese invested billions of dollars in building memory capacity with virtually no returns to show for it.

So, to return to my earlier question, Isn't there a possible danger in overemphasizing the need to leverage core competencies into an all-consuming quest for global leadership? Can that pursuit excuse investing billions of dollars in quest of a core competence that could become available to anybody at commodity prices?

PRAHALAD: Actually, I think you asked seven different questions. And I think it's important to unscramble them because, in any discussion of

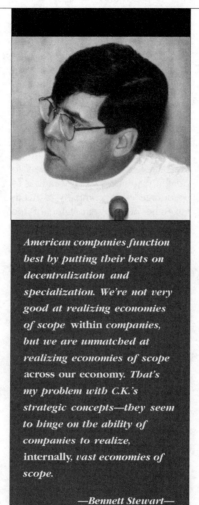

American companies function best by putting their bets on decentralization and specialization. We're not very good at realizing economies of scope within companies, but we are unmatched at realizing economies of scope across our economy. That's my problem with C.K.'s strategic concepts—they seem to binge on the ability of companies to realize, internally, vast economies of scope.

—*Bennett Stewart*—

this kind, unless you are very clear about what issue we are talking about, we can go from one to another almost seamlessly.

The first question you raised was this: Is NEC creating wealth compared to, say, GTE? It's an interesting question. If you look at profitability alone, GTE is probably more profitable than NEC. And I suspect that GTE's shareholders have done better than NEC's, at least in the last five or six years.

But if you think about what I call "wealth creation"—which is to me a much more interesting question—

then I would argue that NEC has put itself into a strategic position with much greater potential than GTE's. NEC, which started off with a much smaller endowment of capabilities and technologies and financial resources than GTE, has been creating a very different kind of wealth over the last ten years. It has achieved global leadership and significant market share in all the major C & C industries. What has GTE done during the same period? Today, they're pretty much back into the telephone operations they started with.

STEWART: Yes, but is that necessarily a bad thing? It seems, judging from GTE's stock price performance in recent years, that the market is applauding that decision to refocus and abandon their earlier diversification attempts.

PRAHALAD: Almost all the debate in the United States centers around stockholders and stockholders' returns. It seems to me an unexamined article of faith, and I'm not at all convinced that it's the only question to ask. I would prefer to put the issue of corporate success in different terms: How well has a company succeeded in creating wealth not only for shareholders, but for its customers and for its employees? Certainly shareholder interests must be served in the process. But, I believe that management's failure to consider customers, employees, and other corporate stakeholders will inevitably lead to the reduction of shareholder wealth over the long term.

In the short term, of course, management can make money simply by buying and selling companies, by functioning as opportunists moving in and out of industries at will. American managers have shown themselves to be very adept at that. But I would like to see the managements of our large companies show greater concern for *long-term* wealth creation.

Over the long term, you cannot short-change your customers and your employees and still create value. You must create a satisfying workplace—one that provides opportunities for people to grow.

So, I'm concerned ultimately about the *continuity* of large corporations—and I believe my view is shared by most societies around the world. For companies that want to survive for 50 or 100 or 200 hundred years, continuity requires a balanced view of wealth creation. If you're concerned solely with shareholders' returns, you'll never make any long-term investments in employees or in customer relations.

So, again, the fundamental issue here is coming up with the proper scorecard for evaluating top management. I'm convinced that, within the next five or ten years, there's going to be a lot of debate in this country on whether we should we continue to worship only at the altar of stockholders. Is there more to running large industrial enterprises than just attending to stockholders? Is it not indeed a position of public trust?

Beyond Shareholder Value?

STEWART: Would anyone on the panel care to respond to C.K.?

WILLIAMS: I think all three groups—employees, customers, and stockholders—are critical to corporate success. But if you want to raise capital for investment in the future, you really have to satisfy the shareholders with a reasonable return. And I frankly have yet to see a business where you can satisfy shareholders without taking care of customers and employees. So I don't see the problem.

STEWART: But that still begs the question: Why should we be concerned first and foremost about shareholders?

WILLIAMS: They're the owners of the business.

STEWART: Well, yes, but I think the explanation is much broader than that. It all goes back to the fact that society's resources are limited. And when I say resources, I'm not talking about just capital or materials or equipment. I am also talking about people, human energy and brainpower—about assets of all kind, intangible as well as tangible. If we can believe Adam Smith, the way to create the greatest social wealth is to encourage every company to maximize the net present value of the enterprise. Maximizing shareholder value is important not because shareholders are especially deserving, but because it is the decision-making rule that leads to the greatest efficiency in allocating resources and, from there, to the greatest economic good for the greatest number. That's why it matters.

PRAHALAD: Okay, let me respond to that by posing an open question. The scorecard for management has always been based on its ability to marshal and allocate resources, and to maximize returns to the scarce resource. Your argument, Bennett, and most American corporate practice, is based on the assumption that capital is the scarce resource. That was true in the past. Indeed, the past success of American business was based on the ability of American managers to marshal and allocate effectively vast amounts of capital.

But, in the future, the truly scarce resource is not going to be capital, but human talent. And if that is the case, then shouldn't we now be using talent accumulation as one of our major criteria for judging corporate success?

WILLIAMS: If the accumulation of talented people were the primary measure of organizational success, then universities would win the competition hands down. But universities can't deliver the goods and services that most of us live on.

PRAHALAD: In fact, our universities may be a much better model for the next round of corporate governance than we think. Now, I know this is a very controversial issue—and I think the first part of this discussion went much too politely and quietly. But, as we enter this new world of global competition, I think we will be forced to re-examine our theory of wealth creation and its assumption of the primacy of shareholder value.

For the game has truly changed from what it was. During the industrial revolution, the accumulation of capital led to productivity increases. And that is why we won the game for the last 50 or 60 years. We were able to accumulate large stores of capital, and then use that capital stock to increase efficiency. In the next round of wealth creation—at least in knowledge-intensive businesses—human talent, or brainpower, may be a more critical resource than access to capital. That is not to say that capital is unimportant, only that it is not a uniquely differentiating factor for productivity improvement.

STEWART: I agree with your last point. But you seem to be assuming that the aim of the corporation is to maximize the *return* on capital. That is not the same thing as maximizing the *net present value* of the enterprise. I agree with you that capital is simply a commodity input to the process. It has a cost, and you have to subtract that cost along with all other expenses. What you try to maximize is what's left over after you've satisfied customers, and fully compensated employees and all the other factors in your business. That is what economists call your economic or *residual* income, that is the measure of the true profitability. What I think you're overlooking, C.K., is that such a measure considers the returns to *all* the resources employed, human as well as material, intangible as well as tangible.

The change you're describing, by the way, was what Alvin Toffler years ago called "the power shift." According to Toffler, there have been three major driving forces in history; he calls them "muscle," "money," and "mind." The Middle Ages were dominated by muscle—by violence and the threat of violence—and serfdom was the governing principle. That gave rise to the Industrial Revolution, where money became important and led to the dominance of large, centrally-directed, bureaucratic organizations. In more recent times, it was the Sears, the GMs—the mass merchandisers, mass marketers, mass manufacturers. And, today, we're going through the information revolution. Brainpower is more important today, and the marshalling of intellectual capabilities, as you said, is the right way to maximize value for companies. There's no question about that.

But, having accepted that premise, companies still have to deal with the fundamental issue of allocating the *proper* amount of resources—not too much, not too little—to any one factor, whether it be human capital or investor capital. The corporation should invest in future capabilities, of course, but only up to the point where the next dollar of investment still yields at least a dollar—adjusted for time and risk—in returns. Focusing on net present value and residual income, on what's left over after all the factors have been fully compensated, is the right way to think about the optimal allocation of resources.

I do agree with you, though, C.K., that the residual should not accrue entirely to the shareholders. A company's managers and employees should be carved into that residual, either through greater equity ownership, or in some other way that also makes them partners with shareholders in creating value.

In the long run, you end up serving your shareholders by serving your customers. In the short run, there are always conflicts between the interests of shareholders and those of customers and employees. Given limited resources, I am forced to make trade-offs among the requirements of these three groups. This, while trying to find balance between the short- and the long-term profit of the business.

—Dennis Eck—

Non-Financial Performance Measures and Communicating with Investors

ECK: Let me bring the discussion down a peg or two from this lofty plane. Things may be somewhat different in the hi-tech area, but in the food retailing business, it seems clear to me that, as one of the top managers of my company, my primary focus must be on my customers, their tastes and requirements.

There are not enough resources or talent—though we have a lot of both—

in our company to give our customers everything they want precisely how and when they want it. In the long run, it's true, you end up best serving your shareholders by serving your customers. In the short run, there are always conflicts between the interests of shareholders and customers. There are also conflicts between the interests of shareholders and employees. Given limited resources, I am forced to make trade-offs among the requirements of my shareholders, customers, and employees. This, while trying to find balance between the short- and the long-term profit of the business.

One of my primary responsibilities is to allocate the resources, the talent and the energy of the organization. However, we must always be pointed toward the consumer. I believe the failure of American business—where it has failed—has resulted from a failure to keep its eye on the consumer.

PRAHALAD: Dennis, it's very interesting that you should say that. For I have yet to see a company that talks about customer satisfaction or presents surveys of consumer opinion in its annual report or analyst presentations.

ECK: Then you should attend one of our analysts presentations.

PRAHALAD: Let me ask another question, then. Why don't customers evaluate the management performance of various business units? We could make customer service an integral part of the evaluation of management.

ECK: But consumers evaluate companies every day. In our business, they do it every day by their purchasing patterns. What they buy, how they buy it, and how they feel about it is a great management scorecard.

WILLIAMS: There is also a downside to using customer satisfaction and other nonfinancial considerations as criteria for evaluating management. I once worked for Federated Department Stores, and the company spent an inordinate amount of money and time trying to measure things that are basically not measurable, such as the churn of people, how many ethnic groups are you employing, and so forth. As head of a division, I was driven crazy trying to figure out just what top management wanted out of me. When they sent me my evaluation forms, the system was so complicated and had so many variables that I simply gave it back to the chairman and told him, "I can't understand this. But if I make any money based on it, just send it to me."

My job as a division manager was to make money. Just let me figure out how to do it, and all the other things will take care of themselves.

And, besides the sheer confusion and inefficiency of it all, there is another real danger to this movement to make customer and employee satisfaction an explicit part of the corporate mission: namely, that uninformed outsiders such as politicians and public interest groups become part of the debate on corporate governance. So my question is, where does this debate take place? Does it take place inside the company as part of running the business? Or does it take place in a larger format with some informed and some uninformed people? And at what cost to management time?

PRAHALAD: I agree that there is a big problem with allowing uninformed people to pass judgments on the quality of a company. But I also think that, in the U.S. system of corporate governance, investors are very underinformed about what is happening inside companies. For that reason, all they can use to evaluate your performance are the numbers you produce at the end of the quarter. And this system gives rise to two different problems. It lets subperforming managements off the hook for a long time in some cases, as in the case of GM. But, in other cases, it keeps some good, far-sighted

managements on too tight a rein, causing underinvestment in capabilities.

For this reason, I think we ought to spend some time asking the question: Are there alternative systems of governance that would enable us to inform our investors in more meaningful ways? In Germany, for example, the large banks that own stock in companies often have representatives that sit on corporate boards. In the Japanese keiretsus, suppliers and distributors have equity stakes and board representation in one another.

It is in the interest of American companies to provide investors with more and better information so they are not forced to make these quarter-to-quarter snap judgments about the quality of management. The result of the current system is enormous volatility, which in turn forces managers to respond in knee-jerk fashion. This is what we have gone through in this country in the last 15 years.

PERRY: Well, C.K., we've only been a public company for one year, and it is all a bit new to us, having been a partnership for over 50 years before that. But what we do each quarter is this: When we announce our earnings, we have a telephone conference with almost a hundred people on the other end. That includes all of our major shareholders and all the principal analysts around the country who follow our firm. During these teleconferences, we'll discuss major issues with them on a fairly informal basis. I was under the impression that most companies did something like this.

THOMPSON: There is a problem with that approach, though. Because of all the laws in this country restricting shareholder communication, and the general litigiousness of our society, we have been forced to filter and restrict our shareholder communications. Everything you say to shareholders becomes part of the public record. And there is a group of law

firms out there that, if you have any change in your fortunes, will immediately slap you with a law suit if they think they can make money out of it. And I have to believe that our legal rules and general litigiousness are seriously restricting the flow of communication between management and shareholders in this country.

PRAHALAD: I agree that we have big legal and regulatory problems with communications between management and investors in the U.S. For one thing, management cannot give information selectively to anybody without going to jail. Nevertheless, even within existing constraints, corporate annual reports and presentations to investors could contain a lot more information on corporate strategies than they do now.

Internal vs. External Economies of Scope

STEWART: C.K., I have what I think is a fundamental disagreement with your analysis on this point. I don't think the market fails to appreciate what management is trying to do. Rather, in many cases, it simply lacks confidence that it will accomplish it. Or, even if management does accomplish the strategic ends they hold up, they are likely to do so in a way that leaves shareholders with an inadequate return on their investment.

A perfect example of this is General Motors. For years, management lamented the level of the company's stock price, proclaiming they were investing for the long term. But, now that the long term has arrived, it turns out that shareholders' concerns were well founded. As another example, when Federal Express announced their intention to introduce Zapmail—a service that was supposed to displace FAX machines—the company's stock price dropped by $8 in a single day. And after Zapmail produced a sea of red ink, the company announced it was abandoning Zapmail, and the stock price shot up.

The academic evidence is pretty convincing in refuting this charge of stock market myopia. As all the studies show, companies that announce increases in R&D and capital expenditures experience significant stock price increases, on average, *upon the announcement*. The single major exception to this was the oil industry during the early '80s, a time of falling oil prices, when announcements of new exploration programs routinely caused sharp declines in stock prices—and rightly so, given the glut of oil that soon followed.

All this leads me, C.K., back to the point you were making about the information revolution. You have suggested that the information revolution is a force driving companies to expand their core competencies across multiple businesses. But I read its import very differently. I think it portends the worldwide breakdown of large organizations, from the overthrow of large, bureaucratic governments to the privatization of enterprises. Industries today are being steam-rolled flat. We are seeing everything from "category killers" like Walmart's taking over retailing, to the niche success of CNN against the major networks, to the flattening of the computer industry through specialization. In general, the restructuring of the 1980s not only streamlined corporate America, but moved it toward greater focus—a movement that, I would argue, has made our companies far more globally competitive than they were ten years ago.

So, it seems to me that what has made the American system work, and the way in which American companies function best, is by putting their bets on decentralization and specialization. In other words, we're not very good at realizing economies of scope

within companies, but we are unmatched at realizing economies of scope *across our economy*. And that's where I have a fundamental problem with your strategic concepts—they all seem to hinge on the ability of companies to realize, *internally*, vast economies of scope. I just think our economy works best when those economies are realized externally.

TOM THEOBALD: I must say, Bennett, that's the first thing I've ever heard you say that I agree with.

STEWART: Well, thanks, Tom. But this may force me to rethink my position.

PRAHALAD: Bennett, I have never said that companies should do everything internally. That's not the point. In the electronics industry today, competition is in fact taking place not among individual companies, but among clusters of companies. The most successful competitors have not integrated vertically, but have developed groups of highly specialized suppliers. And these suppliers operate independently in some aspects, often supplying the competitors of their primary customer.

For example, take the case of charged coupler devices, or CCDs. Sony is one of the leaders in developing CCD technology and in manufacturing and selling CCD products. But they supply everybody, even companies that compete with their own distributors. In the case of spindle motors, 86% of them come from one highly specialized company called Nideq.

So, small companies and specialization play a major role in my view of global competition. Companies need not do everything internally, as AT&T and IBM did for a long time. What they should strive for, however, is to build and dominate a critical number of competencies that allow them, in effect, to exchange hostages with their competitors. There will cer-

tainly be lots of corporate inter-relationships in terms of the supplying of components and sub-components across competitors. But, in order to prosper, you must have something to trade that your trading partner cannot get somewhere else. If you have nothing to trade, you're in a very vulnerable situation.

STEWART: You mentioned that Canon supplies 85% of the laser printer engines for Hewlett-Packard. What does HP offer Canon in return?

PRAHALAD: That's a very interesting question. Hewlett-Packard saw their emerging vulnerability to Canon, and they were smart enough to respond by investing an enormous amount of money in laser printers. They knew they were not going to be able to compete very effectively in laser printing without the help of Canon. But instead of subcontracting the complete customer interface to Canon, they bought the engine instead. They then designed their laser printers around the Canon engine, and this enabled them to retain the direct contact with the customer.

Core Competence and the Threat of Market Power

STEWART: When you say Canon has 85% of the laser printer market, it sounds sinister. It makes Americans say, "Oh, my gosh, they're dominating markets and hollowing out our companies." But isn't the economic reality of this simply that we have a very natural and healthy process of specialization going on? HP has specialized, Canon has specialized, and now they're mutually dependent on each other. What's the matter with that? Why should we view this as a threat to American industry, as so many *Harvard Business Review* articles have done?

PRAHALAD: There is no problem with that, provided American companies have also developed some kind of specialized capabilities. The problem facing many companies, however, is that they have not made the kind of investment necessary to achieve that specialization. Therefore, they cannot enter into a partnership on an equal basis; they have nothing to trade.

For example, take the case of liquid crystal display technologies, or LCDs. In the case of active matrix LCDs, companies such as Compaq, IBM, or Apple have no other recourse but to go to Sharp and Toshiba for LCDs. Nobody makes them here. And that is where I see a problem. In other words, we can get into a very non-competitive situation—one in which the sole suppliers of the product we manufacture or sell are also our competitors. And if we have not created enough of a specialization to trade with, we are then vulnerable.

STEWART: I don't see the problem, I really don't. Take Dell, for example. They go out and buy displays and combine them with Intel chips. Should they be concerned about their dependence upon Intel for their PC chips?

PRAHALAD: I would be extremely concerned with Intel's domination, and for the same reasons everybody is so concerned about Microsoft now. Intel does not yet compete in the PC market effectively, but they could very easily.

CLOUGH: In fact, they have a division that makes PCs.

PRAHALAD: That's right, but they don't call it PCs. They don't have the plastic around the platform. They just give it to you and say, "This is ours."

THOMPSON: Intel is also trying to get into the massively parallel processing business in the commercial marketplace. So they're also positioning themselves to try to get into our business.

PRAHALAD: I would be extremely worried about Intel if I was in this industry.

CLOUGH: Oh, absolutely. They could turn off the faucet for two days and there would be no Dell.

STEWART: But then there would be no Intel, either. Because then who else would buy from them? They would completely destroy their credibility as a supplier. You don't see the mutual dependency in all this? After all, we're not dealing with a Middle East cartel here.

PRAHALAD: The temptation to use market power once you achieve it has nothing to do with the Middle East. It's a human reaction: The Japanese do it and so will we. And that's why everybody is so concerned about Microsoft and Intel. Suppose Intel becomes big at parallel processing, and they also supply Ed at Amdahl. They don't have to say no to Ed, they can just delay shipment for six months. There are all kinds of ways to enforce a cartel. In the electronics business, if you are late by eight months, the game is over.

THOMPSON: That's right, time to market is vital.

CLOUGH: Why did Compaq cancel their agreements with AMD and go back to Intel, when they could have bought that AMD product, the 386, for a lot less? The reason was, they knew they'd no longer be a beta site for the development of next-generation processors, the 486, the 586.

STEWART: Well, let me return to my earlier question. Can the extent of Intel's domination today really be explained as the result of their ability to "leverage" its core competencies across multiple businesses? Their success—to date at least—seems to me a consequence of their choosing to focus only on microprocessors, and not allowing that focus to be diluted by pursuing other opportunities.

PRAHALAD: Bennett, I think you are misunderstanding the core competence framework. It does not say you have to be part of a very large company like NEC. I can give you 25 other

companies that specialize the way Intel has, but without becoming as visibly dominant as Intel in their particular fields. In the case of LCDs, there are two or three companies that dominate that business. But we don't talk much about LCDs in this country. Every time there is a discussion here about whether we as a nation should invest in LCDs, companies talk about how critical it is, but nobody wants to make the investment.

Let me give you another example. For every hand-held device made in the world today, the critical limiting factors are battery life, size, and weight. Can you name one American company that makes miniature batteries that power your laptops and hand-held devices? It is all dominated by one group of companies that also sell the end products as well. All that I'm saying is that the temptation to play hardball in those circumstances is very great.

STEWART: Well, the Japanese companies must be earning fantastic monopoly returns from these products. But that's not what the newspapers are telling us these days. And, if they're not earning monopoly returns, what's the point of being a monopolist?

The same thing was being said about DRAMs just a few years ago. Alarmists like Charles Ferguson were saying, "We don't have an American company other than IBM that can produce DRAMs in quantity, and that's ominous." Yet, today, DRAMs are a commodity in the marketplace and, as I said earlier, the Japanese companies have ended up with enormous overinvestment.

So, my question is, Why aren't the miniature batteries going to become a commodity, too? Japanese companies compete very intensively with one another. How many competitors does it take to drive down the price of batteries until they become widely available? Again, I think we're raising all kinds of sinister flags with this focus on market share. Now, maybe the problem can exist in the product design stage, but I remain skeptical.

PRAHALAD: I'm not trying to create a sinister image. My message is basically just this: Global competition is evolving in a way that threatens U.S. companies because of their failure to invest in continually upgrading their capabilities. We can't keep assuming that companies in other countries will do all the hard work of investment while we continue to make all the money. Companies can show very good returns for a while simply by stopping investment, but that can last only so long. The day of reckoning will come.

STEWART: Well, I for one remain fairly optimistic about current trends in corporate America, and thus about our prospects. And since neither of us is likely to convince the other to change his views in the next five minutes, let's bring this to a close. I want to thank everybody who participated in this discussion. And thank you, C.K., for agreeing to be part of this. We'll see if the debate over shareholder value that you foresee actually comes to pass.

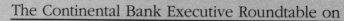

The Continental Bank Executive Roundtable on

CORPORATE STRATEGY IN THE '90s

March 26, 1993 ■ *Boca Raton*

BENNETT STEWART: This morning we were privileged to hear Professor Alfred Chandler, the pre-eminent business historian in our time, discuss the evolution and restructuring of American industry over the past three or four decades. Both in his talk this morning, and in his widely acclaimed books and articles, Dr. Chandler lays major emphasis on the role of large-scale investment in driving the success of large, multinational corporations. As the greater part of his research goes to testify, those companies that had the vision and the resources to make the "three-pronged" investments in manufacturing, marketing, and management capabilities ended up achieving economies of scale and scope that enabled them to dominate their industries for decades.

Hence the title of Dr. Chandler's most recent book, *Scale and Scope.* Published in 1991, this book presents the findings of his study of the growth

patterns of the 200 largest manufacturing companies in the U.S., Germany, and the U.K. from the 1880s, when such firms first appeared, to the beginning of World War II. "The enduring logic of industrial success," he wrote in a *Harvard Business Review* article that came out shortly after the book, is the pursuit of growth "through economies of scale and the development of markets that best fit their distinctive core production and research technologies." From this vantage point, he is able to explain not only the pre-War success of most large multinationals, but also the subsequent failure of many of these same companies in the late '60s and '70s when attempting to expand away from their core capabilities.

The purpose of this Roundtable will be to use Dr. Chandler's insights as a point of departure for thinking about global competitiveness in the 1990s. More specifically, we will at-

tempt to apply these principles of competitive advantage to the particular challenges faced by the companies represented at this table. Dr. Chandler has long insisted that the development of professional management has been a major contributor to U.S. industrial success. In fact, as he wrote in a recent article, "Of all the enterprise's resources, the product-specific and firm-specific *managerial* skills are the *most* essential to maintain the capabilities of its existing businesses and to take the enterprise into new geographical and product markets where such capabilities give it a comparative advantage." I am confident that the group of senior executives assembled here this morning will serve to reinforce Dr. Chandler's conviction on this point.

So, let me now introduce our panelists—in alphabetical order.

ALFRED CHANDLER is the Straus Professor of Business History, Emeri-

tus, at the Harvard Business School. Besides *Scale and Scope*, his two best-known books—and it would not leave much time for this discussion if we were to list *all* of them—are *Strategy and Structure* (MIT Press, 1962) and *The Visible Hand: The Managerial Revolution in American Business* (Harvard University Press, 1977). I was fortunate enough to read *Strategy and Structure* back in the mid-'70s, when I was going through the Chase Manhattan Bank's credit training program, and it continues to be a major influence on my own view of corporate strategy.

DELMONT DAVIS is President and Chief Executive Officer of Ball Corporation. With headquarters in Muncie, Indiana, and roughly $2.6 billion in sales, Ball produces metal beverage containers for brewers and soft drink companies, metal cans for food processors, and glass containers for the food, juice, wine, and liquor markets. Ball also provides aerospace and communications systems and services to government and commercial customers.

DENNIS GORMLEY is Chairman and Chief Executive Officer of Federal-Mogul Corporation. A public company based just outside of Detroit with approximately $1.6 billion in sales, Federal-Mogul is a global distributor and manufacturer of a broad range of precision parts, primarily for automobiles, trucks, and farm and construction vehicles.

DAVID GRUBER is President and Chief Operating Officer of the Wyman-Gordon Company. Based in Worcester, Massachusetts, Wyman-Gordon designs and produces technically advanced forgings and investment castings for heavy-duty internal combustion engines and jet engines, structural aircraft parts, and missiles. It is a public company with approximately $300 million in sales.

RICHARD HUBER is Vice Chairman of Continental Bank, and oversees the global equity, capital markets, and Latin America divisions of the Bank. Prior to joining Continental in 1990, Dick served as executive vice president of Chase Manhattan's capital markets and foreign exchange sector. He also served in various management capacities at Citicorp, including the supervision of Citicorp's Latin American investment bank.

NORM POOLE is Executive Vice President, Chief Operating Officer, and a Director of L.L. Bean of Freeport, Maine. The company, as most of you know, is a leading mail-order outfitter of apparel, footwear, and equipment for outdoor activities. The company today has roughly $800 million in sales.

RICHARD RADT is President and Chief Executive Officer of the Mosinee Paper Corporation. Based in Mosinee, Wisconsin, the company manufac-

tures specialty papers, recycled commercial towel and tissue, and wax-laminated paper. The company has approximately $250 million in sales, and is publicly traded on NASDAQ.

Size and Efficiency

STEWART: I'd like to start off with one question that has been troubling me. Much of Dr. Chandler's writings contain the suggestion that, because of the potential for economies of scale and scope, bigger is inevitably better. "To compete globally," as the bold print in one of your articles says, "you have to be big." But haven't we also been learning that there are major problems associated with excessive corporate growth? My understanding is that much of the corporate restructuring of the '80s was designed to "downsize" companies that had become too large and diverse.

Thus, I wonder if this prescription is still as valid in thinking about competitiveness in the 1990s as it was, say, in the first half of the 20th century. The present predicament of companies like IBM and General Motors might lead us to reexamine this proposition. All your work seems to focus on market share as the primary indication of success. But does market share matter the way it did, say, 50 or even just 15 years ago? Is market share a guarantee of shareholder value added? Or, are we moving toward a somewhat new recognition of the inefficiencies that tend to breed in large organizations?

So, Dr. Chandler, *is* bigger necessarily better?

CHANDLER: Your kind introduction notwithstanding, I think I have been misconstrued. My writings have never suggested that size *per se* is the key to industrial success. In fact, I have stated emphatically that one kind of growth widely pursued by U.S. companies in the late '60s and '70s—that is, diversification away from a company's core capabilities—has been both a disaster and an historical aberration. For the first time in American history, many large U.S. companies decided in the 1960s to grow by *acquiring* businesses in which they had few if any organizational capabilities rather than building businesses from within. In so doing, they compounded the negative consequences of a trend that was already underway since World War II—the increasing separation of top management from the steadily growing number of different operating businesses. Under these circumstances, Bennett, bigger has clearly been for the worse, not the better.

What I do argue, however, is that in the modern world most large corporations are involved in a competition that is becoming ever more *global* in nature. They are competing against overseas companies both at home and abroad. And there is no way to compete globally—particularly in industries where you have a fast-moving technology with a need for large and continuous investment in new product development—without having a lot of people and resources. Though many companies have downsized and some have eliminated layers of corporate planners and middle managers, you still need several levels of management to coordinate and oversee all the different activities.

STEWART: But, Dr. Chandler, doesn't your argument hinge on the ability of companies to continue realizing tremendous economies of scale and scope?

CHANDLER: That's right, they're absolutely key. Economies of scale, for example, explain why we have only a few automakers even to this day. Ninety percent of the automobiles being made today are manufactured by companies that existed before World War II, and most of them well before that. Except for Honda, which was established in 1948, the producers that now account for 90% of the Japanese market were all in production in the 1930s. And the same is true of leading European car manufacturers, with the exception of Volkswagen, the Hitler-sponsored "people's car." So that's evidence of the importance of scale. You're not going to have small entrepreneurial auto companies.

Now, that is not to say that there aren't opportunities for smaller companies in aspects of the auto industry. There are a whole lot of small to medium-sized firms operating in niches of the industry where economies of scale are not critical. In fact, such niches can become pretty big, especially if you're going to be serving them globally.

But, to return to my earlier point, you can't possibly be a global competitor in a major industry without large-scale investment in production, distribution, and other organizational capabilities. It's also important to keep in mind that such capabilities are typically acquired from long experience—from the experience of commercializing new products, scaling up production processes, acquiring knowledge of customers' needs, de-

veloping reliable suppliers, and recruiting and training managers and workers. It is the organizational capabilities that come out of all this experience, generally developed over decades, that make an organization worth much more than the sum of its parts.

This is also the reason that, at least in recent years, long-established companies have played a greater role in the development of new industries than entrepreneurial start-ups. The time and cost of commercializing technologically complex new products and processes is *not* in research, but rather in development—that is, in the long and capital-intensive process of producing goods in large enough quantity and high enough quality to be sold in national and global markets. The commercializing of new products is a continuous learning experience—one that depends on the cumulative organizational experience of developing, producing, and marketing earlier products.

So, although size certainly has some problems associated with it, it is also a source of tremendous benefits.

Differentiating a Commodity: The Case of Mosinee

STEWART: Let me turn to Dick Radt, CEO of Mosinee Paper. Dick, your company is mainly in the commercial towel and toilet paper business. In this sense, your company is like a very small Scott Paper Company; your sales are about $250 million as compared to Scott's $6 billion. How can you possibly compete against a global giant of their size and resources?

RADT: Our basic aim is to differentiate a commodity—and toilet paper

and toweling is about as close as you can get in manufacturing to a pure commodity. It's interesting you mentioned Scott. When I went to the washroom during the break, I found Scott towels—and that's just as I would expect in a big resort like this. We can't really compete for the business of these kinds of places. Scott probably has two or three salesman in Florida alone, and their job is to get Scott products into big places like this hotel. The way they do that is to sell to large paper distributors who then deliver the product to the hotel.

We operate differently. We won't have nearly as many sales representatives. Instead of selling to the paper distributors, we will work out an arrangement with, for example, janitorial supply companies. Janitorial supply companies hire the men and women who come in and clean up after you've gone home from your office. Who better to hang a roll of toilet paper than the people who have swept and vacuumed and cleaned off your desk?

So, we've chosen a special niche of distribution to try and differentiate ourselves from the Scott Paper Company. In fact, we have been living in the shadow of giants for many years. I think our company is the smallest one represented up here, and I must say it has been fun. I've made a career out of competing against large companies, and I have really enjoyed it. You have to live by your wits.

STEWART: But how do you overcome the scale economies problem? This is a classic process industry with lots of stuff coming in and lots of stuff going out. And process industries— be they chemicals, oil, autos, or paper

products—tend to gravitate towards large, centrally directed, bureaucratic enterprises.

RADT: As I said, if you're going to be in a commodity business, you have to find a means of differentiating yourself. We have made ourselves into one of the lowest-cost producers in the industry. In fact, we may now be *the* lowest-cost producer. To that end, we have just finished the biggest capital spending program in our history. We have just completed a brand new facility in Ohio that is the world's fastest toilet-paper manufacturing operation. And though it will undoubtedly be surpassed by some other operation in the next few years, for the time being we are the low-cost producer.

We've also relocated our converting plant from Wisconsin, the site of our headquarters, to Kentucky. The converting plant takes the big rolls of paper and makes them into the little ones you see hung in the washrooms all over America. We moved there to save money on distribution. Because Kentucky is closer geographically to our markets—that is, more central to the U.S. population—we will save about $4 million a year in freight.

We have also invested heavily in a de-inking capability that enables us to recycle used paper. We now produce about 200 tons a day of de-inked fiber, all of which goes into toilet paper and toweling. So we keep the low-cost position by continually finding innovative ways to accomplish traditional functions.

STEWART: Does your company make a profit?

RADT: We're just getting there now. We've just gotten through a period of big spending and ironing out start-up problems, but we expect to do nicely this year.

STEWART: In a normal year, what kind of return on capital do you expect to earn?

RADT: Our target is 20 percent.

STEWART: *After* taxes?

RADT: Yes.

STEWART: Okay, I understand that's your *targeted* rate of return. But what do you really expect to earn, Dick? You can level with us.

RADT: I'm quite serious, Bennett. I think we can achieve 20%, maybe even 25%, at least for a few years. I'm not sure we can do that year after year. But if you can develop a successful strategy, as we think we have, and then replicate your strategy in other locations—perhaps even overseas as well as throughout the U.S.—I feel you can earn high rates of return for quite some time before competition catches up. But you've got to keep finding ways to innovate to stay ahead of the large competitors.

The Case of the Ball Corporation

STEWART: Del, your company is big and getting bigger in the packaging business. Are scale and globalization important objectives for you?

DAVIS: Scale is clearly important to us. But I also think that many of Dick's points about the need to differentiate your business apply in our case.

We are primarily in the packaging business, which is a commodity business. And, as Dick said, to compete in a commodity business, you have to find some way to develop an advantage over your larger competitors. We are about number three in market share in the U.S., but the two companies above us are about twice our size. So, we are a lot smaller than our major competitors.

STEWART: Do you think you suffer because of that?

DAVIS: Well, I don't think we're suffering very much. And we're doing some of the same things Dick just mentioned. We start by making quality and service the hallmark of the company. But, in addition to quality, you also have to be among the low-cost producers to succeed in a commodity business. To be a low-cost producer, you have to spend a fair amount of money on research and development, particularly development. You have to increase productivity and decrease cost continuously to be competitive.

STEWART: Del, there has been a lot of merger activity in your industry. You just acquired Heekin Can; Crown Cork & Seal recently acquired Van Dorn. There seems to be a lot of consolidation going on in your industry. Why is that?

DAVIS: Well, there is a lot of consolidation going on in a lot of industries. I'm not sure I understand why, but I think it's happening mainly for competitive reasons.

I do know a good deal about the case of Heekin Can. They were a regional player in the food canning business, and because they had gotten themselves pretty highly leveraged, they were having trouble expanding the way they wanted. They knew that, by joining with our canning operations, we could achieve enough synergies that we could really make them a more profitable operation.

The acquisition was opportune for us, too, because we were at a crossroads in this particular business. Our first move into the food can business was in 1988, when we acquired American Can's Canadian operations. We had come to a position where we felt we either had to get bigger—to take advantage of scale economies—or get out. Our Canadian operations were too small to support shipping into the U.S.

So Heekin Can's circumstances happened to provide a good fit with our own strategic direction—which is to extend our current focus in metal and glass containers. It will be a mutually beneficial joining of companies. They will probably be a healthier organization, and I think they'll help us a great deal.

Explaining WalMart's Success: Decentralization or Coordination?

STEWART: Both of the businesses we've just been discussing are the kind strategists refer to as "mature" businesses—the kinds of businesses where it's reportedly very tough to make a buck. Nevertheless both Dick's and Del's companies appear to have found ways to be profitable under these circumstances. I would like to suggest that their ability to prosper under these conditions is not that surprising or unusual.

In a recent book called *Rejuvenating the Mature Business*, the authors argue that there is no such thing as a mature business, but only prematurely aged companies or unimaginative management teams. The book cites company after company in tough businesses that has managed to rise above the crowd of its competition. It even goes so far as to claim that profitable companies are almost randomly distributed across different industries.

Perhaps the best example of this is WalMart, which is in retailing, essentially a no-growth business. According to the latest version of our annual Stern Stewart Performance 1000 rankings, WalMart is the most value-adding company on the face of the earth. The last time we looked the market value of the company had reached $60 billion over and above the book value of the business; that is, by our measurement, management

has succeeded in adding about $60 billion in value to shareholders' initial investment. Here is a company operating in a zero-growth business out of Fentonville, Arkansas that has managed to increase sales from $1.6 billion in 1980 to $60 billion in 1992. Their rates of return on capital are 20% to 25% after taxes—*in retailing!*

Norm, as Chief Operating Officer of L.L. Bean, you know a good deal about the retail business. Can you tell us what makes WalMart so successful?

NORM POOLE: WalMart has proven itself to be a wonderful company— and it's one that has followed a very interesting line of development. They started in very small rural communities. And now they are moving much more into urban communities, where they're going to compete—and, I think, very successfully—against the K-Marts of the world. They do face a big challenge, though, in bridging the gap left by Sam Walton. For this reason, I think it will take us some time to see how successful that company will be over the long pull.

STEWART: But what really makes WalMart so successful? What is it that they're doing, *at the operational level*, to make that happen?

POOLE: Well, they certainly have the commitment of their people. If you go into a WalMart, their people actually greet you. If you have questions, they direct you to the right place. They've also empowered their people, at the departmental level, to determine what the customer wants and how much to order of any particular item. That's almost unheard of in retailing. They don't allow a rigid management hierarchy to interfere with their ability to respond at the store level.

They are also, obviously, a fairly low-price outfit. But, if you compare WalMart's prices to others', it's not clear they are competing primarily on price. It's just a very, very well-run company right at the store level.

STEWART: So, the story seems to be one of decentralization, empowerment, and strengthened incentives—carried right down to the level of the individual stores, and to smaller departments within the stores themselves.

DENNIS GORMLEY: Well, there's more to Walmart's success than just decentralization. WalMart, in my opinion, is a logistics company as well as a set of retail operations, and the centralized planning underlying that logistics systems is playing a major role in the company's success.

STEWART: Dennis, would this view have anything to do with the fact that you're the CEO of a manufacturing and distribution company rather than a retail operation? And could you describe briefly the operations of the Federal-Mogul Corporation?

GORMLEY: The answer to your first question is yes, of course. Our business is to make and distribute precision products to auto makers and manufacturers of farm and construction equipment. We have very complex product lines that are highly tailored for specific applications. And we have lots of different products: we currently have 75,000 part numbers. In addition to our sales to OEMs, we also distribute most of our products to the replacement market. One of the critical elements of success in this aftermarket or replacement business is just getting the right part to the right place at the right time.

That, of course, is a logistics problem. And, as I was saying, it's the kind of thing that WalMart does better than anybody else in the retail business.

STEWART: How is that? Their trucks go faster?

GORMLEY: No, it's the entire process, starting with their close relations with their suppliers, getting the product, cross-docking it, getting it out to the marketplace very quickly, and having good information systems to know what is moving. Because they handle this entire process more efficiently than anybody else, they can be more responsive to their customers.

STEWART: So brain power replaces muscle power?

GORMLEY: I have trouble with that formulation. I think bigness is good, all other things equal. If I'm going to recruit a basketball player, I'd much rather have a seven footer than a five foot ten player, given the same athletic ability. And size has its advantages in businesses, too. At the very least, it's an indication of past success—it says that the company was successful under at least one set of conditions.

The problem with size, however, is that conditions can change very suddenly. Take companies like Sears and IBM. They were both once very, very successful companies. We are all prisoners of our past success. We build organizations in which all the paradigms and practices that made us successful in the past become entrenched, and so become obstacles to necessary change. And it is *extremely* tough to change an organization. The bigger it is, the tougher it is to change.

In this sense, sheer size tends to create opportunities for smaller com-

Outsourcing may work in some cases, but it's at best a partial solution to the problem of increasing corporate productivity. There is still a critically important role for central planning, for coordinating all these decentralized activities. At the same time, though, I agree that companies ought to continually keep in mind and focus on their core capabilities. And that's tough to do when you are inside the organization; it takes some real soul-searching.

—Dennis Gormley

panies. To the extent large companies try to be all things to all people, they open profitable niches in which smaller companies can specialize and succeed. But, on the other hand, if you give me a company with good products, a sound strategy, and a well-motivated and responsive management team, then I'll take bigness every time. Economies of scale and scope, as Dr. Chandler says, are major competitive advantages that come with size.

STEWART: So what you are saying is that, to the extent companies can be big *and* yet still manage to retain the focus, the willingness to change, and the incentives we tend to associate with smaller companies, then we have the best of both worlds. You get a company like GE, in short. But the scarcity of companies like GE seems to suggest that there is a difficulty in making both of those happen at once.

GORMLEY: I would agree with that.

CHANDLER: I would just point out that technological change played an important role in both the rise of WalMart and the decline of IBM. In both cases, the crucial change was the development of the computer chip. It was the chip that enabled WalMart to go directly from the retailer to the manufacturer, which is an extraordinary development. As I said in my book *Visible Hand*, manufacturers have historically gone into the wholesaling business, but almost never into retail. Retailers sometimes went into wholesaling, but not into manufacturing. But WalMart's system effectively linked the retailer directly with the manufacturer, thereby eliminating most of the wholesaling function altogether.

At the same time the chip was contributing to the rise of WalMart, it was eroding the value of IBM's mainframe franchise. Advances in chip technology over the past decade or so have caused the cost of computing power to fall by a factor of roughly 200. And with this remarkable drop in computing cost, both the prices and sales growth rates of mainframes have fallen very sharply, leading to huge overcapacity in the industry.

These two cases, those of WalMart and IBM, illustrate both aspects of this process of technological change that Schumpeter called "creative destruction." And this may be the most important difference between global competition today and the period of the late 19th and early 20th century that I have studied most intensively— namely, the incredible pace of technological change. Today things just change so much more quickly than ever before. And this is why the distancing of top management from operations and from an increasingly diverse array of products has had such profoundly negative consequences for so many companies. It's humanly impossible for top management to understand and stay abreast of the problems and opportunities facing all these different operations, especially in technologically complicated businesses. The sheer decision-making overload has made it very difficult for highly diversified companies to respond in an environment of continuous change.

The Case of Wyman-Gordon

STEWART: Some people have noted that changes in organizational theory

tend to reflect changes in our scientific methods and instruments. For example, when the mainframe computer became the dominant tool for scientific analysis in the 1960s, organizational theorists began to proclaim that centralized decision-making was the model of the future. The reigning model then became that of a small group of well-motivated top executives building and presiding over a diverse collection of unrelated companies. Top corporate executives effectively became managers of "portfolios" of different kinds of assets.

But, as the world has moved away from the mainframe and toward the distributed computer processing represented by the PC, organizational theorists have begun to emphasize the virtues of decentralization. The new model is one of fairly loose controls at the top, with decision-making authority pushed down in the company to the people with the most direct contact with the marketplace. At the extreme, we have the neural network form of organization, the *virtual* corporation in which various subcontractors band together to perform specific tasks and then separate when the task is done.

Now, of course, you still need some centralized oversight in even the most decentralized organization. But where do you draw the line? How you retain centralized oversight and controls while pushing decision-making and incentives down in the organization? Dave, as President and COO of Wyman-Gordon, how do you deal with these issues?

GRUBER: Well, we have a somewhat different set of circumstances at Wyman-Gordon. Our business, which

It was not too long ago when information in our company was deliberately safeguarded. Most people below the top ranks of management didn't understand how all the different functions within the company were linked together. But our new teams cut across all these functions, thus eliminating these artificial barriers to information-sharing. Today, we're working very hard to make sure that people have all the information they need to set their own priorities based on the evidence that they see in their customer set.

—David Gruber

is manufacturing precision parts for jet engines for the airline and defense industries, is not just mature—it's shrinking rapidly. Since the year and a half I've been with the company, the market has contracted by roughly a third.

And we have been forced to change along with the industry. As the industry has been shrinking, we have focused on two basic aims: one, reducing our costs and, two, building stronger relationships in the markets that we serve in order to increase our market share. Even as recently as a year and a half ago, Wyman-Gordon was a traditionally structured, very hierarchical company. But since that time, we've transformed ourselves into a customer-oriented, team-based organization. About 80% of our sales come from four or five customers: Boeing, Mack Air, Pratt & Whitney, General Electric Engines. We have responded to the new environment by assembling teams of people in our business that focus just on those customers. So we took people from all these once separate functions—the engineering department, quality department, and even the financial department—and split them all up into cross-functional teams that, as I said, work with directly with the customers. These teams, moreover, have complete decision-making and P & L authority.

And I really think this approach has helped us. It has helped the organization adapt to the new environment. And, if you asked me to generalize from our experience, I would say that adaptability is the critical feature in dealing with the kind of constantly changing industrial environment that

most companies now face. Adaptability to customer requirements—whether it's retailing or industrial—is really the key to success today.

STEWART: Can you tell me more about the benefits of forming these teams? What does that give people that they didn't have before? And how do you make that transition from an organization that was hierarchical, with people always looking over their shoulder for approval, to one where people down in the field really take the initiative and run with it?

GRUBER: Well, to give you a simple example, it became clear to us that we could strengthen our relationships with our customers by having a manufacturing person at Wyman-Gordon talking regularly to a manufacturing person at GE; this way, problems that arise over deliveries or inventories or production schedule shifts can be dealt with much more directly and efficiently. Similarly, on engineering design or whatever other functions, having these people in teams that relate directly and continuously to the customer makes the process far more efficient and makes us far more responsive.

STEWART: I take it your engineers are working with some fairly high-powered work stations. So they're able to design them *with* the customer and then go right into production?

GRUBER: That's right. Now, as you suggest, it does take a while to make this kind of a transition. It takes time for people accustomed to seeking approval to come to terms with their new decision-making power and make the best use of it. It also takes time to coordinate the activities of everybody on the team. To make the best deci-

sions, everyone needs more information than they have had in the past. But, as Professor Chandler was saying about the chip, technological change has revolutionized information flows. It is just so much easier to get information spread throughout an organization than it was, say, five or ten years ago.

And this represents a sharp break with our past. It was not too long ago when information in our company was deliberately safeguarded. Most people below the top ranks of management didn't understand how all the dots were connected, how all the different functions within the company were linked together. But our new teams cut across all these functions, thus eliminating these artificial barriers to information-sharing. Today, we're working very hard to make sure that people have all the information they need to set their own priorities based on the evidence that they see in their customer set. And, together combined with better information, they now have the power to act on that information.

STEWART: Norm, you're nodding your head in agreement. Is team building and empowerment something that's happening at L.L. Bean, too?

POOLE: Yes, and I think it's something that all companies are moving toward today. The whole-team approach is the *only* way to go. As Dave was just suggesting, the functionalization of a company doesn't necessarily work any more—and this has really given American management a tough time. Things are increasingly being organized around process these days. But it's something we're still in our infancy with, quite frankly.

Take, for example, the case of order fulfillment within a retail operation. In the past, that was accomplished by a separate operations department working independently of sales or marketing. But it has become clear that these functions need to be combined to achieve efficiency.

The issue we still have to resolve for ourselves, however, is where to draw the line around responsibilities and this new freedom. I agree that it's important to delegate responsibility and empower people throughout the organization, but you also have to communicate clearly what the boundaries are around their jobs. Although those boundaries are broader than they've been in the past, they still have to understand that there are limits to the kinds of decisions they can make. Without well-defined limits you invite chaos.

Outsourcing and Core Competence: The Case of Continental Bank

STEWART: We're seeing something like the "revenge of the nerds" at work here. It seems to me that large compartmentalized companies lost track of what was going on in their businesses when the accountants took hold, and people started managing by the numbers. All of a sudden, we realized that businesses are a collection of business systems and processes, and that we have to re-engineer those core processes from the bottom up to make them work better.

Let me turn now to Dick Huber of Continental Bank. Is there anything that you've done to re-engineer some of your core processes and systems at Continental?

HUBER: I would venture to say that few companies our size have been *so* re-engineered as the Continental Bank within the past few years. We were a bank of some 13,500 people at our

peak, with total assets of about $45 billion. Today we're very rapidly approaching 4,000 people with assets of about $22.5 billion. So we're today running about half the assets, with less than a third of the staff, we had five years ago.

Bennett, you began by mentioning this issue of size. But it's important to make clear what you are measuring. We don't evaluate our success according to assets or staff size. What we care about are our revenues and, ultimately, our profits and return to the shareholder.

One of the steps we have taken to improve our shareholder returns—and this is something that should be of general interest to this group—is to consider outsourcing. We've been right out on the cutting edge in the whole process of creating what the business schools are calling the *virtual* or *modular* corporation. Now what does this mean? In our case, it has meant going back and defining what our real core competency is—or, alternatively, what our core competency *isn't*.

We discovered that we were reasonably good at being bankers—that is, at serving the needs of our business customers. But we also found that we weren't particularly good at running cafeterias, that we were pretty lousy at running a fleet of vans, and that we probably spent more money managing our building per square foot than almost anyone else in Chicago. We also found that our data center was just so-so.

So what we have done is this: In each function where we felt we had no comparative advantage, we tried to find the best outside provider and then outsource that function from it—often transferring some of our own people to the outside firm. In the case of our data center, for example, we found an outside provider to perform that job whose *only* business function

is to manage data centers. We did the same thing with our telecommunications networks. Even our law department was outsourced.

STEWART: Okay, Dick, so you put the people outside and then you pay for them. What are the real benefits of doing that?

HUBER: Well, we achieved some immediate cost savings. But, more important, we also dramatically improved the quality of some of the services. For example, the people at ISSC, the company to which we outsourced our information technology, have done a *magnificent* job, much better than we did ourselves internally. And they have done it with many of our own former employees; they ended up hiring a lot of our staff.

But that's not surprising to me since it's their *only* business. Because their sole business is managing information technology, we saw a dramatic improvement in the service we get from them—faster implementation of new systems, faster turnaround. As a result, the service we're able to give our own customers is a lot better.

STEWART: So, you're getting more responsiveness from outsiders than you got from insiders?

HUBER: Right.

STEWART: Doesn't that mean you didn't have the proper incentives for the insiders?

HUBER: Probably. But I am not sure you can duplicate those incentives internally. Perhaps the most important change for these people is that we're now important customers for these suppliers. And they treat us like customers.

Also important, our own bankers use these services a lot more intelligently because now it's a hard dollar they pay. This is real money; they actually cut a check. It's not something that gets lost in allocations by the accounting department. So they're much more demanding purchasers of

We've been right out on the cutting edge in the whole process of creating what the business schools are calling the virtual or modular corporation. In our case, this has meant going back and defining what our real core competency is—or, alternatively, what our core competency isn't In each function where we felt we had no comparative advantage, we tried to find the best outside provider and then outsource that function from it—often transferring some of our own people to the outside firm.

—Richard Huber

legal services, information technology services, even buildings and grounds.

STEWART: So would you recommend that every company take a look at those functions that are not really critical to the business, and find a way to outsource them?

HUBER: I wouldn't necessarily go as far as that. But I would certainly look at them, perhaps even put it up for bids to compete with your internal department. It has certainly worked for us at Continental. In virtually every one of the areas we examined we found significant potential for efficiencies, even in those cases in which we ended up keeping things in-house.

You see, we all tend to relegate these support functions to sort of a secondary plane. When we're focusing on marketing our products and dealing with our customers, we tend to forget these *huge* support functions that are embedded in each of our companies. And it doesn't matter what business you're in, these support areas are a big part of the total expense.

STEWART: Dick, your outsourcing policy reminds me of the Japanese keiretsu system. Japanese companies tend to outsource their supplies from independent firms in which they have significant cross-holdings of equity. And the question that has been posed by some economists is this: Does the keiretsu system provide a more efficient way to organize a company than the vertical integration traditionally practiced by American firms? Take the case of Toyota and General Motors. Whereas GM produced 8.7 million cars in 1992 with 365,000 employees, Toyota produced 4.5 million cars with only 65,000 employees.

Dick, your own outsourcing successes seem to provide evidence for the keiretsu system. And I think the root cause driving the evolution of both of these systems is fundamentally the same. It is the power of information technology and the increasing sophistication of markets that is causing this unbundling of companies and this drive toward the virtual corporation.

Dennis, what do you think about outsourcing as a way of increasing shareholder value?

GORMLEY: Outsourcing may work in some cases, but it's at best a partial solution to the problem of increasing corporate productivity. As I said earlier, there is still a critically important role for central planning, for coordinating all these decentralized activities. At the same time, though, I agree that companies ought to continually keep in mind and focus on their core capabilities. And that's tough to do when you are inside the organization; it takes some real soul-searching.

But, again, I don't think the answer is decentralization versus centralization. You've got to have both. Centralization enables you to coordinate certain aspects of the business such as logistics and supplier relations. But if you're talking about servicing your customer and being responsive, or if you're talking about operating a group of somewhat unrelated businesses, then you want them to be sufficiently decentralized that they can be responsive to the changes in the marketplace. If you are too centralized, you tend to become bureaucratic and control too much from headquarters.

Corporate success is knowing what you're about and fully understanding

your business. And that's where bigness, for all its advantages, sometimes gets in the way. The pursuit of growth sometimes leads you to do too many things that aren't related to your core capabilities—things that end up reducing rather than adding value. So, it's not that outsourcing has any magical advantage to it; it's just that it helps restore your focus to your basic activities.

Spin-offs: The Case of Ball Corporation

STEWART: Del, your company recently spun off various businesses to its shareholders. You too are presumably thinking about refocusing on core capabilities, in this case by separating unrelated businesses. Could you tell us more about the thinking behind this spin-off?

DAVIS: We took a good look at our businesses this past year. And this reminded us that, over the years, we had either acquired or developed from within a number of small businesses that were no longer related to our core businesses. We had become, almost without being aware of it, sort of a mini-conglomerate with a number of unrelated businesses. We felt that we would create more shareholder value and be a better company—and Wall Street had indicated this to us, time and time again—if we would concentrate just on our core businesses.

After deciding which operations were no longer essential to our corporate future, we next faced the issue of how to separate these businesses from our remaining core activities. In thinking about this issue, we worried, of

I don't think we've used top-down strategic planning in our company for years. We set general strategic direction and goals at the top. And we monitor the general performance standards we use to evaluate our progress. But, we also lean very strongly towards decentralization and empowerment of people—and also toward the use of multiple, cross-functional teams. Many of the new ideas for improvement come from lower down in the ranks, from people who are continuously finding better ways to do things—in many cases, just by doing them.

—Delmont Davis

course, about how employees were going to be affected—employees who have been very loyal to us for many years. We also worried about losing employees who might bail out before we were able to take action on the company.

When we considered selling the businesses outright, we discovered we had a tax problem: we had a very low tax basis in the businesses we wanted to sell. So, if we sold them to other companies outright, we would not only be losing a lot of employees and talent, but also penalizing our shareholders in the form of large tax payments to Uncle Sam.

Largely for tax reasons, then, we chose to spin those businesses off to our shareholders. We accomplished this by paying a dividend of new shares in those businesses to our shareholders, thus converting those businesses into a separately trading, stand-alone public company called Alltrista Corporation.

STEWART: I'm confused a little bit, Del. You say you want to preserve shareholder value, and yet you passed up this opportunity to book a rather large accounting gain on the sale of these business. Wouldn't that have increased your stock price?

DAVIS: I don't think *you* believe that, Bennett. The market has validated our spin-off strategy in the sense that the combined value of both stocks today exceeds the earlier value of the company; that is, the spin-off has increased our shareholder value.

I might also mention—because Bennett's going to get this out of me sooner or later—that we took about three years to become one of Stern Stewart's disciples. We became an

EVA, or economic value added, company a year ago. I think that once you understand the EVA concept—the idea that it's cash, not earnings, that matters to the market and that all capital has a cost, equity as well as debt—and if you really apply those ideas to the management of your businesses, the answers to these accounting and performance measurement issues become pretty clear. For example, when given a choice between reporting higher earnings (and paying more taxes on it) and having more cash in the bank at the end of the day, we as a firm now choose the cash. And we think the market is smart enough to reward us for doing that.

STEWART: Thanks, Del. I'll buy you lunch, golf, tennis, whatever you want.

But let me get back to the issue we started with? Del, did your core competencies in some sense change over time? Some of the businesses you recently spun off were at least apparently related to your core packaging business at one time, were they not?

DAVIS: That's right. To give you one example, I think everybody in this room knows the Ball home canning jar. Many years ago the home canning jar used to have a zinc cap on it. And we vertically integrated to manufacture that cap in-house. Although that jar hasn't had a zinc cap on it for a lot of years, we were still in the zinc business.

Now, although I think we retain a core competency in that business, it's a business that really didn't pertain to anything else we do. It was a $65 million business that wasn't related to our packaging or aerospace business in any way. But it is still a valuable part

of Alltrista Corporation. And most of the other businesses that we spun off fit that category.

STEWART: I would argue that, even if you have a business in which you have a core competence and it's performing well, it can still make sense to separate that business through a spin-off if it's not really critical to the main operations of the company.

DAVIS: I agree. And there is still another situation where spin-offs can add value. We had some smaller businesses that were in some sense competing with our core businesses. In order to remove that competitive situation, which caused us all kinds of grief, it was best to spin some of these businesses off and then just let them compete without any internal interference.

STEWART: Let me ask one final question on this issue. Although you have spun off a number of these unrelated businesses, you still have a $300 million aerospace business that I'm sure Dave Gruber would love to have his hands on. What is the logic behind retaining the aerospace business, given that you have over $2 billion of sales in packaging?

DAVIS: When we analyzed our businesses, we decided that a company the size of Ball Corporation probably ought to concentrate only in large industries. If you're in a $100 million industry and you have $35 million worth of sales, then you've already got a third of the industry and there's not a lot of room to grow.

So, we wanted to be in large industries, but nevertheless in industries where we had a strong core capability. Besides packaging, we also think we have succeeded in developing a core competence in aerospace. Aerospace is a very large industry. And although it's now shrinking, as Dave mentioned, we have only have about one percent market share, and so we still see lots of opportunity for niche players like us. And we certainly fit that category in aerospace. In fact, we have three major niches in the aerospace industry: telecommunications, electro-optics & cryogenics, and space and systems engineering.

In sum, we have come to the conclusion that we *are able to* manage two unlike businesses, provided we continue to upgrade our capabilities in both.

Decentralization and Strategic Control: The Model of GE

STEWART: It does seem peculiar to me, though, Del, that you've chosen to keep your aerospace operations when a much larger defense company like General Dynamics has decided simply to sell a large portion of its aerospace business.

Dave, you're also in the aerospace industry. What do you think about General Dynamics' sell-off strategy as a way of adding value in shrinking market conditions?

GRUBER: Well, we don't really have much of a choice to get out of the aerospace industry, provided we want to stay in business at all. As I mentioned before, our challenge now is to make our business more efficient so we can weather this downturn in the market, and then come back strong when it recovers. We believe that aircraft engines and airplanes will be made well into the future. But for now, the sudden sharp fall-off in demand has led to overcapacity, and in response the industry is consolidating and some of the marginal players are being shaken out.

Bennett, you said earlier that there's no such thing as mature industries,

only prematurely aged managements. Well, as clearly and widely troubled as the aerospace companies are today, there is some evidence to support your point. For example, we sell to jet engine manufacturers such as United Technologies, Pratt & Whitney, and General Electric. Now, each of these three companies has about the same market share and revenues. And yet, while the first two companies each lost about $500 million last year, General Electric made an operating profit of $1.3 billion.

STEWART: That's a classic example where market share doesn't really matter.

GRUBER: Right. There are clearly important differences in the way these companies are run internally. General Electric, in most of their major operations, has learned to run very lean, pay attention to the right things, understand what is essential to their business, and then cut out the rest. I view GE as holding out a good model for us. It's one that we used to cut our costs while still holding onto our market share.

CHANDLER: It's interesting you mention General Electric. I used to end my business history course at Harvard with the case of GE. It's a fascinating and, I think, very instructive story.

By the 1960s, as in many large, successful U.S. companies, GE's corporate office had essentially lost control because of the size and diversity of the company. Diversification had moved the company into ever more distantly related areas—commercial jet engines, nuclear power, and computers, to name a few. By the end of the '60s, the company had 190 distinct business units, 46 divisions, and 10 major business groups. As a result the planning overload had become overwhelming, profits were down sharply, capital allocations were made without good information or any sensible underlying rationale, and new ven-

tures—especially computers—were doing horribly.

When Reginald Jones became CEO in 1972, he took some measures to restore control. Some businesses were sold, product lines were cut back somewhat, and a moderate level of profits restored. But the problem of decision-making overload, the strategic planning nightmare that set in during the '60s, remained to be dealt with. By the time Jack Welch came in to run the company in 1981, there were something like 200 senior planners at the company. When Welch became CEO, the business plans were being originated from planners in the business units and then passed up to two or three other levels of planners at higher levels of the organization. After they reached the top, and the decisions approved, they were then passed back down to the business units to be carried out.

So the problem Welch faced was that—again, because of the size of GE and the diversity of its product line—the planning and capital allocation process had become completely bureaucratized. The company was responsible for too many units for top management to understand, much less influence their strategies. Welch's solution was to cut back GE's product lines further and to cut planning staff drastically at all levels. Indeed, he ended up bypassing the planning process altogether by having executives in his corporate office talk directly and regularly to the heads of the SBUs.

And, interestingly—and this is a critical point—the amount of direct corporate attention Welch chose to give each SBU varied with *the kind of business*. Early in his tenure, he divided all of GE's businesses into three groups designated "core," "high technology," and "service." The managers of the "core" businesses—the long-established, mature businesses—re-

ceived relatively little planning or attention from the corporate office. These were run instead through a system of tight financial controls based on budgets and budget-based bonuses. The same style was used for the GE service businesses, which required little ongoing capital investment and planning.

The high technology area, however, was run very differently. Here Welch and the corporate office played a large and direct role in strategic planning. By the end of the '80s, GE had reduced its many product lines into 13 different business whose heads now report directly to Welch. Of these businesses, three were high-tech—aerospace, aircraft engines, and medical equipment. It was in these businesses, with their large capital requirements and continuous demand for new products, that the corporate office began to play a major role in strategic planning.

I think this kind of dual top management approach—applying decentralized financial controls to mature businesses and a more centralized form of "strategic" control to capital-intensive, high-tech businesses—has proven to be effective at GE. And I suspect it's a model that could be profitably applied to many other companies.

Two Schools of Strategy: Michael Porter vs. Tom Peters

STEWART: It's interesting you should say that, Dr. Chandler, because there seem to be two prominent schools of strategy today that sort of divide the world between them. One school of strategy I'll call the Michael Porter

school. Michael Porter argues in lengthy tomes that top management should agonize over market conditions and exhaustively analyze industry structure in order to arrive at tops-down strategies. After being designed by an army of strategic planners, such strategies can then be imposed on the divisions and orchestrated from the top.

At the other extreme you have Tom Peters, whose highly decentralized approach is suggested in the titles of his two most recent books: *Managing With Chaos* and *Liberation Management*. Peters's books emphasize the empowerment of people throughout the organization. The basic strategy is really not to have a carefully formulated strategy at all, but rather to have the organizational structure sufficiently loose and managers sufficiently motivated to seize opportunities as they arise. We don't really know in advance what the opportunities will turn out to be, but we want to have the organizational flexibility and incentives to respond when they come. To use one of my favorite expressions, it's "hustle as strategy."

Now, it's interesting to me that the strategic prescription we seem to be arriving at in this discussion aims to combine the experience and capabilities of large organizations with the dynamism and responsiveness of small companies. So, let me put it to the panelists: As you think about your own businesses, which is closer to your own strategic approach: Porter or Peters, mainframe versus PC, centralized versus decentralized, tops-down versus bottoms-up planning?
DAVIS: Well, I think we're somewhere in the middle, but we lean

more towards decentralization. We've always had a feeling that there are certain things in our company that you must control from the top. Certainly we control our treasury and functions of that sort; and general policy-making and performance evaluation must of course be done at the top. But we really try to push down a lot of the responsibility to the operating people.

In one case, interestingly, we decentralized an operation and then later pulled it back under central control. As I mentioned earlier, we have a Canadian operation that manufactures cans, and we also have a U.S. operation in the same business. And both of those operations were managed independently until recently. But, now that we've just acquired Heekin Can, we have decided to consolidate control of their operations under a central management team, in part to realize the scale economies Dr. Chandler was talking about earlier. Those three were separately managed until fairly recently. At the same time, though, this centralized management team for our can manufacturing operations will operate largely independently of headquarters. So, at a second tier, we are centralizing a formerly decentralized function; but that second-tier management has a lot of autonomy from headquarters.

And I suspect our experience is representative of what goes on in many corporations. You experiment with decentralized structures, and sometimes it doesn't work. So, you go back and forth trying to find an equilibrium point, some kind of optimal balance, between the extremes of centralization and decentralization. First, of course, you have to decide what operations you want to be in and what you need to run them. Once you have made these decisions, you then have to ask yourself: Where are the management controls and decision-making authority best located to get the most productivity out of your resources? In some cases, it's at the central headquarters and in others it's at the outlying operations.

But, having said that, we lean very strongly towards decentralization and empowerment of people—and also toward the use of multiple, cross-functional teams that Dave Gruber described earlier. These are things we have been doing for a lot of years. And I think that's also true of TQM and some of the other new buzz words; these are all things we have been doing to one degree or another for some time. In many cases, these are just new names for old ideas.

STEWART: TQM is, in essence, nothing more than the notion of continuous innovation and improvement. And that really has to come from the bottom up, doesn't it?

DAVIS: I think so, at least generally speaking.

STEWART: The real action is in the trenches. It seems to me to the extent that *continuous* improvement is really the key to corporate success these days, then tops-down strategic planning has lost much of its effectiveness. The world is really changing too quickly for a comprehensive vision of a business to be carefully formulated and then just handed down to a set of managerial subordinates to be mechanically executed.

DAVIS: Well, I don't think we've used top-down strategic planning in our company for years. We set general strategic direction and goals at the top. It is of course top management which has determined that we are to be primarily a packaging company,

and we set and monitor the general performance standards we use to evaluate our progress. But many of the new ideas for improvement come from lower down in the ranks, from people who are continuously finding better ways to do things—in many cases, just by doing them.

RADT: This happens a lot at our company. In fact, it happens so regularly that each year we assume in our formal budgeting process that some 10 to 15% of our business will come from completely new sources. And this has actually worked out in practice.

For example, one of our products is sterilizable paper; it's something you would expect to find in hospitals or dentists' offices. The paper is sterilized by folding it up and putting it into a steam autoclave. And one day, somebody in our plant had just an absolutely dumb-wonderful idea. He asked himself: "Do you think there's a marketable use for paper where steam, instead of going *into* the paper, goes *out* of the paper." And the answer turned out to be our biggest product in 1991: microwave popcorn bags. It was just steam coming out of the paper, which causes the paper to expand; it was just the reverse of the technology we used in making sterilizable paper.

So, just because you're in, say, the aerospace business or the auto business, you don't have to limit yourself to that. It's really this principle of economies of scope that Dr. Chandler was talking about earlier. You may be able to make other things using your existing technologies.

A New Role for Top Management?

STEWART: But doesn't this suggest, then, that the really critical role of top management these days is to ensure that its core processes are redesigned

to allow decentralization and empowerment to work? In fact, doesn't it even suggest that top management must now, more than ever, be the servant of the organization instead of imposing from the top down?

In fact, Dr. Chandler, isn't that one of the problems that General Motors had in the 1980s—that the top management tended to manage and direct the organization from the top rather than rewiring the circuits of the company for speed, flexibility, and responsiveness?

CHANDLER: Well, it's more complicated than that, but that's certainly part of the story. I suspect the real source of the problems at GM was the company's domination by financial people. My impression is that financially-oriented executives became influential in the 1970s, and the business began to be run by the numbers. The company became so large that top management attempted to substitute financial controls to compensate for their own distance from and lack of information about operations.

The result was that, as in many American companies, the financial budget became a law unto itself. It was not just one of several performance evaluation tools, but rather the performance standard that became the basis for management promotion within the company. And, because these numbers could be manipulated to hide poor performance, operating heads learned to adjust their data accordingly—and the performance of such companies began to deteriorate.

The really classic story, however, of a company transformed by this management-by-numbers approach is that of ITT. After spending most of its corporate existence as a giant global telecommunications enterprise, the company began to diversify under Harold Geneen in the 1960s. By the mid-1970s, ITT had acquired some 300 companies in businesses ranging from insurance companies to hotels to auto parts.

Geneen was an accountant by training and he set up a system where he required monthly financial statements from every operating unit in the company. As in the case of GM, the numbers replaced all subjective or qualitative judgment about how the divisions were really performing and about which areas deserved more investment. Although Geneen was heralded as a pioneer in business administration in the 1970s, it is now clear that this system did not work. As a consequence, Geneen's successor, Rand Araskog, spent the '80s attempting to transform ITT from an unmanageable conglomerate back into a company with some semblance of a core business—and with only moderate success.

But, to come back to your original question, Bennett, IBM is an even better case for your argument. That's a clear case where strategic planning was held completely at the top, and where the organization accordingly lost its ability to respond to competitive threats and opportunities.

STEWART: To return to my earlier question, though, what is the role of top management? And do you see that undergoing any major change in today's more rapidly changing environment?

CHANDLER: This is something I have thought a good deal about. Investment planning and policy, as I have long argued, is the most important function of top management. Top management will continue to allocate the resources. They still have got to decide where the money is going to go for the next set of investment or the new plants.

The other basic function is monitoring or administrative; it's keeping on top of performance in the ongoing businesses. And, of course, to some extent these two functions go hand in hand, because it's impossible to plan effectively for new investment unless you know how well your existing operations are performing.

STEWART: But, how can top management allocate the resources if they don't really understand the business? How can the top management of IBM *possibly* allocate capital in an organization as large and sprawling as it is? And isn't it precisely the failure of their top management to understand how to allocate capital that has set up the bureaucratic obstacles?

CHANDLER: Well, the whole business of strategic planning has some pitfalls. As I mentioned earlier, GE's Jack Welch basically came in and eliminated layers of strategic planners. In so doing, he effectively restored direct lines of communication and a meaningful strategic dialogue, if you will, between the operating heads and the corporate office. This was something that had been lost during the era of conglomeration.

And I think that IBM should decentralize along the lines that Du Pont and other successful U.S. companies used even before World War II.

The Case of Du Pont

CHANDLER: After all, the current emphasis on decentralization is not a new management insight. Perhaps a useful model for much of what strategists are proposing today was provided by what Du Pont did back in the 1920s. As early as 1921, the top management of Du Pont realized that they had neither the time nor the information to coordinate and monitor day-to-day operations and to devise and execute long-term plans for the company's several product or geographical divisions. The administrative overload, even back in those days, had simply become too great.

So, top management responded to this realization by turning over responsibility for decisions about production and distribution—and, in some cases, even new product development—to the divisional operating heads. The main role of corporate headquarters under this new "M-form" of organization, as it came to be called—and it began to be adopted by multibusiness companies before World War II—was to oversee and monitor these operating heads, and to serve as advisors on strategic matters.

So, under this new arrangement, top management literally relinquished their line authority. Headquarters did not have the authority to step in and interfere with divisional decisions unless something was clearly going wrong. That was decentralization in 1921, and I assure you it's not a new concept.

STEWART: Back in those days, Du Pont had a very clear standard for assessing its performance. It was called return on investment, or "ROI." In fact, as you know, Dr. Chandler, this was known as the "Du Pont Formula." The idea was to break down the ROI calculation into components such as profit margin, sales turnover, and then analyze these components even further. Du Pont had something called the Chart Room, a very large room in which were posted diagrams of the ROI trees for all their businesses.

CHANDLER: The Chart Room has disappeared. But, from the early '20s until well after World War II, the Executive Committee met every Monday in the Chart Room with a division head and his staff to review the operating performance and discuss capital expenditures and the strategic plan of the division. They would evaluate their progress using these ROI diagrams you mentioned. And, as you said, Bennett, the ROIs were broken down into many smaller parts for analysis.

This system worked very well for a time. The company had only eight to ten divisions during the period between the two wars. And the numbers themselves were not viewed as absolutes, but rather as guidelines for understanding the business and as the basis for serious discussion. The purpose of these meetings was in part to allow people to interpret the numbers and thus overcome the limitations that come with managing by numbers alone.

But, over time, and like so many other American companies, Du Pont gradually became too large and diversified for this process to work. Because of the increasing separation between headquarters and the ever larger number of divisions, the statistical ROI data no longer served as the basis for discussion between corporate and operating management; they became instead an inflexible standard of performance.

So, to respond to your earlier point, Bennett, decentralization was not the final answer in the case of Du Pont. Although it worked well when there were only eight or ten divisions before the War, it has turned out to have problems of its own. In an excellent history of Du Pont's R & D program published in the 1960s, a member of Du Pont's Executive Committee was reported as describing the research output of the company as "disgraceful and inexcusably low in proportion to the caliber of the men we employ, the facilities we give them, and the amount of money we allow them to spend." In effect, the Executive Committee admitted that its policy of "departmental autonomy" had allowed it to lose control over R & D productivity.

In fact, I would argue that one of the great problems in the '60's and '70's was that corporations put too much emphasis on basic research, on the "R" in R & D, but too little emphasis on the "D" part, on developing commercial applications. There is no question in my mind they spent too

much on basic R. And many companies, notably IBM, Xerox, and Kodak, are still trying to rationalize R & D operations that just got out of control.

But, to get back to the Du Pont story, authority over R & D spending was eventually handed back to headquarters in the person of Edward Jefferson in 1979. And after Jefferson became CEO two years later, he continued to strengthen the role of the corporate office in both its planning and resource allocation functions.

But this was not enough. In 1991, Du Pont announced a major restructuring that has made the company still more centralized in certain respects. The expressed aim of the restructuring was to break down barriers between divisions and to have top management develop an overall corporate perspective rather than a product or narrowly functional orientation.

So, it's interesting to me that whereas the role and size of GE's corporate office has been sharply reduced in the past decade, the corporate office at Du Pont today has far more direct operating and planning responsibilities than it has had at any time during the past 70 years.

The Limits to Decentralization

STEWART: But I would submit, Dr. Chandler, that the world has changed in the following respect: It may at one time have been possible for top management of even a large company to understand what was happening in their various businesses and appreciate that. But it seems to me the pace of technological and industrial change has accelerated so much that the top management of a company the size and diversity of an IBM or Sears can no longer conceivably understand all that is happening to their businesses. That's what creates the need to decentralize and empower people, to put the information and the responsibility

and the incentive and the accountability down in the field. This way you create a self-managed, self-propelled, self-motivated organization—an organization that, without top management's intervention, senses the problems and responds to them at the micro level instead of at the macro level. Isn't that what we have to get to?

CHANDLER: Well, Bennett, I think we are converging. That's what my own criticisms of the conglomerate have been all about—the problems that arise when top management becomes too divorced from operations. You have to know your business or you shouldn't be in it. If you're just using financial measures, you're going to lose control. This is what happened to General Motors, and to Harold Geneen at ITT. They were just managing by the numbers, meaningless statistics. And, as a consequence of this practice, many firms got too big.

Now, that doesn't mean that large firms can't succeed. For example, the big Japanese companies aren't doing so badly—companies like Hitachi, Fujitsu, and Toshiba. Although large and diversified, these companies tend to diversify only into closely related businesses. And, partly for this reason, they seem to be succeeding in businesses where our electrical companies like GE and RCA have failed. They have managed to become computer and consumer electronics companies, whereas our electrical companies have not. And they have also become semiconductor companies, an area where our small firms have had trouble competing. Unlike our Silicon Valley types, Japanese semiconductor managers are big companies. You don't hear much about Japanese entrepreneurs, but I suspect that's because they have such close ties to the large companies. In the Japanese *keiretsu* system, large companies form the center of a group of smaller companies tied together by cross-holdings and long-term supply contracts. These networks of companies may well be one of the strengths of the Japanese system.

At any rate, my basic point here is that if top management doesn't know what's going in some of their businesses, they should probably sell them to companies specializing in those businesses. It was this separation between top and operating managers that caused much of our problems in the '70s and '80s, and we are still trying to undo some of this conglomeration.

STEWART: In other words, we might as well break companies down into smaller, neural-network-type organizations. Several of the people have mentioned they have spun off unrelated businesses. But where does this process of decentralization stop? Most companies still consist of lots of different business units. And each business unit often consists of different lines of business, which in turn each have different markets. So, at what level does the decentralization and empowerment stop? Have far do you break down the organization into separately accountable parts? Where does authority vest in the organization?

CHANDLER: Well, I would say that what is critically important are the core competencies. Outsourcing represents a partial solution to some of these problems. Instead of being vertically integrated, you can certainly outsource your supplies in certain industrial operations. But you cannot outsource one of your basic capabilities—and this is a very important message. This is what happened to some American companies in their Japanese joint ventures. The end result, in several of these cases, was that the Japanese partners ended up acquiring the basic capability. By outsourcing, say, the production side

of your business, you lose too much control and information.

STEWART: Well, let me stop you there. Let's take the case of Nike. It's a supersuccessful company. They're probably the classic example of a virtual corporation. They concentrate solely on new product design and marketing. The shoes are manufactured in the Far East by a separate firm, and then they're imported by Ishoniwa. They're distributed through independent retailers.

In other words, the company is just a nexus of connections, and it concentrates on just those two functions where they have a comparative advantage—and they're *extremely* successful. In fact, I would submit that the more uncertain a business is, the more fraught with risk, the more of this decentralization and strategic networking needs to take place.

CHANDLER: Well, I'm not sure how far you can generalize from the case of Nike. There is a big difference between selling sneakers and making and selling high-tech products.

STEWART: Well, Intel is very decentralized.

CHANDLER: Yes. Intel did things just right. They didn't pay a dividend, but continued pouring all their earnings back into investment.

STEWART: They also made the decision to drop out of the DRAM business—a business the Japanese overinvested in by a mile. It was exactly the right thing for the American companies to get out of that business. It's become a commodity and, as a result, the Japanese manufacturers are awash in red ink these days while Intel is very profitable.

CHANDLER: Well, I can assure you that Intel did not *intend* to get out of the DRAM business. But they were wise to refocus on microprocessing before Motorola and TI did. For this reason, they are not suffering from the overcapacity in the DRAM business

that now faces the leading U.S. semiconductor producers.

STEWART: Intel may not have realized what they were doing at the time. But, as George Gilder predicted several years ago in his book, *Into the Microcosm,* all the alarmists proclaiming the loss of America's technological and competitive edge were proven wrong. U.S. corporations, he pointed out, were way ahead in digital technology—and so they were bound to win back the TV business they had lost with high-definition TVs—while the Japanese kept sinking billions more into an antiquated analog technology. And this prediction has, of course, proved to be right on the mark.

CHANDLER: Well, Bennett, this may be the exception that proves the rule—although I would point out that the one remaining U.S. producer of TVs, Zenith, is now in financial trouble, and that its best hope remains its joint venture with AT&T.

But my research and experience suggests that the function of headquarters depends critically on the kinds of industries companies are operating in. In more mature industries where the nature of the product is fairly stable, where there is little R & D, or where the R & D is intended primarily for improving product and cost-cutting processes—in these kinds of industries the corporate office can delegate strategic planning to the operating divisions, and then maintain control by setting targets and establishing long-term goals for the corporation as a whole. These are the kinds of industries where decentralization combined with financial controls can be very effective.

But, in industries in which new product development is critical, R & D expenditures are high, and state-of-the-art facilities require major capital investment, the corporate office *must* be closely involved in the strategic planning process. Commercializing a new product is a risky and costly process in which the payoff often does not come for years. Without some centralized oversight and coordination of this kind, companies in technologically advanced businesses will fail to make the fullest use of the competitive strengths of their organization. You just cannot manage IBM the way you run Nike.

Evaluating Performance: Financial vs. Nonfinancial Measures

STEWART: Before we close, I would like to take up one last topic—that of management incentives and corporate performance measures. Alcoa's chairman, Paul O'Neill, was reported in yesterday's *Wall Street Journal* to have received 1992 pay of $1.2 million, including a bonus of $575,000 versus no bonus the year before. You should also know that the aluminum maker posted a roughly 65% decrease in net income relative to the year before. The company said the bonus reflected Mr. O'Neill's "outstanding leadership in achieving non-financial goals for safety, yield, inventory control, and customer satisfaction."

My question is this: To what extent should we allow non-financial measures of performance to become the primary focus of our management incentive systems? Norm, what do you think?

POOLE: Well, I think your example shows the problem with compensating people without reference to financial measures or shareholder value. But let me also say that financial measures are by no means a *leading* indicator of corporate performance. Whether you're in a turnaround business or even in a reasonably profitable business, you better have a lot more monitoring than what is provided by your financial statements.

Companies need to be able to evaluate themselves from their customers' point of view, from their suppliers' point of view, and from their workers' point of view. Financial measures are not likely to send you early warning signals if you're developing problems in these areas.

Now, it's true that your ultimate responsibility is to provide your shareholders—the owners of the business—with an adequate rate of return on their investment. But, to do this, you have to satisfy several different corporate constituencies. For this reason, companies need to have non-financial *as well as* financial performance measures.

STEWART: I grant you that non-financial measures can be useful leading indicators. But shouldn't there still be a hierarchy of corporate goals, one in which non-financial measures are finally subordinated to some measure of shareholder value added? This Alcoa plan is analogous to a bonus plan for a basketball player that rewards him for reaching levels in each of several categories—say, blocked shots, shooting percentage, assists, and rebounds. The problem with these kinds of systems is that they allow you to win statistically while losing the game. Why wouldn't it make sense to compensate people primarily just for winning, and then empower *them* to seek out the most appropriate means to achieve that end. So the question I'm raising is: Do we compensate the means or do we compensate the end?

HUBER: Well, Bennett, I'm not sure the problem is as clear-cut as you seem to be suggesting. I think we would all agree that the days of a simple, single indicator of performance are gone. I see the problem of corporate performance measurement as a simultaneous equation with a whole bunch of variables (and, when I say this, I'm betraying my academic

background as a chemist rather than an economist). The trick here, I think, is to identify and then assign the proper weighting to each of the variables—say, revenue growth, profitability, new customers—that correlate strongly with increases in shareholder value, at least over the long haul. At the same time, though—and I agree with your point, Bennett—the system should have some kind of failsafe override that says in effect: If you don't make at least a certain amount of money at the end of the day, then all these non-financial things do not matter.

But just as shooting and passing both help decide the outcome of basketball games, non-financial things like customer service and satisfaction really play major roles in corporate success. In corporations, you need to find different ways to compensate people in different parts of the organization.

STEWART: Well, I think there is one solution to this problem that can be transported across all industries and across all business environments. And that is: Make managers into owners.

HUBER: I agree. As you know, Bennett, Tom Theobald's policy at Continental clearly reflects that view. He insists that all senior executives at the bank own significant amounts of stock.

STEWART: Yes, but this raises the question of how you go about accomplishing this. How can we make our people into significant owners at a reasonable cost to shareholders and without imposing too much risk on management? You don't want to just hand them the shares.

HUBER: I would think telling people to use their own money to buy shares is a reasonably straightforward and effective approach. That is what we did in structuring leveraged buyouts during the '80s. Although there were some failed LBOs, there were many more success stories. And I strongly believe that much of the success of these transactions—and I was one of those horrible people who facilitated some of these deals—was really due simply to reuniting ownership and control. The value added came in large part from making managers into owners.

STEWART: But you have to remember, Dick, those managers in LBOs weren't buying normal common stock. They were buying highly leveraged stock—in some cases, with 90% debt behind it.

HUBER: That's right. In fact, in the deals I participated in, we insisted that the managers put themselves at considerable risk in buying this stock. We wanted the managers to take out a second mortgage on their house and put real money into that company. We wanted them to face downside risk as well as upside reward. And, in all but a handful of cases, this really helped produced results.

STEWART: But, from what I understand, that incentive structure went by the board starting around 1986. Too many LBO firms got into the game and, to win the business, they began structuring deals that required no upfront investment by management.

In fact, in cases like Interco, managers were selling large blocks of shares without putting any cash back into the deals; they were effectively being bribed to participate. And, as we all know, this arrangement produced some horrible deals.

CHANDLER: I would like to make a comment on the LBO movement. LBOs were remarkably successful in creating value in one sector of the economy—so successful that it prompted a colleague of mine, Michael Jensen, to write an article for the *Harvard Business Review* called "The Eclipse of the Public Corporation." Perhaps because it predicted the eventual displacement of many public companies by private firms, the article received a lot of attention.

But what the article failed to spell out—or at least as clearly as it perhaps could have—was that LBOs have been used only in certain kinds of industries. LBOs during the '80s occurred almost entirely in mature industries with limited ongoing capital requirements, minimal R & D, and highly stable cash flows—industries, in short, where long-term strategic planning is largely unnecessary. Companies in such industries, as I suggested earlier, can be run effectively on a highly

decentralized basis using financial controls alone.

The converse of this point, which Jensen's piece also seems to have obscured, is that the form of the widely held public corporation overwhelmingly dominates in capital-intensive, technologically complex industries—industries such as computers and semiconductors, oil, motor vehicles, chemicals, pharmaceuticals, mining, electrical equipment and electronics, aircraft and aerospace, metals. These are the industries on which most of the nation's economic and industrial growth depend. And there is one prediction that I can make with great confidence as we move toward the 21st century: In these kinds of industries—those that require continuous long-term investment in R & D and capital facilities—the public corporation will continue to be the engine of industrial strength and transformation, just as it has been during the 20th.

STEWART: Well, that's a nice note on which to end this discussion. So let me finish by expressing, once again, my admiration for Dr. Chandler's work and by thanking him and all the panel members for sharing their experiences and insights with us.

LEVERAGE AND
CORPORATE RESTRUCTURING

The Link Between Capital Structure And Shareholder Value

Bennett Stewart | Jay Allen | Cheryl Francis | Michael Jensen | Mike O'Neill | Dennis Soter

Pebble Beach, California   *June 25, 1997*

BENNETT STEWART: Good afternoon, and, on behalf of our hosts Jerry Fair and Bank of America, let me welcome you all to this roundtable discussion of corporate capital structure. I'm Bennett Stewart, senior partner of Stern Stewart & Co., and I will be serving as moderator.

A number of leading business magazines have recently run cover stories on the "return of leverage." "Like it or not," it says on the cover of this *Institutional Investor* that I'm now holding up, "Leverage is back." And the cover story presents two startling facts: In 1996, new junk bond issues reached a record-high $73 billion; and, over the period 1995-1996, leveraged buyout funds amassed $40 billion in new capital. When you put debt on top of that $40 billion—leveraged, say, at three to one—that means there are now $160 billion of funds out there ready to buy your company.

These developments raise a number of interesting questions: Are we witnessing a return to the debt and leveraged transactions of the 1980s? Why would leveraged restructuring come back now? And what does this all say about the optimal, or value-maximizing, corporate capital struc-ture? To put the same question a little differently, are there reliable ways for corporate managers to manage their capital structure so as to add value for their shareholders?

It's also true that equity markets are at all-time highs, and dividend yields are at all-time lows. So it's tempting to think that equity is cheap if not free. But is equity cheap? If you make an acquisition by issuing new shares, is that cheaper than using debt? If so, why? Does it matter whether you use purchase or pool-ing accounting? Does accounting matter? These are some of the questions we'll address this afternoon.

PHOTOGRAPHS BY GARY GEIGER

And because major changes in capital structure are often accompanied by changes in ownership structure—in fact, debt financing is one of the principal means for accomplishing such changes—we will also find ourselves talking about corporate ownership structure. LBOs, of course, involve major changes in ownership as well as debt structure—and so do large leveraged recaps. And while we're addressing the subject of ownership structure, we might also look briefly at the issues raised by spin-offs. Just yesterday, the Whitman Corporation announced its intention to spin off its Hussman and Midas Muffler businesses. The stock rose almost 10%, in spite of an accompanying announcement of bad earnings and more restructuring charges to follow. This is equivalent to saying that when you take a pie and cut it into slices and put them on separate plates, you suddenly have a bigger pie. It's curious; it appears to defy the laws of physics—and of economics as well. But the market reaction to spin-offs, together with the subsequent performance of spun-off businesses, suggests that ownership structure matters. Who owns the assets, the form of the ownership, and the composition of the right-hand side of the balance sheet—all these seem to be capable of having large effects on firm performance and value.

So, these are the kinds of questions that we want to investigate today. We have assembled a distinguished group of panelists to help us explore these issues, and I will introduce them in alphabetical order:

JAY ALLEN is the President of Tosco Corporation, which is the largest independent refiner and marketer of oil in America. Tosco, as we will hear, has been actively acquiring other refining operations and using considerable amounts of debt financing to fund the acquisitions. In the process, the company has seen its stock price go up fivefold in the past four and a half years.

CHERYL FRANCIS is the Chief Financial Officer of the R.R. Donnelley & Sons Co. For the past two years, and with the assistance of Stern Stewart, Donnelley has been implementing an EVA performance measurement and incentive compensation program. Prior to joining Donnelley about a year ago, Cheryl was Treasurer of the FMC Corporation, which undertook a very dramatic leveraged recapitalization in 1986—and I think this audience will find Cheryl's account of this experience an interesting and instructive one.

MICHAEL JENSEN is the Edsel Bryant Ford Professor of Business Administration at the Harvard Business School. Mike has to be at the top of the list of leading academic scholars in the area of corporate finance and its relationship to corporate governance. He will talk at length about the implications of a paper he published in the *American Economic Review* in 1986 setting forth his "free cash flow" theory of takeovers. "Free cash flow," for those of you who are unfamiliar with the term, is the amount by which a company's operating cash flow exceeds what can be profitably reinvested in its basic businesses—and the emphasis here is on the word "profitably." In his 1993 Presidential Address to the American Finance Association, Mike gave this theory new life by arguing that we are now in the midst of a "Third Industrial Revolution"—an era of rapid technological change that, by speeding up product obsolescence, is continuing to create still more excess capacity and free cash flow, and so more demand for leveraged restructuring and downsizing. As Mike will tell us, there are persistent economic forces, now operating on an increasingly global basis, that are making the 1990s look a lot like the '80s—and the resulting pressures on corporate management can be expected to continue well into the next century.

MICHAEL O'NEILL is Chief Financial Officer and a Vice Chairman of Bank of America. As most of you are aware, Bank of America has created an extraordinary amount of shareholder value since Dave Coulter took over as CEO 18 months ago. What is probably less well known is the role financial management has played in the process. Under Mike O'Neill, B of A has been using its substantial "free cash flow" to buy back very large amounts of its stock. And, as Mike I'm sure will also mention, the bank has put in place an innovative performance measurement scheme that draws on and resembles the RAROC system for allocating capital to individual business units that was developed by Banker's Trust. B of A's system also makes use of a measure called "economic profit" that looks a lot like EVA. And, like our EVA system, the bank's new performance measurement system is designed to hold managers accountable for the capital tied up in their businesses.

Last but not least is **DENNIS SOTER**, my colleague and fellow partner at Stern Stewart. Dennis runs our corporate finance advisory activity and also oversees implementations of EVA in middle-market companies. In the past several months, Dennis has served as financial adviser in three highly successful leveraged recapitalizations. The companies executing the transactions were an Indianapolis utility called IPALCO, the engine manufacturer Briggs & Stratton, and auto parts maker SPX Corporation. Each of these three deals involved borrowing substantial amounts of new debt to buy back shares—and two cases involved major changes in dividend policy as well.

Capital Structure and the Theory of Corporate Finance

STEWART: So, with that brief introduction of the panelists, let me just say a few more words to introduce the subject. The beginnings of the current academic thinking on capital structure and shareholder value can be traced to two papers published over 35 years ago by professors Franco Modigliani and Merton Miller, both of whom won Nobel Prizes. The two papers argued that both capital structure and dividend policy are "irrelevant"—that is, incapable of affecting the total value of the firm. In the M & M view, the public corporation is a cash-generating engine whose market value is determined only by the investment and operating decisions that generate the cash flows. These are what economists refer to as the "real" decisions, those that affect the left-hand side of the balance sheet. Capital structure and dividend decisions, by contrast, are merely "financial" decisions—that is, ways of dividing up those operating cash flows among different groups of investors. And if financial markets are doing their job and arbitrageurs are exploiting all profit opportunities, there should be little opportunity for financing decisions to add value.

On the day it was announced that he won the Nobel Prize, Merton Miller was asked during a press interview to explain the M & M theory. After a series of failed attempts to compress the theory into a sound byte, Mert threw out, "Let me give you a *very simple* analogy. Whether you cut a pizza into six or eight slices doesn't change the size of the pie, right? Well, it's the same with corporations." As Mert likes to tell the story, the interviewer then looked at him and said, "And you got a Nobel Prize for *that?*"—and, with that, the press crew took down the cameras and lights and went away.

The message of the M & M irrelevance propositions is that there is no "magic" in leverage or dividends. M & M showed that, if we make some simplifying assumptions—if we ignore taxes and bankruptcy costs, and if we assume managers behave the same way if the firm is leveraged with 10% debt or 90% debt—there is no good reason to expect changes in corporate leverage and dividend payout ratios to affect the total market value of the firm's debt and equity.

One interesting experiment to test the logic of the M & M propositions took place about three years ago. In late 1994, a profitable utility called Florida Power & Light, with counsel from my colleague Dennis Soter, announced that it was cutting its dividend by 33%. No profitable utility had ever done such a thing. The conventional wisdom was that utility investors *require* dividends—and the more the better.

After FPL announced the cut, the stock price immediately fell from about 32 to 27, or about 15%, just as its investment banker had predicted. The banker also warned that the discount might last as long as two years. But, as it turned out, most of the discount disappeared in the following two weeks! And FPL's stock has outperformed the electric utility index since that time.

But the practical import of the M & M propositions is not in these isolated events, but in what they say about why financing decisions might matter. The M & M propositions say, in effect, that *if* corporate financing and dividend decisions are going to increase corporate values, they are likely to do so only for the following reasons: (1) they reduce the taxes paid by the corporation or its investors; (2) they reduce the probability of a costly bankruptcy; (3) they send a positive signal to investors about management's view of the firm's pros-

pects; or (4) they provide managers with stronger incentives to invest wisely and operate efficiently. It is in this sense that the M & M framework laid the groundwork for the modern theory of corporate finance; it showed future scholars where to look for the *real* effects of financial decisions.

It was Merton Miller himself who started the process of relaxing some of the assumptions underlying M & M by exploring issues like the tax benefit of debt and the "signaling effect" of dividends. But the most important attempt to take finance theory beyond the M & M propositions—to show why capital structure and dividend policy matter—was a 1976 paper by Mike Jensen and Bill Meckling called "Theory of the Firm: Managerial Behavior, Agency Costs, and Capital Structure." Mike and Bill Meckling's accomplishment was to focus the attention of the academic finance profession on the potential loss in value caused by the separation of ownership from control in large public corporations. As Jensen and Meckling observed, conflicts of interest between management and shareholders could be controlled—or made worse—by corporate capital structure and dividend choices.

Then, as if to confirm the thinking of Jensen and Meckling, there came the leverage revolution of the 1980s—the expansion of the junk bond market and the remarkable successes of the LBO movement. And, in 1986, Mike published the *American Economic Review* article I mentioned earlier called "The Agency Costs of Free Cash Flow: Corporate Finance and Takeovers." That article, in my opinion, offers the single most powerful explanation of the leveraged takeover movement of the 1980s. Stated in brief, the free cash flow theory says that highly leveraged acquisitions, stock buybacks, and management buyouts of public compa-

I

t is the contractual obligation to repay the debt, the fact that they've borrowed money and pre-committed to paying it back, that forces companies to pay out cash, to sell unrelated businesses, or to take other value-increasing steps they might otherwise be reluctant to take. And there is likely to be another kind of benefit of debt financing in these leveraged transactions: Having more debt and less equity makes it easier to concentrate the equity in the hands of the insiders so that not only do they have the discipline of debt, they have the stronger incentives to create value that come with significant equity ownership.

nies were all adding value by squeezing excess capital out of organizations with few profitable growth opportunities. Jensen observed that managers in mature industries have a natural tendency to hoard capital, to reinvest corporate earnings rather than paying them out to shareholders. And the massive substitution of debt for equity in the '80s provided a solution to this free cash flow problem by converting smaller, discretionary dividend payments into much higher, and contractually binding, payments of interest and principal.

Jensen's free cash flow analysis also does a nice job of explaining the problems with the Japanese economy in the 1990s. As early as 1989, Mike was writing in our *Journal of Applied Corporate Finance* that Japanese managers were in the same position as U.S. managers in the late 1960s. Japanese companies in the late '80s were flush with cash from their successes in the product wars, they were paying only nominal dividends, and stock repurchase was forbidden by law. As a result, they were either overinvesting in their core businesses in misguided attempts to maintain market share, or they were diversifying through acquisition into completely unrelated businesses. In many cases, they were doing both—and both are symptoms of the same free cash flow problem.

In 1991, we ran a piece in our journal by Carl Kester of the Harvard Business School called "The Hidden Costs of Japanese Success" that pointed directly to this problem. And soon after that my colleague Don Chew, who is the editor of the *Journal*, received a visit from four representatives of the Nomura Research Institute, the well-known private Japanese thinktank. The subject they wanted to discuss was stock repurchase. And it appears that the Ministry of Finance has finally taken the free cash flow problem seriously because Japanese stock repurchases were legalized in 1995.

So, it's hard to overstate the importance of Michael Jensen's work on the role of management incentives in corporate financial decisions. And, since he's sitting here with us, let me now turn the floor over to him. Mike, you have written extensively about the debt wave of the 1980s. You have put this into the context of corporate governance. You see an ongoing free cash flow problem coming out of this broad new modern industrial revolution. Can you give us your perspective on the forces that are now shaping corporate capital structure?

The Restructuring of the '80s

JENSEN: Thank you, Bennett, for that very generous account of my work— and I think Bill Meckling would be happy to hear it, too. I have a number of things I want to chat about. I want to begin by talking a little about why capital structure does matter, even though Merton Miller got a Nobel Prize for saying it didn't. Mert, by the way, was one of my teachers back at Chicago. I learned a great deal from him, and he is rightly identified as the "father" of modern finance. Mert, more than anyone else I can think of, has been responsible for whatever claim the academic finance profession can now make to being a hard science.

After I talk about the M & M propositions, I'm going to talk about what I have called "the agency costs of free cash flow." It is an endemic problem in large organizations. Solving that problem has been a big challenge for capital markets and companies for the last 20 years, and it will continue to be a major challenge for a long time. I'll talk a bit about the decade of the '80s, and show how most of the leveraged transactions, although very controversial, served the interests of the U.S. economy by providing a solution to this free cash flow problem.

Then I want to step back and talk for a few minutes about what I call the modern industrial revolution. It has been going on for several decades now; if I had to pick a starting point, I would choose the oil crisis of 1973 and all the changes that set off. This revolution is affecting all of our lives by making products obsolete with incredible speed, generating excess capacity, substantial free cash flow, and the necessity for downsizing. These forces are going to continue to operate in our lives for at least the next 20 years or so.

If there's still time at the end, I will also say a few things about the current environment. The bankers here—people like Mike Murray and Mike O'Neill—are much closer to these issues than I am. But I can at least open up that discussion with a few thoughts. Finally, I will mention in passing how new performance measurement and compensation systems like EVA act to resolve some of these free cash flow issues and in fact substitute for changes in capital structure.

So that's what I'm going to do, all in 15 minutes. We're going to move right along.

Why, then, does capital structure matter? The famous Modigliani-Miller theorems said that, in well-functioning capital markets, changes in capital structure and dividend policy should not have any predictable effects on the profitability and value of the organization. There are a number of restrictive assumptions on which this argument rests—things like perfect information, no taxes or transactions costs, and no bankruptcy costs. But far and away the most important assumption underlying M & M is that corporate real investment and operating decisions are not affected by corporate capital structure and dividend policies. That is, regardless of whether the company operates with 10% debt or 90% debt, and whether it commits to pay out all or none of its earnings, M & M effectively assume that a company's real investment policy and thus the operating cash flows of the organization do not change.

Now, as logical propositions, the M & M irrelevance theorems are absolutely correct. Under those assumptions, changes in capital structure and payout policy should not affect value. But what we know from the 1980s—and from the vast amount of theoretical and empirical work that's been done since the original M & M theory—is that it is precisely this last condition that is not fulfilled. When companies make dramatic changes in their capital structure, their ownership structure, or their payout ratios, we tend to see major changes in the performance and value of those organizations. We see changes in real investment policy, changes in efficiency, and therefore big changes in value, either up or down, depending on how the financial policies are changing. And these real effects of financial decisions, as I said, have

been well documented by studies published in the *Journal of Financial Economics*—the journal I founded in 1973, and which I recently stepped down from as managing editor—and in other reputable academic journals.

So what is this thing called the "agency cost of free cash flow?" It occurs in the following environment: You have an organization generating lots of cash, more than managers can possibly reinvest in positive net present value projects. In that kind of an environment, we have a serious problem in the capital markets, a serious organizational control problem: How do we motivate managers and organizations to get rid of the cash, to pay it back to investors? By the late '70s and early '80s, it reached the point where companies could destroy as much as one half of their value by failing to pay out their free cash flow and instead reinvesting in low-return projects or diversifying acquisitions. The failure of organizations right and left to pay out their excess capital led to the invention—or, more precisely, the "reinvention"—of hostile takeovers and leveraged acquisitions. And it led to the LBO movement in the mid-1970s, which then roared right along through the 1980s.

The net result of the leveraged restructurings of the '80s was close to a trillion dollars worth of gains in the equity market. Ironically, this was all being accomplished at the very time when so many people were saying that corporate America was being stripped of its competitive potential by financial markets. I think most economists and businessmen now understand that what went on during the '80s ended up leaving corporate America lean and mean. But not as lean and mean as it could have been; the process was stopped too soon. But, even so, U.S. companies today are faring very well in the international competitive markets in large

MICHAEL JENSEN

I agree that if you have the wrong business strategy, or if you hire the wrong people, you're going to destroy value. Finance cannot solve those problems. My point is this: You can do all those things right, but if you screw up these financial issues at the top of the organization where the cash comes pouring in, the company can destroy much of the value that's been created on the real side of the business. You can have everything done right at the lower levels in the organization. But if you don't get the right governance structure at the top—and finance can be a critical part of that governance structure—the operating value of the company can be frittered away.

part as a result of the changes that went on then.

So how does debt play a role in this? Think of an organization that has huge amounts of excess cash. Rather than paying out the cash, managers have a natural tendency to spend it on projects that have very low or even negative rates of return. There are several ways to solve that problem. First of all, managers can just pay out the excess cash by declaring increases in the dividend, or by making a large special or one-time dividend. An alternative to dividends is to pay out free cash flow in a regular series of stock buybacks. But a consistent policy of paying out free cash flow is very hard to maintain. There are large organizational pressures from middle managers and others who want to get to bat, who want to have their favorite projects funded—and so we get this gold-plating of organizations at the expense of massive reductions in value.

But now consider what happens when the firm issues a lot of new debt

and uses it to buy back a significant fraction of its stock. In that case, contractual debt service payments substitute for the promised dividend payments. Dividends can be cut—or at least not increased—without too much difficulty. But if you don't make the debt service payments, the trustee can eventually put you into bankruptcy court. So, the use of debt puts some incentives and some bite behind that contract. And that sharpening of incentives to pay out excess cash and capital is an important source of value in leveraged restructurings. It's not the only thing going on in LBOs and other leveraged deals, but it's a very important part of it.

Now, let's look a little more closely at what happens in highly leveraged transactions. One of the things they accomplish is to make the cost of capital both explicit and contractually binding. Before the 1980s, large, mature organizations could operate with 20% debt and 80% equity and think that they were making lots of money—

at least that's what their accounting statements were telling them—when in fact they were destroying value by failing to earn their cost of capital every single year. When dividend yields are low and the cost of equity doesn't show up in the accounting statements, managers can easily get into the habit of thinking that equity is costless when, in fact, it's the most costly source of finance. That was certainly one factor behind IBM's failure to take decisive action in response to competitive threats in the mid-80s, and it is clearly a big part of the problem still facing many Japanese and European companies today. They continue to think that equity is free.

So, in the process of converting most of that old equity into debt, LBOs make the cost of capital explicit. Besides being an actual cash cost, it's now in the accounting statements. And, in this sense, it's very much like Stern Stewart's EVA financial management system. Under EVA, if you don't earn the cost of capital, you don't get a bonus. But there's also an importance difference between the simulated ownership of EVA and the actual ownership of an LBO. If you can't make the interest payments in an LBO, not only will managers' bonuses and equity values be reduced, but there will be some unhappy debtholders or bankers to put you into bankruptcy.

So, what happened during the 1980s was a dramatic increase in leveraged transactions that brought about the exit of trapped equity in organization after organization throughout corporate America. To give you a typical example, let's say you have an oil company with a billion dollars worth of cash floating around in corporate headquarters that is targeted for exploration projects or refineries that the market expects to be worth only $600 million. And we know from our research, by the way, that even though investors generally react positively to announcements of capital spending projects, the market had a systematically *negative* response to announcements of big oil projects in the early '80s.

Now, if the capital market is expecting the firm's marginal investments to generate a net economic loss of $400 million, then the company's share price will sell at a large discount to net asset value. You might recall that oil executives were then complaining that you could buy oil on Wall Street more cheaply than drilling for it. But Wall Street was being perfectly rational by discounting the shares. And this price discounting by the market invited the attention of outside investors, corporate raiders. People like Boone Pickens saw that they could add $400 million in value simply by shutting off the investment spigot.

And this same phenomenon of overcapacity, stock market discounting of corporate assets below replacement cost, and corrective leveraged

restructurings took place in industry after industry in America. Besides oil and gas, it happened in paper and forest products, it happened in tires, in publishing and broadcasting, commodity chemicals, financial services, and the list goes on. So, these leveraged restructurings were by and large a productive, value-adding response by our capital markets to this free cash flow problem—to the excess capacity generated by managers' natural tendency to pursue growth instead of the necessary downsizing.

The 1990s—What Went Wrong?

Then, of course, came the problems with the leveraged deals in the late 1980s. Starting in 1989, there was a sharp increase in the number of defaults and bankruptcies of LBOs. Most of the problems, it turns out, came in the deals done in the latter half of the 1980s. Of the 41 LBOs with purchase prices of $100 million or more completed between 1980 and 1984, only one defaulted on its debt. But, of the 83 deals larger than $100 million between 1985 and 1989, at least 26 defaulted and 18 went into bankruptcy.

So what went wrong with the later deals? The problem started with what I have described as a "contracting failure," a gross misalignment of the incentives between the dealmakers who promoted the transactions and the lenders and other investors who provided most of the funding for the deals. By the end of the '80s, dealmakers like Bruce Wasserstein were essentially being paid just to do deals; they were taking out more in upfront fees than they were putting back into the deals. And this arrangement was a sure prescription for too many deals—for deals that were overpriced and structured with too much debt, or with the wrong kind of debt. Now, as Bennett mentioned earlier,

LBOs are back today, and with a different structure. Sponsors are required to put in much more equity, and the deals themselves are less highly leveraged.

But, having said this, there is also some evidence that a private market correction to this contracting problem was already underway when regulators intervened heavily in the summer of 1989. There was already a general move toward larger equity commitments, less debt, lower transaction prices, and lower upfront fees when S&L legislation like FIRREA and HLT regulations created a downward spiral in high-yield bond prices. And when combined with changes in the tax law penalizing private work-outs, tightened oversight by bank regulators made it virtually impossible to reorganize troubled companies outside of Chapter 11. Few people seem to be aware of this, but private work-outs—many of them by Drexel under Mike Milken—were a common event for the first wave of LBOs during the bad recession of 1981-82. But by the time the troubles in the leveraged markets began to emerge in the late '80s, Milken was under investigation and Drexel was in the process of being "RICO'd" out of existence.

So, as a consequence of the tanking of the junk bond markets, the destruction of Drexel, and changes in the bankruptcy laws, the optimal leverage ratio for corporate America suddenly went way down. And, in fact, Milken saw much of this coming because he was advising companies in the late '80s to put equity back into their capital structures. But because of this contracting problem I mentioned, most of the participants in the HLT markets kept going, pushing purchase prices higher and increasing leverage ratios.

Interestingly enough, by the way, the banks seem to have recognized what was going on, because they responded to the higher purchase prices by funding smaller portions of the deals and accelerating their repayment schedules. As a result, their losses on HLTs were remarkably small—so small in fact that the Comptroller of the Currency dropped the HLT category altogether in 1992. The real losers in the overpriced deals turned out to be the junk bondholders. But, again, you have to keep this all in perspective. Total creditors' losses in all the deals of the '80s probably did not exceed $30 billion— a number that seems trivial when set against the trillion or so dollars of value that was added by leveraged restructurings over this period.

Now, what about the '90s? Coming on top of the new constraints on leveraged lending, we saw state takeover laws that basically shut down the old-style corporate control market. And that sharply limited the capital markets' ability to curb the value-destruction that was going on inside many organizations with too much capital. But other forces then came in to fill the vacuum left by takeovers and LBOs. There was a sharp increase in the activism of institutional investors like CALPERS and the United Shareholders Association. And, although much of this was sound and fury with little significance, some of it succeeded in putting pressure on boards to get rid of underperforming CEOs. About the same time, a lot of companies began to show interest in adopting EVA-type systems that attempt to reproduce internally the capital discipline exerted by takeover markets. And, perhaps most important, there was heightened foreign competition in the product markets, which is guaranteed to work if none of these other forces kicks in.

So, given these different pressures on management for efficiency that are operating today, most companies are now in a situation where, if they don't make the necessary adjustments themselves, they're going to have a hard time just staying in business.

The Modern Industrial Revolution

Now, let me say a little bit about the broader environment within which all of this has been taking place. In my 1993 speech to the American Finance Association that Bennett mentioned earlier, I argued that there are striking parallels between what's happened in America in the past 20 years and what went on in the second half of the 19th century—a period historians have called "the Second Industrial Revolution." In both periods, technological advances resulted in huge increases in productivity and dramatic reductions in prices. But, at the same time these changes were increasing productivity, they were causing massive obsolescence and overcapacity in many industries. After the Civil War, for example, there were reductions of as much as 80% to 90% in the prices of important industrial commodities such as kerosene, aluminum, and chemicals. And much as the great M & A wave of the 1890s served to reduce capacity—between 1890 and 1910, some 1,800 U.S. firms were consolidated into about 150— the leveraged takeovers, LBOs, and other leveraged recapitalizations of the 1980s provided a solution to over-capacity building in many sectors of the U.S. economy.

To give you one modern example, think about what happened in the tire industry in the '80s. The introduction of steel radial tires, which last several times longer than the old bias ply tires, suddenly made much of the tire industry obsolete. And leveraged restructurings, like Bridgestone's takeover of Firestone and James Goldsmith's run at Goodyear Tire, succeeded in removing much of the resulting overcapacity. In fact, every U.S. tire company with the possible exception of Cooper has either merged or been restructured.

But, to give you a more dramatic example, think about what has happened to the price of computer chips and computing power in the last 20 years. If we had seen the same kind of price/performance changes in the automobile industry that we've seen in the computer business since 1980, a $20,000 automobile in 1980 would be selling for about two bucks today. And these advances, coupled with advances in communications technology, have had profound changes on how our organizations are run. You can't have that kind of change in such a basic commodity as computer chips and processors without dramatically affecting the ways in which we live and interrelate to each other, both in the social dimension and in the work dimension. Just ask a lot of the people that used to work for the old IBM or, more recently, for DEC.

So what we're seeing are major changes in technology—and it's not just in computers and telecommunications—that are being implemented over and over again in various organizations. The huge increases in output that are being brought about by such advances are driving down market prices. But many managers are not paying attention to the fact that these changes result in excess capacity and huge amounts of free cash flow. In those industries where the overcapacity is really chronic—and commercial banking comes to mind—a large number of firms will have to go out of business. But, of course, nobody wants to volunteer to leave.

So, today we have the same phenomenon going on that we saw both in the 1890s and the 1980s. But there is also another important factor driving today's restructuring activity— and this one promises to be with us well into the next century. In addition to the burst of technological change that's generating excess capacity, we now have political revolutions taking place throughout the world that are compounding the problem. The decline of socialism as a way of organizing business activity is now pretty obvious. And, with the failure of closed, centrally-planned economic systems, we are now seeing Russia and other nations in central and eastern Europe moving in fits and starts toward open capitalist systems. The same thing is going in parts of Latin America, and in India and other Asian countries.

How does all this translate into excess capacity and a free cash flow problem? Over the next 30 years, we're going to see something on the order of 1.2 billion laborers coming into world labor markets. About a billion of those people currently earn less than $3 a day; 250 million earn less than 10 bucks a day. To put that in comparison, average daily wages in the West are about $85, and the total labor force is about 250 million people. What we have discovered in recent years is that you can take relatively modern, up-to-date technology, install it in developing countries, and get 85% to 100% of the productivity of those same plants in the West. Without larger differences in productivity, you can't have these kind of wage differences across national economies surviving for very long. That's why, for example, so much of the U.S. textile industry has moved to Asia. And it's not just textiles; there are lots of other industries where U.S. and European and Japanese facilities have been made obsolete by these wage differentials. There are big implications in all of this for labor union activity, for political conflict, for trade wars.

So, all of these forces that were in play in the '80s are being intensified by the political revolutions around the world. In the end, the migration of some Western facilities and capital to emerging economies is going to make both the industrialized and the developing economies better off. But it's going to require major adjustments—lots of dislocations and downsizings and restructurings—to accomplish such changes.

What do we see going on in the current U.S. financial environment? Well, LBO's have not gone away. They've come back stronger than ever, as many of us predicted they would. The junk bond market did not go away after the destruction of Drexel and the jailing of Mike Milken. As Bennett said earlier, they're at all-time records. As I mentioned earlier, LBOs have got a somewhat different structure now than they had in the '80s. LBO sponsors are putting up much more equity; and besides having less debt, today's LBOs seem to be making greater use of bank debt than public junk debt, especially in the leveraged build-ups. The rise of the leverage buildup is to me an especially interesting development; it's kind of a new version of the focused conglomerate. They seem to growing up everywhere, and they're changing the industrial landscape in another way by consolidating fragmented industries—and reducing excess capacity in the process.

Now, it's hard to imagine that every industry worldwide is afflicted with this problem of overcapacity. There's got to be growth companies out there exploiting profitable investment opportunities—and this is certainly true of much of the high-tech sector in the U.S. And perhaps there are lots of large, mature companies that are finding ways to "reinvent" their businesses, new growth opportunities that are sufficiently related to their core businesses that they can find uses for some of their internal cash. But it's really hard to find an industry where

at least some parts of the business are not experiencing overcapacity.

Before I close, let me say that EVA is another way of accomplishing the central features of an LBO or leveraged acquisition. I am a big fan of EVA as a performance measurement and management compensation system. It is a way of changing internal management accounting statements to simulate many of the benefits of a leveraged buyout without any of the financial risks. It simply prices out what the capital costs for every division in the organization, and then bases management compensation on the extent to which operating profits exceed the capital costs. Making managers' conscious of the cost of capital in this way can have a huge impact on organizational efficiency and values.

So, there's no reason why our public companies can't imitate the effect of virtually all of these highly leveraged capital market transactions that resolve the free cash flow and governance problems. Even if they can't do an LBO, they can make greater use of debt and use it to concentrate ownership. Or, if debt financing is too risky, they can simulate ownership with an EVA-type system. And I'll stop there.

The Distinction between Overpayment and Overleveraging

STEWART: Thank you, Michael. I can't imagine that everyone in the room feels as warmly as you do about the benefits of debt financing. So let me just play the devil's advocate. Let's take the case of Robert Campeau's highly leveraged acquisition of Federated Department Stores in 1988. The whole deal blew up in his face. How can you say that such transactions are so wonderful when we see a deal like that?
JENSEN: Steve Kaplan has done an excellent analysis of the Campeau case, which was published in the *JFE.*

Contrary to what we were told by the business press, the Campeau transaction—or at least the change of control initiated by that transaction—actually created about $1.5 billion in value. What do I mean by that? When Federated and the associated companies eventually emerged from bankruptcy, the value of the total debt and equity was about $1.5 billion higher—even after adjusting for the time value of money and broad market movements over the period—than what they were selling for just before the Campeau bid was announced.

So what was the problem, then? It turns out that Campeau paid a $4 billion premium over market value for the right to run those companies, and you can't make that up on volume. People confuse the overpayment with the fact that the deal was structured with a very large amount of debt. But one of the beneficial effects of structuring an overpaid deal with debt is that it reveals the mistake very clearly, both to the market, and to the managers and to the board of directors. As a result of the bankruptcy filing, Campeau was forced out and replaced by a highly respected bankruptcy trustee, Allen Questrom, who by all accounts did a very creditable job of restoring the company to profitability. In fact, a *New York Times* article made the point that Bloomingdales had never been run as well outside of Chapter 11.

But now let me give you an example of a deal that was done with equity—a vast overpayment involving massive value destruction even though there was nothing in the accounting statements that would indicate that. It was the Time-Warner merger that took place a number of years ago, which was an utter disaster. The loss of value from that deal never showed up in the accounting statements because it was done with equity.

Now, I'm not saying that you can't overleverage an organization, and I'm not advocating that you do it. But it's very important to keep separate overleveraging from overpayment. If you overpay for anything, as I said before, it's real hard to make it up in volume.

A "Public LBO": The Case of FMC

STEWART: You're saying that it is the contractual obligation to repay the debt, the fact that they've borrowed money and pre-committed to paying it back, that forces companies to pay out cash, to sell unrelated businesses, or to take other value-increasing steps they might otherwise be reluctant to take. And, you've also suggested that there is likely to be another kind of benefit of debt financing in these leveraged transactions: Having more debt and less equity makes it easier to concentrate the equity in the hands of the insiders so that not only do they have the discipline of debt, but they have the stronger incentives to create value that come with significant equity ownership.

And this brings me to a question for Cheryl Francis. Cheryl, in your former life as Treasurer at FMC, FMC went through a very dramatic leveraged recapitalization. Essentially, FMC's management said to its shareholders: "Look, our stock is now trading at $70. We'll pay you $70 in cash for each of your shares and give you one share in the new FMC. But management insiders will get a different deal: for each of our shares, we will get no cash but five and two thirds shares in the new company. This way, if the new shares were to be valued by the market at $15, both groups—outsiders and insiders—will come out with a total value of $85, which is obviously a nice premium over $70."

FMC had to borrow $2 billion to make this cash distribution. And al-

though the company remained public, insiders' ownership increased dramatically in relation to the ownership of outsiders. In effect, FMC did a "public LBO." And, as in private LBOs, you have the combination of the discipline of debt with greater concentration of the equity in the hands of insiders.

Cheryl, from your insider's experience, can you provide us with some insights as to why this transaction happened? Was the expected incentive effect important in your decision? And what were the consequences of this dramatic change in capital and ownership structure?

CHERYL FRANCIS: You explained the transaction pretty well. There were also some nice tax structures that were in place at the time that allowed us to get some extra cash that you couldn't get today—for example, we had a $300 million surplus in our pension fund that we were able to use to pay down the debt.

But the transaction was essentially as you described it, Bennett. FMC basically chose to borrow $2 billion one day and then turn around and pay it out to shareholders the next day. And, within four months of the announcement of the transaction, FMC's share price had risen not to $85, but to $97. So, this transformation of FMC's capital structure and ownership structure ended up creating a lot of value for shareholders.

But let me also mention—and I'm surprised you didn't take credit for this, Bennett—that the leveraged recap was the second stage of a shareholder value program that we started at FMC several years earlier. The first stage was the creation of an EVA-like measurement system—a process that was started in 1979, but not fully implemented until 1982. Our leveraged recap affected the right-hand side of the balance sheet; but the left-hand side is extremely important, of course, and you have to keep the two aligned. The leveraging concept worked well at FMC because our EVA-type system had already forced us to run the company for cash and for value. And I believe that's one major reason why FMC's recapitalization proved to be more successful than several others that came along later.

Running the company for cash flow and value prior to the recap also had the benefit of providing us with valuable perspective when evaluating several strategic alternatives that we were considering at the same time. As alternatives to the leverage recap, we were also looking at three very large acquisitions in related businesses. But, after weighing the risks and expected benefits of each alternative, we chose to do the leveraged recap. That is, we chose to stick with the company that we knew how to run, and to run it even more effectively for cash.

So, it's important to understand that we were embedding the capital charge into the business for at least three years prior to the time that we did the recap. Two years before the recap, we bought back a third of our shares, which means that we were already paying out lots of cash well in advance of the recap. But when we looked forward, we saw that we would have to disgorge far more cash because we did not have profitable opportunities for reinvestment inside the company. Thus, our choices were either to acquire or to lever up. We chose to borrow extensively and give it back to the shareholders—and it was a rewarding experience for management as well as the shareholders.

This brings me to the last part of your question: Did the change in leverage and ownership structure change people's behavior? As Mike Jensen said earlier, the EVA concept gets you *part* of the way there with less of the risk. It makes managers conscious of the fact that capital is costly and that value can be created by running the business for cash as opposed to just earnings. But when you actually go out and put the leverage on, it does two things: You now have the financial risk, and it's staring you in the face every day. As a result, the sense of urgency goes up several notches. The second effect comes from management's highly concentrated stock and option ownership, which gives them a much stronger incentive for value creation.

The Case of R.R. Donnelley

FRANCIS: Interestingly enough, my present company, R.R. Donnelley, has adopted an EVA measurement and reward system. It's been in place for about a year-and-a-half. And, although we are facing less risk, there is also less of a sense of urgency about increasing cash flow and value than if we had a highly leveraged capital structure. So, there is a tradeoff that you make between EVA and high leverage in terms of how quickly you want to bring about the change.

STEWART: Why wouldn't R.R. Donnelley pursue a leveraged recap?

FRANCIS: Well, at some point, we may choose to do that. But we haven't reached that point because we haven't proven to ourselves how much cash can really be generated by the company.

And, this is not an idle question, by the way. When John Walter left us to go to AT&T, our stock was depressed, and we felt vulnerable without leadership at the top. So, with the help of some investment bankers, our finance team at Donnelley spent a very long weekend figuring out whether we were now a target for financial buyers. What we then concluded was that a leveraged recap didn't work for Donnelley at that time. But if we succeed in changing our business model so that we can become much more profitable, and produce much higher returns and cash flows, a leveraged recap may become a real choice for us.

STEWART: Mike Jensen pointed to excess capacity as a cause of much of the leveraged activity. Is excess capacity a feature of your business at Donnelley?

FRANCIS: Very much so. It's happening in our business, and in just the ways that Michael explained it. We have market impacts, and we have technology impacts—and we have them both in spades. These two sets of forces have been affecting the company for five years, and the company is only now catching up with that.

But let me step back and say just a little about R.R. Donnelley so people can put this into context. Donnelley is primarily a printing company. We produce magazines, catalogues, telephone directories, and books. We also do financial printing, but this is actually more of a service than a product these days. The company has $6-1/2 billion in revenues; but though we have some overseas operations, I would not describe the company as "global."

The printing industry is a low-growth industry. And, although it has been that way for the past five to seven years, the internal management team did not view it as such. Instead we continued to invest heavily in new capacity. And, compounding this problem of industry-wide overinvestment, the printing industry has also been impacted by technology in the base business. In fact, as a result of some recent technological advances, the replacement of old presses by new ones has the effect of increasing existing capacity. So, just by replacing assets, managers in the industry are effectively choosing to add significant capacity. And, besides this source of overcapacity, we are facing the additional threat from other technologies that could displace some uses of print.

CHERYL FRANCIS

The leveraged recap was the second stage of a shareholder value program that we started at FMC several years earlier. The first stage was the creation of an EVA-like measurement system. The leveraging concept worked well at FMC because our EVA-type system had already forced us to run the company for cash and for value. And I believe that's one major reason why FMC's recapitalization proved to be more successful than several others that came along later.

STEWART: Why wouldn't you just add fewer presses, then?

FRANCIS: You would do that, if you were acting *intelligently*, or *rationally*.

JAY ALLEN: Yes, but it doesn't pay to be the only rational competitor in an *irrational industry*.

FRANCIS: Well, no industry can be irrational for long periods of time. You're much better off by acting rationally, by attempting to understand the economics of what's driving your business and positioning yourself accordingly.

STEWART: Jay, I don't understand what you're saying. Are you saying that if everyone else is being irrational by adding capacity in a low-growth market, then you should be irrational, too?

ALLEN: I am not saying you should be irrational. What I'm suggesting is that you don't benefit from your own rational behavior if all your competitors are irrational. You have to adopt a different strategy.

STEWART: Well, one strategy would be to buy your irrational competitors and turn them into rational ones.

JENSEN: There's a better strategy than that. *Sell* your firm to your irrational competitors. If they're willing to build excess capacity, they're also likely to overpay for your company.

FRANCIS: Yes, that's the ultimate strategy. But few management teams are willing to volunteer to leave the business.

The Case of Tosco

ALLEN: The industry I'm most familiar with is the oil refining business. It's a business that has long been plagued with overcapacity. It's endemic to the business for lots of reasons, including some regulatory factors. The irrational competitors in our business are happy to build new capacity, but they will not even consider buying *existing* capacity. In fact, Tosco is one of the very few oil refiners that will buy capacity from other companies.

So, yes, there is some classical consolidation going on in the industry. There have been a few mergers among players at public market prices that will result in fewer and bigger—though not necessarily more rational—players. But we know of no one else besides Tosco that is buying up other refineries in private market transactions.

STEWART: Let me ask you this, Jay. Michael's theory would suggest that if you're willing to buy other companies in a mature industry that generates a lot of excess cash, then you want to turn off the investment spigot. And to do that, you should make aggressive use of debt finance to fund those acquisitions. Is that what you've done?

ALLEN: We use a fair amount of debt in our acquisitions. Our industry is not one that generates lots of "free cash flow" as you would typically measure it. The uses of cash are driven by outside forces. The Clean Air Act of 1990 effectively mandated $3 or $4 billion of investment by the U.S. oil industry. California's change in specifications for gasoline mandated at least another $5 billion of investment. And those requirements reduced the amount of free cash flow that could be paid out to investors.

STEWART: Okay, but that doesn't really *eliminate* the free cash flow problem. Let me ask you the following question: Why wouldn't the obligation to make such investments already be reflected in the stock prices of the companies that you buy? And if the prices of the companies are now lower to reflect those mandates, why wouldn't you acquire those companies at the lower prices and still use debt to finance the acquisition? You can still finance the transaction with debt because the current stock price has already been reduced by the future investment necessary to comply with the regulatory requirements.

ALLEN: I agree. In fact, Tosco has bought several companies after they already made those investments. And other companies are choosing to leave the industry rather than make such investments—but these companies are few and far between. So, we borrow to the extent we think is reasonable, which is usually 50%, 60%, or sometimes 70%, of the purchase price. And if you want to include working capital, the leverage gets as high as 80% of the transaction. We use such leverage because we know of no other way to get a decent return on our equity investment.

But you have to understand something about our situation. Mike Jensen said, "Why not sell out to your competitors?" Well, we are buying assets at pennies on the dollar. To give you an example, while we were buying a refinery in New Jersey from the Exxon Corporation and paying $175 million for the fixed assets, Amerada Hess was spending a billion dollars to build a comparable facility that was only about two-thirds the size of the refinery we had just purchased.

Now, why wouldn't Amerada Hess have bought that plant instead of us and saved themselves more than $800 million? Well, you'll have to ask them. But this kind of thing happens all the time in our industry.

JENSEN: That's right, and it's called the agency cost of free cash flow. Many managers don't seem to understand that when you're in an industry that is low-growth, and your competitors are clearly reducing their own value by overinvesting, you can make money by downsizing. Provided you do it rationally, there's always a way to pick up some of the money that's on the table or being poured down an investment rathole.

As I said earlier, the managers of oil companies were all complaining in the early '80s that it was much cheaper to buy oil "on Wall Street" than it was to drill for it. But though managers pointed to this as evidence of market irrationality, it was in fact completely rational. The market was recognizing the amount of excess capacity that was being put in place by unwise competitors by putting a value on the shares that was well below the replacement cost of the net assets. And, in this situation, a value-conscious management ought to be able to buy up its less efficient competitors, even at premiums over their current market value, and then cut down on the capital investment, extract the resources from the industry by letting the assets depreciate, and make a lot of money in the process.

ALLEN: That sounds like a good strategy in a stand-alone industry. But the refining industry is by and large part of a larger integrated business. Our main competitors are not independent refiners, but integrated producers like Exxon, Shell, BP, and Amoco. Those integrated oil companies treat our part of the business—refining and marketing—as merely an adjunct to their basic business, which is to produce and sell

crude oil at a huge margin. And, by deciding to be in the refining business, they are choosing to give up a piece of that margin. They tax themselves by maintaining overcapacity in the downstream side of their business, which in turn kills everybody in the downstream side of the business.

So, for the business to really be rationalized will require the integrated companies to separate their downstream business from their upstream business. If and when that happens, the downstream business will rationalize itself very quickly because there's not enough profit to go around. But, until then, the large integrated producers will simply continue to subsidize their downstream operations and to overbuild capacity in anticipation of some future demand that will almost certainly never materialize. These are all common mistakes that a capital-intensive business with unequaled access to capital can be expected to make. And management doesn't really even need to raise outside capital, or to make a conscious choice of debt or equity. The capital just flows in from the business.

JENSEN: You mean it's internally generated?

ALLEN: It's internally generated. At the same time, though, we are seeing some movement toward a solution. Some of the majors are beginning to say to themselves, "Maybe we don't want to be in a downstream business in the U.S. any longer." The downstream business outside of Europe and the U.S. is highly profitable.

JENSEN: But Jay, in the situation you describe, you should be able to make them an offer to buy some of their downstream capacity that they should find attractive—at least if they're doing their calculations correctly.

ALLEN: Well, we have, and we will continue to do so. Indeed, we have purchased two-thirds of what the company is today from integrated com-

JAY ALLEN

O ur main competitors are not other independent refiners, but integrated producers like Exxon, Shell, BP, and Amoco. For the business to really be rationalized will require the integrated companies to separate their downstream business from their upstream business. But, until that happens, the large integrated producers will simply continue to subsidize their downstream operations and to overbuild capacity in anticipation of some future demand that will almost certainly never materialize. These are all common mistakes that a capital-intensive business with unequaled access to capital can be expected to make. And management doesn't really even need to raise outside capital, or to make a conscious choice of debt or equity: the capital just flows in from the business.

panies that either wanted to get rid of a certain plant or, in some cases, became convinced that they shouldn't be fully integrated. In each such case, we have been able to take that plant and make it highly profitable within our own system.

But, remember, this is not a growth industry. It's a very typical, commodity, low-growth business. And getting the large oil companies to sell their refineries requires nothing less than a cultural change at the very highest level. If I'm CEO of Exxon, I am asking myself, "Why should I sell to these guys who're going to make more money with my assets than I did? We've been integrated like this for 60 years. We invented this business, and so what if I've got some assets that aren't earning adequate rates of return."

But Exxon's not a good example of this thinking. They pay attention to returns on *all* their assets. But a lot of other large oil companies don't.

JENSEN: So, one way to view organizations like your own is as entrepre-

neurs who are going about the business of restructuring the industry.

ALLEN: We're rationalizing our industry, but we can't do it unless they're willing to sell.

JENSEN: And you're making money at it.

ALLEN: We make money at it because we buy cheap. Because of this overcapacity problem, it's almost always cheaper in commodity-based industries to buy the assets rather than build them. So, the strategy in our business is to find the guy who's got a nice asset that you can either talk into selling or a guy who's just thrown his hands up in the air, and says, "I want out." That's what we look for. And when we find what we want, we go to Bank of America and borrow to fund a large part of the purchase.

The Case of General Dynamics

JENSEN: Cheryl said earlier that few managements volunteer to go out of business. And that, of course, is one of

the major sources of the free cash flow problem we've been talking about. In shrinking industries, it becomes a game of musical chairs—and nobody wants to be the first to leave.

But I do know of at least one case where management found a way to maximize value for its shareholders under those conditions. There is a very careful study published in the *Journal of Financial Economics* that describes how General Dynamics created enormous value for its shareholders in a shrinking industry. When Bill Anders took over as CEO, it was shortly after the Cold War ended, not a very auspicious time for defense contractors. Anders saw the implications of reduced government spending on defense—the need for massive downsizing—and he went around and tried to buy up a lot of his competitors in the industry. But nobody would sell to him. As Anders put it, he was "hanged on his own theory." So, he had to go back and rethink his strategy.

His next move was to initiate a strategy to shrink the company. Over a two-and-a-half-year period, General Dynamics went from having 98,000 people to less than 27,000. Anders took a company with a backlog of $25 billion that was selling on the market for $1 billion, and he created $4 billion of additional shareholder wealth over the next three years by downsizing. At the end of the three years, he fired himself because they were too small to justify keeping him on.

STEWART: What sort of incentive compensation plan did he have?

JENSEN: Anders recruited a new management team, and he put in a high-powered incentive compensation plan for the top 18 managers. The price of General Dynamics was at $25 when they approved the plan. The plan specified that, for every $10 increase in the stock price, Anders and his top managers got a bonus that was equal to double their annual salary. And, since Anders was then being paid $800,000, he was promised a payment of $1.6 million for every $10 increase in the stock price that stayed there for five or ten days.

When this plan was made public, it caused a lot of heat because the plan triggered a large payment a week after the stockholders approved the plan. It wasn't very long before it triggered the next payment and then the next payment. And, by December of the year the plan was adopted, the Compensation Committee canceled the compensation plan in the face of fierce criticism from the press and commentators—a group from which shareholders were conspicuously absent.

Now, what happened next is a very interesting lesson for those of us who pay attention to compensation. When the board soon after substituted for the old plan a conventional stock option plan that effectively paid him $1.6 million for every $10 increase in the stock price, the controversy over compensation died out completely. The lesson here is that apparently it's okay if you take performance-based pay in the form of equity, but it's not okay if you take it in cash. The cosmetics of this stuff is very important. You cannot be laying people off, selling divisions, shrinking the enterprise—even though it's very hard to get top managers to do that—and be paying top managers large cash bonuses. It just won't wash in the press.

Managerial Incentives and Debt Capacity

STEWART: Mike, do you think there's a relationship between the amount of money a company can borrow and the kind of incentive plan or stock ownership interest that the management has in the company? Do lenders or rating agencies consider management incentives at all in their decision-making?

JENSEN: I think the capital markets are becoming much more sophisticated in how they respond to compensation plans and management incentives. There are lots of examples in the past where organizations implemented high-powered compensation plans and the capital markets didn't pay much attention to it until the cash flows were delivered in the market. The capital markets now appear to understand the import of an announced change in compensation, and they often reflect that in the stock price well before the improvements materialize.

But, having said that, I still think we're a long way from the capital markets seeing it as well as they should.

DENNIS SOTER: I would put this issue of incentives and debt capacity a little differently. I would argue that the *willingness* of companies to assume debt in the first place is a function of the compensation structures that are in place. I agree with Mike that there has been an increase in the sophistication of institutional investors—and, to a lesser extent, in the sophistication of the rating agencies—in responding to corporate incentive structures. But the willingness of management to take on debt is very much a function of the compensation plan and the incentives it provides.

STEWART: Can you give us some examples of that, Dennis?

SOTER: In 1997, we have been involved as adviser in three highly publicized leveraged recapitalizations. The first involved IPALCO Enterprises, which is the holding company for Indianapolis Power & Light. That was followed by SPX Corporation, which is an automotive components manufacturer in Muskegon, Michigan. And the third was Briggs & Stratton in suburban Milwaukee. In each instance, management is working under EVA compensation plans—and, in the case of both SPX and Briggs & Stratton, management has leveraged stock options as well. So, especially in the last two cases, management has a highly-leveraged compensation plan that is pegged to sustainable increases in the stock price. As a consequence, it was far easier to convince those managements that debt is good—and more debt is even better—than it would have been if their compensation structures weren't so closely tied to increases in stock prices.

STEWART: Let's take the example of SPX. Here's a company that announced a decision to make a permanent change in its capital structure, in its mix of debt and equity. Management was going to borrow money to buy back stock. And they were completely eliminating the dividend so as to retain more cash in the firm to service the debt. When they communicated this new financial policy to the mar-

I would argue that the *willingness* of companies to assume debt in the first place is a function of the compensation structures that are in place. In 1997, we were involved as adviser in three highly publicized leveraged recapitalizations. In each instance, management is working under EVA compensation plans—and, in the case of both SPX and Briggs & Stratton, management has leveraged stock options as well. As a consequence, it was far easier to convince those managements that debt is good—and more debt is even better—than it would have been if their compensation structures weren't so closely tied to increases in stock prices.

ketplace, I think the stock went from $43 to $53 a share.

Now, why did the stock price go up so much? Is the market saying that it views debt as being that much cheaper than equity? If so, why is debt cheaper than equity?

SOTER: Well, let me first say that your question may be as much a subject for psychoanalysis as economic analysis. But the market clearly interpreted the change as a very strong positive signal about the future performance of the company.

SPX is a particularly interesting example because it was already a highly-leveraged company when it announced the transaction. It had one issue of senior subordinated notes outstanding rated "B" and a corporate credit rating of "BB–." Even in these circumstances, we were able to convince management—and later the board—that the company would add value by borrowing an additional $100 million to buy back common stock. And I might add that the re-

purchase, which was structured as a Dutch auction to buy up to 21% of the outstanding common stock, eliminated the entire accounting net worth of the company.

STEWART: That also happened in FMC's case, as I recall.

FRANCIS: That's right. Our accounting net worth went to a negative $600 million.

SOTER: The stock price on the day we priced the Dutch auction was $45-7/8. We set the range at $48 to $56. The transaction cleared at $56, which meant that we were not successful in buying back all of the shares we sought. And the stock continued to go up. In fact, within a few weeks, it peaked at just over $70.

As Bennett mentioned, along with this recapitalization the company also announced that it was eliminating cash dividends. There were two important considerations behind this decision. Because dividends are effectively taxed twice, share repurchases are more efficient from a tax

standpoint. And substituting a major stock repurchase for a future series of dividend payments adds to debt capacity by removing an additional layer of fixed costs. Think about it this way: To pay one dollar in cash dividends, a company must earn about $1.60 pre-tax since dividends are paid with after-tax cash. And if the company can borrow at, say, 8 percent, it means that the $1.60 in pre-tax income that has to be generated to pay $1 in cash dividends could instead service interest expense on $20 of debt. This means that every dollar in dividends paid represents a reduction in debt capacity of at least $20 in today's capital market environment. So, by eliminating SPX's dividend, we effectively increased its debt capacity enough to fund the stock buyback.

A Brief Digression on EPS vs. Economic Profit

STEWART: Let me ask Mike O'Neill a question. Mike, Bank of America

THE STERN STEWART ROUNDTABLES

has been buying back a lot of stock lately. Do you share the conviction that dividends don't matter to your shareholders?

O'NEILL: When we ask them, most of our investors say they want both port and brandy, dividends and share repurchases. But we clearly have a preference for share repurchases because, as Dennis just suggested, for those investors that are not institutional there is a tax advantage to selling your stock and getting capital gains treatment versus ordinary income.

I know you're going to hate this, Bennett, but we also think that stock repurchases help support our stock price through their effect on our earnings per share. This does not mean that we manage the company to maximize EPS, or that we use it as the primary measure for evaluating our performance. But it is something we look at.

STEWART: Why?

O'NEILL: Because our investors look at it. Aren't we strange?

But, again, Bennett, share repurchase is something we do for more fundamental economic reasons. It just happens to have this nice EPS side-effect that can prove useful in certain circumstances—including meetings with some securities analysts.

ALLEN: We too feel that we need to manage the company for EPS. We do that because that's what our shareholders tell us they want. But, at the same time, we are also highly leveraged because the business doesn't generate adequate returns to shareholders if you don't leverage. We understand that equity is expensive. In fact, we find that equity is *super*-expensive, because you're spreading a fixed amount of earnings power over more and more shares.

So when we buy in shares—and we've done a good deal of it in the past—that helps our EPS. And EPS matters. It matters an awful lot.

STEWART: Well, let me ask you a question. Suppose your earnings are $10, you sell for 10 times earnings, and so your stock price is $100. And let's say you earn a five percent return on investment, and you reinvest all the earnings back in the business. This means next year's earnings are $10.50. Now, according to the accounting model of the firm, you should still sell for 10 times earnings, and so your stock price should go to $105.

But what have you really accomplished in all this? The stock price went up by $5, but you invested $10. In effect, you destroyed $5 in value. That's what we refer to as a loss of $5 of Market Value Added, or MVA. It's the difference between the value that you create and the capital that you invest back in the business. Now, Jay, is that kind of growth in earnings per share a good deal for the shareholders?

ALLEN: I agree completely with your analysis. But let me also say that, if you grow the earnings by only five percent a year, you're not going to have a P/E of 10.

STEWART: Well, let me put it a little differently. You can increase earnings per share by earning any positive rate of return whatsoever on your retained earnings. My question is this: Is there some minimum rate of return on capital your company must earn so that your market value will increase by at least as much as the capital you retain in your business? As Warren Buffett put it, any moron can increase earnings. If you just put more money in a savings account, you get more earnings.

ALLEN: Taken to its logical conclusion, though, doesn't your argument suggest that growth in earnings per share is a *bad* thing for shareholders?

STEWART: No, not at all. Earnings per share is simply a misleading measure. It's often the case that when

earnings per share is up, the EVA is up, too.

O'NEILL: That's right. And I think it is possible to triangulate between the two measures, EPS and economic profit, while using economic measures as the driver. But, at the same time, you have to look at EPS because there are people out there—misguided though they may be—who continue to rely on it as their primary measure of performance.

STEWART: We ran an interesting experiment several years ago. We looked at 1,000 U.S. companies and found that, over a three- to five-year period, the change in the company's MVA had a much higher correlation with the change in EVA than with the change in earnings or earnings per share.

O'NEILL: I absolutely agree. We've done the same work.

STEWART: Well, then what's the argument?

O'NEILL: I guess I'm just a little less messianic than you are.

STEWART: Well, when you have a good thing, run with it. But, more seriously, Mike, as I'm sure you're aware, the research departments at places like Goldman Sachs, Smith Barney, First Boston, and Morgan Stanley are now paying a lot of attention to our EVA concept.

Dividends and Stock Buybacks: The Case of Bank of America

O'NEILL: But, as I was saying, in this business of repurchasing our shares, the EPS effect is essentially just a by-product, a sideshow. What we're really trying to do at Bank of America is to manage the company on the premise that equity capital is in fact the most expensive source of funding. Using a now pretty well-established technique called "RAROC"—which is shorthand for "risk adjusted return on capital"—we allocate eq-

Bank of America is now generating about $3-1/2 billion a year in net operating cash flow, and we are investing only about $600 to $700 million back in our businesses. So that leaves us with a large excess. We are in an industry that's been characterized by overcapitalization and overcapacity. In the past, bankers have had the hubris to think that they could all expand and make money across a broad range of financial services and markets. So, the agency costs of free cash flow have been alive and well in the banking industry.

What we're trying to do at Bank of America is to manage the company on the premise that equity capital is the most expensive source of funding. We say to ourselves, "If we can't put this money to use by earning returns above our cost of capital, we're going to give it back."

uity capital to all of our businesses and try to hold the people running those businesses accountable for that capital. If we find a business that is generating returns below our cost of capital, we withdraw funds from that business. At the same time, we invest as aggressively as prudence will allow in the businesses that are generating returns above the cost of capital.

Bank of America is now generating about $3-1/2 billion a year in net operating cash flow, and we are investing only about $600 to $700 million back in our businesses. So that leaves us with a large excess. Like the other companies represented at this table, we are in an industry that's been characterized by overcapitalization and overcapacity. In the past, bankers have had the hubris to think that they could all expand and make money across a broad range of financial services and markets. So, the agency costs of free cash flow have been alive and well in the banking industry. Bankers as a group took their excess

cash and reinvested it, often with pretty poor results.

What we're trying to do today at BAC is to be more disciplined. We say to ourselves, "If we can't put this money to use productively—that is, by earning returns above our cost of capital—we're going to give it back." That is what we have done for the last couple of years at B of A. And the payoff from that strategy has been showing up in our stock price over the last two years.

STEWART: But, Mike, it still sounds like you have kind of a hedging strategy with respect to dividends and stock repurchase. You continue to pay dividends, and you also buy back stock. You're trying to give investors both. But, if you believe there's a tax benefit to buying back stock instead of paying dividends, why wouldn't you do what SPX did and just completely eliminate the dividend? This way you can buy back even more stock, and enhance your debt capacity in the process? If that

strategy works a little, why doesn't it work a lot?

O'NEILL: We are a large-cap company, with a market cap approaching $50 billion. We've got a lot of institutional investors, and a number of them continue to have dividend requirements that we just try to meet. Many of our institutional investors will not invest in a company that doesn't have at least a 2 percent dividend yield. We think there is value to having a broad investor base, and so we attempt to pay the minimum required level of dividends.

But having said that, I will also concede that our largest institutional investors are showing an increasing preference for buybacks over dividends. Fidelity, for instance, is a good example of an investor that likes share repurchases. Now, if I wanted Fidelity as my only shareholder, I might consider eliminating our dividend. But I think it's a value-adding strategy for a large-cap company to attract a broad range of shareholders.

Leverage, Dividends, and Investor Clientele

JENSEN: Dennis, what happened to the shareholder base in SPX after the elimination of the dividend and the leveraged recap? When Sealed Air did a similar transaction and eliminated the dividend, about 75% of its shareholders turned over within a couple of weeks of the announcement of the transaction. And the net effect was a large increase in value.

But Sealed Air had a market cap of less than $1 billion. And I agree with Mike O'Neill that, if you tried this with a company like Bank of America with a $50 billion equity base, the company's market value could take a big hit because of institutional constraints demanding all kinds of things like a positive book value of equity and a minimum dividend yield.

SOTER: Let me first say that if all SPX did was to eliminate the dividend, the market reaction would have been much less positive. Three years ago, as Bennett mentioned earlier, we were adviser to FPL Group, the parent company of Florida Power & Light, when it announced a cut in its dividend. Like many utilities, its dividend payout ratio had crept up over 90%, and management felt that a 90% payout was simply not sustainable in an era of increased competition. We convinced them to cut the dividend by just under one-third.

Now, in that particular case, there was no change in the company's capital structure policy. Upon the announcement of the dividend cut, the stock fell from about $32 to $27-1/2, a drop of about 15%. But, as new investors replaced those who were selling, it took less than three weeks for the stock to recover. And, as Bennett told you earlier, FPL's stock ended up outperforming the S&P electric index over the next year.

JENSEN: What was the total market cap of FPL at the time of the elimination of the dividend?
SOTER: It was probably around $2.5 to $3 billion.
JENSEN: But, as Mike O'Neill was suggesting, if you do that with a company that has a $50 billion market cap, you could take a huge hit during the time it takes for the EPS and institutionally-constrained crowd to drop your stock and for the value-based and cash flow sharpies to move in.
SOTER: But there's a way to limit that clientele effect. It's one that we used when one of our clients, IPALCO, became the second profitable utility to voluntarily cut its dividend. In this case, as with FPL, the cut was about 33% At the same time it announced its dividend cut, IPALCO also announced a Dutch auction stock repurchase that would be financed with additional debt. In effect, management said to its stockholders: "If you don't like our new dividend policy, we're giving you the opportunity to get out at a premium."

And let me share with you an interesting aspect of the IPALCO situation. No industry prizes its investment-grade ratings more than utilities because they are constantly in the marketplace raising capital. In the course of borrowing $400 million to buy back 21% of its stock, we leveraged the company from a debt-to-capital ratio of 42% to 68%. At 42% debt to capital, IPALCO's ratings were "AA–" by Standard & Poor's and "AA" by Moody's. And the fascinating thing is that, when the company moved to 68%, its bond ratings were reaffirmed by both rating agencies. Absolutely nothing happened to the bond rating because we were able to demonstrate to the rating agencies that the book-debt-to-capital ratio had no economic significance. In fact, Standard & Poor's was even considering *increasing* the

company's rating to "AA" because we were able to demonstrate that the after-tax cash savings from cutting the dividend would be significantly greater than the after-tax interest expense that would be incurred in financing the stock buyback.

Now, one question that invariably arises is: How much can you afford to pay when you buy back your own stock? Our answer is this: It doesn't matter how much you pay to buy back your stock so long as after the expiration of the tender offer, the stockholders that don't tender are at least as well off as the stockholders who tender. And, in fact, in all three of the situations that I've described—IPALCO, Briggs & Stratton, and SPX—the nontendering stockholders ended up at least as well off as the stockholders who did tender.

STEWART: And it's important to keep in mind that the managements of those companies were among the non-tendering stockholders. For example, both John Blystone at SPX and Fred Stratton and the top management team at Briggs & Stratton have large stock or leveraged stock option positions. And, especially in such cases, management's decision not to tender their shares can send a very powerful signal to the market.

So one of the reasons why the market price would not go down is that you're buying your stock back at the higher price and management is not selling. What stronger signal of management confidence could you provide to the marketplace?

FRANCIS: Bennett, I think there are some other practical considerations that might keep you from cutting the dividend. At Donnelley I have a problem that maybe you can help me with. Regardless of what the general market thinks about the inefficiency of dividends relative to stock repurchase, 18% of my company's shares are held by the Donnelley family. And, because of restrictions in their trust agreements, they can't sell those shares. They want income, and so reducing the dividend in our case is not likely to happen.

STEWART: Well, you could say to them, "Look, let's calculate the present value of the dividends we would pay for the next five years. And, instead of paying it for the next five years, we'll go out and borrow that amount, and we'll pay you today the present value of the dividend." Now, it's true, that this would force them to pay today the same tax that they would have paid over the five years. But this way the company can borrow money and benefit from the tax deductibility of the interest payments. What's more, the company's financing capacity will not be affected because the additional debt can be serviced by the forgone dividend payments.

So this way the company is better off and the family is no worse. In fact, they will be better off, too, to the extent the stock price is higher as a result. What's the matter with that?

FRANCIS: Well, that's an option we might consider.

STEWART: And this strategy will become all the more attractive if capital gains tax rates are cut. It seems to me that every company in the U.S. will have to reexamine its capital structure and their choice of dividends and share repurchases if capital gains tax rates are dropped in some significant way.

Growth Companies and the Limits of Debt Financing

STEWART: When I visit companies and make the arguments for debt that you have heard this afternoon, some CFOs will say to me, "Well, Bennett, I hear your argument. But, to tell you the truth, we look out over the next three to five years, and we see ourselves generating internally a lot more cash than we can productively reinvest. So, for us, debt is just unnecessary." My typical response to them is, "The less you need to borrow, the more you ought to borrow. Debt is advantageous both from a tax point of view and from an incentive or control point of view. You should borrow money if you're able to, not because you need to."

MICHAEL DE BLASIO: So far, we've only been talking about low-growth companies, about companies that generate more cash than they can reinvest in their basic business. But what about companies that are growing at 30% or 40% a year? Do any of these arguments apply to these kind of companies?

STEWART: About five years ago, we worked with a company called Equifax. They had recently made a number of acquisitions, and it was part of their strategy to continue to grow aggressively through acquisition. But they also had a very conservative capital structure, with only about 20% debt. At the same time, they were paying lots of dividends.

In that case, the company ended up making two major changes: it adopted our EVA performance measurement and incentive compensation, and it did a leveraged recapitalization in the form of a Dutch auction share repurchase. The company's debt to capital ratio went up significantly. And, even though this was a service business without much in the way of tangible assets or other collateral, management was able to persuade the rating agencies that the company's creditworthiness was largely unaffected. True, its bond rating was dropped from A to BBB. But, as Dennis was suggesting, this was likely to be closer to the optimal capital structure than their A-rated structure with 20% debt.

JENSEN: That case is really the essence of the leverage build-up strategy that we've been hearing a lot about lately. These are by some measures very rapidly growing companies that are growing through highly-leveraged acquisitions in the same business. They typically occur in fragmented industries that are consolidating. And they seem to be creating large amounts of value very quickly in industries that are actually shrinking—again, because of the existence of too many players and the need for consolidation.

The leverage is playing an important role in this process. Although leverage build-ups don't operate with the same amount of debt as the LBOs of the 80s—they tend to run with leverage ratios around 50-60%—the debt is soaking up the excess cash flow and thus adding value in these industries in much the same way as the leveraged deals of the '80s. And, as I suggested earlier in the case of Campeau, the use of debt makes it a "razor-edged" strategy in the sense that, if you overpay for those acquisitions, it's going to show up very quickly in the accounting statements and in your ability to make the debt service payments.

DE BLASIO: Yes, but these leveraged build-ups are a very different animal from the kind of classic high-growth companies that I'm thinking about. Take the case of a company whose basic business is growing very rapidly—and let's say the stock is selling at about 40 times earnings to reflect that growth. What is the role of debt, or stock repurchase, in these kinds of situations?

STEWART: Stewart Myers once said that all corporate assets can be classified as one of two kinds: "assets in place" and "growth options." And Stew went on to argue that while assets in place should be financed with lots of debt, growth options generally should be funded with equity.

145

So, I agree with you, Mike, that if much of your company's current value consists of growth options, and if that value is premised on management's ability to "exercise" those options by continuing to make strategic investments, then the high-leverage strategy could end up imposing large costs and destroying value.

And, in fact, some of the best empirical work on capital structure would seem to bear this out. About two years ago, our journal ran an article summarizing a study by Michael Barclay, Clifford Smith, and Ross Watts of the University of Rochester. After looking at both the capital structures and dividend policies of some 6,800 companies—all the companies covered by COMPUSTAT—over a 30-year period, they concluded that the most important factor in determining both a company's leverage ratio and its dividend payout was the extent of its profitable investment opportunities. The study found that companies whose value consisted largely of intangible growth options—as measured by high market-to-book ratios and high R & D-to-value ratios—had significantly lower leverage ratios and dividend yields than firms whose value was represented mainly by tangible assets—as indicated by low market-to-book and high depreciation-to-value ratios.

So, it seems to me we need to be more careful in making distinctions about which kinds of companies will benefit from high leverage. As Mike De Blasio was suggesting, companies whose value consists largely of attractive reinvestment or growth opportunities are going to stay away from debt. For these companies, the tax and control benefits of debt are going to be much less important than the need to maintain continuous access to the capital markets.

Take Yahoo!, for example, a company with the exclamation point built right into its name. That company is so risky that management goes out and raises equity and then parks it in marketable securities. It's really negative debt, if you will. And this strategy has a major tax disadvantage: the returns on those securities are taxed twice, once inside the company and then again on distribution—though such companies typically don't pay much in the way of dividends. But for these companies with vast growth opportunities and high business risk, incurring this tax disadvantage is probably a small price to pay for the increase in financial flexibility.

Do you agree with that, Michael? We're close to Silicon Valley, and I see you've got your Apple computer here for your lecture. Would a lot more debt be good for Apple Computer or a high-tech Silicon Valley company? **JENSEN:** Well, I agree that high leverage can impose big costs on companies with high operating risk and lots of investment opportunities. But such companies, by definition, do not have a free cash flow problem. They have lots of *profitable* investment opportunities. The companies that will benefit most from debt are those that don't have profitable investment opportunities. The problem I see, though, is the willingness of managers to see profitable growth opportunities where they just don't exist—and where the markets are clearly telling them not to do it.

But let me add one more reason to your argument about why companies should be careful in using debt. A company's capital structure can also affect its ability to sell its products. Financial firms like Bank of America operate with very high credit ratings because their customers—their depositors, their relationship borrowers with lines of credit, and their swap counterparties—put a high value on the assurance that the bank will be around to make good on its commitments down the road. Many of a bank's customers have effectively made an investment in the bank, and a high credit rating can help "bond" the bank's commitment to making the payoff.

And the same argument applies to the product warranties provided by some industrial companies. For example, I'm going to hold Apple personally responsible for the decline in the value of my PowerBook 3400 if the company goes under. So, even if the capital markets allowed Apple to borrow a lot, management has got to pay very careful attention to how consumers like me are going to view that financing decision. The capital markets aren't perfect, and in some cases too much leverage can absolutely kill the company by reducing demand for its products.

Capital Structure, Incentives, and Performance: More on Bank of America

SOTER: In the course of advising companies on recapitalization strategies, we've analyzed almost 25 different industries. And in virtually all of those industries, we have found that the optimal capital structure—that is, the mix of debt and equity that results in the lowest weighted-average cost of debt and equity capital—is *below* an investment-grade rating.
FRANCIS: Then why do you suppose there are so few companies operating there now?
SOTER: I think the primary reason has to do with the incentive structures at most large public companies. Most compensation plans don't motivate that kind of behavior on the part of management.
STEWART: Well, let me turn to Mike O'Neill and put that question to him. Mike, what real incentives are there for the chief financial officer, or the treasurer of a company, to promote

this kind of recapitalization? After all, it does appear—at least on the surface—to be a much riskier strategy. It is also often a value-adding strategy, but think of the personal risk if it doesn't work out. What are the incentives for the chief financial officer to push the capital structure and dividend policy issue to the point where you do in fact minimize the cost of capital? What's the dynamic of all this in an organization?

O'NEILL: Generally, the motivating force is self-interest, *enlightened* self-interest. People like to get rewarded for doing a good job. And if you link their pay to shareholder returns, people get on the bandwagon pretty quickly.

We've been at this for a couple of years at Bank of America. It has not been easy because it is a departure from the way things were done in the past. Historically, our mission was to grow. We were very successful in accomplishing that goal under Dick Rosenberg. The investments in expanding our franchise undertaken during that period really laid the basis for our future growth and profitability. But our overarching mission now is the creation of value for our shareholders.

Our biggest challenge in this undertaking has been to impress on our people that capital has a cost—and that if you do not generate returns above that cost, your stock is unlikely to do very well. The beauty of the argument is that when investors believe that you are going to do better, those expectations get built into your current stock price. This way, you are often rewarded even before you have achieved the expectation. So if you do a reasonable job of communicating the strategy and implementing it in the early stages, the market will often give you the benefit of the doubt, particularly in the benign environment that we've been blessed with recently.

STEWART: Mike, it's also my impression that when companies go through major policy changes—such as B of A's move to economic profit or through a leveraged restructuring like the one Cheryl went through at FMC—one of the critical determinants of success is the active involvement and complete commitment by the chief executive officer.

O'NEILL: That has absolutely been the case at Bank of America. In fact, it's really *all* his fault. Dave Coulter has pushed it through, and he's done a terrific job of getting the board and other constituencies convinced that this is the right way to go.

What I'm talking about is our use of "economic profit" to evaluate the performance of our different operations and, to some extent, as a basis for rewarding managers. Like your EVA system, Bennett, our economic profit measures the dollar amount by which the operating earnings of each of our profit centers—and, in some cases, our individual customer relationships—exceeds its capital charge. The capital charge in turn is calculated by multiplying our corporate-wide cost of capital, which we estimate to be about 12%, by the amount of capital that has been assigned to the profit center. What is different for us, as a financial institution as opposed to an industrial firm, is the extent to which the *implicit* capital backing our operations is different from our actual cash or regulatory capital.

So, we are now doing economic value-based management. As far as our capital structure goes, we've got regulators who sort of limit what our capital structure can look like within a fairly narrow range. Moreover, we are involved in a number of businesses where we feel it is essential to maintain a credit posture no lower than AA. This means that, in managing our capital structure, we have a

limited range of options for replacing our equity by issuing more debt. Given the constraints put on us both by regulators and by our customers, we have not found it a good idea to borrow much more than our principal competitors.

But what we have done is to use our cash flow to buy back some of our excess equity, and to get the most out of the equity that we are operating with. And our attempt to maximize economic profit, as suggested, has led us to look at all the businesses that we're in, assign capital based on the risk, and make judgments about where we can and where we can't make a go of it. Based on this analysis, we have also made decisions to get out of businesses where there appeared to be little chance of ever earning our cost of capital.

An Alternative to LBOs: Leveraged Stock Options

STEWART: Well, Mike, you say that you are constrained in your ability to use high leverage. But there is a way that bankers can experience the thrill of victory and agony of defeat of a leveraged buyout without leveraging the bank at all. It's by using a concept called "leveraged stock options," or LSOs.

To illustrate how an LSO operates, consider a company with a current share price of $10. The initial exercise price on the LSO is set at a 10% discount from the current stock price, or $9, making the option worth $1 right out of the gate. But instead of just handing the LSOs to management, managers are required to purchase them—generally with a portion of their EVA cash bonus—for the $1 discount, and that money is put at risk.

Besides requiring managers to make an initial investment, another important difference between LSOs and regular options is that the exercise price is projected to increase at a rate that approximates the cost of capital, less a discount for undiversifiable risk and illiquidity. Now, let's just assume that rate of increase is 10% per annum. In this case, over a five-year period—and ignoring compounding for simplicity—the exercise price will rise 50% above the current $9 level to $13.50. This way, management pays $1 today for an option to purchase the company's stock, currently worth $10, for $13.50 five years down the road.

Only if the company's equity value grows at a rate faster than the exercise price will management come out ahead. In fact, if the exercise price rises at a rate equal to the cost of capital (less dividends), then the LSOs wll provide exactly the same incentives as an EVA bonus plan.

O'NEILL: Bennett, we've done essentially the same thing with our own stock option plan.

STEWART: What do you use as the growth rate for the exercise price?

O'NEILL: We looked at the performance of the S&P 500 banks over the past ten years, and we found that total shareholder returns increased about 9% per year, on average, over that ten-year period. Then we made the simplifying assumption that the next ten years would be like the last ten, and we essentially increased the strike price over the eight-year life of our options by roughly 9%

STEWART: Per year?

O'NEILL: Effectively, yes. We have three different tranches of options, each with higher exercise prices. So these are *premium-priced* stock options. It's a variation on the leveraged stock option. Transamerica has a similar plan. But, to my knowledge, we are the only large bank in America using such a program. And although we put it in fairly recently, it is clearly having quite an impact on the way our people behave.

The Internal LBO

STEWART: Besides leveraged stock options, there's another strategy for replicating the incentives of LBOs within companies that have multiple operating units. Suppose you run a company with lots of different divisions; and, though you would like to use the incentive effect of leverage to motivate your operating heads, you don't want to subject your company to the financial risk. In that case, you can take an individual business unit and have it borrow money nonrecourse to the parent, and then have the unit pay the money out to the parent company. In effect, you're substituting nonrecourse unit debt for corporate debt. And, if you at the same time grant or sell the operating managers an equity stake in the business unit, then you have what I call an "internal LBO."

Why would you want to do this? In the 1980s, I was struck by the fact that KKR and other buyout firms were buying business units from conglomerates and getting fantastic returns. And I asked myself, "Why wouldn't a company want to do that on its own?" What's more, you don't even actually have to borrow the money. You can just simulate the transaction on a piece of paper. You can just pretend that the business unit borrowed the money, and the only real part of this transaction is that the managers of the business unit will be required to buy an equity stake. The value of the unit will be appraised each year according to the firm's success in earning a return over and above the imputed debt service on the fictional debt.

But, again, we're trying to find ways to compete with the KKRs of the world by simulating *inside the firm* what otherwise can be very expensive and risky to do from an external point of view.

O'NEILL: Again, we have done that at Bank of America, at least in a limited way. We have a private equity business with a little over $2 billion of investments. These are KKR-type buyout investments, but obviously smaller than KKR's because of our regulatory limitations. But, essentially, we force the people who arrange the deals at B of A to *coinvest* in the deals that they do. These deals are pretty highly leveraged, and our success rate in this business has been nothing short of terrific.

ALLEN: Mike, how do you manage the cultural differences between the more traditional commercial bankers in your organization, and the investment and merchant bankers you're trying to attract and keep satisfied? How do you manage that cultural diversity?

I ask the question because I wonder what would happen to a lot of corporate divisions if they went through an LBO, or allowed some of their managers to act as if they were LBO'd. Would such changes really affect their behavior? Or would you, in most cases, have to change management? Regardless of which way you do it, though, it seems to me that everybody who isn't in on that type of plan will soon be unhappy with those who are in on it.

STEWART: Jay, you suggested that you might have to change the management if you were to LBO, or even pretend to LBO, a division. Doesn't that suggest that you might not have the right people running your divisions?

ALLEN: My impression is that most of the LBOs were done either with a new management team, or by the exceptional managers that either chose to stick around, or were asked by the buyout firm to stay on. And it's also my impression that those managers who stayed became exceptional performers in large part because they had to shove in their own personal equity.

Now, the question you're asking is: Do we have the right managers for our divisions? It's a question we ask each other every day. But big companies have trouble hiring and firing at great speed, and that can be a big obstacle to doing this kind of internal LBO. And, if you do carve out parts of your company and provide ownership incentives, then you're bound to run into problems in integrating an entrepreneurial LBO culture with the more traditional corporate culture.

JENSEN: I think this issue of mixing cultures is a big potential problem. In fact, it's the one of the major costs of becoming a large organization. Small companies can pick off pieces of large organizations just by paying people in a way that large companies can't because of these pressures for equity in compensation. And, except in cases where there are large economies of scale and scope, we see small companies taking business from large ones all the time.

But even so, I still think large organizations would benefit from doing more of these internal LBOs than they have done to date. And I feel certain that if we required divisional managers to coinvest in their projects, we would see a lot more projects turned down that are now routinely approved based on the typical hockey-stick projections. Because now they're betting their families' wealth on it.

ALLEN: Well, let me give you the other side of that theory. We're old fashioned at Tosco, and we continue to leave the major capital spending decisions to senior management. Division heads can propose but they don't dispose. So the discipline is really the CEO's, and he's already laid down the law on that.

JENSEN: That kind of centralization can work in an industry that's fairly

mature, and where there is little technological change and market conditions are relatively stable. In those cases, the "specific knowledge" necessary to make the right investment and production decisions may well be at the top of the organization. On the other hand, we have all kinds of evidence from studies of Harold Geneen's ITT and other conglomerates that centralized decision-making will fail if you're in a lot of different businesses, and your businesses are highly dynamic. As has been strongly suggested in the case of ITT, too much centralization can easily lead a company to underinvest in potentially profitable businesses while overinvesting in mature businesses.

So, in many organizations, the critical issue has been to get those decision rights out of corporate headquarters and down to the divisions.

ALLEN: What you're saying, at bottom, is that diversified companies typically don't work well because top management is incapable of managing all of them equally well.

JENSEN: That's right, or at least that's one of the main implications. The traditional conglomerate with centralized controls and decision-making is bound to fail in today's environment.

ALLEN: I agree completely. I've seen it in my own life, and I've seen it in others'. We all took on businesses saying, "We're smart people, we can do this." And the typical outcome was that the new operation you thought you could manage ended up taking nine-tenths of your time, even though it was only three-tenths of your total business—and you never made a dent in it. And the worst thing about this kind of diversification is that it forces you to ignore your good businesses.

So, my feeling, based on both my own experience and that of many others I've observed, is that corporate diversification is a bad idea.

Broadening the Issue

ANIRUDDHA ROY: Up to this point, we have been discussing corporate governance as if the resolution of agency costs were the only major problem confronting corporate managers and their boards of directors. But surely there are other issues that are at least as important, if not more important, than paying out free cash flow and preventing managements from overinvesting. Surely management must spend at least as much time thinking about whether they have the right technology and the right supplier networks as they do about having the right dividend and financial policy. Successful managements must devote as much effort to ensuring they have the optimal level and kinds of *human* capital as they do to figuring out the optimal mix of financial capital. As C.K. Prahalad likes to say, capital is not the scarce resource these days; it's human talent and technology that are most likely to distinguish the exceptional value creators from the mediocre.

So, these are all aspects of corporate decision-making that strike me as contributing more to future corporate value than financial policies and whether you choose EVA or some other measure to evaluate your performance. And, what concerns me about this discussion is that an *exclusive* focus on stock price performance or some financial measure can end up reducing value, especially in the case of high-growth companies. Such measures are also likely to discourage mature companies from seeking out new sources of growth and so transforming themselves into growth companies.

JENSEN: Well, I agree with you completely in one sense. And that is, if you have the wrong business strategy, or if you hire the wrong people, you're going to destroy value. My point is this: You can do all those things right, but if you screw up these financial issues at the top level of the organization where the cash comes pouring in, the company can destroy much of the value that's been created on the real side of the business. Top management can go out on elephant hunts—acquisition campaigns that systematically destroy value—or make major investment decisions without actually looking at the numbers. So, you can have everything done right at the lower levels in the organization. But if you don't get the right governance structure at the top—and finance can be a critical part of that governance structure—the operating value of the company can be frittered away.

Now, if you want to push this discussion beyond finance, let me say that I think there are non-financial aspects of corporate governance where corporate America is continuing to make serious mistakes. We tend to have systematically overcentralized organizations. As I said earlier, we now have evidence of the enormous destruction of value by conglomerates before many of them were taken apart in the '80s. And there's still a lot of that centralized, conglomerate mentality lingering in corporate America. What we have found in our field work at Harvard is that, in large diversified enterprises, the decision rights migrate to the top where uninformed people—not stupid people, but *uninformed* people—lose track of what's going on lower down. As Jay was suggesting earlier, although you may have the most intelligent top management team in the world, top management in large organizations can't possibly have sufficient "specific" knowledge to make the right decisions at the division level.

In contrast to large organizations, the LBO associations, private equity

groups, and venture capitalists that I've studied seem to know very well how to assign decision rights so as to strike the proper balance of decentralization and centralization. But, once you start moving into larger organizations, getting the decision-making authority in the right place becomes a very difficult problem. And, again, that's one of the big problems with large organizations. Even after all the downsizing, I would say that we still have too many large, diversified public corporations in this country. After all these years, ITT is still attempting to get down to the right structure.

So, let me endorse your comment that, in a full-ranging discussion of organizational policy, all of those things you mentioned are critically important. I started out my remarks by saying that the reason capital structure matters is not because of any financial alchemy; as Bennett put it, there is no magic in leverage. The reason finance matters is because it affects real operating decisions; it affects what actually goes on at lower levels in the organization.

To give you just one example, I visited FMC about two years after they had done their buyout in 1986. And I was astonished at how the middle managers I was talking to understood, and felt threatened by, the possibility of bankruptcy. My recollection, Cheryl, was that your employees owned about 45% of the company through an ESOP plan...

FRANCIS: It was 40%.

JENSEN: 40% of the company. And that ownership was playing a big role in the decisions that were being made. People at all levels of the organization suddenly became concerned about the level of capital expenditures and began paying attention to expected returns. In fact, I remember being led by a secretary from one meeting to another; and, as we were going down

the elevator, she remarked that yesterday the company's stock price had reached an all-time high. She added that it didn't *close* at an all-time high, but it reached the high during the day. And when I asked her why she was interested in this, she mentioned the ESOP and her concerns about the company's future.

Now, if you walk into the typical corporate environment, you will find that only people at the very top are concerned with those kinds of decisions and their consequences. When you use financial changes to make a significant change in ownership, that can affect awareness and decision-making throughout the organization.

And it is that kind of decentralized decision-making, combined with highly concentrated ownership, that explains the success of LBOs in this country. We've had well over 3,000 LBOs since the mid-1970s. Although the business press gives you the opposite impression, very few of them ever come back public. And very few of them, except for some very large ones at the end of the 1980s, went into bankruptcy. It has been the most successful wave of restructuring in American history. And it continues to go on.

The LBO represents a new organizational "technology," if you will. And those of you in corporate America who are running old-style companies and not paying attention to what this new LBO technology can do for you could be blind-sided by changes in the product market and the competition by people who are taking advantage of the technology. As I said before, public companies can imitate these firms in lots of ways without going private. Besides levering up, they can get more equity ownership, shrink their board size, and even persuade large investors to become long-term owners in their companies, if not part of their board.

The Balanced Scorecard vs. Shareholder Value

ROY: But, I am still concerned about the effect of an exclusive focus on shareholder value. If you look at companies like General Motors, IBM, Phillips, and Wang that have gone through very difficult periods, the stock market was the last to see the troubles that were coming on. The management literature reveals that not only people inside the company, but also some outside observers, foresaw these difficulties long before the market.

So, given that the stock market often seems to function as a lagging rather than a leading indicator, do we really want to rely so heavily on stock prices—and on market-value proxies like EVA—in evaluating managers' performance? Shouldn't we also be focusing on customer and employee satisfaction, and on a whole host of strategic performance variables?

Once a company's stock price crashes, it tends to be a crisis situation. It reminds of something my son told me the other day: As long as he gets good grades, everything's fine. But, by the time the poor performance shows up in his grades, the problem has probably gotten out of hand.

JENSEN: Well, you're making at least one very good point. And let me agree with you while trying to put your argument in a slightly different way. I agree with you in the sense that I feel the U.S. corporate governance system lets companies go on destroying value too long before intervening in a meaningful way. And I'm prepared to accept your view that the capital markets are not always the first to see the problems. But, after all, the capital market investors in our large public companies are *outsiders*. That's the way we've set up our system in this country. And outsiders don't always have the information—much less the

control—to bring about change when it's necessary.

So, for this reason I agree that we don't want to focus on the stock price in the sense that I think I heard you say. But we do want to focus on the stock price in another way. We want to hold up stock price maximization—or, more generally, maximizing the total value of the enterprise—as the main objective function, the overarching goal, for corporate management. If you're interested in maximizing efficiency and social welfare, then total enterprise value is the correct number for managers to aim to maximize. If you pick any other number or any other index or any other multiple of indexes or indices, you're going to screw it up. You will end up destroying value.

This is my major concern over the use of the so-called balanced scorecard. It never puts it altogether in a single overall number. The reason I find EVA so attractive is that it converts what is essentially a "stock" number—that is, the total market value added—into a "flow" number that managers can look at year by year to assess the extent to which they're adding or destroying value.

Now, given that you're going to maximize the total market value added of the company, how do you do that? You've got to look at the business strategy, you've got to look at HR policies, you've got to look at R&D, and the list goes on. These are the things that somebody in the organization actually gets to decide on. But nobody gets to decide on what the stock price is. That is the result of all those millions of decisions that get made in any organization.

So if your point is that the stock price is an imperfect index of year-to-year performance—and that in some cases it can fail to indicate problems where problems exist—then I'm in 100% agreement. But it's the market

value added—which, again, is determined largely by changes in your stock price—that should serve as your longer-run index of success. And what I think we're talking about today is how corporate financial policies—pay-out ratios, leverage ratios, and to some extent ownership structure—can be used to encourage investment and production decisions that increase EVA and MVA. If financial decisions don't end up affecting these real decisions inside organizations, then I agree with Merton Miller that they're essentially irrelevant.

STEWART: To expand on what Michael said, we have an expression that says, "Metrics without mission is madness." And this relates back to the balanced scorecard. A number of years ago, before Briggs & Stratton went on EVA, they would manage according to a process they now describe as "squeezing on a balloon." One month was inventory-management month, and the head office would trumpet out, "Drive-down-inventory day is at hand." And, sure enough, inventories would go down; but then they would have stock-outs of key parts and products. So the next month was total customer satisfaction month. With the marketers in charge, the company extended the receivables, dropped prices, and offered delivery of any part or product anytime you wanted—and, quite predictably, the manufacturing department screamed bloody murder. So the next month was manufacturing efficiency month, and they drove down unit costs of production with long runs of standardized products. But this succeeded only in bringing them full circle to the excess inventory problem that they started with.

And this is a large part of my problem with the balanced scorecard. It has all these metrics and a flat landscape, but there's no measure of total factor productivity.

Another good example of this is Coca-Cola, which is a longstanding EVA company. For years, they sent their concentrates to their bottlers in stainless steel containers. The cost of the containers was written off against earnings over a long period of time, which had the effect of increasing reported profits and profit margins. But, after they switched to EVA, somebody lower down in the organization—and this bears on Michael's point about the difficulty of transferring good information to the top of the organization—came up with a new idea. He said, "What if we switch to cardboard containers? Now, it's true that because cardboard containers are not reusable, they have to be expensed against the earnings, which reduces profit and profit margins. But, because cardboard costs much less than steel containers, our investment on our balance sheet goes way down."

So, the manager faces a trade-off here. The company could have faster inventory turns and higher returns on assets with cardboard, or a juicier profit margin with stainless steel. Which is the right answer?

The balanced scorecard doesn't give you any means for evaluating such trade-offs. If you have to choose between two desirable, but conflicting objectives that are both rewarded by the balanced scorecard—and, after all, this is often what management decision-making comes down to— there's no single scale that allows you weigh those trade-offs?

Coke solved this problem simply by saying that EVA *is* the balanced scorecard. Run the numbers, and tell us what gives us more EVA. And what they found was that when they switched from stainless steel to cardboard, the savings on the balance sheet ended up being far more valuable than what they gave up on the income statement.

So, that's why we feel metrics without mission is madness. But metrics *with* mission is marvelous! If you have a well-defined mission like increasing economic profit, then that can enable you to evaluate the trade-offs among the other less quantifiable goals of the company.

Too Much Stock Ownership?

ROY: Professor Jensen, are you concerned that when senior management has a lot of stock in their own company, such holdings could actually cause them to behave in ways that run against the shareholder interest? We have a client with an outstanding track record based on growth through acquisitions. The managers are people in their late 30s and early 40s who are sitting on $40-50 million of value in their stock. And, although the company would appear to have more opportunities for growth, the managers are saying, "It's time to slow down; we really don't need to take those kind of risks anymore."

So, my question is, can too much stock ownership lead to an undesirable amount of risk aversion on the part of the managers? And are you concerned about this effect?

JENSEN: You're absolutely right; it can have that effect. Gene Fama and I wrote a paper on that very topic that was published in the *Journal of Business* about ten years ago. As we show there, as the total amount of equity by the top management team rises, you can get exactly the effect you're talking about, which is excessively risk-averse behavior.

But the answer to that problem is not to abandon stock, but rather to change the structure of the stock ownership. That's why I love Bennett's leveraged stock option concept. Unlike conventional options, these LSOs involve a sort of sharing at the margin with managers. So, even if you've

already got a large amount of equity in managers' hands, you can put leveraged stock options on top of that to give them incentives to take the right amount of risk.

Now, finding the right amount and structure for equity ownership by managers is a delicate process, and we're never going to get it exactly right. But I agree with you completely that as we move to more and more equity-based and option-based plans, we will need to think carefully about these issues.

And let me also say, by the way, that I would eliminate tomorrow all the traditional executive stock options and replace them with these leveraged stock options. The way conventional stock option plans work today induces very bad behavior on the part of managers. The cost of equity capital that is implied in the typical executive stock option is zero. And, given the way compensation plans are "recalibrated" each year, and new options are awarded with exercise prices at market each year, managers are effectively rewarded for lousy performance.

So, if we could just get rid of conventional stock option programs, we could have a big impact on the way managers behave.

The Effect of Financial Risk on Operating Risk

ROY: On a related issue, has anybody done any studies or simulations of what happens to the performance of EVA companies when the industry or the economy turns down?

STEWART: Well, since our EVA program really took off around 1992, there hasn't been a general bear market, but there have been downturns in various industries. George Harad, the Chairman & CEO of Boise Cascade, is here with us. Boise Cascade is a forest products and paper company that went on EVA several years ago. George, I understand that paper prices fell over 40% last year, which means you're going through a bear market in your business. Could you comment on this question about whether EVA has helped you weather the down part of your business cycle?

GEORGE HARAD: Well, I think there are really two different questions here: How does EVA work in bear markets? And how does it work in companies with volatile markets?

I think focusing on EVA works in either direction; in fact it may work better when your markets are falling away from you. It motivates people to do something, as opposed to just sitting on capital assets while the returns keep falling farther below the cost of capital.

The second question is: How does EVA work in a business or an industry where the volatility of cash flows makes the cash flows very unpredictable. In two of our businesses—the wood products business and the paper business—in the past five years we have seen prices go down as much as 50-60% in a single year, and then go up by as much as 130%. Now, given the size of those price swings, we really have to get on top of the other, more controllable elements of our business. Dealing with that kind of price volatility forces you to engineer close to the edge, and having an EVA system in place has helped us find ways to eliminate other fixed costs in our overall system.

JENSEN: That's an interesting comment. One of the results that we now have from our studies of leveraged transactions is that, when companies lever up and take on high financial risk, the people on the operating side

of the business find ways to reduce operating risk so that the companies are not operating so close to the edge. For example, a study by Steve Kaplan and Jeremy Stein examined the riskiness of the stub shares that remain after the the large leveraged restructurings like the one by FMC. And the measured risk of that equity was much lower than it should have been if the operating risk of the total assets had remained the same. This evidence is consistent with my own observation that the operating risk of the assets just plummets in these highly leveraged deals.

STEWART: Give me an example. How does somebody magically reduce the operating leverage in their business?

JENSEN: Well, in our Harvard field studies, we have found that managers in LBOs find all kinds of ways to reduce fixed costs, or to convert them into variable costs. You can subcontract or outsource a lot of activities. You can substitute stock or options for salary increases. These kinds of changes can have a dramatic effect on the riskiness of the business—one that helps highly leveraged firms to pull through in down markets.

Now I happen to think that these kinds of changes ought to be made by most companies, not just those with high leverage. And I'm not suggesting that companies should never pursue strategies with high operating risk. But what we have learned from studies of LBOs is that managers can generally do a lot more to increase value when given the right incentives and when facing the pressure of debt.

Some of the success stories are really dramatic, and I'll just tell you about one. There was a little company

I studied back in 1987 that did an LBO of 2,000 miles of railroad track in Wisconsin that the SOO Line couldn't make money on. And, as part of a new organization called Wisconsin Central Limited, a group of managers from Northwestern Railroad bought it out with a lot of debt and with some equity from an LBO firm in Boston called Berkshire Partners. And within a year and a half, Wisconsin Central was rated the number one regional railroad in the United States. Wisconsin Central and Berkshire Partners then went on to buy the New Zealand Rail and Shipping System when it was denationalized. They also recently bought a very substantial fraction of the British railroad system.

I should also point out that the LBO sponsor, Berkshire Partners, using the same operating and financial strategies, has also recently made large equity investments in a variety of other businesses such as cable and cellular tower construction. And the remarkable thing is that, while operating all of these different businesses, Berkshire Partners has never had a losing business. But you have to remember that this is not like a conventional U.S. conglomerate. This is a highly decentralized system in which the operating managers of each business get to make the operating decisions—and they own a significant fraction of their businesses. And that, in a nutshell, is why LBO firms have succeeded where companies like ITT have failed.

STEWART: Well, that sounds like a good note on which to bring this to an end. I would like to thank the panel for their participation, and to thank Jerry Fair once again for setting up this event—and for including me in it.

STATEMENT BY
Alan Greenspan
CHAIRMAN,
BOARD OF GOVERNORS OF THE
FEDERAL RESERVE SYSTEM
BEFORE THE SENATE FINANCE COMMITTEE
January 26, 1989

Mr. Chairman and other members of the Senate Finance Committee:

I am pleased to be here today to address issues raised by recent trends in corporate restructuring activity. The spate of mergers, acquisitions, leveraged buyouts, share repurchases, and divestitures in recent years is a significant development. It has implications for shareholders, the efficiency of our companies, employment and investment, financial stability, and, of course, tax revenues and our tax system. While the evidence suggests that the restructurings of the 1980s probably are improving, on balance, the efficiency of the America economy, the worrisome and possibly excessive degree of leveraging associated with this process could create a set of new problems for the financial system.

Corporate restructuring is not new to American business. It has long been a feature of our enterprise system, a means by which firms adjust to ever-changing product and resource markets, and to perceived opportunities for gains from changes in management and management strategies.

Moreover, waves of corporate restructuring activity are not new. We experienced a wave of mergers and acquisitions around the turn of this century and again in the 1920s. In the postwar period, we witnessed a flurry of so-called conglomerate mergers and acquisitions in the late 1960s and early 1970s.

However, the 1980s have been characterized by features not present in the previous episodes. The recent period has been marked not only by acquisitions and mergers, but also by significant increases in leveraged buyouts, divestitures, asset sales, and share re-purchase programs. In many cases, recent activity reflects the break-up of the big conglomerate deals packaged in the 1960s and 1970s. Also, the recent period has been characterized by the retirement of substantial amounts of equity (more than $500 billion since 1983), financed mostly by borrowing in the credit markets.

The accompanying increase in debt has resulted in an appreciable rise in leverage ratios for many of our large corporations. Aggregate book value debt-equity ratios, based on balance sheet data for nonfinancial firms, have increased sharply in the 1980s, moving outside their range in recent decades, although measures based on market values have risen more modestly.

Along with this debt expansion, the ability of firms in the aggregate to cover interest payments has deteriorated. The ratio of gross interest payments to corporate cash flow before interest provision is currently around 35 percent, close to the 1982 peak when interest rates were much higher. Moreover, current interest coverage rates are characteristic of past recession periods, when weak profits have been the culprit. Lately profits have been fairly buoyant; the current deterioration has been due to heavier interest burdens.

A measure of credit quality erosion is suggested by an unusually large number of downgradings of corporate bonds in recent years. The average bond rating of a large sample of firms has declined since the late 1970s from A+ to A-.

CAUSES OF RESTRUCTURING ACTIVITY

To fashion an appropriate policy response, if any, to such extraordinary phenomena, there are some key questions that must be answered: What is behind the corporate restructuring movement? Why is it occurring now, in the middle and late 1980s, rather than in some earlier time? Why has it involved such a broad leveraging of corporate balance sheets? And finally, has it been good or bad for the American economy?

The 1980s has been a period of dramatic economic changes: large swings in the exchange value of the dollar, with substantial consequences for trade-dependent industries; rapid technological progress, especially in automation and telecom- munications; rapid growth in the service sector; and large movements in real interest rates and relative prices. Clearly, such changes in the economic environment imply major, perhaps unprecedented, shifts in the optimal mix of assets at firms—owing to corresponding shifts in synergies—and new opportunities for improving efficiency. Some activities need to be shed or curtailed, and others added or beefed up. Moreover, the long period of slow productivity growth in the 1970s may have partly exacerbated the buildup of a backlog of inefficient practices.

When assets become misaligned or less than optimally managed, there is clearly an increasing opportunity to create economic value by restructuring companies, restoring what markets perceive as a more optimal mix of assets. But restructuring requires corporate control. And managers, unfortunately, often have been slow in reacting to changes in their external environment, some more so than others. Hence, it shouldn't be a surprise that, in recent years, unaffiliated corporate restructurers, some call them corporate raiders, have significantly bid up the control premiums over the passive investment value of companies that are perceived to have suboptimal asset allocations. If a company already has an optimal mix, there is no economic value to be gained from restructuring and, hence, no advantage in obtaining control of a company for such purposes. In that case, there is no incentive to bid up the stock price above the passive investment value based on its existing, presumed optimal, mix of assets. But in an economy knocked partially off kilter by real interest rate increases and gyrations in foreign exchange and commodity prices, there emerge significant opportunities for value-creating restructuring at many companies.

This presumably explains why common stock tender-offer prices of potential restructurings have risen significantly during the past decade. Observed stock prices generally (though not always) reflect values of shares as passive investments. But there are, for any individual company, two or more prices for its shares, reflecting the degree of control over a company's mix of assets.

Tender-offer premiums over passive investment values presumably are smaller than control premiums to the extent that those making tender offers believe that, restructured, the value of shares is still higher than the tender. Nonetheless, series on tender-offer premiums afford a reasonable proxy for the direction of control premiums.

Such tender-offer premiums ranged from 13 to 25 percent in the 1960s, but have moved to 45 percent and higher during the past decade, underscoring the evident increase in the perceived profit to be gained from corporate control and restructuring.

Interest in restructuring also has been spurred by the apparent increased willingness and ability of corporate managers and owners to leverage balance sheets. The gradual replacement of managers who grew up in the Depression and developed a strong aversion to bankruptcy risk probably accounts for some of the increased proclivity to issue debt now.

Moreover, innovations in capital markets have made the increased propensity to leverage feasible. It is now much easier than it used to be to mobilize tremendous sums of debt capital for leveraged purchases of firms. Improvements in the loan-sale market among banks and the greater presence of foreign banks in U.S. markets have greatly increased the ability of banks to participate in merger and acquisition transactions. The phenomenal development of the market for low-grade corporate debt, so-called "junk bonds," also has enhanced the availability of credit for a wide variety of corporate transactions. The increased liquidity of this market has made it possible for investors to diversify away firm-specific risks by building portfolios of such debt.

The tax benefits of restructuring activities are, of course, undeniable, but this is not a particularly new phenomenon. Our tax system has long favored debt finance by taxing the earnings of corporate debt capital only at the investor level, while earnings on equity capital are taxed at both the investor and corporate levels. There have been other sources of tax savings in mergers that do not depend on debt finance, involving such items as the tax basis for depreciation and foreign tax credits. And taxable owners benefit when firms repurchase their own shares, using what is, in effect, a tax-favored method of paying cash dividends. In any event, the recent rise in restructuring activity is not easily tied to any change in tax law.

Evidence about the economic consequences of restructuring is beginning to take shape, but much remains conjectural. It is clear that the markets believe that the recent restructurings are potentially advantageous. Estimates range from $200 billion to $500 billion or more in paper gains to shareholders since 1982. Apparently, only a small portion of that has come at the expense of bondholders. These gains are reflections of the expectations of market participants that the restructuring will, in fact, lead to a better mix of assets within companies and greater efficiencies in their use. This, in turn, is expected to produce marked increases in future productivity and, hence, in the value of American corporate business. Many of the internal adjustments brought about by changes in management or managerial policies are still being implemented, and it will take time before they show up for good or ill in measures of performance.

So far, various pieces of evidence indicate that the trend toward more ownership by managers and tighter control by other owners and creditors has generally enhanced operational efficiency. In the process, both jobs and capital spending in many firms have contracted as unprofitable projects are scrapped. But no clear trends in these variables are yet evident in restructured firms as a group. For the business sector generally, growth of both employment and investment has been strong.

If what I've outlined earlier is a generally accurate description of the causes of the surge in restructurings of the past decade, one would assume that a stabilization of interest rates, exchange rates, and product prices would slow the emergence of newly misaligned companies and opportunities for further restructuring. Such a development would presumably lower control premiums and reduce the pace of merger, acquisition, and LBO activity.

This suggests that the most potent policies for defusing the restructuring boom over the long haul are essentially the same macroeconomic policies toward budget deficit reduction and price stability that have been the principal policy concerns of recent years.

FINANCIAL RISKS

Whatever the trends in restructuring, we cannot ignore the implications that the associated heavy leveraging has for broad-based risk in the economy. Other things equal, greater use of debt makes the corporate sector more vulnerable to an economic downturn or a rise in interest rates. The financial stability of lenders, in turn, may also be affected. How much is another question. The answer depends greatly on which firms are leveraging, which financial institutions are lending, and how the financings are structured.

Most of the restructured firms appear to be in mature, stable, non-cyclical industries. Restructuring activity has been especially prevalent in the trade, services, and, more recently, the food and tobacco industries. For such businesses, a substantial increase in debt may raise the probability of insolvency by only a relatively small amount. However, roughly two-fifths of merger and acquisition activity, as well as LBOs, have involved companies in cyclically sensitive industries that are more likely to run into trouble in the event of a severe economic downturn.

Lenders to leveraged enterprises have been, in large part, those that can most easily absorb losses without major systemic consequences. They include mutual funds, pension funds, and insurance companies, which generally have diversified portfolios, have traditionally invested in securities involving some risk, such as equities, and are not themselves heavily leveraged. To the extent such debt is held by individual institutions that are not well diversified, however, there is some concern. At the Federal Reserve, we are particularly concerned about the increasing share of restructuring loans made by banks. Massive failures of these loans could have broader ramifications.

Generally, we must recognize that the line between equity and debt has become increasingly fuzzy in recent years. Convertible debt has always had an intermediate character, but now there is almost a continuum of securities varying in their relative proportions of debt and equity flavoring. Once there was a fairly sharp distinction between being unable to make interest payments on a bond which frequently led to liquidation proceedings, and merely missing a dividend. Now the distinction is much smaller. Outright defaults on original issue high-yield bonds have been infrequent to date, but payment difficulties have led to more frequent exchanges of debt that reduce the immediate cash needs of troubled firms. Investors know when they purchase such issues that the stream of payments received may well differ from the stream promised, and prices tend to move in response to changes in both debt and equity markets. In effect, the yields on debt capital rise toward that of equity capital when scheduled repayments are less secure.

POLICY IMPLICATIONS

In view of these considerations, and the very limited evidence on the effects of restructuring at the present time, it would be unwise to arbitrarily restrict corporate restructuring. We must resist the temptation to seek to allocate credit to specific uses through the tax system or through the regulation of financial institutions. Restrictions on the deductibility of interest on certain types of debt for tax purposes or on the granting of certain types of loans unavoidably involve an important element of arbitrariness, one that will affect not only those types of lending intended but other types as well. Moreover, foreign acquirers could be given an artificial edge to the extent that they could avoid these restrictions. Also, the historical experience with various types of selective credit controls clearly indicates that, in time, borrowers and lenders find ways around them.

All that doesn't mean that we should do nothing. The degree of corporate leveraging is especially disturbing in that it is being subsidized by our tax structure. To the extent that the double taxation of earnings from corporate equity capital has added to leveraging, debt levels are higher than they need, or should, be. Our options for dealing with this distortion are, unfortunately, constrained severely by the federal government's still serious budget deficit problems. One straightforward approach to this distortion, of course, would be to substantially reduce the corporation income tax. Alternatively, partial integration of corporate and individual income taxes could be achieved by allowing corporations a deduction for dividends paid or by giving individuals credit for taxes paid at the corporate level. But these changes taken alone would result in substantial revenue losses. A rough estimate of IRS collections from taxing dividends is in the $20 to $25 billion range.

Dangers of risk to the banking system associated with high debt levels also warrant attention. The Federal Reserve, in its role as a supervisor of banks, has particular concerns in this regard. In 1984, the Board issued supervisory guidelines for assessing LBO-related loans, which are set forth in an attachment to my text. The Federal Reserve is currently in the process of reviewing its procedures regarding the evaluation of bank participation in highly leveraged financing transactions. The circumstances associated with highly leveraged deals require that creditors exercise credit judgment with special care. Doing so entails assessing those risks that are firm-specific as well as those common to all highly leveraged firms.

STATEMENT BY

Michael C. Jensen

EDSEL BRYANT FORD PROFESSOR OF
BUSINESS ADMINISTRATION,
HARVARD BUSINESS SCHOOL

BEFORE THE HOUSE WAYS AND MEANS COMMITTEE
February 1, 1989

"Active Investors, LBOs, and the Privatization of Bankruptcy*"

The corporate sector of the U.S. economy has been experiencing major change, and the rate of change continues as we head into the last year of the 1980s. Over the past two decades the corporate control market has generated considerable controversy, first with the merger and acquisition movement of the 1960s, then with the hostile tender offers of the 1970s and, most recently, with the leveraged buyouts and leveraged restructurings of the 1980s. The controversy has been renewed with the recent $25 billion KKR leveraged buyout of RJR-Nabisco, a transaction almost double the size of the largest previous acquisition to date, the $13.2 billion Chevron purchase of Gulf Oil in 1985.

These control transactions are the most visible aspect of a much larger phenomenon that is not yet well understood. Though controversy surrounds them, and despite the fact that they are not all productive, these transactions are the manifestation of powerful underlying economic forces that, on the whole, are productive for the economy. Thorough understanding is made difficult by the fact that change, as always, is threatening-and in this case the threats disturb many powerful interests.

One popular hypothesis offered for the current activity is that Wall Street is engineering transactions to buy and sell fine old firms out of pure greed. The notion is that these transactions reduce productivity, but generate high fees for investment bankers and lawyers. The facts do not support this hypothesis even though mergers and acquisitions professionals undoubtedly prefer more deals to less, and thus sometimes encourage deals (like diversifying acquisitions) that are not productive.

There has been much study of corporate control activity, and although the results are not uniform, the evidence indicates control transactions generate value for shareholders. The evidence also suggests that this value comes from real increases in productivity rather than from simple wealth transfers to shareholders from other parties such as creditors, labor, government, customers or suppliers.[1]

I have analyzed the causes and consequences of takeover activity in the U.S. elsewhere.[2] My purpose here is to outline an explanation of the fundamental underlying cause of this activity that has to date received no attention. I propose to show how current corporate control activity is part of a larger develop-

---

*This is part of an ongoing research effort that includes Clifford Holderness, Jay Light, Dennis Sheehan, and John Pound. General research support has been received from the Harvard Business School Division of Research and a grant has been awarded by Drexel Burnham Lambert to the University of Rochester.

1. For the argument that takeover gains to shareholders come from wealth redistribution from other parties, see Andrei Shleifer and Lawrence Summers, "Breach of Trust in Hostile Takeovers," in *Corporate Takeovers: Causes and Consequences*, Alan Auerbach, ed. (University of Chicago Press, 1988). However, no evidence has yet been produced that supports this argument. For surveys of the evidence on the effects of control-related transactions, see Michael C. Jensen and Richard Ruback, "The Market for Corporate Control: The Scientific Evidence," *Journal of Financial Economics* 11 (1983) and Greg Jarrell, James Brickley, and Jeffrey Netter, "The Market for Corporate Control: The Empirical Evidence Since 1980," Journal of Economic Perspectives, (Winter, 1988), pp. 49-68. Lichtenberg and

Seigel (1987, 1989) analyze Census data on 18,000 plants and 33,000 auxiliary establishments in the U.S. manufacturing sector in the period 1972-81 and find that changes in ownership significantly increase productivity and reduce administrative overhead. See F. Lichtenberg and D. Seigel, "Productivity and Changes of Ownership in Manufacturing Plants," Brookings Papers on Economic Activity, 1987, and "The Effect of Takeovers on the Employment and Wages of Central Office and Other Personnel," unpublished manuscript, Columbia University, 1989.

2. See Michael C. Jensen, "The Agency Costs of Free Cash Flow: Corporate Finance and Takeovers," *American Economic Review*, Vol. 76 No. 2 (May, 1986); see also my articles "The Takeover Controversy: Analysis and Evidence," *Midland Corporate Finance Journal*, Vol. 4 No. 2 (Summer, 1986), pp.6-32, and "Takeovers: Their Causes and Consequences," Journal of Economic Perspectives, Vol. 1, No. 1 (Winter, 1988), pp. 21-48.

ment, to provide perspective on how IBOs, restructurings, and increased leverage in the corporate sector fit into the overall picture, and to discuss some reasons why high debt ratios and insolvency are less costly now than in the past Because of its topical relevance, I pay particular attention to LBOs and their role in the restoration of competitiveness in the American corporation.

ACTIVE INVESTORS AND THEIR IMPORTANCE

The role of institutional investors and financial institutions in the corporate sector has changed greatly over the last 50 years as institutions" have been driven out of the role of active investors. By active investor I don't mean one who indulges in portfolio churning. I mean an investor who actually monitors management, sits on boards, is sometimes involved in dismissing management, is often intimately involved in the strategic direction of the company, and on occasion even manages. That description fits Carl Icahn, Irwin Jacobs, and Kohlberg, Kravis, Roberts (KKR).

Before the mid-1930s, investment banks and commercial banks played a much more important role on boards of directors, monitoring management and occasionally engineering changes in management. At the peak of their activities, J.P. Morgan and several of his partners served on boards of directors and played a major role in the strategic direction of many firms.

Bankers' roles have changed over the past 50 years as a result of a number of factors. One important source of this change is a set of laws established in the 1930s that increased the costs of being actively involved in the strategic direction of a company while also holding large amounts of its debt and equity. For example, under the definitions of the 1934 SEC Act, an institution or individual is considered an "insider" if it owns more than 10 percent of the shares of a company, serves on its board of directors, or holds a position as officer. And the 16-b Short Swing Profit Rules in the SEC Act require an institution satisfying any insider conditions to pay to the company 100 percent of the profits earned on investments held less than six months. Commercial bank equity holdings are significantly restricted and Glass Steagall restricts bank involvement in investment banking activities. The Chandler Act restricts the involvement by banks in the reorganization of companies in which they have substantial debt holdings. In addition, the 1940 Investment Company Act puts restrictions on the maximum holdings of investment funds. These factors do much to explain why money managers do not serve on boards today, and seldom think of getting involved in the strategy of their portfolio companies.

The restrictive laws of the 1930s were passed after an outpouring of populist attacks on the investment banking and financial community, as exemplified by the Pecora hearings of the 1930s and the Pujo hearings in 1913. Current attacks on Wall Street are reminiscent of that era.

The result of these political and other forces over the past 50 years has been to leave managers increasingly unmonitored. In the U.S. at present, when the institutional holders of over 40 percent of corporate equity become dissatisfied with management, they have few options other than to sell their shares. Moreover, managers' complaints about the churning of financial institutions' portfolios ring hollow: One can guess they much prefer the churning system to one in which those institutions actually have direct power to correct a management problem. Few CEOs look kindly on the prospect of having institutions with substantial stock ownership sitting on their corporate board. That would bring about the monitoring of managerial activities by people who more closely bear the wealth consequences of managerial mistakes and who are not beholden to the CEO for their jobs. As financial institution monitors left the scene in the post-1940 period, managers commonly came to believe companies belonged to them and that stockholders were merely one of many stockholders the firm had to serve.[3] This process took time, and the cultures of these organizations slowly changed as senior managers brought up in the old regime were replaced with younger managers.

The banning of financial institutions from fulfilling their critically important monitoring role has resulted in major inefficiencies. The increase in "agency costs" (loosely speaking, the efficiency loss resulting from the separation between ownership and control in widely held public corporations) appears to have peaked in the mid to late 1960s when a substantial part of corporate America generated large

---

3. Even the most voracious maximizer of stockholder wealth must care about the other constituencies of the corporation. Value maximizing implies the corporation should expend resources (to the point where marginal costs equal marginal benefits) in the service of customers, employees, communities, and other parties who affect firm value by influencing the terms on which they contract with the organization or through the threat of restrictive regulation or decline in reputation. If this is the meaning of "stakeholder theory," there is no conflict with value maximization as the corporate objective.

cash flows but had few profitable investment projects. With this excess cash, these firms launched diversification programs that led to the assembly of conglomerates, a course since proven to be unproductive.[4] While most attacks on takeovers have been directed at acquisitions by entrepreneurs such as Icahn and Goldsmith, it is the diversification acquisitions by the largest corporations (such as GE, GM, the major oil companies, etc.) that have proven to be unproductive. The recent criticism levied at the KKR takeover seems misplaced given the evidence—especially given the lack of controversy surrounding the Phillip Morris takeover of Kraft which, if past evidence is any guide, will prove to be counterproductive.

The fact that takeover and restructuring premiums regularly average about 50 percent indicates that managers have been able to destroy up to 30 percent of the value of the organizations they lead before facing serious threat of disturbance. This destruction of value generates large profit opportunities, and the response to these incentives has been the creation of innovative financial institutions to recapture the lost value. Takeovers and LBOs are among the products of these institutions. My estimates indicate that over the 10 years from 1975 to 1986, corporate control activities alone (i.e., mergers, tender offers, divestitures, spin-offs, buybacks, and LBOs) created more than $400 billion in value for investors.

Along with the takeover specialists came other new financial institutions such as the family funds (owned by the Bass Brothers, the Pritzkers, and the Bronfmans) and Warren Buffet's Berkshire Hathaway-institutions that discovered ways to bear the cost associated with insider status. Coniston Partners is another version of this new organizational response to the monitoring problem, and so is the Lazard Frères Corporate Partners Fund. These new institutions have discovered ways different from those of J.P. Morgan to resolve the monitoring problem. They purchase entire companies and play an active role in them; in fact, they often are the board of directors.

The modern trend toward merchant banking in which Wall Street firms take equity positions in their own deals is another manifestation of this phenomenon. KKR is much more than an expediter of LBO transactions. It plays an important role in management after the transaction. In general, LBO specialists control the boards of directors in the companies they help take private. They choose the managers of the firm and influence the corporate strategy in important ways. Buyout specialists are very different from the usual outside or public directors that supposedly represent shareholders. Buyout specialists own, or represent in their buyout funds, an average of 60 percent of the firm's equity[5] and therefore have great incentive to take the job seriously, in contrast to public directors with little or no equity interest.

The development of new financial institutions as a response to problems caused by the lack of effective monitoring of corporate managers continues to grow. Such innovation is likely to continue unless handicapped by new legislation, tax penalties, or unfavorable public opinion. The attack on Wall Street and investment bankers that has been progressing in recent years may be the modern equivalent to the populist attacks in the decades prior to 1940 that led to the crippling of American corporations in the 1960s and 1970s.

THE LBO ASSOCIATION: A NEW ORGANIZATIONAL FORM

It is instructive to think about LBO associations such as KKR and Forstmann-Little as new organizational Forms-in effect, a new model of general management. These organizations are similar in many respects to diversified conglomerates or to the Japanese groups of firms known as "keretsu" It is noteworthy that the corporate sectors in Japan and Germany are significantly different from the American corporate model of diffuse ownership monitored by public directors. In both these economies, banks and associations of firms are more important than in the U.S. Indeed, one way to see the current conflict between the Business Roundtable and Wall Street is that Wall Street is now a direct competitor to the corporate headquarters office of the typical conglomerate.[6] Moreover, the evidence on the relative success of the active investor versus the public director organizational form seems to indicate that many CEOS of large diversified corporations have no future in their jobs; one way or the other many of those jobs are being eliminated in favor of operating level jobs by competition in the organizational dimension.

---

4. See Jensen (1986) and Jensen (1988), as cited in footnote 2.

5. See Steve N. Kaplan, "Sources of Value in Management Buyouts," unpublished doctoral thesis, Harvard Business School (March, 1989).

6. A point originally made by Amar Bhide, Harvard Business School.

ONE WAY TO SEE THE CURRENT CONFLICT BETWEEN THE BUSINESS ROUNDTABLE AND WALL STREET IS THAT WALL STREET IS NOW A DIRECT COMPETITOR TO THE CORPORATE HEADQUARTERS OFFICE OF THE TYPICAL CONGLOMERATE.

FIGURE 1
CORRESPONDENCE BETWEEN THE TYPICAL DIVERSIFIED FIRM AND THE TYPICAL LBO ASSOCIATION (COMPETING ORGANIZATIONAL FORMS)

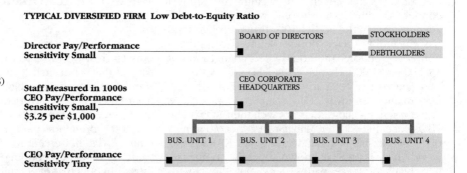

TYPICAL DIVERSIFIED FIRM Low Debt-to-Equity Ratio

Director Pay/Performance Sensitivity Small

Staff Measured in 1000s
CEO Pay/Performance Sensitivity Small,
$3.25 per $1,000

CEO Pay/Performance Sensitivity Tiny

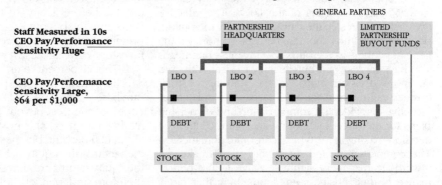

TYPICAL LBO ASSOCIATION (KKR, FORSTMANN LITTLE) High Debt-to-Equity Ratio

Staff Measured in 10s
CEO Pay/Performance Sensitivity Huge

CEO Pay/Performance Sensitivity Large,
$64 per $1,000

The LBO association is headed by a small partnership organization that substitutes compensation incentives (mostly through equity ownership) and top-level over sight by a board with large equity ownership for the large bureaucratic monitoring of the typical corpoarte headquarters. For simplicity, the board of directors of each LBO firm has been omitted. The LBO Partnership Headquarters generally holds 60% of the stock in its own name or that of the Limited Partnership fund and controls each of these boards.

LBO associations such as KKR are one alternative to conglomerate organizations and, judging from their past performance, they apparently generate large increases in efficiency. Figure 1 illustrates the parallels and differences between these organizational forms. LBO associations, portrayed in the bottom of the figure, are run by partnerships instead of the headquarters office in the typical large, multibusiness diversified corporation. These partnerships perform the monitoring and peak coordination function with a staff numbering in the tens of people, and replace the typical corporate headquarters staff of thousands. The leaders of these partnerships have large equity ownership in the outcomes and direct fiduciary relationships as general partners to the limited partner investors in their buyout funds.

The LBO partnerships play a role that is similar in many ways to that of the main banks in the Japanese groups of companies. The banks (and LBO partnerships) hold substantial amounts of equity and debt in their client firms and are deeply involved in the monitoring and strategic direction of these firms. Moreover, the business unit heads in the typical LBO association, unlike those in Westinghouse or GE, also have substantial equity ownership that gives them a pay-to-performance sensitivity which, on average, is 20 times higher than the average corporate CEO. In a sample of LBOs examined by Steven Kaplan, the average CEO receives $64 per $1,000 change in shareholder wealth from his 6.4 percent equity interest alone.[7] The typical corporate CEO, by contrast, is paid in a way that is insensitive to performance as

7. See Kaplan (1989), as cited in note 5.

measured by changes in CEO wealth. In a study I conducted with Kevin Murphy, we found that the average CEO in the Forbes 1000 firms receives total pay (including salary, bonus, deferred compensation, stock options and equity) that changes about $3.25 per $1,000 change in stockholder value.[8]

The proper comparison, however, of the pay-performance sensitivity of the compensation package of the conglomerate CEO is not with the CEOs of the LBOs but rather with the Managing Partner or Partners of the partnership headquarters (e.g., the KKR's of this world). Little is publicly known about the compensation plans of these partnerships, but the pay-to-performance sensitivity (including ownership interests, of course) appears to be very large, even relative to that of the managers of the LBOs. The effective ownership interest in the gains realized by the buyout pool generally runs about 20 percent or more for the general partners as a group. LBO business unit heads also have far less of a bureaucracy to deal with, and far more decision rights, in the running of their businesses. In effect, the LBO association substitutes incentives provided by compensation and ownership plans for the direct monitoring and often centralized decision-making in the typical corporate bureaucracy. The compensation and ownership plans make the rewards to managers highly sensitive to the performance of their business unit, something that rarely occurs in major corporations.[9]

In addition, the contractual relation between the partnership headquarters and the suppliers of capital to the buyout funds is very different from that between the corporate headquarters and stockholders in the diversified firm. The buyout funds are organized as limited partnerships, in which the managers of the partnership headquarters are the general partners. Unlike the diversified firm, the contract with the limited partners denies partnership headquarters the right to transfer cash or other resources from one LBO business unit to another. Generally all cash payouts from each LBO business unit must be paid out directly to the limited partners of the buyout funds. This reduces the waste of free cash flow that is so prevalent in diversified corporations.[10]

THE EMPIRICAL EVIDENCE ON THE SOURCE OF LBO GMNS

The evidence on LBOs and management buyouts is growing rapidly. In general, this evidence shows that abnormal gains to stockholders are significantly positive and in the same range as gains from takeovers. Stock prices rise about 14 percent to 25 percent on the announcement of the offer, and the total premium paid to public shareholders ranges from 40 percent to 56 percent.[11] The recent study by Kaplan, mentioned earlier, shows that for those buyouts that eventually come back public or are otherwise sold, the total value (adjusted for market movements) increases 73 percent from two months before a buyout to the final sale about 5 years after the buyout Pre-buyout shareholders earn premiums of about 35 percent, and the post-buyout investors earn about 27 percent.[12]

This 27 percent return to post-buyout investors, it is important to note, is measured on the total purchase price of the pre-buyout equity and not the equity of the post-buyout firm. The median net-of-market return on the post-buyout equity alone is about 600 percent, but these returns are distorted by the fact that the equity is highly leveraged. In effect, the equity returns are almost a pure risk premium and therefore independent of the amount invested. Calculating the returns on the entire capital base used to purchase the pre-buyout equity, or the fraction of the total wealth gains that go to the pre-buyout shareholders, gives a better picture of the distribution of the total wealth created in the buyout. Average total buyout fees amount to 5.5 percent of the equity two months prior to the buyout proposal.

Some assert that post-buyout shareholders, especially managers, earn "too much" in these transactions, and that managers are exploiting shareholders by using their inside information about the firm to buy it at below-market prices. Kaplan, however, finds evidence that managers holding substantial amounts of equity who are not part of the post-buyout management team are systematically selling their shares into the buyout This is irrational behavior if the buyout is

8. Michael C. Jensen and Kevin J. Murphy, "Performance Pay and Top Management Incentives," Harvard Business School Working Paper #89-059, (1989).

9. See George F. Baker, Michael C. Jensen, and Kevin J. Murphy, "Compensation and Incentives: Practice vs. Theory," *Journal of Finance*, (July, 1988), 593-616. See also Jensen and Murphy (1989), cited in note 8.

10. For a discussion of the waste of free cash flow see my article, "The Agency Costs of Free Cash Flow: Corporate Finance and Takeovers," *American Economic Review*, cited in note 2.

11. Evidence on stock price increases comes from Harry DeAngelo, Linda DeAngelo, and Ed Rice, "Going Private Minority Freezeouts and Shareholder Wealth," *Journal of Financial Economics*, 27 (1984) PP. 367-401. See also Kenneth Lehn and Annette Poulsen, "Leveraged Buyouts: Wealth Created or Wealth Redistributed?," in *Public Policy toward Corporate Mergers*, M. Weidenbaum and K. Chilton, eds. (Transition Books, New Brunswick, NJ, 1988).

12. Kaplan (1989), as cited in note 5. The average total returns before adjustment for market returns are 220% with pre-buyout shareholders earning 47% and post-buyout shareholders earning 128%.

significantly underpriced in light of inside information and if such non-participating insiders have the same information as that of the continuing management team. Moreover, shareholders have many legal forums to press their claims because virtually all announcements of buyouts are followed by suits from the plaintiffs' bar. In addition, buyout firms systematically underperform the post-buyout projections they make in the proxy materials provided to selling shareholders.[13]

If, however, the buyout gains are due to the major changes in ownership and debt that occur at the buyout and the real changes in operations they engender, there may be no alternative but to allow managers to acquire substantial equity interests. These equity interests give them the incentive to make such highly leveraged companies successful and compensates them for the risks they are taking with their careers. One of the major risks, as Ross Johnson of RJR-Nabisco found out, is that a substantial fraction of proposed buyouts fail, and competing bids are an important reason for this failure.

Managers are subject to severe conflicts of interest in buyout transactions because they cannot simultaneously act as both buyer and agent for the seller. The system seems to work well, however, to protect shareholder interests. Directors are liable if they behave inappropriately and sacrifice shareholder interests in favor of managers, and shareholders receive protection from the fact that a bid significantly below the real value of the company (risk-adjusted, of course) is likely to be met by competing outside bids. This is exactly what happened in the RJR case, where the initial management bid of $75 per share was topped by two outside bidders for an eventual stated price of $109 per share, an increase of $7.7 billion. In this case the system worked well to ensure that shareholder interests were served.

There are now several credible studies that have examined the operating characteristics of large samples of LBOs after the buyout and have found real increases in productivity. The Kaplan study cited above finds average increases in operating earnings of 42 percent from the year prior to the buyout to the

third year after the buyout, and increases of 25 percent when adjusted for industry and business cycle trends. He also finds 96 percent increases in cash flow in the same period (80 percent increases after adjustment for industry and business cycle trends).

A study by Abbie Smith also finds significant increases in operating earnings and net cash flows. In addition she documents improvements in profit margins, sales per employee, working capital, inventories, and receivables, and finds no evidence of delays in payments to suppliers. She finds no changes in maintenance, repairs and advertising as a fraction of sales, and no evidence that these items are being cut in ways that harm the long-run health of the enterprise.[14]

Corporate debt rises significantly, from about 20 percent of assets to almost 90 percent after a buyout.[15] Some argue that a major part of the shareholder benefits are simply wealth transfers from bondholders who suffer when their bonds are left outstanding in the new company with its massive total debt. While it is undoubtedly true that some bondholders have lost in these transactions, there is no evidence that bondholders lose on average. Convertible bond and preferred stockholders generally gain a statistically significant amount in such transactions, while straight bond holders show no significant gains or losses.[16] This result is somewhat surprising since, in the majority of cases, the old bonds experience significant downgradings by rating agencies.

The bondholder loss issue has been prominent in the press as Metropolitan Life has filed suit against RJR-Nabisco for restitution of the losses it experienced on its RJR-Nabisco bond holdings. The press, however, has greatly exaggerated the amount of the wealth loss to the RJR bondholders. The original announcement of the Johnson/Shearson Lehman offer occurred on October 20. In the period September 29,1988 to November 29,1988, the bondholders of RJR-Nabisco suffered losses of slightly under $300 million.[17] This loss is trivial relative to the $12.1 billion gain to RJR shareholders (calculated at the stated price of $109 per share).

13. Ibid.

14. Abbie Smith, "Corporate Ownership Structure and Performance: The Case of Management Buyouts," unpublished manuscript, University of Chicago Graduate School of Business, January, 1989.

15. See Kaplan (1988), as cited in note 5. See also L. Marais, K. Schipper, and Abbie Smith, "Wealth effects of Going Private for Senior Securities," *Journal of Financial Economics* (forthcoming).

16. See Marais, Schipper and Smith (forthcoming), cited in note 15.

17. Press reports typically estimate bondholder losses at $1 billion on RJR's $5 billion of debt outstanding prior to the buyout. While it is true that RJR's longest bond fell 20 percent on announcement of the proposal, much of RJR's debt was shorter term, and the effect on the shorter-term debt was much smaller.

In any event the expropriation of wealth from bondholders is not a continuing problem because the technology to protect bondholders from losses in the event of substantial restructuring and increases in debt is available. Poison puts or other covenant provisions that require repurchase of the bonds during such events can be used to eliminate such restructuring risk. One view of the RJR situation is that the Met and other bondholders gambled that no restructuring would occur in order to reap the premium they would have given up if the protection had been included in the bonds they bought in 1988. Having gambled and lost, they are now asking for compensation.

The effects of LBOs on labor have not been thoroughly studied to date, but evidence in the Kaplan study indicates that median employment increases by 4.9 percent after a buyout (although, adjusted for industry conditions, it falls by 6.2 percent).[18] Thus, employment does not systematically fall after a buyout. No data has been found that allows inference on whether wages are cut after a buyout.

There is also concern about the effect of LBOs on R&D expenditures. This concern seems unwarranted because the low-growth, old-line firms that make good candidates for highly leveraged LBOs don't typically invest in R&D. Kaplan and Smith, for example, each found only seven firms in their respective samples of 76 and 58 firms that engaged in enough R&D to report it in their financial statements.

Another area of controversy is the amount of value transferred from the U.S. Treasury in the form of tax subsidies to buyout transactions. The argument is that the massive increases in tax-deductible interest payments virtually eliminate tax obligations for buyout firms. In the year following the buyout, Kaplan finds that 50 percent of the firms pay no taxes. However, because of operating improvements and the retirement of some debt, average tax payments are essentially back to the pre-buyout level by the third year after the buyout. Moreover, these subsidy arguments ignore five sources of added tax revenues: (1) the large increases in tax payments generated by the buyout in the form of capital gains tax payments by pre-buyout shareholders who are forced to realize all the gains in their holdings; (2) the capital gains taxes paid on the sale of assets by the LBO firms; (3) the tax payments on the large increases in operating earnings caused by the buyout; (4) the tax payments by the buyout firm creditors who receive the interest payments; and (5) the increased taxes generated by the more efficient use of the firm's capital.

Direct estimates of the total effect on Treasury tax revenues taking account of all such gains and losses indicate the present value of revenues actually increases by about 10 million under the 1986 tax rules on the average buyout with a price of $500 million Converted to an equivalent annual increase of $11 million in perpetuity, these revenues represent an annual increase of approximately 61 percent over the average $18 million tax payment by buyout firms in the year prior to the buyout. On a current account basis-that is, considering only the tax effects in the year after the buyout-the Treasury gains $41 million over the average pre-buyout tax payments.[19] Conservative estimates indicate that, at worst, the Treasury is unlikely to be a net loser from these transactions. If the value increases are the result of real productivity changes, rather than merely transfers of wealth from other parties, then it is not surprising that the Treasury is a winner. In the controversial RJR-Nabisco case, the $12 billion plus gains are likely to generate net incremental tax revenues to the treasury totaling $3.8 billion in present value terms, and about $3.3 billion solely in the year following the buyout. Before the buyout, RJR-Nabisco was paying about $370 million in federal taxes.

HIGH LEVERAGE AND THE PRIVATIZATION OF BANKRUPTCY

One important and interesting characteristic of the LBO organization is its intensive use of debt. The debt-to-value ratio in the business units of these organizations averages close to 90 percent on a book value basis.[20] LBOs, however, are not the only organizations that are making use of high debt ratios. Public corporations are also following suit as witnessed by recapitalizations, highly leveraged mergers, and stock repurchases.

There has been much concern in the press and in public policy circles about the dangers of high debt ratios in these new organizations. What is not generally recognized, however, is that high debt has benefits as a monitoring and incentive device, espe-

---

18. The increase in employment is statistically significant, and the difference from industry trends is insignificantly different from zero. The data cover only companies without significant divestitures in the post-buyout period.

19. These estimates are discussed in detail in Michael C. Jensen, Steven N. Kaplan, and Laura Stiglin, "The Effects of LBOs on Tax Revenues of the U.S. Treasury," *Tax Notes*, Vol. 42 No. 6 (February 6, 1989), pp. 727-733.

20. Kaplan (1988), as cited in note 5.

IN EFFECT, BANKRUPTCY WILL BE TAKEN OUT OF THE COURTS AND "PRIVATIZED."
THIS INSTITUTIONAL INNOVATION WILL TAKE PLACE TO RECOGNIZE THE LARGE
ECONOMIC VALUE THAT CAN BE PRESERVED BY PRIVATELY RESOLVING THE
CONFLICTS OF INTEREST AMONG CLAIMANTS TO THE FIRM.

FIGURE 2
RELATION BETWEEN
INSOLVENCY POINT AND
LIQUIDATION VALUE
WHEN THE DEBT/VALUE
RATIO IS LOW VS. HIGH

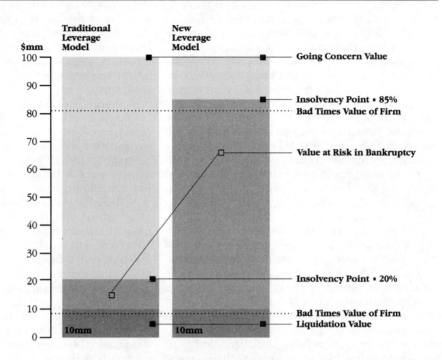

The darkest shaded area represents the liquidation value for a given firm with assumed value of $100 million dollars. Traditionally leveraged, the firm would have about a 20% debt-to-value ratio (on a healthy going concern basis), while it would have about 85% debt in the new leverage model characterizing LBO and restructuring transactions. The much larger value at risk in the new leverage model if the firm should go into bankruptcy, represented by the next darkest shaded area, provides larger incentives to bring about private reorganization outside of the courts.

cially in slow-growing or shrinking firms. Even less well-known, the costs for a firm in insolvency—the situation in which a firm cannot meet its contractual obligations to make payments—are likely to be much smaller in the new world of high leverage ratios than they have been historically. The reason is illustrated in Figure 2.

In a world of 20 percent debt-to-value ratios (with value based on the going concern value of a healthy company), the liquidation or salvage value is much closer to the face value of the debt than in the same company with an 85 percent debt/value ratio.[21] Figure 2 shows a $100 million company under these two leverage ratios, and assumes that the salvage or liquidation value of the assets is 10 percent of the going concern value of $10 million. Thus, if the company experiences such a decline in

value during bad times that it cannot meet its payments on $20 million of debt, it is also likely that its value is below its liquidation value.

An identical company with an 85 percent debt ratio, however, is nowhere near liquidation when it experiences times sufficiently difficult to cause it to be unable to meet the payments on its $85 million of debt. That situation could occur when the company still has total value in excess of $80 million. In this case there is $70 million in value that can be preserved by resolving the insolvency problem in a fashion that minimizes the value lost through the bankruptcy process. In the former case, when the firm is worth less than $20 million, there may be so little value left that the economically sensible action is liquidation, with all its attendant conflicts and dislocation.

21. I am indebted to Mark Wolfson for helping me see this point.

The incentives to preserve value in the new leverage model imply that a very different set of institutional arrangements and practices will arise to substitute for the usual bankruptcy process. In effect, bankruptcy will be taken out of the courts and "privatized." This institutional innovation will take place to recognize the large economic value that can be preserved by privately resolving the conflicts of interest among claimants to the firm. When the going concern value of the firm is vastly greater than the liquidation value, it is likely to be more costly to trigger the cumbersome court-supervised bankruptcy process that diverts management time and attention away from managing the enterprise to focus on the abrogation of contracts that the bankruptcy process is set up to accomplish.

These large poteintial losses provide incentives for the parties to accomplish reorganization of the claims more efficiently outside the courtroom. This fact is reflected in the strip financing practices commonly observed in LBOs whereby claimants hold approximately proportional strips of all securities and thereby reduce the conflicts of interest among classes of claimants.[22] Incentives to manage the insolvency process better are also reflected in the extremely low frequency with which these new organizations actually enter bankruptcy. The recent Revco case is both the largest such bankruptcy of an LBO and one of the handful that have occurred.

LBOs frequently get in trouble, but they seldom enter formal bankruptcy. Instead they are reorganized in a short period of time (several months is common), often under new management, and at apparently lower cost than would occur in the courts. The process has not been formally studied yet, so good empirical data is currently unavailable.

Some assert that the success of LBOs has been ensured by the greatest bull market in history. the story is not that simple, however, because during the last eight years, major sectors of the economy have experienced bad times, and buyouts have occurred in many of these sectors. So although they have not been tested by a general recession, they have survived well the trials of subsectors of the economy in the recent past (textiles and apparel are examples).

In addition, there are indications that organizations such as Drexel Burnham Lambert (which has been most active in facilitating the intensive use of debt) has anticipated these problems They seem sensitive to the potential gains from innovation in the work-out and reorganization process. Such innovation is to be expected when there are large efficiency gains to be realized from new reorganization and recontracting procedures to deal with insolvency.

There is reason to believe, however, that actions by regulatory authorities will generate serious bankruptcy problems among Drexel's clients if its ability to handle the reorganization and work-out process is hampered. Drexel's position in the high-yield bond market gives it a unique ability to perform this function and no substitute is likely to emerge soon.

There has been much concern about the ability of LBO firms to withstand sharp increases in interest rates, given that the bank debt which frequently amounts to 50 percent of the total debt is primarily at floating rates. This problem is mitigated by the fact that most LBOs now protect themselves against sharp increases in interest rates by purchasing caps that limit any increase or by using swaps that convert the floating-rate debt to fixed rates. Indeed it has become common for banks to require such protection for the buyout firm as a condition for lending. These new financial techniques are another means where-by some of the risks can be hedged away in the market, and therefore the total risks to the buyout firm are less than they would have been in past years at equivalent debt levels.

It will undoubtedly take time for the institutional innovation in reorganization practices ton mature and for participants in the process ton understand that insolvency will be a more frequent and less costly event than it has been historically. It is also reasonable to predict that this will be an area of intense future academic study.

It is likely we will discover that debt and insolvency can serve a very important control function to replace what seems to be the failed model in which the public board of directors monitors management and its strategy directly Although I have not studied it in detail, and therefore my conclusions are tentative. the recent Revco bankruptcy seems to be an example Revco's management pursued a strategy to upgrade its drugstores to department stores. The strategy failed, but the high debt load prevented the company from pursuing the flawed project for long because insolvency and bankruptcy allowed the creditors and owners ton replace managers and force abandonment

---

22. See Jensen (1988), as cited in note 2.

of the strategy. Such rapid change in management and strategy would probably not have occurred under the usual public director/low leverage control model of the typical American corporation.

It is interesting that the Japanese system seems to have many of the characteristics of the evolving American system. Japanese firms make intensive use of leverage and Japanese banks appear ton allow a company ton go into bankruptcy only when it is economic ton liquidate it that is, only when the firm is more valuable dead than alive. This appears ton be the norm in the American LBO community as well as leader of the consortium of banks lending ton any firm, the Japanese main bank takes responsibility for evaluating the economic viability of an insolvent firm, and for planning its recovery, including the infusion of new capital and top-level managerial manpower (often drawn from the bank itself). Other members of the lending consortium commonly follow the lead of the main bank and contribute additional funding, if required, ton the reorganization effort. The main bank bonds its role by making the largest commitment of funds ton the effort. Viewed in this light, the most puzzling aspect of the Revco experience is why Revco's investment bankers and creditors let the firm get into the formal bankruptcy process.

CONCLUSION

LBOs are an interesting example of control transfers that highlight the effect of changes in organizational form and incentives on productivity. It appears there is no explanation for most of the gains other than real increases in operating efficiencies. That in itself is interesting because these are generally situations in which the same managers with the same assets are able, when provided better incentives, to almost double the productivity and value of the enterprise. It is also surprising that it is so difficult ton find losers in these transactions. Some middle and upper managers lose their jobs as the inefficient and bloated corporate staffs are replaced by LBO partnership headquarters units. Such LBO associations rely on incentives (created by equity ownership, performance-sensitive compensation, and high debt obligations) and decentralized decision-making as substitutes for direct involvement by corporate headquarters in decision-making.

As major innovations in corporate organization continue, mistakes will be made. This is natural and not counterproductive. How can we learn without pushing new policies ton the margin? the surprising thing to me is that there have been son few major mistakes or problems in a revolution in business practice as large as that occurring over the last decade. Many of the proposed changes in public policy toward these transactions threaten to stifle this recreation of the competitiveness of the American corporation. Perhaps the most dangerous of these policy proposals are those that, like the American Law Institute's, would limit the formation of debt and the distribution of resources from corporations by imposing various tax penalties.[23] Removal of biases towards higher debt in the tax system would be desirable, but not if the proposed solutions create large inefficiencies as the A.L.I.'s now threatens to do.

The best and simplest way ton remove any tax-induced bias toward debt is to eliminate the double taxation of dividends by making them tax deductible at the corporate level. This change would generate large additional efficiency gains in the economy because It would reduce the incentives for corporations ton retain substantial amounts of funds even when they have no profitable projects in which to invest. This change would eliminate some of The most inefficient acquisitions that take place. These acquisitions are frequently engineered by managers flooded with free cash flow they are unable to invest in the businesses they understand but are reluctant ton pay out to shareholders for reinvestment elsewhere in the economy Some of the best examples of this have occurred in the oil, tire, and tobacco industrial industries that have been forced to shrink their operations in the last decade. As in the past, elimination of the double taxation of dividends is likely ton be opposed by corporate managers who wish ton avoid pressure for increased payouts to shareholders Reforming the bankruptcy process ton limit the courts' abrogation of the contractual priority of claims voluntarily agreed ton by security holders is also an important function that policymakers should address.

---

23. The American Law Institute has proposed a minimum tax on corpoaret distributions as an alternative way to accomplish "debt disqualification," American Law Institute, Federal Income Tax Project, Tax Advisory Group Draft No. 18, Subchapter C (Supplemental Study), Part I. Distribution Issues, (November 3, 1988)). This proposal would exacerbate the major free cash flow problem facing the American corporate sector by locking into place penaltied for the distributions that must occur to resolve the problem. See Jensen (1986, 1988), as cited in note 2.

TESTIMONY OF

Lawrence H. Summers *"Taxation and Corporate Debt"*

PROFESSOR,
DEPARTMENT OF ECONOMICS,
HARVARD UNIVERSITY
BEFORE THE SENATE FINANCE COMMITTEE
January 26, 1989

I welcome the opportunity to testify before this distinguished committee on the important subject of the recent wave of corporate restructurings and increases in indebtedness, and its implications for the tax system. While I do not share the fears of some critics that recent trends in corporate debt pose grave threats to economic stability, I do believe they highlight the need to address certain distortions that have long been present in our income tax system.

Today, I shall make four points. First, there is no reason for a punitive reaction to recent trends in corporate indebtedness. To a significant extent, increased reliance on debt has reduced capital costs and improved incentives for managerial efficiency. While increased reliance on debt may be justified in many instances, there is no justification for tax policies which encourage its use beyond the level that an undistorted market would dictate. Second, the cur-rent tax system provides substantial incentives for the excessive use of debt both in the context of corporate restructurings and in the context of ordinary business operations. Claims that LBO transactions benefit the Treasury are misleading in a number of respects. Third, as long as the tax system seeks to doubly tax corporate income, to distinguish between debt and equity, dividends and interest, and interest and capital gains, financial innovation will continue to create substantial problems. Now is not too soon to begin consideration of fundamental changes in traditional tax concepts. Fourth, for the near term the argument for changing tax rules to tax equity that masquerades as high yield debt is overwhelming. Serious consideration should be given to using the revenues to finance reductions in the tax rate on dividends arising from future new equity issues.

ASSESSING CORPORATE DEBT TRENDS

By almost any measure the extent of corporate indebtedness has increased in recent years. Figure 1 illustrates the behavior of one standard measure-the ratio of non-financial corporate debt to GNP. It is evident that there is a long-term trend towards increased corporate reliance on debt which dates back to the end of World War II. However, the increase in corporate indebtedness during the 1980s was almost entirely the result of corporate restructurings. But for the effects of these restructurings, there would have been almost no increase in the quantity of corporate debt outstanding relative to corporate GNP during the 1980s.

At the outset, it is important to recognize that not all LBOs represent the type of public deal that has got. ten so much attention in recent months. Many transactions occur when the owner-manager of a relatively small company approaches retirement, or when it becomes clear that a profitable line of business no longer fits with a corporation's overall strategy. These deals are almost certainly benign, and it would be unfortunate if public policies directed at larger transactions inhibited them to a substantial extent. In the remainder of my remarks, however, I shall concentrate on the large public LBOs that have been the been the focus of recent discussions.

The proliferation of corporate restructurings in the 1980s is primarily a reflection of financial innovation—particularly the development of the high yield, "junk" bond market. These have made it possible for acquirers—whether hostile, friendly, or inside, as in the case of management buyouts finance acquisitions on a scale that was previously impossible. The recent RJR-Nabisco deal, which accounts for nearly 1/4 of the dollar value of all the LBO activity in the 1980s, suggests that the feasible scale of leveraged transactions is continuing to increase. Because large leveraged buyout transactions are a recent development, only limited evidence on their effects is available. Here I offer my interpretation of the available evidence on various questions that are often raised in discussions of the phenomena.

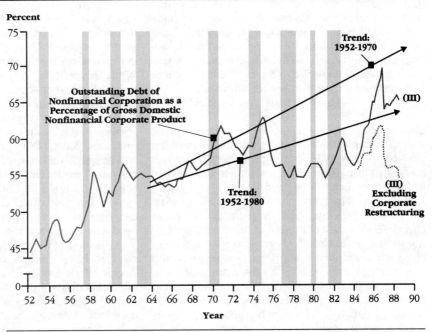

FIGURE 1
CORPORATE DEBT
BURDEN IN HISTORICAL
PERSPECTIVE

Source: Federal Reserve Board. Department of Commerce.
Reprinted from Goldman Sachs, *Financial Market Perspectives*, December 1988.

Why Has So Much Money Been Made by So Few People? In large part, LBOs have succeeded so spectacularly because of general upward trends in the stock market. An individual who bought and held the stock market on 10% margin since 1982 would have earned a return of close to 1000%. Few LBO funds have done better over the last few years. It is always true that those willing to borrow heavily and invest fare well in bull markets. The current experience is no exception. The unlikelihood of another bull market like the one of the last six years, and the increasing competition in the LBO business, means that it is very unlikely that the current generation of deals will pay off nearly as spectacularly as the past ones have.

Much has been made of the size of the fees associated with these transactions and the diversion of talent from other pursuits into the investment banking business. Without endorsing the excesses, it is fair to point out that the number of "doers" diverted into investment banking in recent years is almost certainly more than offset by the reduction in the number of

corporate staff functionaries as leveraged transactions have encouraged managerial efficiency and broken apart wasteful conglomerate structures.

There are legitimate concerns about management's ability to fulfill its fiduciary duty to shareholders when it is also seeking to acquire the company. Accumulating evidence that reported earnings and stock prices frequently decline immediately prior to LBOs and rise thereafter is particularly alarming in this regard. This is an issue of securities regulation, not tax policy. Serious consideration should be given to strengthening the role and independence of outside directors as a safeguard against managerial abuse.

This need is highlighted by the recent RJR-Nabisco case. While public reports strongly suggest that the recent auction of RJR-Nabisco was a fair one, there are suggestions that efforts were made to make it otherwise. According to one report[1] "Johnson spoiled his directors with lucrative consulting contracts and always available airplanes. He had led the

---

1. Corporate Governance Bulletin, (December 1988), p. 147. For further allegations about management and board improprieties see the series of articles in *Barrons* by Ben Stein.

fight to double directors' pay to $50,000 a year... Some were so close that one commentator jokingly described them as Johnson's kangaroo court." Experience suggests that in the future some boards will respond more strongly to the interests of incumbent management than to the interests of outside shareholders unless current rules are altered.

Why Are Acquirers Able to Pay Such Large Premia over Previous Stock Prices? This crucial question continues to be a subject of intense debate among both practitioners and academics. Part of the answer appears to lie in the profitability improvements that managers realize when their feet are held to the fire by large debts, and when a large equity stake sharpens incentives. It is not yet clear to what extent these improvements represent real increases in economic efficiency, and to what extent they represent transfers from other corporate stockholders, such as employers, suppliers, bondholders, and neighboring communities. This distinction is crucial. When more output is produced with the same group of employees, economic efficiency is clearly enhanced. On the other hand, when more employees are put to work collecting receivable more quickly, a company may collect more but only at the expense of its customers. This does not represent any improvement in the performance of the economy.

In many transactions, value is created by divesting assets. In these cases, the value may come from the ability to sell assets to different buyers with higher-valued uses for those assets. Another part of the answer, however, probably lies in the superior information of management. Inevitably, corporate managers know more about their companies than even the most attentive market observers. They will buy when the company looks cheap relative to its fundamental value. The same market misplacing that gives them an incentive to buy makes it possible for them to pay a premium over the going market price.

As I discuss in more detail below, because interest is deductible for corporations and dividends are not, the tax system tends to subsidize transactions which replace corporate equity with debt. In many cases, LBOs can nearly eliminate a corporation's tax liability for several years. An additional tax reason for LBO premia is the need to compensate shareholders for the capital gains taxes they are forced to pay when their shares are acquired.

Do Rising Levels of Corporate Debt Threaten Corporate Performance? The evidence here is quite inconclusive. It appears that in most cases operating profits increase following LBOs even when they are compared with other firms in the same industry. While this reflects, to some extent, inside information on the part of acquirers about trends that would have taken place anyway and efficiencies that come at the expense of corporate stockholders, there do appear to be some improvements in operating practices. Most LBOs occur in mature industries where spending on research is low, so there is not yet much evidence to support claims that R&D is severely cramped by LBOs. There is evidence that in-vestment outlays decline following LBOs. But the data do not permit us to disentangle the productivity of the investments that are forgone.

Because of the strength of the economy, we do not yet have enough experience to assess the degree of disruption that will be associated with LBOs that go bankrupt. It is important to recognize that LBO bankruptcies will differ importantly from traditional bankruptcies. When traditional, lightly levered companies cannot meet their debt obligations, it is a sign of massive failure in the underlying business. This is not true in the case of LBOs, which may be driven into bankruptcy by events that would simply depress the stock of a normal company by 20 or 30 percent. Because the underlying assets are more valuable, the waste associated with LBO bankruptcies may be greater than in the case of traditional bankruptcies. The more than $1 billion in combined losses suffered by shareholders in Texaco and Penozoil during the course of their litigation illustrates how serious financial disruptions can be.[2]

On the other hand, innovations associated with LBOs may reduce the costs of financial stress. Zero coupon bonds permit companies to ride out transitory financial difficulties. More importantly, strip financing and the more general alignment of interests between high-yield debt and equity owners reduce the incentive to force liquidations. It is often remarked that Japanese corporations can tolerate much higher debt equity ratios than their American counterparts because Japanese banks hold equity and are therefore more patient than American lenders. The same may prove to be true of American LBO firms and their clients.

---

2. For a discussion of this episode and its implications see David Cutler and Lawrence Summers, "The Costs of Conflict Resolution and Financial Distress: Evidence from the Texaco-Pennzoil Litigation," *Rand Journal of Economics* (Summer 1988).

DO RISING DEBT LEVELS POSE SYSTEMIC RISKS?

Alarmists regarding the systemic risks posed by increased levels of corporate debt often overlook a fundamental lesson of recent experience. During the early 1980s, the U.S. suffered the steepest post-War recession, saw inflation abate more rapidly than almost anyone anticipated, saw real interest rates reach and remain at unprecedented levels, and saw the dollar gyrate spectacularly; yet with the exception of special situations like Johns Mansville and firms in the energy sector of the economy, there was only a minimal level of bankruptcy among large publicly traded corporations. Financial distress abounded in the banking system, internationally, and for those who had made certain real estate and agricultural investments, but corporations fared remarkably well through very trying times.

It is hardly unreasonable to expect that this experience would lead to some increases in acceptable levels of leverage. As a general proposition, there is little basis for supposing that the total indebtedness of the U.S. corporate sector is far too high at the present time. Claims that numerous companies that are now publicly traded will be driven into bankruptcy during the next recession overlook the increasing ability of the credit markets to sustain "fallen angels" during periods of temporary distress. It remains the case that levels of leverage in the U.S. are well below those in many of our trading partners.

There will no doubt be some bankruptcies among companies that are in the highly levered early stages of LBOs. While this will hurt naive investors who failed to appreciate the magnitude of the risks for which their high yields were providing compensation, it is doubtful that it will have large economic consequences. If another 1982 recession were to come, which I judge to be quite unlikely, problems in the banking system and in the real estate and farm sectors would dwarf any consequences of recent LBOs.

Overall Judgment

There is no basis for punitive efforts to roll back corporate debt-equity ratios. However, efforts to insure that managers fulfill their fiduciary duties should be increased. Furthermore, nothing in either logic or our experience with debt-increasing transactions suggests that they are so desirable as to warrant substantial government subsidies. The benefi-

ciaries of such subsidies are surely affluent and the government deficit continues to be a serious problem. Moreover most of the benefits of debt finance accrue privately. If anything, the social or external costs of debt finance probably exceed the benefits. This suggests the need to examine the incentives provided by current tax policies.

TAX INCENTIVES AND CORPORATE INDEBTEDNESS

Two related aspects of our current tax system lead to a tax bias in favor of the use of corporate debt. First, corporate borrowers deduct interest payments at a much higher rate than lenders pay on interest payments. Corporate borrowers deduct their interest at a rate of 34 percent.

Table 1 presents Federal Reserve estimates of the ownership of corporate bonds. For each category of investors, I have made a crude estimate of the tax rate after making allowance for various kinds of sheltering activity. The average tax rate on the interest income of corporate bondholders is only about 7.

percent. This means that on every dollar of corporate interest paid, the government loses about 27 cents. This figure was probably reduced somewhat by the reduction in the corporate tax rate from 46 to 34 percent in the 1986 Tax Reform Act.

The substantial wedge between the tax deductions on corporate income and the taxes paid give taxpayers a strong incentive to use debt finance. Most obviously, this creates an incentive for companies to replace outstanding equity with debt, and to replace dividend payments with interest payments. This is exactly what is accomplished in LBOs. It is also accomplished by a variety of corporate restructuring schemes such as the recent Shearson-American Express deal. More generally, debt replaces equity when a corporation draws down the cash from its cash holdings and uses the proceeds to repurchase its stock. Of course, beyond transactions that have as their explicit purpose the replacement of equity by debt, the tax law encourages the use of debt finance for new capital investments.

The second inducement to the use of debt finance is the double taxation of corporate equity income, particularly when it is paid in the form of dividends. If dividends were deductible in just the same way that interest now is, and if shareholders had the same low tax rates as debt owners do, there would be no reason for corporations to prefer debt to equity

TABLE 1
TAX RATES ON INTEREST RECEIPTS

	Interest Receipts ($billions)	1988 Tax Rate (%)
Household (Untaxed)	**2.9**	**0**
Households (Taxed)	5.0	28
Foreigners	**13.3**	**0**
Commercial Banks	6.0	15
Savings and Loans	**3.2**	**18**
Mutual Savings Banks	1.2	6
Life Insurance Companies	**32.9**	**20**
Private Pensions	13.3	0
State & Local Govt. Retirement Funds	**11.4**	**0**
Other Insurance	4.6	20
Mutual Funds	**4.6**	**28**
Securities Brokers and Dealers	1.6	34
TOTAL/Weighted Average Tax Rate	**$105.0**	**7.3%**

Sources: Interest Receipts are from the Federal Reserve Board, Flow of Funds. Tax Rates for industries are from Tax Analysts, *Quantifying the Impact of the Tax Reform Act of 1986 on Effective Corporate Tax Rates*, 1986. Rates for households, foreigners and pension funds are based on 1988 tax law.

finance. However, because dividends are not deductible, corporations have a strong incentive to avoid their use. This leads to a bias in favor of debt finance. It also encourages schemes which transform dividends into capital gains and permit securities to be tailored to the tax situation of their owner. Again the Shearson-American Express deal is a good example.

The conclusion that the tax system creates a general bias in favor of the use of debt finance is to my Knowledge almost universally accepted. However, a number of observers have pointed out that the Treasury gains from LBO transactions because of forced capital gains realizations by the shareowners who are being bought out. It also gains to the extent that operating improvements increase profitability and therefore raise corporate tax payments. This has led to claims by some of those engaged in LBO transactions, by the business press, and by some academics that LBO transactions are already tax penalized. The conclusion drawn is that further tax changes that would reduce the benefits associated with these transactions would be inappropriate.

My analysis suggests that such claims are misleading. First, estimates suggesting that the Treasury gains from LBOs are suspect. They do not take sufficient account of the ability of investors who are forced to realize large capital gains to shelter their income in various ways and probably overstate the taxes paid by corporate creditors. More importantly, in many cases they assume that there will be operat-

ing improvements or that after several years assets will be sold at a substantial premium. While this has been the case in recent years, it is much less clear that it will be the case in the future given the strength of the stock market in the past several years. There is also the difficulty that to the extent post-LBO improvements were anticipated by acquirers, they might have taken place even without the LBO. Finally, claims that LBOs help the Treasury do not take account of losses to corporate stockholders which also affect Treasury revenues.

Second, even beyond these arithmetic points, there is a conceptual point. If, as proponents assume, most LBO deals involve substantial efficiency improvements. they would presumably take place without government subsidy. And the government would share in the efficiency improvement just as it shares in efficiency improvements whenever corporations are able to increase their profitablility This does not justify the further subsidy provided by special tax treatment of debt. There is no question that there exist marginal transactions that are profitable only because of the tax benefits of leverage. Modifications of the tax treatment of debt would affect these transactions, but would not, if LBO advocates are correct, eliminate most LBO transactions.[3]

Finally, it is worthwhile to observe that the revenue offsets to increased interest deductions that are suggested in the case of LBOs are not present in the case of other corporate restructurings.

---

3. The point here may be put another way. It has long been thought that certain industries were tax favored—real estate is one example. Demonstrations that the real estate industry pays positive taxes hardly counter this argument. In just the same way, claims that banning LBOs would reduce tax revenues, even if correct, do not justify the conclusion that these transactions are not tax subsidized.

FUNDAMENTAL TAX REFORM

As long as the tax system seeks to distinguish between debt and equity, and taxes equity income from dividends and capital gains differently, there will be strong incentives for financial engineering to exploit the resulting arbitrage opportunities. Current concern over the excessive use of debt finance is only the latest in a long sequence of policy problems posed by the antiquated categorizations we use in taxing the income from capital. It will not be the last.

As the examples of commodity straddles, zero coupon bonds, and mirror transactions suggest, the private sector is capable of finding an endless array of devices to exploit the differential tax treatment of different individuals and types of income. As the pace of financial innovation has quickened and regulatory barriers have eased, the pace at which these devices are created has accelerated. Patchwork, piecemeal fixes will not forever staunch the tide of financial innovation. It is not too early to begin the process of reconsidering the fundamental principles underlying the way our income tax treats capital income.

Fundamental issues that should be given serious consideration include the following. First, should we tax saving and investment income twice as current law provides? Or should we instead simply tax consumption, thereby taxing capital income when it is consumed but not when it is reinvested? Beyond the strong macroeconomic arguments for moving in this direction provided by our 2% national saving rate, movements towards a cash flow tax would eliminate much of the current scope for abuse. Value added taxes are only one way of taxing consumption. A promising variety of progressive consumption tax schemes have been proposed in recent years.

Should the corporate tax be integrated? As capital markets become more and more perfect, the case for double taxing corporate equity income becomes more and more dubious. Must of our trading partners have tax systems that are integrated in some way through either partial dividend deductibility or tax credits to individuals for corporate taxes paid on their behalf. While integration has traditionally been opposed by corporate executives, who do not want increased pressures to pay out dividends rather than undertake investments or acquisitions, this source of opposition may be muted in the current environment, when market pressures are sharply curbing free cash flows.

Third, is there an argument for wealth or property value based corporate taxation? Business property taxes at the state and local level raise substantial amounts of revenue, without generating nearly the complexity that the current corporate income tax system does. Property value based taxation does not distinguish between debt arid equity finance, and has certain other desirable neutrality properties. It is particularly attractive for large publicly traded corporations because the market provides a continuous assessment of property value.

Fourth, can accrual capital gains be taxed on publicly traded securities? The Achilles' heel of the current income tax is the fact that capital gains now are taxed only when realized. This makes it impossible to tax all economic income at the same rate, and creates strong incentives to transform income into the form of capital gains. While taxing real estate on an accrual basis would be difficult because of the problem of valuation, it might well be possible to tax capital gains on listed securities on an accrual basis. This would substantially discourage financial engineering.

It is not realistic to expect new legislative answers to any of these questions in the context of the LBO issue. But this issue is really just the tip of an iceberg. It is high time to begin a fundamental reassessment of our current approach to taxing capital income.

CURRENT POLICY OPTIONS

Drawing precise lines between debt and equity is inevitably difficult in close cases. But some of the securities used in recent LBO transactions do not represent close cases. When debt-equity ratios approach 10 to 1, yields on junior debt approach or exceed 20 percent. debt instruments do nut require any cash payment for five or more years, arid deal participants note that bankruptcy risks are nut large because debt securities represent "equity in drag," it is hard to see the public policy justification fur permitting the deduction of interest accrued but not even paid out. These conditions are all satisfied in many recent LBO transactions. There are strong arguments fur policy changes that tighten up on the definition of debt fur tax purposes.

Criteria for disallowing the deductibility of interest should include some combination of the following elements: (1) the yield to maturity when debt risk premia exceed the roughly eight percent risk premia normally observed on equity securities, there is a case for treating them as equity securities; (2) the extent to which cash payments are not actually made but interest is only accrued or paid in the form of new debt securities when dividends can legally be paid on equity before any cash interest must be paid, it is unclear in what real sense a debt security can be said to be senior; (3) the corporate balance sheet when substantial new debt is being issued and the ratio of outstanding debt to the market value of equity is high, the debt may well represent disguised equity; and (4) the share of operating earnings paid out in interest or the ratio of interest to dividend payments—when either of these measures is high there is a presumption that interest is being used to substantially avoid corporate taxes that would otherwise be paid.

Application of rules based on some combination of these criteria to recent public transactions would probably have eliminated the deductibility of a small part, perhaps 10 or 20 percent of interest, used in financing acquisitions. This would probably have led to somewhat greater reliance on equity financing. If the claims of participants in these transactions are correct, this would not have prevented them from taking place, though it would have reduced acquisition premiums somewhat and probably reduced the profits earned by deal participants. It also would have funneled significant additional revenues to the Treasury.

The challenge in designing tax rules that tighten up on the definition of debt for tax purposes is to avoid throwing out the baby with the bath water. Most high-yield debt is not used in the context of takeovers. Restrictions on all high yield debt would therefore be undesirable. However, it does not appear that high-yield zero coupon securities are extensibely used outside of the takeover context, so criteria (2) above should be helpful in targeting tax rules appropriately. There is the additional complication that limitations on interest deductibility might give foreign acquirers an advantage over their American competitors. This probably is not an important issue for the modest rule changes envisaged here. The kind of extremely high-yield debt used in recent deals is not yet available abroad.

The approach outlined here is preferable to proposals directed specifically at acquisition transactions. The basic problem of equity masquerading as debt is as present in restructurings as it is in ownership changes. Measures which penalized only acquisition

interest would therefore give strong advantages to incumbents in control contests who could take advantage of tax benefits not available to potential acquirers. The available evidence does not suggest the desirability of such a tilt in the playing field. Even if such a tilt were desirable, it is doubtful that it is best implemented through the tax system.

The approach outlined here will not preserve the existing tax base intact. It does not for example, address the erosion of the tax base that occurs when corporations use cash to repurchase shares. Nor does it address transactions like the recent Shearson-American Express deal. These problems probably cannot be addressed short of the sort of fundamental tax reform discussed above.

The existing tax bias towards debt can be addressed in two ways—either by reducing the tax advantages of debt or by increasing the tax benefits for new equity issues. I have concentrated on the former approach because of budgetary realities. But I believe that there is a strong case for using any revenues derived from limits on interest deductions to finance reductions in the dividend tax burden on newly issued equity. Because equity issuance is relatively small, this would not be very costly over the next few years. It would also avoid the problem of giving windfalls to existing shareholders that plagues most dividend relief proposals.

CONCLUSION

Recent increases in corporate indebtedness are probably not primarily tax motivated, and do not pose grave dangers to economic stability. In some cases, they are associated with improvements in economic efficiency. There is, however, little case for subsidizing debt to the extent done by current tax rules. Reforms that tightened the tax definition of debt would have relatively small effects on acquisition transactions if the proponents of these transactions are to be believed. They would raise some revenue, correct some abuses, and probably improve economic performance by eliminating some marginal buyouts and increasing the equity share in others.

For the longer term, recent developments suggest the need to rethink basic questions about our approach to capital taxation, including the choice of the income tax base, the decision to double tax corporate equity income, the use of income rather than wealth concepts in assessing tax burdens, and the taxation of capital gains on a realization basis.

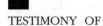

TESTIMONY OF
Alan J. Auerbach
CHAIRMAN AND PROFESSOR,
DEPARTMENT OF ECONOMICS
UNIVERSITY OF PENNSYLVANIA
BEFORE THE SENATE FINANCE COMMITTEE
January 26, 1989

Mr. Chairman and Members of the Committee:

The recent explosion in corporate borrowing and leveraged buyout activity raises significant questions about tax policy and financial regulation. This committee is to be commended for addressing these questions so swiftly. I will begin my testimony by stating my conclusions.

1. Corporate debt-equity ratios have risen sharply in recent years. This increase is largely attributable to increases in share repurchases, cash-financed acquisitions, and leveraged buyouts. Yet cur-rent debt-equity ratios are not unprecedented for the United States, nor do they yet compare to those observed in Japan or in many other industrial countries.

2. The increase in borrowing and merger activity cannot be attributed to changes in tax provisions. While certain incentives to borrow and acquire are provided by the Internal Revenue Code, these have existed for many years and, in some cases, were actually reduced by the Tax Reform Act of 1986.

3. The ultimate aim of tax policy should not be to discourage borrowing in general or leveraged buyouts in particular, but simply to ensure that such activities are not driven by tax advantages.

4. Given the increasing difficulty of telling debt from equity, the only practical way to achieve "neutrality" is to reduce and eventually remove the distinction between debt and equity imposed by the in-come tax. A component of most plans would be tax relief for corporate dividends, but the relief must be restricted in some way to avoid enormous losses of tax revenue.

DEBT-EQUITY RATIOS

There is little question that fundamental changes in corporate financial behavior have occurred in recent years. In every year since 1984, net corporate equity issues have been negative. After appearing to level off at an annual level of about $80 billion through 1987, net repurchases occurred at an annual rate of $109 billion during the first three quarters of 1988, according to statistics compiled by the Federal Reserve Board. The bulk of this decline in equity is attributable to cash-financed acquisitions, although share repurchases have also played an important role.

Over this same period, corporate borrowing has increased. Net annual borrowing by nonfinancial corporations averaged $64 billion during the period 1980-83, $153 billion during the period 1984-87, and $183 billion during the first three quarters of 1988.

Despite this evident shift away from equity and toward debt, the aggregate corporate debt-equity ratio is still not especially high by historical standards or by international comparison. At the end of 1987, the debt-equity ratio of the U.S. nonfinancial corporate sector, measured at market values, was .71. This ratio has hovered between .62 and .76 since 1980, and indeed was higher during the entire period from 1974 to 1979. Measured at book values, the current aggregate debt-equity ratio is higher than during the last decade, but comparable to those of the late 1960s and early 1970s. By comparison, the aggregate debt-equity ratio for Japanese nonfinancial corporations has exceeded 1.0 (more debt than equity) for decades.

These aggregate statistics suggest that current levels of indebtedness of U.S. corporations are not dangerously high. What is cause for concern, though, is the speed with which debt has recently replaced equity and the prospect that the shift may continue at this pace. At some point, the financial stability of U. S. business could become a serious issue. While I can't offer a definitive explanation for recent behavior, I do not believe that changes in tax policy are the cause.

BORROWING AND THE CORPORATE TAX

Corporations deduct their interest payments in computing their taxable income, but cannot deduct dividends. Because of this, companies are encouraged to finance their investments by borrowing rather than by issuing new equity. This is a defect of the system of taxation under which we treat corporations as separate entities, but it has always been one. Little has happened in the relative treatment of debt and equity that can explain recent changes in financial behavior.

The Tax Reform Act of 1986 reduced the corporate tax rate from 46 percent to 34 percent, cutting by over one-fourth the value of the corporate interest deduction. This can hardly explain an increase in borrowing. One must look at the taxes paid by asset holders to get a complete picture of the total tax burden. Marginal tax rates on interest receipts and dividends also fell under the 1986 Act, especially. for high-income investors. On the other hand, capital gains tax rates rose. Since a significant part of the return to equity is typically in the form of capital gains, the net impact of these provisions was to lower the individual tax burden on interest income by considerably more than on total returns to equity. This works against the reduction in the corporate tax rate, and the net impact depends on an investor's tax bracket. Among high-bracket investors, for whom the reduced tax burden on interest payments is significant, the net result has been to encourage corporate borrowing. For another significant class of investors, tax-exempt institutions and pension funds, only the corporate tax changes are relevant, and these discourage the use of debt. If one weighs the effects on different classes of investors, the 1986 Act appears, on balance, to have discouraged borrowing.

A second factor discouraging the use of debt recently has been the decline in the rate of inflation and nominal interest rates. Since the potential tax advantage of borrowing is attributable to the deductibility of nominal interest payments, this decline in interest rates would have reduced the tax advantage of borrowing even had there been no change in marginal tax rates.

As recent changes in tax rules and inflation have discouraged borrowing in general, they have put an even greater damper on borrowing associated with cash acquisitions and leveraged buyouts. I have already described the changes in the relative tax burdens on returns to equity and debt. But to convert equity to debt, corporations and shareholders must bear additional taxes. The increase in capital gains taxes hits equity repurchase transactions with full force, to the extent that shareholders are taxable. This is especially true in the case of acquisitions, because the premia associated with tender offers are fully taxable at the capital gains tax rate. Moreover, the 1986 repeal of the General Utilities doctrine means that the tax benefits of stepping up asset bases are likely to be more than offset by immediate corporate capital gains tax liabilities. On balance, it is very difficult to argue that debt-financed take-overs have been newly encouraged by the tax system. The evidence is very much to the contrary.

Why the increase in borrowing and debt-financed takeovers? I believe there are several causes. One is the macroeconomic performance of the 1980s. The U.S. economy has been growing steadily since 1982. The fear of financial reverses that normally limits borrowing may well have subsided as memory of the last recession faded.

Another important factor is the changing nature of U.S. financial markets. The increasing availability of large pools of funds to finance potentially risky borrowing on a significant scale has helped. There has been considerable debate over the social value of "junk" bonds and whether markets have ad-equately measured the risk they carry. But, in general, innovations that reduce the cost of financial intermediation and make funds more available are technological advantages just as much as discover-ies that reduce the costs of manufacturing pro-cesses. Historically, the development of financial intermediaries has played a significant role in the rise of industrial economies. We hardly should lament the continuation of this process or the changes in financial structure that it brings.

Borrowing has also increased, I believe, be-cause of an increase in the competitiveness of the market for corporate control. Whether involved in a takeover or not, managers are being pushed to borrow more to maintain equity values. In this more competitive market for corporate control, fostered by relaxed antitrust enforcement and the increasing availability of funds, corporations have often been driven to borrow as a way to increase the value of their shares and thereby defend against potential acquisition. Directly or indirectly, the takeover process has spurred corporate borrowing and its associated increases in share values.

Not all of this increase in value has been socially beneficial. Increased borrowing can reduce the value of existing corporate debt, in effect transferring re-sources to shareholders from the owners of outstand-ing debt. Another source of value that is equally un-productive from the social perspective is the reduc-tion in federal tax burden associated with borrowed funds. Even though the tax incentive to borrow has not increased, the pressure to take advantage of this tax incentive has. While perhaps helping shareholders, competition that forces corporations to reduce their tax burden is hardly in the public interest. Evidence on leveraged buyouts from the period through 1986 suggests that a substantial part of the takeover premium can be explained by tax factors. However, such evidence also suggests that companies taken private subsequently reduced operating costs, a result some would attribute to the increased pres-sure of having to meet higher interest payments. The continued growth of LBO activity after 1986 suggests that nontax factors play an important role.

In summary, the tax incentive to borrow has not increased in recent years, though pressure on man-agers to take full advantage of this incentive may help explain increased corporate borrowing. At the same time, the strong economy, the reduced cost of financial intermediation and increased pressure on managers to operate efficiently may also have played a significant role in encouraging corporate borrowing.

THE SOCIAL COSTS OF BORROWING

There is little question that tax-driven borrow-ing is an appropriate target of tax reform. If borrowing has tax advantages, then those who borrow impose a cost on the rest of society by increasing the amount of tax that must be raised from other sources. Some would argue that corporate borrowing, even if not tax-driven, has social costs beyond those recognized by those who borrow, that a "level playing field" is still too generous to borrowing. I do not subscribe to this position, but believe the arguments are worth review.

Restrictions on Monetary Policy

If a significant fraction of the corporate sector is deeply in debt, a credit crunch with sharply rising interest rates would drive many firms into bank-ruptcy. The prospect of such a debacle might impede the ability of the Federal Reserve to use tight monetary policy to fight inflation. Hence, more borrowing might inevitably lead to more inflation.

This theoretical possibility is loot very convinc-ing, particularly given the behavior of monetary policy in recent years. In the early 1980s, the economy experienced the deepest recession since the Great Depression, as a tight monetary policy was successfully used to bring the inflation rate down rapidly. If the Fed is willing to fight inflation with unemployment rates exceeding 10 percent, why should it be cowed by higher rates of default?

Lack of Long-Range Planning

Managers of U.S. firms have been criticized for being too concerned with short-run results, and have been compared unfavorably to their foreign counterparts, notably the Japanese, in this respect. The increased pressure to meet interest payments is viewed by some as increasing the pressure to focus exclusively on short-run results.

There are several difficulties with this line of argument. Perhaps most obvious is that, as I have already pointed out, Japanese firms have significantly higher debt-equity ratios than do those in the United States. Moreover, companies taken private typically have been mature companies. in stable industries with little research and development or long-term spending. There is no evidence to support the related argument that firms involved in ordinary mergers and acquisitions experience a reduction in expenditures on research and development.

Reduced National Saving

There is little doubt or disagreement that the U.S. saving rate is very low, particularly in light of the federal budget deficit. In recent years, private saving has barely exceeded public saving. Corporate saving, via retained earnings, typically has accounted for about half of all private saving in the United States. By substituting debt for equity, corporations are committing themselves to save less. Some fear this will reduce private saving as a whole.

Although this is a worrisome prospect, there is no evidence that increasing distributions of funds from corporations, either through interest payments or increased dividend yields, in itself causes a decline in the level of private saving. The recipients of these funds are not prohibited from reinvesting them. My own recent research on this subject fails to turn up any evidence that changes in corporate financial policy, by themselves, affect the rate of private saving.

THE APPROPRIATE OBJECTIVES OF TAX POLICY

The main problem associated with corporate borrowing-if any problem exists-is the tax advantage of borrowing that remains even after the Tax Reform Act of 1986. Once this advantage is eliminated, no further restrictions on borrowing are necessary. Even if the tax advantage is not eliminated, the imposition of borrowing restrictions represents a poor substitute for the direct solution.

Borrowing Restrictions

Several restrictions have been proposed to limit corporate borrowing. The simplest would be to reduce the deductibility of interest payments on all corporate debt. This is the most general type of borrowing restriction and for many reasons the most attractive. It is the simplest to enforce, for it is easier (though not necessarily easy) to identify debt than to identify debt incurred for particular reasons. Reducing interest deductibility also attacks the underlying problem, which is the tax advantage of debt over equity. Finally, it can be implemented to satisfy other objectives as well, such as raising tax revenue and moving toward a system of taxing real income, with only the real component of interest expense (and not the inflation premium as well) deductible. The main drawback of reducing the deductibility of interest is that it exacerbates the distinction between corporate and noncorporate investment; the latter already enjoys a lower overall rate of tax. It would be better to achieve neutral tax treatment of debt and equity by lowering the tax rate on equity income, for this would also reduce the distortion between corporate and noncorporate investment.

Other, narrower restrictions on borrowing are far less attractive, being harder to implement and more difficult to justify. One type of policy that has been considered seriously in the past would limit the deduction of interest on debt incurred to finance takeovers. Like other targeted borrowing restrictions that have been introduced in recent years, such a restriction would introduce great complexity to the tax system. Identifying such debt would be very difficult, for money is fungible. Even if this problem were overcome, I can see no reason to discourage take-overs this way; what problem is such a measure supposed to address?

Another restriction on borrowing would place a cap on interest deductions based on some relatively safe rate of interest, making the excess interest on high-yield, lower grade bonds nondeductible. Once again, I see both administrative and logical problems with such a policy. From the administrative viewpoint, one would have to identify the interest rate on each obligation. How would one treat bonds that had been downgraded after their issue, for example? One might seek to rationalize this policy by pointing to the fact that it removes the tax advantage of borrowing once there is substantial risk of default. How-ever, the extent to which interest deductions should be denied to produce neutrality between debt and equity depends on the relative tax treatment of debt and equity, not on the riskiness of the debt. An alter-native argument is that once debt becomes risky, it is like equity and should be treated as equity. But the sources of risk for equity and low grade debt are quite different.

Equity Relief

As I have already suggested, the best approach to the unequal taxation of debt and equity is to reduce the tax burden on corporate equity. A simple and straightforward approach, already practiced in many countries, is some form of dividend relief, implemented either through a deduction for dividends paid (also called a split-rate system) or through a shareholder credit (also called an imputation system). The problem with such a plan is also simple: it is very expensive. The Treasury's November 1984 tax reform proposals included partial dividend relief in the form of a 50 percent deduction for dividends paid. It was then estimated that this plan would cost the Treasury $30.9 billion in fiscal year 1990. Little has happened since that would alter this estimate substantially. Such partial dividend relief, and certainly more complete relief, is entirely impractical at present. Even a 10 percent dividends paid deduction would cost roughly $6.7 billion during fiscal year 1990, according to the estimates presented in the president's 1985 tax reform proposals.

These proposals are expensive because they would create windfalls. Most dividends paid during the next few years will come from income on assets already in place. Reducing the taxes on all such income is a very inefficient and (to the recipients of such income) overly generous method of correcting the distortion between debt and equity finance. There are many ways to make this policy more efficient, but each has its drawbacks.

Institute the policy, but combine it with a tax on the windfalls generated. The most straightforward approach would combine a dividends paid deduction with an offsetting tax on some measure of current dividend capacity, such as accumulated earnings and profits. For example, a 50 per-cent dividends paid deduction would be combined with a 17 percent (50 percent of the 34 percent corporate tax rate) tax on accumulated earnings and profits. The windfall tax could be made payable over several years. The logic of this policy is that it would eliminate the net benefit of the deduction for all dividends paid out of past earnings and profits; it would provide a net reduction only for dividends generated by new equity capital. Depending on the timing of the windfall tax, the total package could raise revenue for a number of years. The disadvantage of this policy is not economic but political. The President's 1985 proposals included a similar provision (to reduce the windfalls arising from the corporate rate reduction) that proved to be extremely unpopular, and I am sure this policy would have a similar reception. That is unfortunate, because from an economic perspective it is clearly the best policy.

Institute the Policy of dividend relief only for new equity issues, and combine this with restrictions on the conversion of existing equity to debt or new equity. This is the proposal circulated by the American Law Institute (ALI). The most recent version (dated November 1988) would provide a dividends paid deduction based on the extent of new equity contributions, and would at the same time impose an alternative minimum tax of 28 percent on nondividend corporate distributions, withheld at the corporate level and credited against shareholder tax liability on the distributions.

The ALI proposal is intended to limit windfalls by excluding existing equity from dividend relief Under certain assumptions, this approach would provide the same incentives as the combination of full dividend relief and a windfalls tax. Neither the tax on accumulated earnings and profits nor the ALI proposal would either discourage or encourage conversions of existing equity into debt. This would be true in spite of the new tax on nondividend distributions because this tax (or the ordinary tax on dividends) would apply to any distributions a corporation made in the future. Thus, the tax could be deferred (with interest, since distributions would be greater in the future) but not reduced in value, and so, like the tax on accumulated earnings and profits, could not be avoided.

The ALI plan is a more elaborate way of achieving the tax on windfalls. In effect, the corporation rather than the government decides when the tax is paid; the unpaid balance accumulates interest. The proposal's major "benefit" is that it is less clearly an unavoidable capital levy. While this lack of transparency may make it more acceptable, it also makes it harder to understand and, I would presume, enforce. This is evident from the many drafts through which the proposal has gone. Unlike the more straightforward policy, its effectiveness depends on taxpayers' believing that its provisions are permanent. A permanent tax on distributions may not affect the timing of such distributions, but a temporary tax would. Given the frequency with which tax provisions change any tax on distributions may be perceived as a temporary one. In this case, the ALI plan would strongly discourage share repurchases, leveraged buyouts and other cash acquisitions. It might even discourage dividends, if corporations anticipated that dividend relief would be made available to all dividends in the future.

My conclusion is that the ALI plan's chief distinction is that it is more difficult to comprehend than a windfalls tax. At best, its impact would be identical, but it might very well impose costly distortions as the price for its complexity.

Combine a partial dividends paid deduction with a partial denial of the deduction of interest. Although this approach would raise the overall burden on new corporate investment more than either of the previous approaches (it pays for dividend relief with an increase in the tax burden on debt-financed corporate investment), it would still achieve neutrality between corporate debt and equity without a significant revenue cost. It is a workable approach that does not depend on novel tax instruments or particular expectations about future policy, but it also imposes costs (in discouraging corporate investment) that may outweigh its benefits (removing the distortion of corporate financial decisions).

CONCLUSIONS

In a dynamic economy experiencing financial innovations and more competition for corporate control, it is natural to ask to what extent the changes we observe are for the best. It is not clear that the tax advantage to debt is an important cause of recent in-creases in borrowing, but this distortion has merited correction for many years and might well be addressed now to ensure that it play no part in future behavior. The solution chosen, however, ought to satisfy the ultimate objectives of taxation rather than simply assuage the fears of the moment.

THE ECONOMIC CONSEQUENCES OF HIGH LEVERAGE AND STOCK MARKET PRESSURES ON CORPORATE MANAGEMENT: A ROUNDTABLE DISCUSSION

Sponsored by the J. Ira Harris Center for the Study of Corporate Finance at the University of Michigan

March 15, 1990

IRA HARRIS AND HARRY DeANGELO

HARRY DeANGELO: Good afternoon, my name is Harry DeAngelo. I am Director of the Harris Center, and I will be serving as moderator of today's discussion. The focus of our discussion is a very timely and important issue: the question of how high leverage and other capital market pressures on management are affecting the competitiveness of American corporations and the U.S. economy at large.

The discussion will be held in two parts. In the first part, we will hear from four panelists who have either studied or participated directly in the leveraged buyout movement. After each of the four presents a brief statement of his views, we will then open things up for discussion. The second part will begin with comments by our other four panelists on the role of high leverage and stock market pressures in the management of our *public* companies. Following a second open discussion among the panelists, we will then close with a few questions from the audience.

We are privileged to have with us a uniformly outstanding group of corporate finance experts. I will introduce all of them now in the order in which they will be speaking.

MICHAEL JENSEN is the Edsel Bryant Ford Professor of Business Administration at the Harvard Business School.

Mike's views on leveraged buyouts were set forth most recently in his highly controversial *Harvard Business Review* article called "The Eclipse of the Public Corporation," about which I expect to hear a lot today.

LAWRENCE SUMMERS holds the Nathaniel Ropes Chair in Economics at Harvard University. Larry is a nationally recognized expert on public policy issues and is known for sharp criticisms of LBOs and stock market efficiency.

ROBERT SIEFERT was formerly President and Chief Operating Officer of the Fruehauf Corporation, which undertook a leveraged buyout. He was also Chairman and CEO of Kelsey-Hayes. Prior to the LBO, Bob was President in charge of Automotive Operations at Fruehauf as well as President and CEO of Kelsey-Hayes.

JOHN MORLEY is President and CEO of Reliance Electric Corporation, which was taken private through a leveraged management buyout from the company's former parent, Exxon.

The second part of the discussion will open with statements by our two representatives from public companies, both of which have felt high leverage and stock market pressures to varying degrees.

ALLAN GILMOUR is Executive Vice President of Ford Motor Company and

President, Ford Automotive Group. Allan has been a member of the Board of Directors since 1986. He has been with Ford since his graduation from the University of Michigan in 1960 and, since then, has held the positions of Chief Financial Officer, head of International Automotive Operations, and head of Corporate Staffs.

ROBERT MERCER recently retired as CEO of the Goodyear Tire and Rubber Company after a 42-year career. Our final two participants, although not from public companies, have strong interests in their success.

NELL MINOW is General Counsel for Institutional Shareholder Services, Inc., a private firm based in Washington, D.C. that advises institutional investors on matters of corporate governance.

BENNETT STEWART is a Senior Partner of Stern Stewart & Co., a New York-based firm that advises corporate managements on corporate restructuring, incentive compensation plans, and other methods of generating value for stockholders.

We have one other participant in today's discussion. **IRA HARRIS** is a Senior Partner at Lazard Frères, and it is largely Ira's efforts that have made events like the present one possible through the activities of the Harris Center.

The challenge for all of us today...is to address the problem caused by the failure of the internal control processes within our largest companies. Why is U.S. Steel in its current predicament when it's been clear for so long that something's gone wrong? Why are our companies having such a hard time coming to grips with the need to reform within? Why have we had to resort to our capital markets to make the necessary changes? Are we better off letting many of our companies go through a slow decline and eventual dismemberment by the product markets? Or should we let our capital markets intercede and bring about change—ugly as the process is—and get these organizations back on track as quickly as possible?

The problem is especially critical today because we are again in a position where we are severely limiting the monitoring role of our capital markets. So the burden of change is now back where it was during the 60s and 70s—that is, on the boards of directors and the internal managements. And, to enable our companies to compete in increasingly global markets, they will have to do a much better job than they have in the past.

Will we make the necessary changes, or will we simply sit back and wait for the forces of the international product market to bind? That, in my view, is the major management challenge we face going forward in the 1990s.

—MICHAEL JENSEN—

PART I: PERSPECTIVES ON LEVERAGED BUYOUTS

Two Economists' Views of LBOs and Corporate Debt

DeANGELO: To start off our economic overview of the subject, I will now turn the microphone over to Michael Jensen.

MICHAEL JENSEN: Thanks, Harry. Harry has led me to understand that a good number of people here today, in the audience as well as on this panel, have read a couple of things I've written on the subject of LBOs and the benefits of corporate leverage—one of them most recently in the *Harvard Business Review.* So I won't bother to repeat the arguments I made there. Those parts of the article my fellow panelists disagree with will no doubt surface in the second part of this discussion.

It is a very different world now from what it was a year and a half ago when I was writing that piece. Harry asked me whether I would change anything I said in that article. I might change a few things. But, after re-reading it on my way out here this afternoon, I decided that I still stand by what I wrote. I still think it's right.

LAWRENCE SUMMERS: Mike, my old debate coach taught me a key point of strategy: When *reduced* to the absurd, *defend* the absurd.

JENSEN: Larry, you've already violated the agreement we just made in the back room.

As we all know, the high-yield market has been in turmoil. The yield differential between high-yield bonds and Treasuries is now at an all-time high of 800 basis points. That obviously means the cost of high leverage has gone up considerably—in fact, by some 300 to 400 basis points over what it's been historically. As is true in any market, when the price of a good goes up, people consume less of that good. So, for this reason alone, it makes sense to have less leverage now than it did before. Maybe Larry would interpret that as a change, but certainly nothing I said would imply that managers shouldn't pay attention to prices. But the benefits—what I call the "control benefits"—of leverage are still very much in evidence today.

The takeover market is also very different today than it was a year and a half ago. The fact that money is now so much more expensive means that market pressures—most notably, the threat of takeover—that once forced many managements to undertake defensive LBOs and other financial restructurings are now significantly reduced. So we're going to see a lot fewer defensive recapitalizations. Further reducing the threat of takeover, poison pills and state anti-takeover regulations are now very effective; they are now legally enforceable. And, as a consequence of higher financing costs and these new legal barriers to takeover, we are seeing a substantial shift away from tender offers and toward proxy contests—a shift that I expect to continue. We'll see continued innovation and evolution in the proxy challenge process.

We've also seen the bankruptcy of some fairly major firms, Campeau being the most publicized of them. Steve Kaplan at the University of Chicago has been studying that deal; and it turns out that Campeau provides a good illustration of how important valuation is to the success of these transactions. Contrary to what we have been told by the business press, Campeau has actually created an enormous amount of value in the process of acquiring Federated Stores. As Kaplan reports, Federated's equity and debt were worth about $4.25 billion prior to the Campeau acquisition. In the first year after the acquisition, Campeau sold off half of Federated's assets for over $4 billion dollars while also cutting millions of dollars out of overhead and paying out $310 million to bondholders. In December of 1989, Merrill Lynch valued the remaining half of the assets at distress sale prices of $3 billion. Since the total value created as of December 1989 was over $3 billion (the number is $2 billion when adjusted for market movements over the same period), it looks like this has been a successful acquisition.

Then why has it ended up in the tank? Very simply, Campeau, with the help of some handy investment bankers who have acquired a reputation for urging their clients to do whatever it takes to get a deal done, overpaid by about $1.5 billion. It was also overlevered, of course. But the fact that most of Campeau's investment took the form of debt rather than equity is the principal reason why the story of that acquisition was front-page news for weeks. If the deal had instead been financed by means of a stock swap (like the recent Time-Warner deal), then we would have read little or nothing in the media after the deal. The loss would have occurred, but it would have been borne entirely by Campeau shareholders. In fact the losses would likely have been higher because there would have been less value created, fewer improvements in operating efficiency.

Now, of course, despite this major increase in value, and although the companies are continuing to produce good operating results (pre-interest), Campeau has gone into bankruptcy—a bankruptcy that of course would not have occurred if the deal had been equity financed. And whether the transaction turns out to have been value-creating on net, and thus socially desirable, is going to depend on how much costs are generated in the bankruptcy process. Kaplan estimates that the bankruptcy costs will have to total $2.5 billion in current dollars, or over 80 percent of Campeau's pre-bankruptcy value, to eliminate all value created. This is unlikely because bankruptcies usually generate costs under 10 percent of pre-bankruptcy firm value.

I would like to spend a couple of minutes today discussing something that the editors at the *Harvard Business Review* wouldn't let me talk about (because of space constraints) at the end of my article—what I call a "contracting failure" in venture capital markets. Such contracting problems in the market for LBOs and other highly leveraged transactions almost guarantee that we're going to get "overshooting" and "boom-bust" cycles in the markets for these HLTs. It's a perfectly general phenomenon. We see it in real estate all the time, in REITs, and in oil and gas well drilling. Venture capital itself is going through it at the current time. And if we're not already in it with LBOs, we will certainly get there.

What causes this phenomenon? I think it's reasonably simple. First, you begin with a depressed market or with a market that doesn't really even exist, like the LBO market in the 1970s. In the earliest stage of LBOs, you had this strange animal that investors did not understand. A handful of entrepreneurs, possessing some combination of vision and, in some cases, just dumb luck, figure out a way to do some deals and make a lot of money. Because nobody understands why the transactions work, the entrepreneurs have a tough time getting capital. So they end up having to put in a fair amount of equity themselves.

But, when a few of these deals turn out to earn fabulous returns, investors begin to take notice. As we now know from our studies of LBOs consummated prior to 1986, the annual rates of return for the largest LBOs—those of $50 million or more—have been something like 135 percent per year compounded. This is far more than investors could have gotten by using their margin accounts (even if they could have borrowed 9 times the amount of their own cash investment) to buy the stock of public companies over the same period of time. By any measure you want to look at, these transactions have been generating significant increases in productivity—that is, whether evaluated in terms of year-to-year accounting measures or according to changes in the value of the underlying securities.

Now, the next stage in this LBO process is that the lenders and the other participants in these deals begin to sense the presence of a gold mine. And, as they become less cautious about putting money into the deals, they also begin to demand more of the equity. As a result, the venture capitalists and promoters, the KKRs of the world, suddenly find themselves under pressure to share more of the upside with the creditors. And with all the money chasing after them, the promoters end up reducing the amount of equity that they put in the deal out of their own pocket. At the same time, the rates of return earned on the deals are becoming increasingly publicized by the media. As a consequence, more money keeps flowing in, new dealmakers and lenders enter the business, and many of the good deals get done. And then you start to get to the marginal deals.

Now, the classic economic model would say that, as the prices go up and the deals begin to approach the margin, then insolvencies should begin to appear; and the activity should begin to slow. But, in this case, the expected safeguards do not appear to have operated soon enough. What is it, then, that causes the players in these markets to systematically overshoot, to build too many condominiums, to drill too many oil and gas wells—and probably to do too many LBOs at excessive prices and with too much leverage?

The answer, I think, is that in the final stages of this process, the promoters themselves begin to see that they are getting to marginal deals. So they don't fight as hard to maintain their share of the equity. After all, they still get their standard 20 percent "override," which amounts to a free warrant for 20 percent of the final value of the deal. And together with this free override, they even find themselves able to charge high up-front cash fees—not to mention the ongoing management fees—which they often substitute for the commitment of cash equity.

The result is that, as the process continues, many dealmakers are no longer getting paid *only* on the back end of successful deals. They're now getting paid simply to *do* deals. Even if you ignore all the fees and just think about the 20 percent override, the dealmakers are now in a situation where they are putting up no equity money at all.

What happens, then, at the end of the process, is that the promoters, the venture capitalists, have created an environment in which it pays them to do deals that they know (or should know) at the time are less valuable than the cost of the deal. And the result—and in fact the only force that brings this market into equilibrium—is mounting evidence of deals getting into trouble. But, by the time we reach this terminal stage, the reputation of everyone in the industry has gone into the tank. It has become very unpopular; it has the smell of death about it. The investment banking community has become a favorite target of the press. *Forbes* magazine, for example, published an article referring to Bruce Wasserstein as "Bid 'em up, Bruce." (Although I'm not sure, this may be a well-deserved title. But I would be very interested to know how much equity he's putting into his deals out of his own pocket.)

So how do we solve this problem? Although I haven't solved the optimization problem, there is a simple rule of thumb that would probably prevent many, if not most, of the bad deals we're now seeing. And it's a solution that doesn't rely on better monitoring by the lenders and the limited partners. What can be done instead is to correct the up-front incentives by requiring the dealmakers to put up their own capital, to put their own money on the line. In the venture capital market, the standard contract has the venture capitalist putting up one percent. The real estate market, although more complicated, is much the same; and oil and gas well drilling is also very much the same. I think that if you force the promoter to put up a larger stake, perhaps as much as 10 to 20 percent of the equity—and in cash, not in fees—then the dealmakers will sort out the bad deals themselves and you'll stop the overshooting.

The tendency for overshooting is not a problem, however, that requires regulatory intervention. It is essentially a self-correcting problem—one that will cause lenders, limited partners, and dealmakers to devise better methods of sorting out good deals from bad.

In the meantime, our large public corporations are still experiencing international competition as well as competition from smaller and some now private U.S. firms. So, although the market for highly leveraged transactions is sharply depressed and hamstrung by regulators, we're still going to continue to see our large public corporations facing substantial competitive pressures from new organizational forms like KKR and Forstmann Little. And even if these markets are curbed, international product market competition will eventually force our public companies to shape up or suffer from the competitive disadvantage that arises from the separation of ownership from control.

Let me also mention in closing that, in the article I wrote for the *Harvard Business Review*, space constraints also prevented me from including a final section that would have said the following: Our public companies really *can* get most of those benefits of private companies and LBO associations like KKR by adopting many of the same programs. They can increase leverage, they can cut down the size of the headquarters staff, and they can decentralize. They can also bring in active investors to act as monitors such as Lazard Frère's Corporate Partners Fund, and other organizations like that. The question is, *will* they make these changes without outside pressure?

DeANGELO: Thanks, Mike. Now, for a somewhat different view of the LBO process, let's turn to Larry Summers.

SUMMERS: Thanks, Harry. I've been sitting here wondering whether it was an accident that Harry DeAngelo put me on the far left side of this panel. Then I noticed that, from the audience's perspective, Mike Jensen appears to be on the far left end of the panel—and I appear to be on the right. So, I guess I'm not at all sure.

I want to talk about the question of LBOs and other highly leveraged transactions from the perspective not of

It seems to me that there's a danger of hubris in all this talk about the benefits of restructuring. Mike Jensen's speech today reminds me of a terrifically eloquent speech by Harold Geneen in 1969—in this case, extolling the glories of the conglomerate form and the superiority of internal capital markets. Geneen based his prescription for more conglomeration on the same evidence that Mike Jensen is using today to justify leveraged restructuring: namely, the huge stock market premiums that attended these activities.

—LAWRENCE SUMMERS—

private policy but of public policy. It seems to me that, from that perspective, debating the question of whether leverage is good or bad is like debating the question of whether coal is good or bad. Obviously the presence of coal makes the economy better, and I would make the same claim about LBOs.

The interesting policy questions involve whether we should promote the further use of coal or whether we should take steps to scale back the use of coal, not whether on balance the benefits of coal do or do not exceed the cost. And I think the same thing is true with respect to the use of high leverage. The position that higher leverage is always bad, it seems to me, is an absurd one. The interesting question, I think, is whether or not the tilt of public policy should be to reduce the number of highly leveraged transactions and to reduce the amount of leverage in those transactions that do take place. To answer that question, one doesn't ask about the *average* transaction, one asks about the *marginal* transaction. One looks at the question I think

from two perspectives. First you ask, Is there anything artificial in the system that distorts the market towards too much leverage? The second question you want to ask is, Are there external consequences of high leverage that go beyond the parties to the transaction? If there are external consequences, those could be reasons why public policy might want to have a tilt.

So let me take up those two questions. Are there artificial encouragements to leverage? I think the answer to that question is clearly yes. The tax system gives an enormous advantage to issuers of securities that can be labeled as debt. One can argue that, at the end of the day, highly leveraged transaction may bring about such increases in efficiency that the extra operating income may cause the Treasury to come out ahead. But that's the wrong question. The right question is, if we look at a marginal transaction, a transaction that would not be profitable without taxes, does the tax system encourage such a transaction to be done? And it's easy to see that when corporations are permitted to

deduct the cash they pay out as interest but not as dividends, and when the holders of bonds for a variety of reasons largely escape taxation, then there are large incentives to do deals that could not be justified solely on the grounds of increased operating efficiencies. Based on one reasonable set of estimates that I don't have the time to review in detail here, you could explain close to 70 percent of the premium on the RJR-Nabisco deal by pointing to the tax advantage emerging from the increase in leverage.

JENSEN: Larry, we think a more reasonable estimate is in the neighborhood of 20 percent.

SUMMERS: Well, we can take up that issue further elsewhere. But it's hard to argue that there isn't a tax advantage to debt, and it's hard to see what it is about the use of leverage that says that we should have a public policy that actively promotes the use of more leverage than private agencies would choose if left to their own devices. That point is reinforced when you consider the external consequences of these transactions. Some of the value in these transactions, perhaps much of the value, can be attributed to the people who do a better job of structuring incentives in the new organization. There is no question that that is an important part of the story. But there are at least three other important sources of value which are much more "zero-sum" in character.

First, there are the consequences of high leveraged transactions for other stakeholders. There are the consequences for the employees who lose jobs and for the suppliers who are squeezed more heavily. In such cases, what gains are achieved come at the expense of another group. They represent simply a transfer rather than a net increase in absolute efficiency. And although that's not a reason to ban the transactions, it's certainly a reason why the gains from the transaction to private parties may be far greater than the true social benefit of the transaction.

Second, there is the question of misvaluations. Some of the proponents of these transactions seem to want to have it both ways. On the one hand they complain that companies with an excess of free cash flow are prone to overpay for acquisitions. On the other, they applaud the tremendous increase in efficiency that comes about when some entrepreneur takes a company, breaks apart their divisions, and then sells them to *other* people who overpay for those divisions. Clearly there's no social efficiency advantage in finding someone who will overpay for your division.

Third, there's a question of reduced investment. Now I think too much can be made of this point. When I hear corporate managers talk about how stock market pressures and high leverage have been forcing them to take too short a horizon, I confess I'm sometimes reminded of the attitude we all took towards exams in college. We all complained that exams, by making us study specific material, didn't allow us to pursue our creativity to the extent we wanted; exams made us take a myopic perspective and forsake the long view. Well, that was all true. On the other hand, exams did make us study, which we might not have done otherwise. And I believe the control market is exercising a similar function with regard to corporate management.

Nonetheless, given that we do have a system that taxes corporate investment and therefore causes corporate investment to be inefficiently low, if some people want to invest more than is profitable for them and in the process generate extra tax collections, it's not exactly vast social progress to stop them from voluntarily undoing the disincentives associated with the corporate income tax.

So stakeholder consequences, misvaluation, and reduced investment are all reasons why the private benefit of LBOs may well come at the expense of the rest of society. And these are all reasons why the tilt of public policy should be less supportive of these transactions.

How should current policy be changed? I have two principal suggestions. First, there should be increased limits on the deductibility of corporate interest, particularly on the deductibility of corporate interest on securities labeled debt that are really equity "in drag." I am thinking of your standard 23 percent interest-bearing instrument on which there'll be no cash payments for the next 6 years, but under which dividends will be paid. Congress took a start in that direction last year, but there's room to go further.

Second, although I am not as comfortable in making this prescription, I think there is probably room for much greater restriction on the self-dealing element in management buyouts. I found it hard to read about the RJR-Nabisco transaction without concluding that, if the egos had been different and things had broken a slightly different way, the two factions would have gotten together three weeks and 20 percent earlier on the price. That would have worked substantially to the disadvantage of the existing shareholders of the company. And I suspect that, although sometimes the fight breaks out and there is a competitive auction, there must be many other times when somehow everybody works out their disagreements; and the stockholders lose a substantial portion of the premium.

JENSEN: Let me get this straight, Larry. After complaining about what these high acquisition prices and all this leverage is doing to stakeholders, are you now *also* saying you want to ensure that all the transactions are bid up like Fruehauf?

SUMMERS: I don't want to see people collude to hurt shareholders.

JENSEN: You and I have found something we can agree on, Larry. I too think that there's a bias in the tax system that pushes us towards having too much debt in some deals. I also think we ought to get rid of the tax bias toward debt financing; but I'd prefer to solve the problem in a way that doesn't line the pockets of Washington. The real source of that problem is the double taxation of dividends. What you are proposing, Larry, is that we doubly tax interest as well as dividends.

Second, although I agree with Larry that in principle there could be transfers to stockholders from other corporate stakeholders, there is very little evidence that suggests that the value changes in LBOs are coming out of the hides of labor, creditors, the Treasury, or any other corporate constituency. So far, nobody's been able to find it in the data. I'm sure there have been specific cases of large transfers. In the R.J.R.-Nabisco case, for example, the old bondholders lost about $300 million—far less, by the way, than the $1 billion reported in the press. But the amount appears almost trivial when set against the $12 billion worth of value created in the purchase price increment alone.

On the consequences for labor, the statistics show that employment is not declining, on average, in LBO organizations. In fact, in the deals done prior to 1986 for which we have three years of data, the median employment has actually risen by 4.9 percent. But that measure is probably insignificantly different from zero; and my best guess is that employment in these companies remains essentially unchanged.

On the issue of too many leveraged transactions, I think Larry calls attention to a very important point. But if I can get you back to focusing on the argument about marginal transactions—which I agree is the right focus—then what it sounds like you're saying (and I know you don't mean this) amounts to the following: By restricting leveraged buyouts, we should prevent investors from taking their money out of mature, old-line, corporations flooded with excess capital for which they have no promising investment opportunities—corporations whose inclination to retain capital they don't need is already exaggerated by our policy of taxing dividends twice. Larry, you would surely agree with me that, as a matter of public policy, we ought to be encouraging rather than blocking transactions that channel excess capital out of those declining organizations—where expected returns are only 5 or 10 percent on capital—and into new growth areas in the economy—where returns are expected to be well above investors' cost of capital. Surely, you agree that this process benefits the economy.

SUMMERS: Mike, you raise three points.

JENSEN: There's our debate coach again.

SUMMERS: On the dividends versus interest question, you're quite right that you could equalize things by eliminating either the tax on dividends or the deductibility of interest. But, when I look at the United States with its $150 billion budget deficit, and I contemplate our inability to find more money to feed poor children or help get Eastern Europe back on its feet, then I have to ask whether this nation, in this time, cannot find a higher priority use for $40 billion dollars than eliminating the double taxation of dividends and mitigating the debt-equity bias. Moreover, I'm not advocating the double taxing of *all* interest, just the interest on those bonds that have risk characteristics like those of equity and that indeed function as equity. I'm simply proposing that we tax what amounts to equity in the same way we tax all other equity.

IRA HARRIS: What happened to the old concept of equity-thin corporations that the IRS used to discriminate between debt and equity?

SUMMERS: The IRS has tried to make such distinctions, but they have always failed. It just turns out that Wall Street invariably has better tax lawyers. And, whenever the IRS comes out with a new set of restrictions, the lawyers then go to work devising loopholes. They are very well paid, and they tend to be very effective in reducing corporate taxes. But, having said that, I certainly would support far more vigorous attempts to reclassify some debt as equity.

On the question of stakeholders, I don't think we really know the full extent of the consequences of leveraged transactions. I wouldn't claim all of the value represents transfers from stakeholders. But, if the question you're interested in is how we should tilt the playing field, then all you have to determine is whether the private gains exceed the social benefit. And that will be true, I think,

as long as some of the costs are borne by stakeholders. Given the number of pension fund reversions, for example, I think we can all agree that there's cause for tilting against these transactions—at least somewhat.

On the question of channeling money into growth areas, I am as much a friend of growth areas as Mike Jensen. It's just that I see some of the money that has been forced out of the corporate sector as having gone not into new investments in growth areas, but into increased consumption. The U.S. national savings rate has fallen by 2/3 in the 1980s relative to the 1970s. One of the forces driving that decline has been reduced corporate savings. The cash being forced out of the corporate sector into individual hands has increased consumption rather than saving. I think it's very difficult to find evidence that forcing cash out of corporations through leveraged transactions has increased the availability of capital, or venture capital, for growth companies. Certainly, the rush three or four years ago of all the venture capital companies to get into LBOs does not support your argument. If anything, the movement has been in the other direction.

JENSEN: Well, in the name of full disclosure, you should at least mention that since the mid 1970s, the amount of capital available in the venture capital business has increased many times. It has been enormous.

SUMMERS: I think you'll find that a lot of that increase came in the late 1970s and early 1980s as pension funds decided to invest in venture capital for the first time. I think you'd be hard-pressed to link that increase to the rise of HLTs and LBOs in the 1980s.

JENSEN: We both recognize that, because of the "fungibility" of money, it's impossible to trace funds through different sectors of the economy. But I don't believe it's by accident that this massive increase in venture capital—

SIEFERT

I consider the Fruehauf LBO to have been very risky because of the cyclical nature of the trailer and automotive business, the high capital requirements of Kelsey Hayes, and the large debt that was already on the company. I believe that everyone, Mr. Edelman included, overestimated the value of the real estate and the value of the divisions to be sold. They also failed to see the extent to which future profitability was vulnerable to the changes occurring within the trailer industry. Everyone also underestimated the potential cost of unfunded liabilities and environmental problems...As a consequence, the price paid was too high and the huge debt was not manageable.

—ROBERT SIEFERT—

not to mention the rise of R&D limited partnerships in the last 5 or 6 years—has occurred during the same period of time as massive amounts of cash have been leaving the old-line, low-growth corporate sector.

Two LBO Experiences

DeANGELO: Let me interrupt the dialogue here and try to shift our focus from these broad macroeconomic issues to the micro issues raised by leveraged transactions. So let's now turn to Bob Siefert, who will share some of his own experiences with the LBO phenomenon.

ROBERT SIEFERT: Thanks, Harry. I suppose that I represent a company that successfully defeated a raider by forming an LBO—one that, in the end, did not live up to its expectations. I will comment on why we decided to undertake an LBO, why it did not work out as planned, and how we eventually extricated ourselves from the problems that arose from the LBO financing structure.

In 1986, Fruehauf was the major trailer manufacturer in the world; and

its major subsidiary, Kelsey Hayes, was a profitable components supplier to the automotive industry. Total company sales were about $2.6 billion and profits after taxes were about $71 million.

Early in 1986, Asher Edelman approached management to discuss a plan to increase shareholder value. The plan was strongly resisted, of course, because we felt that any plan proposed by Edelman would result in the selling off of a major part of the company. At this time, management wanted to keep both of the core businesses—that is, both the trailer operations and Kelsey Hayes. The desire to retain both businesses reflected a commitment by management to employees, customers, suppliers, and the local communities.

Accordingly, a campaign was waged to re-elect the management board of directors and defeat the slate proposed by Edelman. The campaign against Mr. Edelman was an emotional one by both sides. Personal accusations and vitriolic language became the order of the day. In fact, the movie "Wall Street" was supposed to have been based on the Edelman-Fruehauf conflict; and I

can assure you that our stockholder meeting was very much like the one portrayed in the movie.

During this time, Fruehauf's management was pursued relentlessly by a New York investment house to form an LBO. Both the New York investment house and the lead commercial bank wanted this Fruehauf LBO to happen because it was one of the first large LBOs in which either of them would have participated. Both institutions were looking to build reputations as LBO dealmakers to compete successfully with other New York firms. Their fees were also large.

The LBO was formed with 70 management participants and Merrill Lynch. After many negotiations and court actions, Edelman decided to stop bidding. And the Fruehauf Company was sold to the LBO at a very high price. In fact, the final price that was offered was $49.50 in cash for 65 percent of the company. The balance of the stock would be purchased for one share of Common B and 1.75 shares of a Preferred Stock issue redeemable at $25.

We had an unusual capital structure in that it had both a Class A and Class

B Stock. Both had equal financial rights, but the A Stock had three voting rights to Class B's one. The A Stock was held only by management and Merrill Lynch. The B Stock traded on the New York Stock Exchange.

The financial structure was as follows: The bank group provided a bridge loan of $425 million to carry us over until certain divestitures could be completed. High-yield bonds were also sold with a face value of $510 million. Also $250 million of preferred stock was issued which was paid-in-kind (PIK) rather than paying cash dividends for the first five years. Equity was $25 million.

To prevent another raider from attacking the company, stringent restrictions were put on all the classes of stock. Any investor group that wanted to make any change in the company now had to obtain the approval of 80 percent of the bondholders, 66-2/3 of the preferred, and 80 percent of the Class A and B holders.

The financial results for the first two years were not encouraging. There were divestitures of the non-core businesses. Kelsey-Hayes almost met its profit targets as projected in the LBO plan. But the trailer and maritime divisions had fallen well short of expectations, mainly because of the changing business environment. The problems were caused by the investor group's and management's failure to respond appropriately to the changes in the industry.

During the third year of the LBO, however, significant changes were made. Excess plant capacity was closed, branches were shut down, and more emphasis was placed on after-market sales and service. There were also significant reductions of management and staff, and a variety of other cost reduction programs were initiated.

At this point, our future business opportunities and projections looked very promising. Our problem, however, was that the company simply could not continue with the heavy debt-service burden imposed by the LBO. So a recapitalization was proposed whereby the bondholders would receive the following package for each $1,000 bond: a new $500 debenture with current interest payments; a second debenture that would begin to pay interest in 1992; and seven shares of preferred stock. Moreover, we offered 3.5 shares of Class B common stock for each preferred share.

During the presentation to the bondholders, however, a Canadian company came in and blanketed the restructuring proposal, offering to better any proposal offered by management. Given this situation, there was no way to complete the reorganization. It was decided to put the company up for sale to get maximum value for the shareholders.

Now I'd like to make a couple of observations about the Fruehauf LBO that might prove to have wider application.

First: I consider the Fruehauf LBO to have been very risky because of the cyclical nature of the trailer and automotive business, the high capital requirements of Kelsey Hayes, and the large debt that was already on the company. I believe that everyone, Mr. Edelman included, overestimated the value of the real estate and the value of the divisions to be sold. They also failed to see the extent to which future profitability was vulnerable to the changes occurring within the trailer industry. Everyone also underestimated the potential cost of unfunded liabilities and environmental problems.

Second: Emotions played a dominant role during the negotiations, with the result that the price of the stock was pushed up too high. Also contributing to the high price were too optimistic projections at a time when the business environment was clearly becoming more competitive. As a consequence, the price paid was too high and the huge debt was not manageable.

Third: It was not wise to issue public common stock. By so doing, we failed to gain one of the major advantages of a management buyout: namely, eliminating the pressure to manage for short-term results and other costs associated with being a public company.

Fourth: The initial LBO placed severe restrictions on corporate flexibility by giving almost complete veto power to all the bondholders and stockholders. Such restrictions caused us a lot of problems in attempting to restructure or sell the company. Management needs to retain as much flexibility as possible in entering into these transactions.

Fifth: It took far longer than anticipated to sell the assets and divisions. Companies must be prepared to respond to the possibility that they cannot get the prices expected for divested assets. And besides planning for reduced prices, they also need to account for the possibility of having to assume past liability problems such as unfunded pension plans, retiree health costs, and environmental problems.

Sixth: After an LBO or acquisition, changes must be made immediately to focus everyone's attention on the primary goal, which is to conserve cash and pay down the debt to reduce interest costs. As I said before, we were three years into the LBO before significant changes were made. Any delay in implementing changes reduces the chance of ultimate success.

In summary, then, high leverage and ownership can be exciting. LBOs present tremendous opportunities for managers and entrepreneurs to run their own businesses, to make their own decisions, and reap the rewards

> From the outset of our LBO, we sought to broaden the sense of employee ownership and participation in the progress and performance of the company. We were able to push direct management investment down through the top 100 managers, including plant and sales management. Management ended up with 20 percent of the equity...
>
> We implemented immediately a cash management award program that involved over 800 managers. The award program tied progressively larger cash bonus pay-outs to the achievement of $80 million increments of cash generation. We achieved five such trigger points during '87 and '88, and paid out a total of $5 million to these 800 managers.
>
> To broaden participation and incentives we have modified our savings and investment program to provide that, beginning in 1990, every participant in the savings and investment plan will build a common stock ownership position in Reliance.

> —JOHN MORLEY—

of their own efforts. But there are also clearly dangers in the process.

The LBO and the raider I've discussed were made possible, of course, only by the availability of capital in the high-yield market. That market is clearly depressed now, and thus it's highly unlikely that large leveraged buyouts similar to the Fruehauf transaction will occur in the immediate future. Nor will corporate raiders have access to the vast amounts of money for raiding.

There will continue to be opportunities for highly leveraged companies. But lending institutions will be more conservative and only support businesses with good business prospects and long-term potential. Money is available for future high-leveraged transactions. The real demand, though, is for operations people who can manage highly-levered companies.

All in all, then, the Fruehauf operation failed not because the company was not a good operation, but rather because the level of debt was too high. Fortunately, we didn't go into bankruptcy. We were able to sell off both the trailer operation and the Kelsey Hayes operations so that the shareholders and the LBO participants didn't take too much of a loss.

DeANGELO: Thanks, Bob. Our next speaker is John Morley, who will talk about his firm's experience with an LBO.

JOHN MORLEY: Thank you, Harry. I may be coming at this set of issues from the other side of the LBO experience, and I will be doing this in the context of the story of Reliance Electric. It's a story that to date has been very successful. But the story is of course incomplete and still unfolding. So what I'd like to do is to begin by establishing our financial and operating progress and then comment on what we call the "lessons learned" from our experience—that is, on those things we did in order to improve our prospects for succeeding in a high-risk environment.

The leveraged buyout of Reliance from Exxon was engineered in the fall of 1986, and was closed in December of '86, with nearly $1.2 billion of bridge financing in place. The principal investors included the Reliance management, Citicorp Capital Investors, and Prudential Bache Securities. With the debt that was existing prior to the LBO, our total borrowings on January 1st, 1987 were $1.263 billion. We basically had zero equity.

During the first quarter of '87 we placed the permanent financing, which consisted of $650 million of senior bank debt, $450 billion of subordinated high-yield notes and debentures, $120 million of preferred stock, and $10 million of common stock. $90 million of the preferred was later exchanged into a junior subordinated debenture. Including the preferred stock, our equity base was 10 percent of total capitalization when we completed the permanent financing.

Let me hit some financial highlights. Our sales have increased almost 30 percent between 1986 and 1989, from $1.1 billion to a little over $1.4 billion last year. Our earnings before interest and taxes in 1989 were more than triple the 1986 level. As a percent of sales, EBIT was increased from 4.5 percent to 12.3 percent. We have reduced our total borrowings by a net of $606 million, or roughly a 48 percent reduction since the outset. Gross repayment of debt in the amount of $776 million was partially offset by the exchange of the $90 million of the exchangeable preferred and $80 million accretion of the subordinated zero coupon debentures.Our securities have generally sold at significant premiums to issue in spite of the fact that the prime rate is approximately 3 points higher today than it was in 1987 when we financed the deal.

We've been profitable in each year of the LBO. We have increased our investment in technology and new product introductions during each year of the LBO. We have increased employment in our continuing businesses, and we believe we've gained market share in each of our principal product lines.

So how did we get here from there? Reflecting on our experience, we have identified six factors that we think are important to our situation and perhaps are portable to others.

First: Be conservative in forecasting. We did not base our financial justication on significant volume increases or aggressively optimistic economic scenarios. In fact, we based our financial projections on average annual sales growth of a little over 4 percent. This tactic reinforced the price paid for Reliance, ensured that it was supportable, and laid the groundwork for developing a high degree of credibility with our financial investors, the rating agencies, and other prospective investors.

Second: Build financial flexibility into the capital structure. We sought out and achieved a blend of variable-rate bank debt, fixed-rate, cash-paying bonds and notes, zero-coupon bonds, exchangeable preferred stock, and permanent equity. This structure gave us the flexibility to continue to invest in the business and be opportunistic with our asset sale program, while

avoiding the need for a fire-sale program to meet debt service. In fact, our financing was achieved with the sale of only miscellaneous assets and did not require the sale of a major business unit. Having said that, though, I must add that we subsequently chose to sell Toledo Scale, a major operating unit, both for business reasons and because we received an excellent value.

Third: Set clear and straightforward goals. To put this as bluntly as possible, cash is king. An LBO is obviously an extremely complex undertaking—particularly in our case, since we had not been an independent company for seven years. We thus had to struggle not only with the risks inherent in high leverage but also with the issue of renewed independence. We felt it imperative—and I believe time has proved it—that we establish and articulate clear, simple commercial and financial objectives.

Fourth: Communicate effectively. The success of our enterprise was achieved through the broad input of our work force of 13,000 people. That input could not have been provided without a broad and clear understanding of where we were going. We invested substantial time and effort to fashion the message and take our goals and objectives to each employee, and to follow up on a scheduled basis, to chart our progress, and to fine-tune the objectives.

Fifth: Create (and I can't overemphasize the importance of this) the strongest possible incentives for management and employees. From the outset of our LBO, we sought to broaden the sense of employee ownership and participation in the progress and performance of the company. We were able to push direct management investment down through the top 100 managers, including plant and sales management. Management ended up with 20 percent of the

equity, Citicorp with 37 percent, Prudential Bache Capital Funding with nearly 20 percent, and the remaining 23 percent was issued with the subordinated debt.

We implemented immediately a cash management award program that involved over 800 managers. The award program tied progressively larger cash bonus pay-outs to the achievement of $80 million increments of cash generation. We achieved five such trigger points during '87 and '88, and paid out a total of $5 million to these 800 managers.

Another critical aspect in our success has been employee involvement in the implementation of our world-class operations program, which is based on the concept of connected production, both in the plant and in the office. The program is built upon the individual and team involvements of every employee at every level. Our employees have come to know that they make the difference. Their creativity, initiative, and brainpower are the catalyst to our competitive success. Perhaps most important of all is their knowledge that their ideas will be heard and acted upon. To broaden participation and incentives we have modified our savings and investment program to provide that, beginning in 1990, every participant in the savings and investment plan will build a common stock ownership position in Reliance.

Sixth: Anticipate the crossover from an almost single-minded focus on debt reduction to a more balanced strategy of business growth and attention to debt reduction. Early in the LBO our incentives, our financial objectives, and our financial tactics were focused on debt reduction. We recaptured significant pension overfunding, we sold miscellaneous assets, real estate, and non-core business units. We implemented the cash award program and we ultimately sold Toledo. But, as we reduced our debt level, we recognized the need to begin working on the longer-term business considerations of growth and future profitability. That process is now underway at Reliance. Whether our timing is correct is yet to be seen, but we are increasing our capital expenditures, our technology initiatives, and new business activities.

These, then, are the six important lessons that I think we learned. I would also add one last comment: There's nothing like good timing and lots of luck. I would also leave you with just a couple of questions in the context of this partnershipping that goes on within LBOs. What will be the make-up of the equity ownership, and how does that structure coincide with the objectives of the different partners? What conflicts of interest will appear among the investors, particularly the financial investors? And finally, how firm a grip do we have on the deleveraging process?

Exploring The Contracting Process: Why Some Deals Go Bad

BENNETT STEWART: As I listened to these stories of Fruehauf and Reliance Electric, I was struck by the thought that Bob Siefert and John Morley, although presumably chosen to represent opposing points of view on LBOs, both ended up taking similar actions after their LBOs. There was a sale of some assets in both cases. There was a renewed focus on the business. Bob Siefert mentioned that Fruehauf shut down redundant plants and narrowed its focus on its trailer business—actions which strike me as being productive. And John Morley listed six steps undertaken by Reliance to improve efficiency.

Given these similarities, it also struck me that the principal *difference*

between the Fruehauf and the Reliance transactions—the reason why one succeeded and the other did not—was really a matter of price. And the thought also occurred to me that the difference in pricing undoubtedly reflects the fact that one transaction was effected voluntarily and the other was constructed as a defense against a raider. If Reliance Electric had been priced at a 30 percent higher level, and if Fruehauf had been priced at a 30 percent lower level, I suspect that Bob Siefert and John Morley would now be taking opposite sides in this debate.

Besides the presence of a raider in the case of Fruehauf, another reason why the Reliance transaction might have been priced more reasonably was that Reliance was a subsidiary of Exxon, and the management of the subsidiary might have been able to negotiate a lower price in the absence of an auction-like environment.

But the success of Reliance as a private company raises the question: Why wouldn't it have made sense for Exxon itself to have sponsored the LBO? Why didn't Exxon retain a 50 or 60 percent stake in Reliance Electric and then allow management—perhaps along with an outside financial investor—to purchase the rest? If it was good for Exxon to buy Reliance in the first place, then why not recapitalize the subsidiary such that the parent can participate in the fruits of the transaction that management and Citibank and Pru Bache are now dividing amongst themselves?

But, to return to my earlier point, I suspect there is a great deal of difference between the likelihood of succeeding in a management-initiated LBO as opposed to a defensive LBO.
MORLEY: I would agree with your observation, Bennett. But let me add just another dimension to the facts I've given you about the Reliance deal. It turned out there were three

separate groups bidding for Reliance; and they were all seeking management participation. An important factor in our case was that each investor group was depending on us for the projections that would allow them to value the operation. Now, I admit that our case wasn't nearly as contentious and adversarial as Bob's situation. But I think in retrospect we did influence to some degree the level of valuation put on the deal.
STEWART: Well, it's clear that in your case the sponsors wanted your management team to participate. And I suspect that, in the case of Fruehauf, Asher Edelman was willing to proceed without management.
SIEFERT: In our case, as I pointed out earlier, our emotional commitment to maintaining control of the business interfered with our economic judgment. Adding to the problem was the intensity of the interest of our Wall Street backers—both the investment bankers and the commercial bankers—in making the deal happen. We based our financial projections on past history while ignoring current changes in the business environment that would make those projections difficult to meet. In 1984 the Fruehauf trailer operations made a lot of money. If we had been able to make in '86 and '87 what we did in '84, we wouldn't have run into problems. In 1984, there were changes in the laws governing the width and length of trailers that gave us a virtual monopoly in that industry. In '86 and '87, however, deregulation came along and truckers began buying the least expensive trailers they could get. They no longer cared about quality, but only about cost. As a result the trailer industry was completely changed.

At the same time, our once profitable maritime business—which involved the repair of oil tankers coming into Florida—also suddenly dried up in 1986 as a result of the Navy's adventure in the Persian Gulf. At that point, there was no longer money available for Navy repair work.

HARRIS: Bob, you said that your financing was premised on the assumption that the future would be at least as profitable as the past. Most of the transactions I've seen go bad are based on the premise that the future is going to far exceed the past. I've seen cases where earnings have been flat for 5 to 10 years and where projections show growth at rates of 15 to 20 percent a year. So, I don't think we can generalize that all LBOs are good or all LBOs are bad. We can only comment on individual transactions. As Bennett said earlier, the critical determinant of success or failure is the price. A good LBO is one that is done at the right price. A bad LBO is one where you take the same transaction and do it at too high a price. The problem with the LBO market, as I see it, was that prices were being determined not by what a business was worth, but rather by your ability to finance the transaction.

STEWART: I disagree with that statement, at least to a certain extent. The transactions in the early '80s were equally financeable, and yet the vast majority of them have worked out extremely well. So why after 1986 do the projections all of a sudden become rosier?

HARRIS: Because too much money started to chase too few transactions.

JENSEN: There's always a problem when you have a corporate entity acting as the promoter as Merrill Lynch did in the case of Fruehauf. But let's set that issue aside for the moment and explore another potential source of the problem. Could you tell us, Bob, how much of Merrill Lynch's money went into the equity? And I don't want to know how much equity they got, but rather how much cash they actually put up to get the equity.

SIEFERT: The deal that we had with Merrill Lynch is that the equity would be $25 million.

JENSEN: Out of the total price of . . . ?

SIEFERT: About a billion and a half.

JENSEN: A billion and a half. And how much of that $25 million did Merrill put up?

SIEFERT: They left that decision to us. They simply said that they would put up whatever part of the $25 million that we didn't. So that if management raised $12.5 million, then it would have control of the company. But if management were unable to come up with $12.5 milion, then Merrill Lynch would have control of the company.

Merrill Lynch put in approximately $10 million. But they also collected large fees for executing the deal, for the divestiture of assets, and for the restructuring.

JENSEN: You didn't actually give us the numbers, but I gather from your statements that they didn't put any *net* money into the deal. They got paid for doing the deal whether it worked or not.

SIEFERT: Absolutely, absolutely.

JENSEN: QED.

DeANGELO: I wonder if there's a representative of Merrill Lynch here? Are there further thoughts on the fee structure problem?

NELL MINOW: I think that story summarizes the fee structure problem.

Recent Trends in the Deal Market

HARRIS: I have been outspoken as a critic of some of the financing practices we've seen in the past few years. A major cause of our current problem stems from the relatively new practice of investment bankers becoming principals in their own deals. Wall street became driven by this frenzy to earn some of the high returns that were being earned by the KKRs and the Forstmann Littles.

So, I think that in the beginning deals were being done at reasonable prices. The concept was a good concept (in fact it still is a good concept). In the early years of the 80s, we weren't leveraging companies to the point where management had two chances of succeeding: slim and none. But then things changed dramatically. To give you some idea of the magnitude of the change, the first raise in the RJR-Nabisco bidding contest—the one from $75 to $90 per share—would have measured up as the 8th largest deal in history. I'm talking about just the raise alone. And that's what started to change.

STEWART: The question I would ask, Ira, is why aren't the transactions being done now. People blame the condition of the junk bond market, but I think that's more a symptom than a disease. Will transactions come back? Will they be as aggressively financed? What will change?

HARRIS: Well, I think transactions will come back. And when they come back, they will come back with real money, with a lot of real people, and the deals will make real economic sense.

STEWART: I thought it was interesting that Ted Forstmann just announced a major transaction—the buyout of Gulfstream Aerospace—which is his first deal in two or three years. Ted has been one of the most outspoken critics of the very highly leveraged transactions—especially of the PIK bonds, which he says are in large part responsible for the overpricing. They allow bidders to bid prices up to levels where the immediate cash flows are not necessary to service all the debt.

But, again, I find it somewhat amusing that this erstwhile critic of HLTs has suddenly re-entered the arena after holding himself above the madness so long.

JENSEN: And this deal is also highly leveraged. I believe there is fifty percent bank debt right off the top.

STEWART: Right. And there is also a mezzanine layer—the part normally reserved for junk bonds—that is being raised from his own mezzanine fund. Forstmann likes to pride himself on his abstinence from junk bonds, but let's face it: this mezzanine layer is the economic equivalent of junk.

JENSEN: It would be interesting to know how much debt was put into the mezzanine fund? It was never revealed in the news reports. Fifty percent of the purchase price was financed with senior bank debt, which is common. How much debt went into the mezzanine fund, does anybody know? It wasn't zero.

STEWART: I think he's read Michael Porter's book and has found a way to develop a comparative advantage in *marketing* his business.

MORLEY: I would like to get back to the question of the parallel interest, or lack of interest, between the various parties in these LBOs.

In our experience at Reliance, we found that at the beginning of the leveraged buyout, there was a strong unity of interest between the financial investors and the management investors. But the moment you reached a point where the financial pressures began to let up and there appeared to be some slack, there was a tremendous pressure from our financial investors to turn the crank again—to releverage and pay out some of the profit. Our incentive, however, was different. We said, "No, we've done that once already. Now let's get on with the prosecution of our affairs." Now, my question is this: How do you plan for that conflict of incentives at the beginning of a deal and then structure the deal to minimize that conflict?

DeANGELO: While still keeping control of the situation?

MORLEY: Well, yes. But there will be negotiations about control running throughout the process, from day one

onward. At some point, of course, management must be prepared to relinquish control.

HARRIS: But why can't corporate management just say no to a recapitalization? I don't know any investment banker that's ever walked into a corporate manager's office and pulled a 38 on him. There's been a certain amount of greed that has also driven corporate management. . . which is fine.

SUMMERS: "Greed is good," right?

HARRIS: No, I can't say that. Last year on this platform I said it was bad. But, kidding aside, I don't understand why corporate management doesn't say to some of the banking firms, "Look, you guys are nuts. You don't have to run this business. You don't know what it's like. We're not going to go beyond a certain point." My suggestion is that corporate America get together and see that each of these corporate raiders actually gets the opportunity to run a company. Then we would see a halt to this nonsense.

DeANGELO: Let me try to rephrase John Morley's question. I think the issue comes down to this: First, should management forecast that, five years after the deal, the financial investors are going to want out? If so, what sort of alternative investor responses are available? In other words, is there room for other investors to step into the breach in the intermediate stages of a buyout and take over from the original investors?

MORLEY: In the case of Reliance, we did have a five-year plan leading to an IPO or other liquidity event for the investors. But the irony of all this is that our success begot an appetite for still more leverage. Our financial investors came to us and said, "Let's forget the IPO. Let's have a major distribution and lever up again."

And, Ira, I want you to know that we said no to that proposal. But,

having made this point, let me also say that there are limitations to the negotiating position that either side has in these deals.

JENSEN: Yes, but isn't this a healthy tension? In any large company, if you've got it structured right, then you must have a certain amount of tension among the various divisions and between corporate staff and the line people in the divisions.

One of the healthy tensions that's been missing in corporate America is exactly the one you're pointing to now. For the last 30 or 40 years, we have had boards of directors that have no financial interest in the organizations they supposedly oversee. These boards are, for all practical purposes, rubber stamps for endorsing management's investment and spending plans. As Larry pointed out earlier, we've had a tax system that is biased against the pay-out of cash. Furthermore, we've had compensation plans that reward managers simply for making our public corporations bigger—not more efficient, not more valuable, just bigger.

The consequence of this lack of control has been the enormous waste—and I mean a really incredible waste—of this nation's resources. Companies in industries with excess capacity have been throwing away cash and other assets on projects that don't make any economic sense. Now, I am not saying this has been true of all organizations. But, what has allowed this waste to continue is the fact there is no effective voice for shareholders in our public corporations.

MINOW: Now, you're singing my favorite song. I think that's exactly right. I want to enlarge on a theme that I've heard from several people here today, and it's something that I believe is critically important. That is, virtually everybody here seems to want managers and dealmakers to put their money where their mouths are. As a representative of institutional share-holders—those people who have over two trillion dollars invested in the economy—I want the people who are running our companies and who are doing the deals to put their own money at risk.

We also need to see major changes in our corporate governance system. Mike Jensen mentioned the compensation issue. Shareholders get only one tiny little look at executive compensation, and that's the result of a peculiarity of the tax code rather than any requirement in our securities law.

JENSEN: But, Nell, I've seen a very mixed attitude on the part of institutional investors with respect to issues like CEO and board compensation. There's a strong bias against large salaries and bonuses, even when they're associated with good performance. There's also considerable resistance to substantial awards of stock options or restricted stock. Now, this is not true of all institutions, but there's a leveling influence coming from many institutional investors that encourages preservation of the status quo. It is not helping to strengthen the correlation of pay with performance in our corporations; and it is therefore part of the competitiveness problem we now face.

MINOW: Well, I agree with you. My own philosophy is that, as long as the interests of managers and directors are aligned with those of shareholders (and I agree they should have substantial investment in the company), and as long as shareholders are making money, then management can make all the money in the world. For example, we supported Michael Eisner's compensation at Disney. The president of my company, Bob Monks, is the director of a company where the CEO has made $50 million based

exclusively on the wonderful things that he's done with the stock. We think that's just great.

What I have opposed, though, are cases of abuse. One case that comes to mind—which we criticized last year—was at Toys-R-Us, where Mr. Lazarus exercised stock options over a three-year period worth $72 million. What bothered me was not the amount of the award (although it is a lot of money), but rather the fact that he borrowed money from the company at 6% annual interest to exercise the options. I don't really call that a stock option plan. I call that a charitable gift of shareholder funds.

HARRIS: That's called estate planning.
MINOW: That's right.

But, in response to Mike Jensen's statement, let me also point out that institutional shareholders are people, and they have instincts and prejudices just like anybody else. For example, if you take a manager in the state pension system—where the salaries are very limited—then it is often politically useful for them to object to $72 million payments to CEOs.

As a representative of the 60 largest institutional investors in the United States, let me also point out a major problem faced by most of them. To illustrate the problem, pretend you are the manager of the California employees retirement system. Because you've got $58 billion under management, you're not going to be moving money around a lot. The transaction costs will kill you. Furthermore, when you do choose to take your eighth of a point, you must (and you may laugh at this) find some other place to put it. And that's not a trivial exercise. They have already invested in just about everything you could imagine. So these institutions are becoming more and more heavily indexed, either *de facto* or *de jure*.

PART II: PERSPECTIVES ON PUBLIC CORPORATIONS

DeANGELO: In this second half of our discussion, we will address the concerns of publicly held companies, both from corporate management's point of view and from that of shareholders in those companies. We will start this second session with Allan Gilmour of the Ford Motor Company.

Two Views From the Inside

ALLAN GILMOUR: Thank you, Harry. It's a little unclear to me whether the second panel is supposed to be the second shift or the minor leagues . . .
ROBERT MERCER: We're batting cleanup.
GILMOUR: . . . But we'll try to be as colorful and controversial as the first panel.

Let me start by saying that LBOs have changed the face of corporate finance in America, at least in the short run. But now that some dust has settled, what fundamentals of business will really have changed? Obviously some companies and industries have been affected, for good and ill. But I believe the basic principles of ownership and management will not have changed that much, on balance.

The "old time religion" (which I learned in this school more years ago than I'm going to admit) warned us of the dangers of excessive debt, particularly in cyclical businesses like the auto industry. We were warned about that for a very simple reason: In economic downturns, excessive debt and the excessive payments that go with that debt increase the risk of financial trouble, disaster, or even bankruptcy.

The "new religion" would ask us to believe that high leverage provides the road to salvation—and financial

> **I believe, contrary to what Professor Jensen has written, that the real discipline in business is the product market, not the financial market. It is the customer, not the banker, who ultimately determines the fate of a company...**
>
> **A company has more constituencies than shareholders or debtholders. It is not enough to maximize the value of their investments—even if we knew how, and we don't. Employees, suppliers, the distribution system, communities, taxpayers, and, once again, customers all have stakes in the success of the company, however success is measured. Take care of these constituents and the shareholders will be taken care of also.**
>
> **—ALLAN GILMOUR—**

reward for the stockholders. The reason for this thinking also is simple: Large interest payments impose a fiscal discipline on management. With large interest payments to make, managers are less likely to develop cases of the "roving eye" and diversify, or as Peter Lynch of the Fidelity Magellan fund said, "deworsify." I would point out, as an aside, that most of these people do not favor high labor costs, for example, as a disciplinary influence on management.

Now debt may have its virtues (and, on this account, Ford was very virtuous in the early 80s). But I've come to believe there are several practical problems with this line of thinking, despite the enthusiasm with which it has been embraced.

I want to take issue with the theory of debt set forth in Mike Jensen's article in the *Harvard Business Review*. And I want to raise three basic objections.

First of all, just as LBOs can discourage bad investment on the part of managers—and I think they can discourage bad investment—they can also discourage good investments. The argument in favor of LBOs is made in terms of "free cash flow"— that is, cash available after all projects with positive net present values have been undertaken. To know how much free cash is available, a manager must decide which projects have a positive net present value and which don't. Now these projects include not only today's, but those that may develop over several years in the future. These are the decisions that Professor Jensen and others believe that those of us in management cannot be trusted to make. Under their proposal, all investment decisions would be handed over to the capital markets. In other words, Ford's management can't be trusted to buy Jaguar, nor can it be trusted to develop a line of luxury cars on its own.

I believe that the expertise for most kinds of investment decisions does reside within our corporations. While Wall Street may have some wisdom to impart, we haven't had much luck there finding expertise in technology or savvy in marketing cars and trucks.

Second, Professor Jensen suggests that companies with excess produc- tion capacity—companies perhaps like Goodyear and Ford—are unlikely to have future investment opportuni- ties. Yet, in the auto industry, despite the fact that some of our competitors' production capacity is greater than their sales, investment in new prod- ucts is a constant need.

Third, the pro-LBO argument rests on a belief that capital markets are highly efficient. Now I recognize the dangers that I'm facing when I say otherwise in an academic setting such as this, but events over the past six months involving Campeau, Drexel, and the collapse of junk bond prices suggest that capital markets, like people (and I suppose capital mar- kets are people, way down deep), are subject to whims, fads, hysteria, as well as euphoria. In short, I am hesi- tant to subject our investment projects to the approval of Wall Street.

What about the role of debt, then? As with anything, there is a proper balance. It's hard to know what the optimal debt-to-equity ratio should be, but I do know that it is not infinite. About a year ago, Ben Stein wrote a column in the *New York Times* urging

There have been too many financial engineers in this country. They have successfully found and exploited a flaw in the free enterprise system. Our administration still thinks that what was going on during the 80s was part of the free enterprise system. Many of us tried to explain that it was a flaw in the free enterprise system...

The popular phrases "enhancing shareholder value" and "unlocking asset values"... unfortunately, have meant cashing in the company. For the Street seems to have reserved its highest reward for liquidation... the net effect of this process was to enhance speculator prices and decrease investors' value.

—ROBERT MERCER—

us all, as individuals, to remodel our lives along the lines of the RJR-Nabisco LBO. "Do a leveraged buyout on your house," he wrote. "Mortgage it to the hilt and put the money in the bank. Sell your cars and put that money in the bank also. Rent your clothes, rent your cars, rent your furniture. Have the kids drop out of school—that will do quite a lot to improve cash flow, too."

If my skepticism sounds thoroughly "out of it," I guess that I prefer it that way. "New eras" in finance make me nervous, not because I'm resistant to new ideas, but because I'm suspicious that many "new eras" in finance are only new packaging.

One final point—and this will ensure that I'm never invited back to a forum on financial matters. There's nothing inherently bad, in my view, about LBOs or high debt. Some of their implications are good, very good in certain circumstances. But that's only part of the story. I believe, contrary to what Professor Jensen has written, that the real discipline in business is the product market, not the financial market. It is the customer, not

the banker, who ultimately determines the fate of a company. (And thank heavens we have more customers than bankers.) The customer doesn't care about our costs—about our interest costs, our labor costs, or any other kinds of costs. But he or she cares greatly about product price. Price is a measure of value, and that's our job: giving the customer what he thinks is value as measured by his value structure. Providing sound value is more than capital structure, and it's more than outside pressure on management for financial results. These aspects obviously shouldn't be ignored. They're important, but they're only part of the game.

Let me conclude by saying that any company has more constituencies than shareholders or debtholders. It is not enough to maximize the value of their investments—even if we knew how, and we don't. Employees, suppliers, the distribution system, communities, taxpayers, and, once again, customers all have stakes in the success of the company, however success is measured. Take care of these constituents and the shareholders will

be taken care of also. I never saw Ford's stock price too high, but I also know that there's more to our success and vitality than that alone.

DeANGELO: Thanks, Allan. Now we'll turn to Bob Mercer.

MERCER: Thanks, Harry. Allan just gave my speech, and far more articulately than I could have. Given our current investment banking climate, I want to start my remarks by mentioning a merger that took place last week. Merrill Lynch merged with Drexel Burnham, and the new firm is going to be called Lynch 'em and Burn 'em.

Now, I retired about a year ago, last April as a matter of fact. And the world has changed dramatically since then. Not only has the Berlin Wall come down, but also the Chinese walls in many of our financial institutions. Unfortunately, this has been given only belated recognition by our enforcement agencies. But at least the fraud and corruption have finally been brought to the fore. What has been made clear by these investigations is that some of our financial institutions have gotten away from what I consider to be their basic job description—that is, creating capital so that our industrial base can grow and our companies compete effectively on a global scale. For we cannot conquer the twin deficits that we are all concerned about when our corporations are saddled with excessive debt.

My own company, for instance, had to spend $2.6 billion to buy back our stock and just stay alive. Today we're spending a million dollars a day to service the debt created by that buyback.

Now compare that with the behavior of a Japanese competitor of ours in this global arena. Bridgestone spent exactly the same amount of money—$2.6 billion—to buy Firestone. (It was reported, by the way, that the acquisition made a good fit because they only had to change half the sign.) But, believe it or not, I was giving testimony at a Congressional hearing and one of the congressmen said to me, "Well, Mr. Mercer, don't you think you would have been better advised to spend that $2.6 billion to buy Firestone yourself, instead of buying the stock back?" I had to remind him that our government would not allow me to buy Firestone. But they certainly allowed an international competitor to do it.

There have been too many financial engineers in this country. They have successfully found and exploited a flaw in the free enterprise system. Our administration still thinks that what was going on during the 80s was part of the free enterprise system. Many of us tried to explain that it was a flaw in the free enterprise system.

And I think you know the story. Financial buyers would find a corporation—and the woods were full of them at the time—with assets under-valued by the Street. Then they attracted the bonds and they marched into battle with a good public relations firm and made tender offers. And then it was all over.

Even the language was loaded with euphemisms and coined words. "Corpocracy" was one that I had thrown at me consistently. Corpocracy was defined by Jimmy Goldsmith as an "unholy alliance of big government, big business, and big labor." Well, let me assure you that if corpocracy did in fact exist in this country, then Jimmy could never have gotten off his yacht.

"Entrenched management" was another catchy phrase. In fact, it's become one word now, like "damn-yankee." There is no such thing as just plain "management" anymore. Other popular phrases are "enhancing shareholder value" and "unlocking asset values." Now, who could be against that?

Well, unfortunately, what it meant was cashing in the company. For the Street seems to have reserved its highest reward for liquidation. The Arbs smell this process and the stock price is driven up.

Now, let me submit that there is an important difference between "price" and "value." "Look what we did for our shareholders," I hear from companies that have gone through this liquidating process. And I reply, "Which shareholders? The ones who sold or the ones who bought?" In the process of being raided, buying back its stock, and liquidating the assets, my company's stock went from $33 to $76. The shareholders who sold off at $75 were speculators. Those who bought were investors, and their paper is now undervalued again at about $36.* The net effect of the process was to enhance speculator prices and decrease investors' value.

To summarize, then, we were treated to the spectacle of a knight in shining junk bonds, leaping out of the Cayman Islands with a wife and two mistresses. And he had the gall to accuse *us* of over-diversification.

Now I really think that those days are gone. LBOs and mergers and acquisitions will continue to be with us, as they should be. But it is the motives for these transactions that will change. And it is the motive behind the LBO or the acquisition that should determine whether or not the transaction is value-adding. Who is to make that determination? I say the board of directors. The tender offer should be outlawed or, at a minimum, the board should be empowered to declare a speculator's stock to be nonvoting shares. We need to have corporations concentrating on customer satisfaction, and not listening for footsteps. Otherwise our industrial base will move overseas to people and countries who are out to swap their standards of living with ours. Thank you.

Two Outsiders' Views of the Public Corporation

DeANGELO: Thank you, Bob. Nell Minow is our next speaker.

MINOW: One nice thing about coming near the end of the program is that I've found something to agree with in every presentation so far. To carry on the metaphor of being seated according to where we are in the political spectrum, I think I kind of like being here in the middle.

I'm here to represent what Ira Harris referred to as "the real people with real money." The institutional shareholders that I work with, as I said before, have about two trillion dollars invested in the economy. By the year 2000, we expect they will

---

* Editor's Note: Over 60% of the difference between the $75 and the $36 is accounted for by the $2.6 billion distribution to shareholders, which amounts to roughly $24 per share when spread over the approximately 109 million shares outstanding at the time of the distribution.

Adam Smith's argument, back in 1776, was that a form of organization where one guy puts up the money and another guy does the work is not likely to succeed against companies where the ownership and control are combined.

But I think Smith has been proven wrong. Our economy has devised a very sophisticated and, I think, a fundamentally sound corporate structure that enables our public companies to combine capital, management skills, and a lot of effort in a way that benefits all parties. What makes the structure of the public corporation work is the same thing that makes our government work...what makes it work is the separation of powers and the balance of authority; it's the accountability of each part to all the others.

—NELL MINOW—

hold more than half of the equity securities in this country. They already own more than half of the stock of many of the Fortune 500.

Like Larry, I think some LBOs are good and some are bad. When I was speaking before the Delaware legislature, in an extremely futile attempt to try to get them not to pass an anti-takeover law, my presentation followed that of a corporate official who was predicting all kinds of dire consequences if they didn't pass the law. One of the stories he told ended with the observation, "and the raider came in and bought the company, *and he borrowed money to do it.*" Then I came next and I said, "You know, I have never been in Delaware before. I don't know any of you, but I'm going to confess a dirty little secret about my life. I borrowed money to buy my house; and I don't think there's anything wrong with borrow-ing money."

The real question, of course, is this: How do we set up a structure that will allow investors to distinguish between the good transactions and the bad ones? And there is an even more

important question of corporate governance—one which is related to the distinction between good and bad deals—that I would now like to address. Even though I don't know the answer, I think it's good to talk about it. In fact I think it's so important that I'm going to ask the question three times in three languages.

The first is the language of public policy. Which kind of accountability best produces competitiveness and productivity in our public corporations?

To illustrate this issue, I'm going to read a brief selection from *Barbarians at the Gate* (which I refer to as my "Bible"). Toward the end of the Bible, Ross Johnson comes out of the meeting where all has been decided; and the reporters yell out at him, "Who won? Who won?" And Johnson replies, "The shareholders."

Now, let's hold that thought for a minute while we go back earlier into the book to the point where Johnson is meeting with Kravis and Roberts for the first time. They chat a little about the company. And then Johnson says, "I don't want to give up my planes. I

don't want to give up my 24 country club memberships." Now, expenses aside, do we really want someone running a company who has to show up at 24 different country clubs? Does he have time?

Roberts says to him, "Well, we don't want you to live a Spartan life, but we like to have things justified. We don't mind people using private planes to get places if there's no ordinary way. But it's important that the CEO set the tone in any deal we do."

Now we get to the critical issue. Johnson says, "I guess the deal I'm looking for is an unusual one. I want to keep control of the company." "No," Roberts said, shaking his head, "KKR doesn't operate that way. We're not going to do any deal where management controls it. We'll work with you but we have no interest in losing control." Then (and I love this) Johnson says, "Why?" "Because," Roberts said, "we've got the money, we've got the investors. That's why we have to control the deal." From the look in Johnson's eyes, Roberts could tell that wasn't the message he wanted to hear. "We'll, that's interesting," Johnson said, "but, frankly, I've got more freedom doing what I do right now."

Okay, now this is the question I want to focus on: Why should corporate management—notice I didn't say "entrenched" management—why should corporate management be more accountable to the debt guys than to the equity guys? Or, to return to my public policy language: Which system of accountability best produces competitiveness and productivity?

Now, let's ask the same question in a different language—in the language of the law. Which accountability reduces conflicts of interest? And a third alternative—in the language of economics—which accountability minimizes agency costs? (I would like to add a fourth language here; and that's the language of the Delaware courts. But I'm afraid I'm not fluent in it. To me that's like trying to learn Urdu.)

Now let's step back and think for a moment about corporate structure. Even Adam Smith, the patron saint of the Republican party (though I'm a Democrat myself, I used to be part of the Reagan administration with all those guys wearing Adam Smith ties)— even Adam Smith did not believe in the corporate structure. He couldn't understand how public (he called them "joint stock") companies could solve this agency cost problem that Michael Jensen has made part of finance theory. Smith's argument, back in 1776, was that a form of organization where one guy puts up the money and another guy does the work is not likely to succeed against companies where the ownership and control are combined.

But I think Smith has been proven wrong. Our economy has devised a very sophisticated and, I think, a fundamentally sound corporate structure that enables our public companies to combine capital, management skills, and a lot of effort in a way that benefits all parties. What makes the structure of the public corporation work is the same thing that makes our government work (and, as probably the only one here from Washington, I do think it works.) What makes it work is the separation of powers and the balance of authority; it's the account-ability of each part to all the others.

Now, what kind of accountability do you get in an equity structure and in a debt structure? I kind of like the equity structure because that way you grow with the company. If you're a bondholder, you have a guaranteed return—which is very nice for an institutional investor with a guaranteed or actuarially defined payout. But, if the company does spectacularly well, then you clearly have a high opportunity cost. In theory at least, then, the shareholder not only grows with the company but has some say in the overall direction of the company; and I think that control aspect of equity ownership is very important.

So one of the things that bothers me about LBOs is that, although shareholders get some premium, I think either management or whoever else comes in and buys the company generally gets the lion's share of the total premium. What I really object to are those companies that go private and then return as public companies five years later. In such cases, there are almost always huge gains to the new investors in the process—much more of which should have gone to the original shareholders. And I particularly object to the self-dealing element in MBOs. I don't think there's any way that you can play checkers with yourself, and that's what an MBO essentially is. An MBO is one guy sitting on both sides of the table, negotiating both for himself and for other people whose interests he's supposed to be representing.

So, I don't like MBOs. And if it were up to me, I would make them illegal.

I would say, "If you want to make a bid for the company, leave and go somewhere else. Open up an office, and come in off the street like everybody else; and, like everyone else, pay the costs if the deal doesn't go through." In the case of United Airlines, the shareholders ended up paying a lot of money for a deal that didn't happen.

Another of my objections to the leveraged restructuring movement is the creation of what Bob Monks calls "junk stock." In cases of highly levered firms that leave what's known as equity "stubs" outstanding, everybody sort of gets in line in front of the shareholders and they're treated very badly.

To go back to my original point, though, some LBOs are good and some are bad. I think an improved governance structure would help the market—the shareholders, the bondholders, and in fact all investors—to make a surer determination between which ones are good and which ones are bad.

My final point is this: As I said earlier, I think everybody involved should have an equity interest in the outcome because that's the single best way that I know to minimize conflicts of interest, the agency costs, in our public companies. Creating that kind of accountability is the key to making the company work.

I will end with one final quote from my RJR Bible. At the end of the book, after some 500 pages, the authors ask, "Did any of this have anything to do with the business of the company?" I'm with my colleague down there from Ford who says, "I'm interested in good products and good companies." And to the extent that these transactions are distractions from that basic aim, I'm opposed to them. But, to the extent that they free up management to make some valuble changes, then I'm in favor of them.

KKR also does not really own companies so much as it leases them. The towering level of debt service is akin to a lease payment. They're really in the business of leasing companies, fixing them up, and discharging them back to the marketplace—a process that is perhaps best described as "buy, build, and harvest." You buy an operation, you install a new management system, a new framework, a new focus, and then you discharge it back to the marketplace.

Viewed in this light, what has been criticized as a shortsighted practice of building companies only to sell them off again is in fact an essential part of the process of creating value. Once you have created as much value as you can by instituting a new management system, there is no need to continue to hold onto it...when the debt is paid down and financial pressures slacken, the organization may lose some of its focus and momentum. In such cases, instead of going public, you often see LBO companies releverage once more and then pass the value back to the marketplace. They are simply rewinding the spring that propels the creation of value.

—BENNETT STEWART—

DeANGELO: Thank you, Nell. Bennett Stewart is our final speaker.

STEWART: Thanks, Harry. Let me begin by saying that I believe that public corporations in America are using their debt improperly. The lesson, I think, is best learned by looking at what KKR does as a model. Although their record is far from unblemished, keep in mind that KKR is now a company that has $60 billion in sales and whose major subsidiary units range from Duracell to Safeway to Motel 6. They own a whole series of completely unrelated businesses, all bought at huge premiums over current value. In amassing such a conglomeration, the number of mistakes they have made seems miraculously small. That KKR has been an engine of exceptional value creation is I think undeniable.

The question is, why does KKR work so well—especially when most of our conglomerates are failing and being dismantled by our capital markets? There are a couple of simple principles behind KKR's success that I believe many public corporations could adapt to their own best purposes.

One is that KKR relies on decentralization as a management approach. They must do so—because KKR itself consists only of some 60 people. Instead of a broad, overarching corporate bureaucracy, much of the operational decision-making is necessarily pushed down into its individual subsidiary units. The company manages by motivation rather than by mandate. It's not a military or command system, but rather a self-motivating incentive system.

Now, it is rare that people in charge can be made to give up a command structure for an incentive structure—not at least without a struggle. Mikhail Gorbachev is finding out how very difficult it is to transform a vast closed bureaucracy into a more open, dynamic organization. You may find the comparison farfetched, but there is certainly some of that same bureaucratic arrogance and resistance to change in our large American companies. I believe that such bureaucratic attitudes would change dramatically if managers had significant equity stakes in the companies they run—and especially if they made a significant commitment of their own savings.

Equity ownership by management, in short, is KKR's *modus operandi*; it is their principal management tool. The operating people who run the major subsidiary units of KKR are required to be significant owners. As Mike Jensen's research has shown, the typical CEO of a KKR subsidiary owns something like 6.4 percent of the unit, as compared to the 0.2 percent owned by the CEO of the typical Fortune 500 company. The difference there is a remarkable one.

The second thing that distinguishes KKR from the typical American company is that not only do they borrow money very aggressively, but, perhaps more important, they borrow money at the subsidiary instead of at the corporate level. They "compartmentalize" their use of debt and equity. It's much like a ship whose hull is divided into separate chambers; a leak in any one of the units will not sink the entire ship. Right now, Jim Walter is in bankruptcy court, other of KKR's individual units are in trouble, and yet life goes on.

This decentralization of debt, if you will, gives KKR tremendous financial flexibility at the corporate level, while imposing the debt burden at the subsidiary level. Now you will pay a higher rate of interest as the result of that decentralization, but the amount of financial flexibility you gain—and the impression you give to the operating people in the units regarding the true cost of corporate capital and the obligation to earn an acceptable return—makes the higher interest rate a small price to pay for that benefit.

The other thing that distinguishes KKR from the run-of-the-mill American company is that they tend to pay their debt down instead of maintaining a relatively fixed ratio of debt to capital. Allan Gilmour mentioned the need to maintain a sensible capital structure, but that's only true when one thinks about debt statically. In fact, our firm for many years advised companies to maintain a reasonably fixed blend of debt and equity. Now, for most companies, it would clearly be madness to maintain a level of debt at 80 or 90 percent of the capital structure.

But the issue here is not the long-run targeted debt level, but rather what happens to most companies when they are forced to pay the debt down. It is the act of paying down the debt that brings into the picture all of the gains from focusing management on cash flow rather than earnings, forcing them to sell businesses that are worth more to others, and giving them a dedication to greater efficiency. These productive changes are what Michael Jensen earlier called the "control benefits" of debt; and such benefits, especially when combined with equity ownership stakes, are the principal reasons why KKR has been so successful in creating value in their collection of companies in unrelated businesses.

KKR also does not really own companies so much as it leases them. The towering level of debt service is akin to a lease payment. They're really in the business of leasing companies, fixing them up, and discharging them back to the marketplace—a process that is perhaps best described as "buy, build, and harvest." You buy an operation, you install a new management system, a new framework, a new focus, and then you discharge it back to the marketplace.

Viewed in this light, what has been criticized as a shortsighted practice of building companies only to sell them off again is in fact an essential part of the process of creating value. Once you have created as much value as you can by instituting a new management system, there is no need to continue to hold onto it. In fact there may well be disadvantages in holding on. When the debt is paid down and financial pressures slacken, the organization may lose some of its focus and momentum. In such cases, instead of going public, you often see LBO companies releverage once more and then pass the value back to the marketplace. They are simply rewinding the spring that propels the creation of value.

KKR also leases talent. They're one of the largest users of executive search firms in the world. For example, they brought in Lou Gerstner from American Express to oversee RJR. They also brought in Karl Van der Heyden from Heinz to serve as chief financial officer. Van der Heyden, incidentally, immediately discontinued the company's absurd practice of "trade loading"—a practice that involved loading cigarettes onto distributors. This practice, whose sole purpose was to inflate accounting profits, actually reduced cash flow by accelerating the payment of income taxes and by offending consumers with stale cigarettes. Van der Heyden also immediately cut out the premier cigarette program—one that, although clearly a failure in test markets, would have been difficult for the former management to eliminate.

The new management team at RJR also scaled back dramatically a $2.8 billion capital spending program for the Nabisco unit whose projected after-tax rate of return was no greater than 3 percent. As John Greeniaus, the head of the Nabisco unit, admitted in the *Wall Street Journal*, "Well, that plan was devised at a time when we were looking frantically for ways to spend tobacco unit cash flow." Given such an admission, incidentally, I'm more than a little puzzled by the concluding statement by the authors of *Barbarians at the Gate* that nothing about the RJR business was likely to have been changed by the KKR transaction. It would probably have been more accurate to say that virtually everything was about to be changed—not the least of which was management's attitude toward creating value—by virtue of KKR's presence.

Now, I don't believe that every company has the gross inefficiencies that characterized RJR prior to the buyout. But many of our public companies can benefit from applying the same principles that KKR is now using to reform RJR-Nabisco.

In fact, I have devised a three-step process whereby any American company can replicate the management incentives and financial structure of a KKR and still remain public if it wishes. I call this a management "buy-in," as opposed to a leveraged buyout. The idea is simple: At the outset, the senior corporate managers of the company and influential members of the board become significant owners of the company. The technique used to accomplish this transfer of ownership is something I refer to as a "leveraged equity purchase plan" (or LEPP). Although management technically owns stock, the equity is leveraged in such a way as to give management a package of in-the-money stock options. For example, if the current stock price were $60, management could be given the right to buy the stock at some future date at a 10 percent discount—that is, for a price of $54. In such a case, management would effectively own a package of call options with an in-the-money component worth $6.

What distinguishes this LEPP plan from conventional corporate stock option plans is that, instead of granting these options to management, management would be obligated to pay for their LEPP shares. More specifically, they would be asked to come up with 10 percent of the purchase price (exactly equal to the in-the-money component) and the company would lend them the remaining 90 percent non-recourse against the value of their shares. These LEPP options would also differ from conventional options in that the exercise price could be adjusted upward every year at some specified rate of interest (or perhaps at the corporate cost of capital), thus mimicking the debt service payments that would be incurred in an actual leveraged buyout.

So, in contrast to normal stock options, which tend to be just compensation in disguise, LEPP options are bought instead of granted. They are in-the-money instead of at-the-money, and they have an exercise price that is indexed to increase at some specified rate of interest. Such an option plan, moreover, is designed to give management an equity claim that is levered 9-to-1, thus dramatically amplifying their ordinary incentives to improve performance. It's just like an LBO for management people without necessitating the leveraging of the company. It is, in fact, precisely identical in payoff to leveraging the company 9 to 1 by means of an LBO or other recap.

MERCER: Let me just interrupt you. I happen to be a member of one of these rubber-stamp boards, and I want you to know that we're now considering putting in a version of that very program you're talking about.

STEWART: I'm glad to hear you say that because, as I said, what you're really proposing is essentially an LBO. You're going to create the equivalent of an LBO environment in terms of strengthened management incentives—but without the corporate debt.

MERCER: It's getting management ownership that you're talking about, and in a way that they can afford it. I have often heard people complain that the CEOs of Fortune 500 company don't own enough stock in their companies. In fact, Boone Pickens used to point at me and say, "This man doesn't even own three tenths of one percent of his company's stock." Well, let me just point out that it would have cost me *$11 million* to own that three tenths of one percent. And, because I wasn't making the kind of money that T. Boone was making, there was no way I could come up with $11 million.

But, again, I think this is a program that is worthwhile and we are looking at it seriously.

STEWART: I agree that the affordability of these options is an important aspect. For example, with as little as a $500,000 investment, a manager could command $5 million worth of stock if it's leveraged 9 to 1 in a leveraged equity purchase plan.

HARRIS: Do you limit the amount of stock that is available to the management in a company?

STEWART: One of the interesting aspects of this stock option plan—again, in contrast to normal stock option plans—is that it does not dilute the holdings of current shareholders *unless* the common stock grows at a rate of interest that exceeds the interest that's being indexed on the option

itself. The fact that the exercise price keeps rising means that a board of directors is justified, in my view, in selling vast quantities of these special LEPP options.

Now, the LEPP option program is only the first step in my three-part program to strengthen incentives in our public companies. In the case of companies with multiple businesses, the second step is to pass the benefits of debt down into the subsidiary units of the company. This can done by means of a process that I call the "internal leveraged buyout."

The first phase in planning an internal LBO is to divide all the company's businesses into two groups. Some of them will be mature and stable, others will have significant growth opportunities. Or, to use the old BCG nomenclature, start by separating your "cash cows" from your "rising stars." Next, you take your mature cash cows and then leverage them up *at the subsidiary level* and pass the cash back up to the parent. In so doing, you will have narrowed the equity stake in the subsidiary to the point where you can now sell the subsidiary's management a significant equity stake, say 20 percent, of the remaining equity in the sub. In other words, the parent company itself will sponsor the leveraged buyout of its own units. Which brings me back to my earlier question I was asking John Morley about Reliance Electric. Why would it not have made sense for Exxon itself to simply walk up to John Morley and say, "John, why don't you guys join us in sponsoring an internal LBO?" All it really amounts to is a sophisticated incentive compensation plan in disguise.

The parent company, moreover, can even provide the mezzanine layer of debt. This way, if the parent company plays the role of the mezzanine lender, and the implicit transaction price turns out to have been too high with the benefit of hindsight, then the parent can solve the problem by renegotiating the contract with subsidiary management—by going through what amounts to an internal corporate bankruptcy proceeding that should result in far lower costs than a Chapter 11 filing.

So the second step, then, is the decentralization of debt through internal LBOs. Such internal LBOs, moreover, are the economic equivalent of the management buyouts of subsidiaries that we saw throughout the 1980s.

One of the reasons I like the idea of internal LBOs is the problem faced by corporate management in constructing meaningful and challenging budgets for the operatings units. In fact, I once had the experience of working with a large, integrated oil company. Our mandate was to examine the performance of the individual operating units. And when we attempted to get numbers on one of the company's chemicals units, we were told we could not have access to information on that unit. Why? Because a negotiation had taken place between the parent and the subsidiary that actually *denied the parent access* to information about its own subsidiary. Corporate management admitted to me that this unusual arrangement (at least, I trust this is not a common practice in our large companies) had created some difficulty around budget negotiation time.

So what an internal LBO is designed to accomplish is to engage the market, to engage lenders, and to engage corporate management in a process of internally bidding up the debt to a point where, in effect, the management of the unit is passing up cash to the parent. The cash passed up to the parent represents a dividending, if you will, of the unit's budget. And the debt that must be repaid by the subsidiary

simply represents a challenging multi-period cash flow budget in which there is no chance for hedging or renegotiation.

JENSEN: I agree with your concept. The tough part, however, will be making those commitments stick without the threat of outside claimants.

STEWART: But, Michael, you've got to remember that the management people in the sub are going to buy into the equity of the plan.

JENSEN: No, no. You see, the internal corporate problem you're struggling with here is how to eliminate the cross-subsidization of unprofitable business units by profitable ones. BCG tried to solve that problem with their growth matrix model—the one in which corporate headquarters would milk their cash cows and transfer the cash to their high-growth stars. That model, in principle, could have worked just as well as the system you're proposing. But it didn't. The BCG system broke down because of the problems in the relationship between corporate headquarters and the divisions.

Now, I like the thrust of your internal LBO concept. It's a way to get the same kind of incentive structures into the corporate environment as do leveraged restructurings. The problem you're going to have, however, is in making these internal corporate contracts binding. These bonded cash budgets, or quasi-debt claims, may not be effective in disciplining management unless they are a legally enforceable claim.

STEWART: Why do you need a legal contract?

JENSEN: As venture capitalists understand clearly, it's very important to force the entrepreneur—and, in this case, subsidiary management—to get additional financing from *outside* sources. The process of bringing in external creditors or other capital sources prevents management from falling in love with its own deals. In so

doing, they protect themselves from wasting large amounts of stockholder capital on pet projects.

Now, how is your system going to guard against the temptation of management to use internal resources to fund uneconomic reinvestment? It seems to me you have to require that the sub get some of its capital from the outside.

STEWART: I'm going to solve the problem by having the management of the subsidiary unit dig into their pockets and buy stock in their subsidiary unit, which is at risk of loss.

JENSEN: That won't solve the problem. The problem is at the *corporate* level. How are you going to get corporate headquarters to shut down the subsidiary's operation if it fails, to force the subsidiary through the equivalent of an internal bankruptcy or even liquidation—rather than just reaching over into division B and transferring cash from B to the failing sub?

STEWART: But, Mike, you're forgetting the first step in the process, the "management buy-in" that should precede the internal LBO. If corporate management already owns LEPP options, then it has every incentive to enforce the deal they make with subsidiary management. If you want corporate management to behave like KKR, and turn their subsidiaries into what amount to self-standing operations, you first have to make the board and the corporate management people into real equity owners of the parent. I'm assuming that's already been accomplished by the leveraged equity plan.

JENSEN: Okay, I see what you're doing; and that helps. But it won't solve the problem completely. Even large equity holders like Robert Campeau can fall in love with a strategy or deal that destroys value. There is still an important difference between your proposal and KKR's financing arrangement. What you haven't mentioned so far about KKR is that their limited partnership agreements with their buyout funds forbid them from taking any cash from Motel 6 and putting it into Seamen's Furniture, or taking from RJR Nabisco and putting it into SCI. In KKR's case, all cash taken out of the individual business must go back to the limited partners.

Now, if we applied KKR's stricture to, say, the Ford Motor Company, it would force Ford to give its free cash flow—once as much as $15 billion, but today about $4 billion—back to its shareholders. This way, if Ford's management then discovered profitable uses for the funds, they would be forced to return to the markets for more capital.

STEWART: OK, but in an internal LBO, the subsidiary would pass its borrowings up to the parent, which could in turn use that cash to make a distribution to its shareholders. Moreover, the parent could still maintain its double AA rating, or whatever, because the new debt would all be nonrecourse at the sub level.

HARRIS: Yes, but remember that in the 1970s, public companies were not able to get high ratings at the holding company levels.

STEWART: But, again, that's because in most cases corporate management did not have a significant ownership stake to begin with. How is it, Ira, that KKR can still obtain unlimited amounts of financing when some of its deals are belly up?

HARRIS: Because each one is financed separately.

STEWART: Right. It's the compartmentalization, the decentralization, of debt.

HARRIS: But you're not looking for a rating on KKR debt. When you think about the conglomerates of the 1970s, very few of them were conglomerates at the holding company level. Also, it sounds like you're almost recommending a conglomerate structure. Wasn't the whole game in the 1980s

to break up these conglomerates and create value for the shareholders?

STEWART: OK, I'm glad you raised that issue. Why is KKR so successful at managing a group of dissimilar companies when conglomerates like ITT and Gulf + Western have failed?

JENSEN: Because of the structure of the contracts KKR has designed.

HARRIS: The structure's important, but also important—and this is where I have a little problem with your proposals—in making these deals "look" so good is the role of leverage in exaggerating rates of return. Many of the transactions, if examined on the basis of return on total assets, or total debt and equity investment, have relatively low rates of return. For example, the Beatrice deal was getting played up as providing a fantastic return to KKR. But this return was calculated on a very narrow equity base. If you look at the total investment (debt plus equity) of $9 billion, and the fact that these same securities were worth $11 billion after two years, that amounts to a compound rate of return on the whole investment of less than 10 percent a year.

STEWART: Yes, but Ira, you have to remember that that 10 percent return was earned on a purchase price to KKR that already reflected a substantial premium over the pre-offer market value of Beatrice. If you use the pre-offer value as your investment base, then the total operating returns were probably improved dramatically over what they were prior to the buyout.

JENSEN: Look, Ira, we now have good numbers on what the operating returns to LBOs have been, at least on the deals larger than $50 million that were transacted through 1986. Let me just remind everybody what they are. If you take the total value of the equity prior to the announcement of the deal, and you follow that value through for those transactions that were actually revalued—either by

going public, being sold to another company, or refinanced—what you find is the following: Three years after the deal, the total package of securities that were used to buy the public equity—that's debt, preferred stock, and the equity of the buyout partners—increased about 100 percent in value (and this is over and above any increase in the general level of the market during that period).

DeANGELO: That increase is over their value as a public company prior to the buyout, right?

JENSEN: That's right. And, Nell, to answer your and Larry's concern about the potential problem of self-dealing in management buyouts, the numbers now indicate that the division of the gains between public shareholders and the buyout investors, including management, is roughly 50/50. So your statement, Nell, that the public shareholders are being taken to the cleaners—although likely to have been true in some cases—has not been true on average.

In the largest MBO ever attempted, for example, the public shareholders of RJR-Nabisco were offered a 50 percent premium over its current stock price by Ross Johnson together with Shearson Lehman. And the premium eventually paid by KKR, which amounted to over $12 billion, was close to 100 percent over the pre-offer value of RJR. And if you look at the past evidence, the $12 billion paid by KKR to the outside shareholders is greater than the value of all the premiums paid to acquire LBOs over the period 1979 to 1986. The big question to me is this: How will KKR be able to create enough value *over and above the $12 billion premium* they paid just for the right to take control of the company? How can KKR earn an adequate rate of return on that enormous total investment? And, although they face some tough refinancing problems ahead, they clearly seem to be succeeding on an operating basis.

Now, these increases in shareholder value are all coming about simply as a result of the private pursuit of self-interest and the auction process. It's the result of people competing for the right to control scarce corporate resources. And let me say that it is a very healthy form of competition—one that promises to keep our economy strong and our companies competitive internationally.

MINOW: But, Michael, let me say that the payment of these enormous control premiums gets back to the point you made at the beginning of this discussion: In some of these deals, although the operation is a success, the patient dies in this process. Remember, you said earlier that lots of value was created at Federated even though the company is now in bankruptcy.

JENSEN: Well, let me remind you that the patient isn't dead by any means. It is now producing over $400 million per year in operating earnings. Also, I think the Campeau transaction was a highly unusual deal, and thus not at all representative of the vast majority of transactions. There have been well over 1500 of these transactions since the late 1970s. As far as we can tell, maybe 20 of them have ever gone into the bankruptcy court formally. They're hard numbers to get and it may be more. But I keep asking everybody that's playing in this market to give me a list and I'm up to about 20. Now, even if the actual number is as much as 50 percent higher, that only brings the number to 30.

Given the leverage ratios, then, I find the record for LBOs and other highly leveraged transactions to be astonishingly good. Of course, such companies get into financial trouble all the time; and they often become temporarily insolvent. But they get

reorganized very quickly, one way or another. Fruehauf, for example, was an extreme case in that it was actually sold. It didn't go into formal bankruptcy like the Jim Walter deal, which is going the route of Johns Mansville. It is fundamentally an asbestos-related problem. In the case of Campeau, I think it's the complexity of the debt structure that has prevented claimants from resolving their problems outside of the bankruptcy courts. In particular trade credit is critical for survival and bankruptcy is commonly used in retailing to preserve ongoing trade while reorganizing the debt claims.

Now, unfortunately, there are some bad things going on today with our bankruptcy law that are going to make formal bankruptcies much more common than they have been to date. I am thinking especially of the recent LTV decision by federal bankruptcy court Judge Liflan in January. Unless it is reversed, it threatens to end voluntary reorganizations and renegotiations. Such private reorganizations are accomplished generally in a matter of months, and they allow the organization to continue operating without much interference.

What that federal bankruptcy judge's decision essentially said was this: "Thou shalt not reorganize the company without first coming to my bankruptcy court." If my understanding of it is right, this decision is a disaster.

The Challenge Ahead

JENSEN: At this point, I would like to go back to the remarks made by Bob Mercer and Allan Gilmour. And I want to challenge the audience and see if I can bring you into this discussion because I noticed the warm response—the kind normally evoked by words like *God, mother,* and *country*—to

the appeal to customers and to product markets.

MERCER: These are our customers out here in the audience.

JENSEN: I want you to know that I love customers just as well. My wife characterizes me as the best customer in the world.

Anyway, let me try and pose what I think is the general issue that we face today. And I'd like you all to think about it, because the future efficiency of our companies depends critically on whether and how we manage to resolve this problem.

The problem is this: As far as I can tell, there are only four major control mechanisms on the public corporation. They are, first, the product markets; second, the internal control processes of the organization itself run by the board of directors, third, governmental agencies—regulatory, court, and legislative; and, fourth and finally, the capital markets. Now, the problem we face today arises in large part from the consequences of legislation in the 1930s and 1940s that largely stripped our capital markets of their power to function as an effective control mechanism. Although Nell hasn't expressed it, I'm sure she has experienced enormous frustration as she contemplates the reality that her clients, with some *two trillion dollars invested in these organizations*, have virtually no power to influence their operation. Barring the takeover market, the only recourse for dissatisfied institutional investors has been essentially to vote with their feet, to take their 1/8 of a point and leave. And when they do sell, as Nell pointed out, they're faced with the problem of finding some other place to put the money.

Now this brings us to the role of the control market and hostile takeovers. What all of this mucking around in capital markets over the last decade and a half has accomplished is this: It has helped to bring about the re-emergence of what I call active investors, which in turn has restored to capital markets the traditional role of active investors as monitors of corporate performance, as an effective control mechanism for investors. Now, I concede that takeovers and the actual process of change that it imposes on companies often is very dirty. It causes things to change much more rapidly than they would otherwise; and, in so doing, it surely imposes costs. But the benefits of this process are enormous.

Now, let me portray for you what the trade-offs are in restricting the takeover market. Look around in your own community. Look at General Motors, which has long faced competition in the product market. The fact is, because of various explicit and implicit import restrictions, GM today faces no serious internal threat. *It is flooded with free cash flow that it has no profitable use for.*

To illustrate the magnitude of its free cash flow problem, consider that General Motors has spent $80 billion on so-called capital investment in the past 10 years. And even after this enormous investment—many observers have called it "waste"—of stockholder funds, GM remains far and away the high-cost producer even in this country; and it has seen its market share plummet by something on the order of 25 percent—or 10 percent of the total market. Now, given this kind of return on the $80 billion—which, after all, could instead have been returned to stockholders—it is disturbing to me that the company is still under no serious threat. Nor does it show any sign of going through a major reorganization. The way it's going today, in fact, I give it less than a 50/50 chance of surviving as we know it without major government intervention.

And look at our steel industry and how it's behaved. It has long been

insulated from competition, and U.S. Steel is still insulated from the control mechanisms of the product markets by the fact that it bought Marathon Oil. Although U.S. Steel may be beyond the point at which efficiency can be restored, Carl Icahn's proposal to separate the steel business from the oil company is probably the best hope for reforming the company. By denying the steel company the cash flow subsidy that now comes out of the oil company, the proposed spin-off would effectively force the steel operation to face the competition from product markets on its own.

And we could go right down the list of sheltered and inefficient industries and companies in this country.

Now, in the 1980s, the capital markets have been playing this role of forcing our companies to become more efficient. They do it in a chaotic way. But, the important question here is this: Do we really want to waste our scarce capital and other resources while we go through a long period of time—probably a decade or better—waiting for the product market forces eventually to come to bear? (And, in this sense, I agree with Bob and Allan—the pressures of product markets will ultimately come to bear.) In the process, these pressures will end up requiring the break-up of our most inefficient companies.

So, to repeat the question: Are we better off letting many of our companies go through a slow decline and eventual dismemberment by the product markets? Or should we let our capital markets intercede and bring about change—ugly as the process is—and get these organizations back on track as quickly as possible?

Now, of course, there are clearly cases when corporations will voluntarily make such changes—cases in which the internal control processes of our major organizations will deal with problems without the motiva-

tion either of the capital markets or of dramatic competition in the product markets. But it is very hard to find major examples of completely voluntary restructurings. One of my colleagues at the Harvard Business School, Gordon Donaldson, has found one he says in General Mills. As Donaldson shows in a case study, General Mills underwent a major restructuring in the early 1980s that didn't appear to be driven either by massive troubles in the product markets or by any serious threat from the capital markets.

Now, before I get off my soapbox, let me close by saying that the challenge for all of us today—for Bob and Allan, and for all of you in the audience who are going to join our public companies after graduation—is to address the problem caused by the failure of the internal control processes within our largest companies. Why is U.S. Steel in its current predicament when it's been clear for so long that something's gone wrong? Why are our companies having such a hard time coming to grips with the need to reform within? Why have we had to resort to our capital markets to make the necessary changes? The problem is especially critical today because we are again in a position where we are severely limiting the monitoring role of our capital markets. So the burden of change is now back where it was during the 60s and 70s—that is, on the boards of directors and the internal managements. And, to enable our companies to compete in increasingly global markets, they will have to do a much better job than they have in the past.

So, will we make the necessary changes, or will we simply sit back and wait for the forces of the international product market to bind? That, in my view, is the major management challenge we face going forward in the 1990s.

MERCER: Well, Allan, as I said earlier, you and I might as well shoot ourselves. I have a few disagreements with Mike I'd like to take up; but I'll let you start things off.

GILMOUR: Well, Mike, I have a very different view of the 1980s. I think that the restructuring movement has been little more than a reaction to another, earlier Wall Street fad. As Ira mentioned, we're seeing the unwinding of conglomerates because the top management of these companies had no knowledge of the businesses other than financial knowledge. Their only interest was in whether they could—or could not, as the case may be—pay off the debt. The primary lesson we have learned from the last few years is that a broadly diversified company participating in a whole bunch of segments doesn't add a lot of value to the shareholders or the economy because there isn't any critical mass. That top management, the top ownership—however you want to describe it—brings nothing but an overview, if you will, a portfolio overview to its group of companies.

So I think many—not all, but many—of the LBOs and MBOs we've seen have amounted to the cleaning up of a structure that 20 or 30 years ago we were told was a grand idea. It was going to be the savior of the future because, of course, we were going to be able to take different kinds of businesses and they were going to offset the business cycle. They were going to give us deep pockets to outspend and outlast our foreign competitors.

Now, I think that a lot of what Mike said is right, because any society or any economy must have self-correcting mechanisms. And I agree that we don't want the government assuming that role. My lord, why in the world you would want them to do anything is beyond me. They can't even run the government. Have you looked at their income statement recently?

What we're talking about here is how we're going to govern big companies. One thing we have learned, then, is that it's important to narrow the focus of a business. Having essentially solved this overdiversification problem, however, I question whether we really want to repeat the process of leveraging up our companies to instill the discipline of having to pay it down again. I have serious reservations about Mike's debt control hypothesis and its role in curbing the free cash flow problem. I somehow rather doubt that, in the absence of debt and other market pressures, we are now all suddenly going to get sloppy, and start spending most of our time at the country club—one of the 24 or however many we all belong to.

JENSEN: Are you getting your share, Allan?

GILMOUR: No. In fact, since I don't belong to any country clubs at all, this panel has been an education for me.

MINOW: Ross Johnson has a lot of time to visit those country clubs now, doesn't he?

MERCER: He's also got a lot of money.

GILMOUR: I continue to believe that boards of directors, in general, amount to something. They do take their job seriously; it's not just fees and lunch. And I do believe that ultimately the product markets are a very key discriminator, if you will, between success and failure. I think that where Mike and I disagree is that he doesn't want to wait that long. I think that some of the LBOs have done a good job, but we seem to subcribe as a nation to the creed that if a little bit is good, a lot has got to be much better. (I used to work for a boss who thought if you took two aspirin and that fixed your headache, then why not take 12; then you'd be really efficient.) That's the concern I think that many of us have with the corporate leveraging and restructur-

ing that we've been talking about this afternoon.

MERCER: Mike, I wish I could take you to Akron and show you some examples of the kind of changes you're talking about when you deliberately get away from the product market. The tire industry, of course, is one that doesn't move all that rapidly. It takes seven years to grow a rubber tree (and nobody can help that but the good Lord).

Now, in the same town of Akron, we had an erstwhile competitor—Firestone, by name. And its board of directors felt they ought to do something about their stock and about the earnings per share. So they hired a very talented individual to come in—an ex-Ford man—and he was given a much different charter than the one I had when I was running Goodyear. His job was increase share price by increasing earnings per share. At the time, Firestone was number two in the world market.

When this new man came on, he closed several plants, put 53,000 people on the street, and bought back a lot of stock. One way to get earnings per share up, of course, is to reduce your denominator. And this all worked very well. As I indicated earlier, Wall Street rewards liquidation; so their shares went up. He was paid $6 million for the job; and then, as a finale, he sold what was left to the Japanese.

Now, in our industry today there are only two home-grown tire companies left in this country—Goodyear and Cooper down in Findlay. And that's it. So, if you want to hold a rubber manufacturers association meeting today, you've got to go to the U.N.

JENSEN: Bob, it sounds to me like Firestone did just the right thing. With the introduction of radial tires, you get three times the mileage that we used to get under the old bias-ply tires. As soon as radials became a generally accepted product, we had three times the tire capacity in the world that was required. All this excess capacity meant that people and resources had to leave the industry. Now, it's a little more complicated than what I've made it out to be, primarily because you can't make the radial tires in the old bias-ply plants. But an exit of capital and people had to occur.

So, in this sense, the guy at Firestone did exactly the right thing; and the market rewarded him for it. And I should point out, by the way, that all mergers for cash or debt force resources to leave the industry. They are an effective means for forcing industries with excess capacity to shrink. We have seen the same thing in the oil business, in paper and forest products, in food processing, and in broadcasting.

So the tire business clearly faced excess capacity. And, Bob, if I understand this right, Goodyear also was forced to close plants.

MERCER: We've closed 25 plants in the last 10 years. But we didn't do it to get capacity down. We actually increased our capacity.

JENSEN: But, for the industry as a whole, capacity had to fall under the new technology. And the question I have raised here is, How do we get that done? Do we really want massive investment of new capacity in an industry where we've already got three times too much?

MERCER: Mike, moving from bias-ply to radial is not a one-to-one swap. You take out about 1-1/2 tires to get one radial. But what you seem to be ignoring is that it was vital to us that we move into that technology. Allan needed it at Ford, the rest of the industry needed it, and all these people out here in the audience needed it. And we responded to that need.

JENSEN: But they're going to get it. And I want them to get it. My question is, How are we going to reduce the excess capacity?

MERCER: Well, my question is a little different: Are they going to get it from the Japanese or are they going to get it from us?

JENSEN: I don't care who they get it from.

MERCER: I do care.

JENSEN: I care about the customer.

Some Predictions

SUMMERS: An economist has been defined as someone who knows the price of everything and the value of nothing. Which brings me to my observation that the question here isn't whether leverage and leveraged buyouts are good or bad. The question isn't even would the world be a better or worse place if the LBO had never been invented. I think most of us on this panel would agree that our economy is better off as a result of LBOs and other leveraged transactions.

I think the question that one has to ask is, Has the process gone too far? And, given where we are, should the process be scaled back? And it also seems to me that everyone on this panel, albeit for rather different reasons, essentially agrees that highly leveraged transactions have gone too far. Mike thinks it's because of the speculative cycle brought on by the incentives of the promoters. Some of the rest of us think we can make a judgement about what the social consequences are going to be. Still others think we have found innovations that will allow us to reform the corporation from within and thereby capture much of the benefits of leveraged restructuring without the associated costs. But, the striking thing here is that we have nine people representing different points of view, all of whom agree that the leveraging of public corporations has gone too far.

STEWART: Well, hold it. I'm not sure I want to be included in that company.

SUMMERS: All right, we have one dissenter, then.

STEWART: No, what Mike Jensen and I have said was not that there has been too much leverage, but simply that the prices of the deals have been too high. I continue to believe that a significant part of corporate America remains underleveraged because companies are not thinking about using leverage in the right way. They still think about using it involuntarily, defensively. In the process, they needlessly sacrifice the financing flexibility of the entire company instead of using the debt strategically, as part of a process to strengthen management incentives to create value.

MORLEY: Well, I do want to take issue with Mike Jensen's point about the noble purpose of the raider. I find that hard to take.

JENSEN: Oh no. Noble effect perhaps, but never noble purpose. I have never suggested that raiders are motivated fundamentally by anything other than self-interest (or what some people call "greed")—a force which, I might add, drives most activity in this world.

MORLEY: But this process is now turning companies into nothing more than financial instruments. They're losing their purpose.

JENSEN: I can tell you that the LBOs that I've had the chance to observe are not in any danger of losing their purpose. And I'll bet if I walked through your own company today, I'd find the same thing that I've found in other LBOs; and that is an enormous devotion to products and customers. Whether it's a regional railroad, a food manufacturer, a machinery manufacturing company, hotel properties, or biscuit factories, what I've found is a major refocusing on the basic business and on the customer. It's true, of course, that the financial rewards at the top are the driving force behind the transactions;

but the changes in control that result are certainly not turning these companies into financial vehicles.

You didn't forget about the customer at Reliance Electric, did you?

MORLEY: We didn't, but we had to remind some of our investors not to forget them.

SUMMERS: I would like to offer a prediction. I predict that, even though the conglomerate form was described as the source of all corporate ills in the 1980s, within three years we will see at least five stories in the major business press lamenting the missing corporate staff. They will complain about all the contingencies that companies failed to plan for because they didn't have enough corporate staff, because all those guys got fired in the last round of restructuring.

It seems to me that there's a danger of hubris in all this talk about the benefits of restructuring. Mike Jensen's speech today reminds me of a terrifically eloquent speech by Harold Geneen in 1969—in this case, extolling the glories of the conglomerate form and the superiority of internal capital markets. Geneen based his prescription for more conglomeration on the same evidence that Mike Jensen is using today to justify leveraged restructuring: namely, the huge stock market premiums that attended these activities.

So, I think we may be making a big mistake to try and make a judgement about what works while using such a short time horizon. If I had to make a guess, I think that some narrowing of the focus was right. But it seems to me the assertion has been made with far more confidence than the evidence warrants. I'll bet we'll see a reversal of a lot of these developments in the next five years.

STEWART: I will make the opposite prediction. I will say that much of what's been happening in recent years has come about because capital mar-

kets are becoming more efficient, more sophisticated. And with increasing investor sophistication, the demand for corporate staff will continue to shrink accordingly. Outside investors are now performing many of the monitoring tasks that were once performed at the corporate headquarters. This has been made possible in large part by the dissemination of information using microcomputers and personal computers, by the ability of someone sitting at a desk to analyze a company and its sources of value. The information revolution has made it far more possible today for an outsider to question the governance of a company than it was when Geneen was running ITT in the 60s and 70s.

One case that comes to mind is that of Fred Hartley, former CEO of Unocal, who committed his company to a synfuels project that would pay off only if oil became 70 dollars a barrel. How Fred could claim that he had a better understanding of the likely payoff from that investment than outside investors I simply do not understand. That kind of managerial indifference to the marketplace strikes me as the real hubris.

In short, I see the world moving toward greater decentralization, and toward greater capital market control over corporate decisions. Even Russia cannot resist this trend. It is a worldwide phenomenon and I believe it can only accelerate.

DeANGELO: At this point, I will turn to John Morley for one final comment; and then we'll close with one or two questions from the audience.

MORLEY: Bennett Stewart has asked me three times why Exxon sold Reliance, and I thought maybe I should attempt to answer him more fully. Let me say, first of all, that I really don't know why; and I certainly wasn't going to ask them to the point of changing their minds. But I think their motive gets back to a point Allan

made earlier about companies reversing their earlier diversification mistakes. Exxon initially bought Reliance because Reliance had an invention they wanted to exploit. The invention didn't develop, however, and they were left with something that really didn't belong in their investment portfolio. So getting rid of Reliance may really have amounted to a kind of corporate housecleaning.

STEWART: But let's suppose—and Allan mentioned this earlier—that you are a multi-divisional company that has pared itself down to a series of businesses that are somehow connected to one another; and that some of these businesses are at the end of their life cycles while others are at the beginning. As I proposed earlier, why not push the debt down into the mature businesses, sell management an equity stake in those businesses, and thus create an internal LBO? This would enable operating management to buy into their operation—and I mean emotionally as well as financially. I'm talking about enfranchising operating management, liberating at a subsidiary level all the creative energies that get trapped in a centralized, bureaucratic conglomerate corporation.

MORLEY: Well, at Reliance, we have done essentially what you're proposing with two of our foreign operations; and it does work.

GILMOUR: Let me give two quick responses to Bennett's proposal. First, it is designed for a multi-product company. While it makes very good reading to say that Ford is a widely diversified company, we're not. The Ford Motor Company is essentially a one-product company; we produce cars and trucks. And, in such cases, the ability to separate a business from the whole organization is very limited. Ford is not a holding company, it's an operating company—at least I hope it is.

My second comment is that we do try to measure profitability in each of our divisions—perhaps not as aggressively as Bennett has suggested, but I think the idea has merit. We attempt to reward operating management according to their division's contribution to corporate cash flow. But having said that, much of our revenues and costs cannot be allocated so clearly among divisions. And thus individual bonuses tend to be tied to overall corporate profitability more than to individual unit performance.

STEWART: I think the issue comes down to how physically separable are the operations that make up your company.

GILMOUR: Separable in a product sense, or in a geographic sense?

STEWART: In a product sense.

GILMOUR: Not very.

STEWART: If that's the case, then what about using transfer pricing among the various divisions to allow better divisional profitability analysis?

GILMOUR: That reminds me of one of my first assignments at Ford 30 years ago. There was a series of articles on how to do transfer pricing in the *Harvard Business Review* back in the late 1950s. And, although they too seemed exciting at the time, we have generally concluded that most of those were impracticable. They could not work in an actual business setting. We concluded what we should be doing is not so much establishing profit centers as focusing on the effectiveness of individuals—and on the success of our specific products. The profit center concept sometimes seems to miss the forest for the trees, and ignores how well the corporation is doing as a whole.

High Leverage and International Competition

DeANGELO: Let's now turn to the audience for a quick question or two.

AUDIENCE: If the benefits of leveraging are so apparent in this country, then why is it that companies in Japan and West Germany, operating in very different market structures, seem able to out-perform American companies? Would overseas companies further improve their performance if they were to turn to leveraged financing? Or is this something that you think is specifically American?

JENSEN: Historically, Japanese and West German companies have been much more highly leveraged than our companies—although that's changing today. And, my forecast is that these changes will have disastrous results for them.

GILMOUR: Well, that's good news. We're hoping for sloppy competitors.

JENSEN: You will get it.

SUMMERS: But, Mike, although they've been more levered, Japanese and German companies have also been much less distracted by our Boone Pickenses and other capital market pyrotechnics. And many people think that somehow they function just fine without having corporate raiders displace managers and without paying their CEOs $60 million a year.

JENSEN: That's not true, Larry. Both Japan and West Germany have had very effective controls from the capital markets. But, unlike our system, it's not coming from the KKRs and Carl Icahns, but rather from the banking system. In both those countries, large commercial banks typically own large equity blocks in companies they lend to. And it has been the banks that make the changes when they become necessary. Glass Steagall and other restrictions have made that impossible in this country. But the role of bank financing has amounted to a very effective form of capital market control.

MERCER: Well, Mike, I want you to know that my archaic company is competitive to the point where we are now shipping tires from this country to Japan and to Korea. Why? Because they are better tires and the public wants them.

JENSEN: But Bob, you got restructured. You did what had to be done.

MERCER: We were successful *in spite of* that restructuring.

High Leverage and Corporate R & D

DeANGELO: We'll take one final question.

AUDIENCE: A recent National Science Foundation Study showed a decline in the growth rate of corporate R&D. Can this be attributed to leverage and other market pressures?

STEWART: Let me address your question by means of an example. Merck & Co. is one of the most R & D-intensive companies in America. It spends some $800 million annually, more than 10 percent of its sales, on R & D. Just for fun, about a year ago I thought about what it would take to do an LBO of Merck. Merck had a market value of about $25 billion; and if you put a typical 30 percent premium on top of that, then you're up in the range of, say, $33 billion. Now, suppose I financed that $33 billion with 90 percent debt. That would require about $30 billion in debt; and if I paid that off in seven years, then my annual debt service payments would be $3.5 to $4 billion. That amount is several times its annual cash flow; in fact, it is roughly equal to Merck's entire capital base; and thus, an LBO would require it to return its entire capital base each year.

Now, the plain lesson here is that not only wouldn't you want to do an LBO of Merck (it would force you to turn off the R & D spigot to service the debt, which would cause the value of the company to collapse), but in fact you couldn't do an LBO of Merck because you couldn't come close to servicing the debt, even if you cut out much of the R & D budget.

Which brings me to the second lesson here: The market handsomely rewards effective R & D programs. And the best protection against a leveraged takeover is to spend lots of money in R & D effectively so that your price is so high that a takeover is inconceivable. As we know from research by the SEC, it is those companies that lag their industries in R & D, and not those that lead, that tend to become takeover targets.

So, all this amounts to a long-winded way of saying that I have seen no evidence of capital market pressures forcing companies to cut back effective investment in R & D—but, again, the key word here is effective.

JENSEN: Joe Grundfest, the former Commissioner of the SEC, has made an interesting comparison between Merck and GM. Although Merck has only $6.5 billion in sales compared to GM's $125 billion, Merck now has a market capitalization of $30 billion, which is $5 billion greater than the market value of General Motors. GM also, incidentally, spends only about 4 percent of its sales compared to Merck's 11 percent.

So, if you look at those two numbers, you just cannot seriously argue that our capital markets are failing to place a value on successful R & D. As Bennett says, it just doesn't make sense to operate R & D-intensive organizations like Merck as LBOs. And, in fact, those kinds of companies are not being LBOed. Of all the LBOs over $50 million from '79 to '86, only seven spent enough on R & D to even report it in their financial statements. And even among those seven cases,

in three of them R & D spending actually increased after the LBO.

MINOW: The problem here, aside from the failure to align management interests with those of stockholders, is that not all R & D expenditures are productive. For example, you can spend a lot of money on research designed to produce a premier cigarette, as RJR did, and make yourself more vulnerable in the process.

JENSEN: But that doesn't mean you can't run high R&D operations in ways that incorporate many of the principles of LBOs. As my colleague Bill Sahlman has pointed out, there are striking parallels between venture capital organizations and the LBO associations I mentioned earlier. The similarities are remarkable. The biggest difference is the absence of debt financing in venture capital.

Now, if you think about what venture capital organizations do, they also use limited partnership buyout funds, and they also have controlling boards of directors with significant ownership interests. Indeed, it seems that the venture capital organization simply takes the governance structure of a KKR and drives it right down to the level of an individual R & D project. In fact, Wall Street is now packaging and selling portfolios of individual R & D projects—projects that used to be done under the corporate umbrella—to both institutional and retail investors. And this technique has been remarkably successful. In effect, it amounts to an LBO of an R & D project financed not by debt, but rather by equity from limited partners.

STEWART: I agree. In fact, that is essentially the third step in my three-part process that I didn't get a chance to complete. The last step, which I call "venture capitalization," involves getting equity, through spin-offs of high-growth subsidiaries, into the hands of the managers of those operations. This could also be accomplished through partial public offerings of stock; but there are likely to be ways to keep this completely "internal" that are even better.

MORLEY: In my comments earlier, I mentioned that Reliance had actually increased its R & D spending after our LBO. But what I think the leverage accomplished was to drive us to use our R & D to reduce the cycle time for product development. This shrinkage of the product development cycle has had a very large pay-off in terms of increased profitability.

GILMOUR: Just to add one contrary comment. Most of the leveraged buyouts have occurred in good economic times. If we experience a sharp downturn, then a lot of these now heavily leveraged companies will be forced to cut their R & D budgets.

MERCER: Let me recommend to this audience that they get the current copy of *Time* magazine. There's an article in there entitled "The Prophets of Doom" that I encourage you all to read. The main point the article makes is that "LBO" means "Large Bankruptcy Opportunity."

DeANGELO: On that note I think we should end this discussion. Thank you all very much for taking part. ∎

■

BANKRUPTCIES, WORKOUTS, AND TURNAROUNDS: A ROUNDTABLE DISCUSSION

Sponsored by the J. Ira Harris Center for the Study of Corporate Finance at the University of Michigan

April 5, 1991

HARRY DeANGELO: Good morning, and welcome to the fifth annual corporate finance forum sponsored by the Harris Center. Our discussion today will focus on the timely subject of corporate bankruptcy and reorganization. Among our principal aims will be to shed some light on the conflicting incentives faced by managers, creditors, and investors in troubled companies.

Serving as moderator of today's discussion is **LEONARD ROSEN**, Senior Partner of the law firm Wachtell, Lipton, Rosen & Katz. Leonard's experience as a leading bankruptcy attorney makes him well suited to reconciling the divergent interests of the various claimants involved with troubled companies. At this point, I will turn the floor over to Len, who will give a brief introduction to our subject matter and our panelists.

ROSEN: Thank you, Harry. I'm very flattered to be here. This is an absolutely all-star cast, and I will start by telling you very briefly who they are.

PETER FITTS is a Division Executive with Citibank. Peter ran the workout group at Citibank for many years until he was elevated above that position. The Citibank workout group is perhaps the premier workout group in the country. They have been doing a terrific job for a long time.

RUSSELL LUIGS is the CEO of a company called Global Marine, which went through a difficult Chapter 11 and re-emerged as a profitable company. Russ was the CEO both at the beginning and at the end of the process, which is highly unusual.

STEVE MILLER is Vice Chairman of the Chrysler Corporation. When Chrysler was having financial problems in 1980, Steve did a brilliant job of pulling together what was then thought to be an impossible group of lenders from all over the world; and he has since risen appropriately at Chrysler to his current position.

MICHAEL PRICE is the founder and president of Mutual Shares Corporation. Michael was one of the earliest investors in the securities of troubled entities. He's been an extraordinarily successful investor, both in the sense of buying for trading purposes and in accumulating substantial blocks of companies.

WILBUR ROSS is Senior Managing Director of the investment banking firm Rothschild, Inc. Wilbur is a household name in the workout world today. He's been involved in almost every workout you can name, generally either on behalf of the subordinated debt or the equity.

DAVID SCHULTE is a Senior Partner of Chilmark Partners, and has spent many years in the business of reorganizing troubled companies. He and Sam Zell, also on this panel, are running a billion-dollar fund that invests equity in troubled situations. The fund was successfully marketed to institutional investors by Merrill Lynch.

GERALD TURNER is a Senior Vice President at Bank of America, where he's been running a special workout group for many years. Jerry was one of the principal architects on the bank side of the Chrysler restructuring.

SAM ZELL is the founder and chairman of the board of Equity and Financial Management Company, a Chicago-based nationwide real estate organization that owns and operates a portfolio of residential and commercial properties. Sam has been through many workouts, taking positions and controlling companies that have emerged from workouts. Most notable among them are ITEL and General American Management and Investment.

This is a truly extraordinary panel, and it has the added virtue of providing four distinct perspectives on workouts and bankruptcy. The perspective of corporate management is represented by Russ Luigs and Steve Miller. The commercial bank perspective is represented by Peter Fitts and Jerry Turner. The subordinated debt and equity are represented by Wilbur Ross. And then you have the investors represented by Sam Zell, David Schulte, and Mike Price. (You're fortunate, by the way, to have only one professional lawyer, who will try to shut up very soon.)

There is no doubt that we've been through a period of great overleveraging in this country, and it is now combined with what I think most people would agree is somewhat of a recession. Our ability to cope with the problems of troubled businesses will be tested as it has never been tested before. Basically, there are two ways to go. You can liquidate or you can work out. And we'll skip liquidation, because that's the fate reserved only for the hopeless.

In terms of the workout process, there are two basic choices. You can work out difficulties outside of the courts or you can go into Chapter 11. Generally speaking, people prefer to do it out of court, and you'll hear many of the reasons why. The problem, however, is that it's becoming increasingly difficult to do it out of court. So Chapter 11 is being resorted to more and more. And this raises the question as to whether Chapter 11 is working well: Is it too easy a place to get to? Is it too difficult, and costly, to get out of once you're in it? How should the current process be changed to make it more efficient?

The discussion will proceed in two parts. We will start by allowing each of the panelists to offer a brief set of remarks. Then, after a short break, we will have an open discussion in which the speakers can have at one another.

So let's begin with Steve Miller, Vice Chairman of Chrysler Corporation, who will give you some of his insights into the workout process.

PART I
Management's Perspective

MILLER: Thank you, Len. I'm glad Iacocca's on his honeymoon this week, so he doesn't find out that I'm consorting with this bunch again.

I want to offer a few observations about this business from the experience I had with Chrysler's problems of a decade ago in connection with the bailout legislation, the Chrysler Loan Guarantee Act. There were, of course, some parallels in our case to other out-of-court workouts. But our case also had some unique aspects—notably, the role of Uncle Sam in bringing new money to the table, which undoubtedly helped us work out our differences with our many creditors. But a successful resolution, which involved lawyers and bankers representing over 400 financial institutions from all over the globe, was by no means assured from the outset.

Interestingly enough, by the way, of all those 400 banks caught up in the Chrysler mess, it was the bank with the longest overdue loan to Chrysler that was the very first to sign its approval of the workout deal. I'm proud to say the bank was from my home state, the First Interstate Bank of Oregon. And I called up one of their senior directors to express my appreciation for their support for Chrysler, and I said, "Thanks, Dad."

One of the great impediments in the workout process is what I would call bankers' "myopia." When Chrysler fell into deep trouble, all of a sudden its principal bank calling officers disappeared from view, and a new breed of bankers showed up. Peter Fitts and Jerry Turner were there—and, I might add, were among the very best. But they were *not* the same guys we had become accustomed to dealing with. And they were surrounded by lawyers—headed, of course, by Leonard Rosen.

Now, what do I mean by myopia? In my view, there was a single-minded focus on the near-term recovery of as many cents on the dollar as possible. I don't think anyone imagined that Chrysler might actually survive; the workout guys don't seem to have that basic orientation. Instead, the aim was simply to devour what's left of the carcass before it's picked clean by others. I believe the banks could have emerged from the Chrysler situation in far better shape than they did if they had been willing to take a longer view, if they had been willing to take more equity and less upfront cash.

I also think the banks would be better served to put more responsibility for getting the money back on the loan officer who made the loans in the first place, instead of handing it over completely to a specialized workout group. If nothing else, the workout experience would be good training for the loan officers.

My second observation is that honesty is the best policy. It sounds trivial, but it's very important to the process. In working out any difficult credit, the confidence of the lenders in the integrity of the debtor is critical. In practice, that means telling a hostile group some bad news; however unhappy that makes them, it's better than having them find out later that you were sitting on something.

My third and last point is that companies should plan for the possibility of financial trouble by reducing the complexity of their credit agreements—because the more complex the credit structure, the more difficult and costly the workout process. It's axiomatic that any company sliding downhill will find ever more creative ways to borrow money. So that, when it hits the workout stage, it's likely to have a bewildering variety of loans and creditors to deal with.

What I learned from the Chrysler workout was that getting a general agreement to do something to help Chrysler was the easy part. But the squabbles among the various classes of lenders themselves were vicious and lasted for months on end. People were determined to settle old scores from other failed credits unrelated to Chrysler. And I became the referee in one of the financial world's great donnybrooks.

What we have done since then is to streamline and simplify our credit lines and reduce substantially the number of lenders by raising the minimum amount required to participate. If we ever get into the soup again, we would much rather be dealing with a smaller, more homogenous group.

ROSEN: Thank you Steve. All right, we'll now hear from Russ Luigs, CEO of Global Marine. Russ, as mentioned earlier, didn't go through a workout but through the true ordeal by fire, Chapter 11.

LUIGS: Let me start by saying that I'm not a specialist in bankruptcy. I've been through it once, and I think I've enjoyed about all that I can stand. In fact, as I've told many people since then, I have never learned so much about something I didn't want to know anything about in all my life.

From a management point of view, what you're really trying to do is to create a turnaround. And the question becomes, Is Chapter 11 a workable means of achieving that end? That's the first question you've got to deal with. And if the answer to that isn't a clear yes, then the right thing to do is to liquidate the company. Chapter 11 is a very expensive process; and if you're not convinced it's going to work, all you're really doing is dissipating the assets you've been entrusted by investors to manage.

The second part of that question is, Do you have at your disposal what it takes to get through the Chapter 11 process? The first requirement is cash.

215

Companies should plan for the possibility of financial trouble by reducing the complexity of their credit agreements—because the more complex the credit structure, the more difficult and costly the workout process. What I learned from the Chrysler workout was that getting a general agreement to do something to help Chrysler was the easy part. But the squabbles among the various classes of lenders themselves were vicious and lasted for months on end. I became the referee in one of the financial world's great donnybrooks.

What we have done since then is to streamline and simplify our credit lines and reduce substantially the number of lenders by raising the minimum amount required to participate. We just renegotiated our corporate revolving credit agreement with our 38 participating institutions. And that group of 38 is down from over 450 ten years ago. With just 38 lenders, you can get everybody into one room at one time.

STEVE MILLER
Vice Chairman
Chrysler Corporation

ests that threaten the survival of the business. As Steve said, the refrain we so often hear from creditors is, "Give me as many cents on the dollar as I can get, and give it to me right now. I don't care about anything else." So, when you're charging down through this white water, you better have somebody with you who has been through there before, and at least understands where the rocks are, and has the ability to provide some degree of guidance.

Commercial Bank Perspectives

ROSEN: Thank you, Russ. We've heard from the company side. Now we'll hear what bankers have to say about the process, and what they think of the companies that get into it. Our next speaker is Jerry Turner of Bank of America.

TURNER: Thank you, Leonard. Last year, I believe the topic of this forum was the consequences of financial leverage—that is, whether leverage is good or bad for the economy. Well, given that this year's topic is bankruptcies and turnarounds, I think we have at least a partial answer—though I may have a somewhat narrow perspective on all this—to this question about leverage.

Years ago, when I first got into the workout business, someone on this panel advised me that the workout game is not a financial numbers game, but rather an exercise in group dynamics. So, this morning, I would like to make a couple of points about how the group has changed, and thus how the dynamics have been influenced.

Back in the 80s, when leverage was fashionable, my industry was doing its share to create the leverage through LBOs and other HLTs. In competing to lead or co-manage such deals, commercial banks would make available large sums of money, typically

And you realize very quickly that there's an enormous difference between being bankrupt and being broke. If you're out of cash, you're out of business and bankruptcy will not fix that.

And, as I said earlier, you've got to ask yourself the question, Is the company worth saving? Even if you can make all your creditors happy, are the fundamental operations potentially profitable enough to justify the costs of reorganizing all the claims? Is there an ongoing, long-term business opportunity that will support the company's existence? To adapt an old

cliche, there's really no sense in reorganizing a buggy-whip company.

So, to get through a reorganization, you need cash. And, second, you need a team of professionals, both inside and outside the firm. You need experienced legal and investment banking professionals to guide you through the bankruptcy process. I like to compare Chapter 11 to starting down through white water rapids. Although you have some general ability to aim the process, you don't have real good control over it. Like the rocks in the white water, there are a lot of people following selfish inter-

running in the hundreds of millions of dollars. If they were successful in getting the business, their intent was then to sell down or "participate" this loan to other institutions so that their exposure would be reduced from, say, $200 million down to a typical selldown target of $25 million, perhaps even zero in some cases. Now, as banks sell down toward zero—and, believe it or not, some large banks did sell down to zero in some deals—you can start to see them lose their interest in managing any problems with the borrower that might develop later.

Another serious obstacle to working out borrower difficulties was the fact that over 70% of the institutions buying participations in HLTs were foreign banks. Many of them had no office in this country. So, questions started to arise: Were they informed buyers? Was there full disclosure? And, indeed, many of the buyers of this debt believed this debt was risk-free because large institutions such as Citibank and Bank of America were selling it.

Well, guess what? When the problems did arise—and here we get to the subject of the group dynamics— these institutions would pick up the phone and tell us, "Gee whiz, we really didn't think that this problem was going to happen, so you can pay us off now." Now, it doesn't take too long to imagine that if you're in the business of selling and participating loans, you're in real trouble if you start buying back the bad ones. So, our answer was, "We're very sorry, but this is a problem that we're going to have to work through together."

Another complication arises from our legal system. There's a widespread feeling in business today that "litigation results are more certain than business cash flow." And this is a sickness that has poisoned the whole workout arena. So, instead of hearing from

the business person or the banker himself, you would most likely get a letter from his attorney saying, "We still think you should buy our debt back." And so, before you could even turn to the complications that the borrowers were experiencing, you had an enormous intercreditor problem—a problem that takes a lot of time, effort, and money to solve. This represents a massive change from the older workout process.

Still another complication today are problems with the banks themselves. As banks became more aggressive in lending, many of them have gotten into trouble. This in turn has prompted the FDIC to step in and take over these institutions. In many cases, the institutions taken over were divided up into the good banks and the bad banks; and those bad banks then became players in our credits.

Now the reason that's affected the workout process is that, when the FDIC takes over an institution and sells it to someone else, the buyer is typically given an incentive program that rewards it solely on the basis of how much cash it collects. So, cash becomes king. Steve Miller earlier told us that the banks in Chrysler's

One of my big fears in the workout industry today is that people are coming to believe that "litigation results" can be more certain than operating cash flow. And this is a sickness that has poisoned the whole workout arena...

Before you can even turn to the complications that the borrowers were experiencing, you have an enormous intercreditor problem—a problem that takes a lot of time, effort, and money to solve. At least 80% of the negotiations that take place in a workout are those that take place among the lending groups, and not with the borrower at all. Creditors often immediately turn to their attorneys, and the attorneys immediately start recommending litigation.

This represents a massive change from the older workout process. If we start trying to resolve our differences within the financial industry through litigation, I think we're all doomed.

JERRY TURNER
Senior Vice President
Bank of America

restructuring would have done better if they had taken less upfront. And though I question that...

MILLER: Still?

TURNER: Yes, even today. Although some bankers are myopic, Steve, they're not all as shortsighted as you're suggesting.

The problem, however, as I was saying, is that you now have banks owned by the FDIC saying they want "nothing but cash"—even when it might be in their best interests to take less cash along with some longer-term debt and equity.

So, given all these complications, the degree of difficulty in reaching a consensus among all these diverging interests has gone up dramatically. It surprises a great number of people when they hear this for the first time, but at least 80% of the negotiations that take place in a workout are those that take place *among* the lending groups, and not with the borrower at all. Steve was not quite accurate when he said that there were 400 banks in the Chrysler situation. There were in fact 454 banks that all had to agree to have a restructuring succeed. It's difficult enough to get five people to agree on anything, much less 454 banks. That was an accomplishment.

ROSEN: Thank you Jerry. Our next speaker is Peter Fitts of Citibank.

FITTS: With all due respect, Jerry, you're correct that there were 454 banks that all had to agree to the restructuring. In fact, only 453 banks agreed. There was one bank that did not agree. It was an Iranian bank. We did not have a phone number, and no one wanted to deliver the documents in person.

I'm going to continue Jerry's line of thought. I agree with almost everything he said, but I'd like to expand on his comments, and maybe get slightly more technical.

From a lender's standpoint, there are major distortions in the workout process that are interfering with out-of-court settlements. As Jerry said, we spend hours and hours arguing among the creditors and very little time dealing with the one source that we look to for repayment, which is the debtor.

Let me give an example that shows the complexity of the syndication process. With the assistance of the legal profession, banks have developed a number of different methods of selling off pieces of their loans to some other entity. The two principal ways are called "participations" and "assignments." Although they are very different from a legal standpoint, the banks really did not take these differences into consideration when they sold them off. For example, both participations and assignments were sold to banks and other investors on a *non-pro rata* basis. In other words, if the debt included a revolving credit and a term loan, some investors may have taken only the revolving credit piece, others may have taken the term loan, and still others may have taken both pieces.

Now, it takes very little imagination to see that if that particular credit gets into trouble, these different positions—even though they all have a common interest in working out the company's problems—will inevitably create conflicts among creditors. The process gets very complicated.

Jerry mentioned his problems with the FDIC, but our biggest problems have come in dealing with a quasi-government agency called the Resolution Trust Corp. They have certainly been a wild card in the whole process. Their fundamental aim is to get their money back now, and they will typically block any attempt at reorganization that does not buy them off.

Jerry also touched on the fact that creditors' balance sheets, as a result of real estate and HLT losses, are in as much disarray as debtors' balance sheets. And because many creditors are thus experiencing a liquidity crunch as severe as their debtors', their ability or willingness to provide new money is much reduced; if anything, they are looking for excuses to call in their loans rather than extend new ones.

Let me mention another major distortion in the process. We have on the panel Wilbur Ross, who represents the sub debt. Now sub debt has been around for a long time; and, according to the debt contracts, subordinated debtholders are not supposed to be paid anything until the senior debt is repaid in full. This rule is called "absolute priority."

In practice, however, we have something called *relative* priority. Which means the following: You better do a deal with Wilbur and the sub debt if you want to get repaid. The sub debtholders have recognized this power that has perhaps always been there, but they are exercising it with great vigor at the present time.

I would make one other comment in terms of looking at distortions in the process. This one's probably a hard one to pin down, but it's certainly something you have heard and read about. There has been in the process a

I think we all see the reorganization process heading toward a more formal, in-court proceeding. And, yet, I think most everyone here would agree that you're going to save investor capital—and, ultimately, you're going to have more jobs and viable companies—by reversing this process and moving things back toward a private restructuring process.

We just got finished restructuring $8 billion worth of debt at the News Corp. And I'm sure the restructuring was expensive. But the cost was infinitesimal compared to what it would have been in the courts.

And I think the frustration here is this: How do we push back out of the courts a process that unfortunately seems to be sliding that way for a lot of reasons?

PETER FITTS
Division Executive
Citicorp

certain lack of integrity throughout the 80s—and that lack of integrity has existed both on the debtors' side and the creditors' side. I do not believe that the system is yet purged of that lack of integrity.

The Sub Debt

ROSEN: Thank you Peter. Now let's turn to Wilbur Ross and the subordinated debt side that Wilbur so often represents.

ROSS: I'm glad to see that the banks are finally acknowledging that the sub debt exists.

TURNER: Only Peter did that.

ROSS: Okay, well we're halfway there, and it's still early in the session.

Sub debt in many ways has the most peculiar problems in the workout process. We have all the regular problems facing other creditors, but we also have a special problem that arises from the fact that our paper trades. The problem is this: When forming a committee of sub debtholders that will represent the interests of the class, many of the holders are reluctant to join the committee because, in so doing, they effectively agree to "restrict" themselves from trading. Many sub debtholders are institutions like open-end mutual funds that are anxious to preserve liquidity. So you often find that a significant group whose interests you are representing cannot be privy to the factual information that their advisers are getting from the company; and, in some cases, they may not even be privy to the negotiations themselves. This peculiar situation creates its own wonderful dynamic when it comes time to decide what sort of a proposal to accept.

Like the banks, the sub debt also has its own set of intercreditor conflicts. Within the group of sub debtholders, you frequently will have two or three tiers. There may be a senior sub piece, a regular sub, and a junior sub. Some of those may be PIKs or deferred-pay instruments while others pay cash; some may have reset features or other exotica that crept in in the late 80s; and all this complexity compounds to a fare-thee-well the intercreditor problems the banks have. On occasion, some of the sub debtholders also end up buying up some of the bank debt, typically at a discount. This creates another set of conflicts.

Another problem we sometimes face is resolving differences between the "par" buyers—original buyers—and the "discount buyers" of the sub debt. There's a whole universe of institutional investors, some of whom you'll hear from in a bit, who routinely buy defaulted paper at a discount. Sometimes their needs and objectives are somewhat different from those of the par buyer. The par buyers, particularly nowadays, are often insurance companies or other entities that have regulatory accounting constraints. Such people, especially today, are likely to have a fondness for preserving the principal amount of their claim, as opposed to making a true fix of the capital structure.

So those are all terrible complications. The biggest complication, though, is that the sub debt usually has no natural ally in the case. The banks tend to look at their documents and try to enforce archaic notions of strict priority. The boards of directors tend to be very shareholder-oriented and cast the sub debtholders into the unseemly role of "junk bondholders," viewing them as perpetrators rather than as the victims they actually are.

Now, as it often happens, the only way out for the sub debt is to take most of the equity in the company. And that then gets you into an adversarial position not just with the people downstairs, but it raises issues that managements find a little sensitive, matters of corporate governance, golden parachutes and things of that sort. And so the sub debt, as mild-mannered as it originally wished to be, frequently finds itself having no alternative but to conduct warfare on several fronts simultaneously.

All this has led the sub debt to resort to a combination of litigation and negotiation as their only means of defending their interests. And this brings us to the new "f-word" in bankruptcy circles, fraudulent conveyance. Fraudulent conveyance, which has become a very popular slogan, is at the center of an effort to try to look back at the original leveraged transaction to see who did what to whom, and who may be available to enhance the recoveries of the public debt buyers who are innocent bystanders in the process. More and more, that effort is also looking toward the original selling shareholders, because they, after all, are the ones who got the money. It has also begun to look toward the professionals who set up the LBO and who got very big fees for doing it. And, finally, it attempts to determine whether it's appropriate for the pecking sequence

of the capital structure to continue to remain what it was at the outset, or whether the existing priority should be changed to put junior claims more on a parity with the banks. All this, of course, has provoked lively discussion among creditors of all classes.

So, the way the world has evolved with the sub debt is that the workout process is now one third litigation, one third negotiation, and maybe one third M & A activity. What's also new is that the sub debt nowadays tends to get itself pretty well organized, and fairly early on in the case. It's not at all infrequent, in fact, for the sub debt to form a committee *before* there's an event of default. A sub debt committee, you have to remember, has no legal standing as such; there is no contractual arrangement among its members of the kind that exists among parties to a bank loan agreement. Rather it exists and functions as a creature of its own imagination in a workout. A few holders get together, who then become the spokespeople for the class; using them as a lever, we try to get everybody into the act.

Before closing, I want to touch briefly on the issue of private out-of-court restructurings versus the formal Chapter 11 process. In the case of companies that have a lot of public debt, it's unlikely that you'll see very many workouts that don't at least technically go through bankruptcy. It may be a very mild form, such as the "pre-packaged," or consensual, bankruptcy that I'm sure we'll hear more about later. One major reason for my pessimism about private restructurings is that the recent tax bill, bizarrely enough, penalizes companies for converting debt to equity if they do it out of court rather than in Chapter 11 (and why the drafters of the tax laws decided to penalize companies that are already struggling is wholly beyond me).

The second problem that will block out-of-court settlements and provoke more Chapter 11 filings is the problem of hold-outs. If you're a public debtholder, important changes to your instrument like lowering the coupon, extending the maturity, or converting it to equity can't be made without the individual consent of every holder. For this reason, a non-consenting sub debtholder in an out-of-court workout invariably makes out better than one who assents to a restructuring. Why? Because the fellow who doesn't go along with the deal gets reinstated, keeps his face amount, keeps the contract rate, gets whatever back interest was due, and is probably creditworthy in large part *only because* of concessions others have made. So we're in the strange business of trying to convince people to go along with us when, if they could be one of the few who are left out, they'd actually be better off.

In a Chapter 11, by contrast, if you get the consent of two-thirds of the holders by amount and half by number, you can impose the solution on everyone. So this "holdout problem" will inevitably lead to more Chapter 11 filings.

One last observation: I think more and more people are going to focus on the notion that maybe there's a contribution for the trade creditors to make in some of these situations. It's very difficult to deal with the trade outside of the courtroom setting. So, for a variety of reasons, I think you're going to see more and more Chapter 11 filings, although I do think a lot of them will take a more benign form, as distinguished from the free-form knife-fights we've become accustomed to seeing in the past.

Investors' Perspectives

ROSEN: Thank you, Wilbur. Now we'll turn to David Schulte, who is on the investor side, and who has also been on the corporate advisory side, of the process.

In the vast majority of cases, Chapter 11 filings reflect the workings of the ultimate meritocracy—a system which winds up identifying our most poorly run firms by forcing them into bankruptcy court. And a lot of these poorly managed companies, especially if they hit the right judge, get away with murder. Judges tend to be very, very pro-debtor. There tends to be a willing suspension of disbelief and an assumption that somehow the miraculous act of filing has imparted good business judgment to people who are not capable of performing properly outside of Chapter 11.

What delays cases, in part, is leaving the debtor in control of the process, sometimes for years... If we made extensions of exclusivity depend on the consent of all creditors, we'd be putting the decision-making power back in the hands of the people who have the money at stake. The problem with management is that they're not owners and they're not lenders. What they have at stake are their jobs, and their bonuses and their golden handshakes.

WILBUR ROSS
Senior Managing Director
Rothschild, Inc.

SCHULTE: Thank you. Let me start with just a word on the organization of this panel, which I had something to do with. To borrow a theme from the wedding ceremony, we have on this panel today "Something old, something new, something borrowed, and something blue." Peter Fitts is certainly representative of the old. Jerry Turner has also been in the business a long time; but because Peter is now an alumnus of the work-out profession, I think he deserves the "old" end of this. Wilbur Ross clearly represents the new breed because the problem of dealing with

the subordinated debt, as I will argue later, is really the problem of the 90s. In terms of something borrowed, between Chrysler and Global Marine you really can't borrow any more. And the rest of us are blue.

I want to start by providing a bit of historical perspective on the workout business. I've been in it since 1980, and we are now in the second cycle I've lived through. And many of the themes we've heard this morning—for example, Wilbur's closing suggestion that there are concessions to be had from the trade credit—resonate back ten years earlier to the days of the

Chrysler game. In that case, the U.S. government imposed something that we called "the scoreboard." Concessions, or contributions to the workout process, were expected to be made by all the constituencies involved. In the Chrysler settlement, everyone had to participate—trade credit had to do something, the banks had to do something, labor had to do something—or else the government would not have written the check. That notion now appears to be coming back around as a governing principle in workouts. So maybe there is nothing new under the sun, maybe it's just a question of remembering the old lessons.

There is, however, one important difference in the workout world between the beginning of the 80s and today. The great Milken has walked among us—and that has really changed everything. In the old days, there was something called credit quality, and the approval of rating agencies then had something to do with a corporation's ability to borrow in the public market. If you were not of investment grade, no right-thinking insurance company or mutual fund would buy your securities, and thus you didn't have access to the public markets.

Practically speaking, that meant, in the old days, that financially weak companies had relatively little public debt compared to their total capitalization—not because they didn't want it, but because they couldn't get it. Companies that had non-investment grade bonds back then had typically issued those bonds when they were creditworthy, and those bonds had since been downgraded as the company's credit quality fell.

So that when I met up with Jerry Turner and Peter Fitts in the Chrysler situation, and then later in the International Harvester case, neither of those companies had measurable quantities of public debt at the parent company level. And, in fact, both of those workouts were accomplished without doing anything to the public debt. In both those cases, the public debt was minimal, it was hard to reach institutionally, so it was left alone.

The truly significant development took place in 1984, when the junk bond machine in Beverly Hills married the leveraged buyout activity on 57th Street in a deal called Storer Communications. That deal really changed the financial world; it meant the public market would now begin to issue high-risk debt. No longer were LBOs and highly leveraged transactions the sole province of the banks and the insurance companies. And the consequence has been that the debt structures of most troubled HLTs today are disproportionately public rather than private.

The widespread substitution of public for private debt has created enormous problems in the workout process. When Jerry Turner and I worked together on a reorganization of our first busted LBO in the early 80s, it was a privately financed company. And there were only, what, about ten banks in the room?

TURNER: Yes, that's right.

SCHULTE: I don't even remember how many subordinate holders there were, but their holdings were trivial. The deal was cut within a conference room much smaller than this room. And although it took time—all deals take time—it was manageable. Secured debt took a seventy-five cent loss, the subordinated debt got wiped out, the ESOP was protected, and the company was restructured. And, yes, the company eventually failed, but that's because the business wasn't so good to begin with.

But my point is, when you have a limited number of institutional players, it's possible to make a deal and have a negotiation. By contrast, if that same leveraged buyout had instead been financed with junk bonds, it would have been institutional anarchy. The Trust Indenture Act has created the only known custodian of the public bonds, the indenture trustee. Indenture trustees serve under an archaic statute that entitles them to do absolutely nothing, and they are not paid to take any risk. As a result, Wilbur Ross exercises far more control in the bond market today than any indenture trustee.

Wilbur used more polite words to describe this state of things, but it is crazy. I'm now privileged to be the financial adviser to the junk bondholders of Revco Drug Stores. I've been at it two years, and it's a dismal failure. The deal was a failure, the attempted workout was a failure, and now the Chapter 11's proving to be a failure; and we can't get out of our own way yet. It is enormously difficult to restructure when you have a broad variety of institutional players—when you have, as Wilbur put it, the par buyers who originally paid a hundred cents on the dollar and the sharpshooters (and Michael Price is the most constructive of that group) who have paid fifteen cents on the dollar. Bridging the gulf between those interests is a major problem even in Chapter 11. And doing it out of court in the absence of any decisional structure or modification rules is almost impossible.

So I agree that there are going to be a lot more Chapter 11s because no one has yet found a way to get adequate quantities of bondholders to go along outside of court. And this brings me to the subject of Chapter 11. The problem I have with Chapter 11 is that it takes a business problem and turns it—forgive me, Leonard—into a legal case. A business then becomes hostage to people who are payed by the hour... and it doesn't go fast.

FITTS: They're paid *a lot* by the hour.

SCHULTE: For a lot of hours. The pre-packaged Chapter 11 is an interesting hybrid that may represent a partial solution. Maybe it's reality, but I don't yet quite believe it. There've been a couple pre-packaged deals used in what I think were unrepresentative cases. And there is one new one pending, the JPS Textiles deal. But even these tend to be preceded by long negotiations.

The one thing that happened to us in the Revco case, though, is still a problem in pre-packaged bankruptcies; and that's a quirk of legal process. We wound up in the Revco case with an examiner even though no party of interest wanted it.

ROSS: One party wanted it.

SCHULTE: That's right, there was one party that wanted it. And the examiner added a year to the case. That kind of a thing can happen in any Chapter 11 case.

In short, Chapter 11 is a legal process, it's dominated by lawyers and judges, and I think that right-thinking people ought to want to avoid it if they can. But I question whether companies with all this public debt can avoid it.

ROSEN: Thank you, David. Let's now hear from Michael Price, who is one of the investors—and, as David just said, one of the nicest "sharpshooters"—in this business.

PRICE: Our angle in this game is investing in what transpires between these people and trying to make a buck. We are essentially arbitrageurs looking to buy undervalued stock. Such companies may be undervalued because they are not well-run, because they are overleveraged, or for a variety of reasons. Now, if they become overleveraged and have to file Chapter 11, they can be reorganized and emerge as profitable companies. And there is always new money coming in in search of profitable opportunities.

> I've always hated bankruptcy. I don't know what a guy who wears a black robe has to offer that the parties in interest can't do privately themselves. So I would suggest that it might be sensible if you could take the bankruptcy confirmation standard—this ability to bind the minority by securing the consent of one half of the creditors by number and two-thirds by amount—and somehow make that an override to indentures. If we could devise a simple way for exchange offers to work outside of Chapter 11, and for bank credit agreements to be amended in the event of a default, investors would be well served and we'd all be a lot better off.
>
> In short, I'd like to have a non-bankruptcy bankruptcy. It's virtually impossible to do an out-of-court deal right now. All in all, 1990 was a very bad year for exchange offers.
>
> **DAVID SCHULTE**
> **Senior Partner**
> **Chilmark Partners**

When you reorganize a company, you shouldn't lose sight of the fact that you really can't *create* any value. A company has a certain intrinsic value. People can disagree about it, but there is a value for a business. How you capitalize and structure a deal may bring out that fundamental value sooner rather than later. But I think people are kidding themselves if they think they can create value out of thin air—as I guess some of the LBOs claim to have done simply by printing up bonds in the 80s.

For example, when Interco went private, it looked like the value being offered was $58 a share; and in the case of Federated, it looked like the value being paid was $75 a share. But it really wasn't. Interco's real value was about $35 and it's lower today; and Federated's value was probably $50 instead of $75. So, although Wall Street may have fooled some people for a while, corporate values eventually reveal themselves and things come home to roost.

Our job as investors is to help put things back in place. Our aim is to try and tailor a package based on our independent assessments of company values. Regardless of what Wilbur

Going to [an English-style, professional trustee] kind of system would be a huge step backwards. They are not nearly as effective at reorganizing companies in England as we are here in the U.S. It's true that Saatchi & Saatchi and WPP just completed reorganizations outside of trusteeship, but it generally doesn't work there.

I think what we're looking at here is a corporate governance issue, a need to strengthen the role of the board of directors. If you need new management, whether before or after a filing date, the board has got to make that decision. Boards are charged by the shareholders to make such decisions. And as a potential creditor, we look at who's on the board and assess whether they can make good business decisions. They were wise in keeping Russ at Global Marine, they were unwise in keeping Boake Sells at Revco.

MICHAEL PRICE
President
Mutual Shares Corporation

four." And it turned out the company was successful in taking that interest forgiveness, building their library, and selling a thousand units. And the stock has done well.

We are typically not control players, and so we trade out of our positions over time. But, to be a successful investor in such situations, you can't just attempt to maximize the value of your own position; you have to consider the total needs of the business. You also have to get into the game early and with a large commitment of cash. As I said earlier, we play an arbitrage role in which we attempt to recognize the values before others. But if you get into situation too late—after there are other significant players in the game—you can get blind-sided, you can get held up in Revco-type litigations.

Because of increased competition, investment opportunities are harder to find today. But, at the same time, the supply of troubled companies has gone up dramatically; and as time goes on we'll continue to see opportunities for investing in senior debt.

There are, however, a few problems in the game today. I think the court system's working pretty well and most of the players are reasonably cooperative. But, as a couple of people have commented before me, there is a major problem with holdouts. There are investment banks that take positions with the aim not of reorganizing the company, but of getting more investment banking business. And I think that runs counter to the goal of the process.

There are also corporate advisers who simultaneously take positions for their own account; and in some cases, these bankers have advised their clients to tender into a reorganization while keeping their own positions. Take the case of the Zapata deal. When the agreement of two thirds of the bonds was necessary to

or the bankers think, we want to see a company emerge. We don't want to just litigate, we don't want to stick around. Time is a very big factor in determining our rates of return. For example, we've been in LTV for almost seven years now. We were in Manville for six years. I don't even want to talk about Revco. It makes me nauseous to think about it (and it's not your fault, David). But the whole idea is to go in there, get the job done, and go on to the next one.

So we look at the nature of the business and design a plan that fits

the business needs. In the case of Storage Technology, for example, we knew that, for every dollar of claims we bought, we could pull out roughly fifteen cents in cash, a note, and a certain amount of common stock. We did have to pay off the sub class, but it was small. We then designed a note to fit the forecast capital needs of the company. The main requirement was for higher R & D expenditures to fund a big computer library. So we said, "Give us half the interest on the note for the first couple of years, and we'll make up the other half over years three and

complete the exchange, we saw most people tendering two thirds of their bonds. But the deal didn't get done. What we saw instead was the price of the held-out bonds rising *in one day* from about 50 to 55 cents on the dollar to about 120 cents. So we've got to find a way to address this hold-out problem, to remove the profits available to the few that block the workout process.

The second major problem is legal and administrative bankruptcy expenses. We've got to speed up the process. In the case of Allegheny International, the judge didn't begin to challenge the lawyers on their fees until six months after we closed the bankruptcy. Why wait until six months after, why not do it early in the process? Or, better yet, why not just pay the lawyers in the same form as the creditors, say, half in cash and half in stock? Why couldn't Wachtell Lipton be given this incentive to make the process more efficient?

ROSEN: We have a rule against taking equity or investing in equity. So we can't oblige you... fortunately.

PRICE: What can we do to cut down the fees that sap these companies? The fees are enormous.

Another source of problems are government agencies like the PBGC and the RTC, and personal injury trusts like the Manville Trust. These parties often act, or fail to act, solely out of political motives; and that creates a major obstacle to reorganization. In the LTV case, five years ago we offered the PBGC $400 million in cash along with half the upside to settle their claim. It was a good deal, one that should have been done on its economic merits alone. But, given the political realities, it's one that never could have gotten done.

As a general rule, then, when the U.S. government gets involved as a major creditor in these companies—and the Chysler case is the notable

exception—it doesn't typically help the process. So, again, there are major obstacles to workouts, and it would be very, very beneficial if we could think of ways to address them.

ROSEN: Thanks, Michael. Our clean-up speaker is Sam Zell, who also happens to be a graduate of the University of Michigan.

ZELL: After listening to everybody else, I want to start by sharing with you some of the oxymorons that have come out of this workout arena. Certainly, "nice sharpshooter" is an oxymoron. "Creditor consensus" is clearly an oxymoron. Others that come to mind are "fast bankruptcy," "relationship banker," and "moderate fees." Be on the watch for such phrases, for buried in them is the source of much of the current problem.

My perspective is quite different from that of most of the gentlemen on this panel, with the exception of David Schulte, who has been working with me for the last year. David and I have been working the equity side of this arena. I also want to distinguish myself from Michael Price. Michael is a *securities* holder, I am an *equity* holder.

And rule number one of being an equity holder is this: Never get partially pregnant. You write the check only as part of the process of completion. The people who bought Revco, for example, were very bright. About three years ago, they bought the subordinated securities for 50 cents on the dollar on the assumption that that purchase price was in fact significantly less than the value of the company at that time. Those assumptions were in fact correct. The problem is, it's now three years later, and they're still holding the securities. If you add an entrepreneurial rate of return to the cost of their investment, their investment now amounts to 120 cents on the dollar while the value of

the securities has fallen from 50 cents to 20 cents on the dollar.

SCHULTE: No, it's nine cents on the dollar.

ZELL: Nine cents, it's even worse than I thought.

When we look at an opportunity, we look at it from a number of different perspectives. First of all, we focus on buying and controlling the company. We put our money up only when we are in a position to control our destiny.

Second, we put our money up with the expectation that we will be rewarded for serving as the catalyst. Now, all of these gentlemen here—again, except for David—are in the process of achieving some form of consensus on some kind of a reorganization. Almost all reorganizations require new capital. My job is to provide the new capital.

Before I provide the money, however, we generally have a battle. The battle that goes on between me and the creditors begins with my trying to get them to face reality. When I walk into the room for the first time, I invariably hear the line, "Sam, you don't understand." I usually respond to that by asking them how much money *they* are going to put up. And that usually gets me through the first understanding.

Second, you're walking into a room that is characterized by despair, failure, and frustration. With all these people sitting together, the first thing that has to happen is the venting of outrage against the schmucks who got them there in the first place. Leonard Rosen mentioned earlier how unusual it is for a CEO of a reorganized company to be there at the end of the Chapter 11 process. But I don't think he laid enough stress on how extraordinary it is for a chief executive to survive the process. The reason it's so extraordinary is the CEO invariably bears the brunt of the blame and is thus among the first people to disappear. It's hard to tank a billion dollars of debt and then offer yourself as the savior to your creditors.

When looking at companies that are in varying forms of distress, it's very important to establish your guiding principle and then stick to it. Our aim is to invest money in *good* companies with *bad* balance sheets. Bad companies with good balance sheets are something we don't want to get involved with; and an awful lot of these companies that do get in trouble are in fact *bad* companies with bad balance sheets.

Dave and I spent six months looking at a company without being able to determine if it was in fact a good company. We could have bought the company for less than its firesale liquidation value, and this would have guaranteed us a good return on our money. But it would have put us in a position where, if we finally reached the conclusion the company itself wasn't viable, we would have been forced to become liquidation experts rather than reorganization experts.

A number of speakers have commented on the negotiation process. But what may not have come through clearly enough is that getting through a reorganization is as much a test of physical stamina as an intellectual challenge. The average length of our transactions, and we've done quite a number of them, is 19 months. Now, that 19-month period begins with denial. Denial is then followed by depression. Depression is then followed by hope, because somebody with no net worth just came in and said he'd overpay you for your interest. When this happens, we have to go through the process where the flake takes the creditor's committee to the circus; and after three or four months of bullshit in that arena, we then come to the point where everybody says, "Oh, I guess he doesn't

have the money; we better go find somebody who does."

Now what you have to understand is that, during this entire period, everybody at the table is getting paid but me. Many of these workouts would more aptly be described as series of creditor lunches. You can often tell what phase of reorganization you're in by the number of lunches that have been consumed in the process. If you've gone from the fancy catered lunch to the sandwiches and the bags of potato chips, you're usually near the end—because the creditors won't come back for more meetings unless the quality of the food is appropriate.

When we get involved in these transactions, we obviously find that it's difficult to get a large group to reach a consensus. But we have also found historically that if you don't set up shibboleths and instead maintain the greatest degree of flexibility, your likelihood of achieving success goes up exponentially.

For example, a number of the buyers who might participate in restructuring financially troubled companies are only interested in participating if they can own 100%. When General Cinema made their bid for Harcourt Brace, one of the major obstacles to reaching agreement was the fact that General Cinema was asking all the creditors to take a hit; but the hit had no "hope certificate" attached to it. The hit they were being asked to take gave them no hope of recovery.

Now, holding out the *hope* of recovery can be very important in helping to actually achieve that recovery. Everybody wants to structure a deal that gives them a chance to come back into the picture and participate in the upside. For this reason, I usually present a deal to the creditors along the following lines. I say to them: "I will buy 30% of the company and put in x numbers of dollars; but

I will also stand ready to buy up to 100% of the company on those same terms. At the same time, I will offer all creditors a choice: You can have my deal, or you can instead take x number of cents on the dollar." And this kind of a deal, I've found, is much more likely to convince creditors to go along with you.

Why is offering creditors a choice important? One reason is the lack of trust among the players that pervades this whole arena. As Jerry Turner and Peter Fitts said earlier, the creditors spend most of their time trying to kill each other. And so, when the entrepreneur walks into the room, the distrust is palpable. For this reason, the whole concept of presenting the creditors with the right to participate in your own deal—which says to them in effect, "if you think I'm getting such a bargain, then come on board"—helps remove this problem.

Now, the creditors often talk a good game about wanting equity without really meaning it. In one case, David and I spent some 15 months negotiating a deal that gave a group of creditors x amount of cash and x amount of stock. The deal finally closed on a Tuesday and the creditors got 20% of the company. At nine o'clock Wednesday morning, I got a call from Bear Stearns telling me the creditors had hired them to get a bid for the same equity they just spent the last 15 months negotiating for.

And who did they end up selling it to? To me, of course. But let me assure you that if I had instead offered to put the same amount of additional dollars into the settlement as I did to buy the 20% back from them, I'd still be sitting there negotiating with them.

Another important element in reaching consensus is devising alternatives that suit different lenders' special situations and preferences. About 10 years ago, I sat in a room with six of the largest banks in America. The Bank of

America was there, Citibank was there, and we ended up negotiating for six months. We couldn't get the deal done because the various creditors in the room had written down the loans to different levels. One guy had already written it down 25%, and he was more than willing to take 75 cents on the dollar in cash. The other guy was carrying the same loan at 80 cents on the dollar, and there was no way in the world he was going to write his loan down. So we ended up creating a special package of cash and notes for Bank of America, and a different package of notes and cash for Citicorp. Both had the same present value, but they appeared different on the two banks' balance sheets.

When looking at the values of these kinds of companies, it's also very important to distinguish the corporate side of the business from the operating side. When we took over ITEL, the company had been in bankruptcy for two and a half years. Although they had 150 people in the corporate office, there was only one operating subsidiary—and that was in the container leasing business. The 150 people were divided into two groups: 75 thought up questions and the other 75 answered them; and then the second 75 came up with new questions for the first 75. And when business really got difficult, the 150 got together and decided the way to improve business was to double the reporting requirements on the one operating subsidiary.

Now this kind of preposterous environment is very common in companies in Chapter 11. The one feature that really distinguishes Russ Luigs' case from most of these situations is that most of them have long ago become leaderless. Basically, the people who are left at corporate headquarters are usually the people that couldn't get a job in the interim.

But that's very different from what was going on in the operating side of

Part of what's wrong with the bankruptcy court is that it has about the least control and predictability of any judicial process we have in this country. Just take a look at the Eastern Airlines case. The judge in that case decided that $600 million of creditor money should be devoted to an attempt to resuscitate and perpetuate an airline that should have been liquidated.

Now, my first question is, Where did that judge get the training to make such decisions? Secondly, if I were a lawyer on that case, on what basis would I be able to predict how the judge would respond to various creditor requests to end this spending of money and return it to the creditors?

SAM ZELL
Chairman
Equity and Financial Management Company

the business. ITEL's container business went through the entire bankruptcy relatively unaffected. The people there stayed because they were container people and this was a container business; the Chapter 11 proceeding was really directed only at the corporate office up above.

So, to repeat what I said earlier, the key to investing equity in reorganizations is to identify companies that have good operating reasons to exist. Those same operating strengths are also in fact the only good reason to reorganize troubled companies. A basically good operating company may be shrouded in debt and other financing problems. You can redesign the balance sheet, but you can't redesign the company's operations.

One last thought: reorganizing companies is an arduous, time-consuming process. The challenge, as I said before, is as much to keep at it as to figure out how to do it. But the rewards are there, because this environment really represents the ultimate definition of an inefficient market; and inefficient markets produce extraordinary rates of return. And that's what this business is all about.

PART II

ROSEN: Thanks, Sam. I'd now like to open up the floor to general discussion. Let me start by asking the panelists if they would like to ask any questions of other panelists.

TURNER: I'll ask one, Leonard. Wilbur, you said that about a third of your time in achieving settlements with debtors and other creditors is typically devoted to litigation. One of my big fears in the workout industry today, as I said earlier, is that people are coming to believe that "litigation results" can be more certain than operating cash flow. Consider the commercial banks and their involvement with small banks and foreign banks. The latter group of banks, although they may be quality institutions, often don't have people with workout expertise. As a consequence, they immediately hire attorneys, and the attorneys immediately start recommending litigation. If we start trying to resolve our differences within the financial industry through litigation, I think we're all doomed.

ROSS: I think there's going to be a trend—and, indeed, it's one I'm trying to encourage—toward appointing third-party examiners to help resolve cases where there are big legal issues; and I mean examiners who are business people, not lawyers.

Take the issue of fraudulent conveyance. There ought to be a way to establish a procedure whereby you appoint a third party who's not just an advocate for the bank side or the public debt side. Such an examiner can then really look at the case and say, "Gee, do I think that there really was a problem here? Was this LBO in fact dead on arrival?" I think this new role for a new kind of examiner could get rid of a lot of problems caused by everybody taking an advocacy point of view. When everybody becomes an advocate, they all tend to make

exaggerated claims to support their own position; and such claims, if repeated long and loud enough, tend to take on a life of their own. This, needless to say, does not create an atmosphere congenial to reorganizing companies.

SCHULTE: I have a big problem with the use of examiners. I think that, in most cases, it will simply work to lengthen the Chapter 11 and add to the expense.

ROSS: I don't think that has to be true. Having a disinterested examiner research the case, establish a body of "agreed-upon" facts, and perhaps even come to conclusions can't be more expensive than having the banks' lawyers, the company's lawyers, the sub debt's lawyers, and the equity's lawyers all researching the same subject matter. I do agree with you, however, that the current examiner reports are not very useful—the kind that just restate the legal issues and then in a discoordinated way recite some findings without coming to precise conclusions.

Fraudulent Conveyance

SCHULTE: Let's take a minute to explain this fraudulent conveyance issue for the audience. Leonard, you want to take a shot at this?

TURNER: I'd like to know what it is, too!

ROSS: You see, if we had a little more litigation, the banks would be better informed on this matter.

ROSEN: Okay, let me briefly try to describe what fraudulent conveyance is all about. In a leveraged buyout, what essentially happens is that money is paid out of the company to the shareholders of the company; those shareholders are bought out. Now, the money to buy out those shareholders comes from some new source, usually it's either from bank

lenders or perhaps public debtholders. Thus, the money that comes into the company then goes out in some form or another (and I'm collapsing transactions here) to the shareholders.

Now, from a bankruptcy point of view, any money that ever goes to a shareholder is automatically for "inadequate consideration." A dividend is inadequate consideration. A redemption is inadequate consideration. In whatever form it goes to shareholders, it is inadequate consideration from a bankruptcy point of view because the company has received no value in return.

SCHULTE: The corporation is a person, in effect, with a life independent of its investors.

ROSEN: Yes, that's right. And, from a bankruptcy point of view, when you're through with an LBO, the company has gotten nothing but a load of debt that it didn't previously have as well as a new group of shareholders. The company itself has lost equity value because assets have gone out to the shareholders.

For this reason, most lawyers think—though I guess there's still some dispute about this—that every LBO is an incipient fraudulent conveyance. And the critical question is this: At the end of the transaction, is the company still solvent? In making this determination, you have to consider not only balance sheet solvency (that is, does the value of the assets exceed the value of the liabilities), but you also have to look at it from a cash or capital point of view: Does it have enough money to continue to function or has it been left with inadequate capital?

Now, there were several cases in which LBO companies were unable to meet their interest payments within a year or two of completing the transaction. And the question that arises is this: Was the deal doomed at the point when the transaction occurred because the company was insolvent or it did not have enough money or capital to function, or did subsequent external events cause the transaction to fail?

And the law provides a remedy. If the LBO is in fact determined to have involved a fraudulent conveyance, then injured parties—typically unsecured and subordinated creditors—may seek redress from the recipients of the transfer. That is, from the shareholders who got the money. The problem, however, is that because shareholders are numerous and perhaps got it in small quantities, it is easier to look to the individuals or the institutions that financed the transactions and to say, "Well, you knew what you were doing, you financed it, you're still around." And they will specifically say to commercial banks, "Because you financed this deal and collected fees for so doing, we want to subordinate your loans, or otherwise do violence to your position, to help those who did not participate in arranging this transaction."

Now that's perhaps an oversimplified description of fraudulent conveyance law as applied to LBOs, but that essentially is the legal challenge that is now being asserted, if not actually fought in the courts. It's a scrap to divide what's left in a different order of priority than originally contracted for because of an allegedly inequitable transaction.

SCHULTE: And the major losers are likely to be the lienholders, the people who thought they had a good lien on an asset.

ROSEN: Yes. And the irony is that the lenders with liens are not, of course, the primary beneficiaries or recipients of the transfer. The primary recipients, the shareholders who sold out, are gone. The banks are the target mainly because they're still there. And they, in fact, are more like co-victims in the process. It was also their money, after all, that went out to pay the shareholders.

I always thought that the purpose of a workout was first to create the biggest possible pot, and then to fight about the division of the pot afterwards. That was the spirit in which workouts used to be done in the old days. By having everybody focus on creating the biggest pot from the beginning, you effectively maximized the value that could then be shared among all the creditors, senior and subordinated.

What worries me about the current use of fraudulent conveyance is that, if creditor fights about the division of the pot start at the beginning of the process, then nobody's probably paying attention to more fundamental questions like: Have we got the right management running the business? And are they making the right strategic and operating decisions? We're starting the fights so early, spending so much energy on the intercreditor struggle, and creating such divisiveness in the process that we're making it much less likely that companies will be restructured quickly and economically.

LEONARD ROSEN
Senior Partner
Wachtell, Lipton, Rosen & Katz

ZELL: Are people suing the investment bankers and lawyers, too?

IRA HARRIS: No, no, no. That's not nice, Sam.

ROSEN: There is talk about recovering fees from professionals.

HARRIS: They're indemnified by the same company, right?

ZELL: Right. As are the directors.

ROSS: There are questions about the usefulness of that indemnification.

ZELL: What good is indemnification? Does that wind up as a fraudulent conveyance as well?

ROSEN: It winds up as probably being unenforceable.

ZELL: I see.

SCHULTE: But Leonard, how many cases have been actually been tried and won? How many have been followed through to a conclusion?

ROSEN: The reality is that this kind of statute has been on the books since the time of the English common law, from which our law was derived— that is, since the 16th and 17th century. There have been very few cases in which that statute has been used to mount a successful attack against a leveraged buyout transaction. The one case that was successful was a case in Pennsylvania in which Jimmy

Hoffa was involved; and there were other factors involved which are not typically present in the normal LBO.

So there is a question as to whether courts will in fact apply this kind of doctrine in a case where a legitimate bank group advanced money in good faith. They certainly are out the money, and the money went out to the shareholders. So will the court later say to those banks, "You ought to be subordinated, or your lien disallowed, because you participated in this transaction"? On the other hand, of course, you could easily argue that application of this doctrine to LBOs wasn't contemplated when the statute was passed in Elizabethan times.

PRICE: Based on pricing developments in the bank loan trading markets, I think we're going to be seeing some fraudulent conveyance cases tried and perhaps even won. We are starting to see a two-tier pricing structure that discriminates between bank loans with representations and warranties certifying that the banks didn't take any security or fees for arranging those loans, and loans without such reps and warranties. We have seen handshake deals fall through when we have gotten to the rep-and-warranty stage. As a result, we've been able to buy certain bank loans without reps and warranties at a 10-20% discount below the normal price of loans with warranties. And that tells me the banks are getting very, very nervous as time goes on.

A New Role for Examiners?

ROSEN: I'd like to respond to Wilbur's proposal about appointing third-party examiners. Like David Schulte, I don't think examiners will ultimately help the process. Our legal system is uniquely based on an adversarial system. You have two parties, they each hire the best guns they can get, and they slug it out doing all kinds of

discovery, and a lot of research and plugging. It takes a long time to resolve a serious dispute under our legal system and it's very expensive.

What troubles me about Wilbur's proposal is its supposition that a disinterested person can do the kind of job in a short period of time that will convince both sides to this controversy. I think you will get a report that will be a perfectly good law review article on what the law says about fraudulent conveyance. But when it gets to the question of whether the examiner has been able to dig out all the facts—about whether he has spent the time and money necessary to do that—I suspect that the examiner will come up short. He will come up with something that is less than what you want, Wilbur. He will not come up with a firm conclusion that will cause all parties to be satisfied that, say, a given LBO was, or was not, a fraudulent conveyance.

ROSS: Well, let's not use the Revco case as any basis for making this judgment. The fact that the examiner in a case like Revco may not have done a job that convinced everyone doesn't mean that examiners can't do such a job. The judge in the Revco case gave the examiner only 45 days to make his report, which is a preposterously short time period to do the work. Since the typical big Chapter 11, as we all know, can last several years, a judge could give the examiner considerably more time without unduly dragging out the case.

ROSEN: I agree that it was ridiculous. He couldn't possibly do the job he wanted to do.

ROSS: So it wasn't the idea of the examiner that was wrong, it was the fact that the examiner wasn't given the proper tools. The court wouldn't retain his financial adviser for more than about three weeks of the month and a half that he had; and the

fraudulent conveyance issue, it seems to me, is largely a financial question. It's a question about whether the deal was based on a reasonable set of assumptions. So, I really don't think we've seen a proper testing of whether examiners can do the job.

I like the idea of the examiner in large part because it's not easy to get discovery, to get to the facts, in these cases. Let me say that "fraudulent conveyance" is an unfortunate term because of its moral connotations. And such connotations understandably increase the resistance of debtors and bankers to the discovery process. So one merit of appointing an independent examiner is that he'll be given better access to the facts by all the interested parties.

Let me also say that fraudulent conveyance isn't going to go away. The reason I think very few of them have been adjudicated is not that it requires Jimmy Hoffa's presence for the victims to prosecute the case. I think the real reason is the difficulty in getting the facts together. An awful lot of people are stonewalling. And because of their ability to do this, the cases usually get negotiated out and then some value changes hands. So it's not just Hoffa and the teamsters, there are *bona fide* claims here.

ZELL: There are a couple of things that I think have to be added to this equation. First, I really think that fraudulent conveyance is not a substantive issue in any deal where there is a perception that a reorganization is in fact potentially successful. Fraudulent conveyance tends to appear on the scene when, as in the Revco case, things have really deteriorated. The deal was originally done for $1.4 billion; then along came a guy who wanted to buy the company for $900 million; and, according to the most recent numbers, the value of the company is now maybe $500 million. So, in effect, there's a direct correlation between hopelessness on one side and fraudulent conveyance on the other.

I also have a problem with Wilbur's examiner idea—and I think it's really relevant to the whole topic we're talking about today. Bankruptcy judges are not the people best qualified to make economic decisions in this country. And the examiners appointed by judges are generally hired not for their competence, but because they have some connection or acquaintance with the judge. So, Wilbur, if we were to adopt your approach and make greater use of examiners, we would need to appoint professional, certified examiners, people with business experience who are independent of the bankruptcy judge.

SCHULTE: I think the problem Wilbur is talking about is really not about losses, it's about money. The reason these fraudulent conveyance cases aren't litigated is that, in the end, people trade dollars against finality.

What I don't understand, though— and let me put this question to Jerry Turner because he's the only active workout lender in the room—is why banks don't negotiate this issue. Let me tell you what I mean by that. As Leonard said, any leveraged buyout that's gone south is arguably, if not for sure, a fraudulent conveyance when measured against the 17th-century jurisprudential standard (and let me also say that I also think it's absurd to apply such a standard to LBOs). But, if you could look into the files of any major bank that's been a senior lender in an LBO, I am sure you would find some memorandum from counsel about fraudulent conveyance.

Now, what the banks have done instead of addressing the problem squarely, and perhaps resolving the matter through negotiation, is to try and insulate themselves from the problem. They have found some streetwalker willing to write them a

solvency opinion. (No accounting firm will do it; in fact there's only about one firm in the United States that will write such opinions.) And so they have gone forward with more leveraged deals and collected the fees, all the while using these solvency opinions to cover their loins.

Then along comes a deal that doesn't work. And we keep coming back to Revco, but it's an example that demonstrates everything that could possibly go wrong. What we have in Revco is a pair of agent banks behaving like vestal virgins. They wrote $320 million worth of loans, and the whole company isn't worth $400 million today. And it's not surprising that the holders of $750 million of junk debt and the holders of $400 million of preferred are looking at those banks and saying, "I want to nick your lien and get some of your money."

Now, what surprises me is that the banks, in order to avoid the possibility of losing the big one in litigation, haven't come to the table and said, "Let's trade."

TURNER: Oh, I think they have, David. First of all, if I could go back to a point that Leonard made, fraudulent conveyance is not litigated in most cases, it's threatened. And I think the reason banks settle is that while we believe the ultimate resolution of a fraudulent conveyance will be favorable to us—and in fact we think that this application of fraudulent conveyance is totally ridiculous— the cost of defending such a case in our legal system would be astronomical. People like Wilbur walk in and mention fraudulent conveyance...

SCHULTE: Politely.

TURNER: ...and it's almost never litigated. Why? Because it's too costly. You're much better off carving out a nickel and passing it over to the sub debt than you are paying a $50 million legal bill.

SCHULTE: Okay, but in the big busted LBOs, has there been a break in the wall? Can you think of a major LBO case where the senior lenders have in effect compromised their principal amount and settled this issue out yet?

ROSS: I don't know that compromising the principal amount is the issue. There have been present value contributions, for sure. And, as Jerry suggests, that's how these things are normally worked out. I'm also not sure that it's wrong to have it negotiated out this way. But, at the same time, I think the banks would be better off if all the facts could be gotten out on the table early on so people would know what they were negotiating around on the fraudulence conveyance issue.

I also think that the former shareholders tend to get off too lightly, because nobody really goes after them. This has been justified in part by this theory that goes, "Oh well, it's all Aunt Nellies who are the stockholders, and you could never track down 82,000 of *them*." But the truth is, by the time most LBOs go through, the ownership of the stock is very concentrated. It's either in the hands of the arbs or it's concentrated in institutional hands. In the case of Revco, I think that something like 70% of the stock was really closely held when the deal was done. So, you may start to see some cases where there's a carveout of those claims against parties like the former shareholders who are not essential to the reorganization. Because of the negotiated environment, they've gotten off far too lightly.

ROSEN: The problem I have with all this, Wilbur, is that our system is supposed to be based on this absolute priority rule that says creditors are supposed to be repaid strictly in the order of their priority. In practice, of course, there is always a tension that pushes those on the lower end of the order of priority to try to get up the ladder. And I think we should view the fraudulent conveyance brouhaha in that context. If it wasn't a fraudulent conveyance argument, then it would be an equitable subordination argument based on banks having control. It would be some form of lenders' liability argument based on some other theory. There have always been these bits of rubber in the system that allow some value to go down to the lower levels. The lower levels are very clever and creative in thinking of theories that justify some contribution from the top level.

The part that bothers me especially about fraudulent conveyance, though, is that the day the department stores were filed, there was immediately action about fraudulent conveyances. It wasn't the kind of situation that Sam described where so much value is gone that you know you've got a lawsuit. Fraudulent conveyance is now being raised right at the beginning of every case.

My problem with this tactic is this: As an economic matter, I always thought that the purpose of a workout was first to create the biggest possible pot, and then to fight about the division of the pot afterwards. That was the spirit in which workouts used to be done in the old days. By having everybody focus on creating the biggest pot from the beginning, you effectively maximized the value that could then be shared among all the creditors, the senior as well as the subordinated.

What worries me about the current use of fraudulent conveyance is that, if creditor fights about the division of the pot start at the beginning of the process, then nobody's probably paying attention to more fundamental questions like: Have we got the right management running the business? And are they making the right strategic and operating decisions? I think we're sort of backing ourselves

into a situation where we're wasting a lot of time and money, thus jeopardizing the future of some companies that could be far more efficiently reorganized. We're starting the fights so early, spending so much energy on the intercreditor struggle, and creating such divisiveness in the process that we're making it much less likely that companies will be restructured quickly and economically.

The Downside of Loan Syndications

FITTS: Leonard, it sounds as though the machinery is starting to break down here. And, if all this wasn't enough, let me mention another potential complication in the process: the Japanese tax code. Japanese banks, it turns out, have a tax incentive to prefer bankruptcy over out-of-court restructurings. In a bankruptcy, they can write off a large percentage of the debt forgiveness, I think it's 75% or thereabouts. Under a private restructuring, anything that they give up is viewed as a non-deductible charitable contribution. This means that if you have Japanese creditors in your bank group, you want to be very careful what you do, because it may very well cause the workout to become a Chapter 11.

ROSEN: Steve, let me try and get at a question you raised earlier. You said that, having once gone through the workout experience with 450 lenders at Chrysler, you redesigned your credit group so that if there were another workout, God forbid, you would not have to deal with 454 lenders.

FITTS: I thought the next workout was already underway at Chrysler. (Oops, I forgot I'm almost in Detroit.)

ROSEN: Obviously, Steve, the company has some control over the composition of its lending group, but it seems to me the agent banks also have a great deal of control. Those

banks could say to you, "We will not let anybody into this credit for less than $50 million. We will not allow further selldowns." They could put in documentation saying that the consent of 80% of the lenders is sufficient to change the interest rate or the maturity instead of requiring unanimity. This would diminish the intercreditor warfare that has made private workouts close to impossible.

In short, it seems that the lessons from the old days have been forgotten. If anything, the potential for intercreditor conflict is worse today than it was years ago. So I would ask you, Steve, what can the company do to prevent these problems from happening again? And is there any hope that the lending industry will do anything constructive about this?

MILLER: Well, to answer Peter's comment first, Chrysler is not in a workout situation, although we did just renegotiate our corporate revolving credit agreement with our 38 participating institutions. And that group of 38, as I mentioned earlier, is down from over 450 ten years ago.

Renegotiating our revolver was also easier because we did not have any small banks. Ten years ago we had banks with exposures as little as $750,000 and we had to accommodate them all. This time we have only major players, with a minimum loan of about $50 million. With just 38 lenders, you can get everybody into one room at one time. And, as you also suggested, Leonard, we built into the documentation a provision enabling things to get done by two-thirds rather than unanimous vote.

For whatever reason, the Japanese banks are almost non-existent in our credit. (It may be that some of our corporate ads have discouraged their participation.) But having learned from our earlier experience, we do value the homogeneity of the bank group. We did not in fact achieve unanimous consent to what we just did. We had a couple of hold-outs in the end, but we had a mechanism in place to deal with that problem.

ROSS: What restrictions did you put in on resale of the loans? Can the banks sell to another $50 million player or can someone divide it up on his own books? And how tightly is the process controlled?

MILLER: I don't know how tight the controls are, and that *was* a problem in 1980. Banks would say, "I would like to help you, but I sold my position out to ten other guys and it's going to take me a while to check with them all." So we couldn't even talk with the actual holders. This time, we have not had that problem. But I frankly don't know whether such restrictions are in the documentation or not.

ZELL: Let me add, Leonard, that I think that saying all that is really wonderful. The problem is that that ain't reality. I've tried to get banks to agree not to "subsyndicate" their positions. It's a very gratifying and wonderful experience. You just bring your kneepads along and, though they say they'd like to help you, they will never hold the loans if they can sell them off.

Why do they do they sell their loans? Bankers are no different than anybody else. This year they're called bankers, they used to be called real estate syndicators, and before that they were called oil deal syndicators. And it all just comes down to the following: The temptation to do a deal when you know you can collect fees and then lay off all the risk is truly irresistible. And I'll bet you that there isn't a major loan in America today—except your loan, Steve—that hasn't been syndicated down without the borrower's knowledge. And only when things get tough will the borrower find out who really owns his paper.

Although the problems that exist today are the result of everybody's efforts, what has happened in the banking system has played a major role. As loans have been shoved down, there has been a growing lack of "responsibility" that is making the business of reorganizing companies far more difficult. We used to work in bank credits; and even in the 70s, if there were, say, 79 creditors, maybe there'd be at most three foreign banks. Today, if you get involved in a deal with 79 banks, half of them are going to be foreign banks. And they're all likely to be subsyndicates of other banks. So, in effect, you end up in situations where it's very difficult to talk to anybody with authority.

MILLER: I think that's true. But one thing I'd like to challenge you on, Sam, is your point about the importance of creating choices for different creditors. Back in 1980, as we tried to deal with the differing appetites of the banks—for example, those who wanted cash now versus those who would take some equity—it seemed natural that you could solve this problem by granting a menu of choices. In fact, however, the bank group absolutely resisted that. It was hard enough for us to get a response to the simple choice of yes or no from the credit committee. It was infinitely more difficult for them to have to choose from a menu. For one thing, the availability of choices would impose career risk: bankers who made the wrong choice between cash and equity could find that decision coming back to haunt them.

ZELL: Then I would raise the question, Steve, as to whether they understood what their choice really was—since they apparently really didn't have a choice between saying yes or no. They simply had a choice between a disaster and a deal that worked. And that's why you were able to get it done.

But I think it's very important to distinguish between a case in which a company works out its problems alone and one in which a new money player comes in. The company itself, for all practical purposes, brings nothing to the table. Management will say, "Here we are, we've got this, we've got that. How about if we do this, how about if we do that." But if the creditors don't go along with it, whatever problems and opportunities are there today will still be there tomorrow.

But when *we* put a choice on the table, what we're saying is this: "Here's the money. If you want it, I'll give it to you either this way or that way. And my third alternative is to go skiing." A company working out its own problems is never in that position; it's only alternative is to file Chapter 11. Now, in theory, the filing of Chapter 11 is not supposed to dissipate assets; it's not supposed to take from the pot that was brought to the table. The practical reality, as we all know, is quite different.

MILLER: I think you're right in that, in our case, the new money was Uncle Sam's. Jerry and Peter and Leonard will all remember one Saturday we spent negotiating with Paul Volcker. Volcker was puffing on his cigar, saying "Listen, I got the money; if you want it, you're going to do things my way." And that was the way it went.

ZELL: That *sounds* like a negotiation with a banker.

MILLER: Volcker used to be a banker.

FITTS: Sam is missing something here. We as bankers would be happy to agree not to syndicate the loans if the borrowers would pay us for the resulting illiquidity. You're effectively asking us to make a liquidity decision. However, I have yet to see any borrowers willing to pay us higher rates for sacrificing liquidity in order to maintain the stability of the bank group.

ZELL: And I have yet to see a bank offer that option.

FITTS: Oh no, we will.

ZELL: I'm just telling you I've never seen it.

ROSEN: Maybe that's a reality we'll get to some day. Maybe borrowers will voluntarily pay a higher price to get a more stable bank group instead of always looking for the lowest possible interest rate.

Management Entrenchment

ROSEN: Let me turn to a question that I think Russ raised when he said that going through Chapter 11 is a very difficult process and management really should ask itself hard questions about the long-term viability of the enterprise. I thought that was a very refreshing statement from a member of professional corporate management; in fact it's not one I would expect to hear from any other management in the country.

What is the panel's general reaction to Russ's statement? Is that the typical attitude of management, or do managements hang on too long? And what are the problems in trying to deal with a management that is entrenched in a troubled situation?

ROSS: I think it's not at all a typical attitude. In the vast majority of cases, Chapter 11 filings reflect the working out of the ultimate meritocracy—a system which winds up identifying our most poorly run firms by forcing them into bankruptcy court. And also I think that a lot of these poorly managed companies, especially if they hit the right judge, get away with murder. Judges tend to be very, very pro-debtor, much more than is warranted by the realities. There tends to be, particularly early on in the case, a kind of willing suspension of disbelief and an assumption that somehow the miraculous act of filing has imparted good business judgment to

people incapable of performing properly outside of Chapter 11.

What delays cases, for the most part, is not so much the fighting among creditors—although that's part of it—but also leaving the debtor in control of the process, sometimes for years. Chapter 11 often offers management the promise of continuity of their employment as well as the possibility of a big golden handshake at the end. Such practices surely represent an abuse of investors, and I seriously doubt whether they add value to any corporate constituencies other than management and bankruptcy lawyers. So I think the pro-debtor, pro-management bias built into our current Chapter 11 process is a very big problem.

ROSEN: You've suggested, Wilbur, that Chapter 11 provides the debtor with more than a fair shot of being reorganized on its own terms, and management with more than a fair shot at staying in power. But now let's consider the case outside of Chapter 11. Is there any sensible vehicle for creditors who are unhappy with management to replace them?

PRICE: Creditors, Leonard, don't have any right to change management; only the shareholders do. It's my understanding that creditors have to be defaulted upon to have a claim.

ROSEN: That's correct.

PRICE: The proxy fight route is the accepted route for shareholders. One of the problems with proxy contests, though, is that once companies file Chapter 11, some judges haven't even allowed annual meetings.

ROSEN: All right, so what we're finding is that corporate democracy doesn't work because even the shareholders can't get to management, can't get to the directors. And creditors don't really have a way to get to management other than to say, "Well, I'm not going to lend anymore," as part of a restructuring after there has been a default.

So it is very difficult to dislodge a management that doesn't have the kind of view that Russ has: namely, to take a cold look at the company and determine whether it does or does not deserve to live on.

ROSS: Well, it's even worse than that. The bankers are frequently worried about equitable subordination arguments. And, when the management is bad, it frequently falls to the sub debt to be the executioner of the management. And that is a problem in and of itself.

SCHULTE: I think it's a lot easier to get the management changed outside of Chapter 11. I agree that Chapter 11 is a terrific entrenchment device. There used to be an airline called Braniff, and there was a chief executive called Harding Lawrence. And, once upon a time, he had to go just because the performance of the company was lousy. And the way that happened, I'm told, is that some bankers paid a call on the board. They very quietly said, "It's got to be."

Now, you can do that when you're dealing with a board of directors that desperately wants to avoid a filing. It may be a little awkward for people, and their lawyers will tell them not to do it; but it has happened.

FITTS: I would disagree with you, David. From a lender's standpoint, I don't think it's even possible to get management changed outside of bankruptcy. Of course, you're going to have some entrenchment within bankruptcy. But how many companies do you see coming out of bankruptcy with the same people who took them in?

SCHULTE: There are some.

TURNER: David, I was also a lender to Braniff, and I don't recall any meeting with the board.

SCHULTE: Well, why did he resign then? I had a feeling there were a couple of people here who remembered those events, but never mind.

DIP Financing:
A Mixed Blessing?

TURNER: Let me go back to Leonard's point that Russ Luigs' case represents a success story of Chapter 11. I think such stories are very few in number. From my perspective, a Chapter 11 filing betokens a failure to restructure outside of the courts, which is typically far more economical than a Chapter 11.

It's also disconcerting beyond the need to change management. I agree with Peter that it's very difficult for a commercial banker to bring about a change in management. So you do the next best thing: you limit management's access to new money. By saying no, you try to show management how to live off the countryside like the Viet Cong. By saying no, you force management to deal with its problems instead of masking them with new money lending.

The problem that we've created among others in the Chapter 11 proceeding—and the banking industry is itself responsible for this—is that we now quickly make money available within Chapter 11 in the form of DIP financing. Banks are actively pursuing that business—so actively they're even out there now bidding down the rates. I question the wisdom of this. Someday this so-called low-risk business of DIP financing is going to blow up in somebody's face.
ROSEN: Let me explain what DIP financing is. DIP stands for "debtor in possession." The debtor in possession is the entity that takes control of the debtor after it files. Essentially it's the same management that ran the company before. The debtor in question is vested with the powers of a trustee in the bankruptcy and it can operate the business of the debtor, including borrowing money.

And, typically, if a company goes into Chapter 11 without a lot of liens,

it can get DIP financing. In fact, it can often get trade credit far more readily *after* filing Chapter 11 than before filing. Why? Because all of the creditors who lend after the filing have priority over all of the unsecured creditors who were there before the filing. For this reason, as long as there are unliened assets, it is usually a relatively easy matter to obtain credit after a Chapter 11 case is started in the form of trade credit or in the form of a DIP loan.

In the last year, DIP financing has become one of the few growth businesses for commercial banks; and Chemical Bank has been leading the pack. The fees for making the lending commitment are relatively high, and the interest rates look relatively high—because the loans, at this moment at least, look relatively riskless with their priority claim and, in some cases, collateral.

The question I think Jerry is raising here is this: Well, now that I have made this great $100 million DIP loan to someone in Chapter 11, and the maturity date has been reached (which may be one year out, and the debtor is not yet ready to confirm a plan), what if I decide I don't want to lend anymore? How do I then get repaid? That question has yet to be answered because the only way to get repaid is to find another lender to replace you. And, presumably, if you want to get out, no one else is likely to want to come in. Your only alternative at such a point would be to try to liquidate the company. And, you as the lender would be at the mercy of the judge, who then decides whether or not to liquidate the company.

And, as Jerry also said, the easy availability of this new kind of credit in Chapter 11 has taken away some of the normal reluctance that a debtor might feel about entering Chapter 11 and being forced to deal with unhappy creditors.

Reforming the Bankruptcy Code: A Look at the English System

MILLER: The assertion here, generally, is that Chapter 11 both rewards and entrenches current management and, in probably far too many cases, continues the life of an enterprise that is worth more dead than alive. If we accept that proposition, then what alternative governance process would you propose? Who can better make those life and death decisions for the enterprise? Who can better hire a new management team to run the enterprise if it is to live in Chapter 11? The group of creditors that we are confronted with, who are engaged in a streetfight amongst themselves, do not seem to be a ready-made governance body for the company.

So, my question is this: If we throw out the old management, then whom do we put in their place?
ROSEN: When the current bankruptcy code was being discussed back in 1977 or so, the question was seriously considered as to whether we should have debtors in possession once there is a filing. The alternative would have been to adopt a system like the English or Canadian system. In those systems, if you file, there is automatically appointed a trustee or a receiver who is then given the responsibility for running the business. The receiver is free to hire the existing management, or parts of it, or he can replace the entire team.

Now, that alternative was explicitly considered and rejected when the code was passed, and the present strong preference for debtors in possession was put into the code. It is true that, under the current code, you can get a trustee apppointed, but to do so you must pretty much prove fraud or *very gross* mismanagement. It's a very tough job. And you don't want to litigate the issue because, while you litigate, the business may die. The trustee remedy is thus not an easy remedy to obtain under our system.

So this raises the question, Should we have an automatic trustee system such as exists in other countries? Have we seen enough grief under our current system that we ought to try to move in that direction?

Let me also point out that one major reason the automatic trustee approach wasn't adopted in the 1978 bankruptcy code was the history of trustees under the old Bankruptcy Act. Under Chapter X of the Bankruptcy Act, the appointment of trustees in cases involving corporate reorganization was automatic. The trustees were appointed by the judge handling the case, and frequently were law partners or acquaintances of the judge. The discomfort with that kind of an appointment process by the judiciary, in which the person appointed would then appear before the very same judge in the case, was very great.

The history of trustees in England and Canada is quite different. In those countries, accounting firms with professional staffs serve as professional trustees. They're unrelated to the judiciary and have extensive experience in managing troubled companies. And, if we could ever surmount the current concerns about the wisdom of automatically providing for a trustee in every case, we might presumably move to that kind of professional trustee system.

PRICE: I think going to that kind of system would be a huge step backwards. They are not nearly as effective at reorganizing companies in England as we are here in the U.S. It's true that Saatchi & Saatchi and WPP just completed reorganizations outside of trusteeship, but it generally doesn't work there.

I think what we're looking at here is a corporate governance issue, a need to strengthen the role of the board of directors. If you need new management, whether before or after a filing date, the board has got to make that decision. Boards are charged by the shareholders to make such decisions. And as a potential creditor, we look at who's on the board and assess whether they can make good business decisions. They were wise in keeping Russ at Global Marine; they were unwise in keeping Boake Sells at Revco.

ROSS: I agree with Michael that automatic trustees are not the solution. I think one little change is really all you need, and that would be to make an automatic end of the debtor's exclusivity period after 120 days unless all the real constituencies agree to an extension. As things now stand, all the debtor has to do is to convince the judge to extend the period; and judges are usually very inclined to grant at least a few extensions.

ROSEN: It's almost automatic in the early stages of a case.

ROSS: So it's awfully hard to terminate exclusivity and I think it gives management and debtors an inordinate degree of leverage.

ZELL: Isn't one of the problems here, Leonard, the fact that the rules governing bankruptcy judges today are probably the most loosy-goosy rules of any judiciary we have? Part of what makes the whole bankruptcy process so difficult is the total unpredictability of bankruptcy judges' rulings. Just take a look at the Eastern Airlines case. The judge in that case decided that $600 million of creditor money should be devoted to an attempt to resuscitate and perpetuate an airline that should have been liquidated.

Now, my first question is, Where did that judge get the training to make such decisions? Secondly, if I were a lawyer on that case, on what basis would I be able to predict how the judge would respond to various creditor requests to end this spending of money and return it to the creditors?

Part of what's wrong with the bankruptcy court is that it has about the least control and predictability of any judicial process we have in this country. Until you first create a more narrow band of rules for the bankruptcy judges, then the question of trustees or examiners basically becomes a lot less relevant.

There was a case last month—I think it was the Continental case—where one court ruled that the debtor didn't have to pay on their leases. And in the Pan Am case, another judge made a completely different ruling. One of the understood rules of the leasing game has always been this: When you file Chapter 11, you make a decision whether or not you want to honor the lease. If you want to honor the lease, you pay. If you don't want to honor the lease, you turn it back. That's always been the rule, until some bankruptcy judge in Denver out of whole cloth came up with his own theory.

ROSEN: It was in Delaware, but she got reversed.

ZELL: I understand that. But, in the world we live in, that decision followed by the reversal probably cost $5 million in fees. And who knows how much it cost in terms of deferring action by other creditors? Perhaps worse still, it also gave management another opportunity not to address the problem.

You see, my real problem with automatic extension of exclusivity is that it creates no urgency on the part of management to solve the problem. David and I have been working with a guy for the last 12 months. We made him an offer to do a deal last May. But because he's continually gotten extensions, he has no incentive to respond to our offer. Now it's a year later, he's paid no interest, he's done nothing; and most important of all, he's had no incentive to come to resolution. Why should he resolve anything? The fact that the estate is now worth maybe 40% less as a result of delaying means nothing to him; he's already broke.

So, our current system puts the fox in charge of the chicken coop. That's what's wrong. And the guy who's supposed to be in charge of the fox is making up the rules as he goes along.

ROSEN: Well, does anybody want to try and answer Sam? I don't.

PRICE: The best results we've ever had in getting a deal done is where the judge stayed away and let the parties negotiate. (And that, by the way, is the fun of the bankruptcy investing game anyway, it's in the negotiation.) But once you bring in this unpredictable third party—and the Southern District of New York is perhaps the worst offender in producing inconsistent rulings—it really puts a kink in the works.

More on Reforming the Bankruptcy Process

ROSEN: Let's go back to your prior comment, Mike, about the superiority of the American system over the Canadian and English systems. The English system really represents a fundamental difference in philosophy. The philosophy of the American system is that reorganization is good, survival is good; and that liquidation—and probably even sales of assets—are bad. Our system contains a presumption in favor of management and companies. The English and Canadian system are based on the assumption that management can't be left in control. And if a negotiated reorganization doesn't happen quickly in those countries, the company is much more likely to be liquidated.

Now, my question is this: Does the American system unnaturally prolong the life of companies to our general

detriment? Sam, I think, has accurately described what occurred in the case of Eastern Airlines, except that the judge did have plenty of advice. He got projections from the debtor and its advisers; and they quite predictably told him that continuing the airline was the right thing to do. And he had another set of projections from creditors that said it was the wrong thing to do. He chose to follow the advice that said it was the right thing to do.

ZELL: But he did not end up being responsible for his decision...

ROSEN: I agree. No question about it.

ZELL: ...and that's what so critically wrong with the process. This guy with no economic training made a $600 million decision about what was in the economic interest of other people; it was *their* money he was committing. He is not an economist, he's a judge.

ROSEN: Okay, but should we change the system to get rid of what I think we would all agree is a bias toward reorganization rather than liquidation? Should we make it a harsher system that requires more immediate action, perhaps by putting in a fiduciary in at the beginning of the process—a process that guarantees that if you don't get results pretty fast, the company should be liquidated?

ROSS: I honestly think that just changing the exclusivity thing would go an awful long way towards solving the problem. If you made extensions of exclusivity depend on the consent of all creditors, you'd be putting the decision-making power back in the hands of the people who have the money at stake. The problem with management is that they're not owners and they're not lenders. What they have at stake are their jobs, and their bonuses and their golden handshakes. So I think you could solve much of Sam's problems by putting control of the reorganization process into the

hands of the people whose money is at stake.

SCHULTE: I have a different suggestion. We ended exclusivity in the Revco case last November. And here it is April, and the world doesn't feel any better to me. We are the creditors and we have a plan on the table, but we're still in the swamp.

Going back to Michael's point, I've always hated bankruptcy. I don't know what a guy who wears a black robe has to offer that the parties in interest can't do privately themselves. So I would suggest that it might be sensible if you could take the bankruptcy confirmation standard—this ability to bind the minority by securing the consent of one half of the creditors by number and two-thirds by amount—and somehow make that an override to indentures. If we could devise a simple way for exchange offers to work outside of Chapter 11, and for bank credit agreements to be amended in the event of a default, investors would be well served and we'd all be a lot better off.

Peter seems shocked, but the government of the United States overrides private party contracts all the time. The tax courts do it all the time.

FITTS: No, I was watching Wilbur's face.

ROSS: We'll do it if you'll do it.

ROSEN: All right, David, so I guess you want a new statute.

SCHULTE: Yeah, I'd like to have a non-bankruptcy bankruptcy. It's virtually impossible to do an out-of-court deal right now. All the exchange offers in 1990 were flops; none of them closed.

ROSS: That's not true.

SCHULTE: How many of them closed?

ROSS: Seaman's and Western Union closed. That's two.

SCHULTE: Yes, but how many of them didn't close that were tried? All in all, 1990 was a very bad year for exchange offers.

ROSS: Yes, but that was because of the LTV decision and the change in the tax code that converts debt forgiveness into taxable income.

SCHULTE: I understand that. And I agree with your earlier statement that, because of the LTV decision, exchange offers are going to be very difficult. There seems to be a general attempt, perhaps encouraged by the courts themselves and the legal profession generally, to make out-of-court deals harder to do. The essential economics of the hold-out problem already make them very hard to do. But, as I said before, if we could accomplish the binding of the minority that formal bankruptcy provides, I think we'd have a far better system.

Pre-Packaged Bankruptcies: A Hybrid Form

FITTS: Leonard, didn't you partially achieve what David is talking about in the Southland bankruptcy, which was a pre-packaged deal. Of course, there were some special circumstances in the deal. There was a lot of new money at the other end—some four or five hundred million dollars—which makes a big difference in creditors' willingness to participate.

ROSEN: Yes, the pre-packaged plan is really close to what David is proposing. A pre-packaged plan is one that a troubled company puts together *before* filing for bankruptcy. You get everybody to consent to your plan, and then you file for bankruptcy; and the process, at least theoretically, goes much faster.

But it's not that easy to execute in practice. One limitation is that you generally can't affect trade creditors; you can only deal with borrowed money. If you try to get the trade to participate, they can stop shipping and thus strangle your business. But your other lenders aren't going anywhere; so you can stop paying them

interest and you can get them to the table and try to do a deal.

FITTS: But, Leonard, my understanding is pre-packaged bankruptcy also works because it changes the voting requirements by actually going into Chapter 11.

ROSEN: Yes, that's right. You say in effect, "I would need 95% of you to agree if we did this deal out of court. But, if I don't get 95% to agree, then I will simply take the same deal, slap a petition for Chapter 11 on it, and file it in court. This way, I will only need 66% in amount and a majority in number of those voting to agree."

And you might be able to get through Chapter 11 in a couple of months. There have been some very quick pre-packaged deals. In the Southland case, there was a little glitch in the voting so it took an extra two months. But it only took four altogether. And I think one deal came out in as little as 45 or 50 days.

ROSS: Lasalle, I think, was just 50 days.

ROSEN: At any rate, a couple of them have come out very quickly. So I think people feel that pre-packaged is a vehicle that can help this process. It's not a panacea, because you can't deal with all kinds of problems. And you still have to do your deal, of course. You have to remember that the Southland workout was negotiated for over a year before reaching a deal. Republic Health was negotiated, I believe, for over two years before they got to the pre-packaged deal; and then they spent 90 days in Chapter 11.

So what's happening in this marketplace is fascinating in that sense. Pre-packaged bankruptcy is really an attempt by the marketplace to adapt to investor demands for a more efficient process; it's an attempt to get around the legal and regulatory obstacles to an efficient economic resolution of creditor and debtor restructuring conflicts. In pre-packaged deals, people are essentially attempting to take only the most valuable aspects of the existing Chapter 11—in effect, to use only one piece of the bankruptcy code—to get the job done as quickly as possible.

Ethics

ROSEN: Let's now turn to another issue, one that Peter Fitts raised in his opening remarks. Peter observed that that there's been a general lack of integrity among debtors and among creditors. And to this group I'm sure we could add some investment bankers and lawyers. Are the ethics of the marketplace getting any better now that the 80s are behind us?

FITTS: There is a prevalent lack of honesty in the process. I think Sam Zell has hit on some of the problems when he described the games that get played. Some of these games are created by the perverse economic incentives built into the system. People in different positions naturally have different aims, and so they're willing to use the distortions in the system to benefit themselves at the expense of the general public. There's no question that we're in a much more complex environment than we ever have been in before, and the game playing that goes on in the bankruptcy process costs enormous amounts of time and money.

ROSEN: One problem I now see is a clear conflict of interest faced by those investment banks that simultaneously give reorganization advice and trade distressed securities. Is this a major problem? And what about the role of lawyers in all this activity? I see problems there, too.

ZELL: Leonard, I don't think you've even touched the surface of what's really going on. You have investment bankers buying junk bonds in one set of companies, and then advising other companies who want to take them over. They say that's not insider trading because the statute says that's not insider trading. But if you'd done the same thing with stocks, that would clearly be insider trading.

ROSEN: Sam, are you saying nothing has changed from the Drexel days?

ZELL: That's right. The only difference between the Drexel days and today is that, in the Drexel days, the Drexel people were the only guys who admitted to wearing a black hat. And now it's become pervasive. It really relates to what I think is a bigger overall issue. It's called trust. In the last year and a half, I have never seen a greater erosion of trust—and not just in reorganizations, but across the whole economy. We have severed the trust tendon.

One important difference between today and the workouts we did in the early 80s was that, in the old days, the guys in the room with you generally had authority. So you'd sit down with Jerry, and you'd yell at him, and you'd throw things at him, and you'd call him whatever names you could come up with. Then eventually he'd give in and you'd make a deal. (Wasn't that the way it was, Jerry?) But the point is, he had authority.

Today, you get things happening to you in deals and you can't even find the guy who admits to making the decision. It's the committee, and you'd think that the committee sits at the right of God and St. Peter in deciding these things.

I also think that the whole LBO business is a testimonial to the difference between the way business was done in this country prior to the 80s and during the 80s. Prior to the 80s, the most important thing about doing business was who you were doing business with. During the 80s the most important thing was, how much can you get out of the deal? What was missing in the 80s was the old sense of

accountability. People weren't thinking to themselves, "Well, I'd betterbe reasonable because I'm going to have to deal with this guy again." Instead, they'd be thinking, "I'll take my shot at the big deal now; and even if the deal doesn't work out, it's my last hurrah. I can bank my bonuses and fees before my reputation catches up with me.

And the results of these kind of short-term incentives—the total lack of long-run accountability that is pandemic in the system—are totally predictable. Just look at all the deals that have been coming apart.

Controlling the Costs of Bankruptcy

ROSEN: As a final matter, let me raise the issue of fees and expense. We seem to be employing too many professionals, and the professionals seem to be too expensive. For example, if you add up the total of the LTV case at a rate of maybe $30 or 40 million a year, you've got well over a $100 million dollars spent on professionals in that case.

In defense of those fees, there are a whole slew of professionals representing parties that have divergent interests. So if an application gets filed in the court to do X, you've got at least five or six lawyers looking at that application to try to figure out whether it's good or bad for their clients. The result is a proliferation of fees that can be absolutely astounding in some cases, and that can really eat up the value of the assets.

Take the case of Judge Pollack, who is now presiding over the Drexel case. There's about $2 billion in value to divide among a large number of categories of claims; and the judge knows that if he doesn't do something quickly to get all the parties into a room and force them to split what's there, the value of those assets will start to shrink very rapidly. The rate

of accumulated expenses in that case has been estimated to be over a $100 million a year. The FDIC is involved, the IRS is involved, many substantial litigations are pending, and there are a number of different committees. They all know that, at the rate of a $100 million a year over a couple of years, the fees will end up making a significant dent in what now appears to be a very large amount of money.

And perhaps all these fees will be earned legitimately by professionals who are just doing their job on behalf of their clients. But does anybody have any suggestions as to what we can do to curb the expense of a Chapter 11 case?

ROSS: I think that, if the fees were tied to the recoveries actually achieved by the constituencies rather than to time denominations, the business would be done differently. And I mean that not just for the lawyers, but for investment bankers as well. If we instead applied some sort of a rule of reason that capped professional fees at some percentage of the recovery ultimately achieved, I think that would cut out a lot of the costly side shows.

I don't think there should be even the slightest theoretical encouragement of people to spend more time rather than less. And I think the whole fee structure is a wrong fee structure for the investment bankers and the lawyers. I really do. People learn to live within constraints. M & A deals get done awfully fast, and they're at least as complex as a typical bankruptcy. How can it be that you can go from the start to finish of a hostile bid in a month or two when it takes five years to do a bankruptcy? You either have to conclude that the issues are fundamentally much more difficult, which I doubt, or that the professionals are all retarded, which I hope is not true. Or that something else is going on.

ROSEN: In fact, those M & A fees are higher fees per hour than the fees bankruptcy lawyers charge.

ROSS: Sure, but I also think the real loss of value in Chapter 11 is not the loss of value from the magnitude of the fees. It's the time. The unsecured creditors are getting no return on their money, and the businesses frequently go straight downhill—that's the real loss of value. And in a case like Drexel's, if you're running a two billion dollar portfolio, the difference between running it right and wrong for a few months would be a lot more than the professional fees.

So I really think that truncating the time spent in Chapter 11 is the single most important reform we could make. The worst thing about Chapter 11 is it takes too long. And I think

every other sin flows from that. And, as I said before, I think we ought to consider tying people's fees somehow to what investors recover.

MILLER: I would despair of having to write the formula for those fees. And would the formula apply only to in-court proceedings or out-of-court workouts as well? I think it would be far better instead to clean up the process so it runs faster.

ROSS: Well, I don't know how you would do that as a practical matter.

MILLER: Well, I don't know how you would set up your formula.

FITTS: But doesn't this sort of bring us back to the theme of this whole meeting? That is, I think we all see the reorganization process heading toward a more formal, in-court proceeding. And, yet, most everyone here would

agree that we're going to save investor capital—and, ultimately, you're going to have more jobs and viable companies—by reversing this process and moving things back toward a private workout process.

We just finished restructuring $8 billion of debt at the News Corp. And I'm sure the expense was enormous. But it was done outside of court. It could have been in a court process no doubt, if it had to be done that way.

ROSEN: But the cost must have been infinitesimal compared to what it would have been in the courts.

FITTS: Yes, infinitesimal compared to what it could have been. And I think the frustration here is this: How do we push back out of the courts a process that unfortunately seems to be sliding that way for a lot of reasons?

EVA, CORPORATE GOVERNANCE, AND MANAGEMENT INCENTIVES

STERN STEWART
EVA™
ROUNDTABLE

Johnson & Johnson
Headquarters

New Brunswick, New Jersey

June 1, 1994

Carm Adimando

Robert Butler

Susan Malley

JOEL STERN: Good afternoon, and welcome to this roundtable on EVA and corporate performance measurement. Before we plunge into the subject at hand, let me take this opportunity to thank the sponsors of this session, particularly Clark Johnson and JoAnn Heffernan Heisen of our host company, Johnson & Johnson, and Paul Koether of T.R. Winston & Company. I would also thank Professor Jim Bicksler and Dean George Benson of the Rutgers Graduate School of Management for their efforts in bringing this meeting to pass.

As many of you know, last September *Fortune* magazine ran a cover story called "The Key to Creating Wealth for Shareholders." The subject of that article was a measure of corporate performance called Economic Value Added, or EVA, that Bennett Stewart and I have refined and popularized over almost 20 years of working together.

The financial concepts underlying EVA were not, of course, invented at Stern Stewart & Co. Economists since Adam Smith have been telling us that the social mission of the individual business enterprise is to maximize its value to its owners. And financial economists such as Nobel laureate Merton Miller have translated Smith's prescription into the goal of maximizing Net Present Value, or NPV. Our aim at Stern Stewart has been to decompose NPV, which is fundamentally a multi-year or long-term capital budgeting tool, into annual (or even monthly) installments called EVA that can be

used to evaluate the periodic performance of corporate managers and their businesses.

The purpose of this roundtable will be to discuss EVA in relation to more conventional measures of corporate performance—to examine its strengths, the advantages it confers over traditional EPS and ROE measurement systems, as well as any potential drawbacks (though I feel obliged to warn you from the start that we have found very few). We will consider EVA not only as a measure of operating performance, but also as the basis for the entire range of corporate financial management functions, from capital budgeting and the setting of corporate goals to shareholder communication and, my favorite subject, management incentive compensation.

To discuss these matters with us, we have assembled a first-rate panel that includes three corporate CFOs (each of whom is now using EVA in their companies), three representatives from the investment and legal community, and two distinguished financial academics. I will now introduce them in alphabetical order.

■ **CARM ADIMANDO** is Vice President-Finance and Administration and Treasurer of Pitney Bowes. As the company's chief financial officer, Carm is responsible for all treasury and pension-related functions, corporate accounting and strategic financial planning, corporate facilities and administrative activities, and investor relations.

■ **ROBERT BUTLER** is Senior Vice President and Chief Financial Officer of International Paper, and has served in that capacity since joining the company in 1988. Prior to that, Bob served as group executive president and CFO of National Broadcasting Corporation—at a time when NBC was a subsidiary of RCA.

■ **SUSAN MALLEY** is the Chief Investment Officer for Citicorp Investment Services. As such she is responsible for economic, equity, and fixed income research, market allocation and investment strategy, bond trading, and product development. Dr. Malley holds a Ph.D. in finance from New York University's Stern Business School, and was previously a professor at Fordham University's Business School.

■ **S. ABRAHAM RAVID** is Associate Professor of Management at Rutgers University. Avri received his Ph.D. in Business Economics from Cornell University, has taught at NYU, UCLA, and Columbia, and published over 20 academic papers in top finance and economics journals. He has done consulting work for the U.S. Congress, the World Bank, and consumer organizations. Before becoming an academic, Professor Ravid was a professional journalist with the Israeli National Radio network.

■ **RICHARD SHEPRO** is a Partner of the Chicago law firm Mayer, Brown & Platt. He advises clients on matters related to acquisitions and other complex business transactions. In 1990, he published a book with Leo Herzl entitled *Bidders & Targets: Mergers and Acquisitions in the U.S.* Rick also holds the position of Lecturer at the University of Chicago Law School.

■ **BENNETT STEWART** is my colleague and founding partner of Stern Stewart & Co. Bennett has been a constant source of inspiration (as well as occasional vexation) throughout the almost twenty years that we have worked together, and I am confident that both aspects of our relationship will reveal themselves during the next two hours.

■ **R. HUTCHINGS VERNON** is a Vice President at Alex Brown Investment Management. Prior to joining Alex Brown in 1993, he previously held portfolio management and research positions at T. Rowe Price Associates, Legg Mason, and Wachovia Bank. In the name of full disclosure, I should tell you that Hutch is a big fan of EVA.

■ **JOSEPH WILLETT** is Senior Vice President and Chief Financial Officer of Merrill Lynch & Co., Inc. Prior to joining Merrill Lynch in 1982, Joe served seven years in the Chase Financial Policy Division of the Chase Manhattan Bank. And since I happened to have been President of the Financial Policy group at the time, I want to extend an especially warm greeting to Joe, and thank him for joining us.

■ **JEROLD ZIMMERMAN** is Professor of Accounting at the University of Rochester's Simon School of Business. He is also the founding co-editor of the *Journal of Accounting and Economics*, a distinguished publication produced at the University of Rochester. Jerry has been among the four or five superstars in accounting research over the last 15 to 20 years.

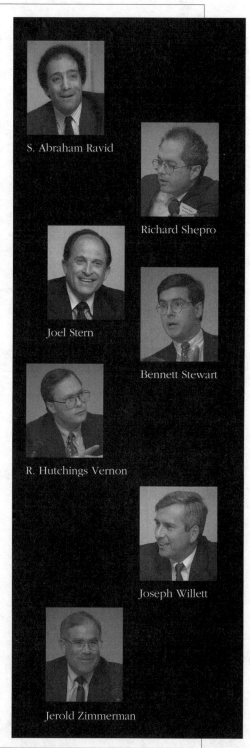

S. Abraham Ravid

Richard Shepro

Joel Stern

Bennett Stewart

R. Hutchings Vernon

Joseph Willett

Jerold Zimmerman

EVA™ and Management Incentives

STERN: I'd like to begin by discussing briefly why it is that an EVA-based incentive system makes managers behave as if they were owners of the enterprise. In most current corporate reward systems, executive pay is so dominated by the "fixed" elements of the total pay package—that is, salary and benefits—that managers behave more like lenders to the firm than the representatives of the shareholders they are supposed to be. By increasing the proportion of the "variable" element of managerial pay—bonuses, stock, and stock options—and by tying that variable pay to a more reliable proxy for shareholder value, an EVA incentive plan can go a long way toward aligning the interests of managers and shareholders.

As our friend Michael Jensen stated the issue in the title of a *Harvard Business Review* article several years ago, "It's Not How Much You Pay, But How." Jensen was so pessimistic about the ability of public companies to solve the manager-shareholder conflict—a conflict he referred to as "the agency costs of outside equity"—that he wrote another *HBR* article in 1989 called "The Eclipse of the Public Corporation." And although we continue to believe that Jensen and his collaborator Bill Meckling will eventually earn a Nobel Prize for their theory of agency costs, our aim at Stern Stewart is to eliminate—or at least to reduce significantly—the agency problem that Jensen and Meckling have identified at the core of the large public corporation. The alignment of managerial and shareholder interests is precisely what an EVA system is designed to accomplish.

But, before I begin telling you what EVA is, let me first attempt to correct a general misconception. The mission of the corporation is not to maximize its market value, as economists like to say, but rather its "market value added," or what we at Stern Stewart call MVA. Although this is a bit of an oversimplification, MVA is essentially the difference between a company's current market value, as determined by its stock price, and its "economic book value." A company's economic book value can be thought of as the amount of capital that shareholders (and, in the technically more correct version of EVA, lenders and all the other capital providers) have committed to the firm throughout its existence, including earnings that have been retained within the business.

Now, all this is not quite as simple as it sounds. Calculating a firm's economic book value, in particular, requires a number of adjustments that I will just mention briefly. At Stern Stewart, for example, we do not use pooling accounting for acquisitions; all acquisitions are treated as purchases—that is, as if they involved outlays of cash. Further unlike the accountants, we do not write off the goodwill that arises from purchase acquisitions of companies for amounts greater than their book value. That goodwill stays on the balance sheet more or less indefinitely, unless there is a real decline of economic value. As an example of another adjustment to conventional accounting statements, we also add back the balance sheet provision for deferred taxes to book equity, because it represents a reserve of cash on which the firm is expected to earn an adequate return. And there are a variety of other adjustments that can be made to get a better estimate of how much investor capital is really tied up in a firm.

To illustrate the importance of this distinction between market value and MVA, consider the case of General Motors. At the end of 1988, the company had a total market value of equity of $25 billion and an economic

---

Our aim at Stern Stewart has been to decompose NPV, which is a multi-year or long-term capital budgeting tool, into annual (or even monthly) installments called EVA that can be used to evaluate the periodic performance of corporate managers and their businesses. But EVA is not only a measure of performance, but also the basis for the entire range of corporate financial management functions, from capital budgeting and the setting of corporate goals to shareholder communication and management incentive compensation.

—Joel Stern—

book value of roughly $45 billion. That is, the company had invested $45 billion of shareholder funds to produce an enterprise worth only $25 billion. GM thus had an MVA of *negative* $20 billion!

Interestingly, Merck also had a market equity value of $25 billion at the end of 1988. But because Merck's economic book value value was only $5 billion (even after adding back a considerable amount of already expensed R & D into the equity base, as our adjustments call for), the company had an MVA of positive $20 billion. So, although Merck and GM had almost the same market value at the end of 1988, Merck's management had succeeded in creating $20 billion of shareholder value while GM's had destroyed roughly the same amount.

To repeat what I said earlier, then, the corporate mission is not to maximize market value—this can be accomplished, as the case of GM illustrates, simply by retaining a large fraction of your earnings and raising more capital from outsiders—but rather to maximize the *difference* between a firm's market value and outside capital contributions. MVA, I should also point out, is the basis for our corporate ranking system known as the Stern Stewart Performance 1,000, which *Fortune* featured in an issue this past December.

Now, how does a company increase its MVA? The short answer is, by increasing its economic value added, or EVA™. EVA is the *internal* measure of year-to-year corporate operating performance that best reflects the success of companies in adding value to their shareholders' investment. As such, EVA is strongly related to both the level of MVA at any given time and to changes in MVA over time. EVA is the "residual income" left over from operating profits after the cost of capital has been subtracted. So, for example, a firm

with a 10% cost of capital that earns $20 million on $100 million of net assets would have an EVA of $10 million.

To the extent a company's EVA is greater than zero, the firm is creating value for its shareholders. As I mentioned earlier, EVA is a kind of annual installment of the multi-year Net Present Value (NPV) that is calculated by using the standard discounted cash flow (or DCF) capital budgeting technique. Like NPV, EVA measures the degree to which a firm is successful in earning rates of return that exceed its cost of capital. But, as my colleague Bennett Stewart and I hope to convince you, EVA is a far better all-purpose corporate tool than NPV or DCF, even though both methods properly applied give you the same answer over an extended period of time.

We have done a number of studies to see which measures of performance are most closely linked *not* with market value, but with market value added—this *premium* value that's being created by management. Measures like earnings, earnings per share, and earnings growth all have some trivial relationship to MVA. When you bring in the balance sheet as well as the income statement—with measures such as ROE and return on net assets, or RONA—the significance of the relationship improves a great deal. But the correlation is not anywhere near as strong as what happens when you use EVA. And one reason for the greater strength of that correlation is that EVA, unlike ROE or RONA, takes into account the amount as well as the quality of corporate investment, corrects for accounting distortions in GAAP income statements and balance sheets, and specifies a minimum or required rate of return that must be earned on capital employed. To have a *positive* EVA, your rate of return on capital or net assets *must* exceed the required rate of return.

I'd like to describe very briefly what happens when you use EVA as a measurement device instead of more conventional measures. A senior manager recently asked me, "Why can't I use just RONA itself as a basis for evaluating and rewarding my people?" I said, "You shouldn't do that, for two reasons. One, if a company or a division is currently earning substandard returns, managers can increase RONA simply by taking projects with higher, but still inadequate returns. In this case, you would actually be rewarding managers for reducing shareholder value and further reducing MVA."

At the other extreme, consider a company with a 12% cost of capital that earns 25% after tax. In such cases, managers might be discouraged from taking on *all* projects below 25% because that will lower their *average* RONA. For that reason, the firm could be passing up value-adding investment opportunities.

Neither of these distortions of corporate investment incentives occurs under an EVA framework. In an EVA system, you improve EVA as long as you take on new projects where the rate of return on net assets exceeds the threshold.

In fact, there are three different ways to increase EVA. The first, as just mentioned, is to grow the business by taking on new investments that promise to earn more than the cost of capital. The second way to improve EVA is by not growing the business, but improving efficiency and so increasing returns on existing capital. And the third way is by getting rid of those parts of your business that offer no promise for improvement. EVA encourages managers to engage in a periodic culling of their businesses, discouraging them from wasting more time and money on clear losers.

Conventional corporate reward systems often do not encourage managers to take such steps. By making the lion's share of managerial compensation take the form of wages and wage-related items, such compensation plans lead managers to maximize not EVA™ or shareholder value, but rather their number of "Hay points." The way you do that is to maximize the *size* of your operation.

Now, the question is: To what extent can we change this kind of behavior that encourages size or empire-building at the expense of profitability? You will not succeed in changing behavior simply by changing corporate performance objectives *without also changing the compensation scheme*. If you set the performance objective with EVA over here, and you set the incentive compensation on some other basis over there, all your people will bow down to the performance objective and then march off in whatever direction the incentive structure calls for.

So, what do you need to do? Without going into great detail at this point, let me just say that there are four properties for any successful incentive compensation system. If you don't have these four properties, your plan won't work.

First, you need objectivity, not subjectivity. Most corporate bonus plans set targets based on negotiations between senior people and their juniors. The result is that the juniors have a tremendous incentive to "low ball" their budgets—because their bonus depends just on beating the budget (though not by too much, because that casts doubt on their credibility in setting the budget in the first place). Instead of stimulating managers to stretch—to expand the size of the pie, if you will—negotiated budgets reward managers for their success in carving out a larger share of the existing pie for themselves, often at the expense of the shareholders.

The second essential quality of an effective comp plan is simplicity. Incentive compensation should be carried down into the organization at least as far as the level of middle management, and many of our clients are extending it to all salaried employees. And the farther down you go, in my opinion, the more dramatic and durable the benefits seem to be.

Third, the plan has got to be significant. That means that the bonus potentials that come from improving EVA have to be large enough to affect people's behavior.

Fourth, the plan must be honored; it must not be subject to *ex post* adjustments. This means that if the board of directors and senior management find some employees doing *very* well and then *very, very* well, they must resist the inclination to pull the rug out from underneath them and change the rules. We have to permit people to do very well, *provided* the shareholders are also doing very well.

There are also three other distinctive features of a Stern Stewart incentive compensation program. One is that there are no caps on the upside. The more EVA people produce, the greater their reward, with no limitation on the size of the bonus awards.

At the same time, however, our system has a hold-back or bonus bank feature. To illustrate, when bonus plans are based on *improvements in* EVA as opposed to absolute EVA, we typically hold hostage as much as two-thirds of declared bonuses tied to EVA. And managers will lose the two-thirds held hostage if they don't at least maintain the level of performance that caused the declaration of the bonus in the first place.

The consequence of this bonus bank feature is to lengthen the managerial decision-making horizon beyond one year. It's very important to think of this as an ongoing cycle of

value creation with one-third payable now, two-thirds later. For a successful manager under this plan, each new year brings steadily increasing payouts, new declarations, and new hold-backs. And if you do the calculations the way we do them, it takes you about six years to get 90% of your bonus declarations fully paid out.

We also have an unusual stock option program. Without going into too much detail, managers are asked to purchase stock options with a part of each year's bonus payments. What makes these options unusual is that they have an exercise price that is adjusted each year for the level of the broad stock market or, if management chooses, an industry group of the firm's primary competitors. If the S&P 500 or industry composite goes up by 10% in a given year, then the exercise price goes up by 10%. This way, shareholders have to get their rewards *before* the managers participate in any gains.

But consider also what happens if the market or industry goes down, even while the firm continues to churn out positive EVA. In those circumstances, the EVA bonuses can be used to buy options at a lower price, thus insulating high-performance operating managers from adverse industry or market events beyond their control. Take the case of our host company, Johnson & Johnson. If J & J's stock price drops because of exogenous factors such as announcements about impending health care reform, those people who are still creating EVA inside the firm will get their just deserts by being allowed to buy options with a lower exercise price.

So those are the major issues of corporate performance measurement as I see them. I'm interested not just in the performance measurement itself, but in how it motivates people to behave differently. Talking about increasing shareholder value and setting the right corporate objectives are necessary but not sufficient conditions for corporate success. Managerial incentives must also be changed along with the goals to make the system work.

With that as introduction, I will now turn the floor over to my colleague Bennett Stewart, who has his own story about EVA™.

The EVA Financial Management System

BENNETT STEWART: Before opening up the floor to our panelists, let me take a little bit more of your time to give you my point of view as to why this is all happening now. Why all of a sudden EVA?

There are some profound changes going on in the world. There's an information revolution that is manifesting itself in many ways. Management hierarchies are flattening, large companies are being broken down into smaller firms, and vertical integration is giving way to outsourcing. Dramatic reductions in the costs of gathering and processing information have led to widespread corporate downsizing and outsourcing. And contracting with outsiders to perform functions once performed inside the company has allowed for a sharpening of corporate focus, for greater specialization and all the associated benefits.

And it's this information revolution that is really driving the whole business process re-engineering movement. Whether it's just-in-time inventory management or time-cycle compression, companies are increasingly recognizing that the real success of business today depends not on having a well-thought-out, far-reaching strategy, but rather on re-engineering a company's business systems to respond more effectively to the new business environment of continuous change. And our contention at Stern Stewart is that just as this information revolution has created a need for business process re-engineering, it has also precipitated a need to re-engineer the corporate *financial management system.*

Now, let me describe what we mean by a financial management system. To us, a financial management system consists of all those financial policies, procedures, methods, and measures that guide a company's operations and its strategy. It has to do with how companies address such questions as: What are our overall corporate financial goals and how do we communicate them, both within the company and to the investment community? How do we evaluate business plans when they come up for review? How do we allocate resources—everything from the purchase of an individual piece of equipment to the acquisition of an entire company to the evaluation of opportunities to downsize and restructure? How do we evaluate ongoing operating performance? And, last but not least, how do we pay our people, what's our corporate reward system?

Many companies these days have ended up with a needlessly complicated and, in many respects, hopelessly obsolete financial management system. For example, most companies use discounted cash flow analysis for capital budgeting evaluations. But, when it comes to other purposes such as setting goals and communicating with investors, the same companies tend to reach for accounting proxies—measures like earnings, earnings per share, earnings growth, profit margins, ROE, and the like. Well, to the extent this is true, it means there is already a "disconnect," if you will, between the cash-flow-based capital budget and accounting-based corporate goals. To make matters worse, the bonuses for

Many companies have ended up with needlessly complicated and hopelessly obsolete financial management systems. For example, most companies use discounted cash flow for capital budgeting. But, when it comes to setting goals and communicating with investors, the same companies use measures like earnings, earnings per share, and ROE. This widespread corporate practice of using different financial measures for different corporate functions creates inconsistency, and thus considerable confusion, in the management process.

—Bennett Stewart—

operating people tend to be structured around achieving some annually negotiated profit figure.

This widespread corporate practice of using different financial measures for different corporate functions creates inconsistency, and thus considerable confusion, in the management process. And, given all the different, often conflicting, measures of performance, it is understandable that corporate operating people tend to throw their hands in the air and say, "So, what are you really trying to get me to do here? What is the real financial mission of our company?"

Take the case of Du Pont. Back in the 1920s, Du Pont had a very clear standard for assessing its performance. It was called return on investment, or ROI. In fact, this was known as the "Du Pont Formula." Du Pont then had "the Chart Room," a very large room in which they posted diagrams of the ROI trees for all of their businesses. From the early '20s until well after World War II, the Executive Committee met every Monday in the Chart Room with a division head and his staff to review the division's operating performance and discuss its capital expenditures and strategic plan. They would evaluate their progress using these ROI diagrams; and then they would break down the ROI calculation into more manageable components such as profit margin, sales turnover, and then analyze these components even further.

But, as the company began to acquire more businesses in unrelated industries, DuPont began to use EPS and EPS growth as its metric for evaluating corporate performance. And that change introduced a new level of complexity into the financial management process. It became impossible to reconcile internal ROI measures used for investment planning on the inside with the EPS measures reported to the investment community.

Then, in 1982, DuPont acquired Conoco, the oil and gas company, reportedly in part to take advantage of a "cash flow play." Operating cash flow became one of the major justifications for the acquisition, and thus another metric of performance further complicated the situation. And so the outcome at DuPont, as in so many large U.S. companies, has been the proliferation of financial measures.

Why is it important to have only one measure? The natural inclination of operating managers in large public companies is to get their hands on more capital in order to spend and grow the empire. This tendency in turn leads to an overtly political internal competition for capital—one in which different performance measures are used to gain approval for pet projects.

Because of this tendency toward empire-building, top management typically feels compelled to intervene excessively—not in day-to-day decision making, but in capital spending decisions. Why? Because they don't trust the financial management system to guide their operating managers to make the right decisions. There's no real accountability built into the system, there's no real incentive for operating heads to choose only those investment projects that will increase value.

So that's really what an EVA^{TM} financial management system is designed to do. And, in this sense, I think the *Fortune* article was somewhat misleading. It seemed to give the impression that if a company simply calculates EVA, and begins to use it as just one of the dials on its financial navigation system, then that's enough to align the interests of management with shareholder value. But, as Joel was suggesting at the outset, that is not enough. EVA is a financial management *system*. It is a *framework* for all aspects of financial management

decision-making that are anchored by the incentive compensation plan.

Besides changing the performance measures, then, establishing an EVA system involves a number of other challenges: changing the capital budgeting process to emphasize the projecting and discounting of EVA instead of cash flow; tracing EVA back to key drivers in the business so operating managers understand how their decisions affect it; adopting continuous improvement in EVA as both the main financial goal internally and in communications with the investment community; and, finally, as Joel emphasized, designing an EVA-based annual cash bonus plan that has the effect of simulating ownership.

Integrating Disciplines in the Business Schools

So, with that introduction to EVA, let me turn to Professor Jerry Zimmerman, who is an expert on accounting systems and organizational theory at the University of Rochester. Jerry, when I graduated from the University of Chicago back in the 1970s, it seemed to me there was an excessive compartmentalization of the different disciplines. There were a number of required courses—corporate finance, investments, accounting, marketing, operations research—but there was no course designed to pull all these disciplines together into a single cohesive system. And that's really, I think, the major challenge that most large companies confront today: How should they go about designing and implementing an integrated, cohesive, but nevertheless simple and readily understandable financial management system?

Jerry, do you think the academic community has missed this point? Where does the issue of aligning business decisions with shareholder value manifest itself in a consistent and integrated way in our business schools?

ZIMMERMAN: Most business schools do not do a very good job of integrating and aligning business decisions with the corporate aim of maximizing shareholder value. Business schools are just starting to try and integrate the various disciplines. Some schools—Stanford, Harvard, and Rochester, to name a few—now offer courses that emphasize the linkage among business decision-making, performance evaluation, and compensation policy. Important research by finance and accounting scholars is beginning to break down the black box we call the firm and to provide insights into these linkages.

But I don't think you want to lay all the blame on the business schools for the failure of the business community to align all the various aspects of the financial management system with shareholder value. In fact, let me say that I don't think Stern Stewart has succeeded in pulling it all together with EVA™. I think you and Joel have solved two-thirds of the problem. You have succeeded in putting the NPV/DCF valuation method we teach in business schools into a form that can be used by some corporations for ongoing performance measurement. But EVA is not right for every company, and we need to gain a better understanding of where EVA works well and where it may cause problems and should not be used.

So, there is still a missing third; there is still a critical element of this problem of integrating systems that I don't believe your approach addresses. And rather than telling you what I think that third is at this point, I'll let you see if you can figure it out. That's the final exam for today.

STERN: But, Jerry, even if we are missing something, and even if it represents one-third, then why is it that when companies today simply

announce their *intention* to go on to an EVA performance measurement and incentive compensation system, they experience substantial increases in the prices of their shares?

ZIMMERMAN: Don't misunderstand me, Joel. I think EVA clearly has the potential to add significant value in many corporate circumstances. At least for some companies, it holds out major improvements over the conventional accounting systems that form the basis for SEC disclosures. But there are other cases—cases that I think will come out in this discussion—in which a straightforward application of EVA to different operating businesses within a large company may create more problems than it solves, raise more questions than it answers.

As an academic historical footnote to this discussion, let me also point out that EVA is not new. I've been able to trace it back to a 1955 monograph by General Electric's management. GE was worried about some of the incentive problems with Return on Net Assets, or RONA, that Joel just described. And the GE people actually proposed a measure they called "residual income," which is operating income less a capital charge.

David Solomons, who had a long and industrious career at Wharton, wrote a 1965 monograph called "Divisional Performance" that is devoted to the subject of measuring residual income or EVA. And all managerial accounting textbooks since then include discussions of RONA versus residual income.

So, EVA is not new. What Joel and Bennett have accomplished with EVA, however, is primarily to make more precise estimates of cost of capital and better adjustments of conventional accounting statements. EVA corrects a lot of the accounting distortions—problems like those that arise from leasing and deferred taxes—that

I think you and Joel have solved two-thirds of the problem. You have succeeded in putting the NPV/DCF valuation method we teach in business schools into a form that can be used by some corporations for ongoing performance measurement. But EVA is not right for every company. There are cases in which a straightforward application of EVA to different operating businesses within a large company may create more problems than it solves, raise more questions than it answers.

—Jerold Zimmerman—

weren't really around when David Solomons wrote his book in 1965.

STEWART: In fact, Jerry, EVA™ actually goes back much farther than 1965. Alfred Sloan's book *My Years at General Motors* describes how in the 1920s General Motors had a system where they set aside a 15% rate of return on net assets as the required rate of return in their business. Ten percent of all operating profits after the 15% capital charge became the bonus pool to be shared by management.

And, much like our leveraged equity purchase plan, GM's managers would then be required to use part of their bonus to buy stock in the company on a leveraged basis. So, in this sense, everything we at Stern Stewart have done to refine and apply EVA is merely an afterthought to a system General Motors had in place in the 1920s. Now, how GM went from that system to their focus on EPS under Roger Smith during the 1980s is a sad story I will not regale you with.

The Case of Pitney Bowes

STEWART: While we're wondering about Jerry's other one-third, let me turn to Carm Adimando, the CFO of Pitney-Bowes. Carm, as a long-time user of EVA, can you tell us about the benefits—and limitations—of such a system?

ADIMANDO: As you know, Bennett, we have been measuring EVA by division for the last ten years. We measure the performance of each operation every month. And those monthly EVA numbers are sent to the board of directors as well as each of the divisional heads.

Perhaps our greatest challenge in implementing an EVA system was convincing our chairman and board of directors to go along with it. But we've been able to accomplish that, and our EVA program has led to

dramatic improvements in the efficiency with which our operating heads manage capital. During the time the plan has been in place, we've had great improvement in our share price, and we've moved up to number 79 this past year on your Stern Stewart 1,000 hit list. Between 1982 and 1992, we averaged a 24.5% rate of return to our investors.

STEWART: Carm, can you offer any concrete examples of how EVA has changed the behavior of operating managers?

ADIMANDO: It has affected not only our operating managers, but our sales managers, R & D personnel, financial managers, and division presidents. When considering a major decision, whether it be a strategic investment, a new product or marketing strategy, or a production plan, our people thoroughly evaluate its projected EVA *before* embarking on the plan. As a consequence, our returns have improved, margins have increased, new products have been more successful—and management bonuses and our share price have increased accordingly.

But, having mentioned the benefits, let me also describe some of the costs associated with starting an EVA program. In addition to selling the board on the merits of such a program, getting your operating people to understand that every little thing they do has an effect on shareholder value is a very difficult task—particularly when you start bringing people in from different companies with different ideas and methods. Take the case of a successful operating guy who has been around for 20 or 25 years and is fairly set in his ways. He knows he has achieved a certain level of accomplishment during those 20 years, and trying to convince him there's a better way is not easy.

The rapid obsolescence of products also makes EVA, or any financial

measurement system, very difficult to apply. Think about the difficulty of convincing people in production that they don't need that old product any more, even though it has been selling like hotcakes, because we've got a new product coming out. At the same time, you've got to convince the sales force that this new product is now the product to sell, when they've spent the last three years learning how to sell the older product and convinced three-quarters of corporate America that the older product is the one they need.

On the finance side, meanwhile, you're trying to guess how quickly the new product is going to cannibalize the old product, and how much profit you're going to sacrifice, especially since you're now producing the old product at the lowest cost in the last three years. Given that the new product will likely be produced inefficiently at the outset, and in the face of all the other uncertainties surrounding this process of substituting new products for old, financial systems don't offer much guidance.

The challenge of top management in such cases is to convince the factory floor person, the manufacturing person, the division head, the head of sales, the head of marketing, and, most important, the sales force that the new product is the way we have to go. If you can sit there and take them through EVA, it may make a lot of sense. But, at the beginning of this process, there are large hurdles. Your salespeople, who are on straight commission, are having a tough time because they aren't allowed to sell the old product any more. The factory floor worker is being criticized by the head of the factory for failing to make the conversion. And the division head is worrying about trying to make up with a new product what he's losing by cannibalizing the old.

At the same time, planning and financial personnel are trying to calculate how much has to be invested, not only in this product, but in the next generation of products. At our company, we have already budgeted three percent of our revenues for R & D over the next five years, and we have no way of estimating—at least not with any precision—what kind of value is being created by this R & D spending.

So, these are some of the uncertainties facing corporate financial management that do not seem to lend themselves to any financial system, EVA or otherwise.

STEWART: Well, I certainly sympathize with some of these problems, especially in evaluating the long-run payoff from R & D expenditures (although we do have a way of handling that, which I'm sure will come up later in the discussion). But let me just address this problem you cited about educating your line managers and employees.

At Quaker Oats, they have really driven their EVA™ program all the way down to the shop floor. In fact, I'm now holding up a picture of a fellow named Steve Brunner. He's a 23-year veteran of Quaker Oats, and here you can see him alongside his granola bars on the shop floor in Danville, Illinois.

The way Quaker has pushed EVA down through the ranks to the factory floor is by introducing a program called EVA *drivers*. This has meant breaking down EVA into its components and linking it, in this case, to variables like machine set-up times, operating up-times, inventory levels, and defect rates. In this way, the EVA drivers create a bridge linking day-to-day actions and decisions with EVA itself and hence with the creation of shareholder value.

And those EVA drivers have allowed people like Steve Brunner to see that if they are willing to incur the costs of setting up their machines more frequently, they can run their machines in smaller batches and so reduce their inventory. Besides the reduced capital charge associated with lower inventory, the greater consistency in the level of inventories also leads to better coordination with suppliers and lower defect rates.

So, the whole focus on EVA and EVA drivers allowed this guy to see how he could make what is essentially an investment—that is, a reduction in his income statement—that had as its principal payoff a benefit that took place largely on the balance sheet—that is, a reduction in the base of net assets under his control.

ADIMANDO: EVA also creates another problem, or at least a challenge, for management. As Joel pointed out, when you announce you're going on an EVA plan, or that you're going to spin off or sell a subsidiary, your stock price is likely to go up. The problem that creates for management is this: Because the stock market is forward looking, that stock price represents expected *future* value. Internally, however, we haven't achieved that value yet. And, given the market's higher expectations, we then have to spend the next two years achieving that expected value just to keep our stock price from falling. If we don't succeed in creating that value, our stock price will fall. The market is always pushing you, in effect asking you what's the next project that's going to push your market value above and beyond the level of shareholder capital invested in the company.

Let me give you another example of a similar problem. Pitney Bowes is part of a group of Fortune 500 computer and office equipment companies. For the last four years prior to this one, we have been ranked first in ten-year total return to investors. And that group includes companies like Compaq, Hewlett Packard, and

> **Y**ou have to push EVA all the way down to the individual operating units to get people's attention and produce results. You've got to convince everyone that increasing shareholder value is the one overarching goal of the organization, and that EVA is the main internal yardstick for evaluating your progress toward meeting that goal. You must also make clear the role of customer satisfaction in sustaining higher EVA—because if you don't have satisfied customers, your market share, your EVA, and your market value will all fall.
>
> **—Carm Adimando—**

Xerox—and half of these companies, incidentally, are now talking EVA™.

But, at any rate, we have achieved very high shareholder returns and a very high MVA. The problem is, our market valuation is so high that, unless we substantially increase our returns or our price/earnings multiple, there is no place for us to go but down in these rankings. And, in fact, this year Compaq, which is a very highly rated firm, achieved number one, and we fell to number two. Not because we slipped on returns—in fact our returns are even better—but because Compaq really got their act together and has created even more value.

Joel suggested that if a company is currently achieving a 25% return on capital, it should accept new projects earning less than 25% as long as they're earning more than the cost of capital. But I want to take issue with that. If you accept returns substantially lower than 25%, then your average return is going to fall. And the more you let projects bring that total return down, the more those returns start getting reflected into your stock price.

STEWART: Well, Carm, I think the problem you face is an enviable one; it arises from your extraordinary success. I'm even tempted to say that your stock price may be in some sense "overvalued." That is, you have done such a good job in the past that you may have succeeded in persuading the market you can continue earning 25% returns for longer than you can. But that's still not a good reason to walk away from new projects that promise to earn 15% or 20%.

But, as you say, the market is forward looking; it's always attempting to capture future profits in current prices. And, for this reason, I can see where having a very high stock price today could create problems for managers being rewarded on the basis of year-to-year stock price returns, or on

the basis of year-to-year changes in MVA. That's one reason we use EVA instead of MVA in measuring internal operating performance; it helps eliminate the unwanted effects of market volatility or unrealistic shareholder expectations.

This problem of market volatility could also affect an EVA system that attempted to mark net assets to market continuously. A sharp and sudden increase in market value, to the extent it was translated immediately into higher capital charges for operating managers, could end up holding those managers to unrealistically high standards of performance. And that's one reason why we typically end up recommending that companies use modified book values of net assets rather than some estimate of fair market values in calculating EVA.

EVA at Merrill Lynch

STEWART: But let me turn now to Joe Willett. Joe, as CFO of Merrill Lynch, you have developed a version of EVA that is designed for a financial institution as opposed to the industrial companies we typically advise. Would you mind describing what you have done and why you did it?

WILLETT: Sure. The standard approach for industrial companies using EVA is to look at the after-tax but pre-interest return on *total* capital in relation to the weighted average cost of capital. For financial institutions levered 25 to 30 times, that approach is analytically messy because the weighted average cost of capital (or WACC) is dominated by the after-tax cost of debt financing, and it will be very low in relation to normally observed market rates of return. For this reason, WACC is not very useful for us as a performance measurement tool.

So the approach that we've adopted—which I think, Bennett, is analytically equivalent to the way you

calculate EVA—is to look at the after-tax, *after*-interest operating returns in relation to the equity capital used in the business. Our performance measurement approach is to look at return on *equity* capital in relation to the cost of *equity* capital as the hurdle rate. For each of 50 or so different businesses in Merrill Lynch, we've assigned equity capital based on the risks of those businesses, and we calculate EVA based on the return on equity, the cost of equity, and the amount of equity capital employed in the business. For each of these businesses, an EVA level of zero is considered break-even economic performance.

STEWART: What do you see as the benefits of such an EVA system?

WILLETT: The appeal of EVA is that it encourages people to look for profitable growth opportunities while, at the same time, looking for ways to economize on the use of capital—not only by reducing capital needs in existing businesses, but also by eliminating unprofitable lines of business. Those are the most important benefits of the EVA approach.

Let me add that I think a good performance measurement system, such as one based on EVA, is necessary nowadays because most corporations have become too big and complex to be managed from one central place, and so you need to decentralize decision-making and controls. This is certainly true of Merrill Lynch, and it's probably true of the other companies represented on the panel. And, if you're going to decentralize the organization—if you're going to have real empowerment down through levels of the organization—then you're also going to have to align the incentives of the operating managers with those of top management and the shareholders. People with line authority are going to have to be focused on the right objectives.

I think it's fair to begin with the premise that individuals will do what they perceive to be in their own self-interest. At Merrill Lynch, we have learned that we get what we measure and what we pay people to do. If you go back in our history, there was a time when we emphasized revenues in our compensation system—and, not surprisingly, what we got then was revenues and not profits. Over time our system evolved to put more emphasis on profits and, ultimately, on both profits and returns, or what amounts to EVA™. Our current EVA system captures both the quantity and quality dimensions of earnings. EVA, we think, gives our managers the proper incentive to achieve the right balance between profitability and growth.

As I said earlier, our company is too complex to be managed centrally. Having an EVA system combined with a compensation system that reinforces the emphasis on EVA allows us to decentralize while knowing that the interests of the people running our different businesses are consistent with those of our shareholders.

STERN: Your comment reminds me of an experience we recently had in working for a large company overseas. In January, they made their decision to go onto an EVA plan effective April 1st. The chairman of the company called me in February and said, "Something has happened, you must hear about this. Back in December, our operating managers submitted $570 million in capital expenditures for this fiscal year. But after we announced we were going on the EVA program, the very same people cut back on their requests for capital by $180 million. Why do you think they did that?"

I said, "My guess is that the rate of return on that extra $180 million of net assets was not going to earn the cost of capital, and that taking on those

extra projects was going to reduce management bonuses."

He said, "I think you're right. In the past, we had about an 80/20 wage-to-bonus structure, fixed-to-variable pay. Under your system, we're going to have 50/50; so our managers can really benefit if they do well and sustain that performance over time. They can't afford to have that extra $180 million dragging down their performance."

And that's the kind of thing that companies can accomplish with EVA. That is, we want a police function that stops dead in its tracks the incentive of corporate managers to overinvest in ways that hurt shareholders.

The Case of International Paper

STERN: Let's now turn to Robert Butler, CFO of International Paper? Bob, could you tell us a little about your experience with EVA?
BUTLER: One of the major attractions of EVA for us is that it's simple. That's what I especially like about it. During my own career, I've experimented with a variety of performance measures. For example, for years we tried to relate the returns on individual facilities with shareholder returns. We assigned debt-equity ratios to all divisions and calculated divisional returns on capital. We have also tried to allocate some part of earnings per share to all our businesses.

But I think EVA accomplishes this aim much more effectively. With this system, you simply say to the person running the facility, I want you to deliver $100,000 of EVA. So, if the facility has net assets of, say, $1 million, and the cost of capital is 10%, then the guy knows he's got to produce $200,000 of operating profit to earn his bonus. Nothing could be more straightforward. So, our experience with EVA is that it is very easy to budget and understand—it's just the

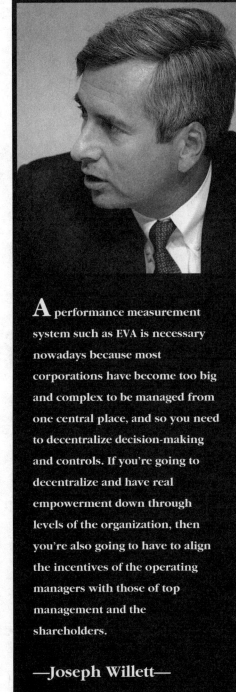

A performance measurement system such as EVA is necessary nowadays because most corporations have become too big and complex to be managed from one central place, and so you need to decentralize decision-making and controls. If you're going to decentralize and have real empowerment down through levels of the organization, then you're also going to have to align the incentives of the operating managers with those of top management and the shareholders.

—Joseph Willett—

There are a number of factors that go into corporate investment decisions that are difficult to handle with EVA. If you're thinking about building a new paper facility, you're going to base your decision on some assumptions of economic growth—and, as the result of globalization, the relevant growth measure today is worldwide rather than just domestic or U.S. growth. But you also have to factor in the response of your competitors. We don't announce our plans—and the Justice Department doesn't encourage us to talk to our competitors about these matters.

—Robert Butler—

amount that you're going to contribute over and above the company's cost of capital.

STERN: Bob, could you tell us what the response of the operating people has been to this new performance measure?

BUTLER: As you know, Joel, we have only recently introduced EVA™ into our performance measurement system, and we are using it on an experimental basis. At this point, managerial compensation isn't tied to EVA; we're just trying to get our managers comfortable with and accustomed to using the measure. But I think our EVA system is going to work well for us, and tying managers' compensation to EVA is a likely next step.

I can also tell you that over two-thirds of my company is producing negative EVA right now. The paper industry is highly cyclical and, as you know, we've been in the down part of the paper cycle for the last three or four years.

STEWART: I'm kind of fascinated by your industry because it does go through these cycles, and some part of that cyclical market behavior seems to be self-inflicted. When times are tough, the industry as a group tends to hold back, thus causing demand to rise very abruptly. Then, when demand does rise, all the companies tend to throw piles of money into new capacity in attempts to maintain market share.

Now, Bob, let's suppose you're back at the top of the cycle, demand is outrunning supply, and prices are rising, and it's time to consider reinvesting in the business. But you also know that if you invest along with everybody else, you face the following prisoner's dilemma: If you don't invest, and many other companies choose the same strategy, you will end up losing out on a profitable investment opportunity; but if you do invest, and everybody else follows

suit, then you will all suffer together from excess capacity. How do you think you're going to handle that situation under an EVA framework?

BUTLER: Well, I don't know; that's hard to answer. If you're thinking about building a new paper facility, you're going to base your decision on some assumptions of economic growth—and, by the way, as the result of globalization, the relevant growth measure today is worldwide rather than just domestic or U.S. growth.

What we never seem to factor in, however, is the response of our competitors. Who else is going to build a plant or machine at the same time? We don't announce our plans—and the Justice Department doesn't encourage us to talk to each other about these matters.

There are also a number of other factors that go into corporate investment decisions, particularly when you're dealing with very large companies, that are difficult to handle with EVA. In our industry, cutting capital expenditures could be very counterproductive. In the first place, you've got to maintain the plant. That's sort of a given, because you're not going to get any EVA after a while if the mill roof comes in on you.

And what about the expenditures necessary to comply with environmental regulations? We have to spend a lot of money these days on non-return projects to meet new regulations of all kinds. How does EVA evaluate those expenditures? And how does it take into account things like accidents in the plant, lost work days, incident rates, and so forth. Minimizing these things must be part of the corporate reward system.

STEWART: There are clearly costs to safety and environmental compliance that end up showing up in your financial results. But, given that you're making these expenditures, there must be potential benefits—a strong plant safety record, for example, which would help you attract better employees—that are not being reflected in your financial statements.

In one of our consulting assignments, we actually devised a measurement system as part of an EVA™ program that would take account of not only explicit costs of unsafe plants such as higher workmen's compensation premiums, but also implicit costs such as lost time. We asked management to rank different kinds of safety infractions and then built penalty surcharges for such infractions into the EVA calculation. And we could do the same thing for a failure to comply fully with environmental laws—that is, establish penalty surcharges at levels top management viewed as appropriate to encourage the desired kind of behavior.

So, under this system, if managers spend money on improving safety or reducing environmental violations, then there really is a return to them from so doing. Having such a measurement and incentive system forces the corporate debate to focus on the right issue: Namely, what is the real marginal cost/benefit tradeoff of spending an additional dollar to improve safety. And it's important that this calculation be part and parcel of the overall performance framework, as opposed to the common corporate practice of putting these outlays into a separate category called mandatory expenditures. I feel very strongly that putting these expenditures *within* the framework of managerial financial accountability and incentives is the right way to go.

EVA and Corporate Governance

STEWART: Let me turn now to Richard Shepro. Rick, as a partner of the law firm Mayer Brown & Platt, you get involved in advising boards of directors on questions of proxy contests, takeovers, and all the other legal aspects of corporate governance. What do you think about the potential of an EVA financial management system for helping to eliminate the so-called U.S. corporate governance problem?

SHEPRO: Well, the main problem in corporate governance that people have been talking about for at least the last decade is how to align managers' interests with shareholders' interests. And that's a very, very difficult thing to do. The recent court decisions in takeover battles that have surprised so many people have all been the result of the courts' continued interest in the conflict of interest between managers and shareholders.

There are a number of ways for companies to assure the courts that the conflict of interest is being minimized. One is simply having managers hold a lot of stock, because courts tend to focus on the manager-shareholder conflict at the top of the organization. But, from a business perspective, you don't want something that just minimizes the conflict of interest, you want something that also produces profits for the company over the long run. And that's where a system such as EVA can have a real benefit. The courts respect companies that have a long-term point of view, and that are able to provide a credible explanation of why their policies were put in place.

In fact, that's one of the major reasons the courts reacted so differently to Paramount's attempt to challenge the Time-Warner merger and to its subsequent attempt to lock up its deal with Viacom. The critical difference between the two cases was that Time and Warner were able to articulate a long-term strategic vision in which their shareholders would ultimately benefit—and Paramount and Viacom were not.

So, long-term planning is just one more one way of demonstrating busi-

To the extent EVA does a better job of reflecting economic reality than GAAP accounting, it may provide a better language for communicating with institutional investors. It's a second set of books, in effect—one that gives management much more latitude to discuss the expected future payoff from its current investment policies. Having this alternative accounting framework should encourage more and better communication both between management and shareholders and among shareholders themselves.

—Richard Shepro—

ness judgment to a court, and having an EVA™ plan in place may well be construed as evidence of long-term planning.

STEWART: Rick, what do you think will be the effect of the new rules allowing institutional shareholders to talk to one another and make their voices heard? And can EVA play a role in dealing with investor activism?

SHEPRO: A system like EVA produces very different results from the SEC accounting rules, which are based on GAAP. To the extent it does a better job of reflecting economic reality, EVA may provide a better language for companies to use in communicating with institutional investors. It's a second set of books, in effect—one that gives management much more latitude to discuss its policies and the expected future payoff from its current investment policies. Having this alternative accounting framework should encourage more and better communication both between management and shareholders, and among shareholders themselves.

STEWART: I agree with you, Rick. You see, there seem to be two prominent schools of strategy today that divide the world between them. One school of strategy I'll call the Michael Porter school. Michael Porter argues in his tomes that top management should agonize over market conditions and exhaustively analyze industry structure in order to arrive at top-down strategies. After being designed by an army of strategic planners, such strategies can then be imposed on the divisions and orchestrated from the top.

At the other extreme you have Tom Peters, whose highly decentralized approach is suggested by the titles of his two most recent books: *Managing With Chaos* and *Liberation Management*. Peters's books emphasize the empowerment of people throughout the organization. The basic strategy is

really not to have a carefully formulated strategy at all, but rather to have the organizational structure sufficiently loose and managers sufficiently motivated to seize opportunities as they arise. We don't really know in advance what the opportunities will turn out to be, but we want to have the flexibility and incentives to respond when they come.

This devaluation of strategic thinking and emphasis on organizational responsiveness has important implications not only for how companies evaluate and reward their managers, but also for how they communicate with investors. What really matters to investors today is not corporate strategy, but the management *process* and the incentives that go along with it. For this reason, I think companies could benefit greatly just by focusing their disclosures on how they manage, what their goals are, how they monitor their progress in meeting those goals, and what their incentives are to bring it all off.

So, it's not the specifics of strategy that are important—indeed, in some sense, a company's strategy is changing every day—but rather the corporate process that would give investors a sense of management's alertness and incentives to respond to continuous change.

STERN: One way to promote such communication is simply to send a special letter to your shareholders from the chairman or chief executive officer spelling out the details of your EVA program in a page or two. Another method—used by firms like Coca-Cola and Quaker Oats—is to devote part of your annual report to explaining your results and expectations in terms of EVA. For example, the firm might attempt to show the correlation between their past five years' EVA and MVA as part of an explanation of why they are adopting an EVA program. And, once having

started the program, they can then report their EVA results on a regular basis along with the earnings measures required by the SEC.

SHEPRO: Given the new requirements on disclosure of executive pay and stock price performance, I think the SEC would welcome those additional kinds of explanation.

EVA and Investors

STEWART: Well, instead of our prating on about what might be done in the area of shareholder communication, why don't we consult our two representatives from the investment community? Susan, as Chief Investment Officer and head of research at Citicorp Investment Services, what do you think about EVA and its potential role in communicating corporate strategy to investors?

MALLEY: I'd like to comment on this from two perspectives. One is from the perspective of a corporate manager, the other is from the perspective of a securities analyst.

As some of my colleagues have mentioned, the ideas of net present value, discounted cash flow, and residual income have all been around for a while. But I think that EVA's contribution from a managerial point of view is that it has provided a method of taking those concepts and turning them into a simple, "actionable" framework that can be pushed down into the corporation.

Now, the flip side of that is the securities analysis perspective. Based on my knowledge and experience, analysts have always attempted to look at cash flow rather than earnings.

STEWART: Really?

MALLEY: Yes. In fact, I think that most analysts understand clearly that earnings are basically serving as a proxy for cash flow. But what I think EVA does for securities analysts is provide them with a look at the *process* of corporate decision-making. The most difficult problem in securities analysis is estimating the cash flows beyond two years or so. Creating a common language that would allow management to communicate its decision-making process could go a long way toward solving this problem, toward overcoming the information gap between managment and investors with regard to decisions that are being made today that will affect cash flows in the future.

Aside from EVA™, there's really no financial language that allows management to communicate its longer-run prospects. When securities analysts are probing for this kind of information, they tend to ask: "What's the business strategy?" And I think EVA could help corporate managements provide a useful answer to that question.

So, I think EVA can make two important parallel contributions. On the managerial side, it takes an unconventional performance measure designed to promote capital efficiency and makes it simple and straightforward enough for use by operating people. On the securities analysis side, it provides a new language, if you will, that allows for discussion of longer-term corporate decision making and strategy.

STEWART: Are you now having more or better dialogue with companies that are using EVA? Or is this something you expect to happen?

MALLEY: I think it's already happening in certain cases. What remains to be done, though—and I understand you folks are addressing this to some extent—is to make EVA analysis available in automated form in standard data bases. This will allow EVA to become part of the ongoing evolution of the financial analyst community toward quantitative processes. If EVA isn't integrated into the data bases and information infrastructure, the quants

will ignore it and so will many fundamental analysts.

The second important missing element is what I would call "measures along the way." Although companies may say they're adopting EVA, there can still be major disagreements between management and analysts about the company's future prospects, implementation issues, and the intensity of competitive pressures. Take the case of high-technology firms like Intel, where analysts are always asking about the future payoff from research. Analysts want to know, for example, when the Pentium chip is going to take off, how much of the market it's going to win, and what the competitive response is going to be.

There is likely to be considerable uncertainty, and thus considerable disagreement, among analysts about the answers to these questions. And I think interim performance measures could help resolve part of this uncertainty.

STEWART: One of the companies that we're looking at right now is Polaroid. When Polaroid sells a Captiva camera, the company does not make an acceptable profit on that sale. They are willing to use camera sales as a "loss leader" because they expect to make it back on subsequent film sales. Under EVA, and in contrast to conventional GAAP accounting, we don't penalize them for selling more cameras; we make an internal adjustment to capture the expected payoff from those sales.

So, how would you and most analysts look at a company where the more cameras they sell in the fourth quarter of the year, the lower their reported returns? Does the market make this EVA kind of adjustment, or does it just take the accounting numbers at face value?

MALLEY: Most securities analysts, I think, would view the camera sales as producing a future stream of film

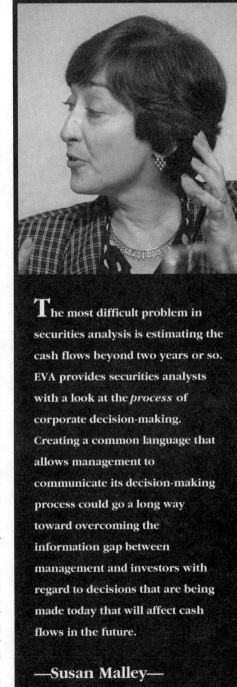

The most difficult problem in securities analysis is estimating the cash flows beyond two years or so. EVA provides securities analysts with a look at the *process* of corporate decision-making. Creating a common language that allows management to communicate its decision-making process could go a long way toward overcoming the information gap between management and investors with regard to decisions that are being made today that will affect cash flows in the future.

—Susan Malley—

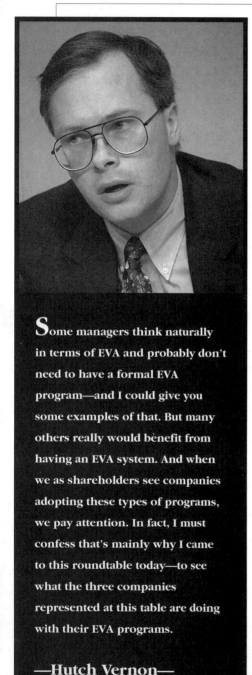

profits. And I think the market clearly understands the limitations of conventional accounting in such cases.

But let me change the subject and say something about the relationship between EVA™ and total quality management, or TQM, because I've heard people say that the two disciplines are incompatible. I don't think they're incompatible at all; in fact, I think that EVA actually reinforces and strengthens TQM. EVA provides management with a financial decision-making framework—one that deals very well with the management of *financial* capital. TQM deals effectively with management process and implementation—that is, with the management of *human* capital. So, when you put EVA and TQM together, I think you get a much more substantial management system.

BUTLER: Like EVA, TQM depends on empowerment. TQM works only if you've empowered your employees to improve themselves and the quality of their work.

STEWART: We try to make TQM and EVA parts of the same message. TQM largely boils down to the continuous improvement of products and processes. The goal of an EVA financial management system is, of course, continuous improvement in EVA. So, we too think that the goals of EVA and TQM are highly consistent with each other. EVA motivates and reinforces the TQM quest for operating efficiencies. An EVA system that focuses on incremental improvement allows the organization to relish its progressive successes and so institutionalize the dynamic of continuous change.

Another Investor Perspective

STEWART: Let me turn to our other representative of the investment community, Hutch Vernon of Alex Brown in Baltimore. Hutch, what's your interest in EVA?

VERNON: The reason we like EVA is that it encourages the kind of behavior among managers that we, as investors, like. We think the primary job of management is to produce a high return on the capital that has been entrusted to them by the shareholders. If the company is performing well, management must continue making the investment necessary to create high returns in the future. If the company is performing poorly, they need to make the changes, however painful, that will bring the return on capital back to acceptable levels. Or, if they've completely exhausted the possibilities of earning their cost of capital, then they should return that capital to the shareholders so that we can put it to some other productive use.

Some managers think naturally in terms of EVA and probably don't need to have a formal EVA program—and I could give you some examples of that. But many others really would benefit from having an EVA system. And when we as shareholders see companies adopting these types of programs, we pay attention. In fact, I must confess that's mainly why I came to this roundtable today—to see what the three companies represented at this table are doing with their EVA programs.

STEWART: You say some companies don't need EVA because there's an instinctive focus on value at the top. Can you give me examples?

VERNON: We like companies where the folks that run them think like owners.

STEWART: Is that because they *are* owners?

VERNON: Because they are owners or that's just their nature. Now, that's a small percentage of the population, but that's the way some people are.

STEWART: Can you give me a good example?

VERNON: Warren Buffett is one.

STEWART: He's a big owner.

VERNON: Travelers.

STEWART: Sandy Weill is a big owner.

VERNON: Well, I can think of some companies where managers also have significant ownership, but they really don't understand capital efficiency and shareholder value. One of the benefits of an EVA™ program in a situation like that—whether management owns the stock or not—is that it forces them to do the right thing by its shareholders.

STEWART: In your way of looking at companies, if a firm simply managed its assets more efficiently, or began to turn its assets faster or speed up its cycle times—even if that didn't show up in higher earnings—how would that cause you to increase its value?

VERNON: One way is by returning cash to the investor. If a company in a sorry business manages just to speed up the asset turnover and so produce some cash, and they can get that cash out of the company and into my hands, then I can plow that cash back into a company with better prospects. This kind of transfer of capital from mature to promising businesses, and from inefficient to more efficient managements, not only increases returns to private investors like us, but it has the social benefit of increasing the overall growth of the economy.

EVA vs. Cash Flow

STERN: We haven't heard yet from Professor Ravid. Avri, as a financial academic, could you tell us what you think of this EVA business?

RAVID: As Jerry Zimmerman was saying earlier, EVA is not new. In fact, the analysis of EVA is part of a much broader analysis I've been teaching in various universities for the last 15 years under the name of discounted cash flow and net present value. And, in fact, if you look at some other

people who are trying to implement a similar kind of analysis, you see that the market reacts the same way. For example, my friends at McKinsey have discovered a very high correlation between changes in discounted cash flow and changes in market value. So EVA is really just a kind of discounted cash flow analysis.

The concept of market value added, or MVA, is also not new. It is very similar to the concept of Tobin's Q, which is the ratio of the market value of assets to their replacement cost or book value. So, it's very nice that people are finally using these methods that we've been teaching our students for the last 20 or 30 years. If they buy it as EVA, that's great. And if they buy it as DCF, that's okay, too. Furthermore, nobody can argue with goals such as making better use of capital and getting rid of unproductive assets.

At the same time, however, one should also remember that EVA has the same problems that we have always had with discounted cash flow. For one thing, getting a precise estimate of the cost of capital is very difficult, especially in decentralized companies with many different business units. Also, estimating expected future cash flows is more of an art than a science. Because you are investing today and hoping that something will happen a few years hence, there is a great deal of uncertainty about those estimates. You can't escape this imprecision, whether you use EVA or discounted cash flow.

STEWART: In answer to your first objection about imprecision in the cost of capital, let me say this. From a practical perspective, we have found that just by charging managers for the use of capital, and by making their bonuses depend in a big way on covering that capital charge, that step alone goes a lot farther in motivating efficiency than in making subtle dis-

EVA has the same problems that we have always had with discounted cash flow. For one thing, getting a precise estimate of the cost of capital is very difficult, especially in decentralized companies with many different business units. Also, estimating expected future cash flows is more of an art than a science. Because you are investing today and hoping that something will happen a few years hence, there is a great deal of uncertainty about those estimates. You can't escape this imprecision, whether you use EVA or discounted cash flow.

—Abraham Ravid—

tinctions among levels of risk and cost of capital.

In fact, these days when people ask me what's the cost of capital, I often tell them just to use 12%. Why? Because it's one percent a month.

STERN: The other problem with DCF, as I mentioned earlier, is the difficulty in using it to come up with an interim or periodic performance measure. That is, if you have large cash outlays in time period zero, and the benefits begin in years two, three, and four, you need some way of holding people accountable for their performance on a year-by-year basis.

Under an EVA™ framework, we attempt to solve this problem by putting large capital expenditure items into a suspense account that, instead of being amortized on a standard depreciation schedule, bears interest at the required rate of return. The operating head responsible for the outlay is given what amounts to a customized, back-end-loaded amortization schedule built into his or her year-to-year performance measure that avoids penalizing large investments with heavy upfront depreciation charges. At the same time, however, the operating heads still have the incentive to bring the revenues onstream as quickly as possible because, in so doing, they reduce the interest costs for all that capital tied up in the suspense account.

And I think this ability to use EVA as an interim performance measure makes it far more useful than DCF.

STEWART: I would go farther, Joel, and say that not only is discounted cash flow not the answer, cash flow is *the problem*. Companies typically cast their capital budgets in cash flow terms. The problem, however, is they can't use cash flow for any other corporate function; it doesn't work as a year-to-year performance measure nor does it provide a useful basis for incentive compensation.

In most companies, the only time all the numbers in a capital budgeting exercise are ever put down on one piece of paper is when the project is first proposed. After the project is launched, the capital gets buried back in the balance sheet and no one gives it a second thought. At that stage, managers are not being held accountable for their use of additional capital but are being judged instead largely on the basis of the profit target negotiated in their budgets. The original discounted cash flow capital budget is just totally divorced from everything else that's happening in the financial management system.

For this reason, I think that the companies that use EVA most effectively are those that literally rewrite their capital budgeting manuals, valuation procedures, and strategy reviews from scratch so as to emphasize the projecting and discounting of EVA instead of cash flow. You're going to get the exact same NPV either way; but if the bonuses are also based upon increasing EVA, then you will have a completely integrated financial management system, including an automatic post-audit of project performance versus expectations.

Another virtue of EVA is that the calculation is based on earnings, which makes it easier for operating managers to grasp. To get a monthly EVA for an operation, you simply take sales, subtract all operating expenses, and then subtract a capital charge equal to one percent times the net assets employed in the balance sheet. The one percent represents a corporate charge to the operating head for renting him the assets. And what's left over after the capital charge is EVA.

So, EVA is simpler, it's more focused, and it's integrated. And that's why I tell companies to abandon discounted cash flow.

RAVID: But, Bennett, don't you think managers would quickly learn to

understand discounted cash flow if their bonuses were based upon it?

STEWART: It wouldn't work. Wal-Mart, which by our estimates was perhaps the biggest wealth creator in corporate America during the '80s, had a negative cash flow during the entire decade—they were investing more than they were earning. In fact, there's likely to be a *negative* correlation between contemporaneous changes in corporate cash flow and market value because companies that are investing the most to build their business sell for the highest prices.

RAVID: But there is surely a strong positive correlation between current market value and *projected* future cash flow.

STEWART: But that's precisely my point; that's why you can't use cash flow as a measure of interim performance. It's useful only looking forward, not backwards. EVA is useful looking forward and looking backwards.

Rewriting the Corporate Constitution

SHEPRO: Joel stated in his introduction that an effective compensation system has to be perceived as objective. But think about your Polaroid example, the case where the company loses money on each camera, but makes it up on subsequent film sales. My question is, When you make these accounting adjustments to capture future benefits from film sales, don't you risk introducing a new kind of agency cost? We know that conventional accounting understates the future benefits of the film sales, but what prevents operating management from overestimating those benefits in order to win bigger bonuses for themselves, at least in the short term?

STEWART: Well, that's an excellent point. What we're really calling for is rewriting a company's constitution.

It's a one-time exercise of sitting down, understanding the business, understanding the accounting, and literally rewriting a set of ground rules that are not renegotiable.

And you're right. The integrity of the accounting system depends upon a careful thinking through of as many as 164 different EVA™ performance measurement issues. How do you account for acquisitions, start-ups, joint ventures? How do you account for inventories and depreciation? What about warranty reserves and overfunded pension plans? There's a whole laundry list of items where our conventional GAAP accounting system clearly fails to capture economic reality.

WILLETT: Bennett, what happens if you get your new system up and running, and then you suddenly discover you overlooked something? Do you then open up the system to further renegotiation?

STEWART: No, you just have to live with it.

STERN: I would answer you differently. When we take on an assignment with a firm, we typically start by looking at the historical performance of all the units to get some idea as to how far down into an organization EVA can be constructively and reliably measured. You can only carry the new incentive structure as far down as you can sensibly identify and measure separate EVAs or EVA drivers.

The second stage of our work is to set up a steering committee to work with us—one that represents every major discipline in the firm. In the case of a manufacturing firm, the committee would include representatives from operations, manufacturing, sales and marketing, human resources, finance, and the CEO. And we would hold several all-day sessions in which we explore all the major issues that go into the process of measuring EVA.

WILLETT: But, Joel, I thought one of the virtues of the system was that it was supposed to be simple. What happened to simplicity as an objective?
STERN: Well, although the analysis is complex and time-consuming, the final product is simple. The accounting adjustments that end up being introduced into the system are only those that have a material impact on performance. For example, in the case of a company like Johnson & Johnson, the two biggest adjustments would be for advertising and R & D. Although these are both major sources of future value, GAAP forces the company to write them off completely. But that makes absolutely no sense from an economic measurement standpoint.

Under EVA, the people at Johnson & Johnson would capitalize their R & D and write it off over a more sensible period. We would turn to the head of R & D and ask, "What do you think is the right period for amortizing R & D? Give us some average number that you can live with, is consistent with shareholder value, and will be approved by the compensation committee of your board." And we would come up with an adjustment on that basis.

We're actually doing this for a pharmaceutical company at this moment. And I think Professor Zimmerman would agree with the logic of what we're proposing here.
ZIMMERMAN: Well, yes and no. I agree that investments in both advertising and R & D have future payoffs that are not reflected in GAAP accounting. But, at the same time, you've got to keep in mind why GAAP has this conservative bias. As I said in an earlier Stern Stewart roundtable, GAAP accounting was not really designed to help shareholders value companies; its fundamental purpose was to help people such as creditors monitor debt agreements and to establish liquidation values, not going-concern values.

But what happens, Joel, if you put in this EVA program and the Clinton plan succeeds three years from now in turning the whole pharmaceutical industry on its head—or if the FDA changes the whole new drug application process, either shortening or lengthening it in such a way that it makes all of those prior assumptions that you built into the capitalization of R & D totally obsolete. Do you go back and reopen the discussion?
STERN: I would say yes, because the world has been changed and managers should be insulated against these kinds of shocks. You see—and I'm about to disagree with my colleague Bennett Stewart on this one—I don't necessarily believe that corporate managers should have large stock holdings in their company. The problem with having a large block of stock in their hands is that somewhere between 50% and 75% of changes in value are not company specific, and I wouldn't want managerial rewards to be determined largely by factors that have no relationship to their own efforts or decisions. For example, if the connection between managerial effort and stock returns becomes tenuous—as it has become in the case of Johnson & Johnson and Merck over the last 18 months or so—we feel that it's important for managers to spend their time doing what they know how to do best.
STEWART: But, Joel, what happened to our conception of managers as owners with payoffs aligned with those of the shareholders? If there's an external shock, shareholders don't get to reopen the discussion about the value of the stock. I think you want to aim at establishing a rule of laws, not a rule of men.
STERN: You're missing an important point, Bennett. If you rewrite the laws to reflect the new circumstances, managers will not be penalized for

events beyond their control, but they will still have the right incentives *going forward*—that is, on all new investments. And I think it makes sense even from a shareholder perspective to offer that kind of protection to management.

STEWART: Yes, but Joel, there's no need to go in and rewrite the system a second time. Under our EVA™ improvement system, a major shock will lead to a one-time drop in EVA, and management will forgo its bonus in that year. But, as a result of that reduction in EVA, the level of future targeted EVA will be reduced accordingly, the bonus will effectively recalibrate itself from the new lower base, and the company will be able to reward continuous improvement *after adjusting for that shock.*

And that's precisely what happens to the shareholders in those circumstances. They take a one-time hit and, after the share price adjusts downward, the future is fair game. Why treat managers any differently from shareholders?

ZIMMERMAN: A similar debate has been going on in the accounting and organization literature for the last 50 years, and it has to do with a problem that every controller has probably had to deal with since we invented something called standard costs. When do you revise the standards? Does anyone here ever reopen the standards in the middle of the year?

ADIMANDO: We would change standards in mid-year if we added, let's say, a new component at a significantly lower cost.

ZIMMERMAN: Okay, but once you allow the standards to be reopened, then you run into the problem that Bennett is alluding to. You create a set of incentives for managers to avoid accountability every time the world changes.

BUTLER: We don't change standards in the middle of a year.

ZIMMERMAN: Okay, so Carm changes standards, but Bob doesn't. You're facing essentially the same issue of accountability with respect to changing standard costs that Joel and Bennett have just been debating in the context of changing asset amortization schedules. And I suspect if I asked a hundred people, I'd get roughly the same split of opinion. Unfortunately, there is no single right answer to this question.

If you don't allow *any* flexibility to change the system, you create inaccuracies and inequities. But once you allow flexibility, you give rise to what economists call "influence costs," the costs people impose on organizations in trying to change the rules of the game. Once people know the rules are flexible, they will work hard to change them if it serves their interests to do so.

A Role for Subjectivity

WILLETT: Well, I think it's possible to build too much objectivity into the system, and so I would argue there is a lot of room for the exercise of judgment by top management in performance evaluation and compensation. Even with the most careful planning in the world, when you put into place a system that has 164 components, it is likely that you will discover that you forgot one or two. And it seems to me that you ought to build in a fair amount of subjectivity not only into the measurement system, but also into the compensation system that reinforces the measurement system. This will allow you to make the inevitable adjustments that you're going to want to make once the system is put into place.

STEWART: Well, the most objective measure of all is the stock price. Take the case of a company operating in one line of business in which management and employees own all the stock. In that event, the stock price would be the perfectly objective measure; you wouldn't need surrogates like EVA in that case.

WILLETT: That's true, Bennett. But if you're managing a large and somewhat diverse collection of businesses under rapidly changing circumstances, the current stock price is certainly not going to provide a useful indicator of the performance of the person running one of the businesses.

STEWART: Well, for that same reason, I say that the right answer is not to pay for performance, but to make managers into owners. Pay-for-performance schemes are based on the notion that you can somehow isolate what it is that management is doing from everything else that's happening in the world around them. But what often happens with such systems is that somebody will come in and say, "It's true we had a bad year last year. But we were digging ditches, we were draining swamps, we were shooting crocodiles, we never worked so hard in our life— and we deserve our reward." And, to the extent you allow this kind of ex post adjustment, you leave room for endless debate and the discipline of the whole system is lost.

So I think you want to push this idea of surrogate ownership as far as you can. You say to your operating heads, we've thought about all the excuses, and they're built into the system. And if something horrendous happens, you'll lose that year. But the target will automatically adjust to give you a level playing field in the following year. If you don't like bearing the risk of ownership, there's the door. And that's what works, that's why LBOs have worked so well.

SHEPRO: Yes, but that's an awful lot of risk to impose on a manager. If you're an owner and things turn bad, you no longer have the option of moving to another company.

STEWART: Yes, that's true. But we are also offering a total compensation with a considerably higher *expected level* of compensation than the typical plan, because we're asking people to assume more risk. Most companies have both too little risk *and* too little reward. We want more risk and more reward.

In most companies, they not only debate the annual bonus targets, they even allow changes in the time horizon of already established plans. Even in the most far-sighted companies, a bonus plan generally lasts no more than three years. So what you find is that the bonus plans all end up being deferred, but guaranteed, compensation in disguise. There really isn't any sense of ownership understood as a fixed, long-term interest in a company.

Now, there is an entire spectrum of management incentive plans ranging from loose pay-for-performance schemes with lots of subjectivity on the one end to highly rigid and objective schemes on the other. Probably the most disciplined and objective form of managerial ownership is that achieved by an LBO. In that case, the capital charge in our EVA™ system becomes a contractually binding commitment to meet an *unyielding* schedule of interest and principal. If you don't pay it back, you're out; you've lost your investment and maybe your job.

Of course, that is likely to be too much risk for most managers, especially those operating in growth companies with lots of investment requirements. But the right question to ask is this: Where along that spectrum of flexibility and rigidity, of subjectivity and objectivity, is it optimal to design a management incentive system for this particular company? And while it will almost certainly vary from company to company, I feel very strongly that most companies err on the side of subjectivity and too little

risk-bearing. In the vast majority of companies, there are too many ways for corporate managers to earn bonuses that are not justified by shareholders' returns.

You see, what we're really attempting to achieve with EVA is a unified, coherent financial management system. And systems always involve trade-offs. That is, you establish policies designed to handle the most likely cases, even while recognizing that there will always be cases that might cause you to want to deviate from that policy. But, you have to maintain the discipline of the system; you don't want to be constantly changing the rules of the game.

The Missing Third: Accounting for Synergies

STEWART: But let me return to the point Joe Willett was making about accounting for the performance of different businesses. When you examine a large corporation, when you take the lid off the pot and look inside, you'll many times find a complex organization with lots of different product lines. In such cases, there will be shared costs and benefits, with the need to make transfers of costs or revenues among them. And while this is not specifically an EVA issue, it begs the question: How far down in an organization can we calculate individual EVAs until we begin to undermine any sense of common cause within the organization?

ADIMANDO: To make EVA effective, I think you have to push it all the way down to the individual operating units to get people's attention and produce results. And the best way to do that is to give them some level of targets, including an EVA target.

And, by the way, Bennett, I disagree with your characterization of EVA as just a financial management system; I think it's a way of life. You've

got to convince everybody that increasing shareholder value is the one overarching goal of the organization, and that EVA is the main internal yardstick for evaluating your progress toward meeting that goal. You must also make clear the role of customer satisfaction in sustaining higher EVA— because if you don't have satisfied customers, you won't be able to increase prices; you won't be able to sustain the market share you've achieved; and your EVA and market value will fall. I think stock market analysts, and especially the institutions that invest their money in public companies' stock, clearly understand this.

So, I think EVA has got to go down to the level of the operating units; they all have to buy into the plan.

STEWART: Can you measure EVA at the level of the individual plant?

ADIMANDO: Yes, you can. But, rather than go through 164 adjustments, you have to start off with something very simple. You take the assets operating people are familiar with—things like receivables, inventory, fixed assets, and rental equipment—and then figure out the cost of capital for that business. The cost of capital becomes the minimum rate of return they have to achieve on these working assets they have under their control. A given unit's EVA is its net profits minus the capital charge.

Once division heads and plant managers become accustomed to the process, you can begin using more sophisticated adjustments to get a better measure of operating cash flow and net assets employed. If you're a division manager or plant manager in our company, you're held responsible for creating EVA on the company's investment in your operation.

ZIMMERMAN: But how do you recognize profitability or value at the level of the plant?

ADIMANDO: By the value of the products coming out of that plant. We measure that value by setting our actual production costs against our standard costs.

ZIMMERMAN: I agree that you can measure the plant's performance using standard costs. The question is: Do you get a number that really tells you anything? It's very difficult to come up with standard costs that provide a useful basis for measuring profitability, especially in cases where there are joint costs or benefits associated with the product.

Just think about a very simple firm that has two divisions. Presumably, you have one firm with two divisions as opposed to two separate firms because there are some synergies between the two operations. There are either some joint costs that are being shared, or there are joint benefits that would not be realized if the operations were independent. To illustrate the difficulty of accounting for joint costs or benefits, take a company like Coca-Cola with a lot of brand-name capital. How do you charge each of the product lines within Coca-Cola for that joint benefit?

Or consider the hamburger and hide problem of joint costs that appears in virtually every accounting textbook I've ever seen. The cow walks in the door and gets bopped over the head, and so you have a pile of hides and a pile of hamburger. Do you allocate the costs of raising the cow to the hamburger or the hides?

The accounting system can do that allocation, right down to the penny. But the answer will be wrong; it will be at best meaningless and it may even cause you to make bad business decisions. Allocating costs to the hides and the hamburger based on weight, for example, might cause you to decide to stop making hamburger. But, if you do that, you will suddenly discover that hides have become much less profitable than you thought they were.

And that's ultimately the conundrum that you have with EVA™ or any other performance measure. You can allocate costs down to the penny, and they will be right in an arithmetic sense. But they don't tell you anything about the real economic profitability of producing that joint product. Neither EVA nor any accounting system is set up to handle this kind of problem that arises from synergies.

But let me go back to the beginning of the discussion, because we're closing in on this missing third that I mentioned earlier. In his opening remarks, Joel described EVA as a performance measurement *and* a compensation scheme. He said that putting in EVA as a performance measure without changing the compensation plan "isn't going to buy you anything."

But, as I stated earlier, I think Stern Stewart's got the problem two-thirds right, but there's one critical element missing from the story. The other third, which has been floating around in comments here and there, has to do with the notion of empowerment. Bennett earlier showed us a picture of a Quaker Oats plant manager on EVA. But what Bennett failed to mention is that when this guy sets up his machines, he is now able, perhaps for the first time, to determine the batch sizes. The *Fortune* article on EVA also mentioned that, after putting his company on an EVA program, the CEO of AT&T *starting last year* encouraged his operating heads to divide their businesses into profit centers resembling independent companies. And Joe Willett also mentioned the notion of empowerment in connection with Merrill Lynch's 50 different businesses.

My point, then, is that when you think about using EVA, it's not just a matter of linking performance measurement to the comp plan. For EVA to be effective, you have to be willing to decentralize the firm and "em-

power" the operating managers. If you put in an EVA performance measurement system and incentive plan but keep all the decision rights at the top of the organization, then an EVA system may not accomplish much.

For some firms, however—particularly those in stable, mature, low-tech industries that are not facing much competition—decentralization is probably not optimal. The agency costs associated with delegating decisions to line managers in such cases probably outweigh the benefits. In these cases, you don't want to go to EVA—because lower-level managers just don't have the decision-making authority.

STEWART: Well, I agree with you that there's an iron triangle between decentralized decision-making, accountability, and incentives. And, as I said earlier, the information revolution and globalization are driving the need to decentralize decision-making, to vest decision-making closer to the action so that the organization is flexible, responsive, and really takes continuous improvement to heart. If that's the case, then to decentralize decision-making without also decentralizing the risk and reward of ownership is a formula for empire building as opposed to value building.

ZIMMERMAN: I agree with you, Bennett, that there's a lot more outsourcing and downsizing going on as companies realize that the costs of doing everything internally, of being a fully integrated firm, often outweigh the benefits. But there are still lots of large companies that operate in a variety of different businesses. Johnson & Johnson is one. And Merrill Lynch, as Joe said, has some 50 operating divisions that are each presumably more valuable as part of Merrill Lynch than as independent businesses.

So, there is still lots of evidence of valuable synergies in the corporate world. You can measure the EVA of the whole firm. But when you try and divide it up, you've got the classic hamburger and hide problem of joint costs. And activity-based costing won't solve that problem. It's not just the allocation of the joint costs, it's the allocation of the joint benefits as well, such as Coca-Cola's brand name capital. It's a very contentious matter, and it's bound to involve subjective judgment by top management overseeing the entire organization.

Think about your own firm, Bennett. Stern Stewart is basically a two-part firm: it has the consulting side of the business, as represented by you and Joel. And it has the *Journal of Applied Corporate Finance*, which is edited by Don Chew.

STEWART: That's an oversimplification. In fact, we have about ten lines of business.

ZIMMERMAN: Let's just keep it to those two for my example. Now, why do these two activities exist within the same firm? Well, presumably, because there are joint benefits. In fact, there are synergies that are evident in this room right now: the *Journal* benefits from the reputation of the consulting practice and its ability to bring practitioners into this kind of meeting, and the consulting side benefits from the prestige and advertising value of the *Journal*.

Now, how do you measure the EVA™ of the *Journal*? Does Don Chew have an EVA target?

STEWART: Yes, in effect.

ZIMMERMAN: And how do you allocate the joint benefits of having them both in the same firm?

STEWART: As I said, we have about ten different product lines. And if we get a consulting assignment, that consulting revenue can be divided up into five different pies internally.

ZIMMERMAN: But is it garbage in, garbage out?

STEWART: No, I determine the proper allocation—and, as you know, Jerry,

I have an automatic marginal cost calculator in my head.

ZIMMERMAN: Well, Bennett, that just goes to prove my point: there is likely to be an important role for subjectivity and judgment by top management, particularly in cases involving joint costs and benefits.

STEWART: Well, perhaps my answer was oversimple. A good example of what I have in mind is what AT&T has done with Bell Labs. Bell Labs, as you know, has been a fountain of basic and applied research that has benefitted the reputation and profitability of the entire firm. As such, Bell Labs was treated entirely as corporate overhead. Under their new EVA system, however, only basic research remains in overhead, while all the engineers and researchers working on applied research must now "sell" their services to internal operating units, with explicit goals and deliverables clearly spelled out. The cost of those services are charged to the operating unit or units, and this has transformed Bell Labs' applied research into an EVA center—one that is accountable for generating economic profits. And this in turn has led to a more effective allocation of those research resources to promising uses.

More on Synergies

RAVID: I would like to ask a somewhat technical question. When you measure EVA, how do you measure the value of net assets? Is it historical accounting cost, or is it replacement cost? If you're using replacement cost or market value, then EVA is telling you something about how much absolute economic value you're creating. But, if you're using historical costs—which, in one sense, are sunk costs—then you're really better off just asking managers to increase their economic earnings or cash flow.

STERN: This is an important issue: For example, what do you do with a mining company most of its assets you acquired a hundred years ago? Our answer would be that it depends on how large the differences are between historical and replacement costs. If the differences are not material, or there's no way of confidently establishing replacement costs, then we recommend using historical costs.

STEWART: In the case of the mining firm with 100-year-old assets, you may actually be better off setting up a performance measurement system by assuming there is *no* balance sheet and hence *no* capital. Then you would simply define EVA as the operating earnings. And you would charge people only for new capital that goes in, while giving them a credit for any additional capital that comes out.

You see, if you keep the old balance sheet and attempt to correct that on a piecemeal basis, you then fall prey to the fallacy that sunk costs are relevant; but they are not. That's why if you merely get people to focus on the *increase* in EVA, then it really doesn't matter if you haven't gotten the value of the assets correct the first time. It doesn't matter where you begin; only that you maintain consistency after beginning the measurement process.

RAVID: But that wouldn't tell me how to make a decision on the initial investment—whether the economic earnings were adequate to justify buying the assets in the first place.

STEWART: That's true. But consider this: If you sell an asset and you recognize a book gain or loss, that gain or loss does not go through EVA. In our system, that book gain or loss is taken off the income statement, and put back onto the balance sheet. In this sense, we're using cash accounting.

ZIMMERMAN: But, Bennett, that statement gives me even more concern about how you handle this issue of synergies. Take Coca-Cola again, with its huge investment in its brand name. It's an intangible asset; it can't be sold to a third party without selling the whole firm and the products that go along with it. It's not like a plant, it's not like a deposit of ore that they can sell.

Let's assume that Coca-Cola has just two product lines: Diet Coke and Classic Coke. How does your system work? Assuming there are no assets in Coca-Cola other than its brand name, how do you value its capital stock? Do you value the brand name?

STEWART: No, we don't care about that.

ZIMMERMAN: You don't care? But if I'm running Diet Coke on an EVA plan, I could earn large bonuses at the expense of Classic Coke by making low-quality Diet Coke and cutting back on advertising. I can enrich myself while ruining the brand name and imposing a large cost on Classic Coke.

STEWART: Yes, I know. There you have a joint product, so what you have to do is to create a keiretsu-like structure with what amounts to cross ownership among products. That is, you have to say that while the larger part—say, 70%—of your bonus is based on your own operation's EVA^{TM}, the other 30% is based on the EVA of the entire firm.

ZIMMERMAN: But that won't make the problem disappear. Think about advertising decisions. This is also a case where if I decide to advertise Diet Coke, I'm also advertising Coca-Cola's name, which is going to add to the value of that corporate name.

STEWART: Right. So what we would do in such a case is to figure out what is a reasonable apportionment of value among divisions. For example, we might say that two thirds of the advertising costs in that case are borne by Diet Coke and the remaining third is unallocated and held at corporate. At any rate, you can address this problem by devising some sensible allocation rule.

In Closing

STERN: Well, I don't think we're going to solve this problem in the next five minutes. In bringing this discussion to an end, I would just like to offer a modest proposal—one that holds up EVA as a means of taking a step toward not just managerial ownership, but employee ownership throughout a large organization.

Because of its simplicity, one of the great benefits of EVA is that it can make employees throughout an organization conscious of what they're doing and why they're doing it. If you "incentivize" people on a clear and simple basis, you can impound the corporate objective into their very being. And even if some individuals don't get it right away, peer pressure alone should compel most to behave as value-maximizers.

We instituted an EVA plan at a government agency in South Africa in July of '93. The agency spent four months implementing this program, which included our participation in a two-hour tape that was shown to 11,000 employees—principally laboratory technicians. More than 85% of the employees have not graduated from high school, and we were told they would never be able to understand this.

And we were amazed at the outcome. Their EVA for the first six months exceeded by five times what they had forecast for the entire year. And they are now planning to pay out bonuses to all 11,000 employees that are more than twice what they originally expected.

The lesson from this experience appears to be that, in many cases, all you have to do to improve people's performance is to get them to understand how superior performance can have an impact on themselves. Their performance measure is not a consolidated measure. These people are deep down in their units. But once a month they get a line from the CFO telling them how well their unit is doing on EVA year-to-date. And, as the director of the agency told me, that is the day of the month when these employees tell their families they won't be home for dinner; instead they sit around the table at work trying to figure out what they can do to improve things even more.

So, from the implementation side, I'm not concerned about employees' ability to understand the concept of EVA. I recognize that there are some issues and mechanics of getting it done that we have not addressed in the last two hours—particularly, the issue of empowerment and the problem of accounting for synergies that Jerry Zimmerman was raising at the end. But these are issues that can be resolved, as Bennett was suggesting, through cross-ownership schemes and—as reluctant as I am to concede this—perhaps even some subjective judgment by top management. But, having made this concession, let me say that our ultimate aim with EVA is to eliminate altogether the need for subjectivity in the financial management (and incentive) system.

EVA^{TM} is a trademark of Stern Stewart & Co., New York, NY.

EVA AND SHAREHOLDER VALUE IN JAPAN

Sponsored by the

Mitusi Life Financial Research Center

at the University of Michigan

Business School

Keidanren Kaikan, Tokyo

May 10, 1996

Koshiro Sakata

E. Han Kim

E. HAN KIM: Welcome to the Fourth Mitsui Life Symposium on Global Financial Markets. My name is E. Han Kim, and I am Director of the Mitsui Life Financial Research Center at the University of Michigan Business School. It is my pleasure to introduce the two speakers who will open the proceedings of this symposium.

We are privileged to have in attendance the President of Mitsui Mutual Life Insurance Company, Mr. Koshiro Sakata, whose generous gift has endowed the Mitsui Life Financial Research Center at the University of Michigan. President Sakata will be followed by Joe White, the Dean of the University of Michigan Business School. I would like to thank both President Sakata and Dean White for finding time in their very busy schedules to join us this afternoon.

KOSHIRO SAKATA: Thank you very much, Professor Kim. Today we are very pleased to welcome so many participants to the Fourth Mitsui Life Symposium. The relationship between Mitsui Life Insurance and the University of Michigan dates back six years to when Professor Kim of the University of Michigan and Professor Wakasugi of the University of Tokyo proposed this program. The University of Michigan, needless to say, is one of the top universities in the United States. I have had the opportunity to visit the University several times, and have seen many students with promising futures engaged in their studies and research. In addition to the scholarly atmosphere, I was also impressed by the natural setting of the campus, with all its greenery and flowers.

It was in 1990 that the professors Kim and Wakasugi came to us to propose a plan designed to raise the level of research on financial systems and capital markets in different countries around the world. We wholeheartedly endorsed their proposal and agreed to contribute the funds, and so the Mitsui Life Financial Research Center was established at the Business School.

In 1991 the first symposium was held at the University of Michigan. The second symposium was held in this same hall we are in today at Keidanren. For the third symposium, the setting was once again the University of Michigan, and the meeting was attended by many prominent scholars from the United States. I am pleased to learn that the research results supported by the Center have been widely reported in the financial and business communities as well as in academic circles.

The theme of today's symposium is EVA and shareholder value creation. Although it is a new concept to me, EVA is now considered to be one of most basic themes of capitalism, and it is indeed a timely topic for the symposium. So I am confident that today's discussions will be useful and meaningful to all of you. I would like to thank all of the participants for taking the time to attend the symposium. In fact, I have been told that there are also participants from our neighboring country Korea—and we are very pleased to have them. I would also like to express special thanks to Dean White and the

other members of the University of Michigan as well as the panel members and lecturers.

JOSEPH WHITE: Thank you, Mr. Sakata, both for your kind remarks and your consistently generous support of the activities of the the Mitsui Life Center at the University of Michigan. I would also like express my gratitude to Professors Tak Wakasugi of Tokyo University and Han Kim of the University of Michigan. As co-directors of the Mitsui Center, they have presided over an important program of research, visiting scholars, and symposiums over the last six years. And today's event should be an impressive addition to this record. Professor Wakasugi is the ideal person to speak to us on EVA from the Japanese economic perspective. I am also grateful for the participation of Mr. Toru Mochizuki, Mr. Mark Newburg, and Mr. Virgil Stephens, the chief financial officers, respectively, of Coca-Cola Japan, NCR Japan, and Eastman Chemical Company. They will provide their senior management perspective on this important matter.

Finally, I am also grateful to Mr. Joel Stern, managing partner of Stern Stewart & Company for his participation today. His work on the subject of EVA has gained international recognition. EVA is playing a major role in the successful efforts of many U.S. chief executive officers to revitalize the financial performance of their companies.

This leads to interesting and important questions: How and why does EVA work? Why don't all companies adopt it? Is it culturally limited—that is, applicable only in the U.S. or in the West, but not in Japan and Asia? Will EVA turn out to be just another management fad, or will it prove, like total quality management, to be an enduring management focus and tool? With Mr. Stern, Professors Wakasugi and Kim, and our executive panelists, we have just the right

people to answer these questions. I look forward to a very stimulating and informative symposium.

KIM: Thank you, President Sakata and Dean White, for the kind remarks. The topic of the symposium, as mentioned, is "Economic Value Added and Shareholder Wealth." To discuss this topic, we have assembled a distinguished group of speakers, representing both academic and corporate perspectives that reflect Japanese as well as U.S. experience.

At our last symposium here in Tokyo three years ago, the theme was corporate governance in Japan and the United States. In selecting that theme we were fortunate in anticipating the rise of interest in corporate governance in Japan. One issue that is closely and directly tied to corporate governance is the issue of shareholder rights as owners of corporations, and how their ownership interests are represented in managerial decision-making. Economic Value Added, or EVA, is a management tool designed to encourage managers to do a more effective job of representing the shareholder interests. In recent years, EVA has been adopted by a large number of American companies, and it has been given a lot of credit for increasing the shareholder value of many of these firms.

Professor Wakasugi, who is the co-director of the Mitsui Center as well, will start off this symposium by discussing the current state of Japanese corporate governance, and the potential role of EVA in improving Japanese corporate performance. Professor Wakasugi is a well-respected international scholar in financial economics. He has frequently served in an advisory capacity to the Japanese Ministry of Finance, the Ministry of Posts and Communications, and the Government Policy Investment Council. I will now turn the floor over to Professor Wakasugi.

EVA and the Japanese Corporate Governance Problem

WAKASUGI: Thank you, Professor Kim. And, before I begin, let me acknowledge a very large debt to Professor Kim, for much of what I am now about to tell you reflects his insights into U.S. and Japanese corporate governance issues.

As Dean White and Professor Kim have mentioned, EVA is now central to the thinking of American management. EVA is a management tool—more precisely, an internal performance measurement and incentive compensation system—that can be used to represent the shareholder's viewpoint within the organization. In the United States over the past several years, the EVA approach has become very popular. Many of the companies that have adopted EVA as an internal performance measure and as a basis for incentive compensation have experienced significant operating improvements and increases in stock price.

Japan's experience with corporate governance is one in which—historically at least—the interests of shareholders have been subordinated to the competing demands of other corporate stakeholders. In recent years, however, there has been increasing concern about the issue of shareholder representation. Indeed, we are now, I believe, on the threshold of a national acknowledgement that greater concern for shareholder interests may be the only way to reinvigorate our depressed capital markets.

So, before discussing EVA and its potential for increasing shareholder wealth, I will review some of the historical factors in Japan that may prove instrumental in leading Japanese companies to adopt this new American management tool. Please keep in mind that I will be presenting EVA from a Japanese perspec-tive. That is, my version of EVA and that which will be presented by the American managers on the panel may involve some slight differences—differences that reflect differences in the corporate cultures of the U.S. and Japan.

Most of you will recall that, in the 1980s, Japanese companies became very prosperous, very rich. They used their new-found wealth to diversify into new business areas. The primary focus of Japanese corporate managements was on growth—growth in sales and assets, growth in earnings, and growth in market share. New business ventures and rapid expansion of existing activities were two common ways of pursuing such growth. Moreover, in both domestic and foreign markets, the scope of Japanese companies' investment activities was expanded to include investments in real estate and financial assets as well as the more traditional investments in plant and equipment. Growth was the watchword, as the managers of these companies were convinced that large scale and market dominance would be the keys to success in the future.

Implicit in this strategy was the assumption that capital was an unlimited and free resource. In pursuing growth at any price, no consideration was given to the cost of capital. This way of thinking is easy to criticize in hindsight, but recall that at that time Japanese managers won plaudits not only at home but also in foreign markets for their long-term planning horizons and their willingness to sacrifice current earnings for future growth and market share. From the vantage point of these managers, moreover, it was easy to fall into the trap of treating capital as if it had no cost—for it certainly gave every appearance of being free. Only a tiny fraction of internally generated cash flows were distributed to shareholders as dividends and yet share prices continued to scale new heights year after year. Additional external capital could be raised with convertible bonds issues offering rates as low as two or three percent; and if such bonds were issued in foreign denominations, the yen appreciation sometimes brought the effective cost down to zero or less. So, the perception of free capital helped to justify the long time horizons of Japanese companies—planning horizons that became known, and were indeed widely celebrated, as "Japanese-style management." Whether this was all correct or not is something that we now have to reconsider.

At the same time the Japanese management style was commanding worldwide respect, managers of U.S. companies were being criticized for focusing on cost-cutting and short-term earnings performance. As the globalization of product markets increased, the competition from imports faced by U.S. firms intensified. Achieving production efficiencies and paring product prices became crucial to survival for many U.S. firms. Thus, while Japanese companies were on an expansion binge, American companies were encouraged, if not compelled, by U.S. capital markets to engage in downsizing, divestitures, and decentralization. Inside these companies, individual units began to be treated as profit centers, and each of the units was required to reach adequate levels of profitability.

This new sense of urgency in restoring efficiency and profitability required that American managers turn away from traditional performance measures such as revenue growth or earnings. Each unit had to justify its existence and to do so required that they also justify their ongoing use of the companies' capital resources. EVA, unlike popular performance measures like earn-

Until recently, the primary focus of Japanese corporate managements was on growth—growth in sales and assets, growth in earnings, and growth in market share. In pursuing growth at any price, no consideration was given to the cost of capital. Implicit in this strategy was the assumption that capital was an unlimited and free resource.

But all this is changing. We are now, I believe, on the threshold of a national acknowledgement that greater concern for shareholder interests may be the only way to reinvigorate our depressed capital markets.

Takaaki Wakasugi

ings per share and EPS growth, recognizes that capital has a cost and that a business unit can justify its use of capital only if what it earns exceeds that cost. Thus, the competitive pressures that led to demands for decentralization and greater operational efficiency were also the primary catalyst for the adoption of the EVA methodology by American firms.

Where does this leave Japan? In the 1990s Japan has experienced a serious and protracted recession—and its stock market has stagnated along with the general economy. There has been a growing awareness that the poor performance of the Japanese stock market is attributable in large part to Japanese companies' emphasis on growth at all costs and neglect of shareholder returns—both of which can in turn be traced to the overall governance system's lack of adequate representation of shareholders' interests. As one sign of this new awareness, there has been increasing interest among

Japanese managers in recent years in measuring corporate performance with return on equity, or ROE.

And, in fact, a simple comparison of ROEs over the past decade can serve to highlight the current difference in performance between American and Japanese firms. In every year during the period 1985-1995, the average Japanese ROE was lower than the average ROE in the U.S. Although part of this difference can be explained by more conservative Japanese accounting methods, much of it reflects the difference in managerial priorities. For example, whereas in the U.S. we observed an increase in corporate ROEs throughout the 1990s, in Japan there has been a significant decline of ROEs from peak levels in 1989. At present, the average company in Japan is reporting an ROE of *only about 2%.*

As Joel Stern will tell you later, ROE is not the ideal economic yardstick for evaluating managers' performance—and the EVA measure is designed in part to overcome the shortcomings of

ROE. But ROE nevertheless provides a good indication of whether capital is being used efficiently inside organizations—and, on this score, the difference between Japanese and U.S. firms has become painfully clear.

And such diverging trends in operating profitability, as mentioned, have been clearly reflected in the divergence of stock prices in Japan and the United States. Throughout the 1980s, Japanese stock prices increased in systematic fashion. In the first years of 1990s, however, the Nikkei index lost close to half its value, a plunge that many observers attributed to a speculative "bubble." Perhaps even more troubling, however, has been the stagnation in prices that has continued since the large drop in the early '90s. The Nikkei index continues to trade in a 20,000 to 22,000 range, as compared with a peak of nearly 40,000 at the end of 1989.

In contrast, the Dow Jones Industrial Average in the U.S. continues to break new records every year and currently stands at 5500. During the 1980s, when comparing the progress of the Nikkei average in Japan with the Dow average in the U.S., the rule of thumb was that the Nikkei would be ten times the Dow average. That is, if the Dow was 3000, the Nikkei would be in the 28,000 to 32,000 range. Using that rule of thumb today, the Nikkei should be above 50,000. But today the index is well below half of that level.

So, if you compare the two countries in the past decade, we see that the Japanese approach of limitless expansion has been accompanied by a very large decline in shareholder wealth. In contrast, the American strategy of reliance on capital management tools to guide restructuring in the face of global competition has produced a significant increase in shareholder wealth.

Countervailing Forces to Shareholder Value Maximization in Japan

Despite such differences in managerial focus and behavior, however, Japanese and American corporations are fairly similar in terms of their legal organizational structures. And, given such legal or structural similarities, it is pertinent to ask what accounts for such significant differences in behavior and performance. For whom, or for what purpose, is the Japanese corporation being managed?

In terms of corporate governance systems, the Japanese company, like its American counterpart, in principle belongs to the shareholders (or, at least, the shareholders have claim to the "residual" value after all other claims have been satisfied). Therefore, as in the U.S., the logical objective of Japanese management should be to attempt to maximize the wealth of the shareholders. In practice, however, there are several countervailing influences in the Japanese system that allow or even encourage managers to sacrifice the interests of shareholders in order to satisfy the competing claims of other stakeholders in the corporation.

For example, Japanese corporations are noted for the practice of cross-holding of shares between companies. The stated purpose of such cross-holdings is to build and maintain business relationships between, say, manufacturers and their suppliers. But, in practice, the cross-shareholders do not behave like value-maximizing shareholders, and they exert very little influence on corporate management. Moreover, because such a substantial portion of Japanese companies' outstanding shares are permanently held by other firms, these companies are not subjected to the rigors of the market for corporate control. In the American market, the shares of companies with poor managements can be acquired at depressed prices, which in turn attracts hostile acquirers who often end up replacing the incumbent managers. The Japanese system of cross-shareholding prevents the takeover mechanism from operating and leaves underperforming management in place. And, so, in the absence of the threat of takeover, shareholder interests are unlikely to play a significant role in corporate decision-making.

Some corporate finance scholars have argued that there are substitute governance mechanisms that perform the disciplinary role of takeovers in the Japanese economy. For example, Japanese corporations have traditionally maintained close relationships with one or more large banks in the Japanese "main bank" system. Because banks have for a long time been the major suppliers of external financing, including equity as well as debt, it is the banks, and not the other shareholders, that exert the strongest influence over the companies' management. But, although bank ownership may in some cases end up working to shareholders' advantage, there is a major problem with this corporate governance solution: the banks' interests are not entirely consistent with those of the outside shareholders. For example, it is in the banks' interests as debtholders that their corporate borrowers both avoid risky projects and provide an ongoing source of loan demand in periods when loanable funds are readily available. Neither of these objectives is necessarily consistent with maximizing shareholder profits.

The claims of employees are another source of conflict with the shareholders' interest. In defining its priorities, Japanese corporate management places greater emphasis than U.S. managers on the welfare of corporate employees. In particular, Japan is noted for its system of "lifetime employment" and wages based on seniority. While both of these features can be justified as very long-run investments in employee training and morale, neither is necessarily conducive to increasing shareholder profit. And, finally, as I mentioned earlier, Japanese companies tend to emphasize market share over profitability as the key measure of operating success. In so doing, Japanese companies are said to place relatively greater emphasis on customer satisfaction.

Another important difference between the Japanese and U.S. systems—one that helps explain why shareholders are higher on American companies' list of priorities—is the active role played by pension funds in the United States. Owing to their increasing volume of share transactions, U.S. pension funds have become a decisive factor in valuing corporations. And, as the size of pension funds has grown, they have begun to attempt to influence management decision-making more directly through various kinds of activist governance initiatives. As a result, shareholders in the United States have another means of representing their interests that is not available to shareholders in Japan.

Japan and the United States can also be distinguished from each other by a fundamental difference in attitudes about the proper social role of the corporation. This difference is based in turn on a difference between Japanese and U.S. managers' willingness to accept the assumption that the market mechanism is working (or should be allowed to work) in every field. In the United States, most of the economy has been liberalized and the market mechanism is functioning in virtually all markets, including markets for labor as well as consumer prices. In such a free-market environment, the maximization of shareholder value is more or less accepted by American society as the primary goal of the public corporation. Stockholder interests can be pursued by U.S. corporate managers, and this pursuit is reinforced by an active market for corporate control that ensures that the system operates with reasonable efficiency.

In Japan, by contrast, we are currently far from the point where we can claim that our entire market system is functioning freely. In order for us to address the current sluggish economy and depressed stock market, it is necessary to reform our entire capital allocation system. The maximization of shareholder value is a fundamental part of that reform, and EVA has the potential to help implement it. So let me give you a brief overview of the concept.

A Potential Role for EVA in Improving Capital Allocation

As individual investors investing in equity or debt, we require a rate of return that is commensurate with the risks associated with the investment. In the case of a corporation, the risk-adjusted return it must offer in order to attract new financial capital is called the "cost of capital." The greater the riskiness of the firm's business activities, the greater will be its cost of capital.

Thus, a problem arises when earnings per share or ROE is used to measure corporate investment performance. Because neither of these traditional measures takes into account the firm's risk-adjusted cost of capital, it is impossible to say whether any given level of EPS or ROE is acceptable to investors. A company's real economic profit is the amount it earns *in excess of* the cost of capital— a cost that appears nowhere in the balance sheet or income statement used to calculate EPS or ROE. The

current demand for EVA is thus based in part on one simple idea: you simply cannot know whether your enterprise is creating wealth for your shareholders until you subtract the cost of capital from income.

From the perspective of the overall firm and its risk-adjusted cost of capital, the relevant cost of capital is the *weighted average* cost of both its debt and its equity capital. In order for a company to create value for all its capital suppliers (debtholders as well as shareholders), its return on total capital must exceed the weighted average cost of capital, or WACC. EVA, then, is just the dollar amount by which a company's pre-interest, but after-tax net operating income (or NOPAT) exceeds the charge for total capital (WACC multiplied by debt plus equity). For example, if a firm with a WACC of 10% earns a NOPAT of $20 million on $100 million of total capital, its EVA is $10 million. To the extent EVA is positive, the firm is adding value for its shareholders. But if a company's EVA is negative, the firm is destroying shareholder wealth *even though it may be reporting a positive and growing EPS or ROE.*

So, the cost of capital plays a crucial role in implementing an EVA standard. The lenders who lend money to the corporation and the investors who purchase its equity all expect to receive at least the risk-adjusted rate of return. Without positive EVA performance—or without at least the expectation of such performance in the future—this is not possible.

Some people have objected that, although EVA may be superior in theory, it is difficult to apply in practice. There are three main aspects of an EVA system—"planning," "execution," and "evaluation"—each of which is necessary to make EVA an effective operational management tool. Management must begin by making a plan formulated in terms of expected EVA;

the plan must then be carried out; and management's success in meeting the plan must be measured—again, in terms of EVA—and the managers held accountable.

But, in order for this three-part management decision-making cycle to function effectively, there are four conditions that must be met. These four conditions are very important from the standpoint of the shareholders. First, it is important to have a well-defined managerial objective (say, earn a positive EVA, or at least increase EVA each year). Second, appropriate criteria must be used in selecting investment projects (accept only positive-EVA projects, those expected to earn at least their cost of capital). Third, companies must evaluate the actual performance of their investment over regular time intervals—again using EVA to measure the resulting wealth creation or destruction from the standpoint of the shareholder. Fourth and finally, the managers responsible for the capital allocation decision must be provided incentives—say, in the form of year-end bonuses tied to EVA—that encourage them to make decisions consistent with shareholder objectives.

This, in brief, is the management approach based on the concept of EVA. One of the great strengths of the system is the consistency it maintains throughout the three management phases of strategic planning, performance measurement, and managerial compensation. Before going onto an EVA system, many U.S. companies would use the discounted cash flow method when making their investment decisions, but then use traditional measures like EPS or ROE when evaluating performance after the investment. The resulting inconsistency in the criteria for capital budgeting and performance evaluation would then lead to conflicting priorities and internal confusion among managers.

EVA, however, is a measure that can be used for each of these three functions—strategic planning, performance evaluation, and incentive compensation. By achieving consistency across these three functions, managers are provided incentives both to make value-increasing investment decisions and to operate as efficiently as possible.

Thank you for your attention.

KIM: Thank you, Professor Wakasugi. Now Joel Stern will tell us about his recent efforts to extend EVA outside the U.S. and discuss how it works in actual corporate settings.

An EVA Primer

STERN: Thank you, Han. It is a pleasure to return to Tokyo. Since my last visit several years ago, I have read with great interest a number of academic papers that have been published by professors here. And I hope that you find of some interest what I am about to tell you.

Economic value added, contrary to what you may have heard, is not just a U.S. phenomenon. With the help of Stern Stewart, companies have been implementing EVA in South Africa for the past ten years. We are also presently working with companies in Canada, the U.K., Germany, France, Sweden, Australia, New Zealand, Mexico, and—as I will mention briefly in closing—Singapore. Moreover, we are advising companies operating in a broad range of industries—everything from consumer products and industrial companies, high-tech and pharmaceutical companies, to regulated companies such as banks, insurance companies, and public utilities. In fact, the list has recently expanded to include a number of not-for-profit and government-owned organizations.

So, our focus at Stern Stewart is not just on increasing *shareholder* returns and *shareholder* wealth. We are inter-

ested in making sustainable improvements in the productivity of *all* kinds of organizations. My favorite example is the United States Postal Service, which this past year adopted EVA with our help. U.S. postal workers now have a new arrangement with the American public—it's a deal that says they will receive bonuses for improvements in EVA, but with a significant portion of the bonuses deferred and held at risk to ensure that such improvements are not temporary. Everybody who works for the postal service is a partner in this effort.

But, to return to my earlier statement, EVA is not limited to America, and it is not limited to profit-seeking corporations. EVA has the potential to help a wide variety of organizations both evaluate their own performance and do a better job of identifying value-increasing ways to invest their scarce capital. As just one example, EVA can be used by an acquiring company when setting the maximum price it is willing to pay for an acquisition target. Our feeling is that, if you understand EVA, you will know when to walk away from value-reducing opportunities to invest funds.

The real payoff from an EVA financial management system comes from the direct linking of a better performance measure with incentive compensation. Some companies, I have been told, are using EVA for strategic planning and evaluation purposes, but not for incentive pay. That is a big mistake. If you measure performance on one basis, but pay bonuses according to another, most people will pay lipservice to your stated goal and manage the variables that affect their bonuses. What we want to do is get the right measure of performance and make that the basis for the incentive scheme.

Let me also point out that when we devise an incentive scheme, bonuses are generally based not on the absolute level of EVA produced by a

manager or an operation, but rather on the year-to-year *improvement* in EVA. The financial management goal is continuous improvement in EVA. One advantage of tying bonuses to improvements in EVA is that such bonuses effectively come at no cost to the shareholders. That is, the management bonuses earned under an EVA system are effectively paid for out of the much larger increases in shareholder value that accompany such EVA improvements.

Another important feature of our incentive compensation system is what we call the "bonus bank." We pay only one-third of the declared bonus upon declaration; the remaining two-thirds is held at risk and is subject to loss if you don't sustain the improvement. In other words, in order to receive the full award, you must both increase your EVA and at least maintain that new level of EVA for the next two or three years thereafter.

Besides strengthening management's incentives in a way that does not dilute the shareholder interest, yet another important potential benefit of EVA is that it can help companies communicate more effectively with the investment community. We have found in the U.S. and in the U.K.—and now in Germany as well—that institutional investors want to buy shares in companies that announce they are adopting EVA. Why? Because an EVA system acts as a policeman to make sure that corporate resources are not wasted.

One of the biggest problems with highly diversified or conglomerate forms of organizations—and I understand there are still a great many of them in Japan today—is that when excess cash is generated by one business, it is very often transferred as a subsidy to others that are not doing so well. And this cross-subsidization of negative-EVA by positive-EVA businesses often ends up reducing the

*J*apanese companies today seem to be in essentially the same position as U.S. companies in the late 1960s and early '70s. The U.S. firms were then flush with cash and capital from their product market successes in the '60s, and they too could not resist the temptation to grow through diversification. And American firms were then forced by the tough economic environment of the '70s and the shareholder pressures of the '80s to restructure, to return their excess capital, and to focus on their core businesses.

Joel Stern

value of the entire enterprise. This problem was identified by Harvard professor Michael Jensen as the "agency costs of free cash flow." What does that mean? It means that the excess capital, instead of being returned to shareholders who can reinvest it elsewhere, is being reinvested inside the company at unacceptably low rates of return. The managers are supposed to act as "agents" for their shareholders by making the most efficient possible use of resources. But we know from the U.S. experience with conglomerates in the 1970s and early '80s that managers don't voluntarily distribute excess capital unless they are under great pressure from shareholders—or they are operating under an EVA system.

And, in fact, as Professor Jensen argued in our *Journal of Applied Corporate Finance* as early as 1989, Japanese companies today seem to be in essentially the same position as U.S. companies found themselves in back in the late 1960s and early '70s. The U.S. firms were then flush with cash and capital from their successes in the

'60s, and they too could not resist the temptation to grow through diversification. And the U.S. firms were then forced by the tough economic environment of the '70s and the shareholder pressures to restructure, to return their excess capital and focus on their core businesses.

And this same free cash flow problem faced by U.S. companies 15 or 20 years ago appears to be one of the major problems in Japanese companies today. Their policies of very low dividends and, until very recently, no stock repurchases means that excess capital has effectively been *trapped* inside the companies. An EVA system will encourage manager to find ways to return that excess capital to shareholders, who can then reinvest in more promising growth opportunities in the Japanese economy.

The Link Between EVA and MVA

But I have a confession to make. EVA is not the ultimate measure of corporate success. The most reliable

measure of management's long-run success in adding value is something we call "Market Value Added," or MVA. And perhaps the best way to define MVA is to start by telling you what it is not. Contrary to what you may have heard from some economists, the mission of the corporation is not to maximize its market value, or its total market capitalization. Instead, the aim of corporate management should be to maximize the dollar amount by which the company's market value exceeds the capital supplied by the firm's investors—hence, the name *market value added*, or MVA.

Although this is a bit of an oversimplification, MVA is essentially the difference between a company's current market value, as determined by its stock price, and its "economic book value." A company's economic book value can be thought of as the amount of capital that shareholders (and, in the technically more correct version of EVA, lenders and all the other capital providers) have committed to the firm throughout its existence, including earnings that have been retained within the business.

To illustrate the calculation of MVA, let's take the case of General Electric, which was the top U.S. performer at the end of 1994. The total market value of GE's debt and equity at the time was $101 billion. And since the *adjusted* book value of that capital (and I will describe some of the adjustments in a moment) was only $46 billion, GE's market value *added* amounted to $55 billion. Coca Cola, which ranked number two that year, had only $61 billion in market value. But since Coke's management had achieved that valuation with just $8 billion of investor capital, its MVA was $53 billion, or only $2 billion less than GE's. (And I might add that, at the end of 1995, our results put Coca Cola in first place, $10 billion ahead of General Electric.)

But, to see why total market capitalization is a misleading indicator of success, let's now look at IBM at the same time. At the end of 1994, when IBM's shares were trading at $48 (since then, of course, the price has more than doubled), IBM's total market value was $52 billion, or $17 billion *below* its adjusted book value of $69 billion. Those people who are interested only in market value or size might say that IBM is not doing so bad; after all, it's only $9 billion behind Coca Cola. But that would have missed the point. The point is that IBM's investors put in $69 billion, and the market says that investment is now worth only $52 billion. Before Lou Gerstner came on board, IBM's management succeeded in destroying $17 billion—and actually much more, given the premium value the company once commanded.

Now, the calculation of MVA is not quite as simple as it sounds. Calculating a firm's economic book value, in particular, requires a number of adjustments that I will just mention briefly. At Stern Stewart, for example, we do not use pooling accounting for acquisitions; all acquisitions are treated as purchases—that is, as if they involved outlays of cash. Further unlike the accountants, we do not write off the goodwill that arises from purchase acquisitions of companies for amounts greater than their book value. That goodwill stays on the balance sheet more or less indefinitely, unless there is a real decline of economic value. As an example of another adjustment to conventional accounting statements, we also add back the balance sheet provision for deferred taxes to book equity, because it represents a reserve of cash on which the firm is expected to earn an adequate return. And there are a variety of other adjustments

that can be made to get a better estimate of how much investor capital is really tied up in a firm.

Corporate balance sheets, you see, are really designed for creditors; they are meant to provide an estimate not of going-concern value, but of the value of the firm *in the event of liquidation*. Take the case of research and development. The accountants write off 100% of R&D in the year it occurs, which distorts conventional accounting statements in two ways: it understates the economic earnings of the company (because R&D is expected to have a payoff down the road) and it understates the amount of capital contributed by investors. For this reason, we recommend to our pharmaceutical company clients that they not expense but instead capitalize R&D—that is, put a large portion of it on the balance sheet and add it back to the income statement—and then write it off over a period of time that reflects the useful economic life of the investment. For Coca Cola and other consumer products companies, we suggest doing the same with advertising and promotion. We put that on the balance sheet and write if off, though more quickly, of course, than research and development.

I should also mention that MVA is the measure we use for the the the Stern Stewart Performance 1000 ranking that has been published in *Fortune* Magazine in each of the past four years. This last year we also put together a Stern Stewart ranking of the largest 500 U.K. industrial companies that was run in the Sunday *Financial Times*. In fact, we have now performed MVA rankings for the public companies in a total of eleven countries around the world. The two most recent examples are the performance rankings for Mexico and Canada that will be published in the next few months.

EVA: The Best Internal Performance Measure

So, if we can calculate MVA, why do we need EVA at all? There are a number of reasons. MVA, for starters, cannot be calculated for privately held firms or non-profits because they do not have traded shares. And, even for most large publicly traded companies, MVA is a useful performance measure only at the very top of the organization, at the level of the consolidated firm. As you move down into the individual units, there is no measure of MVA (unless some of the firm's units are also publicly traded).

So the challenge is this: How can we measure the efficiency of an organization that ultimately leads to improving MVA? Or, to put the matter more directly, how does a company increase its MVA?

The short answer is, by increasing its economic value added, or EVA. EVA is the *internal* measure of year-to-year corporate operating performance that best reflects the success of companies in adding value to their shareholders' investment. As such, EVA is strongly related to both the level of MVA at any given time and to changes in MVA over time. EVA is the "residual income" left over from operating profits after the cost of capital has been subtracted. So, for example, a firm with a 10% cost of capital that earns $20 million on $100 million of net assets would have an EVA of $10 million. To the extent a company's EVA is greater than zero, the firm is creating value for its shareholders.

EVA can also be thought of as a breaking down into "annual installments," if you will, of the multi-year Net Present Value that is calculated by using the standard discounted cash flow capital budgeting technique. (Technically speaking, MVA is equal to the present value of all future EVAs.) Like NPV, EVA measures the degree to which a firm is successful in earning rates of return that exceed its cost of capital. But EVA is a more useful all-purpose corporate tool than NPV or DCF, even though both methods properly applied give you the same answer over an extended period of time.

We have done a number of studies to see which measures of performance are most closely linked *not* with market value, but with market value added—this *premium* value that's being created by management. Measures like earnings, earnings per share, and earnings growth all have some trivial relationship to MVA. When you bring in the balance sheet as well as the income statement—with measures such as ROE and return on net assets, or RONA—the significance of the relationship improves a great deal. But the correlation is not anywhere near as strong as what happens when you use EVA. And one reason for the greater strength of that correlation is that EVA, unlike ROE or RONA, corrects for accounting distortions in GAAP income statements and balance sheets, and it specifies a minimum or required rate of return that must be earned on capital employed. To have a *positive* EVA, your rate of return on capital or net assets *must* exceed the required rate of return.

I'd like to describe very briefly what happens when you use EVA as a measurement device instead of more conventional measures. A senior manager recently asked me, "Why can't I use just ROE or RONA as a basis for evaluating and rewarding my people?" I said, "You shouldn't do that, for two reasons: One, if a company or a division is currently earning substandard returns, managers can increase ROE simply by taking projects with higher, but still inadequate returns. In this case, you would actually be rewarding managers for reducing shareholder value and further reducing MVA."

At the other extreme, consider a company with a 12% cost of capital that earns a 25% ROE. In such cases, managers might be discouraged from taking on *all value-increasing* projects with expected returns below 25% because that will lower their *average* ROE. For that reason, the firm could be passing up value-adding investment opportunities.

Neither of these distortions of corporate investment incentives occurs under an EVA framework. In an EVA system, you improve EVA as long as you take on new projects where the rate of return on net assets exceeds the threshold.

In fact, there are three different ways to increase EVA. The first, as just mentioned, is to grow the business by taking on new investments that promise to earn more than the cost of capital. The second way to improve EVA is by not growing the business, but improving efficiency and so increasing returns on existing capital. And the third way is by getting rid of those parts of your business that offer no promise for improvement. EVA encourages managers to engage in a periodic culling of their businesses, discouraging them from wasting more time and money on clear losers.

Conventional corporate reward systems often do not encourage managers to take such steps. By making the lion's share of managerial compensation take the form of wages and wage-related items, such compensation plans lead managers to maximize not EVA or shareholder value, but rather their size or market share. So the question is: To what extent can we change this kind of behavior that encourages size or empire-building at the expense of profitability? You will not succeed in changing behavior simply by changing corporate performance objectives without also changing the compensation scheme. As I said earlier, if you set

the performance objective with EVA over here, and you set the incentive compensation on some other basis over there, all your people will bow down to the performance objective and then march off in whatever direction the incentive structure calls for.

So, what do you need to do? Without going into great detail at this point, let me just say that there are four properties for any successful incentive compensation system. If you don't have these four properties, your plan won't work.

First, you need objectivity, not subjectivity. Most corporate bonus plans set targets based on negotiations between senior people and their juniors. The result is that the juniors have a tremendous incentive to "low ball" their budgets—because their bonus depends just on beating the budget (though not by too much, because that casts doubt on their credibility in setting the budget in the first place). Instead of stimulating managers to stretch, negotiated budgets reward managers for their success in carving out a larger share of the existing pie for themselves, often at the expense of the shareholders.

The second essential quality of an effective compensation plan is simplicity. Incentive compensation should be carried down into the organization at least as far as the level of middle management. And, in fact, many of our clients are extending the plan to cover all salaried employees. Using something we call "EVA drivers," EVA can in some cases be calculated all the way down to the shop floor. The farther down you go, in my opinion, the more dramatic and durable the benefits seem to be. (It is for this reason, by the way, that an EVA plan is potentially far more effective than the stock options that are given out in many U.S. companies. Such programs make no sense to me at all. They may work at the level of the CEO—and perhaps for a few people who report to that person—but below that level they have almost no motivational value. Stock options are, in most cases, give-away programs.)

Third, the plan has got to be significant. That means that the bonus potentials that come from improving EVA have to be large enough to affect people's behavior.

Fourth, the plan must be honored; it must not be subject to *ex post* adjustments. This means that if the board of directors and senior management find some employees doing *very* well and then *very, very* well, they must resist the inclination to pull the rug out from underneath them and change the rules. We have to permit people to do very well, *provided* the shareholders are also doing very well.

There are also three other distinctive features of a Stern Stewart incentive compensation program. One is that there are no caps on the upside. The more EVA people produce, the greater their reward, with no limitation on the size of the bonus awards.

At the same time, as I said earlier, our system has a hold-back or bonus bank feature. To illustrate, we typically recommend to companies that they hold hostage as much as two-thirds of declared bonuses tied to EVA. And managers will lose the two-thirds held hostage if they don't at least maintain the level of performance that caused the declaration of the bonus in the first place.

The consequence of this bonus bank feature is to lengthen the managerial decision-making horizon beyond one year. It's very important to think of this as an ongoing cycle of value creation with one-third payable now, two-thirds later. For a successful manager under this plan, each new year brings steadily increasing payouts, new declarations, and new hold-backs. And if you do the calculations the way

we do them, it takes you about six years to get 90% of your bonus declarations fully paid out.

We also have an unusual stock option program. Without going into too much detail, managers are asked to purchase stock options with a part of each year's bonus payments. What makes these options unusual is that they have an exercise price that is adjusted each year for the level of the broad stock market or, if management chooses, an industry group of the firm's primary competitors. If the S&P 500 or industry composite goes up by 10% in a given year, then the exercise price goes up by 10%. This way, shareholders have to get their rewards *before* the managers participate in any gains.

But consider also what happens if the market or industry goes down, even while the firm—or some parts of it—continues to churn out positive EVA. In those circumstances, the EVA bonuses can be used to buy options at a lower price, thus insulating high-performance operating managers from adverse industry or market events beyond their control. If a company's stock price drops because of uncontrollable market or industry factors, those people who are still creating EVA inside the firm will get their reward by being allowed to buy options with a lower exercise price.

So those are the major issues of corporate performance measurement as I see them. I'm interested not just in the performance measurement itself, but in how it motivates people to behave differently. Talking about increasing shareholder value and setting the right corporate objectives are necessary but not sufficient conditions for corporate success. Managerial incentives must also be changed along with the goals to make the system work.

Let me also mention that the amount of time it typically takes to

implement an EVA system, even in very large companies, runs between nine months and a year. This tells me that people inside organizations can adapt to changes. We have special work groups that we send out to our clients, and the mission of our people is to educate our client companies' trainers so that they can in turn show the company's managers and employees how this entire system works. It has been a very interesting and edifying experience to see the resulting changes in organizational behavior.

And let me just close with a brief story. One of our clients is among the largest companies in Singapore. But, before we were hired for the assignment, the chief executive officer of the firm said to me, "We don't know if we should adopt your EVA model, with its emphasis on capital efficiency, or the Japanese model, with its emphasis on growth and market share. What would you do in my position?" I said to him, "I am not going to answer your question. I do not pretend to be able to change the culture of a country. My aim is more modest: I am simply trying to improve the effectiveness of private decision-making. I am trying to get people to act as if they actually own what they do. The most motivated people in your firm are likely to be the sales force, because they often get paid mainly on commission. They get a percentage of what they do. I want to give the rest of your employees the same thing—not a percentage of turnover, but a percentage of the discretionary value that they create."

Thank you very much.

KIM: Thank you, Mr. Stern. That brings to an end the first half of our symposium. After a short break, we will hear from three senior financial executives who will discuss their corporate experiences with EVA.

EVA at Eastman Chemical

KIM: The first of our next three speakers is Mr. Virgil Stephens, who is the Senior Vice President and Chief Financial Officer of Eastman Chemical Company. Following the company's spin-off from Eastman Kodak in 1994, Mr. Stephens has helped Eastman Chemical to gain notable recognition in the U.S. investment community, in part due to the company's active and successful implementation of EVA.

STEPHENS: I am honored to be here to speak to you today. I would like to thank the sponsor of this symposium, the Mitsui Life Financial Research Center, for inviting me.

We at Eastman have found the concepts of economic value added, or EVA, to be very useful in evaluating our performance and in determining which opportunities have the best potential to add value to our company. But before I tell you about our EVA journey, I would first like to tell you a little bit about Eastman Chemical Company.

Eastman is a global company with 1995 sales of $5 billion. We manufacture a wide range of chemicals, plastics, and fibers that our customers in turn use in producing thousands of consumer products. As Professor Kim pointed out, prior to 1994 we were a division of Eastman Kodak Company. But, at the beginning of 1994, we were spun off from Kodak and are now a separate, independent, publicly held company.

Eastman Chemical is the world leader in plastics for PET bottles, a major supplier of cellulose acetate fiber, and a leading supplier of raw materials for the coatings industry. We also make many specialty chemicals and plastics. Our products are in many items that you use everyday— in your foods, in your toothbrush handles, in the paint on your home, and in automobile parts, electronic

components, packaging, cigarette filters, and many others. Moreover, Eastman has had a presence in Japan since 1983. Today we have a sales office here in Tokyo, and a technical service center and research and development office in Osaka.

Why is EVA important to Eastman? You have to be careful about what you measure in large organizations, because what gets measured gets managed. Now I know Japanese companies are experts in quality management tools and measurements. Eastman is the only major chemical company to win the United States Malcolm Baldridge National Quality Award, an award that is comparable to your prestigious Deming Prize. As a quality award-winning company, we at Eastman realize you simply must measure anything you deem important. So, it is important that you get the right measure.

EVA has been the result of an evolution of thinking that has taken place over the past 40 years or so at Eastman. Years ago I suspect that when people wanted to know how well they were doing, they simply looked at the quantity of products that they sold as a primary indication of performance. How many tons of products have we shipped today versus last year?

But, as the number and kind of products produced by the company increased over time, it became apparent that tons of product shipped was not a good measure. A ton of one product was not necessarily worth the same as one ton of another product. So then sales revenue, along with market share, became the most important measures of how well we were performing.

But, when it became apparent that just sales revenue and market share were not by themselves sufficient to represent performance, the focus turned to accounting earnings. But

there turned out to be a problem with earnings, too. If you wanted higher earnings, all you had to do was pour more capital investment into the company. And, as Professor Wakasugi and Mr. Stern have just finished pointing out, too much investment can be equally effective in destroying shareholder value as too little investment.

So, we at Eastman have experienced a natural progression in our performance measures that has brought us to where we are now. Today, we believe that the best measure of how well we are performing is economic value added, or EVA.

At Eastman, moreover, every person in the company is being exposed to EVA concepts. For example, everyone is taught how we calculate EVA. There are two ways of doing the calculation, both of which give you the same answer. One way is to subtract taxes from the operating profits and arrive at net operating profit after taxes, or NOPAT. Then you subtract the company's charge for capital from NOPAT to get the EVA.

To illustrate this calculation, in 1995 Eastman's pre-tax operating profit was some $978 million. Subtracting taxes of $370 million left us with a NOPAT of $608 million. From that $608 million we next subtracted a capital charge of $262 million (our 10% weighted average cost of capital multiplied by our $2.62 billion of total debt and equity), which left us with an EVA of $346 million.

Another way to calculate EVA is to take the difference between our return on capital (which in 1995 was 23.2%) and the cost of capital (10%), and then multiply that 13.2% by our $2.6 billion of total capital. Doing it this way you come to the same answer, $346 million. Either calculation is straightforward and fairly simple— and that is a big part of the appeal of EVA. Because the calculation is so straightforward, it is easy for most people in the company to understand. And, in fact, we want *all* of our people to be able to pick up a financial statement and calculate our EVA.

The Uses of EVA

Now that we have looked at how we calculate EVA, let me describe how we apply the concept in our business.

First of all, EVA is the primary report card for each of our ten major business units that we produce each quarter. The EVA numbers provided in these reports tell us which businesses are creating value and how much, and which business units, if any, are reducing value. And we don't look just at the absolute numbers, we examine the trend over time to see if progress is being made. We look at whether our businesses with negative EVA are making improvement and moving toward the positive side—and whether those on the positive side are at least sustaining their levels of EVA. These quarterly EVA reports, incidentally, are reviewed not only by a management committee, but also by the Board of Directors of the company.

Another use of EVA at Eastman is as the basis for incentive bonuses for all of our 17,500 employees around the world. All employees have 5% of their pay "at risk." This means they take an initial 5% pay cut, but can earn back that 5% plus a bonus that is based on the size of the spread between our company-wide return on capital and our cost of capital. This payout for all 17,500 employees can vary from zero to as much as 30% of annual salary.

In 1995, for example, we had a very good year, and all our employees received the top award of 30%. The first 5% of that 30% goes automatically into an employee stock ownership plan, thus making all employees shareholders of Eastman.

B y giving managers and employees incentives to use capital and assets as efficiently as possible, we find that we no longer have to dictate decision-making from the top. Although many companies have instructed all their businesses to reduce inventories, our experience under EVA has shown us that some of our businesses find that the best way to increase their value is to make sure they never deplete their inventory. Our corporate charge to the business units is simply to grow EVA. How they do so depends on their strategy and their plans.

Virgil Stephens

Tying the EVA measure to employees' compensation and making them shareholders in the company have been important steps in educating our employees. You can imagine the increase in the level of interest when employees have this kind of earnings potential. If you could overhear the conversations that now take place in our company laboratories, on the plant floor, in offices, you would often hear lively discussions about how certain decisions or practices are expected to affect Eastman's return on capital.

For our 600 or so higher-level managers, we use the absolute dollars of EVA earned by the *entire company* as the basis for incentive pay. These managers have much more than 5% of their pay at risk; indeed, our most senior managers have as much as 40% of their pay at risk. And, last year, the variable pay at Eastman for the senior management turned out to be greater than the fixed pay.

EVA is also an important tool for analyzing our investment and dives-

titure opportunities. For example, we recently acquired two small companies. Our analysis of Eastman's ability to create value with those companies in terms of EVA was a major factor in our decisions to make those acquisitions. Likewise, we recently divested ourselves of three businesses. Those businesses were not earning the cost of capital and were not likely to do so anytime in the foreseeable future. So our management team determined that the capital that those businesses were requiring could be put to much better use in other investments.

Now, what are the potential drawbacks of using EVA in your company? First, let me point out that when I say "drawbacks," I really mean "concerns" or "cautions." When properly used, there are no serious drawbacks, nothing that should keep you from using EVA.

One word of caution is that, if misunderstood or used improperly, EVA can create an excessively short-term focus—similar to what happens if you look at year-to-year profits or cash flow. Even in an EVA system, if you really wanted to make one year's numbers look good, you would be tempted to neglect such things as training for your employees or maintaining your equipment. Of course, if you neglect those things very long you won't have much of a company left. So you must discipline yourself, and provide the appropriate incentives to make these types of investments for long-term success.

EVA may also not be the best measure to use in evaluating a start-up or new business. In the first years of such businesses, you are bound to be investing more than you are getting out of them. So what you want to look for with new businesses is improvement over time. You want to set up an agreed-upon timetable with the operating manager that will allow you to monitor the progress of the business in creating enough value to make up for the first lean years.

Now, let me come back to the benefits Eastman has experienced by using EVA.

First of all, EVA has changed the environment in which we make management decisions. By giving managers and employees incentives to use capital and assets as efficiently as possible, we find that we no longer have to dictate decision-making from the top of the organization. And the greater decentralization of decision-making allowed by EVA has in turn increased our flexibility in ways that can add value.

Let me offer an example. Given the recent popularity of "just-in-time" inventory systems, many companies have instructed all their businesses to reduce their inventories. Our experience under EVA, however, has shown us that some businesses may find that the best way to increase EVA is to make sure they never deplete their inventory; and so they may choose to *increase* their capital investment in inventory. Others of our businesses have found just the opposite—that the best way to increase their EVA is by reducing capital invested in inventory.

The point of my story is this: The optimal decision may differ from business to business, and the best trade-offs are likely to be made where the greatest knowledge exists. In our case, a blanket corporate-wide decision to reduce inventories would probably have ended up reducing overall value. Our corporate charge to the business units is simply to grow EVA. How they do so depends on *their* strategy and *their* plans.

A second important benefit of EVA is that it has changed the behavior of our managers and employees in important ways—and at all levels of the company. We have more people thinking about return on capital in their decision-making process than we have ever had before. And EVA has been critical in aligning employee interests with those of our outside shareholders. Our employees now understand very clearly that if Eastman creates value for shareholders outside the company, those who are shareowners inside the company will share in the rewards. EVA has been integrated into the company's overall metric system so that everyone can tie into it.

Thank you.

KIM: Thank you very much Mr. Stephens. Our next speaker is Mr. Toru Mochizuki, Director and Vice President of Coca-Cola Japan. Mr. Mochizuki is a life-long employee of Coca-Cola and has had operating experience in both Japan and the United States, where he worked in the finance division. Besides describing Coca-Cola's successful experience with EVA, he will also discuss some of issues involved in internal training programs.

EVA at Coca-Cola Japan

MOCHIZUKI: Thank you, Professor Kim. I have been working for a very long time with Coca-Cola Japan. We are a fully owned subsidiary of the Coca-Cola Company, and what I am about to say reflects the thinking of not only Coca-Cola Japan, but the entire Coca-Cola Company.

Coca-Cola Company is widely regarded as the first company to use the concept of EVA. In our company, all major decision-making is guided by EVA. According to a recent *Fortune* Magazine article, Coca-Cola is also the "most admired" company in the United States. I for one believe that these two distinctions are not wholly unrelated.

But let me be a little bit more specific. The people working for the Coca-Cola Company have a very clear-cut mission. In February of 1994, the Coca-Cola Company issued a statement to all of its employees that was entitled, "Our Mission and Commitment." Under the title was written the following words: "*We exist to create value for our shareowners on a long term basis by building a business that enhances the Coca-Cola Company's trademark.*"

The key insight of EVA is that, to create value for our shareholders, the company must generate returns in excess of the cost of capital in all of the business segments. But this does not mean that we take a short-term view of profitability. While we pay close attention to current EVA, we also look at all our businesses over a long-term time horizon as well. Our financial goal is to increase our EVA steadily over time.

My definition of EVA, I should start by pointing out, is a little different from that of the previous speakers. At Coca-Cola we refer to net operating income minus capital charges as "economic profit." EVA, in our definition, is the period-by-period *increase* in economic profit. So, what we mean by EVA is roughly equivalent to what Mr. Stern called the "improvement" or year-to-year increase in EVA.

And we at Coca-Cola have worked very hard to increase our economic profit. For example, in 1981 Coca-Cola's economic profit was just under $100 million. Thirteen years later, in 1994, we were able to achieve an economic profit of $2 billion. So, over this 13-year period, our annual average growth in economic profit was 26%. During the same period, our stock price increased from $2.90 (adjusted for splits) in 1981 to $51.50 at the end of 1994, for an annual rate of increase of 25%. (Moreover, in the past 16 months, our stock price has risen another 60% to over $80, accompanied by a large further increase in economic profit.) So, judging from our case alone, EVA and stock prices appear to be highly correlated. To create economic profit and to increase EVA are the means by which we create additional shareholder value.

At the Coca-Cola Company we also have a "Share-owner Value Model" that shows how various "drivers" of performance contribute to higher economic profit. According to this model, there are three principal ways of increasing shareowner's value. One is by maximizing the rate of return in existing businesses, say, through increases in operating efficiency. The second is by continuously reinvesting in both existing businesses and promising new opportunities. The third is by minimizing our cost of capital.

Let me say a little more about each of these three factors. The first is fairly self-explanatory. It says that existing operations should be run as efficiently as possible so as to maximize the firm's investment on its capital currently in place. The second guides the firm's investment policy; it says by all means reinvest in the business, or

invest in new businesses, but only when the investments are expected to generate returns at least equal to the cost of capital. The second rule also tells us to find ways to reduce operating capital—by eliminating assets, if necessary, that do not meet the cost-of-capital standard. And the third rule instructs us to manage our capital structure—in particular, by using dividends and share repurchases to pay out excess cash and capital—so as to minimize our cost of capital.

Let me illustrate our investment rule with an example. Last year, the Coca-Cola National Sales Company of Japan was established through an investment by each of the 17 independent Coca-Cola bottlers in Japan. (Nine of these independent Coca Cola bottlers, by the way, are publicly traded companies.) The Japanese market is changing very rapidly, and we came up with the idea of a national sales company to improve the ability of our bottling company partners to respond to an environment of increasing change. We have also invested heavily in vending machines, which has also contributed greatly to the success of our bottlers.

Like most companies, we focus on increasing sales volume and market share as a means of increasing profitability. But we also pay close attention to the efficiency of business operations. And the focus on EVA encourages us to eliminate underutilized assets and excess capital whenever possible. As one example of this rationalization process, over the past four years Coca-Cola Japan has consolidated three bottling plants into one and, in so doing, substantially reduced fixed costs.

The reduction of operating capital can also be achieved through better inventory control. With the aid of computers, we have developed an advanced inventory management system that not only controls our inven-

tory, but provides valuable marketing information as well. And, as we approach the year 2000, we are continuing to invest heavily in upgrading this and other information systems.

Implementing EVA

Now, having explained some of the efforts we have been making to increase EVA, let me talk briefly about what is involved in translating the theory behind an EVA system into effective changes in corporate actions and employee behavior. The key to the power of EVA to produce results is its ability to change the mindset of the employees. It is a question of getting the most out of the company's *human* resources.

At Coca-Cola, we have extensive employee training programs. For non-financial managers unfamiliar with accounting and finance, we have a two-day intensive course covering basic principles of financial statement analysis and providing instruction in how to apply EVA in day-to-day operation. As is likely true of most companies, marketing and technical people seem to have an aversion to accounting or financial matters. But we feel that all of the people connected to the Coca-Cola Company must incorporate EVA into their daily activities. And this is the purpose of the training program.

For newly hired finance staff, we also have a more specialized three-to-four-day program focusing on EVA. And, in accordance with the concept of cross-functional teams, we have also redesigned our organizational structure in ways that spread accounting and financial expertise throughout the company. The responsibility and role of these financial people is to help the marketing and operating people in implementing EVA. As a result of this move to cross-functional teams, our marketing and other non-

Competitive changes are forcing all companies, including Japanese companies, to establish pay-for-performance incentive plans. The seniority system has existed in Japan for many years. But it is my view that those companies that continue to adhere to that system will lose out to their competitors. To be rewarded for one's performance is not only an important source of motivation, it is also the fairest way—and most people recognize this. If it is not that way in Japan, it should be that way.

Toru Mochizuki

finance people have become much more interested in and knowledgeable about the balance sheet, inventory management, and operating efficiency. In short, a greater EVA awareness seems to be spreading throughout the company.

One major reason why our training sessions are so effective is because our managers and employees know that their performance evaluations and bonuses will be determined in large part by EVA. At the beginning of every year, each of Coca-Cola's business units set performance objectives expressed in terms of EVA. And it's not only the business units that set goals, but also individual departments within those units, and individual managers within the departments. For middle managers and above, EVA is a major factor in determining incentive bonuses. But it is not the only factor. In Coca-Cola Japan, for example, we are rewarded for increased sales volume and increased net profit as well as increased EVA.

And let me offer one final comment in closing. In yesterday's newspaper, I saw an article saying that there is now a movement in the U.S. away from an exclusive focus on shareholders and toward greater profit-sharing with employees. At Coca-Cola, we already have such a system in EVA—and we have an employees' stock ownership program as well. Both of these programs have given our employees a feeling of participating in the decision-making and success of the company. In fact, Coca-Cola may be thought of as a "Japanese" as well as a U.S. company in the sense that employees really do feel that the company—along with its commitment to increasing EVA—is their own.

Thank you very much.

KIM: Thank you, Mr. Mochizuki. Our last speaker will be Mark Newburg, Senior Managing Director and CFO of NCR Japan. Mr. Newburg was formerly employed as the CFO of AT&T Japan until the break up of AT&T. He has lived and worked in Tokyo and Hong Kong continuously since 1989. He will present AT&T's experience

with EVA, and focus particularly on the issues of implementation and financial planning.

The Case of AT&T Japan

NEWBURG: Thank you. As the final speaker, I will skip the fine points of the theory and focus in somewhat more detail on what was done at AT&T to put EVA to work. As Mr. Stern said earlier, companies have gone from nothing to having EVA in a period of nine to twelve months. This was about the amount of time it took us to install an EVA system at AT&T in 1992. In 1993, we began to report and use EVA for AT&T's worldwide organization.

As Mr. Stern also pointed out, measuring and reporting EVA for the company is one thing, but driving it down into the organization to change behavior is much more difficult. To get EVA to work effectively, you have to give the people who are making day-to-day decisions a tool they can use. You also have to allow them some time to experiment with that tool to see how it works. And, besides lots of training and support, an effective EVA system must also be linked to incentive compensation. If you don't tie compensation to EVA, people's behavior is not going to change.

Our first step in the implementation process was to set up six different implementation teams. The "deployment" team had the responsibility for overall management of the process. They met weekly to ensure that all the other five teams were on track—because once again, we were trying to implement the program in a nine-month period. In order to do that you have to stay on top of the process all the time. You have to set up clear milestones and then try very hard to meet them.

The second team was called "training and communication," and their

Mark Newburg

job was to educate managers and employees so they understand exactly what the tool is and how it can be used to improve performance. That kind of information must be communicated clearly and continuously to all levels of the organization.

The third team is the methodology team. It would be an extraordinary event to get everything right the first time out, so this team's responsibility was to continuously monitor and refine the process.

Fourth was the "tax" team, which was made up of corporate tax people. Because EVA requires that you look at your results on an after-tax basis, you need to push some knowledge about taxes down to the operating levels.

Fifth was the "compensation" team. As I said, you have to link EVA performance to compensation for an EVA system to work. Figuring out the best way to make that linkage was their responsibility.

Sixth, and finally, was the "shadowing" team. Their job is to develop systems for monthly reporting of EVA for each AT&T unit around the world.

As I mentioned, these implementation teams were set up in early 1992. In May of that year, the concept of EVA was incorporated into AT&T's planning process for the following year. (We had to incorporate the EVA implementation into the May plan of 1992 because we wanted it to have an impact on 1993 compensation.)

Beginning in June of 1992, managers of AT&T's were given an EVA tool to be used to "self-monitor" the effects of their own decisions on a day-to-day basis to see whether they were creating positive economic value. So, for approximately six months in 1992, we said, "OK, let's pretend we are now evaluating your performance based on your economic value added to the company." EVA thus became the baseline for evalu-

ating a proposal to a customer, a decision for an investment, a decision to acquire a company, or a decision to divest a company or sell a division. In short, EVA became the primary criterion for all major decision-making—and each unit was assigned someone whose only responsibility was to track this activity. Then, in 1993, after we had already been reporting EVA on a monthly basis for six months, we began linking EVA to compensation.

Each of our six implementation teams remained in place throughout 1993 to take care of questions and problems as they arose. Our training program also continued, both in the finance organization as well as for non-financial people. We had comprehensive training courses designed to communicate to our people what they have to do to be effective EVA managers. Using a spreadsheet, for example, a manager could simulate the potential effect on both EVA and more familiar performance variables of various decisions across a number

of different scenarios. That is, for each of the different scenarios and management decisions, the model would calculate EVA as well as a number of other internal measures that we also pay attention to at AT&T.

I should also mention that this management tool was supported with a 24 hour-a-day on-call EVA advisory service. As I said, we were going around the world with this implementation. And our primary targeted users, once again, were management people, not the finance team.

So, I believe that comprehensive training and support, together with a direct link to compensation, are the keys to success in using EVA. And this brings me to the compensation part of the AT&T story.

Beginning in 1993, the company announced that the AT&T performance award and merit award would be given only in those years in which the company as a whole had positive EVA results. If there was no positive EVA result, there would be no reward. If you were a member of a unit that had a very good year in terms of EVA generation, you had the opportunity to "overachieve." And since positive EVA for the entire firm was a necessary condition for any awards to take place, it was in everyone's own interest to make the best decision for the company using EVA as the measurement tool. Whether it was lower-level managers, directors, or senior managers, they all became accountable for our EVA.

So, what happened at AT&T as a result of moving to EVA and changing the compensation system? What we saw was a dramatic improvement in the condition of the balance sheet and a significant increase in cash flow. EVA prompted people to begin to think what they personally could do to add value to the organization, in no small part because doing so would result in added personal value.

In closing, I feel strongly that a successful EVA roll-out must have the following three elements: training, communication, and compensation. An EVA program must be accompanied by very detailed training; you have to devote a lot of resources to training as many people as you can. And, along with comprehensive training, you have to communicate the program to everybody over and over again, and using many different vehicles. You have to get the word out so everybody understands it, and everybody feels part of it. Finally, you have to tie the compensation to performance. For no matter how good the communication is, no matter how good the training is, it is not going to work without the reinforcement of EVA-based rewards.

EVA and Employee Welfare

KIM: Thank you, Mr. Newburg. Now we open up the discussion for a brief question-and-answer period among the panelists. And, to get this part of the discussion started, I would like to comment on a statement made by Joel Stern, and then ask him to respond.

Joel, when you were describing your experience in Singapore, you cited an executive who was attempting to choose between the EVA model and the Japanese model of corporate governance. Presumably the EVA model would mean a model that would try to maximize shareholder wealth, while the Japanese model emphasized employee welfare as its highest priority. My question for Mr. Stern is this: Are these two models mutually exclusive? Must maximizing shareholder wealth necessarily mean sacrificing employee welfare? Or can the two goals be made to co-exist and reinforce each other?

I raise the question for the following reason: By making more efficient use of capital, EVA is a system designed to increase the size of the total pie. My thinking is that the larger pie, or larger firm value, that results from increased productivity can then be divided in different ways among the different constituencies, including a larger share for employees. For example, I am pretty sure the panelists representing Coca-Cola, Eastman Chemical, and AT&T would agree that implementation of EVA designed to maximize shareholder value also ended up increasing employee welfare.

So, the point I would like to make is that the EVA model and the Japanese model are not necessarily in contradiction with each other. In fact, because of the chance it offers employees to participate in increases in company value, I would think that the EVA model could easily be adapted to the Japanese corporate culture.

STERN: I agree with your argument, and I think most micro-economists would agree with it, too. But I would also add to your comment that EVA has the power to transform a corporate culture just by changing employ-ees' attitude toward their jobs. It has been our experience that a greater sense of accountability, reinforced by monetary incentives, can do wonders for employee morale; they can truly be made to feel like partners in the enterprise.

For example, several years ago we implemented an EVA system in a state-owned enterprise outside the U.S. And when we did, I told the chief executive that he had to become the champion of the program to make it succeed. He said, "I intend to do that. But I am going to have a big problem with risk. Although our people's expected rewards are higher, a much larger percentage of their total compensation will also be put at risk. And our people have a different attitude toward risk-taking than you seem to think they have."

As things turned out, however, the employees in this state-owned enterprise outperformed everyone's expectations, including those of the senior management team. And, for this reason, I am very skeptical of the argument that EVA is culturally bound or conditioned. People everywhere will respond if given the proper training and incentives.

And let me say this: If senior managers in one nation believe that EVA may work in the U.S., but not in their own country, then there is only one logical outcome—ever larger trade barriers to protect those people who have decided that they don't want to adopt this type of process. Because, as I said earlier, companies in countries like Australia, New Zealand, Germany, and Scandinavia—and in regions like Latin America and Eastern Europe as well—are now moving in this direction.

MOCHIZUKI: I think there is suspicion about the EVA system and its possible negative effects on employees. But these concerns can be overcome by education. And when the training is combined with a proper incentive system, employee morale and participation can both be very strong. This has been our experience at Coca-Cola Japan.

STERN: Last year, I met with Mr. Goizueta, the CEO of the Coca-Cola Company, and I asked him, "What do you like best about EVA?" He said, "It has developed a winning attitude among our employees." And he went on to say, "Have you ever noticed that teams that win in sports often continue to win even beyond their initial capability because they believe they can be winners? That is what EVA has done for our people."

Finally, he said to me, "I also want you to know, Joel, that I checked with the people at Equifax here in Atlanta. They have had much the the same success with your EVA program as we have had with ours. They were good before, but now they have a culture that could be called exceptional."

Is Japan Ready for Pay-for-Performance?

KIM: In Japan and in many parts of Asia, the group is considered more important than individuals. And the culture may not be as receptive to the idea of individual bonuses based on individual initiative as it is in the United States. So if we have this resistance to merit-based individual compensation, how would you go about motivating the management and the operating people to change?

MOCHIZUKI: Before I answer that question, let me make a more general comment about managing cultural differences. Although Coca-Cola Japan is a 100% subsidiary of the U.S. company, virtually all of our managers and employees are Japanese. We have worked very hard to overcome international differences in corporate culture. Our feeling about all of our employees, whether they are Japa-

nese or expatriates, is that they must familiarize themselves with two cultures, and eventually become bilingual as well. And I don't mean to limit this to just Coca-Cola Japan and to the Japanese and American cultures. Coca-Cola's worldwide philosophy is that it is both desirable and necessary for its overseas employees to master another culture in addition to their own. And this bi-cultural approach has contributed to the company's success abroad.

But, having said that, let me also say that there is no debate inside Coca-Cola about the appropriateness or effectiveness of merit-based pay in Japan, or anywhere else for that matter. Moreover, I do not believe that EVA has been successful at Coca-Cola Japan because is it part of an American corporation. Whether we like it or not, it is the competitive changes that are taking place around us that are forcing all companies, including Japanese companies, to establish pay-for-performance incentive plans. The seniority system has existed in Japan for many years. But it is my view that those Japanese companies that continue to adhere to that system will lose out to their competitors. To be rewarded for one's performance is not only an important source of motivation, it is also the fairest way—and most people recognize this. If it is not that way in Japan, it should be that way in Japan. That is my personal view.

NEWBURG: There are a couple of comments I would make on this issue of group versus individual performance. One, an EVA system, if properly implemented, has the potential to make an organization more cohesive; it should encourage more than it discourages teamwork. To create this cohesion, we have in our company something we call "visualization stands." They are exhibits set up in the company cafeteria, and next to the vending or coffee machines, that show

everyone how we are doing compared to our EVA commitment for this year. It helps everyone understand where we are and the work that we all have to do to achieve this year's goals.

I also think the idea of individual merit pay is coming very rapidly to Japan. I think we see more and more companies setting up pay-for-performance systems. And, as I said earlier, EVA gives you a very good tool for rewarding those individuals that add value to the company.

STERN: I would like to make a number of comments on this issue. The first is that I do not view an EVA program as primarily a method for rewarding *individual* behavior. In most cases, that is not what it is designed to accomplish. There are one or two exceptions to that rule, such as in merchant banking where certain types of individual behavior are critical to the success of the company. But an EVA program is designed to have a measurement system that rewards group, and indeed company-wide, behavior.

How do we do this? In most cases, we suggest to companies that about 70% of an individual business unit's incentive award be based on the performance of that unit, with the other 30% based on the performance of other units in the firm at the same level. The reason we do that is to address two issues. One is diversification of risk. If we are not doing very well this year, we could be carried this year by somebody else and we will help them out next year or the year after. The other reason is that if you come up with a very good idea in your unit, we want you to be motivated to share that good idea with people who are quite a distance away from you. If 30% of your award is based on how everybody else is going to do, you are going to develop a communication system that enables other people to benefit from that idea.

Capturing Synergies

KIM: That comment leads nicely into my next—and final—question: Namely, how far down in the organization should you go in calculating separate EVAs? In making that decision, you must consider that there are joint costs that are being shared, and there are joint benefits. In the technical jargon, there are synergies that would be lost if the operations were run independently. And, the farther down in the organization you go, the greater is this problem of joint costs and the shared benefits.

So, my question is: How do you trade off the benefits of decentralized decision-making, and better-defined accountability and incentives, against the costs arising from the potential loss of coordination among different EVA centers? And, if you do decide to push EVA performance evaluation well down into the organization, how do you encourage people to capture potential synergies within your system?

STEPHENS: As I mentioned earlier, at Eastman we have ten different business units and we calculate EVA for each of those business units. EVA is the report card for each of our businesses, and that is what we want to see continue to grow. But, as far as the compensation system is concerned, that is determined by the performance of the *entire* company. We have found that the optimal compensation plan is to pay everyone based on the performance of the entire company.

About five years ago we experimented with a 70% total-company, 30% individual-business unit allocation. But we found that we got suboptimal behavior under that system; people were not acting in ways that allowed us to take advantage of potential synergies among our different operations. All of our businesses are in the chemical industry, and so there are lots of shared costs and potential synergies from a more integrated approach. So we went to a 100% company-wide compensation system, and that seems to work best for us.

STERN: I think that the issue Professor Kim raised is one of the most important with respect to EVA. I don't have a definitive or scientific answer for you, but I am going to tell you how we try to overcome the problem that you identified.

No two firms have the same EVA system. Each program is tailor-made to the individual company's culture, preferences, history, and the form in which they choose to do business. Every firm that works on this EVA implementation is asked by us to set up a steering committee. The steering committee includes the CEO; he is the chairman of the committe. There is a vice chairman, usually the head of human resources or the chief financial officer, and then everybody else on the committee is a senior operating executive.

Our program is thus driven by the operating side of the business. So, when issues of cross-unit coordination and synergies come up, we at Stern Stewart are not conducting the orchestra. The steering committee meets once a month over a six- to eight-month period. And, during these meetings, the operating people discuss the problems—and we listen and offer suggestions.

At these meetings, the issue of shared costs and benefits invariably comes up. By listening to their description of how their businesses interact, we help guide them in making the trade-offs and in deciding how far down in the organization to drive the measurement system.

And our recommendations will generally be based on how they *really* manage the business—as oppose to what their annual report says. When you read an annual report that says a company is in the following five businesses, the company may not be managed that way at all. Rather than being managed as five distinct product lines, the company may in fact be divided up along geographic or functional lines—and so having five different EVA performance centers based on product lines would make no sense. So, the specific design of the EVA program really comes out of this process of interaction with the steering committee.

KIM: How do you deal with such problems, Mr. Mochizuki?

MOCHIZUKI: I think better coordination of activities among business units is one of the most important challenges facing most businesses today. Activity-based costing systems, or transfer pricing, is one possible solution to the problem. Although there are often difficulties in arriving at the right measurements, the use of ABC or transfer prices can help solve some joint cost or benefit problems inside companies. But perhaps a more promising solution to this problem is greater use of cross-functional teams that I mentioned earlier. By combining the different skills and experience of people throughout the organization, companies may discover new ways of making the whole company worth more than the sum of the parts. At the very least, our compensation systems must find a way to encourage—or at least not discourage—a fairly fluid organizational structure in which numerous teams can interact and operate across the old boundaries.

In Closing

KIM: Since it has been a rather long day, let me conclude very quickly. Clearly EVA offers an important decision-making and performance evaluation criterion. It reminds managers that capital is not free, and that one of their primary responsibilities—if not indeed their main one—is to represent the interest of shareholders. In the long run, moreover, corporate employees' are likely to find that their own best interests are closely tied to those of the shareholders.

Nevertheless, the varied experiences of our panelists described to-day show that there is no single recipe for making EVA part of the management culture. The critical first step is coming to an understanding of the potential benefits of EVA and of how to translate this understanding into a consensus of purpose within the corporation. Taking this step prove to be the greatest challenge for EVA in gaining acceptance by Japanese corporations.

So, let me bring this discussion to a close by thanking our panelists for their excellent and insightful presentations. And let me say, once again, how grateful I am to President Sakata and Dean White for their support of our activities. Last but not least, I want to thank Professor Wakasugi, my fellow co-director at the Center, for all of his efforts in making this symposium a success. Thank you all very much.

---

*The editor would also like to thank Dan Ebels for his help in editing the transcript of this symposium.

Sponsored by the University of Florida and Stern Stewart & Co.

ROUNDTABLE DISCUSSION OF

CURRENT ISSUES IN COMMERCIAL BANKING:

BENNETT STEWART: Good morning, and welcome to this discussion of strategic and financial issues in commercial banking. I am Bennett Stewart, Senior Partner of Stern Stewart & Co., and I will serve as moderator. Our session will divide into two parts of roughly equal length. For the next hour or so, we will consider strategic opportunities—or new sources of value added—in commercial banking. After a short break, we will then explore how internal performance measurement and incentive compensation systems can be designed to encourage bankers to make the most of such opportunities to add value for their shareholders.

In the first half of the discussion, we will address questions like the following:

■ Changing technology and deregulation have enabled banks to provide more services to their customers in an increasingly efficient manner. What portion of your bank's value added now comes from traditional banking services like deposit-taking and lending, and what part comes from new, off-balance-sheet financial products and services? What are these relative portions likely to be five years from now?

Deregulation and technological advances are also blurring the distinc-
tion between commercial banks and other providers of financial services, while subjecting the industry to increased competition. What do you see as your organization's chief strengths, or "core competencies," in competing against nonbanks? Are these core strengths sufficiently different from those of nonbanks to base your strategy on preserving or even sharpening the distinction between banks and nonbanks? Or is this distinction likely to prove meaningless over time?

■ What trends do you see developing in retail delivery systems and distribution channels? Which of the recent innovations—ATMs, supermarket branches, Internet banking, loan machines, or telemarketing—is likely to prevail? Or will they all peacefully coexist?

■ As the industry continues to evolve, it seems clear that banks will need to become more flexible to adapt to changing circumstances. In one sense, this would seem to require more coordination and thus greater centralization of some activities to ensure that all parts of the organization move in the same direction. On the other hand, a changing environment should also increase the value of greater decision-making autonomy for and entrepreneurial behavior by bank
managers and employees. To what extent are these two demands contradictory, and how do you manage the balance between them? How do you decide which decisions and processes are to be centralized and which to be decentralized?

■ What kinds of people will your bank need to hire and develop in the years ahead? Do you perceive a need for more "specialists"—people who can master the technical aspects of specific products and thereby enable your bank to develop particular niches? Or do you see a demand for "generalists" with a broad understanding of the various banking functions and how to realize the possibilities for achieving synergies among them?

In the second part of the discussion, we will consider the import of these strategic questions for issues of internal performance measurement and evaluation, including the allocation of risk capital to different business activities and the design of incentive compensation plans. Here we will explore questions like the following:

■ The move toward fee-based businesses and the increased concern with risk management have led many banks to devote considerable effort to capital allocation and management. On what basis does your bank allo-

STRATEGIC PLANNING, PERFORMANCE MEASUREMENT, AND INCENTIVE COMPENSATION

cate economic capital to its different business activities? What are the strengths and weaknesses of the capital allocation techniques you use?

■ Has your bank made any recent changes in organizational structure and in the way it compensates people? Is your organizational structure consistent with the goals you have held out, or do you see changes in structure and performance evaluation in the near future?

■ Many regional banks are consolidating some of their activities such as small and middle market lending. This consolidation process, together with the growth of investment products, has decreased the amount of influence that the CEOs of bank subsidiaries exercise over the bank's overall earnings. What changes in performance evaluation and compensation are likely to result from this consolidation?

■ The expansion of bank product offerings to both consumers and businesses has made the management of customer relationships more challenging. One problem that arises in this context is how to promote teamwork among a changing group of product specialists. What changes in performance evaluation and compensation policies has your bank made to deal with this problem?

To discuss these and other issues, we have assembled a distinguished group of senior bank executives representing six of the largest commercial banks in the U.S. So let me now introduce our panelists—and I will do so in alphabetical order:

FRANK GENTRY
is Executive Vice President of Corporate Strategy and Planning at NationsBank.
JIM HATCH
is Senior Vice President of First Union Corporation.
CHRIS JAMES
is the William H. Dial/SunBank Professor of Finance at the University of Florida.
CHUCK NEWMAN
is Chief Financial Officer of Barnett Banks.
MIKE O'NEILL
is Chief Financial Officer of BankAmerica.
JOHN SPIEGEL
is Executive Vice President and Chief Financial Officer of SunTrust.
JOHN WESTMAN
is Senior Vice President of BancOne, with responsibility for the bank's ongoing EVA project.

We are also fortunate to have in our audience a number of bank securities analysts—including Ron Mandle of Bernstein & Co. and Chip Dickson of Smith Barney—as well as a number of money managers with strong interest in the financial services sector. I have invited these people to offer their comments during the second part of this discussion, particularly as they bear on issues like the best measures for evaluating bank operating performance and how such measures should be disclosed to the investment community. My hope in inviting such commentary is to stimulate a dialogue of sorts between our bank executives—those people that control the allocation of capital *inside* banks—and the analysts and buyside people who influence bank share prices and so affect the terms on which banks can raise *outside* capital.

Are Banks Dinosaurs?

With that as introduction, let me start by turning to our bank scholar, Chris James. Chris, as the SunBank Professor of Finance at the University of Florida, you have been a student of the banking industry for many years. About a year ago *Fortune* magazine published an article suggesting that banks are dinosaurs on the verge of extinction. What do *you* see as the future landscape for bankers and banking? Is your position about to become extinct?

JAMES: My position is *endowed*, Bennett. So whatever my concerns about the banking industry, they are not personal ones.

There is a lot of confusion about where this industry is going. Much of this confusion stems from a focus on what I'll refer to as the old "asset-based" view of commercial banking. That view basically says that a bank is an institution that collect deposits and uses those deposits to fund loans. And, if you take that narrow view of what banks are and do, then, yes, it's very clear that the industry is declining. Banks' share of total loans has fallen from over 40% in 1960 to around 25% today, and this trend is likely to continue.

But that asset-based focus misses much of the change that's going on within the industry. In particular, it completely ignores the move to off-balance-sheet or fee-based activities that has been going on for the past 15 years. And this shift away from asset-intensive activities has huge implications for both how strategy is formulated within this industry and what banks focus on in terms of maintaining and strengthening their competitive advantages. Moreover, as we will discuss later this morning, this shift in strategic focus is greatly affecting how banks assign "decision rights" within the organization—that is, whether they

decentralize or centralize various business functions—and how they measure performance and reward people.

The shortcomings of traditional measures for evaluating bank performance—especially earnings per share, but also ROA and ROE—are now becoming apparent. The problems with EPS are, of course, well-known. In banking in particular, EPS gives managers too much latitude to "manage" earnings by manipulating the loan loss provision and other reserves. And, perhaps more important—and this is true of all industries, not just banking—the use of EPS fails almost completely to hold managers accountable for their use of capital.

Measures like ROA and ROE help to overcome some of the problems with EPS by giving bankers some responsibility for the assets and capital at their disposal. But both of these measures were designed for and well-suited to the evaluation of a *funding-based* set of activities, to those activities where the amount of the banks' capital at risk could be identified with a reasonable amount of confidence.

Once bank activities began to migrate off the balance sheet, ROA and ROE started to lose much of their meaning. It becomes very difficult to measure how much of the banks' capital is actually supporting each of the individual activities. And this means that banks must now come up with new internal performance measures and incentive compensation systems—that is, a new basis for evaluating performance that does a better job of reflecting the economic reality of where banks are putting their capital at risk, and whether the rates of return they are earning on their different activities are high enough to reward their shareholders.

So, to respond to your original question, Bennett, I don't think commercial banks are going the way of

the dinosaur. The industry is, however, in the midst of tremendous changes. Though many banks will not survive into the next century, many others are "mutating," if you will, in ways that are making them more competitive. So, far from dismal, the prospects for many commercial banks are actually fairly bright. There are good reasons why bank stock prices are as high as they are today. As Sandy Rose commented recently, U.S. banks have been forced to respond to their crisis in the late '80s and early '90s by accomplishing what amounts to a "professionalization of management." And, to longtime observers of the industry like me, these changes are all pretty exciting.

STEWART: Why is the industry changing, Chris? What are the fundamental forces that are causing this change?

JAMES: Well, there are at least two major factors. Certainly changes in the regulatory environment have allowed banks to engage in lots of off-balance-sheet and non-asset-based activities that were prohibited before. That's number one. The second important factor are the changes in technology and information systems that have enabled banks to "unbundle" financial products and services that were effectively embedded in traditional deposits or loans. For example, whereas banks traditionally originated and then held their loans and mortgages until maturity, today they are just as likely to sell those loans. This unbundling allows them to specialize in origination and servicing, but at the same time to lay off their interest rate risk to the capital markets.

Toward a New Definition of Banking

STEWART: Let me turn to Frank Gentry. Frank, from your vantage point at NationsBank, how do see the industry evolving? Do you agree with Chris

Once bank activities began to migrate off the balance sheet, ROA and ROE started to lose much of their meaning. Because of the difficulty in measuring how much of the banks' capital is actually supporting each of the individual activities, banks must come up with new performance measures that do a better job of reflecting the economic reality of where banks are putting their capital at risk, and whether the rates of return they are earning on their different activities are high enough to reward their shareholders.

Christopher James

that it's primarily changes in regulation and technology that are driving changes in commercial banking?

GENTRY: Well, I agree with Chris that banks are changing greatly. But I would not put as much emphasis on the importance of regulation as a force for change. In fact, I would argue that technology and information flows have been the *primary* drivers of change, while regulatory changes have tended to lag behind. That is, the regulators, when they are not actively inhibiting change, are usually just trying to catch up with changes in business that have already taken place.

Part of the confusion about banking, though, Bennett, comes from the increasing difficulty these days in defining just what a bank is. To me, the only definition of a bank that makes any sense is *that collection of products and services that most banks end up providing*. And that collection of products and services is changing virtually every day. Certainly the relative emphasis among the various products and services is undergoing continuous change at many banks.

In the past, banks have been distinguished from other financial service companies by the fact that they accept deposits that are backed by federal insurance. And this is the way most people continue to think of banks. But, our role as insured depositories is becoming an increasingly less important part of our overall business

activity. Deposit-taking remains important in the sense that it continues to be a source of profits, but it is a shrinking source of profit. Like most of the banks represented here, we have a huge base of depositors that we are trying to "manage down" in a way that preserves the greatest income and value for our shareholders.

Unfortunately, besides being a source of profit, our status as insured depositories also gives the regulators and Congress the opportunity to treat us differently than almost any other industry. They regulate us because they need to protect the government treasury with respect to the insurance fund. Being an insured depository is thus a double-edged sword. It's the source of a nice subsidy, but it's also a ball and chain.

So, gathering deposits is no longer what commercial banks are really all about. It's not nearly as important, for example, as loan origination, risk management, and payments processing.

A Revenue Strategy: The Case of Barnett Banks

STEWART: Are banks moving more towards common strategies? Or are there a variety of strategies that can be successful? Chuck, do you want to take a stab at that question?

CHUCK NEWMAN: I think that banks today are pursuing a number of different strategies. One popular strategy is

consolidation—that is, the acquisition of other banks or financial service companies in similar or overlapping markets with the idea of reducing duplicate effort and so taking out costs. Some good examples of this are the recent mergers of Chase with Chemical and First Interstate with Wells Fargo.

In contrast, many other banks, including Barnett, are pursuing what is known as a growth or *revenue* strategy. To a much greater extent than in a consolidation strategy, a strategy aimed at achieving revenue growth must be based on developing a better understanding of your customers and markets. In the past, banks traditionally offered all products to all customers. Today, there's much greater emphasis on developing strategies based on your core competencies. And, having decided on what products your bank does the best job of providing, you can then use the new information technology to segment your customers in ways that enable you to market those products so as to maximize profits.

So, in addition to understanding more about your customers, there is considerably more emphasis on specializing in what you do best. At Barnett, for example, we have come to the conclusion that we don't have to offer every financial product and service now being offered by banks. Nor do we have to *own* every business line that we offer our customers. That is, we now feel comfortable outsourcing, or accomplishing through joint ventures, at least parts of the process of delivering a product or service that we used to perform internally. For example, we recently announced a joint venture with Bank of Boston and two equity partners to create HomeSide Lending, which is now the seventh largest mortgage servicing company in the nation. This new venture will be highly competitive in this rapidly consolidating industry where scale is essential to lowering our servicing costs per loan. We also think this venture will improve the quality of our service to our mortgage customers.

But, to return to your question, Bennett, the strategies of different banks vary greatly. And I think you'll see that the strategies of individual banks will change continuously over time. As I suggested, you will see more joint ventures in the near future. And banks like Barnett that have focused on revenue generation will continue to invest heavily in information technology to penetrate their markets *all the way down to the level of the individual customer*. The goal of such investment is to develop strong, and profitable, long-term relationships with a carefully targeted customer base.

The Case of BancOne: Centralizing the Uncommon Partnership

STEWART: John, your bank, BancOne, has had a growth-through-acquisition strategy over the years, and that seems to be changing in a number of ways. Could you give us some historical perspective on the strategy of BancOne, and on how and why that strategy is now changing?

WESTMAN: Well, I think the "why" for our recent change is that stock market analysts and investors stopped

appreciating the old strategy. The sharp drop in our P/E ratio in the past few years suggests that our old strategy has lost much of its appeal for the market.

To provide a little background, BancOne was able to grow from being a very small bank based in Columbus, Ohio (in fact, 30 years ago we were number three in Columbus) into the ninth largest bank in the country today. We were able to use our high stock price as a form of currency to acquire other banks in stock-for-stock deals. We were able to grow through acquisitions into what amounted to a "mutual fund" of banks. In implementing our concept of the "uncommon partnership," we created a highly decentralized network of some 69 separate banks and nonbanks operating in eleven different states.

For a number of years, that strategy succeeded in generating consistent earnings growth, which in turn raised our stock price to levels that would support further acquisitions purchased with our own shares. But, once we got to a certain size, it became apparent we could no longer produce sufficient earnings growth with 69 different data processing systems and 69 different customer application systems.

Our new strategy calls for internal consolidation, for centralizing certain functions such as data processing, item processing, and other "backroom" functions. Besides allowing us to capture scale economies that a number of the banks in this room have already achieved, our move toward greater centralization and coordination of some activities is also designed to promote more cross-selling of our various product lines by our different business entities. In the past, as I mentioned, the uncommon partnership represented almost total decentralization. Today we are moving toward a system that, instead of focus-

ing solely on business unit profitability, places equal if not greater emphasis on the profitability of each of our individual *product lines* as they cut across our different business units.

So, our primary focus today is on consolidating operations, rationalizing our product line, and achieving greater coordination among our different business units in marketing those products and services where we think we can be most successful in adding value.

STEWART: John, do you agree with Chuck that increased specialization is the wave of the future for banks, as opposed to banks' past inclination to be all things to all people?

WESTMAN: Well, yes and no. Most of the large commercial banks are probably offering a broader range of products and services today than ever before. But even those banks will increasingly be forced to make some choices. That is, among all those different product lines, they will be forced to increase their investment and spending in certain areas while pulling back in others.

So, yes, in one sense we should expect to see greater specialization by most banks. But, even with this kind of specialization, banks will never be just single-product companies. Much of the potential value of a commercial bank, as we have discovered at BancOne, comes precisely from our ability to offer *a range* of products and services to the same customers or in the same markets.

Let me also say that it would be nice for banks to be able to do a better job of leveraging their areas of specialization. In a number of our acquisitions, we have been able to acquire activities that were in some way or another in a leadership position in their segment of the industry. In our acquisition of Marine Bank in Illinois, for example, we gained a special capability in ACH processing—that is, in

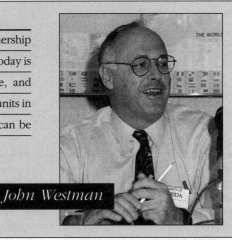

In the past, BancOne's concept of the uncommon partnership represented almost total decentralization. Our primary focus today is on consolidating operations, rationalizing our product line, and achieving greater coordination among our different business units in marketing those products and services where we think we can be most successful in adding value.

John Westman

insurance debit processing. Our acquisition in Arizona gave us a dominant position in real estate banking. Part of our plan is to leverage these highly specialized capabilities by putting them to greater use in other business units or by acquiring other operations with similar capabilities.

Strategic Focus and Core Competencies

STEWART: Well, let's focus a little more on this issue of a bank's "core competencies"—and let me turn to Mike O'Neill here. Mike, does BankAmerica's top management think in terms of core competencies, and in terms of building those core competencies?

O'NEILL: Yes, absolutely. The present-day Bank of America comes out of a tradition of Manifest Destiny. It was a big bank on the West Coast, and for a long time its main goal was to get bigger both nationally and internationally. Big was good, and bigger was better—and that approach worked pretty well for a number of years.

But, like the management of BancOne, Dave Coulter and the new management team at Bank of America have been taking a careful look at the industry, and we are now asking ourselves: Can we continue to do all the things that we have done in the past—and, more to the point, can we do them well enough to provide

acceptable returns for our shareholders? Or should we narrow our focus to just those activities that we do *exceptionally* well?

And our answer has been that we need to get more focused. We need to focus on execution rather than on expansion. So, at this stage in our development, it's really going to be execution and applying the skill set that we've got—the core competencies, as you call them—to fewer situations.

STEWART: Jim, does the top management at First Union feel the same way as Bank of America about the need for greater strategic focus? And can you tell us a little about the role of new financial products and services in First Union's strategy?

HATCH: Ten years ago, the old-line traditional banking services of deposit-taking, lending, and so forth were virtually 100% of our business at First Union. Today, the traditional activities represent 80% of our business, with the other 20% taking the form of things like off-balance sheet activities, derivatives transactions with customers, capital markets, and mutual funds. These new products and services are all beginning to grow very rapidly. And by the year 2000, I believe that the ratio of traditional to nontraditional activities will be close to 50/50. That is to say, 50% of our business will be accounted for by products and services that essentially did not exist ten years ago.

And, if you asked me for a model of what commercial banks will look like in the next century, I would hold up an organization that is essentially a hybrid between a traditional bank and a full-service brokerage and investment banking house like Merrill Lynch. If you stir up all these ingredients in a pot and pour them out, you will get a variety of financial service companies that will end up offering a very broad range of financial products and services. And, as John Westman suggested, much of the value added in these new enterprises will come from the synergies achieved by offering all these products from a single source. But, at the same time, individual financial service providers will also want to focus on building niches, on making targeted investments designed to create and leverage their really distinctive capabilities.

GENTRY: I personally don't find the distinction between traditional banking and new financial services to be very helpful. As we become less regulated, and as the technology gets better and better, banks are being allowed to make choices about what activities to emphasize. In "the bad old days" of tight regulation, the products we offered were precisely those that the government said we could offer. And if the government all of a sudden said, "You can offer a new product like an all-saver's certificate, then *all* banks offered it—immediately. There was no choice. There was no decision to make. You just did whatever the government said you could.

What I find ironic today is that so many banks are choosing to pursue essentially the same activities. For example, we all seem to be buying mortgage companies and selling corporate trusts. At some point, the participation of too many players in the same field will force banks to identify and invest heavily in just those activities where they really do have some kind of competitive advantage. As a couple of people have suggested, most large banks will probably continue to *offer* a fairly complete menu of products and services. But many of these offerings will be justified only insofar as they serve as "loss leaders" for other products. So, in this sense, I agree with Mike O'Neill's statement that banks are going to have to narrow their focus to only those things they do very well.

The New Role of R&D in Retail Banking

STEWART: Let's now direct our focus to the retail banking sector. How is that going to evolve over the next five or ten years? John, what do people at SunTrust think about this issue?
SPIEGEL: As Chris James said earlier, changes in regulation and technology have enabled banks to separate products and services that used to be combined. And Chris cited as an example the fact that many banks are no longer choosing to hold the loans they originate.

This same process of unbundling and specialization is now happening in the retail sector. To support and help guide this process of specialization, there is also a great deal of R&D now going on inside banks that is aimed at identifying the market demand for various financial products and services, and the demand for the different ways of delivering those products and services. We're seeing this now in the case of Smartcards and new types of ATM machines. And we're seeing it with kiosks and with home banking. Each of these new developments represents an opportunity for retail customers to decide how, where, and when they want to do business with banks.

Some of these new delivery systems will pay off in a big way, and some will not. Some firms will end up becoming third-party providers of these systems to the smaller banks, which means that the inability of these banks to spend huge amounts of money on technology will not mean an end to their useful life. For larger banks, though, the challenge in retail will be to invest in ways that allow them to profit from the eventual outcome of this competition among different delivery systems. And let me say that our ultimate aim is not necessarily just to preserve market share throughout all these changes. From our standpoint, making enough money to provide adequate returns for our shareholders is still finally the end of the game.
STEWART: Let's explore a bit more this issue of research and development at commercial banks. Banks, of course, are never going to look like pharmaceutical companies. But, is bank R&D spending increasing, say, as a percentage of your overall revenues? Mike, do you have any thoughts on this?
O'NEILL: R&D is not a term that bankers have historically used very much. But there's a lot of that activity going on, and most of it is focused on the retail side. After decades of stability and people saying what a wonderful business retail banking is, I think the whole equation has changed. As John just suggested, people want to be able to access banking products in a variety of locations and in a variety of ways. And it is the customers who will ultimately choose which of those channels they like best.

At this point, we at Bank of America are very reluctant to herd the consumer into one area or another. What we're really doing is studying all the various options, from telephone banking to ATMs to traditional branches to interactive banking. I don't think any of these possibilities can be ignored because they are all helping to change the landscape. Banks are investing today in these different delivery systems without really being able to do the traditional kind of capital budgeting analysis—the kind where you project the amount and timing of your expected payoffs as well as your outlays. Our investments in these areas can all be seen as providing us with "strategic options," if you will. Some of these options may prove worthless, but others are going to pay off by positioning us for the future. In other words, the payoffs from each of our investments in each of these different retail channels are all highly uncertain when considered alone. But, when we view them together as a *portfolio* of projects, we feel pretty confident about the eventual payoff.
STEWART: But, in a world of finite resources, surely you have to make choices? Are you literally going to attempt to place bets "across the board?" Or are you eventually—say, three to five years down the road—going to find yourself having to choose one or two of these channels in which to specialize? And won't your degree of astuteness—or perhaps just blind luck—in choosing the right delivery mechanisms have a major effect on the future value of your bank?
HATCH: These decisions are going to be made in large part by drilling down into our different businesses and understanding which components of the businesses are adding value and

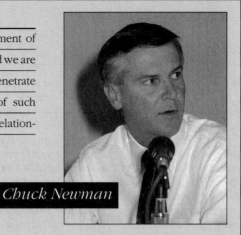

At Barnett, we have succeeded in bringing our measurement of profitability down to the level of the individual customer—and we are continuing to invest heavily in information technology to penetrate our markets all the way down to this level. The goal of such investment is to develop strong, and profitable, long-term relationships with a carefully targeted customer base.

Chuck Newman

which are not. That kind of analysis is going to drive our investment choices, our decisions to spend large amounts of money on developing new technologies, expanding businesses, or whatever.

Another important function of this R&D, however, is external or market analysis—discovering more about our customers in order to improve service and increase the profitability of our relationships. Like other banks, we are now engaged in a statistical analysis—a process of "mining" our data on our customers—that is designed to figure out which of our products and services should be targeted for which kinds of customers. This kind of analysis is expected to increase the cost-effectiveness of our marketing efforts.

So, I think there are two important objectives in banks' recent investments in information and technology. One is knowing more about the customer to exploit opportunities for cross-selling and enhanced revenues. The other is knowing more about your businesses in order to be able to fine-tune the management of the different components of the businesses. So instead of just saying, "We're going to set aside $300 million in capital appropriations this year for across-the-board allocations among all the various divisions, and then let them spend it however they wish," we are going to use our information technology to direct the process and so raise the payoff from our investment dollars.

STEWART: But, to return to my earlier question, are not banks, somewhere down the road, going to have to choose among the various technologies that are now available? Won't they have to make a fairly definite choice to focus their resources on, say, the telephone banking systems or the Internet systems?

NEWMAN: I disagree, Bennett. Bank R&D budgets have grown tremendously over the past five to 10 years, and most large banks are spreading their R&D dollars across the board to figure out which of the different delivery channels are going to win out. What choices we ultimately make among these different delivery systems will be driven by customer demand and by the profitability of the relationships.

It's amazing to me to think that as little as five or ten years ago we never thought of measuring the profitability of our relationships with individual customers. Even in those days we had more information about our customers than any other industry. We just never used it.

At Barnett, as I mentioned earlier, we have succeeded in bringing our measurement of profitability down to the level of the individual customer. What we have learned from this analysis is that we have some customers who are very profitable, and that these customers access our delivery system in a variety of different ways. To offer just one example, we put in

telebanking and automated response telephones in 1988, and we had 250,000 phone calls in that first year. Last year we had 50 million calls. Similarly, our number of monthly "hits," or requests to look at a page, on our Internet website has increased more than 500% since we launched our site in October of 1995.

So I don't think you can just make one bet on delivery systems. And in fact we are reluctant to take any one of them away from our customers. We feel that we have to participate in all of the possibilities. It may turn out that one system prevails over all the others—and you certainly want to be prepared for that possibility. But it seems more likely that several of these channels will remain in demand. And if that's the case, we will probably want to be able to offer our customers all of them.

GENTRY: What we're really trying to do is to manage down a very expensive existing infrastructure for distribution at the same time that we place bets on several different alternatives. My children wouldn't think of going into a branch, but my mother wouldn't think of doing it any other way. So, we're going to have to manage that transition very carefully so that we don't lose very attractive, very profitable customers whose only real interest in our services can be met by going to the branch.

So, it's a balancing act. It's not a matter of which bank makes the best bet one way or the other, but rather who does the best job of balancing the imperatives of reducing costs in the branch system and preserving their customer base. Over time, we will inevitably end up with a less expensive delivery system. The branch will still be part of it, but there will just be a lot fewer of them. And there's enough money in the branch system today to fund every other system you could conceive of, provided you manage the transition process wisely.

STEWART: Frank, do you think that branches will still exist and have a role ten or even 20 years down the road?

GENTRY: Yes, I do. Consider that Charles Schwab today is in the process of opening more branches. Why is Charles Schwab opening branches as a discount broker? Partly because brand is going to be very important, and brand identification and stability come in part from having signs in buildings. And, there will always be people who want to come face-to-face with a real person—whether it's across their kitchen table or in a branch—when they begin their relationships or make major changes.

STEWART: But all these services will presumably have to command a price. Do you see a price differentiation growing between the electronic channels and the personal channels over time?

GENTRY: I see pricing being refined every day so that it is more and more tailored to any particular situation. Customers are increasingly being asked to pay for the value of the individual services they are receiving—services that have been bundled together in the past. And our assessment of that value is based on large part on our marginal cost of providing that particular service.

And, let me be a little more clear about what I think is happening more generally in the industry. Five years from now, there's no question but that

the entire industry will have fewer people, less bricks and mortar, and less capital than it has today. But that doesn't mean the industry will decline in its ability to add value for its customers or its shareholders.

STEWART: Jim, what do you think about the future of retail banking?

HATCH: I agree with Frank that branches will continue to exist, and that there will be fewer of them. But the branches of the future will be different. They will look much more like marketing centers than the traditional deposit-taking centers or check-cashing centers. And this means that the types of people and skills in the branches are going to be fundamentally different.

STEWART: Do you think the locations will change?

HATCH: The locations will change because it will become more strategically important to locate where people can get in and out easily. Shopping malls, for example, are likely to be good strategic locations.

NEWMAN: That's right, if you're going to be a sales organization, you want to be where there's a heavy flow of traffic. And, for some customers, the bank branch may no longer be a destination on its own.

Branding and Relationship Banking

STEWART: Frank Gentry just mentioned the possibility of banks establishing themselves as brands. Can banks really accomplish this? And, if so, what will be the basis for establishing those brands? In an increasingly competitive marketplace, can banks really harvest value for their shareholders while investing heavily in building a brand name?

WESTMAN: Well, I think there are opportunities for branding in banking, but they are limited. Although our clients do show some degree of loy-

alty when we deliver value to them, they are also increasingly inclined to shop around for the best deal. My view is that banks should put greater emphasis on developing a strong reputation for just a handful of their specific products and services, and not necessarily for the entire organization.

STEWART: If you look at distributors of hard goods like Wal-Mart, Penney's, Sears, and Neiman-Marcus, there are obviously lots of different strategies at work. Do you see the same thing happening in banking, or is there instead likely to be a single winning strategy? Will a Wal-Mart strategy win the day?

WESTMAN: Well, let's take the case of mortgages. Some bank may offer an everyday low price for mortgages as a loss leader to get customers in the door. And if they're successful with that approach, then maybe they will succeed in establishing a brand and so become the Wal-Mart of financial services. But, to the extent that customers are going to shop any of our banks and other nonbank companies for mortgage products, I think it will be very difficult to create and leverage a brand name.

STEWART: Mike, do you feel the same way? Is it possible to make a brand out of Bank of America?

O'NEILL: First of all, there are 10,000 banks in the United States. And that alone tells me that many different strategies can be made to work. Indeed, they have been made to work.

But, when a bank has large market shares in each of a variety of related products, like most of the banks at this table, life gets more complicated. You can't walk away from something that's worked in the past as quickly as you can fund a supermarket process. If you don't have any share, it is easy to pick a segment and go for it.

The people at this table have a more complex task because we've got clients of different ages and demographics—and that includes lots of people who do their banking in a traditional way. Taking that away from them too early is a shareholder value-destroying proposition. But staying with it too long is also a shareholder value-destroying proposition. Timing is absolutely critical here. Knowing which of these approaches to push at which time is going to be the key to success for a large bank.

STEWART: When do you see that happening? When will there be enough clarity about the future that banks will be able to commit themselves to one or a few strategies?

O'NEILL: It will happen only gradually over time. But, again, I think the key to success for banks will be their ability to shift their investment gradually to the winning strategies.

STEWART: Well, I'm not sure I agree. In the merchandise retailing business, "category killers" like Home Depot and Wal-Mart have succeeded in revolutionizing their businesses by using new methods. In both of these cases, an innovative company seized an opportunity to take business from more traditional competitors. I'm not hearing the bankers here this morning acknowledge that this could be a possible development in banking. Couldn't some unknown competitor— most likely a nonbank—make a huge investment in just one of these delivery systems and end up walking away with the lion's share of the business?

O'NEILL: Well, you've certainly seen that happen in some areas. Credit cards is one area where some "category-killers," to use your term, have done pretty well. But, as a number of people have already pointed out, most banks are engaged in lots of different businesses at the same time. So, I'm not sure you can really apply your "category-killer" argument to the entire industry. There are just too many different businesses for a single competitor to dominate.

JAMES: That's right. In the retail banking business alone, there is a great variety of different products, and these differences won't lend themselves to any specific strategy across the board. And, in my view, most of the value added by commercial banks will consist precisely in their ability to offer so many related products, to take advantage of potential synergies among these different businesses.

GENTRY: What we have tended to see is someone not in the industry coming in with a new strategy that takes off in one particular business segment. But, as Mike said earlier, that's a rational strategy only if you're a new entrant into a market. In that case, you've got nothing to lose because your success will not cannibalize any of your existing products. But for large banks with market share, as Mike also pointed out, that kind of strategy may end up destroying value.

But there is certainly some truth in what you are suggesting, Bennett. One of the biggest challenges facing the large banks represented here is to figure out ways to compete with ourselves without alienating customers and destroying value. In other words, we have to be willing like Procter & Gamble to offer multiple brands or multiple approaches that overlap in some ways. But we can't do it in such a way that destroys our annuity from our traditional services. It's an annuity that, although shrinking, still represents a good part of our current value.

WESTMAN: Ben, in thinking about category killers, I think that part of our experience in working with your firm—and this is not meant to be a commercial for Stern Stewart...

STEWART: No, go ahead, John. It's okay.

WESTMAN: The experience of working with your firm has caused us gradually to come to the conclusion that there is a strong correlation between the development of category-

killers like Wal-Mart and the use of entrepreneurial incentive compensation systems. In our company and in our industry there are very few such compensation plans. The successful credit card companies, on the other hand, have put in place highly entrepreneurial incentive programs. And I think that's something we all need to consider if we would like to see some of our own businesses become a lot bigger, perhaps become category-killers in their own right. The entire banking industry may have to rethink how it attracts and rewards people.

The Threat of Microsoft

STEWART: Well, I can't help but agree with you, John. And I think we will get to the issue of compensation later in the discussion. But let me just continue with my category killer line of thought just a bit longer.

To what extent will the industry continue to unbundle its products and services? I ask the question because the more unbundling that is possible, the more categories within banks that will become vulnerable to nonbank competitors. On the other hand, if there are economies of scale or scope that make bundling more efficient than specialization, then a broader-based strategy of size and diversity will continue to be valuable. So I guess my question comes down to this: How important are size and economies of scale and scope in banking today, as opposed to the gains from focus and specialization?

NEWMAN: Scale economies are critical in some businesses, particularly in commodity-like businesses where pricing is virtually the only consideration. Take mortgage servicing, for example. Three or four years ago, we were a fairly large servicer with an $11 billion portfolio, but we felt we had to grow the portfolio to reach critical mass. Through several acquisitions, we reached $33 billion last year. Still, we saw scale getting away from us. So, we joined with Bank of Boston to form Homeside Lending, which now has $75 billion in servicing and much better potential for profitability and growth.

To give you a better sense of the increasing importance of scale in that industry, two years ago there was no single player larger than $100 billion. By June of 1995, there were two; and by the end of '95, there were five players over $100 billion.

GENTRY: Bennett, I think your category-killer argument breaks down in this case because you are trying to make banking into a single industry. It isn't; it's many industries. If you want to insist on drawing an analogy to Wal-Mart, then banking can be viewed as the distribution of *all* financial products and services, whether those products are our own or others'.

And there are lots of developments in the banking industry that are making it more competitive. Consolidation, as Chuck has suggested, is one of them. The financing of automobile dealers, for example, is quickly coming to be dominated by just a handful of players because the real source of competitive advantage in that business is information and technology.

So, I don't think the threat of category killers looms as large as you seem to think. I'm sorry we're not following your script, but I just don't think the real world is moving that way.

STEWART: Well, even I can see I'm not making much headway here. But let me try one last approach. When Microsoft proposed to acquire Intuit and its software product, Quicken, there was talk that this was putting fear in the hearts of bankers. If Microsoft ends up getting into your business sometime down the road, is that a big problem? And, thinking more broadly, what sets of industries

are converging and how does that shape your thinking, both defensively and offensively in terms of alliances and so forth? Who are your potential competitors?

O'NEILL: Well, again, I think you need to look at individual products.
STEWART: I'm talking about just retail banking right now.
O'NEILL: Oh, *only* retail. Forgive me, Bennett, but that doesn't narrow things down much for most bankers.

There's no question that technology is becoming very important. Someone in our technology group said the other day that technology in the next century is going to be what credit was in the last century. It's going to be absolutely vital to success in banking. But the question is: How quickly, and in which direction is it taking us?

So, yes, I think it's fair to say that Microsoft and Intuit do send fear into the hearts of bankers. But we are not sitting here gnashing our teeth. We are actually taking actions to deal with this threat. We have a terrific competitive advantage in many ways. We've got trust that's been established over many years. We've got convenience. And I'm not at all convinced that the world is going to move into cyberbanking from one day to the next. This is going to be gradual, and I think we've got some time—though not an eternity.

Now, as this issue relates to areas other than pure retail banking, deposit-taking, and payments, I think life gets pretty complicated. You've got the credit card business, which has some very successful nonbank competitors. You've got the mortgage business, which ten years ago was dominated by thrifts and banks and which is clearly not dominated by them anymore. Can the same thing happen to what is really the core of the banking business—that is, payments and deposit-taking? It's possible. But I don't think the threat is

nearly as great as people suggest. It is clearly, however, something that we need to keep our eye on.

Outsourcing

STEWART: Well, having failed with one analogy, let me try another—and this one comes from the computer industry. For years computer companies were characterized by vertical integration. They would build the hardware, they would provide the systems, and they would provide service. Over time, the industry has fragmented. As Andy Grove at Intel has described it, the industry has vertically "delayered." Some companies now focus on chips, others on software, and still others on just service.

Do you see banks specializing more in various aspects of the entire process? Or do you still think the full-service strategies are going to be the winners over the long run?

WESTMAN: Let me respond to that by building on Chuck's earlier comments about mortgages. It appears as if there are very wide differences in the value created by the different stages of the mortgage process, from origination to funding to servicing. And this leads me to believe that specialization has got to win out over the fully integrated provider. As Chuck was suggesting, you don't need to be able to do everything to be successful. You can actually increase your value—that is, limit your capital investment while preserving or even increasing efficiency—by entering into joint ventures or outsourcing certain activities or functions.

JAMES: How do you make the decision whether to outsource a particular activity as opposed to keeping it in-house? If you are operating in a certain business, I would think you might worry about how outsourcing might impair the relationships you've established with customers.

Although wholesale banks were pronounced dead several years ago, they are finding new ways to make money from their corporate clients. For many unrated companies, banks have been able to transform themselves into a one-stop shop for all kinds of financial products. And, if you talk to some of the investment banking houses today, they will tell you that Chemical Bank, Bank of America, and a handful of other commercial banks are their toughest competitors in parts of the corporate business.

Frank Gentry

O'NEILL: Do you have any examples of where outsourcing has impaired the relationship? Although that's a common criticism of outsourcing, we did a lot of outsourcing in a prior life of mine, and we did not find that to be a problem.

STEWART: At Continental Bank, Mike, I understand you went to the point of outsourcing the receptionists, the legal department, the data processing department, and so forth. Can you describe your experience with that?

O'NEILL: It's really quite odd when you outsource something that used to be done internally. All of a sudden these service providers actually treat you like a client (and, yes, I know that sounds tough to take). So, I have heard people express concern about losing control over quality and thus hurting relationships. But I agree with this only to the following extent: You don't want to outsource the crown jewels. For example, I don't think American Airlines would want to outsource its SABER system.

But let me also say that too many people ascribe crown-jewel status to too many activities that are effectively just commodities. The key consideration in the outsourcing decision is cost. Level of service is obviously important, but I think a given level of service can generally be duplicated by lots of different providers. So, the issue really comes down to what is the most cost-effective way of delivering the service. And my own experience

suggests that people who specialize in some particular task tend to be pretty good at it—and they know how to hold down their costs.

NEWMAN: We look at a number of things when considering outsourcing. In each case we ask ourselves: What would be the effect of outsourcing be on our customer value added and, ultimately, our shareholder value? And we have come to the conclusion that there is a potentially important difference between a vendor-client relationship and a partnership. For example, our experience with outsourcing and joint ventures suggests that joint venture partners tend to be more reliable than outside vendors. For that reason, the reliability of the outside partner is one of the things we examine carefully when considering outsourcing or other kinds of joint efforts.

Take our mortgage venture that I mentioned a moment ago. That partnership was designed to help us achieve economies of scale. Our partner in that case was a firm that had strong mortgage servicing expertise; and by partnering with them we achieved the scale that is so important in this business. But we also retained the exclusive right to market to our customers, because we don't want to outsource the relationship with the customer.

So, there's a lot of opportunities that can come from these arrangements, especially if they're set up as a

partnership of equals, and I think we'll see more of them in banking. We are also seeing collaboration among banks in their R&D efforts, which is highly unusual for the industry. For example, there are now groups of banks getting together to look at the best way to deliver over the Internet.

GENTRY: I would like to use this outsourcing issue to go back to the Microsoft threat we touched on earlier. I think the reason that some banks were quite concerned about Microsoft is that we thought that allowing someone else to provide the link with the customer was the equivalent of outsourcing management of the relationship—and, in my view, the relationship is the crown jewel of banking if there ever was one.

The concern was this. Let's say Microsoft wired your PC so that you could just click on financial services and then be presented with 25 different names and rates for bank cards, for mortgages, for credit cards, for the entire range of products. Now, if all the customer is interested in is rates, then we are all going to have a tough time competing with Microsoft.

There are only two ways I know of for banks to overcome that threat and to prevent ourselves from becoming a purely commodity business. One is to maintain the relationship so that customers think of themselves as your customers and will consider your offering first. And, in that context, let me mention that we now have a joint venture with BankAmerica and some other banks that aims to preserve our relationships with our most technologically advanced customers by giving away the software and the connection with the PC in order to give those people a direct link with our bank. The only other strategy that can prevent banking from becoming a commodity business is establishing a brand.

So, in this sense, I think the future of commercial banks rests in large part on their ability to preserve and strengthen their relationships. I would consider outsourcing anything else, but not the relationship with the customer.

STEWART: But, when you get right down to it, what is it that makes the relationship to the customer so valuable?

GENTRY: The fact that they trust you and would consider your offering first. And, as long as it's reasonably competitive, they won't shop it further.

STEWART: But how do you build that degree of trust? As Ronald Reagan used to say, "Trust, but verify." I don't trust you because I trust you. I trust you because you're doing something for me that I think nobody else can do better.

For example, let's say I can go to that computer screen and get a whole list of options and prices. This is a world that is close to the perfect information that economists dream about. In that setting, it seems very difficult to see the value of a relationship.

Today, if you want to get a mortgage, you still have to call around to five or six institutions and check the terms and rates. It's true you can hire mortgage brokers to do this. But these people are intermediaries; they essentially put together a screen of rates for you; and, of course, they will charge you a fee for this service. But there's a tremendous inefficiency in that shopping process—and, hence, there is an opportunity for gains from

streamlining the process and lowering search costs.

So, if some high tech vendors can collect, standardize, and present all this information in a simple format, then they will accomplish the disintermediation of retail banking. We've already experienced the disintermediation of wholesale banking. Will we see the disintermediation of retail banking, too? It's nice to say that you have a brand and strong customer relationships. But what will those things be based upon?

HATCH: Well, the key for banks will be knowing enough about their customers to be able to figure out what it is you ought to be offering them. The key to success will be highly selective marketing to your customer to maximize your share of his wallet, your share of his total spending on financial services and products. So, it's better use of information, greater knowledge of the customer, and a strong sales and marketing orientation that will make banks succeed in the future. In the past, we essentially just sat behind the counter and took deposits and made loans.

NEWMAN: Bennett, if you take your example to its extreme, then you don't need any stores *of any kind*. Everybody will buy everything from a catalogue. But people are not like that; they place a value on relationships, and on their dealings with other people. Many of our customers want to go into a branch and sit across from somebody—they feel most comfortable that way. And many of our customers also demonstrate the importance of our relationship with them by bringing all their business to us rather than going out and shopping for each and every product or service.

GENTRY: Nobody at this table is suggesting that you can charge a noncompetitive price and compete. But, as long as prices are in a narrow range—which I think they are bound

to be in a market as competitive as ours—there are going to be lots of people for whom convenience and a human contact matter. You mentioned mortgages. The person who can make the mortgage application process simpler, easier, and faster because they already know the customer is going to get the first look. And we have good evidence to support this. Even in direct-mail campaigns for our bank cards and other commodity-type products, we always get a higher response rate in those parts of the country where we've got NationsBank signs all over the place than in places where we don't. And that tells us that our brand is partly established.

NEWMAN: We've sent out credit cards with and without the Barnett brand name and found the same thing. That is, you get a better response from campaigns carrying your brand.

SPIEGEL: At Suntrust we have discovered that some of our most active competitors, when soliciting our customers for credit cards or mortgages, actually ask our customers, "What's the name of your bank?" The question itself suggests that there is a strong sense of relationship—that there is a covenant, if you will, between an individual and his and her bank. It suggests that we have been successful over time in convincing our customers that there is a real commitment on our part to help them when they need financial services. And, as Chuck was suggesting, there is a highly personal or human element in all this. People get a feeling of security and protection from dealing with other people.

So, maybe we really need a psychologist as well as an economist to help us predict the future of banking.

STEWART: Well, to get back to the more mundane world of the economist, I think that people's willingness to shop products will depend on the perceived costs of switching banks. And if switching costs become lower, in part because people have more information about alternatives, then these psychological factors may well become less important.

GENTRY: Bennett, you're coming at this from the perspective of someone who has no fear at all of being turned down for a loan. But, in many, many cases, people want to believe that if they need money, they can go to their bank and they'll get it. They think that because they know people at the bank, or because they've been a depositor for the last 15 years, they're more likely to get the loan. And, historically, they have not been disappointed. This is the way things have worked in the past.

Now, as we get more automated and develop more sophisticated credit-scoring methods, that may change somewhat. But the belief persists, and it's one that banks will use to their advantage.

Wholesale Banking

STEWART: Let's turn to the wholesale banking arena now. Wholesale banking has gone through a tremendous disintermediation over the past 20 years as companies have found the financial markets more willing and able to provide direct conduits for them. Commercial paper has provided a new source of very-short-term money. Mike Milken has displaced some longer-term bank loans with junk bonds, and there have been various other forms of disintermediation in the wholesale market. What do you see as being the future or the evolution of the wholesale banking industry in this country?

O'NEILL: Well, let me take that one on. When talking about "wholesale" banking, most people find it useful to distinguish between at least two major segments—large corporate and the middle market. There is considerable change going on in the whole-

sale bank market—especially in the middle market area—and things are going to continue to sort themselves out for some time.

Large corporate is clearly a tough game, and you need scale and scope to play that game. You also need to be very aware of your costs and to monitor very carefully the profitability of your various products and geographic markets—and even of individual relationships. As in most businesses, 20 percent of the relationships generally end up producing 80 percent of your profits. And, so, you've constantly got to be on the lookout for relationships that are not generating high enough returns to justify the amount of the bank's capital that is supporting the relationship. And, when you find these unprofitable relationships, you've got two choices: either find ways to make them profitable or let them go. So, attention to detail, having good information, and aggressive follow-through are all likely to be critical to success in the wholesale business.

STEWART: But, is banking to large corporates still profitable *in an economic sense*?

GENTRY: It depends on how you do it. The technological changes and resulting efficiencies in the securities market have clearly made the capital-raising process both less profitable for banks and more efficient for the companies raising capital. In fact, these efficiencies have reduced profits for all intermediaries, not just the commercial banks. And this development has been good for the customer, and good for the health of the overall economy.

But what I find particularly interesting is that although wholesale banks were pronounced dead several years ago, they are finding new ways to make money from their corporate clients. In the case of many unrated companies, for example, banks have been able to transform themselves

into a one-stop shop for all kinds of financial products. Although they may no longer need your basic loan products, today you can provide them with a bank line to back their commercial paper. You can underwrite an equity issue. You can underwrite a mezzanine debt issue. You can place their securities. If you talk to some of the investment banking houses today, they will tell you that Chemical Bank, Bank of America, and a handful of other commercial banks are their toughest competitors in parts of the corporate business. But, again, the basic corporate lending business will never be as profitable as it once was.

NEWMAN: I agree. And, although the credit side is very thin, the noncredit side can be quite profitable.

STEWART: Are you talking about risk management activities?

NEWMAN: I'm talking more about access to the payment system, cash management—those types of services.

STEWART: What about risk management products and services? Are they becoming a more important part of what banks offer to their wholesale customers?

O'NEILL: It's not becoming, Bennett. It has *become*. It is now a very important part of wholesale banking. But, unfortunately, like other product innovations, the large early profits invite imitation by competitors, which in turn leads to reductions in pricing and profits. So, although some of the more exotic or structured products can be quite profitable, plain vanilla swap activity is no longer terribly profitable. And that's essentially the challenge of wholesale banking— continuously finding new products for which you can charge premium prices.

WESTMAN: I would second Frank's comment about unrated companies. Products like mezzanine debt can really serve to anchor a relationship, especially in the middle market. This kind of product amounts to a solution that is tailored to the unique circumstances of that company. And it is through the provision of such customized solutions—and this is true of retail as well as wholesale banking—that we are going to be able to add value for our customers and make the most money. To the extent banks can succeed in making themselves into solution-oriented instead of product-oriented companies—in large part by their ability to bring a full basket of products and broad market expertise to the table—we stand a very good chance of getting the business.

O'NEILL: I too like mezzanine debt, but you've got to watch the risk-reward relationship in that game. It's easy to argue that it's very profitable. And, indeed, when you put the loan on, it *looks* very profitable. But guess what? There are more defaults on mezzanine credits than on senior debt.

So, it's a complex game and something you've got to monitor on an ongoing basis. There is no substitute for careful monitoring.

GENTRY: Yes, but mezzanine debt is one of those products that plays to our core competencies as bankers.

O'NEILL: I agree.

WESTMAN: Let me share with you one way we have found to manage the risk of our credit portfolio. We have spun off about 20 percent ownership of our mezzanine debt funds to our own officers and employees. A loan officer doing mezzanine financing at BancOne must own part of the fund as a condition of employment. So, in a sense, risk management is simplified because it becomes more entrepreneurial. It becomes very personal.

STEWART: So, John, you're saying that ultimately risk management and performance measurement and incentive compensation are all inextricably bound together. Risk management methods without the right inter-

nal performance measures and without the right incentives are not likely to work.

WESTMAN: It's much easier to manage somebody who is part owner of the business than someone who is not.

The State of Risk Management in Banks

STEWART: Have the banks represented here developed more sophisticated risk-management techniques to the point where you now feel you have what you need? Or is there still a lot of room for improvement in this area?

SPIEGEL: I've noticed that there are a number of senior regulators and examiners in the room. *And so, for you ladies and gentlemen, let me say that we are all just fine!*

More seriously, though, I think the industry's internal processes for risk management have not kept up with the challenges of some of its new products. In my opinion, the industry has a long way to go yet in developing techniques for the measurement and evaluation of risk—and for evaluating the profitability necessary to justify taking a given level of risk.

GENTRY: In the past we used to respond to our uncertainty about the risk of new products just by overpricing them. So if we were wrong, we had enough of a cushion that it would be okay. But, as the markets have become more and more competitive, we have lost most of our ability to overprice. And this means an increase in the probability that some banks somewhere are going to end up taking large losses on unfamiliar products. In so doing, those banks will demonstrate to the rest of us just what the risks are. And we will all then use this knowledge to raise our prices and otherwise do a better job of managing those risks. But then other new prod-

ucts will come along, prices will get too competitive, and the whole cycle will repeat itself.

So, in this sense, I think risk evaluation and management is a never-ending spiral. It's in large part a matter of trial and error, and of some people getting too confident and too aggressive. But we all learn from others' mistakes, and so the system improves over time.

NEWMAN: One of the things that amazed me was that a number of CFOs from banks actually met a couple of months ago to discuss these issues. We discussed questions like: What do we do to control risk in the future? What amount of capital is required for certain kinds of risk? How do you go about assigning that capital to certain activities? And how do you go about measuring something as nebulous as business or operations risk?

We typically don't have these kinds of discussions among different banks until we have to react to a problem. But, in this case, we were actually anticipating the problems. So, in this sense, I think we've come a long way. But I agree with John that we've got a long way to go.

SPIEGEL: At that meeting Chuck just mentioned, there was almost unanimous agreement that the aspects of banking that are putting us all at greatest risk are the new products and new processes. In the case of our more traditional products, we now feel that we're pretty good about our risk control and risk/reward measurement systems. But not with new products and processes. And there are so many of those today that risk management is really an important issue.

Centralization vs. Decentralization

STEWART: Let's go back to the question of centralization versus decentralization that we mentioned earlier.

John's bank, BancOne, was for years very decentralized. Now it's beginning to become more centralized. Is there a consistent pattern among banks in terms of which decisions are increasingly likely to be centralized and which are going to be decentralized?

HATCH: Banks clearly have got to get their costs down to the extent possible, and so in many instances centralization will be necessary to increase efficiency by reducing duplicate activities. In order to get paid for taking risk and providing services, we will have to centralize certain functions to get the cost down to the absolute minimum in order to be competitive.

We are currently using a performance measure called RAROC—short for Risk Adjusted Return on Capital—to evaluate the value added of each of our different businesses on a stand-alone basis in a way we never have before. And that analysis has caused us to centralize some of our decision-making by combining previously separate activities. This kind of RAROC analysis effectively forces you to think in aggregate fashion, because if the analysis is to be useful, the value of the individual components must add up to the total value of the bank. The very act of doing this kind of analysis uncovers ways of improving the coordination of all our different activities. And an obvious way to get greater coordination is to combine some activities and so centralize decision-making.

STEWART: But, are you really going to redesign your processes to make them more efficient? Or is re-engineering in banking just a euphemism for cutting costs by consolidating activities?

WESTMAN: Well, in the case of BancOne, re-engineering has meant process redesign as well as consolidation. You can talk about choosing the right strategies and executing them

well. But it also helps to be lucky. And we were very lucky to acquire the Great American Savings in Arizona, which had a branch system embedded in about 36 grocery stores. That acquisition ended up providing the impetus for a form of re-engineering that has become known throughout our organization as "BancOne Express." That redesign ended up limiting the number of transactions we would perform in these grocery store facilities and greatly reduced transaction time.

But we also took advantage of that acquisition to re-examine all of the steps that we go through to complete a transaction. In so doing, we were able to sharply reduce the time required to complete a transaction by eliminating unnecessary ones or finding other ways to manage risk in completing a transaction. As a result of those discoveries, and of implementing those changes throughout our system, we have seen about a tenfold increase in the volume going through all of our branches.

So, I think re-engineering is real; it's more than just cost-cutting. We absolutely had to get rid of a lot of our old practices and start over if we wanted real improvement.

NEWMAN: In the past five years, we have accomplished a major centralization and re-engineering of our backroom operations. In the process, we have gone from having 32 banks to just seven today. And, although you get a lot of costs out of the system from this kind of centralization, you also get a much better product.

Before we made these changes, we had 32 different individuals in 32 different banks doing essentially the same job. Now, let's assume that each of these 32 people has a special talent for some part of the job they're asked to do. By having all 32 people spreading their time and energies across all the different responsibilities of this

job, you force them to spend much of their time on some things that they don't do as well, such as regulatory paperwork. Reducing the number of banks from 32 to seven has allowed us to reassign responsibilities in ways that allow our employees to specialize in what they do best. It means, for example, that a lot of people who once spent much of their time on regulatory paperwork can spend more time out in the field and function as a more effective sales force. In the process of consolidating operations, you also find yourself discovering what are the best practices within your own company, and you can make these practices the new standard for your remaining banks.

So, we have gotten major improvements—and not only cost savings, but really a better product—from this change in organizational structure.

GENTRY: NationsBank and First Union have probably got the reputation for being the most centralized as well as the first-to-centralize of any of the large regionals. For example, we are now down to five banks nationwide because we just merged all of Virginia, Maryland, D.C., the Carolinas, Georgia, and Florida. And our experience has been much as Chuck just described it. It is really remarkable what people can do when you allow them to specialize. We not only have lower costs and better controls, but we also do some things much better than we did before.

But we did find that we had to make one major adjustment in the process. Although our local managers were freed from much of their paperwork, there was a tendency among them to continue their old practice of operating "according to the book." And this caused them to be less aggressive and innovative than we had hoped. But, for the past two years, we have been working hard on a campaign to empower our local managers to seek out

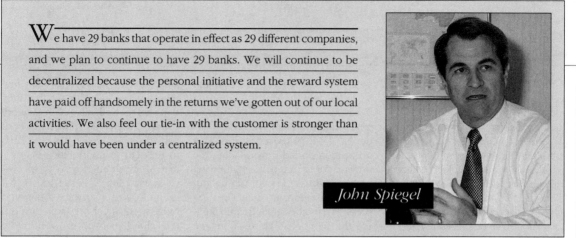

We have 29 banks that operate in effect as 29 different companies, and we plan to continue to have 29 banks. We will continue to be decentralized because the personal initiative and the reward system have paid off handsomely in the returns we've gotten out of our local activities. We also feel our tie-in with the customer is stronger than it would have been under a centralized system.

John Spiegel

continuous improvement, particularly in matters concerning the customer. Today, for example, they now have the ability to look on the screen and see whether the customer is profitable or not; and if the relationship is not adding value, they have much more latitude in deciding what course of action to take. And, as I said, the payoff from these changes has been extraordinary.

The Virtues of Decentralization: The Case of SunTrust

STEWART: John, how do you things at SunTrust?
SPIEGEL: Sun Trust is on the other end of the spectrum. We have 29 banks, and we plan to continue to have 29 banks. And they're all located in only three states: Georgia, Florida, and Tennessee. Although we have centralized a number of back-office functions, we operate in effect as 29 different companies.

So if you come to our bank here in Orlando, all the decisions with respect to your business will be made by people in the Orlando office. They decide what loans to make, and how to price them. And they determine what other services to offer. It's totally in their hands. At the same time, as I said, the back-office operations, the clearing of items and so forth, are all centralized and performed by our service company, which is owned and monitored jointly by all our banks.

Now there are two big problems with this kind of decentralization. One is lack of liquidity. There are significant costs involved in moving monies between banks. And, to the extent you can pull your enterprise together into one bank, you facilitate the movement of funds.

The other problem is decision-making. When you are a highly decentralized organization, and you want to standardize or make changes in certain practices, you have to go through a long and costly process of getting agreement from each of the 29 different decision-makers. The problem is not that you end up making the wrong decisions, but that you spend so much time in getting the buy-ins before the decisions are finally made. For example, each of our 29 banks gets to decide whether or not to deploy the technologies that have been created and developed inside the service company. As a result, a number of our banks have very little in the way of new tools and techniques, while others have the most advanced.

But we plan to continue to be decentralized because the personal initiative and the reward system have paid off handsomely in the returns we've gotten out of our local activities. We also feel our tie-in with the customer is stronger than it would otherwise have been under a centralized system.
NEWMAN: In our case, John, the CEOs of our 32 banks finally came to

us and said, "Let's consolidate." So, at Barnett, centralization wasn't something that was imposed by the holding company. It was the individual banks that initiated it.

Now, in order to provide the right incentives and reward systems, we do have a profitability measurement system. But we no longer measure the profitability of each of our different legal entities, as we did when we had 32 banks. We now focus most of our measurement efforts on determining the profitability of each line of business.

But, again, it did amaze me that here were these 32 independent CEOs coming to us and saying, "We need to consolidate and coordinate." And a big part of this had to do with reducing the burden of regulatory compliance.

Human Resources

STEWART: How does this emphasis on empowerment affect the kind of people that you need to hire? Frank, you mentioned that you took branch managers who were accustomed to relying on policy manuals and attempted to make them more entrepreneurial. But can you really take those people and change them? Can you change the culture? Or do you see a need for changing the type of person that's going to be effective in the new world of banking?
GENTRY: I think the answer to your first question is yes. We have been

very, very pleased with how people have responded to our program. It was a breath of fresh air, and in many instances it has really improved relations between headquarters and the outposts. And, though it's clear that some of our local managers are not going to make the change, most welcomed their new powers.

STEWART: But do you see hiring different kinds of people in the future?

GENTRY: I think we have been hiring differently for a long time. For example, we used to hire people primarily from schools like the University of Florida, Duke, and the University of Virginia. And if we sent them to a farming town in eastern North Carolina, we found, lo and behold, they didn't stay! So now we hire people from a much broader range of colleges with the idea that they're going to be community bankers who stay in the community.

And, in response to John's comment earlier, I don't buy the idea that a decentralized community bank will necessarily know their customer better than an out-of-state bank that's part of a holding company. The technology has gotten to be so good that if one of our customers from Florida walks into one of our branches in western North Carolina, our person in Carolina can know just as much about that customer as our person in Boca Raton. We can take their deposit just because we are one bank.

STEWART: Do you find that more and more training is required to give people the necessary skills?

GENTRY: It's actually less today. We now don't have to train so many people to do all this ridiculous paperwork. Instead we can focus most of them on how to sell.

HATCH: What we are finding, though, is that the sales skills on our retail side need work. Those people who in the past were tellers are having trouble turning themselves into the Customer Service Reps that we want them to be. Having been through one training program, many of these people are being sent back for more training. And, as Frank suggested, some people are not going to make that adjustment.

NEWMAN: We have had the same experience. It has taken us four or five years to convert our employees from primarily order-takers into effective salespeople. And I would say that about half of our people were able to make the transition. The others have been shifted into non-sales positions that make better use of their skills.

PART II: PERFORMANCE MEASUREMENT AND INCENTIVE COMPENSATION

STEWART: Welcome back to part two of this discussion. Now we are going to shift our focus from the strategic changes in banking we've just been discussing to the import of these changes for internal bank performance measurement and incentive compensation. That is, given the major changes in the opportunities for banks to add value in recent years, how do we need to think about redesigning our performance evaluation and reward systems to encourage value-adding behavior by bank managers and employees?

And let me start this part of the discussion by turning to Mike O'Neill of Bank of America. Mike, your organization has done quite a bit of work over the past couple of years in developing and refining a performance measurement system that is built around the concept of what you call *economic profit*. Your concept of economic profit, as I understand it, is quite similar to a measure that we at Stern Stewart have developed and popularized as *economic value added*, or "EVA." EVA, in brief, is an attempt to establish a more effective measure of performance in essentially two ways: Number one, it charges line managers for their business's use of capital, equity as well as debt. And number two, it eliminates accounting distortions of economic reality that can encourage managers to "game" the system—say, by manipulating reserves, or cutting back on R&D or new product promotion—in order to meet their earnings targets.

So, I am curious, Mike, as to what you have been doing with the concept of economic profit, and what your experience has been thus far in using the concept to change behavior.

Risk Measurement and RAROC at BankAmerica

O'NEILL: Well, first let me say that we are very much in midstream in this effort, and I don't want to sit before you and tell you that we've got all this figured out. Bank of America is now in the process of making a major change in the emphasis of its activities. Thanks to our prior CEO, Dick Rosenberg, we have inherited a strong franchise. As I said earlier, the primary objective over most of Bank of America's history has been to get bigger. And, as a result of our past growth, our new management team has inherited a large, complex, far-flung network that gives us real scale and scope.

In our past drive for growth, however, there were times when we did not focus as much as we should have on creating value for our shareholders. What we are attempting to do at this stage is to look at our various activities and, for each of those activities, to determine the answer to three different questions: How much risk are we taking? Are the returns providing the bank with adequate compensation for the risk? And how much value are we adding for the bank's shareholders through our participation in that business?

At Bank of America, we believe that economic profit is the performance measure that makes the most sense in terms of creating shareholder value. We also think it's very important that the same measure be used for incentive compensation and strategic planning as well as performance evaluation. For a performance measure to be effective in changing behavior, you need to reward people on the same basis that you measure performance.

Mike O'Neill

Now, although the concept of risk measurement is actually fairly simple, it often turns out to be quite difficult to put in place. One thing that I think is absolutely critical when you adopt an economic profit approach for measuring performance is to make these concepts accessible to the people that are actually out there doing the business. Finance types and statisticians love to wrestle with these issues, and their solutions can get very esoteric. And, by the time they're finished, you may have an academically pure solution to the problem you set out. But, that solution is also likely to be incomprehensible to most of the people that need to use it. So, there are some shortcuts that need to be taken—some compromises with intellectual purity that need to be made for the greater good so that people understand what it is that we're expecting of them.

Our model for measuring the risk of an activity is essentially the same as the RAROC model that Jim Hatch mentioned earlier—and it's one that is now being used by a number of the other banks represented in this room. That model says, in effect, that we will allocate capital to a business in proportion to the risk contribution of that business. So, a business that is riskier than another will have more capital allocated to it, and therefore the income that it generates must be higher in order to generate the same return on capital as the business with lower risk.

As I suggested, this is a fairly simple notion. But how does one actually measure the risk in practice?

We have broken risk down into four categories. One of the four categories is *credit risk*. The second is *country risk*, which can be viewed as a subset of credit risk. We are active in 36 countries and so the economic performance of the countries in which we operate can affect our performance. But, as it turns out, country risk accounts for a relatively small proportion of the total economic capital that we assign to most of our businesses.

Our third category is *market risk*, which is the possibility that price movements such as changes in interest rates, FX rates, or commodity prices will affect the profitability of our trading or capital markets activities. And, finally, we attempt to measure something we call *business risk*. Basically it is the risk of something going wrong that is not credit or market risk. Things like fraud, faulty controls and unauthorized trading, and failure to satisfy responsibilities as a fiduciary are all examples of business risk.

And when I say we "measure" our business risk, I use the term very loosely. While everyone recognizes that there is business risk, there is no precise way of measuring it. By contrast, it's relatively straightforward to measure credit risk and market risk. For example, in measuring credit risk

at Bank of America, we can rely on very detailed data on our credit portfolio—data that go back 10 years and so cover a couple of credit cycles. Using that data, we can calculate expected losses for each of the different rating categories in our credit portfolio.

Now, once we have measured the risk of an activity, how do we measure how much capital we allocate to it? Our stated policy is to have enough capital supporting any given activity to cover 99.97% of the *unexpected losses* in that business. We may be very confident that the losses on our credit portfolio will *average*, say, 1% per year over a long period of time. In that case, 1% represents our *expected* loss. But, in order to determine how much capital we need to support a business, we also have to know a lot about the *volatility*—or, in statistical language, about the distribution—of our potential losses. That is, how large can these losses get in any one year?

So, to recast my earlier statement, the basic idea here is to determine how much capital we need to cover our losses in all but 0.03% of the possible scenarios given our current portfolio.

STEWART: 99.97! That sounds ivory pure to me!

O'NEILL: That part is indeed ivory pure.

Now, how did we arrive at this 99.97? It's the amount of capital coverage of the probability distribution of losses that is consistent with a AA credit rating. And we are looking for the same degree of coverage and protection for all of the risks we've identified.

As I mentioned, getting good information about market risk is pretty easy. It's available externally in the form of published histories of past price movements. Estimating credit and country risk are also both fairly straightforward. But measuring business risk is tough. What you're really trying to measure here are your *unexpected* losses from a Herrstatt-type of occurrence. There's a very low probability of this kind of event occurring; but if it happens, it's Chernobyl. So it's not a risk that you can ignore. It's just very tough to measure. We have developed a number of techniques, but none of them is completely satisfying.

Using this process I've just described, then, we have quantified each of these four sources of risk for all of the bank's activities. And this in turn has produced an estimate of the total amount of economic capital that we think we need to support all of those activities. Now, some of you may find this surprising—and I believe it is somewhat serendipitous— but when we have gone through this analysis we have discovered that this estimate of our required economic capital is not significantly different from the capital that we have been told we need by the regulators. Our economic capital is somewhat lower than our regulatory capital, but not much lower as it turns out.

At the same time, however, this level of economic capital is *quite a bit* lower than the GAAP capital that we now have. So, our objective over time is to try to bring our GAAP capital and our regulatory capital more in line with the economic capital that we think we need.

Now, having said all this, let me offer one qualification. If we were absolutely sure that all the statistical analysis that we were doing was 100% accurate, we would move aggressively to reduce our Tier I capital and our GAAP capital to our economic capital. But since, as I've already told you, the measurement of business risk is very tough to do with any degree of confidence, we have decided to err on the side of conservatism and to leave a cushion. We have decided to continue to operate with our current Tier I regulatory capital of 7.3%. And that 7.3%, as I said, can be thought of as our required economic capital plus a cushion for business risk.

Now, although that 7.3% is significantly above the "well-capitalized" levels prescribed by the regulators, it is also somewhat below that of other participants in the industry. But, given the diversity of our income stream and the fact that we have a lot of goodwill that is deducted from the Tier I capital calculations (we think there's some value in that goodwill), we feel comfortable operating at 7.3%.

Beyond RAROC, or Choosing the Right Performance Measure

O'NEILL: So, that's our approach to measuring our capital requirements. Now how do we apply those measurements in making our business decisions?

Like many other banks, Bank of America over the years has used a lot of different measures to evaluate both its overall performance and that of its individual business activities. Revenues was a popular one; somebody who had generated lots of revenues was a good guy in many businesses. Other people looked at it and said, "No, revenues is wrong. It's revenues minus direct expenses—that is, it's contribution to general overhead that

matters." Return on assets, or ROA, also became popular as a measure of efficiency in employing bank assets, and it continues to be used quite extensively. And ROE, or return on equity, has also long been used to measure performance at a large number of banks.

But, as the business of banking has changed over the years, we have become increasingly dissatisfied with these traditional performance measures. And, in recent years, we have developed and put in place a performance measure called Risk Adjusted Return on Capital, or RAROC. The risk measurement method I've just finished describing provides us with the basis for allocating capital to an activity. And RAROC is simply the net income from that activity—with a few adjustments for interbank charges and expected losses—divided by the amount of supporting economic capital.

STEWART: Jim, does First Union calculate RAROC in the same way?

HATCH: Yes, it's essentially the same approach. You take each of your business units, and subtract from its revenue not only all its cash expenses, but also a cost for expected losses for the credit risk component for those businesses. Then you allocate a certain amount of capital based on the volatility and other risk components of those businesses. And, finally, you divide your adjusted measure of income by capital.

STEWART: So RAROC, then, like ROE and ROA, is a rate-of-return measure?

O'NEILL: Correct. And, for that reason, RAROC alone does not provide the best measure of performance. One cannot make the assumption that a business with a higher RAROC is adding more value than a business with a lower RAROC. To make that determination, you need to take one more step in the analysis.

STEWART: That's right. To illustrate the problem with RAROC or any rate-

Y̲ou have to be careful how you use the RAROC measure in performance evaluation. Like Bank of America, we believe that maximizing RAROC is not a useful objective, not at least for any business that has any control over its own investment spending. RAROC should instead be thought of as a tool that enables you to measure your economic profit or EVA—or what we call "SVA," or shareholder-value-added.

Jim Hatch

of-return measure, let's say you have a business unit that's earning a 25% RAROC and that has opportunities to expand that promise to earn a 20% RAROC, which is still very attractive relative to a cost of capital of, say, 15%. The problem with using RAROC as a performance measure is that it will encourage managers to reject that 20% project. In this way, an exclusive focus on RAROC can lead to corporate underinvestment—to the rejection of positive NPV projects.

O'NEILL: I agree. And that's one of the main reasons why our ultimate operating goal at Bank of America is not to maximize the RAROC of any given activity, or of the bank as a whole. It is rather to maximize economic profit. You arrive at economic profit by taking adjusted net income and then subtracting a capital charge. This way, managers are held accountable for their use of capital without destroying their incentives to pursue all value-adding projects—that is, all activities that promise to earn at least their cost of capital.

HATCH: We also feel that you have to be careful how you use the RAROC measure in performance evaluation. Like Bank of America, we believe that maximizing RAROC is not a useful objective, not at least for any business that has any control over its own investment spending. RAROC should instead be thought of as a tool that enables you to measure your economic profit or EVA—or what we call

"SVA," or shareholder-value-added. And, let me say that we have found that SVA is the best measure of corporate performance, particularly if used over a longer-time horizon of, say, three to five years.

O'NEILL: Let me make one last point on our economic profit calculation. We calculate the capital charge for each business simply by multiplying economic capital by our corporate-wide cost of capital (which we estimate to be about 12%). Now, ivory-pure academic analysis would tell us we should be assigning different costs of capital or hurdle rates for different lines of business. But this is one of those compromises with academic purity we feel justified in making. We think that we get enough management discipline in using capital just by being reasonably precise in our allocations of capital among different activities.

So, to summarize, our governing objective at Bank of America is to maximize shareholder value. And we believe that economic profit is the measure that makes the most sense in terms of creating shareholder value. Or, to put it another way, economic profit has fewer flaws than any other short-term or single-period measure of performance. What you would ideally like to reward people on is the performance of their businesses over a complete cycle. But, since we need to motivate and hold people accountable on at least a year-to-year basis,

we don't have the luxury of waiting that long. So, we use economic profit.

And, by the way, we place more emphasis on how economic profit changes from year to year than on absolute levels. This way, you not only minimize the effect of any mistakes in measuring capital, you also give your managers a level playing field, if you will. By paying people for improving economic profit or reducing economic losses, you give managers in turnaround situations the same opportunities for large bonuses that you hold out to people who run your best performers.

Let me also say that we think that it's very important that these same techniques be applied not only to historical performance measurement, but also to strategic planning and to incentive compensation. For these measures to be effective in changing behavior, you need to reward people on the same basis that you measure performance. And if you are rewarding people according to economic profit, they are going to consider economic profit when deciding whether or not to pursue different business opportunities. Economic profit has the advantage of being useful looking forward as well as backward.

The Power of Accounting Illusion

GENTRY: At NationsBank we have done analysis that is similar to what

Mike has just described. And we find that some of our activities, such as those operating in our Section 20 subsidiary, require considerably less capital in relationship to assets than most others. And, when we attempt to add up the capital requirements of all of our businesses, we come up with an answer that says we have plenty of equity. The problem is, the regulators still insist on a certain measure of equity against total assets. And, if the regulators *require* us to operate with excessive levels of capital, how can we justify assigning less than pro rata shares of our regulatory capital to individual operations? I'm not sure I see any way around the dilemma that this puts us all in.

O'NEILL: Frank, I'm not convinced that it is just the regulators who want this extra capital. I think the analyst community also looks at our accounting numbers to derive their own conclusions about how profitable banks really are. Academic purists may say that accounting numbers don't matter when it comes to the valuation of securities, but I am not in that camp. Maybe the accounting treatment is fiction. But, as Dean Acheson said, "Fiction perceived as reality is real in its consequences." Analysts look at the rate-of-return measures that come out of our accounting statements; and if those numbers cause them to think that we are not making good choices in terms of asset selection, that perception will be reflected in our stock prices.

Let's talk about Section 20 for a second. That business operates in a real strange way. Glass-Steagall essentially says that banks can't engage in underwriting activity. But there is an exception to that rule. In practice, what that exception means is that for every $10 of so-called "ineligible" revenues you generate, you've got to have $90 of "eligible" revenue. The best way to generate eligible revenue

is to put on a matched book of Treasury securities, which generates spreads of at most four or five basis points.

Now, because there is absolutely no risk in this business of manufacturing eligible revenue, the amount of economic capital you need to support that activity is zero. And, so, from an economist's perspective, the process of generating eligible revenue should have a positive effect on the value of the firm. The return is small but the transaction itself imposes no additional *economic* capital requirement on the bank.

However, the *accounting* effect of putting on a matched book of Treasuries can be considerable. Given our present asset levels at Bank of America, every billion dollars of matched book we put on reduces our net interest margin by two basis points. And this means that the better we get at generating ineligible revenues, the lower is our reported net interest margin.

Now, Bennett would say, "Who cares?" But, Ron, as an analyst who follows banks, do you care if our net interest margin goes down for this reason?

RON MANDLE: Well, if you took the pains to explain it to us in the way you just have, that would make the reduction *somewhat* palatable.

O'NEILL: It's that "somewhat" that I worry about.

BENNETT LINDENBAUM: I'm a fund manager at Basswood Partners; and, in the case just presented, I would not care if the margin went down. If there's a rational explanation for that margin reduction—and if that reduction is allowing you to do other things that increase shareholder value—then I would not be troubled at all by that accounting effect.

And I'm more than a little uncomfortable with the suggestion that we analysts and money managers are all morons who respond completely

mechanically to earnings numbers. The investment community is getting more sophisticated all the time, and I think corporate actions and disclosure policies should increasingly be based on that assumption. My feeling is that if you make decisions on an economic basis, and you communicate what you are doing, the market will take care of you.

STEWART: It's interesting you should say that. Just yesterday I happened to be visiting some people at Fayez Sarofim, which manages about $32 billion in equities. While making a presentation about EVA, I mentioned problems with more conventional measures like profit margin and rate of return. And the people were all nodding their heads in agreement, as if to say, "Of course. Who could be so foolish as to think that we are taken in by accounting conventions?"

O'NEILL: I absolutely agree that making decisions that maximize economic profit as opposed to reported accounting profits is the appropriate course to follow. I'm simply making the point that when the economic course of action gives unfavorable GAAP signals, you need to explain why your actions are sensible or you'll be penalized by the market. Remember, they only see GAAP results.

EVA at BancOne

STEWART: John, BancOne is also fairly well along in the process of adopting economic profit in the form of EVA. Can you give us a little perspective on what has motivated you to go in this direction?

WESTMAN: We have always sought simplicity in our internal measurement systems. Measures like ROA and ROE are fairly easy to calculate and understand. And, for many years, BancOne was operated on the premise that maximizing shareholder value could be achieved primarily by maximizing our ROE. But, since it's very difficult to allocate equity to individual business units, and fairly easy to allocate assets, John McCoy felt that he could drive the bank's ROE higher by rewarding managers for increasing their ROAs. And that strategy worked well for a time. But, then the bank began to pile up more and more equity, often by issuing new stock to fund acquisitions. And, at a certain point, improvements in ROA stopped driving our ROE.

John also became concerned that the budgeting process in which we set performance targets had become too politicized. He felt that the whole process of *negotiating* budgets with line managers was making it more difficult for him to get a clear sense of what individual business units might be able to produce if they were really pushed.

STEWART: Wait a second. Are you saying that the ROA and ROE targets that went into your bonus plans were set by negotiation, and not according to some corporate-wide objective?

WESTMAN: That's right. Incentive compensation was based upon achieving budget. So, if a manager was not feeling particularly ambitious that day, he would walk in and say, "Here are all the reasons why we're not going to do real well next year." And so we were getting this "sandbagging" effect. Our managers were getting paid basically just for doing a good job of managing headquarters' expectations; they were being rewarded just for climbing out of a hole they had dug for themselves.

So, there was a staleness associated with our internal goal-setting and compensation process that had worked so well for so many years. And John McCoy was looking hard for some way to jumpstart or energize the managers of different lines of business, and he came to believe that something like EVA could become as powerful as ROA had been in the past.

STEWART: The hard part about applying EVA in this case, however, may be dealing with the fact that the bank as a whole has so much capital. As Frank Gentry just suggested, if the bank as a whole has too much capital, that may make it difficult to measure the capital required at lower levels of the organization—that is, by the individual business units whose performance you want to evaluate. Are you encountering the same kinds of measurement problems that Mike was describing at Bank of America. And, if so, how have you begun to address those kinds of issues?

WESTMAN: Well, first of all, let me say that "midstream" is also really the best way to describe our progress to date in resolving some of these internal capital allocation and measurement issues. Our determination of the capital to be allocated to our various businesses has taken a couple of different forms. For those of our businesses that have stand-alone or "pure-play" competitors, like the credit card business, the mortgage business, and the investment or trust business, our method has been simply to apply the capitalization of our competitors to those lines of business. You can really zero in on these kinds of measures, and the handshakes on capital allocations from our managers of these lines of business have come pretty quickly. And that's been encouraging.

But, on the credit side of the business—the parts you might think of as the core bank—reaching agreement on the capital to be allocated to the business units has been much more difficult. We would like to be able to look at historical earnings volatility as a proxy for risk. The problem is, some of those numbers really get very shaky because so many of our operations have short operating histories and have experienced such rapid growth

rates. In these cases, volatility measures are not necessarily reliable indicators of underlying risk.

The years 1989, 1990, and 1991 were, of course, particularly difficult ones in terms of commercial loan losses. And, because many of our acquisitions are so recent, we have been forced by our lack of history with these businesses to overweight the experience of those years in our risk measures. And our line managers, with some justification, have been slow to accept our risk measures as representing a full cycle. So, we've got a lot of internal debate going on right now about how much capital is really enough to support many of our core operations.

But we have taken a number of important steps in moving toward resolution of these issues. First, we have resigned ourselves to the fact that the historical data is not going to get any better. We can't go back and study the data more carefully unless we invest massive amounts of money, and we don't see the payoff from doing that. Second, we have decided that in going forward to implement the new system we will continually examine our results to see if the capital allocated to a line of business is consistent with the kind of volatility it is now producing. And third and last, we are winning over people by showing that what we really want to achieve are not high *absolute levels* of EVA, but rather—as Mike O'Neill said of BankAmerica's new emphasis—significant growth or *improvement* in EVA. This means people running our various lines will not be penalized by our initial allocations of capital. As long as they are moving the EVA in the right direction—that is, making it more positive or less negative—then people will be rewarded.

So, by focusing on improvement in rather than absolute levels of EVA, and by making a promise that we will look at future earnings volatility to adjust capital levels, we are getting some buy-in. But there are still obstacles.

Performance Measurement at Barnett Banks

STEWART: Chuck, you've mentioned that Barnett Banks has devised a system for measuring profitability at very local levels. Can you tell us a little more about it?

NEWMAN: We have accomplished two things that together have really enabled us to get a handle on the economic value of our different operations. One, we have put in a new management system. And, two, we have succeeded in bringing profitability measurement down to the level of the individual customer.

Our management system is based on assessing market potential for each line of business, and then working together with the line managers to establish performance targets based on those assessments. That system was put together through a process of collaboration between our line managers and our functional and finance people. The aim has been to determine the principal revenue and expense drivers for each business line, and then to use that analysis as the basis for coming up with mutually agreed-upon performance targets.

One of the real benefits of this analysis, as I mentioned earlier, is that the process of comparing similar markets really gives you a wonderful opportunity to discover the best practices inside your organization. Through this step alone—identifying and then standardizing some of our procedures—I would estimate that we increased our overall earnings by at least $30 million during just our rollout period.

In the past, our performance measure was always the amount of improvement over the past year. But this new system gives us targets that we all believe are more realistic. For example, you may have somebody who's really outperforming their market and can't do any better. In that case, you want to reward them well just for maintaining current performance.

Our second advance in performance measurement, as I said, was to bring our analysis down to the level of each individual customer. The only way to accomplish this is to have a record of every transaction the customer does with you, and advances in technology have allowed us to capture this information in an economical way. Every time a customer comes into an office, we know whether they went to a teller, whether they went to a drive-in, or whether they went to an ATM. We even know how many times they call us on the phone. We have costs for each of those activities that are assigned to the individual customer.

And we make extensive use of that information, not only for evaluating the profitability of the relationship, but especially in our marketing efforts. For example, our local managers use that information in setting up their plans each year. And, on the basis of that information, we will reach an agreement on how their bonus will be determined. Part of it will be determined by sales, part of it by customer retention. Sales, which is the major determinant of each manager's bonus, is measured through a mechanism that we call "customer value added." Using this process, we estimate the value of each product sold to a customer based on the cash flows generated by that product over its life.

With this kind of information at their disposal, our local managers have four possible strategies for managing customer relationships. One is simply to retain the customer, and keep things as they are. A second is to expand the relationship through marketing and sales efforts. A third is to acquire new customers. And the fourth is to seek the appropriate level of service for the price being paid by the customer.

We have five different categories of customers. It's our Customer Ones who make most of the money for us. They represent a very small percentage of your customer base. And you're probably not going to be able to grow those relationships very much. They do a lot of business with you, and what you want to do is retain it.

The real opportunity is to take your Customer Twos and Threes and to move them up by aggressively selling them products. And, so, our sales force now has a tool that identifies who those customers are. In fact, our system will even tell you which one of our products a given customer is most likely to buy next.

So, on the basis of this kind of information, our local managers today can come up with a market plan that says I'm going to retain 10 more customers this year than I did last year. I'm also going to sell products to these Twos and Threes, and so move up 15 of these customers into higher categories. And all this activity can be measured and summarized in a measure of customer value added for the bank. And our people are paid on that basis.

STEWART: Is the profitability measure itself expressed as an operating margin? Or do you attempt to allocate and charge for capital in that process?

NEWMAN: We have not yet attempted to allocate capital at that level. We would like to be able to do that eventually, but for now we want to make it as simple as possible. We want our people to feel that they can understand and have some control over all the key variables in the equation.

But, when we move up to business line profitability, we use a system that is much like those being used at Bank of America and BancOne. We do allocate capital at that level.

STEWART: So you presumably believe that as long as the people at the business unit level are focused on managing return on capital, the activities at lower levels will be managed to support that goal.

NEWMAN: That's right. The people who run our lines of business are responsible for coming up with the strategies, for making investment decisions, and for managing capital efficiently. They worry about the return on the capital. The people in the field are focused on execution and profitability at the local level.

Performance Measurement at SunTrust

STEWART: John, would you mind describing for us your performance evaluation process at SunTrust, and how you think that's working?

SPIEGEL: Our system is very simple. And fortunately—or unfortunately, I'm not always sure which—capital is *not* a limiting resource to SunTrust at this point.

STEWART: Why is that?

SPIEGEL: You see this bottle of Coca Cola I'm holding? It's because of this that we have all the capital we need and more. And, as I like to say to people, whether or not you drink one today, please at least open one.

When the Trust Company and Sun Banks came together to form SunTrust about ten years ago, we had $120 million worth of Coke stock. And today that stock is worth $2.3 billion. So, we have more capital than we need, and we're buying back our own stock as fast as we can.

STEWART: I'm disturbed, though, John by something you seem to be implying. It seems that you're saying that because you have a lot of capital, that capital is free.

SPIEGEL: No, I'm not saying that at all. We are acutely aware that capital has a cost. In fact, we know a lot about

EVA because of our close relationship with Coca Cola. And Coke, as I'm sure you know, has been one of the pioneers in the use of EVA for performance measurement.

STEWART: Are there board-level connections between the two companies?

SPIEGEL: Their chairman's on our Board. Ours is on theirs. And ours also heads Coke's Finance Committee of the Board.

So, yes, we have studied EVA, and we have monitored our performance on that basis. But, what we have decided to focus on, at least for the time being, is consistency of earnings. We have not yet spent a lot of effort to determine whether or not we have different risk exposure within lines of business or with certain products or customers. Instead we have attempted to discover what factors really protect the flow of and growth in our earnings stream. And we reward our line and product managers on that basis.

Now, this is not to say that we don't believe that these new performance measurement techniques are capable of adding value. We think they can. But, in every quarter since Trust Company and Sun Banks came together, we have never failed to make as much money as we made in the quarter before. We have not had any down periods. And so we feel that, at least for the moment, managing the growth and the flow of earnings is more important today than managing the risk that is associated with any particular line of business, and translating that risk measure into a return on capital. Over the longer term, however, we may very well move toward a system based on things like RAROC and EVA.

Purchase vs. Pooling

LINDENBAUM: In all of these various performance measurement systems,

what is the measure of income that you use to get to return on capital? Is it accounting income, or is it some measure of cash flow? I raise this issue in part because Wells Fargo's recent acquisition of First Interstate has really added fuel to this old debate. In that case, Wells Fargo has defied many conventional analysts by going ahead with a "purchase" acquisition. Critics of the deal have argued that the amortization of goodwill will depress Wells' earnings and hence its stock price for years.

SPIEGEL: Well, for most all of us, earnings and cash flow move pretty much together. Purchase accounting in acquisitions can give rise to some major differences, as you pointed out in the case of Wells. And differences in depreciation and certain kinds of leasing activities can also result in large differences. But over time the differences between the two measures are not all that great for most banks.

LINDENBAUM: Well, in the case of Wells Fargo, NationsBank, and Bank of America, I think there are significant differences between earnings and cash flow. So, my question is: What would *you* do if you were evaluating the profitability of an acquisition like Wells' deal with First Interstate? Would you decide on the basis of expected future cash flow, or are you concerned mainly about earnings effects?

SPIEGEL: Well, I think we would have to consider both. I agree that, at least in theory, we ought to look at cash rather than earnings effects if the two are going to be very different. And if the Wells case ends up proving that the investment community can see through the accounting to cash flow, then we might all begin to lose part of our preoccupation with earnings.

GENTRY: In one of the analyst's reports that I particularly liked, the

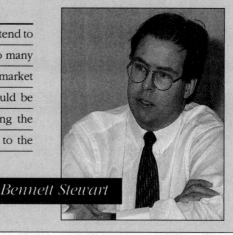

I don't agree with the statement that earnings and cash flow tend to be the same, especially in an industry like banking where so many people feel that the accounting is so obscure. And because the market pays a discount for uncertainty, not a premium, there should be opportunities to add value in banking simply by improving the amount and quality of the information that banks provide to the investment community.

Bennett Stewart

analyst praised Wells for doing the acquisition on the basis of cash flow. And the report went on to show how multiples of cash flow provide a better explanation for bank values than conventional P/E ratios using earnings.

But, you see, for a long time we felt the pressure to do poolings was coming from the market. It seemed very difficult to explain to the investment community why poolings and purchases were economically equivalent. And we think Wells has done the industry a great favor in showing us the way, and in demonstrating that the market can get the message if you make the effort to communicate. This may be particularly important in light of recent SEC restrictions on poolings. We are going to see a lot more purchases, and so I think we're going to see a lot more acquiring companies trying to explain their decisions very much as Wells has done.

LINDENBAUM: What about when you are evaluating the profitability of your different businesses? Do you look at cash flow or earnings measures?

WESTMAN: When we calculate EVA at BancOne, we begin with book earnings and then make a handful of adjustments to arrive at a measure of economic earnings. And the adjustments are really very few—things like adding back deferred taxes and the loan loss provision (net of charge-offs) to our P&L and balance sheet. As John Spiegel was just saying, most of

the differences between book earnings and economic profit are timing differences, and so over time those differences tend to wash out. I would also mention that we are not yet reporting these adjustments to earnings. But, analysts can easily do those calculations for themselves with the information we provide.

STEWART: John, I'm not so sure I agree with your statement that earnings and cash flow tend to be the same, especially in an industry like banking where so many people feel that the accounting is so obscure. For example, besides the purchase vs. pooling differences, there can be very large differences between book taxes and cash taxes paid. And those differences, in our view, ought to be added back to both income and capital in measuring cash returns on capital. And the same is true of the large depreciation tax shields in leasing, and the differences between the loan loss provisions and net charge-offs that you mentioned.

And take the case of research and development. For some industrial companies, we recommend taking R&D off the income statement, putting it on the balance sheet, and then writing it off over five years. Clearly, in the case of a company like Merck today, it would be meaningless to measure their returns without capitalizing and carrying forward their R&D spending. And, as R&D spending becomes a more important part of the

banking industry, banks may want to consider capitalizing part of their R&D in their internal performance evaluation systems.

Improving Disclosure

STEWART: So, as I suggested, there is a great opaqueness to the banking industry. And because the theory suggests that the market pays a discount for uncertainty, not a premium, there should be opportunities to add value in banking simply by improving the amount and quality of the information you provide to the investment community. And since we have some bank analysts in our audience, let me ask the question: What kinds of information could banks provide that would enable analysts to better measure performance and value? Ron, what do you think about this?

MANDLE: Well, I for one find it incredibly difficult to try to get at the cash flows behind bank accounting numbers. In other industries, particularly in the case of LBOs, there is a common practice of estimating cash flows by adding back things like depreciation and amortization of goodwill.

STEWART: You're talking about EBITDA, earnings before interest, taxes, depreciation, and amortization.

MANDLE: Right. Analysts are able to calculate that number in other industries, and then use that to assess the quality of earnings. And I really don't understand why banks don't give you enough information to be able to compute that number.

LINDENBAUM: I agree. And I think investors' demand for this kind of information is only going to grow. As I said, I think the markets are becoming more sophisticated all the time.

STEWART: Or, the market may have been fairly sophisticated all along. For example, everybody seemed to believe that Wells Fargo would be punished by the stock market for making such a large acquisition using purchase accounting. But Wells did it— and, lo and behold, the stock price responded as the theory predicted it would.

O'NEILL: We didn't have that belief at Bank of America. In fact, we have done a number of purchase acquisitions, including Security Pacific and Continental. So, I guess we're really breaking some new ground in San Francisco.

STEWART: Let me turn to Chip Dickson of Smith Barney. Chip, as a bank analyst, what do you think about bank disclosure? And how do you feel about economic profit measures as opposed to accounting profit?

DICKSON: When I value companies, I do a discounted cash flow analysis on all the companies that I follow in the industry. I value them, rank them according to their perceived level of undervaluation, and then make my recommendations on that basis.

STEWART: Is your measure of cash flow roughly the same as the economic profit we have been discussing?

DICKSON: Well, in looking for differences between GAAP accounting and cash flow, I actually focus more on the balance sheet than the income statement. My feeling is that the really significant distortions in bank accounting are in its measurement of cash capital. Because of things like pooling accounting, loan loss provisions, and deferred taxes, many banks

are dramatically understating the amount of investor capital that has been committed to their businesses— and this means that their profitability ratios, their returns on capital, have been greatly overstated. When I see banks doing things like artificially boosting their ROEs through poolings, or smoothing their earnings by manipulating the loan loss provision, my inclination is to reduce my assessment of their value.

STEWART: It's a funny thing about the loan loss provision. You hand a banker $100 and the banker says, "Whoops, I lost a buck or two. Do you mind?" A normal person would respond, "Of course I do." The banker responds, "Yes, but it's risky to make loans and we have to set up a charge." But, as a bank shareholder, I would say, "We realize that you're going to lose money on some of your loans, but we assume you're charging a high enough rate on the ones that pay you back both to cover the losses and to give me my money back with a return. So, if you are going to pre-book your losses on losers, why would you not also pre-book your earnings on winners?"

The reason we do all this, of course, is accounting conservatism. "When in doubt, debit" is the governing principle.

I was visiting with the CFO of a finance company a while ago. And he said, "Bennett, we're very conservative in our accounting here. We take 1 or 2% right off the top for expected losses." And then he went on to say, "Now, you may think this is a fairly harmless practice, but it has some real effects. In the latter half of every year, the interest we book on our loans is lower than our provision for losses. As a result, the reported earnings and the bonuses go down. And, for this reason, our people will often say to their clients, "We'll give you a better interest rate if you start on January 1st."

So, there are huge motivational

problems that can arise from taking accounting numbers at face value. A lot of fee income in banks strikes us as equivalent to providing their clients with puts or calls of various kinds. Now, should that fee income all flow through the income statement in year one, or should the resulting exposure to the bank be put on the balance sheet and then written off as the exposure goes down over time? And take the issue of gains and losses on banks' trading portfolios. This is a wonderful device for earnings management. In our system, those capital gains and losses go to the capital account. They don't flow through earnings.

So, John, I'm afraid to say I have to disagree with you. There are many, many aspects of bank accounting that are highly misleading. And we would hope over time that the quality of the economic information provided by banks would improve.

SPIEGEL: Well, I too think it would be nice to improve disclosure in the banking industry. But one of the problems that we've got with disclosing more information—and it's a big one—is the SEC. We could put out a good deal of internal information about the profitability of our different lines of business, and about our expectations for different investments. But, when you do that, you effectively make a commitment to the SEC that you may not want to keep. If your techniques for measuring return change, then you could be in trouble. Once you provide a certain kind of information, you are committing yourself to continuing to provide that information.

STEWART: Are you saying that you feel restrictions on your ability to disclose additional information that you would *prefer* to disclose?

SPIEGEL: Absolutely.

WESTMAN: We too have the same concern.

Incentive Compensation

STEWART: Well, what about communicating the extent of management's commitment to raising the value of the shares by discussing managerial stock ownership and, more broadly, your bank's overall incentive compensation plan? Is the theme of making managers into owners one that resonates with you?

HATCH: At First Union we have moved very much to performance-based compensation for middle and upper management. For most of our middle and top managers, only one-third of the total compensation package is base salary. Another one-third is stock-based compensation, and the remaining third is incentive-based compensation. So, we believe very strongly in turning managers into owners.

STEWART: How about at Bank of America, Mike?

O'NEILL: The issue of incentive compensation is certainly one that resonates with me. In the last couple of years, significant share ownership has been mandated for the senior people. For the senior people, appreciation in the value of our stock is the single most important source of total compensation.

Now, have we designed our stock programs as well as we could have? The answer is probably not—and we are still in midstream on this issue, too. The traditional stock option mechanism has generally resulted over time in management doing pretty well for itself; but I'm not convinced that it has resulted in shareholder value creation. So, we are now working on a system that will more closely align the interests of management and shareholders. And we are also working on pushing these incentives into lower levels of the organization.

STEWART: There's an irony at work, though, in much of the current compensation programs that I run across

these days. Jim mentioned this pay mix of one-third, one-third, one-third. On the surface, that appears to be very aggressive, and maybe it is. But you also find that how you administer that program can make a huge difference in the extent to which a manager's total compensation is actually at risk. For example, if your incentive-based bonus is tied to targets that are essentially negotiated, then lousy performance can allow targets to be negotiated down so that even substandard managers end up being big winners.

And the same thing is true of the traditional stock option plan. Many plans are set up so that if the stock price goes down in a given year, managers are actually rewarded for poor performance by being given more options than if the stock price had instead gone up. A classic case involved John Akers at IBM. As IBM's stock price kept falling lower and lower, Akers's stock option grants kept getting larger and larger. And, so, by the end of his tenure, had Akers been able to get IBM's stock price anywhere close to where it was when he started, he would have made a fortune.

That's why we recommend things like front-end-loaded, fixed grants of options. We also recommend use of what we call leveraged stock options, or LSOs. These options have an exercise price that rises at a rate equal to the cost of capital to ensure that managers get paid only if shareholders are winning.

John, I know you like to keep things simple at SunTrust. Do you just hand out stock?

SPIEGEL: Fourteen percent of our stock is owned by employees and directors. A big part of this is the result of employee savings plans in which the money goes right back into the company stock. And let me also say that we don't have the kind of annual stock option grants that you were describing.

WESTMAN: One of our current crusades at BancOne is actually to restrict our use of stock options. That is, we want to stop taking them so far down in our organization, and instead find other ways of compensating those people in ways that have a more direct link with their own performance. Nobody at BancOne quarrels with the idea that having managers become owners is a good thing. The question that we're struggling with is this: What exactly should managers own? And what we think they should own is some kind of equity participation in the activity that they're running. That kind of participation can be accomplished through phantom stock whose value reflects the operating performance of a business unit. It could also make use of your "internal LBO" concept, Bennett—the one where you create the illusion of a stand-alone operation and give people an ownership stake in that fictional entity.

STEWART: Well, I like the way you're thinking, John. But we're out of time, and we'll have to leave that issue for another day.

In closing, let me thank all the panelists for taking time out of their busy schedules to participate in this discussion. Let me also thank Chris James and the University of Florida for their hosting and orchestration of this event. I certainly have learned a lot here today. For example, Mike O'Neill has impressed upon me that the term "retail banking" no longer means what it meant during my training days at the Chase Manhattan Bank. I have been very impressed by the stock market performance of banks in recent years. And I am also quite impressed by the efforts of the banks represented here to bring more economic logic into their organizational structures, and into their performance measurement and incentive systems. And I would encourage you all to continue these efforts.

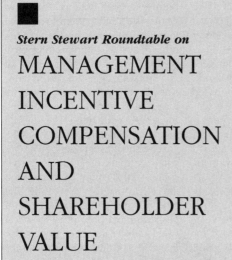

Stern Stewart Roundtable on

MANAGEMENT INCENTIVE COMPENSATION AND SHAREHOLDER VALUE

April 29, 1992 ▪ New York City

JOEL STERN: Good morning, and welcome to this Roundtable on incentive compensation. In keeping with the aim of the *Journal of Applied Corporate Finance*, the main purpose of this discussion is to bring the findings of current academic scholarship to bear on the compensation practices of U.S. corporations both large and small, public and private. At the same time, we want to take advantage of the presence of our distinguished group of senior corporate executives to bring about a dialogue between theorists and practitioners on the subject.

We intend to take up issues like the following:

▪ Is the level of compensation received by American top management excessive, as some

critics claim? Is it true that year-to-year executive rewards bear little relation to annual stockholder returns? Is it true that firm size, for example, is the major determinant of compensation levels? And if so, is this a serious problem?

▪ How are management compensation contracts typically designed? How prevalent, for example, are EPS and EPS growth as measures of performance and what explains their popularity? What problems have you seen arise from the use of such measures? What is the ideal measure of performance for evaluating managers?

▪ Are corporate compensation committees, as sometimes alleged, largely under the thumb of top management, or do they exercise an important independent monitoring function on behalf of stockholders? Should corporate directors be completely disinterested observers, as many contend, or would shareholders benefit from requiring directors to have significant stock ownership?

▪ What lessons have we learned about executive compensation from the successful LBOs of the 1980s? What sort of compensation programs were adopted by companies going private? And what are the barriers to importing such innovative compensation schemes into public companies?

▪ Are money managers ruining corporate America by forcing management to focus on the short run to the detriment of longer-term corporate interests? If so, how can management contracts be structured to overcome this problem?

With us today to discuss these issues are a group of senior corporate executives and outstanding scholars in the field of financial economics. In setting up this discussion we have departed from precedent by attempting, where possible, to pair a corporate CEO or senior operating official together with the top human resources person from each of the companies represented. So let me start by introducing our corporate representatives.

WILLIAM SMITHBURG is Chairman, President, and CEO, and **DOUGLAS RALSTON** is Vice President, Corporate Human Resources, of the Quaker Oats Company.

STEPHEN BUTLER is the Chairman, and **RICHARD WOODHAM** is Vice President - Compensation, Benefits and Personnel, of the W. C. Bradley Co. The Bradley Company is a privately-owned diversified consumer products company based in Columbus, Georgia with roughly $200 million in sales.

JACK CASHMAN is Chairman and **ALEKSANDAR ERDELJAN** is President of R. P. Scherer Corporation. Jack and Alex jointly function as CEO. R. P. Scherer is a leading international developer of drug delivery systems, and is the world's largest producer of softgels for the pharmaceutical, nutritional, and cosmetic industries. The company was taken private through a leveraged buyout in 1989 and then re-emerged as a public company last year.

DENNIS LOVE is President, and **MICHAEL HEMBREE** is Vice President—Finance & Administration, of Printpack Inc. Printpack is a privately-owned specialty printer based in Atlanta with about $400 million in sales.

JAY PROOPS is President and Chief Financial Officer of the Vigoro Corporation, a manufacturer of agricultural chemicals and lawn care products. With two principal colleagues, he consolidated and integrated numerous acquisitions and then took the company public in 1991.

MICHAEL MURRAY is Executive Vice President, and **JOSEPH THOMPSON** is Chief Human Resources Officer, of the Continental Bank.

MICHAEL MAUBOUSSIN, who recently moved to First Boston from County Nat West, is our representative securities analyst. Mike covers the food industry for First Boston.

Now let me turn to our distinguished group of financial academics.

MYRON SCHOLES is Frank E. Buck Professor of Finance at Stanford University Graduate School of Business, and a Research Associate at Hoover Institution. Myron is the co-originator with Fischer Black of the well-known and widely used Black-Scholes option pricing model. In recent years, Myron has also become a Managing Director of Salomon Brothers, advising them on incentive compensation as well as a variety of more general strategic management issues.

YAKOV AMIHUD is Professor of Finance at New York University's Graduate School of Business Administration, and has done some very interesting work on LBOs and stock market liquidity and valuation.

BERNARD BLACK is Professor of Law at Columbia University's School of Law. Bernie has written extensively on corporate governance issues, and his most recent publication is called "Agents Watching Agents: The Value of Institutional Investor Voice," which appeared this year in the *UCLA Law Review*.

Also taking part in this discussion are my colleagues at Stern Stewart, **BENNETT STEWART**, Senior Partner, and **DONALD CHEW**, Editor-in-Chief of the *Journal of Applied Corporate Finance*.

The pay-for-performance ratio [at Quaker Oats] has become much more steeply sloped in the sense that the payoffs are more directly tied to our "Controllable Earnings" measure of shareholder value added.

—William Smithburg, Quaker Oats

Accounting vs. Economics: The Case of Quaker Oats

STERN: Our main purpose today, then, is to discuss this issue of how to reward corporate managers to give them the strongest possible incentives to increase shareholder value. Since almost all of the companies represented in this room are currently using some variation of our measure of corporate performance called Economic Value Added, or EVA for short, I would like to begin by using this occasion to see whether the use of such economic or cash-flow based performance measures can really make a difference in motivating more economic behavior.

In fact, let me start things off by asking Bill Smithburg a question. Bill, in your experience as CEO of Quaker Oats, to what extent do management incentives based on maximizing longer-term, cash-flow returns conflict with management objectives based on maximizing quarter-to-quarter earnings? And when such conflicts arise, how does your board of directors typically react to your making sound investment or financing decisions that reduce current EPS?

SMITHBURG: The quarterly earnings report is a ritual required in our society. Earnings per share is simply an accounting measure—meaningful to some extent, but by no means an infallible measure of value added. The real test of a company's success in building value is producing sustainable, long-term, cash-flow rates of return on investment that exceed the cost of capital. It is this measure that largely determines shareholders' return on investment over time.

At Quaker we recently adopted a measure of periodic operating performance similar to your concept of EVA—one we call "Controllable Earnings"—and it now serves as the basis for performance evaluation and incentive compensation throughout the com-

pany. In fact, we take this kind of performance evaluation all the way down to the level of our individual operating units, where I think it's especially important.

Now, it's true that if you make the right decisions over the long haul, there really is no conflict between accounting earnings and economic earnings. Eventually both systems of measurement will give you the same answer. The problem, however, comes from the potential for conflict in the short run. Reliance on accounting measures in the short run may cause you to make decisions that reduce long-run value. But, as managers charged with maximizing economic value and share returns, we try to keep our eye on the long-term target. So, if the short-term quarterly earnings don't necessarily swing in the direction the analysts want, that doesn't really matter to us. We feel the market will recognize what we are doing and reward us for it.

BENNETT STEWART: Bill, it was announced a couple of weeks ago that Quaker's earnings would be off this quarter, in large part because of the company's decision to discontinue its old practice of "trade loading." The aim of this practice, as I understand it, is to cram as much product as possible into the distribution system at the end of the quarter to give an artificial boost to reported earnings.

And trade loading is apparently a highly addictive practice—one that RJR-Nabisco had fallen into in a very big way before it was taken over by KKR. It was estimated that trade loading was forcing as much as a billion excess cigarettes into the distribution system, thus leading to excess inventories and stale cigarettes. But, when RJR went private, the company immediately ended the practice of trade loading, and took a $160 million charge to earnings in the third quarter of the year. Karl Van der Heyden,

the new CFO, announced that this was a very positive indication that the company would henceforth be managed to maximize cash, not earnings. And by ending trade loading, RJR would also benefit from smoothing out its production, reducing the burden on its distribution system, and deferring the payment of the considerable excise taxes it was effectively volunteering to pay well ahead of time.

So, Bill, I was wondering if the discontinuance of the trade loading of breakfast cereals by Quaker was done for similar reasons. Is this a result of the company's new focus on economic as opposed to accounting performance, or is this something you would have done anyway?

SMITHBURG: Well, you haven't left me much room to answer the question. But, the answer is yes, I think our new focus helped us to make this decision. Trade loading is an industry-wide practice that creates large artificial peaks and valleys in demand for our products. These peaks and valleys in turn generate significant extra infrastructure and extra inventory costs—all things you really would like to get rid of.

Now, we didn't end up cutting back on our total trade promotion expenditures. We just decided to spend the money more evenly across the year, thereby getting rid of the peaks and valleys, and reducing our inventory costs significantly. While this change did cause a temporary decline in our quarterly earnings, it clearly increased the economic value of our operations. And that, I'm convinced, is the right thing to do.

STEWART: As I recall, your comment in the *Wall Street Journal* was that "Our guys better get these earnings back soon."

SMITHBURG: Our operating earnings will be off $50 million, or about 40 cents a share, for our fourth quarter

What we're trying to create [at Salomon Brothers] is, in some sense, a partnership between the employees and the shareholders—one in which the employees share both the gains and the losses with shareholders. The difficulty we face, however, is to get enough "equity" in the hands of the employees that they will really suffer along with shareholders.

—Myron Scholes, Stanford University and Salomon Brothers

ending in June. But we expect all of that to come back to us in the next two quarters. In fact, we adjusted the incentive payments to our operating managers so as to force them to recover those earnings before they start earning their bonuses.

STEWART: Essentially, you were asking your managers to co-invest with shareholders in this program.

SMITHBURG: We were not asking, Bennett; we were telling.

Designing Executive Compensation Plans to Minimize Taxes

STEWART: Another area where increasing corporate cash flow can mean reporting lower earnings is deferred compensation. I want to take advantage of Myron Scholes's presence to ask him about the design of executive compensation schemes. Myron has just written this marvelous new book called, *Taxes and Business Strategy,*[1] which I can't recommend highly enough. There is a nice chapter on taxes and executive compensation. And I was wondering, Myron, if you could comment on a few examples of situations where companies are volunteering to pay extra taxes by choosing kinds of comp plans that don't penalize near-term EPS. To what extent are companies allowing accounting rather than real economic considerations to dictate the form of their compensation packages?

SCHOLES: Well, the most interesting question here has to do with stock options. There are three basic forms in which options can be made available to management: non-qualified stock options, incentive stock options (or ISOs), and stock appreciation rights. And it turns out that granting stock appreciation rights is

the most tax-advantageous way to get stock options into managers' hands.

STEWART: By tax-advantageous, you mean it minimizes taxes for both the corporation and managers combined?

SCHOLES: That's right. The most tax-advantageous strategy minimizes the government's tax revenues. And, on this basis, as I said, stock appreciation rights are the best strategy because, like salary payments, they result in taxable income to the executive each year as the stock appreciates, but the corporation realizes a deduction of the same amount in the same year.

The next best alternative is non-qualified stock options. In that case, the corporation receives a deduction, and the individual is taxed, when the options are exercised. While the executive may have to pay additional tax on future stock-price appreciation, the company cannot deduct that appreciation from its taxable income.

The worst alternative, from a tax standpoint, is the incentive stock option. Managers prefer them because they don't pay any taxes until they actually sell the shares, but the corporation receives no deduction at all. For this reason, in my view, many U.S. companies would benefit simply from replacing their ISOs with non-qualified options.

In terms of the accounting treatments of these three option forms, the situation is exactly the reverse. Because each year's stock appreciation is deductible, stock appreciation rights are expected to produce the lowest reported earnings. The economic consequences of ISOs and non-qualified options currently do not affect earnings per share. Converting ISOs to non-qualified options at the time of exercise could reduce the government's tax receipts, but would also have nega-

tive accounting consequences. And I suspect it is largely because of these accounting consequences that so few public companies seem to use stock appreciation rights or convert their ISOs to non-qualified options.

STERN: So, Myron, would you agree that what companies ought to be doing is to set up their compensation schemes so as to maximize cash flow by minimizing reported earnings and taxes paid?

SCHOLES: That's right. But, as I said, most companies don't seem to be following that principle. They must believe it's more beneficial on the whole to report higher earnings per share than to minimize taxes.

STERN: That reminds me of an interesting experience I had just the other day. In discussing a possible IPO with one of our corporate clients, the firm's investment banker expressed great concern about the reduction in reported earnings resulting from a deferred bonus plan the company recently put in place. According to that plan, which we had a hand in designing, performance must be sustained over several years for the bonuses to be paid out—that is, they represent a contingent liability.

But, according to the conventional accounting treatment, all of the bonus declared in a given period, even if not paid, will have to be expensed against the current year's earnings. The investment banker said that the resulting earnings reduction would have a negative effect on the value of the firm in the IPO market. And he therefore recommended to the company that it eliminate the new deferred comp program.

We of course disagreed with the investment banker. But let me defer here to Mike Mauboussin. Mike, as our representative securities analyst, would

---

1. Myron S. Scholes and Mark A. Wolfson, *Taxes and Business Strategy: A Planning Approach*, Prentice Hall, Englewood Cliffs, NJ, 1992.

Some of our managers have clearly changed their focus. People who were once interested primarily in sales growth and market share have suddenly become much more concerned about managing their own resources more efficiently and holding down their fixed costs.

—Dennis Love, Printpack, Inc.

you be concerned about the charge against current year's earnings for bonuses to be paid in future years—and then only if management continued to generate positive results?

MAUBOUSSIN: Well, my short answer is no, I would not be concerned about this EPS effect. It would not cause me to reduce my estimate of the IPO's value.

STERN: How would most of your investment banking or corporate finance colleagues at First Boston answer this question? Are most of them believers in cash flow or earnings when the numbers go in different directions?

MAUBOUSSIN: I continue to be shocked by the mechanical way in which many investment bankers still respond to reported EPS numbers. In fact, I met with a company considering an IPO just last week. At that meeting the head of the syndicate explained to me that two months ago the market was valuing companies based on cash flow. But, in the last couple of weeks, it seems, the IPO market had reverted back to its old practice of using earnings per share as its primary criterion. So there's more than a little bit of confusion among investment bankers, and securities analysts as well, about what constitutes shareholder value and how it should be measured.

But the real financial management issue goes back to what Bill Smithburg was just saying. The aim of management should be to identify and focus on those factors that really contribute to long-term value, and to ignore short-run considerations when they're just obscuring long-run trends. Clearly, in cases where there's a discrepancy between cash flow and earnings, the market I believe will follow cash flow. And I think corporate policy should thus be governed by the principle of maximimizing long-run cash flow, not earnings.

STERN: Mike, are you continuing to recommend the shares of Quaker Oats in part because of the new management incentive compensation program they've put in place? Or is that just because of the free cereal they now send you?

MAUBOUSSIN: The new economic-based incentive plan plays a major role in our recommendation, there's no question about it. But, at the same time, I don't think that much of the investment community really understands when management talks about "controllable earnings" and "return on invested capital relative to the cost of capital." Most of the sell-side analysts are not as yet fully capable of understanding these concepts.

But, if you look behind the numbers, I think you're starting to see Quaker's program paying off. Asset utilization and returns on capital have improved, and I'm pretty confident this plan will show significant results over the longer term. Ultimately, in spite of some short-term EPS bumps, these things are what smart investors and the markets reward.

Private Ownership and Management's Time Horizon

STERN: With respect to performance measures, I've long argued that public companies ought to be run with the same indifference to reported EPS as private companies. So let me turn to Dennis Love, who runs a privately owned company called Printpack. Dennis, what has been the impact on motivation and morale of adopting EVA as your basis of profitability? And what made you think your people would find this kind of economic value program to be an appropriate one?

LOVE: Well, let me see if I can answer the second question first. About a year ago, when we first looked to you to help us with our incentive compensation plan, we had undergone a major reorganization of the company. We had seen significant growth and were continuing to grow, but we were managing as if we were still a smaller company. So we divided the company into a number of profit centers, each with a somewhat different business focus and requirements.

So, when you came along, Joel, we thought we needed a different compensation scheme to go along with these changes in our organizational structure. We've had a mishmash of different compensation schemes over the years, and we felt we needed something to pull all of the new units together and drive people in the same direction.

We are now in the first year of testing our new comp plan with a group of nine or ten corporate executives, as well as the general managers of our different business units—which makes a total group of about 16 managers. And, to tell you the truth, we haven't had a great year, so it's hard to say exactly what sorts of benefits we've gotten out of it so far. What we have seen, however, is that some managers have clearly changed their focus. People who were once interested primarily in sales growth and market share have suddenly become much more concerned about managing their own resources more efficiently and holding down their fixed costs.

STEWART: Dennis, let me ask you a different question—one we run up against all the time in this process of trying to make managers think and behave more like owners. How long do you need to keep a manager in a given position to be able to evaluate her or him properly, and for the company to realize the fruits of its investment in that business? My feeling is that it's got to be a period of at least three years, maybe more like five years.

If you have continuity at the top..., that continuity enables you to make the kind of cross-function moves appropriate for development of more junior people... To be an effective general manager, you need to have a business perspective that extends beyond your own functional area.

—Douglas Ralston, Quaker Oats

I'd also make the general observation that the managers of private companies tend to stay in place for a longer period of time, and thus have a greater commitment to their operations, than what I have observed in larger public companies. In public companies, the emphasis seems to be placed on career development and mobility. Public companies seem to develop what amounts to an internal labor market with its own set of rules and objectives. And the constant movement around the company that this system encourages does not seem to me to allow for effective performance measurement; it doesn't give managers the opportunity to really build a business and be evaluated and rewarded over a long enough period of time.

Dennis, do your people tend to stay put, or do you move them around a lot?

LOVE: We haven't had a lot of turnover in our management team. For example, our senior sales managers and senior plant managers have been with us, on average, about 12-15 years; and we expect that many of them will be with us until retirement. This expectation is only reinforced by our new compensation scheme, both because of its equity-like payoffs and deferred bonus aspect.

STERN: Mike, how far down does your incentive compensation plan go at Printpack, and what effects of the plan have you noticed to date?

MIKE HEMBREE: Right now, it covers just the top management people. But next year we'll take it down to the next level, which in our case would be plant managers, sales managers, divisional controllers and human resource managers, and others on the general management team at each of the profit centers. Ours is a capital-intensive business and the most significant impact of the plan has been in management's attention to capac-

ity utilization and how that relates to future capital expenditures. We were far more likely in the past to invest in new equipment even when we had relatively underused equipment that might have done the job. Overall, the plan has generated better asset management decisions than would have been possible for us in the past.

STEWART: But increased asset efficiency is not the only expected benefit. What this new plan also means is that if managers do something that's going to reduce near-term performance measures, but they feel it's going to pay off big in five years, they may be much more likely to make the investment. In that sense, they are much more like owners of the businesses they run.

Now, let me put the same question to Doug Ralston. Doug, what would be the typical turnover rate or experience of the key managers at Quaker Oats?

RALSTON: Well, I think the key word here is "balance." We aim to achieve a balance between career development, on the one hand, and building businesses that add value for shareholders. For this reason, although we try to expose people to different parts of the total organization, we're also serious about trying to keep people in businesses long enough to promote a long-term planning horizon.

So the ultimate aim of an effective human resources program is to develop an internal development process that weighs these two considerations and comes to an appropriate middle point. In evaluating the appropriate career development program for a given individual, for example, we will sit down on an annual basis and ask questions like: How long has he or she been in this current assignment? Have they been in the assignment long enough to have provided a return for the company and the shareholders? What alternative

assignments are available, and what career development path makes sense both for the individual and for the company. Over the past several years, we've shifted the pendulum toward longer assignments because we've become convinced that both the individual's personal development and the company's business needs are best served by having peoply stay in a job long enough to achieve mastery of a function. You have to resist the temptation to create a long "daisy chain" of people moves each time a vacancy occurs. We've found that the annual Human Resources Review process I mentioned earlier is a good way to keep ourselves on track.

Now, you'll find that this paradigm for internal development varies somewhat across the different functional areas of the company. But, again, in most cases, it's a matter of balancing these two concerns: the desire to increase the number and variety of assignments against the value added by keeping a manager in a given job.

STEWART: But once you get to the top levels of management, do you find that, like Dennis Love, you're able to keep people for 10 to 15 years?

RALSTON: I think it would be rare to find a high-level Quaker manager that hadn't been with the company for that length of time. We believe that senior managers by definition need to be broad-based business people. To develop that kind of perspective, you need to have people exposed to a variety of business situations during their careers. But the time to make those development moves is at the more junior stages of a person's career. As you move to more senior levels in the organization, the amount of time you spend in one assignment will typically get longer. If you have continuity at the top—say, the president of a division or vice president-marketing—that continuity enables you to make the kind of cross-function

We had to put something in place that gave the new managers opportunities for gains comparable to those we earned as an LBO. Our aim, in effect, was to replicate the LBO model in a public company setting.

—Jay Proops, Vigoro Corporation

moves appropriate for development of more junior people.

The last thing in the world you want is to have all your key people off on a "development" assignment at the same time—you just couldn't get the work done. But we do attempt to have our top marketing people spend time in finance, and finance people learn something about marketing. To be an effective general manager, you need to have a business perspective that extends beyond your own functional area.

Extending the LBO Model to Public Companies: The Case of Vigoro

STERN: Jay, what's been your experience so far at Vigoro with EVA-based management? And how long has it been in place?

PROOPS: Although we've been talking about it for some time, we didn't put our new plan in place until just after we went public, which was on May 30, 1991. In fact, it took us quite a long time to tailor the plan to our specific circumstances and needs. But, since then, we have found the plan to be a tremendous boon to us by strengthening management incentives.

First of all, we have found that our operating managers understand the plan—although we did take considerable pains to go out and explain it to them. We have also found that the plan has an important effect on their expectations, and thus presumably on their level of motivation. In fact, we made this discovery when we offered our managers a choice: we asked them to choose the degree to which they wanted to be tied to the plan. And in almost all instances, we found people wanted the maximum possible exposure to the plan in terms of their earnings capability. I'm not sure if that's because they knew they were going to have a big year

this year, or they really felt that good about the plan. But it's very clear our operating managers like the plan and want to be part of it. The real magic about it for them is that if they do extraordinarily well, their bonuses are literally uncapped.

STEWART: Jay, before going public last year, your company went through a leveraged buyout. And you obviously achieved important improvements in management incentives when you first went private—in that case, by means of all the stock ownership you spread out among your management team. Why didn't you just stick with what you had? What is different now from what you had before as a successful LBO?

PROOPS: Until going public last year, we had a compensation system that was quite typical of LBOs. The handful of people who started the company, including Joe Sullivan and me, purchased the group of eight companies that today make up the Vigoro Corporation. In buying each of the eight companies, we typically gave significant amounts of stock to the top two or three key managers in each company.

STEWART: Stock in their own businesses or stock in Vigoro as a whole?

PROOPS: Stock in the businesses they were running, not the overall company. And we ended up with a relatively small group of people who became quite wealthy in a very short period of time.

The next year, the new managers we were bringing in said to us, "We want to have the same opportunity." And, Bennett, after your people came in and explained your EVA plan to us, we then took that plan and explained it to this group of new managers. And they responded very positively. "That's the way to do it," they said. And it really was—because we had to put something in place that gave the new managers opportunities for gains

comparable to those we earned as an LBO. Our aim, in effect, was to replicate the LBO model in a public company setting.

STEWART: When you went private, your managers were handed stock in one of the eight units they were running. But what happened to those shares when the entire company went public last year? How did you convert or cash out the units' shares?

PROOPS: We rolled those people up on the basis of the number and appraised value of their unit shares in proportion to the actual IPO value of the entire company.

STEWART: So that the final exit value for the operating managers was based upon the appraised value of their units, with the proviso that the appraised values of the eight companies had to sum to the *actual* market value of the overall company when the company went public last year?

PROOPS: Yes, that's basically the idea.

YAKOV AMIHUD: I'm very curious to know why, in an LBO, you would ever deviate from a compensation plan based simply on ownership of stock and stock options. Why bother resorting to these interim cash-flow or EVA measures at all?

PROOPS: Our people clearly wanted stock. But, at the same time, you can't wean them entirely from their desire to have some money in their pocket on a yearly basis. So we designed our system to accomplish those two purposes, providing both current cash income and longer-term equity appreciation. And, for a private company with no stock price, the annual cash awards obviously have to be based on some internal measure of annual performance.

But the thing to keep in mind is that, in our system, the payoff from both sources is based entirely upon the same measure of shareholder value added. The number of shares of stock they are awarded in their

Ours is a capital-intensive business and the most significant impact of the new compensation plan has been on management's attention to capacity utilization and how that relates to future capital expenditures. The plan has generated better asset management decisions than would have been possible for us in the past.

—Michael Hembree, Printpack, Inc.

own unit is determined by the same formula that governs their cash compensation; the whole plan is tied directly to the economic value added for shareholders.

AMIHUD: But you can always design a scheme in which managers can redeem part of their stock for cash to meet their own cash needs. In a public company with a quoted stock price, there is of course no problem. If it's a private company, then you can have the stock redeemed at an imputed price.

PROOPS: That's correct. But I think there's another important aspect to this issue. My personal feeling is that there are people beneath the senior management ranks of the company who can really influence shareholder value. And these people, for whatever reason, seem to have a strong preference for cash payoffs.

STEWART: That explains why you have to have *cash* compensation. It doesn't explain why you have cash *incentive* compensation. In other words, why wouldn't you just pay people cash, and they would get stock in addition to that? Why not do that instead of paying them cash, adding a layer of cash bonus based upon some measure of performance, and then putting a layer of stock on top of that.

PROOPS: Our feeling is that cash payoffs tied directly as possible to a measure of shareholder value added are an effective surrogate for actual stock ownership.

STEWART: Well, do you really view the cash bonus as fixed compensation, or is it truly variable pay based entirely on superior performance? For example, is the cash bonus likely to be zero in certain circumstances?

PROOPS: Absolutely. We took a very firm stand that, at the top management levels at least, the cash bonus is related strictly to the value that they add to the company. If there's no

value created in a given year, there is no cash bonus.

Now, we did decide to have a transition year. We used that to wean people off of the old system, so that all of a sudden there was not a sharp plunge in their earnings. But, in the following year, if the top layer of management fails to create value, they won't get any portion of that incentive compensation.

SCHOLES: I would guess that one reason you use cash compensation as well as stock has to do with the fact that you have eight different divisions. Since it may be difficult for division managers to understand how the performance of their division relates to the value of the overall enterprise, it is likely to be far more effective to tie a division manager's incentive pay to the longer-run earnings of that division than to the corporate stock price.

DON CHEW: I agree, and I think Jay's system at Vigoro also may represent the best of two worlds. That is, it uses divisional cash flows, or EVA, to measure the near-term profitability of operations while using stock prices to evaluate their longer-term performance. Operating managers often object to having their performance measured solely in terms of stock prices, in large part because of their volatility. So, one of the benefits of the Vigoro plan is that it insulates managers from that price volatility—or at least from that part of stock price volatility that exceeds the volatility of operating cash flows.

At the same time, stock prices still function in that system as the ultimate arbiter of value. When Vigoro's operating managers come to cash in their long-run equity interest, say, five or ten years down the road, the company's overall stock market value will determine the total amount that's going to be cashed out by the group of companies. The only remaining

difficulty will be to determine the relative contribution of each of the companies to that total—but that's what the divisional EVA numbers can be used to measure.

So, in this sense, Jay's system avoids the measurement problems arising from market volatility by using accounting measures in the near term; but at the same time it preserves the incentive benefits and discipline of using stock price appreciation to measure and reward longer-term performance.

STEWART: Well, I think there's another special benefit of Jay's system. If a manager owns stock in a company, and if he or she hasn't been through a Stanford Business School program in recent years, it may not be obvious to all these people what they have to do to create value. For that reason, it may be useful to set up a measure of performance like EVA that at least points them in the right direction. And if you tie the bonus directly into that measure, then the measure itself becomes the focal point, the overriding object of the entire financial management system—of the whole process of setting goals and measuring performance and budgeting capital for investment.

The Ratcheting Effect (or Declining Performance Standards)

BERNARD BLACK: Let me play devil's advocate and express some skepticism about cash-flow-based pay-for-performance schemes. Consider a case where an operating management team has a down year; and even though it works hard, it doesn't receive any bonuses. Suppose that happens again the following year and again the managers get no bonus. I can imagine that system working for maybe two years, but not much longer. Good managers will leave the company.

To the extent you allow managers to negotiate their standards downward to accommodate past poor performance, you just invite the sandbagging of compensation plans that goes on at many public companies.

—Bennett Stewart, Stern Stewart & Co.

Companies recognize this problem. As a result, what tends to happen when they fall on hard times is that bonus standards get "ratcheted down" and you end up seeing bonuses for mediocre performance.

STEWART: Or, maybe you see a new set of managers.

BLACK: Well, maybe. But I'm not sure that happens in the vast majority of U.S. companies. I see some companies underperforming year after year, and the top people more often than not stay in place. If the stock price goes down, the compensation committee will often reward these managers for their substandard performance by granting them a new set of stock options with lower exercise prices.

STEWART: You raise an interesting issue about how stock options tend to be granted. They tend to be granted with an exercise price equal to the prevailing stock price. If the price falls, and if there is a fixed dollar amount of compensation that has been targeted by the compensation committe for this purpose, then the top executives will be granted ever larger numbers of options at lower and lower strike prices. And, if this goes on long enough, and the exercise prices fall far enough, then management is bound to win eventually—provided, of course, they manage to hang onto their jobs.

Take the case of U.S. Surgical, which performed poorly for ten years. Over that period the company kept granting management more and more options at lower and lower prices. And when the stock finally just recovered to its former levels, management received a huge payoff.

One way to circumvent this problem, and inject some pay-for-performance leverage into the system, is to use a formula to set the exercise price of the options. Say your current stock price is $100 and it falls to $80. In that case, instead of issuing stock options at $80, you could offer options with an exercise price of $90, or halfway down. This way management isn't effectively being rewarded for contributing to the firm's lower stock price—which is what many corporate option grants do. By the same token, if the stock price rises to $120, the exercise price of next year's options grants would be $110, only halfway up, so as to provide an extra reward.

We address this same problem, by the way, when setting EVA targets. In most turnaround situations, it may be difficult to require a manager to earn his cost of capital. So, you instead might reward him for making his economic earnings, or EVA, significantly less negative than before. This way at least you force the manager to stretch. But to the extent you allow managers to negotiate their standards downward to accommodate past poor performance, you just invite the sandbagging of compensation plans that goes on at many public companies.

SCHOLES: Bennett, I agree with much of what you're saying about how stock options are granted in practice. But there is always this identification problem with the granting of options. Are they being granted as a reward for past performance, or to serve as an incentive for future performance?

If the option grant is just designed to make managers whole for the past, and then the company just keeps granting more options as the stock price goes lower, then management is effectively being provided a floor on their total compensation. Providing a floor is obviously not an effective management incentive system.

STEWART: What you're saying is that, in such a case, options are functioning simply as added compensation rather than strengthening incentives.

SCHOLES: That's right.

The Case of Salomon Brothers

STERN: Myron, one of the reasons I understand you're now associated with Salomon Brothers is that the management at Salomon Brothers was interested in making some changes in the way they compensate their managing directors and other employees. Is it true that you recommended to them that they have a system based primarily on stock ownership?

SCHOLES: Yes, that's right. A couple of years ago, we decided there was very little ownership of stock in the company, and that shareholders would benefit from a compensation plan that put more stock into the hands of management and employees. And, as you said, Joel, it was not a stock option plan, but rather just straight stock ownership.

Employee stock ownership, moreover, was the first leg of a two-part program. The second leg was to establish an incentive system based on group or division profitability. But it will not be based on short-run performance, but rather on longer-run performance. In the securities industry, you can make a large amount of money in one year by taking large bets and then lose it all in the next year. For this reason, the bonus is effectively put into escrow and paid out over time.

STERN: Would those bonuses then be subject to negative charges in future years if the division's performance deteriorates, or is this just the equivalent of a restricted share program where you get your payoff just for staying on the job?

SCHOLES: The employees will be penalized in the event of future losses by having the amount of their escrowed bonuses reduced. This way it's not just a one-sided arrangement in which management and employees get all the upside and shareholders bear a large amount of the down-

A good compensation system ought to start with the directors. Then we could have more confidence that the directors would design an executive compensation scheme that's good for the stockholders.

—Bernard Black, Columbia University

side risk. What we're trying to create is, in some sense, a partnership between the employees and the shareholders—one in which the employees share both the gains and the losses with shareholders. The difficulty we face, however, is to get enough "equity" in the hands of the employees that they will really suffer along with shareholders.

So, we don't believe in just adding on to current cash compensation. Stock ownership and performance plans can only be justified insofar as they really build incentives.

STERN: But your chairman has a reputation of saying that people ought not to get paid the kinds of sums investment bankers get paid. Would this new plan of yours substitute stock ownership for some of those very large cash payments in current years?

SCHOLES: I think our interim chairman has been misunderstood. What he said was that he doesn't mind paying for superior performance, he doesn't mind paying a lot of money for .300 hitters. What was unconscionable to him was the idea that particular investment bankers, regardless of what was achieved, were receiving what amounted to very large fixed salaries. They were receiving huge payoffs while essentially taking no risk in the operations of their specific businesses.

STERN: I'm curious about one other thing, Myron. You are the co-founder of the Black-Scholes option pricing model, and have written extensively in the area of option pricing. Why did you choose ordinary common stock rather than some form of option to provide incentives for Salomon's management and employees?

SCHOLES: We had considered using options, but we ended up concluding that a direct stock program was a more efficient way of accomplishing our aims. For every dollar of declared cash bonus, we decided to have em-

ployees give us back up to 50 cents to be placed in a deferred compensation program that would be invested in common stock. So, we were effectively asking the employees to give up part of their current pay.

We also felt they would be willing to put more of their compensation in common stock because it is a less leveraged form of investment, and thus considerably less risky, than investing in options. If we had instead chosen to make them put their money into a stock option program, we'd have to figure out a way to undo the leverage. We wanted to encourage more ownership.

BLACK: An important aspect of Myron's program is that both parts have significant downside risk. In establishing the right incentives, downside risk may be as important as the potential for gains. But, when I look at the compensation systems of most public companies, I don't see much downside.

In theory, you could achieve downside risk using options as well as stock. But it's often not achieved in practice with option packages. The worst that happens to poorly performing managers is that they earn their base salaries and, if the stock price drops, the exercise price for new options is lowered. The managers can't help but receive a significant payoff sooner or later. Some companies even cancel *existing* out-of-the-money options and reissue them with a lower exercise price—so-called "reload" stock options. Options plans like this have only upside, and no downside.

Is Executive Pay Too High?

STERN: The separation of ownership from control, the lack of a common interest binding management and shareholders, is an issue that seems to be very much on the minds of editors

of financial publications these days. These issues were also being raised in the early 1980s, especially when LBO firms such as KKR and Forstmann Little were finding ways to improve the alignment of interests between managers and shareholders. With the spectacular performance of some of these LBO companies, the large institutional shareholders began to say to the managements of public companies, "When are you going to do this for us? We're not involved in the LBO deals, but we'd like to benefit from these kinds of improvements, too. In the meantime, you managers seem to be getting paid in ways wholly unrelated to shareholder value."

So why has it taken so long for executive compensation to become a focus of concern?

BLACK: I think what's driving the publicity is not the compensation systems that are filtered down into the organization, but rather the levels of pay at the *very top*. Over the past 15 years, average CEO compensation (including options) has tripled in real dollars at a time when everyone else's pay has been basically flat. And profits haven't gone up nearly as fast as CEO pay.

At some point, the disparity between CEO pay and line worker pay got sufficiently large that it grabbed people's attention. And I think rightly so. Because at the upper regions, the pay numbers coupled with lack of pay-for-performance are just very, very hard to understand or explain.

STEWART: How do we *know* that CEOs are overpaid now? Maybe they were underpaid before? One of the achievements of LBOs is that managers made huge returns for delivering superior performance. And thus one of the arguments that's been made for LBOs is that they enabled companies to pay managers what they're really worth *provided they're able to create value.*

BLACK: We don't *know* that CEOs are overpaid. What we do know is that they're paid a whole lot more than they were 15 or 20 years ago and we don't seem to be getting extra performance out of them. And if they don't have the kind of downside risk of someone who owns a big slug of stock, then they're clearly getting an awfully good deal.

So I might turn your question around and say, How do we know CEOs were underpaid 15 years ago? Let's go back to the average pay levels of 15 years ago, cut the average CEO compensation package by a factor of three—that is, the total of salary, bonus, and incentives—and start over from there. If we did this, is there any reason to think we would get any less performance on net from our CEOs? I think you'd still have plenty of incentives, and you wouldn't have the perception problems that we have today.

And I think perception matters. It's good to make managers think like owners. But there are limits. If you've got a penny-pinching business, as many have been forced to become in recent years, most employees don't like to see a CEO on some magazine cover making $5 million for his great job of laying off their co-workers. That's real tough for them to accept. It has to affect morale, and morale affects profits.

SMITHBURG: But this is precisely the problem in conducting these discussions in the mass media. They automatically see a problem if a CEO does well for himself and his stockholders while plant workers are being laid off. But I frankly don't see the problem here. Plants get to be 70 or 80 years old and they need to be shut down after they stop being efficient enough to add value.

Now, I agree that if you have to lay off plant workers, they are entitled to things like re-education, out-place-ment, healthcare, and severance pay. But most large corporations attempt to provide that. And that's the way the system ought to work.

ALEX ERDELJAN: I too want to voice my strong disagreement with Professor Black. To paraphrase Michael Jensen, the important problem with CEO pay today is not the level of pay, but how it's being paid. The problem is the lack of any significant correlation between pay and performance.

The other issue I would raise here is this: Who really has the right to determine whether levels of executive pay are too high or too low? I believe that decision is best entrusted to shareholders, to private market forces. For example, I don't think there are many shareholders of Walt Disney who would complain about Michael Eisner's millions—because they were based on the *billions* in value added for shareholders. But shareholders may have legitimate complaints about companies like Time Warner and Chrysler, where the enormous payoffs have not been justified by consistently superior performance.

So, again, I don't think that the important issue is how much a CEO gets paid, but whether that pay is really reflecting superior performance.

STEWART: One problem here is that it's very difficult to measure the actual sensitivity of pay to corporate performance on a year-by-year basis. The only way you can really do it is to look at executive pay and shareholder returns over a fairly long time period—say, five years. So that, for example, if the CEOs of companies whose shareholders beat the market by more than 50% over the period from 1985-1990 received significantly more in total compensation than CEOs of companies whose stock simply mirrored the broad market, then that would constitute evidence of a pay-performance correlation. But, in general, it's very difficult to associate a given year's pay for a CEO with how that company's stock performed in that year.

ERDELJAN: The issue that people really don't seem to understand has to do with the exercise of options by executives. I would be surprised if two percent of the total population really understood that a properly structured stock option plan represents the payoff for years of superior performance.

And perhaps the level of misconception is not all that surprising. After all, the accountants treat the entire payoff as coming all in one year; and the popular press has certainly done very little to shed light on this issue. But the consequence of all this confusion is that if you have done a superior job for a number of years, and you choose to exercise your options, you suddenly find yourself one of the least desirable people in the country.

SCHOLES: I agree that this misconception is a major source of the current problem people are having with the compensation "excesses" of the 1980s. Of course, much of these large option payoffs resulted from the strong stock market. But what hasn't been recognized is that such grants were originally attended with a great deal of risk; that is, their payoffs were conditioned on superior future stock price performance. This fact is obscured in part by the "lumpy" way in which compensation is reported: the entire appreciation is reported as compensation in the year the option is exercised. In reality, as you suggest, the payoffs from options often represent value that is built up over time through sustained management effort.

Pay-for-Performance: The Cases of R. P. Scherer and Quaker Oats

JACK CASHMAN: I think we're getting to the heart of the issue here—which is the popular misunderstanding of how these compensation grants are being made. At R. P. Scherer, we

*We want to make the game really worth playing by holding out a large upside potential. And if
we find a manager who we feel is a good manager but is not prepared to play the game, he's not
the one for us. Our people have got to be prepared to participate in the risks as well as the
rewards.*

—*Jack Cashman, R. P. Scherer Corp.*

believe very strongly in maintaining both the perception and the reality of pay for performance within our company. Maintaining that perception is important to our shareholders and investors, and it's also important to managers in the organization. We don't believe in high salaries. We believe in paying the right salaries, and in paying high incentive compensation on top of that—both in cash and shares—when performance is good.

In our original LBO, there were a number of people who received share options. We were successful and then we had an IPO. And what we're really trying to do with our new compensation plan, much like Jay Proops at Vigoro, is to simulate the pay-for-performance system of an LBO while operating as a public company. We can't have a share options scheme with 200 people because there are simply not enough share options available. So we have a share option scheme tied to EVA for approximately 18 managers around the world. And those managers in turn use the EVA scheme to evaluate and reward their own people, but in the form of cash rather than share options.

So everybody's now focusing on EVA and shareholder value. And thus we've moved away from the annual process of negotiating budgets with operating managers. There are tremendous problems, as Bennett mentioned, with that whole process of making budgets and then negotiating performance standards on the basis of the budget. So we don't do that anymore. And this change has really come about as a result of seeing how effectively we were able to perform as an LBO, where the requirement to service debt really dictated the performance standards. By charging managers for all capital, equity as well as debt, the EVA system really accomplished the same objective. It ensures

that our performance measurement and incentive system is tied much more directly to shareholder value.

STERN: Why couldn't you have an options scheme that went fairly far down into the organization, but where the options were instead paid using phantom stock?

CASHMAN: Theoretically, we could. But, as much as we are believers in the concept of EVA and incentive compensation, our shareholders would object to granting too many options. I think it's a matter of educating shareholders as to the benefits of this kind of program, and this may well happen a few years down the road. But, if it was up to top management alone, we would have considered spreading more options throughout the system.

STERN: I think there may be another reason at work here. For example, Bill Smithburg rewards the senior managers of Quaker Oats on the basis of the company's new "controllable earnings" policy. Now, I don't know whether or not management bonuses are capped, but let's assume they are not. And let's consider the case of someone who was fortunate enough to be running the Gatorade business, which did spectacularly well. How would you feel, Bill, if that manager got paid twice what you did in a given year?

SMITHBURG: I would be delighted if the president of one of our divisions made twice what I did. And, by the way, our bonuses are uncapped. Now, as a practical matter, in a 12-month period somebody's not going to make four times the earnings of Gatorade we projected. But it would be wonderful for everybody if it happened. Because all our managers would benefit from the resulting increase in our total incentive pool. They would all see increases in their year-end cash compensation, and in the value of their long-term incentive plan as well.

But let me tell you a little more about how our system works. We start by paying competitive salaries to put bread on the table. The second layer is an annual cash bonus award that, over the past ten years, has become a much higher percentage of the total package. The pay-for-performance ratio has become much more steeply sloped in the sense that the payoffs are more directly tied to our "Controllable Earnings" measure of shareholder value added.

The third part of our incentive scheme is our long-term incentive plan, or LTIP, which consists of stock options and various versions of a stock option program combined with an ESOP. In fact, we've even allowed our managers to take 20% of their cash bonus and invest it in company stock (with a partial matching grant in restricted stock) from the company. The restricted stock match vests over five years, but only if the manager retains his original investment in Quaker stock.

In short, much more of a person's total compensation is now built on measures related to real economic value for shareholders.

RALSTON: We have also begun pricing half of our stock options at a "premium" of 25% over the market price on the date of the grant. These premium-priced options mean that management has to earn a "hurdle rate" for shareholders before they can exercise the options for gain. We think this is appropriate because it puts management and shareholders on a more common economic footing.

The Case of Commercial Banking

STERN: I'd like to ask Mike Murray about the commercial banking industry—an industry that does not seem to have distinguished itself as an innovative leader in compensation practices.

Given the reality that most large money-center banks are now in the process of downsizing, and being rewarded by the market for doing so, I strongly doubt that most bank managements are still pursuing growth just to increase their own compensation.

—*Michael Murray, Continental Bank*

MURRAY: Well, Joel, we've certainly *financed* our share of innovative deals. But on this compensation issue, I think Bud Thompson ought to answer that question. And, when Bud explains it to you, I think you'll find it is not quite as backward as you make it sound.

STERN: I'm not suggesting that what applies to the banking industry in general is true of the Continental Bank. On the contrary, given Tom Theobald's large percentage ownership stake in the bank, at least your CEO's compensation has a very high pay-for-performance sensitivity.

What I'm concerned about is the large correlation between size and executive pay in banking—something which I think could be a major obstacle to the downsizing that still needs to take place in that industry. For example, North Carolina National Bank recently merged with another very large bank. And it was interesting for me to observe how quickly the reported salaries of the very senior people increased—as if in direct proportion to the increase in assets under management. That well-documented historical trend, to the extent it's continuing, just cannot be good for bank shareholders.

So, Mike, I'd like to get some idea from you and Bud Thompson why it would not be in the interest of the executive committees of the banks to engage in a major merger wave just to get their own personal compensation up. Because if their salaries go up and their retirement income is based on an average of the last five years of their income before retirement, it is in their interest to have ever larger organizations—while shareholders' returns sink lower and lower.

MURRAY: That is obviously rational behavior on management's part if what you say continues to be true about the relationship between size and compensation in banking. But to the extent senior management and directors have at-risk money, then I think you will see something quite different. In fact, given the reality that most large money-center banks are now in the process of downsizing, and being rewarded by the market for doing so, I strongly doubt that most bank managements are still pursuing growth just to increase their own compensation. To the extent it may still be going on at some banks, though, I agree that it's bad news for shareholders.

STERN: Well, it seems pretty clear that our commercial banks as a group have destroyed enormous amounts of shareholder value in recent years in their quest to increase assets under management.

MURRAY: That was true of the money-center banks—at least until fairly recently—but many of the nation's largest regional banks have done quite well by their shareholders in the last ten years or so. But let me turn the floor over to Bud Thompson, our Director of Human Resources, who is our expert on compensation issues.

THOMPSON: Well, I think this concern about the extent to which sheer size dictates levels of executive pay in banking is certainly a valid one—or at least it was until just a few years ago. The aggregate data would undoubtedly have supported your contention, especially if they were concentrated in the '70s and early to mid '80s. But, as the downsizing of the industry progresses, I suspect that the correlation between size and pay is gradually becoming less pronounced.

At Continental, we have tried to make a clear distinction between the *quantity* or *volume* of an individual loan officer's activity, as measured in loans originated and outstandings, and the credit *quality* and hence *profitability* of those relationships. In so doing, we are attempting to ensure that the only kind of asset growth we encourage is profitable growth. So, we're no longer rewarding growth for growth's sake—and in fact I doubt we ever did, although there was once clearly greater emphasis placed on generating loan volume rather than profitability. And, in many cases, increasing profitability may mean shrinking rather than expanding volume, at least for a time.

So, I think current developments in commercial banking compensation, however true of the past, are changing today. Some banks, especially the more successful regionals, are still looking to grow aggressively, and they may well be rewarding their executives largely on the basis of asset growth. But many of the other large bank mergers, especially those involving the large money-center banks, are adding value by consolidating redundant operations. Such mergers are allowing the industry to shrink, and I very much doubt that CEO and senior management salaries are growing rapidly while workforces are being cut—in some cases by as much as 30% or 40%.

Director Compensation

STERN: I'm a director of a company that's just about to go public. And we announced yesterday that some three times the amount of each director's cash compensation will be granted all the directors to purchase out-of-the-money options with exercise prices about 40% above current stock prices. You see, we want to make sure that if our chief executive officer doesn't do his job, the directors will have enough at stake for themselves to be very responsive to the shareholders. We want them to be selfish on their shareholders' behalf.

So my question is, Why don't more companies find a way to get options in the hands of their directors?

At Continental, we have tried to make a clear distinction between the quantity or volume of an individual loan officer's activity, as measured in loans originated and outstandings, and the credit quality and hence profitability of those relationships.

—Joseph Thompson, Continental Bank

MURRAY: I'll go one better than you, Joel. Why don't you instead require directors to *buy* the options with cash out of their own pocket, or at least use the cash part of their directors' fees to do so?

STERN: Mike, I'm not suggesting that ours was the best of all possible solutions. But I can tell you that the directors were amazed that even my modest proposal was actually being put on the table. We intend to put this information into the registration tape that we file with the SEC in three weeks, and I think it will have a favorable impact on the IPO price.

MURRAY: But, Joel, if you instead put in the S-1 that you and the other directors were also buying a significant number of shares at the current offering price, wouldn't the impact be even more favorable?

STERN: Would the Continental Bank lend me the money to do that?

MURRAY: When we were financing leveraged deals back in the early days of the LBO, we also regularly lent money to the managers involved to buy stock in their own companies. Those were the days when managers were required to hock their houses and take out a second mortgage. It was a much riskier proposition for them; they actually had to dig into their own pockets and leverage themselves on an individual basis.

But much of that discipline was lost. As the business evolved and became much more competitive among the various deal firms, managers in some cases were almost *given* the stock. I remain puzzled why so few companies require their managers to dig into their pockets and buy shares—or at least make them use their cash bonuses to buy shares. As a potential lender, it would certainly give me more confidence in companies' ability to support debt if their managers were also required to own significant stock.

STERN: The Bradley Company has actually done just that. The company has a declared bonus, only part of which is paid out annually while the rest accumulates in a "bonus bank." Besides deferring a significant portion of the declared bonus, the company requires that some 20% to 33% of the annual *paid* bonus automatically go to purchase out-of-the-money options on the company's shares.

In fact let me take this opportunity to ask Steve Butler or Rick Woodham to comment on this plan. Steve, can you tell us what reaction you have had since putting in the new plan?

BUTLER: For those divisions where we put this program into place in 1991, we had awards ranging up and down the ladder. We had very positive reactions from everyone, both to the concept and the measurement and incentive system. Today, it's virtually impossible to have a discussion, at almost all levels of the organization, without somebody talking about business activity in terms of returns on capital employed and EVA.

STERN: Rick, how far down does the EVA plan go at W.C. Bradley?

WOODHAM: We carry our program all the way down through the management ranks. That's about 220 people in all, including even our entry level management trainees.

STERN: What about people who have no background in accounting or finance? Do you find that they are able to understand this?

WOODHAM: I think it's fair to say that most of our managers now understand the concept of EVA, how to calculate it, and how it connects to the value of our overall enterprise. We spent a lot of time educating them, and we continue to report EVA-related information to them on a quarterly basis.

STERN: In effect, this means that managers and employees are putting their own money on the line.

SCHOLES: To get back to your proposal for directors, Joel, one of the problems I see with directors—or managers or employees, for that matter—owning shares in significant concentration, and using their own resources to buy them, is the extent of managerial risk aversion. Managers are likely to attach significantly more value to a given level of cash than to the same expected level in stock or options because they can use that cash to buy a diversified portfolio of common stocks, bonds, or whatever. But, as you force managers to reduce their cash compensation while making a larger investment in their own firm, you're asking them to bear more risk—risk that cannot be diversified away by holding other stocks and bonds. And because that risk cannot be diversified, companies will be forced to pay their executives disproportionately more in total compensation to compensate them for bearing this nondiversifiable risk.

So, my concern is that the beneficial incentive effect of management stock ownership will be outweighed by the greater costs associated with forcing managers to hold undiversified portfolios. What I'm suggesting, Joel, is that there's likely to be an optimal level of risk to impose on managers. And some of your proposals may be pushing people beyond that optimum.

STEWART: I wonder, though, if the costs of forcing managers to hold undiversified portfolios will not typically be outweighed by the gains not merely from stronger managerial incentives, but also from managers' ability to *control* the outcome of the investment. Unlike passive shareholders, share-owning managers are in a position to influence the value of the firm, and they have the information necessary to do so. To paraphrase Mark Twain, the best prescription for success may in fact be to put all your

Today, it's virtually impossible to have a discussion, at almost all levels of our organization, without somebody talking about business activity in terms of returns on capital employed and EVA.

—Stephen Butler, W. C. Bradley Co.

eggs in one basket and then watch that basket very carefully.

SCHOLES: Well, I still think there's a huge amount of risk aversion on the part of individuals, and we have to find a way to deal with it. So, I find myself torn between two opposite concerns about current compensation plans. On the one hand, I think many corporate plans just provide executives with extra pay without providing much incentive to improve performance. On the other hand, I worry that some of these LBO-type plans are imposing perhaps too much risk on corporate managers. It's not clear that you always gain from indiscriminately heaping more risk on managers.

AMIHUD: There is a natural tendency for managers to undertake risk-reducing investments or to engage in conglomerate mergers in order to diversify risk. This is probably inconsistent with shareholder interests because shareholders, being well diversified, are better able to bear risk. Giving stock options to such managers may counter this tendency because the value of stock options increases with the volatility of the underlying value of the firm.

CHEW: I'm very skeptical that senior corporate managers are really taking on more risk in the aggregate. I think the great majority of American CEOs are not taking much more risk today than they did 10 years ago. The findings of Jensen and Murphy's study showed, rather forcefully I think, that the total compensation of CEOs of U.S. companies is less at risk than that of their own rank-and-file workers. The average CEO's total compensation changes by less than $3 for every $1,000 change in shareholder value.

For this reason, I think Bill Smithburg's program at Quaker Oats is not at all representative of what's taking place in corporate America. And I wish somebody here could tell

us how many companies are adopting programs like Bill's—schemes that are really forcing the CEO to take a risk.

SMITHBURG: Let me respond to this comment by telling you a little more about the changes we have made at Quaker Oats. We have gradually improved our incentives in what I often refer to as an "evolutionary" process. After making some changes at the top management level a few years ago, we then made a concerted effort to get our incentive plans for the next levels of management—encompassing the top 400 or 500 people in our company—more closely aligned with our shareholders' interests. In the last couple of years, with the help of Stern Stewart, we have taken some steps forward in this respect. And there's undoubtedly much that still could be done to improve incentives.

But let me address this issue about whether executive pay is really at risk. I can't speak for the average Fortune 500 company, but I can speak for other companies in our industry. In the food industry, we have not seen this alleged phenomenon of persistently substandard corporate performance accompanied by steady increases in executive rewards. So, I really wonder if the pay-for-performance problem is as bad as it's been made out to be in this country.

It may be true in some cases, but let me give you an example of what now happens in our company. Our executives' annual compensation consists basically of salary, cash incentive bonus, and payments into a long-term incentive plan (LTIP). Now suppose we had a year in which our controllable earnings declined by, say, 25%—and that's not the end of the world, our cash flow would be good and we'd still have a good balance sheet. In that event, a senior executive would still get his salary, but his bonus would be zero, and the

value of his cumulative LTIP—which is a kind of bonus bank—would actually be reduced significantly. So it's possible that, if you added up the effect on all three components, our people at the top level could actually have negative income for that year!

So, I think it's pretty clear that the total compensation of our top executives has significant downside risk.

STERN: Bill, I'm impressed with what you've done. But, now that you understand the approach and you've used it successfully, how come your board isn't part of the plan? After all, the directors on your comp committee had to approve the plan in the first place.

SMITHBURG: Again, I think improving compensation is an evolutionary process. We've taken a number of steps in the last two years that I think have been very significant. We've only been on this new program I just described for one year. But, once we get everybody trained—and we have gone all around the country talking to everyone in the company about this new plan—I would hope that this could evolve further, perhaps in a way that directors would also participate.

One thing we have done with our directors is to tie them more and more into the stock. Our directors' retirement program, for example, is funded entirely with company stock.

STERN: Let me ask Mike Mauboussin how he, as a securities analyst, would respond to an announcement by Quaker Oats that their directors were increasing their stock ownership appreciably.

MAUBOUSSIN: I respond positively any time senior managers and directors volunteer to align their own interests more closely with those of shareholders.

BLACK: I see a lot of promise in directors being compensated in the form of stock. An ideal plan might be to give directors a mix of cash and

It seems that creditors are far more effective in bringing about necessary change than the boards that are supposed to represent shareholders. And, although boards may exercise their power to fire management, I suspect it's not done nearly as often or decisively as it should be to enforce a strong managerial discipline.

—Yakov Amihud, New York University

stock, with just enough cash to pay the taxes triggered by the grant. If you required directors to hold that stock for as long as they serve on the board, that could lead to significant holdings over time. And those holdings might wonderfully concentrate the directors' minds. I know they do in the case of the one company I'm a director of. I *care* how the company does.

So, a good compensation system ought to *start* with the directors. Then we could have more confidence that the directors would design an executive compensation scheme that's good for the stockholders.

Management Dismissals

AMIHUD: We have heard throughout this discussion that the managements of U.S. public companies seem to face little downside risk. But we have not touched on one important consequence to executives of poor performance: the increased probability of losing their jobs.

There have been two recent studies of management turnover rates that I would like to mention. Steve Kaplan at the University of Chicago has compared management turnover between the U.S. and Japan. And, for all the claims that Japanese management tend to focus more on the long term, it seems that Japanese CEOs are, if anything, more likely to be fired than their U.S. counterparts in the face of a downturn in earnings. Overall rates of management turnover, however, are about equal in the two countries.

Now, this does not mean that CEOs are fired as often or as promptly as they should be—either in the U.S. or Japan—to make management dismissals a valuable disciplinary threat for shareholders. In fact, there was another recent study that suggests that management dismissals do not take place quickly or often enough. That

study looked at NYSE and ASE companies whose stock prices had fallen by more than 50%, and divided this group into two samples: those in which poor performance was accompanied by default on debt contracts and those in which it was not. What the study found was that management dismissals were more than twice as likely when the firm defaulted on its debt.

Now, that's an interesting finding because, remember, shareholders suffered equally in both cases; in both cases the firms lost roughly 50% of their value. But, it seems that what triggered the management dismissals was not action by the board, but rather pressure from creditors. So, from this piece of evidence alone, it seems that creditors are far more effective in bringing about necessary change than the boards that are supposed to represent shareholders. And, although boards may exercise their power to fire management, I suspect it's not done nearly as often or decisively as it should be to enforce a strong managerial discipline.

And this leads me to ask the following question: To what extent do the CEOs in this room exercise their ability to fire their senior operating managers when performance is substandard—because this would constitute an important incentive to perform well.

ERDELJAN: We've been fortunate that, during the last three years, the company has performed exceedingly well and nearly all of our operating units turned in excellent performance. However, in instances in which we felt an individual's performance was below our standards and expectations, whether at the staff or operating level, we acted as decisively as we could to replace those managers. In some cases with operating people, the replacements were made even *before* the unit's results deteriorated.

CASHMAN: I think that's absolutely right. Somebody earlier raised the question: What happens if a manager has a series of bad years? Well, our response is that, by the time you get into the third bad year or so, it's time to replace the manager. We can't tolerate any of our divisions around the world producing persistent underperformance, even if it's a small one. Because it means somebody has got to outperform exceptionally well to make up for the poor performance.

So we do have zero bonuses. And if they carry on, we have zero people as well.

SMITHBURG: CEOs of large public companies also regularly exercise their power to make layoffs, although I doubt your studies would be able to detect that power being used. A smart management team will take *preventive* action to guard against build-up of excess overhead. For example, we took 400 jobs out of our company a few years ago, and we did it without major layoffs. We did it in advance of what we thought was going to be a tough business climate. And I suspect that many CEOs run their companies in this manner.

BLACK: That may well be true, Bill. But, to play devil's advocate again, I'm not sure that logic applies to the boards of most Fortune 500 companies and their ability to fire top management. Lots of companies have one bad year after another, and the top management manages to stay in place.

STEWART: You weren't, by any chance, thinking of GM?

STERN: I don't think it's useful to single out specific companies here.

STEWART: Well, I disagree. I single out GM because that is probably the prime example of management failure. It would be hard to identify a company that has performed so poorly, and stuck to the same failed strategy for so long, without the board finally taking action. And so I'm won-

Most of our managers now understand the concept of EVA, how to calculate it, and how it connects to the value of our overall enterprise. We spent a lot of time educating them, and we continue to report EVA-related information to them on a quarterly basis.

—Richard Woodham, W. C. Bradley Co.

dering whether Bernie's comments are intended generally, or are they specific to certain highly publicized companies like GM. I'm not as convinced that the problem is as pervasive as Bernie's making it out to be.

SCHOLES: One of the things I think you're forgetting, Bernie, is that there is a market for executive labor. And if an executive does a poor job in one company, then his next position is likely to be a big step down. So it's not as though managers just have this free option, an upside with no consequences for poor performance.

CASHMAN: There's also increasingly another important source of discipline on management at work today, and that is the growing power of institutional investors. In the past five or six years, there has been a fairly dramatic change in the make-up of shareholders. The power of the institutions to raise these issues is quite real today, and is growing rapidly. I also suspect there will be increasing pressure from institutions on corporate boards of directors to take action—or to change management or the board. I think we'll see quite a bit of this activity in the next two or three years.

Independence of Compensation Committees

STERN: I'm curious to ask the chairmen here the extent to which they feel the compensation committees of their companies really operate as independent bodies? Or are they subject to your own influence in setting the terms of the compensation packages for top management?

SMITHBURG: I am chairman of the compensation committees of the two other corporate boards on which I sit, and I'm familiar with the working of our own committee. And a couple of things are common to each of these three committees. First of all, all mem-

bers of the compensation committee, including the chairman, are *outsiders.* I regularly read in the press that the CEO tells the compensation committee what he wants to make and then the committee acts as a rubber stamp. Now, clearly there has to be information shared between the CEO and the committee, and it is a dialogue for sure. But never in any of my experiences has the CEO been permitted to say, "Here's what I ought to make." There is also typically an independent consulting firm hired to evaluate the CEO and company's performance in a competitive framework relative to other companies in the industry.

Now, I'm not saying that insiders have no influence on the process. But there is some outside discipline at work here. The system is not perfect, but it seems to me to function reasonably well.

As for this ratcheting effect we have heard about, this granting of stock options at lower and lower prices, I have never seen that happen in our industry. But I saw that argument made fairly convincingly for a microchip company. In that case, management was not responsible for a 60% drop in the price of stock, and they were likely to lose good managers unless they granted a new set of options.

SCHOLES: There's an interesting issue about the consequences of using independent compensation advisory firms. I too have often heard people talk about this "bootstrap" or "ratcheting" effect that seems to lift corporate salary and bonus levels year after year. The story goes as follows: The compensation firm is hired to present the human resources people and the compensation committee with the *average* pay levels for senior managers in the industry. But the human resources people supposedly like to respond, "Our people are clearly better than average; or if they're not, they should

be. And maybe we should adjust our pay scales to make it that way."

As a result of this experience, the consulting firm comes back the following year with a new compensation survey with the average levels ratcheted up by their corporate clients' insistence on paying above-average salaries. And, from what I understand, most of this analysis justifying these above-average salaries is not based on stock price or EVA-type measures of corporate performance. So, it seems quite plausible to me that this practice of hiring compensation advisory firms to provide industry-wide surveys could be ratcheting pay levels up above optimal levels.

SMITHBURG: I'm not saying the system's perfect. Some of this kind of ratcheting may well take place. But the salary and bonus levels are based on an analysis of internal measures and competitive performance, one that uses a whole range of variables to consider when evaluating performance that could leave room for subjective judgments like this.

Compensation Plans as an Executive Screening Tool

PROOPS: I too think this ratcheting effect has been going on for a while in corporate America. When it goes too far, then a popular reaction like the one we're now seeing will set in. And maybe the rates of salary growth will be cut back sharply as a consequence.

And, in my view, that may not necessarily be a bad idea. I think we need to get back to paying executives a base salary that basically meets their living needs. This way, for example, people don't get paid a lot of money simply for rising to the rank of CEO. Our compensation philosophy is to pay our top executives a base wage of, say $200,000 or $300,000 and then provide large additional rewards based on their ability to generate EVA.

What this kind of EVA system accomplishes, as I said earlier, is to create a compensation model very much like that held out by LBOs. Our experience has been that only a very small percent of the managerial population is willing to stand up and say, "I'm willing to accept below-average fixed compensation and take on a lot of risk with the prospect of large rewards." For this reason, the EVA system becomes a very effective *executive screening* device.

To illustrate, let's say I had two people competing to run one of our companies; and I said to both, "We're going to pay you a modest salary, but you will have enormous upside potential that will be tied directly to performance; in fact, almost everything is on the upside." Now, if one guy is far more willing than the other to accept that arrangement, I will take the risk-taker every time.

STEWART: Your approach reminds me of a comment I recently heard by a very senior executive of the Blackstone Group, one who is currently running a large business for them. When I asked him, "How do you compensate your operating heads?," he said they use a three-part plan. They start by asking, "What do you guys need to live?" And he said that usually comes to around $250,000. And then they put on top of that a cash bonus plan based on some measure of economic profits (like our EVA). And the third piece is based on the increase in the appraised value of the operation.

They also use an interesting method in appraising those values. They take the current capital structure of the overall company—roughly 90% debt and 10% equity—and assign a pro rata level of debt service to each of the subsidiaries. On that same basis, they also create a phantom stock interest and then simply grant the operating heads an amount of stock

that would represent a 10% to 15% interest in the upside stock potential of their particular unit.

Bob Kidder, the CEO of Duracell, also uses a similar scheme. In a Roundtable similar to this one, Bob said that Duracell has three distinct layers of executive compensation: a base salary, strong cash incentives on top of that, and participation in the long-run equity value that is expected to amount to 15 to 20 times the level of annual salary plus bonus. I think these models have real merit. They ought to be given serious consideration as an alternative to the current system in which CEO salaries and bonuses are just ratcheted upward with the help of conventional compensation firms.

SCHOLES: Let me return to Jay's statement that he wants managers to "self-select" by volunteering to bear tremendous risk. There could be lots of terrific managers who, for whatever reason, are reluctant to take large risks and who would thus prefer a lower overall level of compensation but with higher guaranteed payments. Your policy means you will have to forgo these risk-averse managers. Do you think that's a potential problem with your policy?

PROOPS: No, I don't.

SCHOLES: You think that everyone that steps up to the plate is the right manager, and that everyone who refuses ought to be rejected?

PROOPS: No, but I think this is the best management selection method for us. The percentage of U.S. managers that we're looking for to run our businesses—the kind of people who really have the capability and drive to create tremendous value—is a very small percentage of the total population. We're all engaged in the search to find such people. And we all know it's a very, very difficult process to find and attract them. So, although we will undoubtedly pass up some

good managers, we feel we can find and attract such people far more reliably by holding out relatively low fixed pay combined with the potential for huge, basically unlimited, rewards for superior performance.

And that's one of the most important things we have learned from the LBOs in the '80s—namely, that people who are willing to accept more risk along with unlimited value creation opportunity will predictably be more effective managers of assets than others unwilling to do so.

AMIHUD: We have academic evidence that, in LBOs, many managers who were offered the choice of participating chose not to do so. So you really could have an effective self-selection process at work here.

PROOPS: It's true that some people have claimed that the success of LBOs was the result of low interest rates and the general prosperity of the 1980s. But I believe the success of LBOs was essentially unrelated to the business cycle. In our own case, we happened to buy into our industry when it was depressed; and it continued to be a depressed industry for a number of years after we bought in. But our people found a way to add value in spite of those conditions.

And, for this reason I think the academic community would find it an interesting study to look at successful LBOs in terms of economic cycles. That is, were managers in LBOs able to lift their companies out of an industry recession in large part because of the different set of incentives they faced? I tend to think that when the incentives are there, management will find a way to get the job done.

CHEW: There is some interesting academic evidence that supports this notion. Steve Kaplan of the University of Chicago and Jeremy Stein of M.I.T. looked at what happens to the risk of debt and equity in cases of

The findings of Jensen and Murphy's study showed, rather forcefully I think, that the total compensation of CEOs of U.S. companies is less at risk than that of their own rank-and-file workers. The average CEO's total compensation changes by less than $3 for every $1,000 change in shareholder value.

—Donald Chew, Stern Stewart & Co.

corporate recapitalizations like LBOs. What this study finds is that the total operating risk of these companies falls dramatically after the recap. In effect, the total amount of risk in the corporate securities goes down and value thus increases significantly. What this suggests to me is that managers facing tremendous financial risk combined with a large equity stake will try harder to find ways to reduce fixed costs and operating leverage.

I would also point out here the similarity between management selection practices in the LBO market and the conventions of the venture capital market. Venture capitalists—those people who raise money from limited partners and then place that money with entrepreneurs they choose to back—use similar self-selection techniques in evaluating the business plans of entrepreneurs. They offer entrepreneurs in effect a menu of financing choices offering varying levels of risk-reward trade-offs. And they interpret the entrepreneur's choice as a signal of his or her level of confidence. The more risk the entrepreneur is willing to impose on himself, the more confidence the venture capitalist is likely to put in the business plan.

SCHOLES: It's a difficult position I find myself in now—one that's quite different from the position I usually find myself in. My usual position is to say that managements are not bearing enough risk; there's too much fixed compensation and not enough variable pay at risk. So I am accustomed to saying, let's have stronger incentives and get away from the ratcheting effect of option grants and move toward a more linear relationship between pay and performance.

But let me just try to restore a little balance to this discussion. As I suggested before, there is an optimal level of risk-bearing for managers and I think some of these schemes

may be pushing managers well beyond that optimum. You've got to keep in mind here that all people are basically risk averse; they will demand higher expected returns for bearing greater risk. And, at a certain point, the costs to shareholders in terms of higher required pay from imposing greater risks on management begin to outweigh the benefits.

STERN: Myron, we're saying that we recognize that the managers under an EVA system do bear more risk. And therefore, the prospective returns have to be a great deal larger than otherwise. But I don't see that there's necessarily any conflict here with creating value.

CASHMAN: I agree with Jay Proops' position. I recognize that there are good managers who are risk averse and unwilling to submit themselves to the risks involved in an EVA scheme. But, like Jay, we too want to make the game really worth playing by holding out a large upside potential. And if we find a manager who we feel is a good manager but is not prepared to play the game, he's not the one for us. Our people have got to be prepared to participate in the risks and rewards.

STERN: When you started your new program, you already had a group of men in place. You said to them in effect, "Today we begin under a new plan." And then not a single one of those people turned to you and said, "I want no part of this"?

CASHMAN: That's right. And one of the reasons they didn't object is that they had already participated in the share options in our LBO, which was very successful. They had already got a really good feel for how this program could work out.

Lifetime Achievement Awards

STERN: What would you think about paying a CEO an enormous reward

for outstanding performance upon retirement? I have in mind the recent award of some $24 million by Philip Morris to its retiring CEO, Mr. Hamish Maxwell.

STEWART: The general question you're asking is whether it ever makes sense to pay people after the fact. For example, we recently saw Roberto Goizueta of Coca Cola being granted some $80 million in stock, ostensibly as a reward for the extraordinary performance of the company over the past 10 years.

STERN: Bennett, there was an important difference. Roberto Goizueta is going to remain as CEO of Coke for some time. Mr. Maxwell is finished.

BLACK: I think these stock grants are similar, and so is the recent package given to Tony O'Reilly by Heinz. There's still some incentive going forward for O'Reilly and Roberto Goizueta, which isn't true for Hamish Maxwell. But these stock grants are all forms of *ex post* compensation. For me, they have the same problems as stock options—they are upside only with no downside. Such *ex post* awards have the additional disadvantage that you may not even know ahead of time that you're going to get this award. To the extent these awards are unanticipated, you don't even get an upside incentive effect. It's just an outright wealth transfer from shareholders to the CEO.

STEWART: I agree. You can't have pay for performance after the fact.

STERN: I don't necessarily have a problem with these lifetime achievement awards. Philip Morris, after all, did finish number one in the 1991 version of our Stern Stewart 1000 rankings. And such an award may mean that all future CEOs of Philip Morris will think to themselves, "If I become a Hall of Famer—not just an All-Star player, but a Hall of Famer—then I too may be eligible for this kind of award on my way out."

We want to make sure that if our CEO doesn't do his job, the directors will have enough at stake to be very responsive to the shareholders. We want them to be selfish on the shareholders' behalf.

—Joel Stern, Stern Stewart & Co.

In this sense, a lifetime achievement award may turn to be an effective motivator. And I'm not being completely facetious when I suggest that Mr. Maxwell may have felt he was doing Philip Morris' shareholders and all future CEOs a favor by taking this money and establishing a precedent.

STEWART: Well, I think Goizueta's case has an important difference. When he was granted the $80 million in options, he already owned stock worth about $175 million that he had accumulated over the last ten years of exceptional performance.

ERDELJAN: I still think this was a bad decision by the Coca Cola board. It sets a very bad precedent, particularly in the current environment.

STERN: I don't agree with you, Alex. In fact, I might be in favor of lifetime achievement awards. Think about a newly appointed chief executive who might be, say, 45 or 50 years old at the time he's appointed and who thus might be in office for up to the next 20 years. He may say to himself, "If I bring enormous value to my shareholders, I may have a huge gift waiting for me."

SCHOLES: Joel, we don't have enough facts about these cases to really judge the effectiveness of these awards. But, as Bernie suggested, the effectiveness of the incentive really depends on the extent to which the awards are anticipated. If they are anticipated, they could perhaps serve the shareholders' interest.

BLACK: If these awards were really a cost-effective motivator, then CEOs ought to take less compensation in the earlier years of their career to reflect that expectation. But I don't think that happens. That leads me to the following question: Granted Coca-Cola's shareholders have done wonderfully in the last 10 years, did they really get $80 million of value from the recent grant of $80 million *more*

of restricted stock to Roberto Goizueta. I'd be surprised if this was an efficient form of compensation, as opposed to giving him a smaller amount of stock ten years ago and then letting that can grow to $80 million in value if Coke does well.

STEWART: But they also did that; his early grant ended up being worth $175 million.

BLACK: My other question is about Tony O'Reilly's recently awarded package: Why did his board give him a compensation package with enormous upside and with a floor such that the worst he's going to do is get $50 million over the next 10 years? I fail to see how this arrangement serves the shareholders of Heinz.

In Closing

ERDELJAN: One of the problems that we now face is that, having been a very successful LBO and returned as a public company, what do we do for an encore? How do we create sufficient incentives as a public company to carry on our past success? The complication today arises from all the public discussion about fairness, equity, and the like—from all the public guilt and recriminations that now surround the issue of executive rewards.

And I'd like to ask somebody like Bill Smithburg to what extent this public debate has really affected CEOs' compensation packages. After all, who really should care about this issue? Is it truly a matter for *Business Week* or *Fortune* or the U.S. Congress to decide? Or is it a private matter concerning just shareholders, the board, and the people in the company? When we went private, our shareholders were perfectly happy to give us tremendous incentives. But if we exercised our options today, we'd have everybody down on us. So whose business is it anyway?

SMITHBURG: Well, first of all, my experience is that when you have a

public debate about complex economic issues, as this surely is, there is going to be significant distortion of the arguments by all the different interest groups. If it involves economics, the media are going to have trouble getting it right. And the current debate about CEO pay at Fortune 500 companies has certainly received a high level of attention—and distortion.

The job of the CEO, however, is to look past all the rhetoric in the press and elsewhere and just make sure that the company is continuing to build value for its shareholders. We want to ensure that we have the best management team we can put together and then provide them with the strongest possible incentives to create value. And I know I'm preaching to the choir when I say this here—but if you want to have the best CEO or COO or CFO, you're going to have to provide him or her with real financial incentives. The current debate is not going to alter that reality in the least. You're going to have to pay him a salary that pays his bills and a lot more on top of that that's tied to performance.

And these decisions, by the way, are still being made in an essentially free market. It's still a free market system so far. But if some of the current proposals to regulate CEO pay actually become law, then I feel quite confident in predicting that such regulation will succeed only in reducing the competitiveness of most U.S. companies.

STERN: Well, one way to head off such regulation is to respond to the critics of executive pay by demonstrating the social benefits of creating shareholder value. As most of you know, we at Stern Stewart have done an extensive study of corporate performance; and we have found a very strong correlation between our measure of EVA and a measure of superior stock market performance called market value added, or MVA.

Fortune magazine also recently published its rankings of "The Most Admired Companies in American Industry." These rankings were based a number of so-called qualitative measures—things like "integrity," "quality," and "innovativeness." And what I found fascinating was the strength of the correlation between *Fortune*'s rankings and our Stern Stewart Performance 1000; there's an extremely high correlation between the two. All of which tells me that not only shareholders, but society at large, should be extremely happy with those companies that are "incentivizing" based on an EVA system. Higher stockholder value, it appears, often goes hand in hand with qualitative accomplishments that even the most financially unsophisticated among us are capable of appreciating.

STEWART: Your assurances notwithstanding, Joel, I think the issue of CEO pay is only likely to become more contentious as we move through the 1990s. I think the disparity in pay between CEOs and lower level employees, far from shrinking, is actually going to grow progressively larger. This disparity is being driven at bottom by the increasing intensity of international competition in product markets. The American worker is increasingly in competition with the Mexican worker, the worker in Canada, and with workers overseas. So I think we're going to see even more pay

disparities as borders continue to open up and trade talks progress.

This in turn will further increase the premium commanded by highly skilled and educated people—by the marketers, the technological people, and the financial innovators—the people that really create the value. At the same time, it reduces the value of unskilled labor. So, for better or worse, I think the gap is going to continue to grow, and it's going to cause severe turmoil in this country.

Also, with increasing international competition, I think the issues of effective incentive compensation will become only more critical to corporate success, and to the competitiveness of U.S. companies. As Bill Smithburg said, government regulation of this process would almost surely be a big step backward. On the other hand, there is clearly a lot of room at most public corporations for improving executive pay practices to achieve greater sensitivity of pay to corporate performance and shareholder returns.

In my view, moreover, one of the important new developments in incentive compensation will involve applying the lessons we learned from LBOs in reforming the pay practices of large public corporations. Take the case of ARA Services, a firm that went private through a leveraged buyout in 1985. At the time managers had 28% of the stock. Three years later they paid down the debt to the point where

they could have gone public, but they instead elected to recapitalize the company, giving outside equity investors cash and insiders more shares in the company. The result is that management and employee ownership of the company is now over 70%, and has reached much farther down in the ranks of the company.

Interestingly enough, the company also makes a market in its own stock. Managers and employees are invited to tender up to 10 percent of their shares to the company. And it is the company's policy to stand ready to buy in those shares at appraised value. And if people leave the company, they get 10% of the appraised value down in cash, and the other 90% value is paid out over 10 years.

I also envision highly leveraged pay-for-performance schemes in which the managers of individual business units effectively buy into the shares of their own units—somewhat along the lines that Jay Proops was describing today. Many large diversified U.S. companies—I refer to them as the "LDCs" of the 1990s—will use such measures to reform themselves from within.

Anyway, I'll brake my enthusiasm and turn the floor back to Joel.

STERN: How thoughtful, Bennett. Let me end by thanking all of you very much for participating in this roundtable, and I hope you found it as stimulating as I did. I also hope we can make this an annual event.

CEO ROUNDTABLE ON CORPORATE STRUCTURE AND MANAGEMENT INCENTIVES

April 18, 1990 ■ *New York City*

JOEL STERN, Moderator: On behalf of our host, the Continental Bank, I want to welcome you all to this discussion, and to thank you for taking a morning out of your busy schedules to tell us a little about how you run your companies. Our general aim is to explore issues relating to the structure of organizations, financial policies, internal control systems, and management incentives. We want to find out from you how and why differences in structure and incentives affect corporate performance and, ultimately, stockholder value.

But before plunging into the subject, let me introduce all of our panelists and tell you a little more about how this meeting was conceived. The 1980s was a decade of vast experimentation in organizational structure. And each of the CEOs assembled around this table is intended to represent a somewhat different variation on the theme of corporate organization.

ROBERT KIDDER, for example, is the CEO of Duracell, a privately held LBO firm with sales of $1.3 billion that is owned 87% by KKR and 13% by management. Bob also ran Duracell when it was a division of Kraft, and the contrast between the performance of the company as an independent private firm today and as part of a conglomerate should prove interesting.

TOD HAMACHEK, CEO of Penwest, is likely to provide similar insights. In 1984, Penwest was spun off by Univar, the multi-billion dollar Seattle-based chemical distribution company, by means of a pro-rata distribution of new Penwest stock to Univar stockholders. Since becoming a separately traded public company, Penwest's stock price has increased more than fourteen times—which amounts to one of the highest rates of appreciation, Tod tells me, of any spin-off in corporate America during the 1980s. (As you can see, we choose our participants carefully.)

JOHN BURNS is CEO of Vista Chemical, which also has an unusual history. Formerly a division of Du Pont, the company was taken private in a leveraged management buyout in 1984. In 1986, it re-emerged as a public company through an IPO. And, in the summer of 1989, management then bought back one-third of its public shares in a major leveraged recapitalization. We will ask John to explain why his firm can't seem to decide, once and for all, whether it really wants to be a public company.

EUGENE APPLEBAUM is CEO of Arbor Drugs, which has shown a similar ambivalence toward the public form. In 1986, Gene took the company public, but nevertheless continues to own more than 60% of the stock. Sales have grown since then from $150 million to over $500 million, and earnings have grown at a 30% clip per annum.

RICHARD SIM is CEO of Applied Power, a public company with $445 million in sales that has done exceptionally well over the past three years. At least part of the company's success can be attributed (or so we would like to think) to an unconventional incentive compensation plan Dick put in place back in 1986.

JOHN JOHNSTONE, who is CEO of the Olin Corporation, may be the only "normal" CEO in the room. Olin is what is often referred to as an "old-line" chemical company; and although conservatively financed—at least when compared to Vista Chemical—it has done quite well by its shareholders in the past few years.

ROBERT ("SHELL") EVANS is CEO of the Crane Company, an NYSE firm that is probably the closest approximation in this group to a conglomerate, a group that came under considerable pressure during the 1980s. We'll see if we can get Shell to defend his company's current structure and show us how conglomerates are devising new ways to respond to the challenge of creating value for stockholders.

In addition to our group of CEOs, we are also fortunate to have with us two distinguished academics, a corporate investor relations specialist, and the head of corporate finance from the Continental Bank. I'll start with the two gentlemen from the world of scholarship.

MICHAEL JENSEN is the Edsel Bryant Ford Professor of Business at the Harvard Business School. Mike has gone on record many times—recently, in a controversial *Harvard Business Review* article called "The Eclipse of the Public Corporation"—to maintain that the "form" or ownership structure of the corporation can have a profound effect on performance. More pointedly, he has argued that because of serious deficiencies in the

management incentives in our public companies, the public corporation is likely to be supplanted by private companies in mature sectors of our economy. He has also published, even more recently, another *HBR* piece entitled "CEO Incentives—It's Not How Much You Pay, But How," which offers a powerful indictment of corporate compensation practices. And I suspect he will be sharing some of his findings with us today.

Our other representative from the academy is **JOHN GOULD**, who is Distinguished Service Professor as well as Dean of the University of Chicago's Graduate School of Business. Jack is unusual in that, besides being an able administrator, he is an outstanding microeconomist. He is also a director of several industrial corporations.

MICHAEL MURRAY is Executive Vice President and head of corporate finance at the Continental Bank. Mike has been involved in the execution of LBOs, and in corporate restructuring transactions generally, since their beginnings in the early 1970s. Mike also supervises a range of activities that includes M & A, ESOPs, asset-based lending, and receivables purchase.

CLAUDIA ZANER is an adviser to public companies—as well as to those planning to go public—on investor relations. Claudia, perhaps more than anyone I know in this field, is expert in showing corporate management how to reach the "lead steer" investors that matter in the pricing process.

Last, but not least, is my colleague **BENNETT STEWART**. His mention shall be accompanied with only faint praise—largely because he has acquired the annoying habit of interrupting me and holding me to something like "reality" throughout these discussions.

The LBO Experience

STERN: Now, that we have made it around the table, I want to start things off by asking Bob Kidder of Duracell to share with us some of his experiences in running a private company. Bob, Duracell is an LBO that is owned 13% by management and 87% by KKR. Do I have these numbers right?

ROBERT KIDDER: Yes, that's right.

STERN: Given that you don't have a stock price, how does KKR evaluate your performance? And how do they feel about your performance to date?

KIDDER: To take your second question first, I would say that they're quite pleased—mainly because we have managed to invest in our strategic commitments while still generating the cash flow necessary to meet our financial targets. We have been able to maintain a high level of investment in our future while making our interest payments and paying down the principal.

STERN: Let me ask you a somewhat technical finance question. Would you have been able to accomplish both these goals if the returns that you earned on net assets were just above the borrowing rate? I raise this issue because many corporate CFOs I've encountered believe that public companies can increase their share prices simply by borrowing lots of money and then earning returns that exceed the borrowing rate—even if they don't come close to earning an adequate rate of return (one that we call the "cost of capital").

To rephrase my question: Is an LBO's ability just to service its debt a reliable sign of success in adding value?

BENNETT STEWART: Joel, you're not putting the question in quite the right way. In evaluating whether such transactions are really *adding* value, you've got to remember that the LBO

already took place at a significant premium—often as much as 50%—over the previous value of the company. To get a good sense of the value *added* by an acquisition or LBO, you really want to measure current operating cash flow against the old, pre-acquisition value of the assets. And this means, for example, that when evaluating managers' performance, you should add the goodwill premium into the capital base only gradually over time.

But I'm digressing from the point that Bob Kidder just made, which is an important one. Bob said that the way KKR evaluates performance, at least as a crude first check, is primarily in terms of whether the debt schedule is being repaid and basic investment commitments are being met. This is very different from the headquarters of the typical public company, which evaluates business units in terms of meeting short-term budgetary goals. These goals, unlike a debt repayment schedule, are negotiated between a parent and sub on a rolling basis. This budgetary process, I am convinced, is deeply flawed; it ensures mediocrity by encouraging managers to produce cautious budgets and smoothly rising earnings instead of exceptional performance.

In the case of an LBO, by contrast, the debt repayment schedule represents in effect a demanding, multiperiod, cash flow budget in which there is no chance for hedging or renegotiation. In this sense, an LBO allows an outsider like KKR to *impose* a budget with a reward for the management people based solely on its ability to meet the debt repayment schedule.

KIDDER: Well, I agree, Bennett, that the debt schedule is very effective in forcing management to attend to profitability in the near term. But, let me emphasize that *another* impor-

tant consideration—in some sense more important than short-term cash flow—is carrying through on the strategic commitments I mentioned earlier. There is a widespread public misconception that because you're an LBO, you have to do everything possible to generate short-term cash flow; and that LBOs thus simply represent a means of sacrificing future profit for immediate gain.

But let me use a simple case to illustrate why that kind of "short-term" behavior makes no economic sense. Suppose our current level of annual operating cash flow is $300 million, and assume further that we're able to maintain a solid strategic position by investing an additional $10 million in R&D, new products, or marketing. Now, that investment will reduce our near-term cash flow by $10 million. And if the company is valued by the outside world at, say, six times our annual cash flow—and let's just assume the market is short-sighted enough to give us no credit for that investment, at least at the outset—then our value would have been $60 million higher if we chose not to invest in our future. On the other hand, if our investment decisions are successful enough to convince the outside world to raise our multiple from six to seven times, then maintaining our strategic commitment will have increased our company value by $300 million. And, if you compare that value added to the $60 million increase that comes from cutting out $10 million in annual corporate overhead, it becomes clear that the real payoff is coming *not* from a series of modest cost-cutting measures, but rather from effective long-term investment.

Now, I don't mean to suggest that we don't do everything possible to reduce waste and cut costs. That is clearly important, especially at the beginning of the process. But, when I

When I talk with Henry Kravis at lunch, we don't spend our time talking about cost reductions. We talk about how we're increasing the strategic value of the company—and by that I mean our long-term cash flow capability....

When managers become owners, they begin to think a lot harder about taking money out of mature businesses and investing in growth areas. And I think that happens as a fairly natural
consequence of greater ownership. It's certainly not happening because all of a sudden we put in new controls at headquarters. In fact, today we have fewer controls than we had as part of Kraft. What's different is that the proposals for change are coming from the bottom up rather than from the top down.

— Robert Kidder —

talk with Henry Kravis at lunch, we don't spend our time talking about cost reductions. We talk about how we're increasing the strategic value of the company—and by that I mean our long-term cash flow capability.

STERN: Bob, would it have been possible to accomplish many of these objectives without undertaking a leveraged buyout? And what is the role of all this debt financing, if any, in the value creation process? Do you think a company like John Johnstone's Olin Corporation could benefit from adding significantly more leverage to his company's modest debt-equity mix? John, incidentally, has told me that he thinks this whole LBO and management buyout movement is crazy.

JOHN JOHNSTONE: The word I've used is "immoral," Joel.

KIDDER: I do not believe it's immoral, but nor do I believe it's the solution to all corporate problems. The primary role of the high leverage was to provide us with the means of gaining our independence from Kraft. We're clearly far better off now as an independent company. Debt financing also allowed us to concentrate the equity sufficiently so as to give management a significant ownership stake.

And that also has made a big difference.

The Leveraged Recap as an Alternative to LBOs

STEWART: John, do you think LBOs are immoral because managers are buying at prices that subsequently enable them to reap excessive rewards?

JOHNSTONE: No, I think they're immoral because they deprive the current shareholders of the long-term intrinsic value of the corporation. The shareholders have no choice in the matter. They are forced to sell into the offer.

You see, I begin with the premise that a public company has "long-term" prospects that are being evaluated by "long-term" shareholders. The management buyout, by fixing the buyout price today, effectively denies those shareholders the right to participate in the future value of the company.

STEWART: Well, then, would you be more in favor of a leveraged recapitalization like the one done by FMC? That transaction left some equity in public hands while giving management a large stake.

JOHNSTONE: Yes, I would, at least in the sense that it offers shareholders a way of continuing to participate in the future of the company. And, in some of these recaps, shareholders have been granted options, which also gives them a stake in the company's future. With options, the shareholders can either choose to sell or retain their ownership rights.

STEWART: That's true. But, at the same time, we haven't seen many *voluntary* recaps—the kind initiated by management. Most have instead been defensive—and, in fact, desperate—responses to hostile tender offers. So, why don't we see more of these leveraged recapitalizations? They seem to offer the benefits of concentrated management equity ownership without the "self-dealing" taint of an LBO. Are people afraid of putting their company "into play"?

JOHNSTONE: Yes, I think so. There's no question that a recap proposal from management puts the company into play.

STEWART: Maybe it does. But there is not a single instance of a *management-initiated* recap proposal, in the absence of a clear and present threat of takeover, that resulted in the company's later being taken over by a third party. In fact, in the FMC case, the recap plan was submitted to a shareholder vote. Almost a year went by from the start to the finish of the deal, the recap went through, and the company today operates as a profitable, independent entity.

RICHARD SIM: Bennett, I am sympathetic to John's position on management buyouts. There is a fundamental conflict of interest when the management team proposes to buy out the public stockholders. And even in the case of recaps, when the management team suddenly shows up one day and says it wants to buy back a lot of the stock for itself, then they're clearly at that point no longer speaking for the shareholders. They're clearly interested in doing a deal because they think they're going to profit from it. In that sense, I find MBOs and leveraged recaps a little disquieting. People ostensibly hired to serve shareholders are at bottom acting in their own behalf.

But, at the end of the day, the issue really turns on how the board handles such a clear conflict of interest. That, I think, is the key as to whether it's an immoral or a proper process.

STERN: But what if it's the very act of giving management ownership that makes the company more valuable? If that is the case, and the higher valuation on the shares would not result otherwise, then public stockholders are arguably major beneficiaries of proposals by management to take companies private. In this case, the only responsibility of the board is to conduct an auction to prevent management from "stealing" the company. So, unless bidders are somehow discouraged from competing with management's offer, then I'm hard-pressed to see how stockholders suffer from the process of management buyouts.

SIM: I would agree with you, Joel, at least in theory. But, in practice, you often see poorly performing managements using recapitalizations to entrench themselves at the expense of their stockholders. For example, when we initially explored an offer with the Barry Wright Corporation, the management team—which was really derelict—came forward with a recap plan that would have given them much more equity and hence much more control. And the company had a weak board that went along with the proposal. Those kinds of transactions, where you are entrenching a poor management, really turn my stomach.

But, having made this objection to recaps, let me also say that there is nothing inherently wrong in the bidding process itself and with a freely functioning corporate control market. And I am certainly not against attempts to improve management incentives by getting management more ownership. But there are a number of ways you can accomplish the same end that don't involve the entrenchment possibilities of a leveraged recap.

STEWART: Was that recap proposal a response to your takeover offer? Or did the proposal come before your bid?

SIM: We talked to them before they made their proposal. But they started working on the proposal before we became really serious and made our formal offer.

MICHAEL MURRAY: So, they had heard footsteps, then, had they not?

SIM: Well, they were doing so badly that they were hearing footsteps behind them and saw a brick wall in front of them.

Making Management Pay for Its Equity

STERN: Well, Dick, one thing puzzles me about this case you've brought up. Why would a poor-quality management like the one you've just described be willing to risk a significant chunk of their own personal net worth to buy an equity stake in their company? Isn't that what happened in the case of Barry Wright?

SIM: No, management didn't offer to put up any of its own money to buy back the stock.

STERN: They didn't have to pay anything to be included in the deal? I suspect that the board of directors of Barry Wright would probably have provided sufficient protection of the public shareholders' interests simply by making certain that the management group was laying out a significant amount of its own capital.

MURRAY: I agree with you, Joel. But, in most of the leveraged transactions I've seen in recent years, management has not put new money into the deal; instead they have simply been asked to trade in their existing stock or options. And, in some cases, they are even allowed to carry forward their old option programs while also receiving substantial new equity—all this without contributing any new cash.

This practice, which became the rule in the deals done in the mid-1980s, was in sharp contrast to what went on in the early days of the LBOs. In the first KKR deals that we participated in back in the 70s, management was forced to put significant amounts of their own capital at risk. In fact, besides providing senior debt in these early deals, we at Continental also used to do separate financings for the individual executives in our private banking area. In those days, managements would typically hock their houses and really put themselves on the line. But all that was lost when the dealmakers began to compete for the attention of management to win the deal.

The consequence, then, has been that managements have been able to get their equity stake, if not for free, then simply by rolling over their old options. And this means that the downside risk to management, which was an important source of security to creditors in these deals, has been lost

In the first KKR deals that we participated in back in the 70s, management was forced to put significant amounts of their own capital at risk. In fact, besides providing senior debt in these early deals, we at Continental also used to do separate financings for the individual executives in our private banking area. In those days, managements would typically hock their houses and really put themselves on the line. But all that was lost when the dealmakers began to compete for the attention of management to win the deal....

In most of the leveraged transactions I've seen in recent years, management has not put new money into the deal...And this means that the downside risk to management, which was an important source of security to creditors in these deals, has been lost.

— Michael Murray —

along the way. As creditors, we like the fact that management has hocked themselves to the gills and is not going to sleep well at night. The fact that they can get rich from a transaction is of interest to us. But, as bankers, we are much more interested in their willingness to share the downside risk—the one we bear disproportionately in such deals.

MICHAEL JENSEN: Let me just add something here to this point Mike Murray has made. It is something that is absolutely critical, I think, to understanding what has gone wrong with a number of the leveraged deals we saw in the last years of the 1980s. The failure of not only management, but also the deal-making firms themselves—the Wassersteins & Perellas of the world—to put significant equity into their own deals has dramatically increased the probability that deals are overpriced and, as a result, overleveraged.

Just look at the structure of the Interco deal, a transaction in which management was essentially *paid* to do the deal. Far from putting money into the deal, the Interco managers, who held about $12 million in equity prior to the deal, actually *took out* $30 million—roughly half in cash and half in debt. They ended up with only about

4% of the equity of the restructured company—an unusually small amount—which was worth only about $6 million at the high trading price of $3 7/8. These facts go a long way toward explaining Interco's subsequent difficulties.

Capital Scarcity?

STERN: A number of observers have told me, "Joel, there's just no money available for deals anymore." Now, is that because there really is no money available for deals, or is it just because people are not willing to hock themselves the way Mike Murray wants them to?

MURRAY: There's plenty of money available for *good* deals. Forstmann Little recently announced its Gulfstream Aerospace deal; and it was done promptly. There were plenty of buyers for that paper in the secondary market as well. But they did not use junk bonds. Instead they used their own funds to provide the mezzanine or subordinated debt layer.

JENSEN: But, in that case, Forstmann Little already had the funds.

MURRAY: They had the subordinated debt, but they had to go out and get the senior money.

JENSEN: Yes, that's true. But, it certainly is my impression that money for these deals has dried up substantially.

MURRAY: Yes, absolutely.

JENSEN: And it's not just economic factors that are causing this capital shortage. There have certainly been problems with some leveraged transactions. But these problems—which I think are best left to the market to sort out—have been greatly compounded by the intervention of the regulators, by the pressure that's coming from the various banking and thrift regulatory authorities, in the form of the new HLT disclosure rules and a whole variety of new oversight measures.

We are in a position now, it seems to me, where credit is no longer being allocated primarily on the basis of price but is in fact being allocated—to put the case most starkly—on the basis of fear. We are moving to a situation where making a bad bank loan will get you fired and maybe even put in jail as a criminal. That has major implications for the future prosperity of this country. If any single factor is capable of putting us into recession, it will be the restrictive effect of regulators blocking transactions and otherwise restricting credits that private parties would choose to engage in—that is, if they

THE FAILURE OF NOT ONLY MANAGEMENT, BUT ALSO THE DEAL-MAKING FIRMS THEMSELVES—THE WASSERSTEINS & PERELLAS OF THE WORLD—TO PUT SIGNIFICANT EQUITY INTO THEIR OWN DEALS HAS DRAMATICALLY INCREASED THE PROBABILITY THAT DEALS ARE OVERPRICED AND, AS A RESULT, OVERLEVERAGED.

— MICHAEL JENSEN —

were being allowed to act on a strictly economic basis.

MURRAY: Well, I agree with you, Michael, that money is in shorter supply. The hurdle rates on new investment are higher and the discipline in lending is tighter. And the capital structures today are going to have as much as twice the proportion of equity they once had. But, frankly, I think much of the change is a needed corrective to past excesses. There's no question, at least I think in most people's minds, that the so-called "due diligence" process has been terrible for the last two or three years. And that's why you've got so many deals coming unraveled.

But I also believe that for the right deals there's plenty of money available. It's a little harder to get. But that's because the insurance lenders, the Prudential Baches of this world, are now lying low, waiting for the price of credit to come up to acceptable levels.

JENSEN: I agree that there is plenty of money out there. That's not what I'm saying. I'm saying that it's being allocated by Washington and not by Wall Street.

MURRAY: You could almost say, Michael, that it's now being *allocated*. Over the last few years most of the discipline in the allocation process was lost.

JENSEN: I agree that there have been problems with a number of the large deals done in recent years. But, as I said earlier, most of those deals would never have been done at those prices if the dealmakers and the managements had put up a significant piece of the equity. We don't need the regulators to solve this problem by telling banks and insurance companies where they can put their money. The dealmakers will sort out the good deals from the bad when they are forced to commit their own capital. And I believe much of that was already happening before the bank examiners stepped in.

The Case of Arbor Drugs

STERN: As long as we are talking about large equity ownership stakes, let me steer the discussion toward Gene Applebaum, who is the majority stockholder as well as the CEO of a company called Arbor Drugs. I had the pleasure of meeting Gene back in August of 1985, when his company was still privately held. As I mentioned earlier, his sales were then just a bit above $150 million. The company consisted of 41 drugstores sprinkled around the state of Michigan.

In 1986, the company went public by means of an IPO. Gene today runs a company with sales that are well over $500 million, and with some 91 stores. And, Gene, if my understanding is correct, you are the majority shareholder, are you not?

EUGENE APPLEBAUM: Yes, I own 65% of the stock.

STERN: Although that pretty much rules out the possibility of a hostile takeover, the size of your ownership would seem to me to be very effective in convincing outside investors that you have a strong interest in the company's performance. But, how do you manage to transmit that ownership incentive to the managers in your company?

APPLEBAUM: Well, when I was private, I didn't have stock options. Now, as CEO of a public company, I have an ability to give stock options to the right players. It's really helped a great deal. Those stock options have become the driving force behind the profitability of Arbor Drugs. The management team is committed to making a success of the company.

STERN: We're going to focus more directly on incentive compensation later in this discussion. But, let me take this opportunity to ask you about your capital structure. Because Arbor Drugs has such a modest amount of debt, it seems to me the company is paying an

awful lot more in corporate taxes than it really has to. Why have you chosen not to have a higher debt-equity ratio and thereby shelter more of the corporation's income—especially given that you're entitled to 65% of the tax savings through your own equity stake?

APPLEBAUM: Our principal reason for restricting our use of debt is to preserve our opportunities to invest in future growth, which generally means making good acquisitions when they become available. If we run out of growth opportunities, then we may reconsider and perhaps look at the possibility of a leveraged payout to investors. But, for the time being, we are very comfortable with what we're doing, growing and picking up opportunities while staying within our core business of operating drugstores.

STERN: Mike, you are one of the principal lenders to Arbor Drugs. Do you think the company could operate comfortably while using a considerably higher level of debt? Assume for the sake of argument that they raised their debt-equity ratio by 20 to 25 percentage points. Would you continue to lend to that company?

MURRAY: Yes, I would. The company clearly has excess debt capacity, if you will. But, if I understand Gene's argument, the company's primary interest is in retaining its growth options rather than, say, tax-sheltering the greatest amount of income possible. And I think that's fine. If you take a look at the S&P 400 today, I suspect you would find a good many companies in a similar position—that is, sitting on large amounts of cash plus unused debt capacity. In any marketplace, cash is always king; and it's a triple-crowned king today. So, it doesn't surprise me a bit that companies like Gene's are sitting on cash while waiting to capitalize on some good strategic investment opportunities.

Now, if such opportunities are not likely to come along, and thus the firm

Our principal reason for restricting our use of debt is to preserve our opportunities to invest in future growth, which generally means making good acquisitions when they become available. If we run out of growth opportunities, then we may reconsider and perhaps look at the possibility of a leveraged payout to investors. But, for the time being, we are very comfortable with what we're doing, growing and picking up opportunities while staying within our core business of operating drugstores.

— Eugene Applebaum —

has no real growth prospects, then I agree with you, Joel, that a leveraged recap might be entirely appropriate.

JENSEN: Are you saying that if Gene uses up his debt capacity today, and a good acquisition comes along, he won't be able to make that acquisition?

MURRAY: Banks typically want to maintain the discipline that comes with having the existing debt paid down before making another major lending commitment. But, if the right acquisition comes along, the banks are also typically flexible enough to restructure the existing debt—especially if the acquisition is able to service the interest and principal payments out of its own cash flow.

APPLEBAUM: In a number of recent acquisitions we have been looking at, some of the players have been forced to drop out because they could not get any more financing.

JENSEN: I'm not surprised to hear that, Gene, and I suspect that the inability to raise the financing has a lot to do with the political and regulatory factors that are restricting money for leveraged transactions.

MURRAY: But, Mike, once again, it is not only the work of bank regulators that is causing banks to become more cautious. In many cases, they are reassessing the risk-reward trade-off on new loans after having been burned on a number of bad deals in the last few years. So, it's not only regulatory politics that are at work here, but also the fundamental economics of sound lending.

In almost all of these discussions of capital structure, we tend to take only extreme cases. We typically start with a company that is grossly underleveraged by any imaginable standard. And, from that starting point, we inevitably seem to propose moving to the opposite extreme—namely, taking on so much leverage that the company's operating options are compromised.

So, there are certainly a number of intermediate positions between having an AA rating and becoming an HLT. But, for reasons that escape me, there seem to be very few companies that have chosen to take this upper middle road to capital structure. Rarely do I see companies attempting to make what I would call a *judicious* use of debt finance. Adopting such a strategy would give you much of the tax advantage of high leverage without endangering the company's investment options.

STEWART: On this issue of leveraged companies' abilities to fund acquisitions, consider the case of Triangle Industries—a company that first acquired National Can in a highly leveraged transaction and then turned around and acquired American Can's canning business in a similarly highly leveraged transaction. There are also many examples of LBO companies making significant acquisitions *after* going private. Owens Illinois went through a leveraged buyout and then soon after acquired Brockway Glass in another leveraged buyout.

JENSEN: O.M. Scott did the same thing.

STEWART: All of this suggests to me that if a highly-leveraged company is performing well, and if the businesses they buy stand on their own merits as acquisitions, then the ability to use debt in those transactions is probably going to be there as well. Indeed, the mere fact of having all that leverage may serve as an important test of the expected value of a proposed transaction. If the company is already highly leveraged, then it will be less likely to make use of its excess debt capacity to fund an overpriced acquisition. And, as shown by an important SEC study, those companies that made overpriced acquisitions in the 1980s were likely themselves to become the next takeover targets.

THERE MAY BE AN OPTIMAL LEVEL OF MANAGERIAL EQUITY OWNERSHIP THAT IS WELL BELOW 100%—ONE THAT, ALTHOUGH GIVING MANAGEMENT A SIGNIFICANT OWNERSHIP STAKE, FALLS SHORT OF CONFERRING ABSOLUTE CONTROL OF THE COMPANY.

— MICHAEL JENSEN —

JENSEN: Bennett, I would have agreed with you if we had been holding this discussion a year ago. But the world has changed significantly. Economic merit is no longer enough to get a deal done on a stand-alone basis. We are no longer dealing with just economic forces, we are also facing constraints imposed by the political sector.

And viewed in this light, what Gene is saying makes some sense. He's seeing his competitors drop out of the bidding just because they can't get the money.

Too Much Equity Concentration?

JENSEN: I want to raise a separate issue with regard to Gene's company. I'm a well-known advocate of higher equity holdings by managers. But I do think we have to be sensitive to the fact that when those holdings amount to an effective control position, it's not at all clear what the minority interest holds. I'm not sure it's wise to make the public a minority stockholder in any business. I say that because even people who have a very large fractional interest in their companies are liable to make big mistakes and refuse to change. The best evidence of this is the now well-documented finding that the stock prices of companies currently run by their founders often rise sharply when those founders die unexpectedly.

The point I'm making is that there may be an optimal level of managerial equity ownership that is well below 100%—one that, although giving management a significant ownership stake, falls short of conferring absolute control of the company. I think you still need some kind of external monitor looking over management's shoulder—like the role that KKR plays at Duracell.

We now have some statistical evidence, based on a reasonably large sample of firms, that demonstrates that as the percentage of management

equity holdings rises from zero to 100%, the average "Q" ratio (which is somewhat like the price-to-book ratio) of the companies tends to rise along with it and reaches a peak when management ownership reaches a level of around 40 to 45%. As you get closer to 50%, the Q ratios begin to fall and continue falling after you go through the 50% level.

What this evidence suggests to me is the following: When the CEO of a company has an uncontested controlling position, there is no outside influence on his actions other than what comes through the bankers and the covenants. The controlling owner may prove much more willing to pursue interests other than increasing stockholder value when minority stockholders amount to a passive, silent business partner. In such cases, the minority interests are forced to rely on nothing more than the controlling owner's professed commitments to them.

TOD HAMACHEK: I think that's a good point—one that I see clearly reflected in the performance of some of our competitors. Our weakest competitor, for example, has averaged a 2 or 3% return on its equity over the last six or seven years. The CEO has over 50% of the stock. And they have two classes of stock, one voting and one nonvoting. Management controls the voting, needless to say, while the outside stockholders bear much of the brunt of the company's poor performance. That situation is absolutely pathetic.

JENSEN: Yes, that's what can happen when you turn the public into a minority stockholder. And, for this reason, I would recommend that Gene consider reducing his holdings below 50% before too long.

APPLEBAUM: Well, let me say that Arbor Drugs has achieved the highest return on investment and stockholder return in the industry.

HAMACHEK: It isn't just the question of your ownership. Also important is

your ability to motivate your management team.

APPLEBAUM: As long as I'm motivated, the company will be motivated. But, to answer Mike's point, I do have to think of the time when I'm not going to want to do this anymore. We control a large part of the market here in Michigan. But there are a number of other drug chains, like Walgreen, CVS, and Rite-Aid, that want to come into the state. So, the opportunity is there to sell the company to a corporate buyer. Or, when the stock market improves, I may choose to sell more of my stock to the public.

The Case of Vista Chemical: Life After an LBO

STERN: As a counterpoint to Gene Applebaum's strategy at Arbor Drugs, let me turn now to John Burns. John runs Vista Chemical, a company that was sold by Du Pont to management in an LBO in 1984. After performing well and working its debt down for two years, the company went public again in 1986. Since returning to public status, the company has continued to perform exceptionally well. In fact, about a year ago I recall that the company's return on net assets was running almost as high as 40% after taxes; and the remaining debt was being paid down very rapidly.

So, having gone private and then returned as a public company—and having done extremely well for himself and his shareholders in the process—John said to me, "What you don't understand, Joel, is that we are not as sharp as we were a year or two ago when our debt levels were much higher than now. My people are not running their businesses quite as efficiently as they were before. Should we do a leveraged recap and get the debt back to what we were accustomed to seeing during our LBO?"

Although we were currently earning very high returns on our assets in place, we felt there was little prospect of earning adequate returns on *new* investment. Our business has historically been a cyclical one. And because most of our competitors were in the process of adding extra capacity, we felt that prices in our industry were likely to fall in the next year or so. For this reason, the return on whatever additional capacity we added would have been well below our cost of capital....

Some companies may have incentives to expand capacity that have nothing to do with increasing stockholder value; but maintaining growth per se is not part of our basic mission. One of the great benefits of debt financing is that it forces management to make a clear distinction between the sometimes contradictory goals of creating value and growing the company.

—John Burns —

The company decided to undertake a leveraged recap in the summer of 1989, buying back 33% of its stock and raising its debt-to-capital ratio to about 60%. John, would you tell us more about what you were thinking when you decided to do a second major recapitalization?

BURNS: Our principal reason for doing the recap was to find the most effective use for the substantial cash flow we were generating in our business. We had essentially two choices: We could continue to make fairly significant investments to give us additional capacity in our chemicals business—while at the same time gradually increasing our dividend payout and continuing our modest program of buying back shares on the open market. Or we could execute a decisive, one-step transaction that would accomplish several important goals. Probably most important was that it gave us a means of returning our excess cash to stockholders, but it also allowed us to increase the equity ownership of management. It also enabled us to establish a major ESOP plan for our employees. At the time of this transaction, we had a very generous company matching savings plan. When we instituted the ESOP, we ended our plan of contributing cash and substituted contri-

butions of company stock. This stock was, of course, restricted in the sense that it could not be sold for some time except under unusual circumstances.

As a result of the leveraged transaction and the substitution of the ESOP for the old company cash matching plan, stock ownership by management and employees increased from 15% to over 25% today. At the same time, the recap solved the problem of our people sitting around having meetings about what to do with our excess cash. The result has been an improvement of our management focus, and our current operating results have already begun to reflect that improvement.

STEWART: John, can you tell us more about the kind of pressure you saw as a CEO to spend the company's free cash flow? The company had paid its debt down and was continuing to throw off large amounts of cash that could not be profitably reinvested in the basic business. Was there sort of an organizational imperative to begin dreaming up ways to spend the money that would not have arisen in the absence of the ready cash at hand?

BURNS: Well, we had a lot of cash and we needed to come up with a plan for using that cash. Our choices, as I mentioned, were basically either to

increase our dividend, increase internal investment, or make acquisitions. In fact, we looked at a number of possible acquisitions, but found it difficult to justify the prices that were being paid. So there were really few attractive alternatives for creating shareholder value with our cash. And thus our excess cash had become a major problem.

STEWART: But why not invest in new capacity? After all, you were currently earning 40% rates of return.

BURNS: That's right. But although we were currently earning very high returns on our assets in place, we felt there was little prospect of earning adequate returns on *new* investment. Our business has historically been a cyclical one. And because most of our competitors were in the process of adding extra capacity, we felt that prices in our industry were likely to fall in the next year or so. For this reason, the return on whatever additional capacity we added would have been well below not only our current rates of return, but also below our cost of capital. And such investments, as you and Joel have been arguing for years, would reduce shareholder value.

JENSEN: Bennett, John's distinction between his current returns and his expected returns on additional capac-

IN THE EARLY 1980S, THE OIL COMPANIES WERE EARNING HIGH AVERAGE RETURNS ON THEIR EXISTING CAPACITY, EVEN AS THE MARGINAL RETURNS ON NEW EXPLORATION AND DEVELOPMENT HAD TURNED NEGATIVE...THAT IS WHY YOU COULD BUY OIL MORE CHEAPLY ON "WALL STREET" THAN YOU COULD PRODUCE IT IN THE FIELDS.

— MICHAEL JENSEN —

ity is just the simple difference between a company's *average* return on investment and its *marginal* return. A failure to pay attention to this difference is exactly what got the oil industry into trouble in the early 1980s. At this time, the oil companies were earning high average returns on their existing capacity, even as the marginal returns on new exploration and development had turned negative. The stock market clearly recognized this problem; and that is why you could buy oil more cheaply "on Wall Street" than you could produce it in the fields. There was an enormous overinvestment problem, tremendous excess capacity, in the oil industry. And until hostile takeovers solved that problem by getting rid of the overcapacity, the oil companies continued to pour their massive amounts of free cash flow into investment ratholes.

STEWART: Well, John, does this mean that you believe that your competitors that did add capacity will ultimately not earn attractive returns on that investment?

BURNS: That's right. Of course, we may prove to be wrong. But, given the pace of the expansion we have seen, we have strong doubts about whether our competitors' investments will turn out to benefit their stockholders.

Now, some companies may have incentives to expand capacity that have nothing to do with increasing stockholder value; but maintaining growth per se is not part of our basic mission. One of the great benefits of debt financing is that it forces management to make a clear distinction between the sometimes contradictory goals of creating value and growing the company.

The Case of Olin Corporation

STERN: John, as CEO of Olin Corporation, when you observed what Vista Chemical was doing—using a much higher debt-equity ratio, strengthening

equity incentives for the management group, and instituting an ESOP plan— did that not raise questions in your mind as to how Olin was serving its shareholders?

JOHNSTONE: Well, Joel, we ended up doing nearly all of the same things. But, unlike Vista, we kept our shareholders in the game. We did the ESOP, we bought some shares back, we sold off businesses to sharpen our focus, and we also made some very cost-effective acquisitions. Some people have complained about our inability to expand our chemical business. But, as John Burns just suggested, the multiples on chemical companies have been so high that we too have refused to make those kinds of acquisitions.

Because we are a multi-industry business, however, we have been able to take advantage of acquisitions away from the chemical side. But, let me hasten to say that we are not a conglomerate and do not consider ourselves to be a conglomerate by any means. The reason we don't is that there are technology links across all our major businesses. Our managers have a good understanding of our three or four key businesses, and of how to manage the connections among them.

But, to respond to your question, Joel, I did watch the recapitalization of Vista Chemical, and also the recap of FMC, with great interest. And, partly influenced by those cases, we consciously chose to let our debt-equity levels go up. So, as a matter of fact, I'm now sleeping less at night because our debt-equity ratio is slightly over 50%— although we do have an asset sale pending at the Federal Trade Commission that should get us down to around 45%. But we can survive at this level. And, although our current credit rating is not in any danger, I would like to see us get back down below 45%.

In short, Joel, although we have taken on more debt, we have also left our shareholders in place. Over the

past few years, we have raised our ROE from 10% to 18%. The stock has gone up—and I have gotten lots of nice letters from the shareholders.

STERN: But, let me ask John Burns whether there isn't still a considerable difference between the debt ratios of Vista Chemical and Olin.

BURNS: Well, interest coverage ratios are probably the only way to make a direct comparison. Our own coverage ratio today is around two times pre-tax earnings. And we feel quite confident in our ability to operate on that basis.

JOHNSTONE: Although I'm not accustomed to thinking about our debt in terms of interest coverage ratios, I would guess our cash flow-to-interest ratio is running around seven times. I am certain, however, that we are well within our covenant levels.

More on Debt and Free Cash Flow

JOHN GOULD: In listening to these arguments about the relationship between debt financing and cash flow, I'm having trouble distinguishing between cause and effect. On the one hand, I have heard several people say that the use of debt helps the company generate more cash, whether by saving on taxes or by forcing management to cut costs. At the same time, I have heard that companies that have too much cash flow are precisely the kind that are most in need of debt. The reasoning seems circular to me.

So, I'm not quite clear what is the motivation for all this debt? What is it in your case, John?

BURNS: Well, let me put it this way. We began by recognizing that our high level of operating cash flow was creating a problem for us—because we couldn't profitably reinvest it. A company that is generating a lot of cash flow and that has no debt and no plan for profitably reinvesting that cash is a sitting duck for a takeover.

I did watch the recapitalization of Vista Chemical, and also the recap of FMC, with great interest. And, partly influenced by those cases, we consciously chose to let our debt-equity levels go up.... We did the ESOP, we bought some shares back, we sold off some businesses to sharpen our focus, and we also made some very cost-effective acquisitions....

But, unlike Vista, we kept our shareholders in the game.

— John Johnstone —

We accomplished several major aims in one fell swoop by means of a major recapitalization that replaced equity with debt. We effectively increased our level of operating cash flow in two ways: by reducing our reported earnings and hence lowering our tax bill; and by creating greater pressure to manage for efficiencies. At the same time, the fact that the higher cash flow is now committed to interest and principal payments has eliminated the reinvestment problem that drove us to do the transaction in the first place.

STEWART: Another important benefit of debt finance is that it allows for a narrowing of the base of equity behind the company's assets. For example, as I'm sure Bob Kidder will tell you, if you have a business that has a $100 million market value and it's financed exclusively with equity, to get a 10% stake in management's hands would require either that management come up with $10 million or that current shareholders suffer a $10 million dilution of their current value. But, if the corporation is financed with, say, 80% debt and 20% percent equity, then management can purchase a 10% equity interest with only $2 million—an investment they may be more able to finance.

So debt financing changes the risk-reward profile in such a way as to allow a much more significant equity holding by management. It also allows an ESOP to provide stronger incentives for employees. An ESOP in a highly-leveraged company is likely to be far more effective than a plan with the same dollar amount in an all-equity firm of the same size, simply because the percentage ownership will mean much more at the margin to the employees.
JENSEN: Can I expand on that point for a minute? I think this point is enormously important and widely misunderstood. I have often heard people say that the most important motivating factor in a CEO's compensation plan is the fraction of the CEO's personal wealth invested in the stock. But, while I think that is important, what really matters in the end—and I believe this is the only useful way to think about this problem—is the percentage of the equity of the company that the management or the CEO owns. It is that percentage that will most heavily influence corporate investment decisions at the margin—say, whether or not to go ahead with a "strategic" acquisition that is clearly overpriced.

If that number is very small—below 1%—then we've got major problems.

In such cases, when presented with a choice between maintaining corporate growth and increasing profitability by forgoing investment and perhaps even shrinking the size of the firm, management will almost always choose growth—unless, that is, the takeover market presents a credible deterrent. But when that number gets to about 5% for the CEO, and, say, 20% for the entire senior management team (and, obviously, some of these numbers must be scaled to the overall size of the company), the evidence we're now seeing suggests that such organizations are behaving in a fundamentally different way. In such cases, profitability rather than growth appears to become the major corporate objective.

Now, as Bennett suggests, one of the very important functions that debt has served over the last decade has been to reduce the size of that equity "nut," thereby enabling managers either to purchase—or, in some cases, to be granted—significant equity stakes. And, based on the research we now have on LBOs and some other evidence I've cited earlier, I think there's a wide range of companies in this country whose value would increase dramatically if we could overcome the political problems associated with do-

A COMPANY THAT IS GENERATING A LOT OF CASH FLOW AND THAT HAS NO DEBT AND NO PLAN FOR PROFITABLY REIN-VESTING THAT CASH IS A SITTING DUCK FOR A TAKEOVER.

— JOHN BURNS —

ing a correct scaling down of the equity nut and then, if necessary, just turning over an equity interest to management. At the same time, though, I agree with Mike Murray's argument that it would be even better if management paid for the equity and thus carried some downside risk.

But, again, even if we just gave management a substantial equity stake, I believe that the performance and value of the companies would improve so greatly that shareholders would be more than compensated for the dilution they would bear in simply turning over 10% of the stock of the company. But such stock, of course, would have to be granted with the constraint that it not be sold.

CEO Compensation: The Current State of Affairs

JENSEN: One of the things that puzzles me a lot is that I seldom observe any constraints put on the equity holdings that managers get through stock option and other typical compensation plans. I think this arrangement is crazy. Here we have compensation committees setting up equity compensation plans for managers. But they simultaneously turn around and hire investment advisers whose mantra is "sell and diversify." Such equity plans thus amount to nothing more than a revolving door, a subterfuge for giving management higher cash compensation. After the stock has been awarded to management and then sold, it obviously does nothing to provide incentives.

One CEO I was talking to recently told me that he's independently arrived at this 20% rule. He runs a small, highly profitable company, and he wants to see his employees holding about 20% of the shares of the firm. And they're putting in stock option plans and various ways to get stock in the hands of their people. He also has

laid down an informal rule that you won't continue to work for that company if you sell the shares without his permission. Because there are only a couple of thousand employees, it's not hard to monitor compliance with that rule. He does allow them to sell their stock in special cases—a financial emergency, the kids are going to college, or something like that. But he expects them to come and explain to him why they want to sell the stock. And not very many people even bother to come.

Now, why don't we observe these kind of policies more widely practiced? Or am I wrong?

BURNS: I think in part you're wrong. If you lived in Houston, you would have seen an enormous amount of wealth tied up in the oil and collateral industries just vanish overnight. All those people with all that stock that they thought was wonderful today wish they had sold and diversified. One day they were worth $50 million and, if they didn't sell, the next day they were broke. I am talking about people who worked for 10 or 15 years, amassed some wealth, and, for whatever reasons, didn't sell their stock. Now they're broke, they've had to sell their houses, and their kids are borrowing money to go to college. That, to me, is crazy.

JENSEN: Well, John, let me say that I haven't forgotten my lessons about portfolio diversification from a personal standpoint. But that is a separate issue from what we're dealing with here—and I think it is very important that we not confuse your issue of personal diversification with corporate compensation policy.

Let me explain what I mean here. I am beginning with the assumption that we're already paying market wages for managers and then we're simply adding stock to the existing compensation plan. That is, on top of those market wages we want to put a pure "incen-

tive" system that gets stock into the hands of the managers. If the system is set up in this way, I see no reason to let managers follow diversification rules and untie their wagon from the company. If I am chairman of the board, and I have granted them stock *solely* to provide them with stronger incentives to perform, I don't want them to untie their wagon. I want them to understand—even if they're in Texas—that if this thing turns down, an important part of their job is to get the firm's capital out of this industry.

And who knows? At some point, drugstores may not be so good in Michigan. Gene Applebaum needs to know that he, as well as the people under him, are wise enough and have financial interest enough to try and anticipate that possibility.

APPLEBAUM: Yes, you're right.

JENSEN: His people need to have a reason to overcome the natural tendency to continue going down the same road, even when it becomes clear that that road is reaching a dead end. And that, in my opinion, is exactly what executives in the oil industry failed to do. For them, it was just business as usual even as marginal returns on new investment were going lower and lower.

BURNS: Mike, while I agree with your analysis of the overinvestment problem, I'm not sure I share your understanding of the structure of executive compensation. You implied that your top officers would be paid market wages, and then receive an incentive package over and above the normal level of competitive wages. But that is not really how corporate compensation works, at least in my experience.

My understanding is that, as you move up the executive ladder, a greater percentage of your compensation is at risk; and that the salary and the bonus and the incentives are all part of the expected compensation package. And what we want to discuss here, it seems

Kevin Murphy and I have just completed a four-year study on executive compensation, covering roughly 1,000 of the largest companies in the country....What was shocking to me, first of all, was our finding that these bonuses were almost completely unrelated to corporate performance. But what was perhaps even more shocking is that...our CEOs' total compensation packages are at no greater risk than the total pay of our workers on the bottom rung of the corporation.....

What we've experienced since the 1930s in this country is a massive change in the structure of executive compensation, a dramatic widening of the separation of ownership from control that Adolph Berle warned us about back in the 1930s...The median CEO of the largest 120 NYSE companies today owns less than .03% of the stock of his company. In the 1930s, that number was more like 0.3%.

—Michael Jensen —

to me, is what portion of that total package ought to be at risk, and for how long—whether it's a one-year period, a four-year period or whatever.

JENSEN: Well, John, let me give you some facts—because I too was under the impression that much of a CEO's total compensation is "at risk." My colleague at Rochester, Kevin Murphy, and I have just completed a four-year study on executive compensation, covering roughly 1,000 of the largest companies in the country. Consistent with what you just said, we found that bonuses run on average about 50% of salary. And for about one fourth of the companies we examined, the ratio of bonus to salary was even higher, running at about 75% of base salary.

BURNS: Is this just for CEOs?

JENSEN: Yes, for CEOs. Now what was shocking to me, first of all, was our finding that these bonuses were almost completely unrelated to corporate performance (and I'll come back to that point in a minute). But what was perhaps even more shocking—although it's clearly related to the first finding—is that the fraction of an executive's total compensation at risk does not increase as you move up through the corporate hierarchy. This is what we discovered when we com-

pared the percentage changes in annual CEO compensation—salary plus bonus plus incentives like options—to the changes in compensation experienced by two large samples of ordinary workers. We found that the percentage variability in the total compensation of CEOs is indistinguishably different from that of ordinary workers. That tells me that our CEOs' total compensation packages are at no greater risk than the total pay of our workers on the bottom rung of the corporation.

More on the Need for Pay-for-Performance

SIM: Mike, I think we all know that CEO compensation is done badly in this country. It's done badly in the sense that every survey that I have ever seen shows that CEO pay is correlated only with the size of the company. There is no evidence that CEOs, on average, are penalized for poor performance, short of eventually losing their jobs.

JENSEN: Even that rarely happens. The probability of a CEO's ever being dismissed, which is very low to begin with, rises only slightly when you move from the top-performing to the worst-

performing companies in the U.S. As Joe Grundfest, former Commissioner of the SEC, has commented, "The odds of a chief executive being fired by the board of directors is lower than the probability of a congressman's being indicted."

SIM: The other side of the problem is that rarely are CEOs allowed to participate significantly in the value they create for their shareholders. And this ridiculous state of affairs clearly reflects the established practice of corporate compensation committees. When reviewing executive compensation plans, the practical reality is that the compensation committees of our largest corporations let themselves be guided by the pay scales and incentive plans used by their peers, by corporations of comparable size. And that practice, of course, perpetuates the problem.

But, let me comment on your point about cash bonuses, Mike, because I'm not sure how well it applies to our case. In our company, we intentionally pay a base salary that is about 90% of the market salaries for comparable jobs. And our cash bonuses are also designed to be somewhat below market. They typically run as high as 30% of salary, whereas the average firm often

IF I AM CHAIRMAN OF THE BOARD, AND I HAVE GRANTED THEM STOCK *SOLELY* TO PROVIDE THEM WITH STRONGER INCEN-
TIVES TO PERFORM, I SEE NO REASON TO LET MANAGERS FOLLOW DIVERSIFICATION RULES AND UNTIE THEIR WAGON FROM
THE COMPANY.

— MICHAEL JENSEN —

pays bonuses as high as 50 to 60% of salary. But, we then attempt to bring our total package up to market by granting stock options. Such options cannot be exercised, however, until you've been with the company for five years.

Now, this somewhat deferred structure does have its problems. My own management team is a little younger than most, and we all have something of a cash flow problem. We're theoretically rich on paper; and our bankers are happy to lend us money against that paper. But I have people who work for me who have young children; and they would like to have a little bigger house. We're not paying them in salary, we're giving them stock instead. But eventually they will want to have more liquidity.

I personally would prefer to borrow from the bank with the stock as collateral, and pay the bank 10 or 11%. Because, if we continue to succeed, the value of our stock is going to continue to appreciate a hell of a lot faster than that. But, my point here is that, by substituting restricted stock for cash, you do impose liquidity problems on your employees; and you have to take that into consideration. But, having said that, I also believe that our vesting process does a good job in binding people to the company. Unless they're in it for the long haul, they will get discouraged and quit; and that's, quite frankly, just the way I want it.

JENSEN: That reminds me of another finding of our study. Over the roughly 50-year period between the 1930s and the 1980s, proportional CEO equity holdings in their own companies have fallen by a factor of ten. That is, the average CEO today owns less than one tenth of the percentage of his company's stock that he owned in the 1930s. And even the dollar value of CEO equity holdings, when adjusted for inflation, has also actually fallen over the same period. So, even as the market value of the equity of our corporations has in-

creased by a factor of three or four times (again, adjusted for inflation), the dollar value of CEO equity holdings has actually fallen. And the consequence of these two developments is that the median CEO of the largest 120 NYSE companies today owns less than .03% of the stock of his company. In the 1930s, that number was more like 0.3%.

Another important finding of our study, which is consistent with the CEO stock data I just mentioned, is that the pay-performance sensitivity for CEOs has also fallen by a factor of 10 since the 1930s. That is, the relation between year-to-year changes in a CEO's total compensation and changes in the market value of his company's stock is today less than one tenth what it was 50 years ago.

So, what we've experienced since the 1930s in this country is a massive change in the structure of executive compensation—a dramatic widening of the separation of ownership from control that Adolph Berle warned us about back in the 1930s. And let me say that I focus on CEOs not because I think because CEOs are the whole ballgame, but because they represent an important signal to people lower down in the corporate hierarchy. Their compensation is a reflection, however exaggerated, of what's going on in the lower levels of the organization.

There is one aspect of CEO compensation, however, that has changed surprisingly little since the 1930s. Given all the outcry we hear in the press about the level of executive pay, I found it interesting that the inflation-adjusted average pay of the top quartile of CEOs was actually higher in the 1930s than it was for the top quartile of the New York Stock Exchange in 1988. So, the charges carried by the *Wall Street Journal* and *Fortune* that our CEO pay is obscenely high and out of control simply does not comport with the facts—that is, if we're willing to use the period 1934-38 as a benchmark.

BURNS: I think you have a good point. But I think the extreme of having gains on stock options locked in until you're 65 years old is probably not workable. Companies could instead adopt a compromise policy—one that allows you to sell off, say, half of your holdings over time, while keeping the rest until you retire. Such a compromise seems more reasonable to me.

JENSEN: Yes, or some other variation of this system that provides some flexibility. For example, you could encourage people to hold their stock simply by means of moral suasion, without a formal requirement. As Dick Sim pointed out, there will be emergencies, legitimate reasons for people to convert at least part of their holdings into cash. And you want to accommodate those cases whenever possible. Enforcing this rule through moral suasion rather than through a rigid requirement has the benefit of establishing a culture within the organization, of fostering a tradition that effectively makes it a matter of disloyalty—at least, in most circumstances—to sell one's stock.

HAMACHEK: I agree with you very strongly on this point. We have a written policy that no officer of the company can sell stock without my permission. And we in senior management represent about 10% of the stock. Below the senior management level, we use your approach of moral suasion to encourage people to hold onto their stock. We have allowed people to sell who had good reasons. But I can count those people on one hand. We frankly consider it "disloyal" for our management or employees to sell their shares unless there is a emergency.

JENSEN: It would have a huge effect on the performance of American corporations if these kinds of schemes were widely adopted.

HAMACHEK: It does have a major effect on our performance. There is no doubt in my mind about it.

By substituting restricted stock for cash, you do impose liquidity problems on your employees; and you have to take that into consideration. But, having said that, I also believe that our vesting process does a good job in binding people to the company. Unless they're in it for the long haul, they will get discouraged and quit; and that's, quite frankly, just the way I want it....

I'm very confident about the long-run economic future of this country. And I am confident about our future *not* because of our large public corporations. My confidence lies in our venture capital industries, and in our small to medium-sized companies, many of which are privately owned or have the kind of unusual corporate structures that are represented by people sitting around this table. These are the kinds of companies that are creating jobs and that are innovating.

— Richard Sim —

One other observation: We don't use options the way most companies do—that is, as part of the annual compensation award. Instead, we have awarded large blocks of stock options that either don't start vesting for five years or vest only gradually over a 10-year period.

At present, we're going through the process of designing a long-term incentive plan for our middle management group. And it's probably going to take the form of performance-driven stock options. We have two major aims here: (1) to base the payoff from the options on a manager's ability to achieve returns on assets in excess of our weighted cost of capital and (2) to make the award large enough so that it provides a meaningful incentive.

Equity Ownership by the Board of Directors

KIDDER: Another major problem with large corporations is that corporate boards of directors rarely own significant amounts of shares. So, given their own reluctance to own company stock, there's very little hope that boards are going to design a compensation program that features major equity holdings by management. And that is a very important difference between a private LBO company like Duracell and our public companies. Our board of directors represents pretty close to 100% of the shares in the company.

JENSEN: Economically, solving the board incentive problem in our public companies is a trivial one. But emotionally and culturally, it's a major issue. Some of my colleagues at the Harvard Business School are convinced that it's inappropriate for directors to have any financial interests in the companies whose boards they serve on.

STEWART: What is the basis for that point of view?

JENSEN: It comes from the notion that a director's job is to be an impartial, aristocratic representative of all the "stakeholders" in the corporation. And God forbid he or she should have an actual interest in the welfare of the shareholders. I think this view is wrong. It's an example of "stakeholder" analysis run amok. When you begin to interfere with public corporations' primary mandate—that is, to maximize the wealth of its shareholders—then you lose sight of what creates wealth and improves the standard of living in this society.

Now, I concede that there are some problems with monopoly and some externality issues that will require government intervention to set things right. But, I think most economists for the last two hundred years have understood very well that what we want our corporations to do is to maximize their own value, their long-term equity value. It is precisely by allowing our corporations to concentrate on that aim that the long-run interests of all other corporate stakeholders—of employees, creditors, taxpayers, suppliers, and so forth—will ultimately be best served.

STERN: John, when you had your recapitalization last year, the directors of your company, with one or two exceptions, had practically no equity interest in the company. Why would you expect them to vote for this kind of a plan when you were making the company riskier and thus increasing their potential liability as directors without offering them any of the upside they would get through stock ownership?

BURNS: Well, yes, Joel, our board was reluctant to approve our recap plan, and perhaps for that reason. As you say, they were moving into a more risky scenario and it was clearly not going to benefit them.

JENSEN: John, why don't you set up a plan that encourages your board

OUR BOARD OF DIRECTORS REPRESENTS PRETTY CLOSE TO 100% OF THE SHARES IN THE COMPANY....AND THAT IS A VERY IMPORTANT DIFFERENCE BETWEEN A PRIVATE LBO COMPANY LIKE DURACELL AND OUR PUBLIC COMPANIES.

— ROBERT KIDDER —

members to acquire and keep equity in the company?

BURNS: Well, I frankly don't understand how to accomplish that. Assuming a director is paid $30 or $40 thousand a year, even if you insist they take that amount entirely in stock instead of cash, their stock ownership is never going to amount to a significant fraction of their wealth.

STERN: Well, I've been thinking a lot about this issue ever since that time, and one suggestion I would offer is that there be much larger potential cash awards for the board. And I would further recommend that the cash awards then go toward the purchase of deep in-the-money options with very long time horizons—somewhere between five and ten years. If they owned lots of these options, the board members would see a tremendous leveraging of their investment as well as very large payoffs if their companies did very well over that time.

STEWART: The options shouldn't be *deep* in the money, Joel. Instead, they should be only about 10% in the money, because that's what gives you the leverage. Options that were just 10% in the money would give you a 10-to-1 leveraging effect. But, if you made the options, say, 20% in the money, then you would get only a 5-to-1 leveraging of the manager's investment.

The model for this use of in-the-money stock options was provided by the Henley Group in San Diego. The company was a collection of money-losing operations spun off by Allied Signal. Its chairman, Michael Dingman, devised the idea as a way of replicating the incentives of an LBO for management without requiring the leverage of an LBO. The top 23 executives of the new company invested $11 million of their own capital on top of $97 million in non-recourse notes from the company (secured by the value of the securities) to buy $108 million of the company's stock. Management's eq-

uity stake, which amounted to 10% of the company's value, was effectively levered at about 10 to 1.

The interest rate on the corporate loan to management was analogous to the role of the company's cost of capital in the standard capital budgeting process. That is, management would come out ahead only if the market value of the company grew at a rate that exceeded the rate of interest on the loan. So this represents an effective way of turning managers into significant owners without diluting the interest of investors, and without imposing the burden of leverage on the company.

JENSEN: Although I haven't given much thought to the specific parameters, I would also endorse this proposal that management and the board buy in-the-money stock options. I think the notion of selling people in-the-money options, and even doing it on a levered basis, is a brilliant suggestion. It would allow you to separate the issue of how much leverage the corporation should bear from the problem of getting significant equity in management's hands. In this case, the executives themselves would be bearing most of the financial risk while insulating the rest of the corporation.

As Bennett explained earlier, one of the important advantages of LBO financing is that when you lever the company to 90%, it then becomes possible for managers to have 10, 20, or even 30% equity stakes, thus giving them enormous incentives. Now, if you can sell people in-the-money options for, say, $5 on a $50 stock, and if you also adjust the exercise price so that it rises at a rate equal to the cost of capital over time, this allows you to give your board of directors and your management a contract with very high pay-for-performance sensitivity without handing over a big chunk of base wealth. This is a proposal that is very different from the typical stock option

grants, in which case you're simply diluting the shareholders' claims in the hope of improving performance incentives. With these leveraged options, you're giving management a contract that represents almost pure pay-for-performance sensitivity.

Where Has the Risk Gone?

GOULD: I'd like to raise an issue that I haven't heard anyone comment on— and I think it's an important one. One of the basic principles of financial theory is the conservation of risk. That is, there is a total level of risk that goes along with a set of business projects and activities. And one of the important functions of our capital markets is to spread the risk among investors so it's a little bit easier to take.

Leveraged restructurings have dramatically changed the way risk is allocated among investors. Besides shifting more risk to creditors, leveraged restructurings are also shifting more risk onto management's shoulders. My concern is that, at some point, we may be shifting too much risk away from well-diversified investors and onto our banking system, our managements, and our employees.

From our conversation so far, I'm not sure whether the incentive schemes you're now proposing would push us further down the road of excessive *financial* risk-taking. I'm concerned that financial risk-taking may be reducing the amount of *investment* risk-taking that our companies ought to be doing to remain on a sound footing with their international competitors. Will managements with levered equity stakes be more or less likely to take a chance on expensive new technologies and other risky innovations?

JENSEN: There's an interesting study underway at the moment that bears directly on this issue. Steve Kaplan, one of the members of your faculty at Chicago, along with Jeremy Stein, one

Leveraged restructurings have dramatically changed the way risk is allocated among investors. Besides shifting more risk to creditors, leveraged restructurings are also shifting more risk onto management's shoulders. My concern is that, at some point, we may be shifting too much risk away from well-diversified investors and onto our banking system, our managements, and our employees.

I'm not sure whether the incentive schemes you're now proposing would push us further down the road of excessive *financial* risk-taking. I'm concerned that financial risk-taking may be reducing the amount of *investment* risk-taking that our companies ought to be doing to remain on a sound footing with their international competitors. Will managements with levered equity stakes be more or less likely to take a chance on expensive new technologies and other risky innovations?

— John Gould —

of my colleagues at Harvard, have looked at what happens to the risk of debt and equity in cases of corporate recapitalizations—that is, when large amounts of new debt are issued to buy back equity or to pay out a large one-time dividend. What this study finds is that the operating risk of these companies falls dramatically after the recap. In effect, the total amount of risk in the system goes down and the value increases significantly.

GOULD: Why does the risk go down?
JENSEN: We don't know at this stage. Our conjecture is that people are managing differently.

GOULD: How do you measure changes in risk?

JENSEN: By looking at the variability of the market value of the equity. And that variability is far lower than what we would expect to see, given the amount of new debt that has been placed on top of it.

GOULD: On the basis of that evidence, you can't really say that the risk of the *business* has gone down. All you can say is that the risk of the *securities* has gone down. You're making the assumption that the total risk of the securities accurately reflects the total risk of the business itself. I don't think you can make that assumption in this

case because your method captures changes only in the risk of one security relative to another. That is, the "beta" of the market is always going to be one, even if the risk of the average security in the market has increased by a significant amount.

So, I'm not convinced that your study addresses my concern that all corporations are absorbing more financial risk.

JENSEN: No, no, it does address the issue you're talking about. We could go through the details later.

BURNS: Well, as the CEO of a company that has gone through a leveraged recap, I think I understand the point Mike Jensen is making. Our use of leverage turned out to be self-correcting in the following sense. Even though we were operating with a capital structure that was 60% debt, we are, as I like to say to people, a "very conservatively-run" company. The reason we're a conservatively-run company is that management and employees on the plant floor own 25% of the company. We don't risk that ownership foolishly.

Now, from the point of view of the 1950s, people looking at our current balance sheet would fall off their chairs. But we feel it's very conservative in

terms of interest coverage. We don't think of ourselves as playing a risky game. I guess you could say that we have reduced the total risk of our operation by virtue of the fact that we're playing with our own money.

JENSEN: That is also representative of what I've been seeing in the LBOs I've been inside of. I've observed that the managers work hard to change the way they operate the business. Given that they have this tremendous financial risk and large ownership stake, they really strive to reduce their operating risks.

STERN: Bob, is that something you experienced after your LBO?

KIDDER: Well, because we started out with a debt-to-equity ratio of six to one, there is no question we began by trying to figure out how to reduce our risk by streamlining all aspects of our operations as much as we could. We immediately tried to improve our understanding of the sources and uses of our cash flow—and of the risks inherent in that cash flow. We wanted to understand our downside.

But, as major shareholders, we also gave considerable attention to the upside. Our compensation arrangements were structured such that, for every share management paid for in

I GUESS YOU COULD SAY THAT WE HAVE REDUCED THE TOTAL RISK OF OUR OPERATION BY VIRTUE OF THE FACT THAT WE'RE PLAYING WITH OUR OWN MONEY.

— JOHN BURNS —

cash, we were given five more shares in the form of options. And this, I think, is simply a variant of the in-the-money option scheme Bennett was talking about earlier. And I can tell you that such a program really does work.

But now that we have succeeded in managing our financial and operating risks, and have gotten our debt-equity ratio down to more moderate levels, we are faced with a somewhat different issue. John Johnstone earlier said that he wanted to get his debt-equity ratio down to about 45%. My question is, how did he determine that 45% was the amount of debt he wanted to live with? I'm curious because, as we pay off more and more debt, we're headed toward becoming a more financially conservative company just kind of naturally, without any conscious capital structure target in mind.

STEWART: So, you're wondering just how risky this financial risk has really been. You don't feel uncomfortable with the level of debt you've got now, do you?

KIDDER: No, not at all.

STEWART: And does it have a lot to do with the stability of your business and the cash flows it generates.

KIDDER: Yes, but again, our track record—the current level and stability of our cash flows—is not independent of the fact that management has such a major ownership stake. So, like John Burns, I believe that managers with the right incentives can take actions that effectively reduce the operating risk of their companies.

Conglomerates and Spin-Offs: The Cases of Crane and Penwest

STERN: Let me turn now to Shell Evans, CEO of the Crane Company, which is about to make a significant change in its incentive compensation program.

EVANS: That's right. We're redoing our whole incentive plan to make the managers of our different units feel and act more like owners of those individual units. We want to tie their rewards more directly to the returns on their businesses.

STERN: I took the liberty of saying earlier that your company was more like a conglomerate than any of the other companies represented here. Is that a fair description?

EVANS: I think that's correct. We used to report five or six segments as a public company. For this reason people said we were a conglomerate and too diversified. So I said to myself (rather cynically), I'll fix that problem just by reporting two instead of six segments. So now we have just wholesale distribution and industrial products; we're not a conglomerate anymore, we're now very focused.

But, seriously, we have some 30 different business units. And I think it's important that we view our company in this way. That is, we are breaking down our businesses as far as possible into self-contained units. We want to have a separate management team that feels responsible for the performance of each of those units.

STERN: Well, I can think of one good reason why you might *not* want to put these leveraged equity options in a company like yours. If you went any distance below the level of the very top management, stock options on the firm as a whole would not have much effect on the incentives of people running the 30 different units. The impact that each of these people would have on the aggregate market value of the company would necessarily be quite small.

For this reason alone, would you give some consideration to having some of your units publicly traded, thus allowing your operating managers to have an ownership stake in the activity they run?

EVANS: I don't think the spin-off structure you're proposing is an eco- nomic one. Spinning off a subsidiary to the public just to improve management incentives doesn't seem worth the costs in terms of being a separate public company and complying with the disclosure requirements. I think there are other, subtler ways of accomplishing the same end by using the bonus program more effectively.

STEWART: You may be right, at least in the majority of cases. The partial public offerings Joel is talking about are really only appropriate in a special set of circumstances—that is, cases where the business unit is growing much more rapidly than the rest of the company and can therefore benefit from direct access to capital. In the typical conglomerate, investor capital flows through a "Pachinko machine" of competing internal uses that greatly reduces the odds that the capital will flow to the operations with the most profitable uses for it. Investors are well aware of this problem; and that is one good reason why conglomerates often sell at substantial discounts to their break-up values.

An example of a well-designed partial spin-off is the McKesson Corporation's partial public offering of its profitable Armor-All unit. Up to that point, Armor-All was sort of lost within McKesson, which is a $6 billion distributor of beverages, drugs, and pharmaceuticals. And when McKesson announced its intention to take part of Armor-All public, McKesson's stock price rose from $59 to $65 a share.

HAMACHEK: I would like to respond to Shell Evans's comment that the costs of creating two or more separate public companies out of one are likely to outweigh the benefits. In 1984, I was part of a company called Univar that was trading for around $24. Since then, what was once Univar has been split up through spin-offs into four separate companies. The total value of the four public companies that once comprised Univar is today about $84. Now I can

With 30 different businesses, then, it's my job to make sure that the management of each one of those business units is focused on maximizing the value of that business unit. I don't try and run the 30 different businesses. We have a very small corporate headquarters. We'd be kidding ourselves if we thought we could actually run 30 businesses....

In the past, operating management would submit a plan that would generally be accepted by headquarters. And their bonus would be tied to their ability to exceed their plan...In place of that system we are now saying that your compensation will be based on both the level of returns in your operation and your improvement in these returns over time. According to your success in meeting both of these measures, you will build up a nest egg over time that will also have partial payouts each year. If your performance suffers, however, the size of your nest egg will actually be reduced—that is, bonuses already awarded can be lost if future performance is substandard.

— Shell Evans —

tell you, with some confidence, that the benefits of breaking up our old company have dwarfed the costs of having four separate public companies. In the case of my company, Penwest, we have increased our market value by a factor of 14 since going public in 1984.

What such spin-offs accomplish—and I think partial public offerings do pretty much the same—is to focus management and its board on their basic business. It forces management to concentrate on satisfying its customers, which is really the key to running a successful business. They can do it more effectively than when inside a conglomerate because of the simple fact that headquarters can't pay careful attention to 30 different businesses at once. And the line operating managements are not likely to have strong enough incentives to overcome the obstacles put up by headquarters. It simply doesn't pay them to rock the boat.

STEWART: But, wait a minute. KKR runs a successful conglomerate.

HAMACHEK: Well yes, but they've created separate companies and given their line management a major stake in the businesses they run.

EVANS: Well, although people might still regard us as a conglomerate, let me

point out that we have also used spin-offs for certain of our businesses. We spun off 100% of our cement company to our shareholders in 1988. And that's been very effective—in large part because it is a very different kind of company than the other businesses we're in, which are primarily engineered industrial products. The capital markets look at the cement business very differently from the way they view our other businesses. And that was our principal reason for making a stand-alone company. The fact that operating management now has a lot of equity in that business is an additional benefit, but it was not the primary motive.

With 30 different businesses, then, it's my job to make sure that the management of each one of those business units is focused on maximizing the value of that business unit. I don't try and run the 30 different businesses. We have a very small corporate headquarters. We'd be kidding ourselves if we thought we could actually run 30 businesses.

JENSEN: How many people are in your corporate headquarters?

EVANS: We've got a total of about 65, and that includes secretaries.

JENSEN: What's the total size of your organization?

EVANS: A billion five.

JENSEN: Billion five? You're fat.

EVANS: Excuse me?

JENSEN: KKR has 65 people who handle $58 billion.

EVANS: It depends on what you're doing at headquarters, though. KKR is basically just bankers, financiers. They don't need accountants and tax attorneys to comply with public disclosure requirements.

The Flaw in the Corporate Budgeting Process

STERN: Shell, how do you go about providing incentives for the people who run your 30 different units? And what percentage of their base salary is the maximum bonus in all forms that they can expect to receive?

EVANS: In the past, the ceiling has been about 100% of base salary, based on the performance of that unit. We used to determine the bonuses according to the return on equity or total capital employed in the business. We're now changing those measures to reflect cash flow rates of return on investment. Also, we have eliminated virtually all "overrides" and options on total corporate performance below the top level of management.

In 1984, I was part of a company called Univar that was trading for around $24. Since then, what was once Univar has been split up through spin-offs into four separate companies. The total value of the four public companies that once comprised Univar is today about $84....In the case of my company, Penwest, we have increased our market value by a factor of 14 since going public in 1984....

Our success has raised the question: How many operations can you spin off and how much smaller can you make your company before you fall below the optimal size? The conclusion I've come to is that, in the absence of significant economies of scale, smaller is likely to be better. If you want to maximize investors' return on capital, then a collection of independent companies that are clearly directed at distinct market segments is probably going to be much more effective than a large conglomerate.

— Tod Hamachek —

So, with the benefit of hindsight, we now recognize there were major problems with our old plan. In the past, operating management would submit a plan that would generally be accepted, perhaps with some modification, by headquarters. And their bonus would be tied to their ability to exceed their plan.

But we have now discarded that procedure. In place of that system we are now saying that your compensation will be based on both the level of your actual returns in your operation and your improvement in these returns over time. And, according to your success in meeting both of these measures, you will build up a nest egg over time that will also have partial payouts each year. If your performance suffers, however, the size of your nest egg will actually be reduced—that is, bonuses already awarded can be lost if future performance is substandard. And if you get fired or leave, then you lose the entire accumulated bonus.

STEWART: I've given a good deal thought to this issue of how companies like Shell's go about negotiating objectives with their different business units. The typical process in such cases is that once the parent negotiates a budget with a unit, the budget then becomes

the basis for the bonus. And they are also typically structured such that the budget kicks in when, say, 80% of the budgeted performance is achieved; and the maximum bonus is earned when management reaches, say, 120% of the budgeted level. There is thus virtually no downside and very limited upside.

Now, because the budget is negotiated between management and headquarters, there is a circularity about the whole process that makes the resulting standards almost meaningless. Because the budget is intended to reflect what management thinks it can accomplish—presumably without extraordinary effort and major changes in the status quo—the adoption of the budget as a standard is unlikely to motivate exceptional performance, especially since the upside is so limited. Instead it is likely to produce cautious budgets and mediocre performance.

So, because of the perverse incentives built into the budgeting process itself, I think it's important for a company to break the connection between the budget and planning process on the one hand and the bonus systems on the other hand. The bonuses should be based upon absolute performance

standards that are not subject to negotiation.

KIDDER: Absolutely.

STEWART: And, as I said earlier, that's really what an LBO does. It imposes an external performance standard, which in turn does not discourage operating management from devising an ambitious budget.

KIDDER: Abandoning the budgeting process may also allow management to take a longer-term view.

STEWART: Yes, that's right. If you establish absolute instead of relative or negotiated performance standards, then management is not going to be concerned about "banking" its bonus, or smoothing its earnings over time to meet a series of short-term hurdles—each of which has no memory, no relation to what came before. That's a critical difference, I think, between the way a company operates as a division of a public company and as a self-contained company after an LBO.

KIDDER: I agree with you completely, Bennett. In fact, after Duracell went private, our people started negotiating targets *up*, not down. It was a complete reversal of what typically goes on in large companies.

STEWART: Yes, and this change in the budgeting process has got to show up

AFTER DURACELL WENT PRIVATE, OUR PEOPLE STARTED NEGOTIATING TARGETS *UP*, NOT DOWN. IT WAS A COMPLETE REVERSAL OF WHAT TYPICALLY GOES ON IN LARGE COMPANIES.

— ROBERT KIDDER —

in operating improvements. The incentives to make beneficial changes is just so much stronger.

JENSEN: Another way to accomplish the same end would be just to give the line manager some fraction of the residual income or cash flow from the business. One of my colleagues who has been studying the Japanese system has found that before World War II it was common for Japanese CEOs to get between 5 and 10% of the income of their company in their back pockets.

In this country, I know of one very successful conglomerate that does that with no upper bound on compensation. I had a conversation with the operating head of one of the divisions of that conglomerate—a man who also used to be the CEO of the business before it was bought by the conglomerate. He told me that he was now making five times as much as an operating head as he made as CEO of an independent company. But, the key to success in this case is the fact that this operating head was getting a bonus equal to a certain fraction of the division's earnings above a certain level, and with no upper bound.

But there are also, of course, major political obstacles to establishing pay-for-performance plans. Think about Paul Fireman, the CEO of Reebok, who gets roundly chastized every year for having such a compensation plan. And Michael Eisner of Walt Disney got a large payoff in a similar plan. There's a lot to be said for such plans, especially in the cases of conglomerates where there are no stock prices to reflect the performance of individual units.

Now, that isn't to say that the conventional structure of the conglomerate will never work. But, in the absence of strong incentives for the line managers, it requires an enormous amount of information and people at headquarters to process that information. When you contrast that with how Warren Buffet runs Berkshire Hathaway—he runs his company out of Omaha with fewer than 20 people—then it's no wonder that our conglomerates are in trouble.

Do Investors Care About Management Incentives?

STERN: Let me turn now to Claudia Zaner, who has had many years of experience in dealing with money managers. Investor uncertainty, as we all know, translates into lower share prices. And investors are clearly not reassured by the sight of managements' rewarding themselves with large bonuses unrelated to corporate performance and stockholder returns.

Claudia, how do you think money managers would respond to the announcement of an incentive scheme wherein corporate management pays for in-the-money options with a rising exercise price?

CLAUDIA ZANER: If the rationale is communicated properly, they would probably respond by increasing the value of the shares. There is a common misconception among managers that the bottom line is all the smart money pays attention to—and that therefore the lead investors ignore the structure of the incentive package. (Some managers I know would even consider it none of investors' business!)

The misconception arises mainly, I think, from the fact that there is very little open discussion among analysts and fund managers of incentive compensation. But, to take an extreme example, it would be naive to assume that just because a money manager doesn't openly question a CEO about his personal integrity or intellectual capabilities, that money manager isn't making any judgments as to whether the CEO is a liar or a fool. By the same token, just because investors are not discussing a compensation scheme doesn't mean they're not assessing its impact on performance.

Even the most vocal investors rarely come right out and tell the CEO they don't approve of the form of incentives or compensation. Yet, because it's my job to obtain candid (and thus typically anonymous) feedback, I've heard countless times how angry it makes money managers to see golden parachutes and other perks given to senior managers who own very small amounts of stock. Investors become livid when they believe management is only paying lip service to the concept of increasing shareholder value.

My experience also suggests that professional investors generally share the view that managers of LBOs strive to reduce *operating* risks because of the financial risk they've assumed together with the potential rewards from their large ownership stake. And they've seen the results of those efforts in situations like Vista—to name just one example. This becomes important in the valuation process, in part because of investors' practice of comparing a "typical" public company's performance against that of its "peer group," which often contains spin-offs, reverse LBOs and other situations where management's personal risks and rewards are tied much more strongly to performance.

So, if companies could establish a more direct linkage between management and stockholder rewards—whether through your EVA schemes or in-the-money options, particularly if the managers are putting up their own funds—then I think such changes would reduce the smart money's perception of the risk involved in investing and raise their assessment of the shares' future performance.

More on Investor's Perspectives: The Case of Applied Power

STERN: Dick Sim, as I mentioned earlier, is the CEO of a company called Applied Power. When we first took a look at the company's performance

PUBLIC DISCUSSIONS OF CORPORATE PERFORMANCE CONTINUED TO BE MIRED IN TRADITIONAL GAAP ACCOUNTING CONCEPTS—EARNINGS PER SHARE, PRICE-EARNINGS RATIOS, BOOK VALUES—ALL OF WHICH TEND TO BE IRRELEVANT IN EVALUATING A COMPANY'S CONTRIBUTION TO SHAREHOLDER WEALTH.

— RICHARD SIM —

back in 1986, the company was earning substandard rates of return on net assets. Using the terms of the performance measurement scheme we devised at Stern Stewart, the company was producing a negative "Economic Value Added," or EVA for short. But, since that time, the company's operating rates of return have improved dramatically, and EVA has become significantly positive.

Now, if I'm not mistaken, Dick, you have put in place a cash bonus approach that's actually tied to your managers' success in generating EVA—that is, in achieving rates of return that exceed the cost of capital.

SIM: Yes, we have both a quarterly and an annual cash bonus program that is based on a measure of Economic Value Added.

STERN: Also interesting to me is the extent to which you actually talk about your use of EVA and your commitment to shareholder value in your annual report. It is featured prominently on the very first page, and then discussed in some detail later in the report.

Do money managers really understand value-based concepts like EVA, and does the quality of the questions you hear from analysts improve when you attempt to communicate on this more sophisticated level? Or do the security analysts continue to be obsessed with earnings per share?

SIM: In general, we run across few analysts who have understood and "internalized" the performance measures that we try to lay out very clearly. On occasion, I have encountered analysts who say, "Gee, I really like your annual report." And, when you start to talk to them, you discover that they are really, indeed, value-based investors that look at cash flow rather than earnings.

But, for whatever reason, there seems to be a reluctance among most analysts and fund managers to proclaim publicly that the market is driven by these economic, as opposed to accounting-based, factors. These investors are making money using this cash flow methodology and they don't want to wear it on their sleeve. So I sometimes find myself receiving these unsolicited confidences, together with strong endorsements; but they invariably come about in private settings—and they involve only a few, though very sophisticated, money managers.

At the same time, public discussions of corporate performance continue to be mired in traditional GAAP accounting concepts—earnings per share, industry-wide price-earnings ratios, book values—all of which tend to be irrelevant in evaluating a company's contribution to shareholder wealth. Obviously, there's a large herd of analysts who are not capable of doing much more than responding passively to that set of information. So, as a CEO, I tend to spend much of my time dealing with people within this very traditional and limited framework.

But, Joel, to harken back to your theory of the "lead steers" dominating stock prices, let me say that I do believe they are out there. They exist. We have argued about this concept over the last three or four years. And over that time I've become increasingly convinced that you're right on this issue. But, such investors rarely go public with their methods and insights. Going public in this way would only undermine their own comparative advantage in pricing securities.

The Politics of Finance

STEWART: I want to ask Mike Jensen a question. The takeover market has certainly subsided in the past year as a result of a number of factors we've talked about. At the same time, we're seeing increasing activism by pension fund and other institutional investors. Proxy fights now seem to be breaking out all over the place. How effective will the proxy process be in putting pressure on boards to respond to shareholder grievances?

JENSEN: As you say, much of the control market activity has shifted away from takeovers and into the proxy dimension, into the voting mechanism. It's the result of a number of factors, the most important of which are regulatory pressures that are basically shutting down the funding markets for certain kinds of transactions. The so-called "financial" players—the value-maximizing players that used to be able to raise money when they found a profitable opportunity—have essentially been driven out of this market.

The days of the hostile takeover, at least with large companies as targets, are over. And that's true for various reasons. State anti-takeover legislation, very effective poison pills, and strong antagonism in the courts are all powerful deterrents to takeover today. The Time-Warner court ruling, for example, will provide a major obstacle to corporate restructuring. One interpretation of that decision is that it reinforces Martin Lipton's "just-say-no" defense. It has one very important provision that is going to make change in corporate America much more difficult. It says in effect that you can just say no provided you have a plan in place and you're following it. But God forbid you should deviate from that plan.

There will continue to be transactions. But so-called "strategic" transactions like the Time-Warner deal—those designed to build corporate empires *at the expense of* shareholders—will become the rule rather than the exception. The financial transactions, especially those attempts by corporate raiders to break up larger companies, will all but disappear.

As for the proxy mechanism, my prediction is that we will get a lot of activity in the near term until we find out how inefficient that process is—

Because it's my job to obtain candid (and thus typically anonymous) feedback, I've heard countless times how angry it makes money managers to see golden parachutes and other perks given to senior managers who own very small amounts of stock. Investors become livid when they believe management is only paying lip service to the concept of increasing shareholder value.

My experience also suggests that professional investors generally share the view that managers of LBOs strive to reduce *operating* risks because of the financial risk they've assumed together with the potential rewards from their large ownership stake....This becomes important in the valuation process, in part because of investors' practice of comparing a "typical" public company's performance against that of its "peer group," which often contains spin-offs, reverse LBOs and other situations where management's personal risks and rewards are tied much more strongly to performance.

— Claudia Zaner —

how biased it is toward incumbent management. There's some research being done by my Harvard colleague John Pound that carefully documents the history of the regulation of this market. Pound demonstrates how the SEC proxy regulation and disclosure mechanisms have destroyed a private market in information among investors.

Unless you're familiar with the process, you cannot imagine the constraints on free speech that exist as a result of the SEC proxy regulations. For example, if you're involved in a proxy fight, you literally cannot say anything to a shareholder without the SEC's prior approval of the script.

GOULD: I think you make too strong a statement, Mike. There's considerable legal debate on this issue. It is true that, if you're trying to get the voting power for a block, you have to be very careful. But the First Amendment still applies. There's a lot of testing going on at the margin.

JENSEN: I recently served as a proposed director on a dissident directors slate. And I'm just telling you the way the lawyers currently advise their clients on the process. I've been told what I can say and what I can't. And the extent of censorship is dramatic.

GOULD: Let me just say that there are lawyers who will take the opposite position.

JENSEN: Well, it may be that there will be legal decisions down the road that free up this process. I'm not saying the system will never change. But, I predict it won't change substantially for the better.

In fact, today we are going through a period of time that has a strong similarity with the 1930s, a period in which the political sector seized control of a lot of private economic activity and shut down a substantial amount of control market activity—not to mention parts of the investment banking community. Just as it did in the 1930s, this political intervention today is preventing what I call "active" investors from having the substantial influence on corporate decisions they were able to exercise over the last decade and a half. By active investors, I mean the Carl Icahns, the KKRs, and the Forstmann Littles of the world who were able to get around the constraints on large institutional owners imposed by Glass-Steagall and other regulations passed in the 1930s.

Prior to such legislation, our commercial banks and insurance companies routinely took large equity positions in the corporations they lent

money to. But, with the passage of Glass-Steagall and other acts, legislators widened the rift between ownership and control of our corporations. And the effects on corporate performance, as best exemplified by the stock market performance of our companies in the 1970s, were disastrous. During that period, the real returns to stockholders were actually negative.

In effect, then, it took some 25 or 30 years for the problem of the separation of ownership from control to become big enough—and for corporate values to get low enough—to give financial entrepreneurs incentives to figure out how to innovate around those constraints. But, with the destruction of Drexel Burnham and the stricter intervention of the banking authorities (which now also threatens to spread to the insurance sector), the future sphere for active investors and financial entrepreneurs has narrowed dramatically.

So, as I said earlier, we're going to see more activism in the short run on the part of pension funds, and they'll be part of this proxy process.

ZANER: But pension funds, for some of the reasons you've described, typically view the proxy process only as a last resort after all else has failed.

THERE WILL CONTINUE TO BE TRANSACTIONS. BUT SO-CALLED "STRATEGIC" TRANSACTIONS LIKE THE TIME-WARNER DEAL—THOSE DESIGNED TO BUILD CORPORATE EMPIRES *AT THE EXPENSE OF* SHAREHOLDERS—WILL BECOME THE RULE RATHER THAN THE EXCEPTION.

— MICHAEL JENSEN —

JENSEN: I'm confident that proxy contests will not replace hostile takeovers any time soon as an effective control mechanism. And, in fact, there are disturbing signs of political attempts to curb pension funds as well. With the Cuomo report in New York, we are seeing the beginnings of an attempt to constrain pension funds' abilities to put money into LBO pools or to finance hostile takeovers. Jesse Jackson is running a campaign to force public pension funds to invest 10% of their funds (and this is just a foot-in-the-door approach) in infrastructure investments, public works projects, and the like.

One of the ways pension funds could be coerced into accepting such conditions is through the threat of greater regulation and taxes. For example, there are now proposals to tax gains that are deemed to be "short-term." At the extreme, Marty Lipton has now taken to arguing that any profits earned on a transaction that turns over within five years should be taxed at *100%*. (He not only wants institutional investors to be powerless in influencing boards, he wants to prevent them even from selling their shares!) But, Lipton's grandstanding aside, most proposals are starting out with small tax rates. And if they really want to accomplish their mission, that's the way to do it.

The one thing going in our favor—that is, those of us concerned about corporate efficiency—is that capital markets are now global. As a consequence, we can no longer take the kind of regulatory measures we did in the 1930s without driving a major fraction of our industry offshore. And the more restrictions we put in place to protect our companies from pressure towards efficiency from the capital markets, the greater the likelihood that these protected industries are eventually going to be subjected to direct competition from the international product markets. The problem with waiting this long, however, is that many companies will become only more inefficient and a lot more value will have been destroyed in the interim.

Is Efficiency Enough?

GOULD: I want to talk about an impression that I'm going to walk out of this meeting with, and it may be a wrong impression. And if it is, then I'd like to get it clarified.

Some of my colleagues describe me as a person who used to be an economist—but I'm not sure even that label fits as comfortably as it once did. As Mike Jensen's remarks should tell you, economists pay an enormous amount of attention to efficiency. They almost never talk, however, about things like innovation and growth and development. They have little wisdom to impart as to what industry the company should be in, and what strategy the company should follow to achieve its goals. These things are not part of the lingo, because economists don't have any good models to handle those considerations.

People have been concerned about capital markets because of the number of complaints from CEOs that shareholders and analysts are forcing companies to focus too much on short-term results and not enough on long-term competitiveness. Now, some people in this discussion today have suggested that LBOs, by increasing the concentration of ownership in the hands of management, have helped address this problem caused by short-sighted investors. But the fact is, I haven't heard much concern about long-term performance in this discussion. If anything, I'm seeing an even greater preoccupation with short-term results. Because once you have put a lot of debt on your balance sheet to concentrate the equity ownership, you've then got to worry about generating immediate cash flow to service that debt.

To repeat my concern, all of the discussion seems to be focused on efficiency. I don't get the sense that there's any attention being paid to innovation, to trying more risky projects with long-term payoffs. And my feeling is that, in many ways, that's the name of the game for the future. The success of the Japanese has a lot to do with their willingness to innovate. The Japanese succeed a lot because they are willing to take more chances. I don't get the impression that American business is thinking about the long run these days.

KIDDER: I strongly disagree with what you say, at least in my own case. At the beginning of this discussion, I tried to illustrate why Henry Kravis and I spend our time talking about strategic investments and not cost-cutting measures. As I said—and I'll repeat it once more for emphasis—we were faced with a choice: We could have invested $10 million in Technology A every year for the next few years in order to be competitive in Markets B, C, and D. Or we could have chosen simply not to invest and save that $10 million a year. Now, as I explained earlier, if we do invest and we're successful enough just to increase our multiple by one point, then we have increased the value of our company by $300 million. So, given the market's inclination to reward successful investment by placing higher multiples on current earnings, it clearly pays for companies to follow through on investments that have a reasonable probability of success.

STERN: Excuse me. But isn't it impossible for you to get the valuation benefits you're talking about when you're privately held?

KIDDER: Well, yes and no. The markets are pretty much interchangeable, I would say. They work on the same fundamental principles of valuation. And nobody's convinced me we should go public just to get credit for that higher valuation in the form of a published stock price.

STERN: Well, it's sometimes valuable to have outsiders appraise your firm and put their seal of approval on your efforts. This may help you attract even more high-quality people to join your company.

STEWART: Well, I'm not sure you need to go public to accomplish even that end. Avis, for example, is a 100% ESOP-financed LBO, and it publishes valuations put on the company by outside appraisers. It's public knowledge that their market value increased from $5 to $15 a share in one year. And that's had tremendous benefits in recruiting.

So, I would argue that you can privatize even the appraisal process. In short, I see no reason why Duracell should consider going public—not at least until management wants to cash out and diversify its portfolio. And even in that case, going public is not necessarily the best solution. You can just borrow more and have a major distribution. You can do what John Burns and Vista Chemical did, only without going public as an intermediate step.

KIDDER: I agree with you, Bennett, on that point. But let me just follow up on what I was saying earlier.

Our senior managers number roughly 350 out of 8,000 employees. Their compensation is structured in such a way that, as before in the Kraft days, they receive a salary that pays for the groceries. They also have an annual incentive that, unlike the Kraft arrangement, is based on the cash flow generated by their business—and that helps them buy the diamond ring. And, finally, they have an equity piece, which comes either through their stock ownership or related options, or through equity appreciation rights. This equity piece will amount to somewhere between 10 to 20 times whatever they could possibly earn on salary plus bonus in a good year.

So when these senior managers make their decisions, those decisions are unbiased; there is no reason for them to prefer short-run gains to the long-run payoff. The incentives are designed to encourage long-term considerations in two ways: one, nobody's going to leave. We've got the A-team on the field for the next few years. And, two, they know what's putting the serious capital accumulation into their bank account.

JENSEN: Well, Bob just gave us a pretty good answer to Jack's question. But let me add my own comment as an economist. When I use the term "efficiency," what I mean encompasses what I think Jack means by "innovation." Innovation is an important part of the process that yields greater efficiency.

Now, I've done some research in the field to try and find out what goes on inside these LBOs. And I'm not observing the shortsightedness that Jack has complained about.

Let me give you an example that comes out of a stodgy industry. In 1987, Berkshire Partners did an LBO of Wisconsin Central Ltd., a railroad company that owns roughly 2,000 miles of tracks located primarily in Wisconsin. And it's absolutely astonishing what management has done with the business. They have come up with a new way of running a railroad. By using a fairly massive computerized information system, they have created what amounts to a just-in-time inventory system. By having all their cars arriving and leaving on very precise schedules, they have eliminated the need for railroad yards, thus reducing their overhead and their operating risk. And besides the computer system, they have also had to make radical changes in marketing their services in order to keep their trains continuously in motion. I have seen pictures in Chicago newspapers of engineers parking their 20-ton locomotives and getting down to call on customers.

In fact, the company has been rated number one among regional railroads in the country by its customers in terms of service. Prior to the LBO, this company was essentially 2,000 miles of track and rail cars that were headed for the scrap heap. It was systematically losing money.

KIDDER: In our company today, people are making explicit decisions that previously might have been implicit or not taken at all—or, at least, they would not have been treated with the same sense of urgency. For example, we had a factory producing a product that had a stable demand pattern, but one for which the supply far exceeded the demand. There was clearly too much capacity. Now, if we were still operating as a division of Kraft, we might have been willing to sit with that product for some period of time before taking decisive steps to reduce capacity.

But, as a private, stand-alone company, we had far stronger incentives to take a real close look at what we were getting from the product. And when we did the analysis, we noticed that our variable cost of production was greater than the cost of buying it outside. So, having made this discovery, we immediately sold that asset and used the cash not to pay down debt—although we could have done that—but to invest in products with growth potential.

When managers become owners, they begin to think a lot harder about taking money out of mature businesses and investing in growth areas. And I think that is as a fairly natural consequence of greater ownership. It's certainly not happening because all of a sudden we put in new controls at headquarters. In fact, today we have fewer controls than we had as part of Kraft. What's different is that the proposals for change are coming from the bottom up rather than from the top down.

So, again, there's something natural happening here as a result of the new incentive system provided by ownership. I haven't changed. I ran Duracell for three or four years as a division of

I SEE NO REASON WHY DURACELL SHOULD CONSIDER GOING PUBLIC—NOT AT LEAST UNTIL MANAGEMENT WANTS TO CASH OUT AND DIVERSIFY ITS PORTFOLIO. AND EVEN IN THAT CASE, GOING PUBLIC IS NOT NECESSARILY THE BEST SOLUTION.

— BENNETT STEWART —

Kraft before we went private. Now, you could ask me why we didn't make all these changes two or three years before.

STERN: Okay, why didn't you do those things before?

KIDDER: Well, my short answer is that it doesn't have anything directly to do with our being an LBO. But it does have a lot to with the fact that we were part of Kraft rather than an independent company.

STERN: You're saying it doesn't have to do with the LBO?

KIDDER: It has mainly to do with independence and ownership.

JOHNSTONE: It has to do with leadership.

STEWART: But, John, you have the same leader here in front of you. Bob was running the company before and after the LBO.

HAMACHEK: Same leader, but he probably became a leader in a very different sense as a result of the LBO.

KIDDER: Well, yes, I have more degrees of freedom today. As part of Kraft, I had no say in my own compensation structure, nor in the compensation structure of the people reporting to me.

JOHNSTONE: Yes, but that's different. You weren't really the boss when the company was under Kraft. All I'm saying is that I think much of the improvements are a matter of better leadership. Now, if the LBOs are a way of getting better leaders to run our businesses, then I don't disagree with the argument.

More on the Long-Term versus the Short-Term

SIM: In response to Jack Gould's skepticism about the long-term focus of American companies, I want to say that I'm very confident about the long-run economic future of this country. And I am confident about our future *not* because of our large public

corporations. My confidence lies in our venture capital industries, and in our small to medium-sized companies, many of which are privately owned or have the kind of unusual corporate structures that are represented by people sitting around this table. These are the kinds of companies that are creating jobs and that are innovating.

When you look at the Fortune 500, the record is not nearly as good. Management has an insignificant equity interest. The compensation is mainly cash up front, with almost no risk. They're being paid like bureaucrats. As a consequence, they are subject to too many distractions from their basic mission, which is to create value for stockholders.

But although I agree with Mike Jensen's assessment of the compensation problem in our large companies, I do not share his pessimism about the future of hostile takeovers in this country. He's absolutely right that some of these state laws are abominable; they are the worst sort of shelter for inefficient companies. And, in fact, it is predictably only the most inefficient companies that are choosing to be protected by such statutes; companies concerned about their stock price are choosing to opt out of such measures.

But in spite of such new barriers to takeover, money still talks. It is now true that acquirers will have to choose their shots a little more carefully. But if a company is so poorly run that its market value represents an obvious opportunity for an acquirer, and if that acquirer can bring enough money to the table to offer a large premium to the shareholders, the offer should blow right through most of these new artificial barriers. You may face higher legal fees, to be sure. But, if the economics are there and the funding is available, I don't see how acquirers will be stopped.

STEWART: I, too, think there is a silver lining in the dark cloud painted by Michael Jensen. I believe that many managers looking back on the 1980s have come to recognize that there was something very positive going on in many of these LBOs. They have recognized the strengthening of incentives and the decentralization of control that led to an enormous amount of new wealth. I can't tell you how many companies we visit where people grudgingly shake their heads and acknowledge the truth of stories like Bob Kidder's account of Duracell's transformation as an LBO. That is, you take a sluggishly performing unit that was part of the parent company; and once you set it up on its own and give management a large equity stake, it suddenly performs much better.

I also sense that, in some cases, the new impediments to takeover may end up providing a more conducive environment for our large public companies to set about deliberately adapting the principles of restructuring to their own situations. What I'm talking about is taking a multi-business company and transforming it into a publicly-traded, KKR-like organization. This could be accomplished in two or three steps.

First, as we've discussed earlier, senior managements and boards ought to be encouraged to buy in-the-money stock options, perhaps with money borrowed from the corporation.

Second, in the case of multi-business companies, management should separate its mature businesses that have excess capital from its growth opportunities. The mature cash cows should be made to borrow non-recourse against their value and pay out their excess cash to the parent. The parent can then sell up to 20% of the equity in the unit to the management people while still continuing to consolidate for tax purposes. This arrangement is what I call an "internal LBO"—one in

IN OUR COMPANY TODAY, PEOPLE ARE MAKING EXPLICIT DECISIONS THAT PREVIOUSLY MIGHT HAVE BEEN IMPLICIT OR NOT TAKEN AT ALL—OR, AT LEAST, THEY WOULD NOT HAVE BEEN TREATED WITH THE SAME SENSE OF URGENCY.

— ROBERT KIDDER —

The new impediments to takeover may provide a more conducive environment for our large public companies to set about deliberately adapting the principles of restructuring to their own situations. What I'm talking about is taking a multi-business company and transforming it into a publicly-traded, KKR-like organization....

In the case of multi-business companies, management should separate its mature businesses from its growth opportunities. The mature cash cows should be made to borrow and pay out their excess cash to the parent....The growth businesses should be financed with equity and possibly be allowed to issue equity directly to the public.

In either case, operating management will be given the opportunity to have a major equity stake (and a freer hand) in running their own business. In other words, the parent company functions like a KKR in dealing with its mature businesses and like a venture capital group [with its] growth opportunities.

— Bennett Stewart —

which the parent company, perhaps together with an outside investor, plays the role of the LBO sponsor.

The growth businesses, by contrast, should be financed primarily with equity and possibly be allowed to issue equity directly to the public in a partial public offering.

In either case, operating management will be given the opportunity to have a major equity stake (and a freer hand) in running their own business. In other words, the parent company functions like a KKR in dealing with its mature businesses and like a venture capital group in re-allocating cash from the mature businesses to the growth opportunities.

HAMACHEK: I, too, want to respond to Jack Gould's question about competitiveness; and, in so doing, I want to pick up on Dick Sim's point about the importance of small and medium-sized companies in the U.S. economy. I strongly agree with Dick's argument that the real incentive to innovate and take chances is strongest in our small and medium-sized companies.

What disturbs me is that I don't feel that the incentive, the motivation, is there in the Fortune 500. When I read *Barbarians at the Gate*, it reminded me of what it was like to work for a

large company. I know it's not fair to tar all large companies with the same brush, but there is a tendency in all large organizations—a tendency that can be resisted only by exceptionally good management—to become like RJR, to develop the kind of appalling inefficiencies that were displayed in that book.

So, although *Barbarians* may present a somewhat extreme case, as a portrait of the incentives facing a corporate bureaucracy it is probably more representative than not. And that is in sharp contrast to what I've experienced in running a much smaller, stand-alone company. In such cases, management typically bears a lot of risk, but also stands to receive much greater rewards for success. For this reason, our smaller companies have shown themselves much more willing to be innovative, both in product and service. They really focus on their customers. They realize that they sink or swim with those customers.

And I don't think that same sense of urgency prevails in most of our larger companies. Even if top management feels a strong commitment to customers and shareholders, it may be difficult to transmit that attitude down into

the individual units. And that's the real problem: How do you motivate the operating people to become more innovative and take more risks, and thus to overcome the inertia that besets our large corporations?

One Last Look Back at Public Companies

STERN: What lessons have been learned from your successes by the management committees of the parent companies of which you were once a part? John, what has happened at your old parent, Du Pont, as a result of your success at Vista Chemical as an independent company? Has it had any effect at all?

BURNS: Shortly after our LBO, we had a long discussion with some people at Du Pont about some other ways of running this kind of business. In their view, however, our methods were inappropriate for their other 79 businesses. And they had no interest in changing then.

But, let me also say they have taken some positive steps in the last few years. They have eliminated two layers of management and introduced some interesting pay-for-performance programs at the divisional levels.

ALTHOUGH *BARBARIANS AT THE GATE* MAY PRESENT A SOMEWHAT EXTREME CASE, AS A PORTRAIT OF THE INCENTIVES FACING A CORPORATE BUREAUCRACY IT IS PROBABLY MORE REPRESENTATIVE THAN NOT.

— TOD HAMACHEK —

What if it's the very act of giving management ownership that makes the company more valuable? If that is the case, and the higher valuation on the shares would not result otherwise, then public stockholders are arguably major beneficiaries of proposals by management to take companies private. In this case, the only responsibility of the board is to conduct an auction to prevent management from "stealing" the company. So, unless bidders are somehow discouraged from competing with management's offer, then I'm hard-pressed to see how stockholders suffer from the process of management buyouts.

— Joel Stern —

STERN: Tod, what has happened at Univar as a result of your success at Penwest? Have they done anything about this?

HAMACHEK: In Univar's case, they have done quite a lot. They have continued to break up Univar into smaller units through one spin-off after another. One of the spin-offs has even gone on to spin off a piece of its operations, thus becoming even smaller. And that's raised a question that keeps lurking in the back of my mind: How many operations can you spin off and how much smaller can you make your company before you fall below the optimal size?

The conclusion I've come to is that, in the absence of significant economies of scale, smaller is likely to be better. If you want to maximize investors' return on capital, then a collection of independent companies that are clearly directed at distinct market segments is probably going to be much more effective than a large conglomerate.

STERN: Do you think there's a benefit to your firm to being publicly traded as opposed to being privately owned?

HAMACHEK: Well, I've given this a lot of thought, and I've waxed and waned on the whole issue. Putting up with a bunch of analysts and money managers is sometimes a pain in the neck. But, at the same time, I think there is one major benefit. If you're doing well and the public recognizes it, then it serves as a magnet for your organization. People want to be part of a winning team. It's also easier to attract a high caliber of people if you can somehow offer them a significant opportunity to participate in the equity. But, of course, the larger your company gets, the harder that becomes.

In Closing

STERN: Well, we have come to the end of this discussion, and we're left with the question with which we started: How important are management incentives in improving corporate performance and the competitiveness of American corporations? Can it possibly be just a matter of equity ownership, profit-sharing, and freeing people to run their own operations? Does it really just come down to the issue of organizational structure and incentives?

STEWART: What if it were actually that simple, Joel?

JENSEN: Why can't it be that simple?

BURNS: It's not just money. Incentives have to do with issues that are a lot broader than just the money. It's really a matter of changing the entire operating environment, the general attitude of management and employees toward adding value.

STERN: I'm beginning to feel, as I often do at the end of these discussions, the beginnings of a religious experience. And I want to thank each of you high priests for helping to bring about this revelation. ∎

BENNETT STEWART: Yesterday, we heard Michael Jensen talk about the role of the board of directors in creating shareholder value (though after listening to Michael, I suppose we should really think of it as the board of "accommodators"). Professor Jensen identified four main roles our boards *ought* to play in public companies, but in many cases do not. Stated as briefly as possible, they are the hiring, firing, counseling, and compensating of top management. In today's discussion, we will further explore the role of the board with a distinguished panel of senior executives and directors brought together by the Continental Bank.

Current compensation practices are clearly one area where boards seem to be failing—and we will likely talk a little about that today. But there are also more fundamental issues about the relationship between professional management and corporate boards, such as:

- Who really should nominate the board of directors?
- Is it appropriate for management to sit on the board?
- Should the CEO of the company also fulfill the role of the chairman of the company?
- How can we improve the dialogue and decision-making that takes place as a result of the board process?

It would also be interesting to hear the panel's assessment of the import of some current trends. For example, there are a number of public companies that are beginning to feel more pressure from institutional investors to reform the role and function of the board. It can't have escaped anyone's attention that various shareholder interest groups have risen up in recent years to express their dissatisfaction with managements and boards.

Robert Monks, for example, has formed a firm called Institutional Shareholder Partners whose aim is to act with major shareholders to help—or, in some cases, prod—companies into creating shareholder value. You may recall that Monks waged a well-publicized proxy contest with Sears a while back that was designed to serve as a catalyst for change. The United Shareholders Association (USA), a group started by Boone Pickens and now run by Ralph Whitworth, has achieved some modest successes in influencing the corporate governance process. For instance, after a vigorous campaign, USA managed to change the compensation plan of the chairman of ITT; and there are intimations that perhaps more dramatic changes in the overall structure of the company may be forthcoming. So it would be interesting to speculate here about the expected impact of the increasing activism of institutional investors on corporate managements and boards.

To discuss these issues this morning, the Continental Bank has assembled a really first-rate panel. Let me now introduce the panel (and I will do so in alphabetical order).

JAMES BIRLE is a General Partner with The Blackstone Group, the well-known New York investment firm. One of his principal responsibilities at Blackstone is to serve as the co-chairman and CEO of Collins & Aikman Group, Inc., formerly the Wickes Companies, an organization I would describe as a $3 billion conglomerate. Jim also serves on a variety of boards, including that of Transtar, a railroad business acquired by Blackstone in a leveraged buyout from USX. Given that Jim also spent 30 years with General Electric, I expect him to give us some insights as to how internal corporate governance mechanisms differ between public companies and private companies run by so-called financial investors like Blackstone.

WADE CABLE is CEO and a director of the Presley Companies, a prominent California homebuilder. The company went through an initial public offering of stock this past October, largely because of the difficulty most

---

February 29, 1992 ■ *Beaver Creek, Colorado*

CONTINENTAL BANK ROUNDTABLE ON

THE ROLE OF CORPORATE BOARDS IN THE 1990s

real estate developers have today in convincing their banks to lend to them. So Wade is living proof of the credit crunch.

MICHAEL JENSEN, whose name I've already mentioned several times, is the Edsel Bryant Professor of Business Administration at the Harvard Business School, and among the most vocal and controversial critics of corporate governance in the U.S.

trial installation. Like John's former employer, Johns Manville, the Fibreboard Corporation faces a massive potential liability from asbestos litigation—which, I'm sure, has made John's current job most challenging.

BILL ROPER is Senior Vice President and CFO of Science Applications International Corporation, which claims to be the largest employee-

and governance structure—one that may have valuable lessons for our public companies.

JOHN TEETS is Chairman, President, and CEO of The Dial Corp. John presided over a radical restructuring of the company in the 1980s— one which included the sale of the Armour meat-packing business in 1983, the sale of the Greyhound bus lines in 1987, and the recently an-

ROGER LEE is Senior Vice President-Finance and Administration, as well as a director, of Caesars World, a company which fought off a hostile suitor by undergoing a leveraged recap about five years ago. Roger will thus provide the perspective of—and presumably defend—the management and directors of our public companies.

JOHN ROACH is the Chairman, President, and CEO of the Fibreboard Corporation, also a publicly traded company. The company has approximately $300 million in sales and focuses on wood products and indus-

owned company in America. The company certainly represents an interesting paradigm for us to consider this morning. The firm has approximately $1.2 billion in revenues, and is involved primarily in systems development work.

FRED SIMMONS is a General Partner of Freeman Spogli, an investment company that has been very successful in executing LBOs of 15 companies in a variety of industries, including seven supermarket chains. As I suggested earlier in introducing Jim Birle of Blackstone, Fred also represents an alternative ownership

nounced spin-off of Greyhound Financial Corporation, or GFC, to its stockholders. It should be interesting to hear from John about this process, and about the role of the board in overseeing this restructuring.

I am **BENNETT STEWART**, Senior Partner of Stern Stewart & Co., a corporate finance advisory firm that specializes in valuation, restructuring, and management incentive compensation. I'm not a director of any major company, which is probably the surest sign of the failure of our corporate governance system.

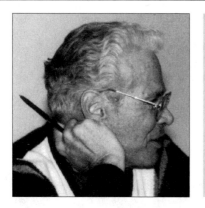

The Case of Dial Corp

STEWART: Let me begin this discussion with John Teets. John, as I just mentioned, last October your company announced its decision to spin off Greyhound Financial Corporation to its shareholders, which caused the firm's stock price to increase from $35 to about $41 a share. And your share price now trades in the vicinity of $50, if I'm not mistaken. The company must be doing something right.

Would you share with us the dynamics of that decision to spin off GFC? And what role did the board play in that process?

TEETS: Well, the decision to sell Greyhound Financial was really made several years ago. At that time we decided The Dial Corp would pursue a strategy focused on consumer products and services. So we knew then that GFC was not part of our long-range plan.

But it turned out to be very difficult to get out of the finance business. We let Salomon Brothers try to sell it for over a year. Then we gave the job to Merrill Lynch, which also had it for over a year without success. GFC has a good record, five years of 15-20% growth in earnings, and a $2 billion portfolio with only 3% non-earning assets. But no one was interested in paying 100 cents on the dollar for a $2-billion portfolio.

Some time later, we realized when we wanted to divest Verex, our mort-gage insurance business, we were not going to be able to sell that operation either. In this case, we also faced a tax problem. The business was carrying a $100 million investment tax credit going forward that would have been triggered by a sale of the business. Our solution, which we devised with the help of Gleacher and Company, was to package GFC together with Verex and spin them off to our shareholders. In fact, the new securities will begin to trade on March 4 this year.

What was the board's role in this decision? For the past nine years, we have apprised our board that we want to keep moving into the consumer products and services area. That is our long-term strategy, and our board has been kept informed throughout the process. In the course of this nine-year program, we have sold close to 20 businesses for about $3.2 billion, and have bought others worth about $1.4 billion.

So we have been moving slowly in the direction we want to go. It's been like moving a giant, but we're finally reaching a point where it's starting to pay off.

STEWART: Well, John, your stock has gone up quite dramatically. Is that something that the board is pleased about? Or do they just not care?

TEETS: Our stock has gone from $13 when I took over to almost $50 today. Our board does not sit around looking at the stock on a daily basis, if that's your point. But they have played, and continued to play, an important role in the company's success in adding value for stockholders.

Let me also add here that I think statements like Professor Jensen's that boards are incapable of bringing about necessary change are greatly exaggerated. For one thing, boards often exercise their power to fire CEOs. And most boards understand their responsibility to monitor management and represent stockholders' interest. Now, there are clearly some cases where the board doesn't function and the system doesn't work. We all know the companies that are not performing. But that is probably true in no more than, say, 20% of American companies today. So, the system *is* working.

In my own case, *all* my board members are outsiders and they are all CEOs of other companies. And they are very thorough in their examination of proposals. For example, when we proposed the spin-off of GFC and Verex to our board last August, what was scheduled to be a one-hour meeting turned into a four-hour meeting. And the proposal was not approved at that meeting, but only after further research and discussion.

So, in our case, the governance process works quite well. And the board has been pleased with what we've succeeded in accomplishing for our stockholders. Some of our board members have also participated directly them-

selves in our shareholder gains. We give our board members the option to take their fees in stock or cash. And one of our directors recently reminded me that he has now accumulated a million-dollar's worth of our stock through this program. So he is, I think, quite aware of the fact our stock price is significantly higher today than it was six months ago.

STEWART: John, you mentioned a one-hour meeting that turned into a four-hour meeting. I'm just interested in the kinds of questions and concerns that surfaced during that dialogue.

TEETS: Professor Jensen yesterday objected that the code of politeness that prevails in board meetings prevents serious disagreements from being aired. But that's misleading. It's true that directors don't go to meetings with the idea of antagonizing the CEO, but nor are they the rubber stamp that Jensen suggests. They ask tough questions. They debate important issues.

As I mentioned, our plan to spin off some of our businesses clearly raised questions and concerns among the board. In fact, our original proposal called for combining our bus manufacturing operation along with the finance companies. One important issue the board was especially concerned about was the funding of the spun-off company: They asked questions such as: How could this new entity be financed so as to satisfy the banks and stand up to the scrutiny of S&P and Moody's. How could the banks and

rating agencies be made to accept what amounts to a mini-conglomerate? Wouldn't it be too complicated to understand? (You can't be too careful, I'm told, in explaining these matters to bankers.)

So, it was only after a lot of thought and a long debate that we ultimately decided to spin off GFC and Verex together, and then either sell or spin off the bus manufacturing company as a stand-alone operation. And our board members played an important role in helping us reach this decision.

The Case of Caesars World

STEWART: John mentioned that all of his company's board members are outsiders except himself. Now let me turn to Roger Lee. Roger, you are the Senior Vice President and CFO of Caesars World, as well as a director. Is the composition of your board like that of John's company?

LEE: No. We have a nine-person board that consists of four insiders and five outsiders. We are probably tilting too much to the inside. I personally think there should probably be at least two outsiders for every insider on the board, maybe more. Other companies I've served on have had at most two insiders on the board.

STEWART: Do you think that difference affects the quality of the dialogue that takes place between the board and top management?

LEE: I think it can reduce the amount of dialogue and may tend to create some passivity on the part of the board members. It makes the outsiders more reluctant to take on such a solid nucleus of people in one room at one time.

STEWART: Roger, Caesars World went through a defensive, and fairly dramatic, leveraged restructuring a number of years ago. Can you tell us a little about how what happened, why the company recapitalized itself the way it did, and what the role of the board was during this difficult process?

LEE: We were the target of a hostile takeover bid. The board responded by introducing an in-depth review of values and alternative courses of action, using both management input and several consultants. Based on the specifics of our situation, it was determined that the bid price was considerably lower than the company's value. Further it was believed that an alternate approach—a corporate restructuring using additional leverage to fund a large one-time cash dividend—could deliver more value to shareholders while preserving their proportional ownership in the company.

We aggressively pursued this alternative, eventually gaining shareholder approval and forcing withdrawal of the opposing bid. But one of the casino control commissions that regulate our industry unexpectedly refused to permit the restructuring. The board then investigated alternative courses of action, and decided to use substantially less leverage and repurchase approximately one-third of the outstanding common shares in a Dutch auction—the kind of auction that calls for each shareholder to name his own price within a range of values specified by the company.

Throughout this entire sequence of events, the board was the focal point for initiating, evaluating, and taking actions. It was a difficult task accomplished under enormous pressure.

The Case of the Presley Companies

STEWART: Wade, your company has recently gone public. Could you give us a little background on your company, and tell us how it got to be where it is now? And do you think the corporate governance process and the role of the board will change much as a result of your transition from a private to a public company?
CABLE: Our company was in fact a public company from 1971 through 1984. In 1984 it was acquired by what was then Pacific Lighting. They have since changed their name to Pacific Enterprises. So I've seen a public board of directors at work in a very large, diverse company.

Michael Jensen would probably have some fun looking at how the board of Pacific Lighting performed. As as example, consider the decision the board made in voting to sell the Presley Companies, along with its other real estate companies. At about the same time, Pacific Lighting decided to buy Thrifty Drug Stores for something in the neighborhood of $870 million. To give you a rough sense of how these two transactions affected the shareholder value of Pacific Lighting, Thrifty Drug Stores made approximately $35 million the first year they owned it. The Presley Companies would have made approximately $100 million in the first year we owned it, had it still been owned by Pacific Lighting. Recently, Pacific Enterprises completely elimi-

nated its dividend to shareholders and announced very large losses as a result of its decision to divest their retail businesses. This is a board that, at least in this instance, did not do well by its shareholders.

When we completed our LBO of the Presley Companies from Pacific Lighting in 1987, the deal was reported to be leveraged with a debt-to-equity ratio of 57 to 1. Actually, the entire deal was leveraged, with the equity piece being subordinated debt. We were able to pay down the debt very quickly; and in just two years following the close of the deal, we had a company with a debt-to-equity ratio of less than 4 to 1. We thought this was terrific, feeling that we had hit the home run of all times.

The problem we ran into was that the world changed and suddenly FIRREA-regulated commercial banks changed their view of what constituted an acceptable amount of leverage for a real estate developer. As a consequence, we chose to take our company public in October 1991 in an effort to access other capital markets.
STEWART: What was the role of the board in this decision to go public?
CABLE: Extensive. As a private company, we had a board that was composed entirely of insiders and manager-owners who were very active in the decision to take the company public. On the subject of the role of the board, I was never once asked by potential investors, "Who's on your board?" I don't think institutions that invested in this company really gave a damn. I think they looked at the management and said, "What can you do and what can't you do?" Their decision to buy stock was based on the company's track record and the perceived ability of the management to perform.

Now consider our current board, which is made up of a broad spectrum of people that includes insider owner-managers, our largest shareholder, a university president, other business executives, and an investment banker. I am

confident this board would have taken equally as active a role as our former board in vital decisions such as going public. Our current board is a very astute group of people with a wide variety of backgrounds and expertise; and I am confident that we, as a company, will benefit from their involvement. For example, we currently have an investment banker on our board. This is significant because in our industry the major problem today is capital and how to access sources that we have traditionally not had relationships with.

STEWART: Are you assuming that unless you have an investment banker on your board, you would not be able to get access to capital?
CABLE: No, but we've been forced to educate ourselves very quickly about raising capital from sources that we have had no experience in dealing with. Two years ago, financing in the residential real estate business was pretty simple. We simply asked ourselves, "To which commercial banker were we going to give the honor of making us this loan?" They were lined up outside the door. The only question was, "Who was going to provide the most credit at the lowest rate?" There was little negotiation required, and frankly, our biggest problem was that we could not satisfy all the lenders we had three years ago.

But credit availability has now changed drastically. In the past, profits from our business accrued almost totally to the developer. Now the capital providers are demanding a much larger share.

So, in answer to your question, we could obviously hire an investment banker. But because we had so little experience in this area, we felt it would be advantageous to have someone on our board who could provide us with the benefit of his experience and ideas. Our strategy was not simply go public, pay the banks down, and go on with business as usual. Instead, we viewed going public as a major first step in a long-range

> *We were able to pay down the debt very quickly; and in just two years following the close of the deal, we had a company with a debt-to-equity ratio of less than 4 to 1. We thought this was terrific, feeling that we had hit the home run of all times.*
>
> *The problem we ran into was that the world changed and suddenly FIRREA-regulated commercial banks changed their view of what constituted an acceptable amount of leverage for a real estate developer.*
>
> —*Wade Cable*

strategy to make our balance sheet match the future capital requirements of our business. To do that effectively, we thought it would be helpful to have an investment banker on the board.

STEWART: But don't you think this investment banker might have an agenda with you as far as maximizing his bank's wealth, possibly at your expense. Doesn't that give you cause for concern, Wade?

CABLE: No. On the contrary, I always like to have somebody whom I know is motivated by profit. This way his motivation is the same as our company's. And if we do another offering, which is something we undoubtedly will explore in the future, his company may or may not be part of that offering.

FRED SIMMONS: So, Bennett, you're suggesting that perhaps Wade should hire a firm like Stern Stewart as his financial adviser, one that couldn't take

him public—so this way there couldn't be any conflict of interest?

STEWART: Well, I must confess the thought did flit through my mind, but only for an instant.

CABLE: Gee, Bennett, I didn't realize that's what you were driving at. I think I'll stick with my investment banker.

The Case of Fibreboard

STEWART: Well, let's change the subject. Let me turn now to John Roach, CEO of Fibreboard. What makes John's company especially interesting, as I mentioned earlier, is that the company is dealing with a major asbestos litigation problem. The stock price, as a consequence, is down to $3 a share. There are four million shares outstanding, so the company has a total market equity capitalization of $12 million.

John, I'm just wondering how the board of your company responds to an obviously very challenging situation— one where you have what appears to be a viable operating business on the one side of the balance sheet, with this terrific liability on the other. All of this would seem to increase the threat of legal liability for the board.

ROACH: At Fibreboard the majority of the board has turned over in less than a year. Four out of seven of our current directors are brand-new, including myself. I am the only insider, and I believe

very strongly that all board members should be outsiders unless there are special circumstances—say, heavy ownership by an individual in the company or by a family. Another likely exception is when a company makes a major acquisition. It then may want to have the CEO of the acquired company on the board. But, aside from these special circumstances, I find it difficult to believe that insiders who spend every day dealing with management and management issues could have an independent perspective on things like executive compensation and the hiring or firing of the CEO.

But, in the case of Fibreboard, as I said, four board members are new. The reason I'm there now is that the prior board finally pulled the plug on the prior CEO. That was an action brought about rather dramatically by some angry shareholders. They were able to put one person on the board. And I have put two new representatives on the board, both CEOs of other firms. Like John Teets, I think the value of having other CEOs on the board is enormous. They understand the issues, they're rarely shy individuals, and they understand the pressures the company is facing. And in this case we needed that kind of experience.

STEWART: John, you mentioned that there was a group of shareholders who were instrumental in tossing your predecessor out of the company. How did that happen?

ROACH: Most of them were from New York, like you, and were very vocal.

STEWART: That's shocking—and how unlike my fellow New Yorkers!

ROACH: So, it wasn't really through the normal process of governance, it was just by being vocal.

STEWART: How much stock did the group own? Was it a formal group of shareholders?

ROACH: It wasn't a formal group. At least they didn't file anything formal. But their combined holdings were on the order of about 30 percent. They had a sizeable ownership stake, and they forcefully expressed their view that there was a need for change at the top. So they triggered the change. And when they brought me on, I then had to rebuild the board.

A somewhat similar experience occurred at Manville Corp., a company that also had an asbestos exposure problem. When Manville finally came out of its Chapter 11 proceedings in November of 1988, 11 out of the 13 board members were replaced during the next two-year period. In both these situations, there were unusual opportunities to transform boards into effective agents for necessary change.

But, in both of these cases, it was a crisis, the great sense of urgency, that allowed the changes to take place. Short of a crisis, however, it seems to me very difficult to get boards to assume the role of initiators of dramatic change. But, in these two cases, the new boards were not constrained by the old rules, by the old ways of doing things. It was clear the board was there to enact change. In these two cases, both the board and management had a strong common interest in getting out of a difficult situation and doing what was best for the company.

Now, there are cases where what may be best for the shareholders—or, at least certain shareholders—may not be what's best for the long-term value of the company. I firmly believe that the job of management and the board is to increase the total value of the firm, or the value of the enterprise. There is, however, a secondary issue of how you get that value into the hands of the shareholders; and this is one area where conflict can arise between even conscientious managements and shareholders, and between long-term owners and short-term speculators. This conflict I have in mind really comes down to a matter of financing. Whereas shareholders might prefer a large increase in the firm's debt-equity ratio, perhaps

combined with a major share repurchase program, management may want to capitalize the firm more conservatively—perhaps to protect the value of the firm's human and organizational "capital" from the costs of financial trouble. So, the issue of value maximization gets more complicated when you consider the corporate obligations to creditors, employees, and other constituencies.

But, with that qualification, I do believe the boards of public companies can and should be integrally involved in increasing that shareholder value. This is not to say that the board should initiate

At least once a year management ought to share with the board its long-term view of the company's strategic plan. And there ought to be periodic updates detailing the company's progress in executing the plan. Such meetings should serve to define the corporate goals and performance parameters that Mike Jensen was insisting on yesterday.

—John Roach

or implement policy; they should not attempt to manage the company. But they should have a voice in questions of long-term strategy, in matters like major divestitures, acquisitions, and capital expenditure programs.

At the same time, I think top managements, particularly the CEOs and the CFOs, could do a far better job in educating and informing their boards. I wrote an article a couple of years ago arguing that the CFO, the comptroller, and the financing staff should not view themselves as simply bean counters and opportunistic fund-raisers, but rather as strategic architects who help the CEO do his job better. That same process is an opportunity to provide the board with the kind of information that would enable the board to help evaluate strategic direction and

major decisions to allocate corporate resources. In many companies, top management simply does not provide enough information to the board to allow the board to do its job.

STEWART: As we discussed earlier, John Teets's company spun off Greyhound Financial. John, you have a destination resort that doesn't seem to fit in your kind of company. Now, if you were to consider divesting or spinning off this resort, would you expect the board to *initiate* a discussion about such an opportunity to restructure the company? Or is the board's role simply one of responding to management's proposals?

ROACH: First of all, let me say that we currently have no intention of divesting or spinning off any of our businesses. Our objective is to enhance the strategic value of each of our businesses and, in so doing, maximize the value of the company.

In response to your question, I think the board should feel free to initiate any idea that management is not smart enough to initiate on their own. It's the management's responsibility, but if management's dragging its feet and doesn't bring that idea forward, any board member should feel completely free to do so.

STEWART: Is that what typically goes on, in your experience? Let me give you an example. Suppose management brings to the board's attention a major capital project for approval. At that point, it's almost too late, it seems to me, for the board to understand all of the factors that could affect the economics of that project. So, given the process, the board is almost put in a position of rubber-stamping a decision that management has initiated. So I'm just wondering whether the board *can* really play an effective role.

ROACH: If that's the way the board is run, they don't have an opportunity to add value. But there is another way—one that I recommended when I was a strategy consultant, and one that we now use at Fibreboard. And that is to have the

company review once a year with its full board the long-term strategy of the company and its individual businesses.

Now, that doesn't have to be more than a quick update if it's been done in great depth before. But, at least once a year management ought to share with the board its long-term view of the company's strategic plan. And there ought to be periodic updates detailing the company's progress in executing the plan. Such updates should tell the board what management expects to accomplish during the year, given the state of the economy and the current competitive environment. Such meetings should shape the board's expectations, it should serve to define the corporate goals and performance parameters that Mike Jensen was insisting on yesterday.

And all this has got to be done within a broad strategic context. So, for example, if management is contemplating a major acquisition in consumer products, the acquisition should not come as a surprise to the board. The same holds if management decides it wants to sell a major line of business. The board should be prepared for such decisions, and should be prepared to understand them as part of a larger strategic plan.

Managements often make the mistake of presenting their boards with acquisitions and then asking them for approval—all during the same meeting. I believe very strongly in putting major projects in front of the board well before a decision is required. Boards ought to be given the opportunity to be educated about such decisions. They should be given the chance to consider and discuss such issues without the pressure that comes from an impending vote.

Governing Private Companies

STEWART: Let me turn now to Fred Simmons. Fred, as a general partner of an LBO firm like Freeman Spogli, you have a very strong ownership interest in the companies on whose boards you serve. To a far greater extent than in the case of public companies, you and your fellow partners have the power to shape the board and to make it what you want it to be. So, given this power, do the boards of your companies end up working differently from what you've heard John Teets and John Roach describe?

SIMMONS: It was very interesting for me to listen to Mike Jensen's comments yesterday about corporate governance by LBO firms—I believe "LBO associations" was the term he used for firms like KKR, Forstmann Little, and our own—because the model of governance Jensen sets forth really does a nice job of describing how Freeman Spogli functions as a firm.

I was struck especially by his discussion of the intensity of the due diligence process that takes place when we first consider investing in companies. As Jensen suggests, the process generates a tremendous amount of research and information about questions that corporate managers are supposed to be asking themselves all the time: Are assets being used correctly? Is management focused in the right problem areas in the business? Is the company spending too much or too little on capital expenditures? Are we financing our assets in the best way possible? Are we in the right businesses? Are we dealing with the competition successfully? Such issues are all looked at in great detail initially upon doing the transaction.

Once our investment is made, the role of the board then becomes one of continually monitoring the company's progress. You continually revisit all those kinds of issues to make sure that the original design is being carried out as was originally planned. And you also re-examine the original plan: Is it still the proper course, or do you need to modify the plan in light of new information?

In putting together our LBO deals, we follow the industry standard of projecting cash flows five or six years into the future. Those estimates determine both the price we are willing to pay and the capital structure we will use in funding our investment in the company.

Another critical determinant of the price we pay for companies—indeed, of our willingness to invest at all—is the extent of the management team's willingness to invest in the deal (and you have to keep in mind that, because of the amount of leverage involved, management's investment is very highly charged equity). If management doesn't want to invest, we get very worried. But if they do want to invest we get very excited. That is a real bellwether for us, an important signal of management's confidence in its ability to achieve projected levels of performance.

STEWART: Fred, do you often see sharp conflicts between the board and the management? Or is it better described as a collaborative interface?

SIMMONS: We try, and generally succeed, in keeping things as collaborative as possible. Of course, there are always issues where there's a natural conflict of interest between management and the board—for example, when it comes to management's compensation. But our philosophy as a firm is that when management invests side by side with us in the equity of the company, then those conflicts are minimized; the goals and interests of the investors and managers are pretty well aligned.

STEWART: How do you combine management ownership with the issue of setting goals and rewarding performance in the company? And what role does the board play in the goal-setting process?

SIMMONS: As majority owners, we clearly call the shots and set the goals in our companies. But before describing our governance process, let me try to explain our investment philosophy. First of all, we try to buy premium companies, well-run companies. We're not in the business of breaking up conglomerates that have problems coordinating all their businesses, nor are we in the business of engineering turnarounds. Our aim is to buy premium companies and then put a lot of capital into them and make them even better.

In the process of investing, we initiate a dialogue with management in which we attempt to come up with a mutually agreeable five-year plan. And, as I mentioned, in our average deal, management typically is asked to buy 5 to 10 percent of the equity of the company up front. They typically buy half of it for cash and half on a full recourse loan. And the company lends them the money at the prime rate of interest, payable quarterly.

So the management has highly charged equity. If the company is lever-

aged, say, 3 to 1, and management borrows to fund half its equity purchase, then management has highly leveraged equity. And this equity is also supplemented by performance options that vest over a five-year period. So we feel that management is in there with us with both feet. They're committed to making good on their projections.

STEWART: But because the projected payoffs are highly illiquid—the payoff on their options is at least five years down the road—it also forces management to take a somewhat longer view of the firm's performance. It's forces them to consider longer-run investment as well as near-term efficiency.

SIMMONS: That's right. If the company were sold in less than five years at a premium, the performance options might well vest in part or in full.

STEWART: And this effect is actually quite different from that of the standard stock options given to the managements of most public companies. In most of our public companies, management has an incentive to exercise their options and sell the stock as soon as the options have significant trading value. And this, needless to say, only reinforces whatever pressures management may feel to increase short-run value at the expense of the long term.

Fred, do you ever consider having just regular options as part of your compensation program?

SIMMONS: No, I don't see any purpose to having straight options. The way they're often granted by public companies causes them to be much less efficient than options tied to performance. Let's face it, management can increase earnings, and thus the value of vested options, on a short-term basis. But this may well be to the detriment of medium- or longer-term shareholder value.

ROACH: As long as we're on the subject, let me say a word on behalf of stock options. We have just adopted an unusal option program for senior

management. As I mentioned earlier, our longer-term mission at Fibreboard is to deal effectively with our asbestos litigation problem. But if we can find a solution to the problem, and increase the profitability of our basic operations at the same time, then there's a tremendous potential upside. Our stock price, as mentioned before, is down to $3.

In order to avoid diluting shareholder value, and yet provide management

strong incentives at the same time, we have decided to set up our option plan so that the prices at which the options can be exercised are considerably higher than today's price of $3. Specifically, one third of management's options will be exercisable if the price hits $10, a second third if the price hits $15, and the final third if the price hits $20. So, our option program will not really pay off unless until our shareholders experience a significant—for example, a five-fold—increase in their wealth. I think that's a good plan, given our current situation. Although I agree that stock options may be abused by some public companies, this is a good use of stock options.

SIMMONS: I agree, John. Although we have not used escalating option prices, that arrangement would seem to create much the same effect as options tied to medium-term or longer-term performance.

The Case of the Blackstone Group

STEWART: Let me ask Jim Birle, who comes from a similar organization, The Blackstone Group, to comment on his views of the governance process. Jim, as both a general partner of The Blackstone Group and co-chairman and CEO of the Collins & Aikman Group of Companies (or what used to be called the Wickes Companies), what do you

> *One critical determinant of the price we pay for companies— indeed, of our willingness to invest at all—is the extent of the management team's willingness to invest in the deal. If management doesn't want to invest, we get very worried. But if they do want to invest we get very excited. That is a real bellwether for us, an important signal of management's confidence in its ability to achieve projected levels of performance.*
>
> *—Fred Simmons*

view as the principal function of the board of directors?

BIRLE: I'm a great believer in the principle that accountability is what makes delegated authority legitimate. In the case of LBO boards, the board delegates to the management of the company the responsibility for managing the enterprise. The board's job is to set the goals for the company and then keep track of whether those goals are being met. If they are not, then it is the board's responsibility to intervene and get things right.

One of the differences between our LBO boards and those of public companies is that if one of our companies fails to meet goals, the consequences to the board members are very significant. We are in the business of investing money on behalf of insurance companies and pension funds. The contractual duration of our fund is 10 years, which means there is a specified time frame within which we have to provide our investors

with a competitive return on their invested capital. If we fail to provide adequate returns within the time frame, then we are going to have a hard time raising capital to fund our next set of investments.

And the fact that time is really working against us in terms of providing returns creates a tension between management and the board. The pressure to ensure that the goals are being met is just far greater than that which exists in most public companies. At the same time, this sense of urgency does not prevent us from setting and pursuing long-range goals and encouraging long-term thinking. We spend considerable time and effort analyzing how to strategically reposition some of the Collins & Aikman businesses and we undertake major reinvestment programs—programs that, in some cases, will not pay off for several years. Our goal is maximizing shareholder value, and you can't command a high price for a business if all you've been doing is liquidating its assets and failing to invest in its future earning power.

But to return to my original point, if the management of one of our companies fails to meet its goals, there's a degree of tension at our board meetings that I think is very healthy—and quite different from some of my prior experiences with public companies. Unlike LBO groups, public companies have

the staying power that may permit them to accommodate a standard of performance that is significantly below what would be considered satisfactory by The Blackstone Group or other similar merchant bankers.

STEWART: Jim, can you tell us a little about your role as CEO of the Collins & Aikman Companies, and what you have done to turn things around there?

BIRLE: In the case of Wickes, I am in the unique position of being co-chairman of a board in which the partners are a combination of Blackstone General Partners and Wasserstein Perella General Partners, all of which are major stockholders and thus directly affected by the performance of the company. I'm CEO of the Holdings Company to which the individual operating units report.

When we acquired Wickes in December of 1988, it was an overleveraged and underperforming conglomerate comprised of a diverse group of retail, distribution, and manufacturing components. We immediately set up a holding company structure and reassigned to operating managers the functions necessary for them to operate these businesses as self-standing enterprises. Through the divestiture of 25 units, we paid down $1.5 billion in debt during the first two years of ownership. At the same time we also brought in stronger operating executives who put in place new investment and growth strategies for the strongest units. Having a knowledgeable and involved board made it possible to effect tremendous changes in a troubled company in a short period of time.

STEWART: What kind of periodic performance measures do you use in evaluating operating management's performance?

BIRLE: We have much a tighter performance measurement system, by necessity, than most public companies I'm familiar with. In collaboration with management, the board sets both yearly targets as well as longer-term growth goals.

STEWART: What is the nature of the goals?

BIRLE: There are basically two: growth in operating income and return on capital employed. Both of these measures are formulated in terms of cash flow rather than earnings and both are used in evaluating long-term as well as short-term performance. Since management are major equity holders in the company, we are confident that they are constantly attempting to balance short-term versus long-term goals in creating value.

STEWART: Does the board set the goals, or does it instead just ratify goals that have been set by the management in a negotiation throughout the company?

BIRLE: I would say it's more of a negotiation. But, unlike the boards of many public companies, our board members come to the table already knowing a great deal about the operations and the expected behavior of the businesses in various economic and competitive situations. This knowledge comes from the extensive due diligence process we have conducted just prior to the acquisition. So we are able to determine when management has really gotten off the track far more quickly and confidently than most public company directors.

Although we do allow the CEOs to present their own budgets to be ratified by us, there has already been a vigorous dialogue between the CEO and the board when the CEO's plan is presented for ratification. We try and work together with operating management in framing the boundary conditions for performance. For example, what should we expect if the economy turns down? And if the CEO and his management team exceed their targeted goal, they're handsomely rewarded.

STEWART: Is there a cap on the bonus?

BIRLE: For the top guys, yes, there's generally a cap on annual awards. It's roughly twice their base salary. But if

they miss on the downside, then their bonus will be zero. So it's very much a pay-for-performance system. Our system is designed such that the people who really perform can make themselves a lot of money in the short term. And the ones who don't perform are really made to feel the pain of failure. To supplement these short-term programs, we put in place long-term capital accumulation programs

where clearly superior performance really translates into significant wealth accumulation.

Employee Ownership and the Case of SAIC

STEWART: Let me just finish my tour of duty here by asking Bill Roper to describe what is probably the unique ownership structure of his company. It may even have considerable value as a model for the future.

ROPER: I am the CFO of a company called Science Applications International Corporation, or SAIC for short. The company was founded in 1969 by four scientists who wanted to do some interesting work with the government. One of their aims was to generate enough revenues to be able to pay themselves a reasonable salary and live in La Jolla, California.

We just completed a year in which our revenues were about $1.3 billion. We

have about 14,000 employees. We've grown at an average compound rate in the high teens; and although the rate of growth is slowing a little bit, it still is in double digits. The company has had revenue and earnings increases in every year of its existence. We are primarily a government contractor; we do almost two thirds of our work for the government.

The company was founded as an employee-owned company, and it has

> *We are in the business of investing money on behalf of insurance companies and pension funds. The contractual duration of our fund is 10 years, which means there is a specified time frame within which we have to provide our investors with a competitive return on their invested capital. And the fact that time is really working against us creates a tension between management and the board. The pressure to ensure that the goals are being met is just far greater than that which exists in most public companies.*
>
> *—James Birle*

remained that way since 1969. Some 10,000 of the 14,000 employees directly own stock in the company. By that, I mean they have either written a check or have had money withheld from their paychecks to purchase stock or exercise options. Virtually all full-time employees own stock through our retirement programs as well.

STEWART: What price do the employees pay for the stock? As a private company, SAIC doesn't have a stock price. So is the purchase price based on some kind of periodic appraisal?

ROPER: The shares are sold for a price based on a formula. There's a quarterly setting of value of the company that is determined by a formula that relates to earnings, book value, and market comparables.

I think an important component of our company has been from the beginning that most employees, and every member of the management team from middle management on up, make a significant financial commitment to own stock in the company. Our stock programs—which, again, consist of options, direct purchases, and voluntary contributions to retirement programs—encourage key managers and employees toward greater ownership as they rise through the organization. The higher paid you are, and the faster that you move through the organization, the more

the system forces you to forgo current cash for future earnings from your ownership.

STEWART: Are you saying that as people move up through the company they're *obligated* to buy stock?

ROPER: Not obligated technically, but the system drives you to do that. For example, we have a bonus system that covers about 40% of all employees. Bonuses are typically paid out half in stock and half in cash. The stock is vested immediately, so it's taxable. So if you get 50 percent of your bonus in cash and 50 percent of it in stock, you don't have a lot of cash left over after you pay the tax liability.

But it's a great wealth accumulator. I wish I had brought a chart showing the rise of our stock value; it's the most beautiful parabolic curve you've ever seen. Our stock has probably grown about 20 percent a year compounded over 20 years.

STEWART: So the higher you go in the organization, the more stock you're *allowed* to buy?

ROPER: That's right. It's not an obligation, it's a privilege. But it would be very unusual to have any senior management members who didn't have a substantial ownership stake in our firm.

STEWART: But isn't this somewhat of a Ponzi scheme—something that works as long as it works?

ROPER: We joke a little bit about that around the shop. The system recycles a lot of money. When people leave the company and the company repurchases their stock, it recycles a lot of money. So, if there is a sharp downturn, then there will have been a transfer of value from the people still in the system to those who have left. But, as long as the company remains profitable and growing, it pays for people to forgo current cash for future earnings, and the system works. It's all driven on the fact that the company is profitable and growing.

STEWART: To what extent do you think the company's success is due to employee ownership—or is the combination of ownership structure and success just a coincidence?

ROPER: It's very easy to see that widespread employee ownership and significant senior management ownership of the company drive an awful lot of things that we do. It is clearly responsible for a good amount of the success of the company.

STEWART: Can you give us an example where people inside the company sit down and have an informal, "mini-shareholder" meeting to make an important decision? By the way, is that an accurate description of the process?

ROPER: That's essentially correct. The management philosophy is very decentralized; it is slightly to the right of anarchy. Many meetings are very contentious. People at all levels feel free to tell you what they think about how you are spending *their money!* Perhaps the most forceful objection to a proposed management decision is the statement, "Well, as a major shareholder, I disagree with your proposal to spend my money this way."

So it's an interesting environment. There's an awful lot of challenge and an awful lot of accountability. It ranges from issues as trivial as how much you spend on your office furniture to major expenditures and acquisitions.

MICHAEL JENSEN: Bill, let me ask a question about your plan. Take a middle manager who's been in the company for, say, 10 years. What kind of money would he or she have invested in the stock, and what would the value of that stock be worth today?

ROPER: Well, let me change your question a little, and let's take the case of a hypothetical senior scientist in our company—because scientists, along with engineers and computer programmers, are really the guts of our company. We don't have a lot of management types.

Let's say a typical scientist has been with the company for 15 years, and is making a base salary of $80,000 along with a cash bonus of $10,000. Over the years, that person has likely put into the company in one form or another—exercising options, payroll deductions, or just direct cash purchases, as well as some retirement contributions—that person is probably out of pocket about $100,000. And the stock purchased by that cash is today probably worth half a million. That seems to me to be a representative case at our firm.

STEWART: Are there any openings at your company?

Well, Bill, your company seems to function as a largely self-regulating, self-governing company. In your case, the role of the board of directors has got to be much less important—because the internal control mechanism is literally woven into the share ownership of the key people throughout the company. Would you agree with that statement, especially in view of the other public companies you've been associated with?

> *The management philosophy of SAIC is very decentralized; it is slightly to the right of anarchy. Many meetings are very contentious. People at all levels feel free to tell you what they think about how you are spending their money! Perhaps the most forceful objection to a proposed management decision is the statement, "Well, as a major shareholder, I disagree with your proposal to spend my money this way."*
>
> *—William Roper*

ROPER: That's clearly the case. I think that's a very wise observation. In thinking about the subject of this panel, and especially Mike Jensen's comments yesterday, it became clear to me that our board does not really fit the model Jensen was holding out for public companies. We have a large board. It's composed of 23 members, six of whom are insiders. They meet quarterly for a few hours. I think it's virtually impossible on a quarterly basis to communicate a lot of detailed information about a very complex company. Now, there are other forums where the board members learn about the company. There's a lot of informal contact with them. But our board clearly does not exercise the kind of oversight that, say, the principals of LBOs or venture capital firms do. And yet we have a company that for 23 years running has been phenomenally successful.

So there seem to be two possible answers here: Either we were just lucky for 23 years in a row, or you guys are all full of hot air and we need to have more unwieldy boards packed with insiders. More seriously, I think we are successful largely because of the internal mechanisms and the management ownership structure that the company has maintained throughout its existence. This makes the board's job fairly easy.

STEWART: Bill, I was struck by the similarity of your company to one that I have some familiarity with, Arthur

Andersen. I would also describe that company as a self-governing, self-regulating organization. There are 2500 key partners who own the company. The company is extremely successful; it has been quite profitable even in the face of a shrinking market for public accounting services. It's also extremely entrepreneurial. For example, they built the immensely successful Andersen Consulting from nothing. And they're now a competitor of yours.

ROPER: Yes, and I wish they weren't.

STEWART: And that company too is controlled chaos. In the early 1980s, we made a presentation to a group of top partners in the company; and they were extremely enthusiastic about the possibility of adopting our corporate finance program throughout the organization. So I said to one of the top partners, "We have to find a way to get others in Arthur Andersen to hear this message; so why don't you just send out an edict throughout the organization?"

And the partner said to me, "Bennett, you don't understand the way it works around here. We have offices throughout the world, and they are each run by the partners in charge of those offices. There's nothing that comes from the top down. It's kind of a neural network in which proposals within the organization are transmitted from the outlying areas to the center. And when they reach the center, there are ad hoc

committees and structures put in place to evaluate them."

What's also interesting about Arthur Andersen—and most of the other accounting firms, too—is that without the pressure of external capital markets, the public accounting industry has gone through a major restructuring and rationalization over the past 10 years. It is no longer the Big 8, it's now the Big 6. And maybe it will be the big five at some point. So this partnership model can work in mature, no-growth industries as well as growth industries like Bill's.

So, Bill, perhaps we can view SAIC as pointing the way towards a new kind of organization—one that reduces the importance of the board in the monitoring process and replaces it with widespread ownership.

JENSEN: Well, Bennett, I'm not sure how far you can extend the application of this model. Both of these companies, Arthur Andersen and SAIC, seem to me classic examples of companies that can't be run any other way than by diffusing ownership throughout the company. In the case of the typical law firm or professional consulting organization, you can't have a complicated control mechanism in which decision initiatives are bucked up a hierarchy—because by the time they get there, the chance to exploit the opportunity has already passed. The specific knowledge that is required for many impor-

tant corporate decisions often lies deep in the organization in small teams. The decisions often have to be made there, and they have to be made quickly.

So, if you tried to take either of these companies and turn them into public companies, it just wouldn't work. You could try and substitute the complicated control mechanisms used by public companies, but they wouldn't work very well in that kind of situation. The substitute for those complicated mechanisms is, as Bennett suggested, to push the equity ownership or partnership shares down and throughout the organization. (Besides the two companies you've mentioned, Gore Associates is another good example of this employee ownership model; and it's an industrial company rather than a consulting operation.)

And let me explain why I asked Bill how much money the typical manager has at stake. If people have a significant investment in the firm, you can be much more comfortable turning them loose to make their own decisions because they are going to be motivated not only by their own financial interests, but by their colleagues' financial interests as well. And it's not just money. It's the fact that they've got the right orientation; they have got the interest of the organization at heart. This is really the only way you can run people-intensive as opposed to capital-intensive organizations.

STEWART: Bill, do you think the kind of employee ownership structure that you've put in place would work for, say, a diversified consumer products company?

ROPER: It's really hard to say. Our main asset is our people. While we do make some products, our principal business is technological consulting, systems development and integration, and other things like that. For this reason, our main asset is the brains and experience of our people. Our company is organized around, and driven by, the need to find and retain good people—getting them on board, motivating them, and rewarding them.

JENSEN: I don't know your company, but I would also predict that this kind of employee ownership works best when you have a technology that's not very capital intensive.

ROPER: That's correct. Over the years, we have had lots of debates about going into capital-intensive businesses. But there's only so much capital that you can aggregate among the body of people that work for you. And so it does work better for those businesses that don't require a lot of capital.

JENSEN: I'm not talking about just your ability to raise large amounts of capital. I'm thinking more about what happens to management incentives after you succeed in raising the capital. If you have a lot of capital assets lying around, partnerships and organizations like yours

with lots of owners run into big problems. Companies with highly decentralized ownership structures will likely start to have major internal conflicts when making decisions about what to do with large capital assets. When do you sell such assets, if ever, and distribute their value to partners? Even owning buildings causes partnerships big problems over issues like this. Having lots of owners with different time horizons makes the decision-making a lot harder.

For this reason, partnerships and 100% employee ownership are well suited for companies that don't invest in major capital assets, but that have a sort of constant flow of capital in and out of the business.

Shareholder Activism and Corporate Accountability

STEWART: Let me ask our representatives of public companies whether they are feeling more pressure to be accountable to their shareholders as a result of some of the increasing shareholder activism that is taking place? John, what about The Dial Corp?

TEETS: The only instance of shareholder pressure I can think of has come from Boone Pickens's group—I think they call themselves the United Shareholders Association. My sense is that Boone got burned pretty badly by the Unocal decision; and after he ran with his tail between his legs, he decided to start this shareholder voting project. So, because Boone has decided he doesn't like poison pills, we now have a vote every year on whether or not to rescind our poison pill. And that's okay. Members of Boone's group own a small amount of our stock, and they are entitled to propose measures like this and to vote on them. That's the way the system works.

But we have not had any pressure from any of the major funds that own our stock. We have excellent relationships with all of them, and we invite them every year to meet our management team. They are allowed to voice their concerns, and we attempt to respond to them as best we can.

STEWART: But my sense is that the role of most institutional investors is really to try to figure out how much the company is worth and not to make recommendations for change. We have this peculiar state of affairs in this country where institutional investors are looked upon as short-term investors on the one hand, and yet are expected to behave like owners. Or, at least, when they behave more like speculators than owners, people profess to be disappointed by their "short termism."

So my question is the following: How do we turn investors—people who are inclined to short the stock if the company does poorly—into owners interested in participating in the effort to maximize long-run value? It seems to me that our current system does not allow, much less encourage, institutional investors to become owners in that classical sense. For one thing, they don't have board representation.

So, John, would you encourage institutional investors to nominate and elect a minority of independent directors to your board? This way they might be more inclined to become long-term holders.

TEETS: Any shareholder has the right to nominate a director and vote for him or her. So it's not whether I agree or disagree, that's the way the system is set up.

Would I want to have an institutional investor on my board? Our board is picked by consensus, and I doubt very much that any of the ten outside board members would even consider having someone who is in the business of managing funds sit on our board and tell us how we are supposed to run the business to increase shareholder wealth. But, then again, I can't really speak for my board on this. We've never had the issue on the agenda and we've never discussed it.

STEWART: John, you took a proactive role in restructuring your company several years ago. Do you feel that boards are going to become much more active in the future in terms of initiating restructurings to increase shareholder value? For example, do you think they'll be more aggressive in recommending the increased use of leverage for underleveraged companies? I personally think that boards today are much less likely to view a triple-A rating as a unambiguous sign of corporate success. What are your views in terms of the initiatives that corporate boards will most likely be taking in the future?

TEETS: I can't speak for other boards. But our board often challenges our direction. We go into great detail on both the targeted and the realized return on assets of each of our subsidiaries. Our board members also participate in regular on-site visits in which they meet and question the managers that run those businesses.

In fact, I am skeptical about the idea that boards are becoming *more* challenging today. I think they have always been challenging. The average tenure of a CEO is about six years in the United States. CEOs are fired by their boards all the time. It's not like being a tenured professor in a university—a system that guarantees a job for life. (Let me also say

that I think the colleges and universities in the United States are among the most poorly run group of organizations in the country, particularly in how they nominate their board and how they function. It's almost impossible to function within their own system.)

I think some boards are becoming more proactive today. There are clearly companies that have not performed well, and where boards have failed to act. And we all know which companies

they are; they are in the newspaper every day. At the same time, of course, we never read about the vast majority of companies in which the boards do a good job.

STEWART: John, what is it that makes a board function well and what makes a board function poorly? What are the key ingredients for success in creating a board that will add value?

TEETS: Well, I think it's important for the CEO to make the best use of the board. He should regularly seek the counsel of the board and listen to their suggestions. Board members have exceptional talent and experience, and the CEO ought to make the best possible use of them. They really do bring different kinds of expertise to the table. They see things I don't see, and I think it's important to have advisers like that.

So I think it's up to the CEO to draw out the expertise of the board. At the same time, though, the board members are the bosses. They have the power to hire and fire top management. If the board does not exercise this power when the company is doing poorly, then there can be a problem. As our professor friend suggested yesterday, this is a very complex issue because each company and board operates differently. Let me also say I just don't think consultants and college professors—that is,

But there are a couple of things running through my mind that maybe you can help me understand. I'm sure there are many CEOs who behave exactly the way you say they do; they make a conscientious effort to use their boards properly and to do the right thing by their shareholders. But even in these cases, there's a potential problem. CEOs get older, they may tend to get set in their ways, but meanwhile the world moves on. We

problem we face in these organizations is how to put in place a control mechanism that creates a healthy tension between management and the board—one that ensures that when management does begin to go off-course, the correction happens sooner rather than later.

Let me tell you about a conversation I had when returning from a board meeting with a fellow member on an airplane. There had been some frank discussion during the meeting, some disagreements with the CEO. This board member is also a very senior executive on the board of his own company, and he was one of those who voiced sharp disagreement with the CEO during our meeting. And this board member explained to me that such frank discussion and disagreements would never happen on his own board. His own CEO would simply take the person aside who asked the hard questions, and then make it very clear that either he was going to get on the same track, or one of them was going to leave. And it was also clear which one of them was going to leave.

We've all seen boards operate this way, John. So what can be done about it?

TEETS: Let me remind you that, although the board can fire the CEO, the CEO cannot fire a board member—or not at least without the approval of the other board members.

JENSEN: But how will you make this organization work so that the CEO will get a message he doesn't want to hear? Because that's when it counts. It's not when the CEO understands that the world is changing and that the corporation has to change with it. It's the opposite situation; the one when the company is off on the wrong track, and the CEO wants to persist with the old strategy. That is precisely when the unpleasantness has to occur, and that is where our current system breaks down. Under the current governance system,

> *With the threat of raiders largely gone, many companies now seem to be looking seriously for new models of corporate governance. In many cases, they are looking for ways of bringing about voluntarily some of the productive changes that were forced upon them during the '80s. One solution is to make the managers and the employees in the company into significant owners. By adopting this self-governing, self-regulating model of governance, we wouldn't have to rely on the capital markets or on the board to bring about change.*
>
> *—Bennett Stewart*

people who are not active in running businesses themselves—are likely to make good board members. They are not fighting in the war, and they thus have a tendency to be less proactive in many cases than people who are out there facing the competition every day.

JENSEN: John, can I push you a little on that?

TEETS: You're *asking* me?

JENSEN: It's only rhetorical.

STEWART: He's gonna get back at you, John.

JENSEN: By the way, John, I completely agree with your comments about the governance of universities and the way they function—and also about the value of the university tenure system. In fact, I should tell you that I have resigned my tenure at both of the institutions that have granted it to me by submitting unconditional letters of resignation.

all see the world through our own eyes, and it's a very natural and understandable human tendency for people to fail to see the need for radical change.

Now, the problem that troubles me arises when the CEO or the management team begins to get off track—and organizations do this all the time. If the burden is on the CEO and top management to seek out the flagellation from others that will force them to face up to the truth, then we have a serious problem with our system. That is just not going to happen—or not until the deterioration has gotten so bad that it's almost too late to save the organization. (This, incidentally, is my feeling about what has happened recently at General Motors—and maybe even IBM, too, although the organizational changes they just made give me hope for them.) The

the company has to confront a crisis before the board will intervene. GM had to lose several billion dollars in a single year before management was forced to recognize the need for radical change. And Digital Equipment had to lose about 80% of its market value before its CEO was finally removed by the board.

TEETS: I've sat on a number of boards. And although some disagreements are brought up at board meetings, I generally think it's better practice to take up major issues privately with the CEO first. Then, if they come out at the board meeting later, some of the defensiveness of the CEO will have been removed.

But let me say that I don't have the answer to the problem you're talking about. This issue of the board and the CEO is very complex. Obviously, some boards work and some don't. You can see well-publicized cases in the *Wall Street Journal* where boards are not working. On the other hand, you see many cases where they're working very well. I would also insist that there are a lot more CEOs who are canned than we know about because they generally resign. It looks better that way.

JENSEN: But the research on total CEO turnover suggests that, even when companies perform poorly, the likelihood of a CEO being fired is less than one in ten. And these numbers attempt to include all those cases where the CEO seems to resign. In fact, a couple of years ago former SEC Commissioner Joseph Grundfest used to say that it was more likely for a Congressman to be indicted for cheating than for a CEO to be fired by a board. But, with the recent cases at GM and DEC, things seem to be changing somewhat.

Information and Accountability

BIRLE: Michael, my opinion is that the current governance system of public companies is based on two important premises—adequate information and

accountability—neither of which is likely to hold for the boards of many public companies. If the board is not properly informed, they are really operating in the dark. If they don't understand there is a problem in the first place, then they are not going to be able to take the appropriate action with the CEO.

One of the advantages that Fred Simmons and I have, as controlling owners of private companies, is that we do the due diligence on the companies we buy. We understand the quality of management, the corporate strategy, the operational plan, the competitive environment, the balance sheet issues—we have a good working knowledge of all those factors that differentiate between success and failure. And then after we make our investment, performance factors are very closely monitored by the board as we go forward.

In public companies, by contrast, board members are brought in with little, if any, knowledge of the company. It's really a ceremonial invitation. And, as I said, if that board member does not really understand what is going on inside the company, his ability to add value is limited. So I think it's up to the CEO to make sure that he gives the board members opportunities to add value at both the committee and full board levels.

As John Roach suggested earlier, issues should be presented to the committees as possible steps under consideration, not as final decisions to be ratified. And as the board becomes more informed about what's going on at the committee level, the discussion at the general board meetings becomes much more constructive and proactive. Armed with greater knowledge, board members will not be as reluctant to penetrating questions. Asking such questions may in turn stimulate a lot of dialogue in the full board meeting. And, as a consequence, even more information comes to light, and the

board can then begin to do its job of holding management to something like accountability. As a party to the decisions, the board members are also likely to feel a greater sense of responsibility to shareholders about the outcome of corporate decisions.

So, again, in my way of looking at it, it's just really a combination of information and accountability. I think you have to build that accountability within your board. It's not something that happens automatically.

STEWART: Besides information and accountability, couldn't financial incentives also serve as an important contributor to board effectiveness? Incentives are likely to make the board work harder to get the necessary information from management; and, once having the information, then to act on it.

Bob Kidder, the CEO of Duracell, said something very similar to your point, Jim. He said that just the process of going through the LBO gave him and his management team a great deal of new insight into their business; it completely changed how they ran the company after the LBO. There were also tighter financial controls put on management; but he also stressed the importance of financial incentives, the carrot as well as the stick, in motivating improvements in performance.

When I was later working with a very large, extremely diversified company, I suggested that they go through a kind of "practice" LBO in order to discover where the value was coming from in their own businesses, and how things might be improved. I even suggested that management put together a mock prospectus saying that a tender offer had been made for the company, and that each one of the units of the company would be challenged to come up with its own plan to maximize value under the new corporate structure.

Initially, top management was extremely enthusiastic about the whole idea. But then the general counsel of the company stepped in and killed the idea. This was several years ago, before the deal market fell apart; and uncovering break-up values was likely getting too close to reality.

There has, however, been one important benefit from the eclipse of the junk bond and takeover markets. With the threat of raiders largely gone, many companies now seem to be looking seriously for new models of corporate governance. In many cases, they are looking for ways of bringing about voluntarily some of the productive changes that were forced upon them during the '80s.

ROACH: Bennett, I'm not so sure the issue is governance. I think there are two structural problems that don't have ready-made solutions. I think the majority of companies are run by CEOs who are genuinely interested in their shareholders and clearly want the board to play the role of active counselors. They solicit board members who are very talented and directed individuals.

But what if you have a company where the CEO is neglecting shareholders and doesn't really want counsel from his board? He's perfectly happy flying around in his Gulfstream, and the directors are perfectly happy collecting their directors' fees, and not getting involved in conflicts. The issue then becomes: Who is going to intervene on behalf of the shareholders to correct such a situation?

The other problem I don't have a solution for has to do with the time horizon of shareholders. Many managements are skeptical about the ability or willingness of shareholders to give them credit for their long-term investment strategies. Now, if management were confident they had a set of classical owners interested in maximizing the long-term value of the firm, then they might be much more enthusiastic about entering into a more collaborative relationship with institutional investors. But what happens if most of your shareholders are speculators? Do you manage the company to maximimize the next quarter's EPS, or do look to strengthen the company's competitive position for the long haul? I don't see any obvious way out of this dilemma.

STEWART: Well, one solution, John, is to make the managers and the employees in the company into significant owners. By adopting such a self-governing, self-regulating model of governance, we wouldn't have to rely on the capital markets or on the board as forces for bringing about change.

For example, in the case of CSX, some 160 of the company's top managers came together as a group to purchase a large number of shares. The typical person invested $35,000 to buy stock leveraged 20 to 1. This meant that a typical CSX manager virtually overnight became the owner of $700,000 worth of stock. To avoid diluting the public stockholders, moreover, the exercise price was indexed to the company's borrowing rate. Since this plan was put in place in 1990, the stock's gone up 50 percent. The other perceptible consequence is that you have to look both ways before you cross the railroad tracks because they only run express trains now.

The Search for More Permanent Owners

JENSEN: I would like to go back to John Roach's comment about the effect of speculators' stock holdings on management's investment decision-making. If John had raised this issue ten years ago, I would have said, "You don't understand financial economics. Short-term prices reflect long-term values." But I think that some financial economists are now coming to understand that the point you're making may be an important one.

Michael Porter, for example, is now arguing in his Council on Competitiveness project that there's a good chance that we have gotten the wrong corporate ownership and governance system in the United States. Another Harvard colleague of mine, Amar Bhide, has partly convinced me that we as a nation have put too much emphasis as a matter of public policy on having highly liquid securities market with lots of disclosure and constraints on insider trading. This emphasis on liquidity and disclosure requirements has combined with a whole set of laws enacted since the Great Depression to make it very costly for either individuals or institutions to both hold large amounts of stock in single companies and to become involved in the strategic direction of the firm.

Such legislation and public policy have led to a progressive widening of the rift between ownership and control over the past 50 years—a period, incidentally, in which CEOs' percentage ownership of their companies' stock fell by a factor of 10. This separation of ownership from control has in turn created enormous information and agency costs for investors, who have basically been shut out of the governance process. With imperfect information, and little ability to intervene and change the corporate direction if things go wrong, our institutional investors have been forced to keep management on a short tether, selling shares when earnings turn down.

And this of course creates a problem for management: How can management really make long-term value-maximizing decisions when all they've got is a bunch of transitory shareholders that the law prevents them from communicating effectively with?

By contrast, the Japanese and the Germans have legal and regulatory structure systems that encourage strong relationships and information-sharing among management, the company's major banks (which often hold large equity stakes in the companies they lend to), and other major shareholders. It's difficult for management to build trust and informal agreements with a constantly churning group of outside investors who really don't know (or care) very much about what's going on inside the company.

At the same time, there are institutions that have said to me, "Look, we know we're making long-term investments, but we have no way to talk to management or to enter into a contract, and we're certainly not getting an adequate return for placing long-term money." So this is a real problem. It lies at the heart of the problems that show up with large organizations like General Motors where our governance system seems to be failing us.

As I have also argued, the LBO association model that firms like KKR and Forstmann Little have borrowed from the venture capital industry—one in which a principal equity investor controls the board and represents the interests of the major debtholders as well—is at bottom an attempt to deal with these information and agency problems that now bedevil our public companies. As another example, institutional investors delegate to the Blackstone Group, to people like Jim Birle, the job of being their representative, their active investor. Warren Buffett does something quite similar through the vehicle of Berkshire Hathaway (of which he is the 45% owner). And so does Lazard Freres' Corporate Partners.

So, given the demonstrated effectiveness of these kinds of investors, it may be time for major changes in our legal system and in the structure of regulations of our capital markets. Let me also say, however, that the proposed changes to the current system being put forward by Porter and others are not ones that most CEOs are likely to welcome. They call for larger stakes and greater involvement by investors in return for less emphasis on diversification and liquidity.

LEE: Mike, I think our system may already be evolving somewhat in this direction, even under the current legal and regulatory structure. In the past few years, I have seen a pronounced change in the way institutional investors are exerting their influence over corporate management. Caesars World is a publicly held company. Management does not have a major stake collectively; it's only a 4% position in the company. We also have about 75% institutional ownership.

Five years ago, when financial engineering and leveraged restructuring was reaching its peak of activity, we found out that the time horizons of our institutional owners were very, very short. In one 10-day period, we discovered that our stock had moved almost entirely into the hands of the arbitrage community, whose time horizon was between 15 and 20 seconds. That was a real learning experience for us. As I mentioned earlier, we managed to exit from that predicament only by restructuring the company and making a healthy offer to let the arbitrageurs sell their shares. All this happened 21 days before the market crash. And, although our shareholders ended up very happy with the consequences, we took on considerable leverage in order to deliver that value to shareholders.

We now are back up to 75% institutional ownership, but we have noticed a profound change in their behavior. We now appear to have a solid base of fairly long-term institutional investors. They spend the time to come out and talk with us at length about the long-term strategy of the company. And a number of them seem to understand it fairly well and to have done a lot of homework. We were pleasantly surprised at the amount of time they spend studying us. They often have contrary ideas on what we should be doing in order to maximize value; so we have nice, lively discussions. These institutions, I should also point out, are not for

the most part the ones you read about in the newspapers, the ones who have the strong vocal positions on the top 25 corporations in the country.

So our institutional investors are proving to be a very constructive force. My only objection is that, despite their lip service to saying management should have larger shareholdings, several of them have refused to vote for authorization for issuing more stock. So it's not clear to me the how theory and practice of maximizing shareholder value are going to come together—at least on this issue. But I do really detect a much deeper involvement and sense of purpose among institutional shareholders than I did five and ten years ago. It's been a major change.

TEETS: We have had a very similar experience with our institutional investors. For example, representatives of the Delaware Fund, which own almost 10% of our stock, come out to visit us regularly. They've held the stock now for eight years. They've been long-term holders. Fidelity is another. In fact, I could list ten institutional shareholders who have held our stock for a long time, who regularly come out to confer with us, and whom we also visit on a regular basis.

We are very much open to having such investors. They can talk to whomever they want in the company, we open our books to them. They spend time with us, and we have an excellent relationship with all of our institutional shareholders. They have made a lot of money from investing in our stock, and we have made believers out of them. So, by demonstrating good performance and an openness to your institutional investors, I think it's possible—and indeed quite valuable—to build strong relationships between management and investors.

STEWART: Well, let me end our discussion on that positive note, and add my own wish that such a trend continues. Thank you all for participating.

V
RISK MANAGEMENT AND
INTERNATIONAL FINANCE

■

BANK OF AMERICA ROUNDTABLE ON

DERIVATIVES AND CORPORATE RISK MANAGEMENT

Kiawah Island
South Carolina
May 13, 1995

ROBERT McKNEW: Good morning, and welcome to this discussion of derivatives and corporate risk management. My name is Bob McKnew, and I am an executive vice president at Bank of America. As head of the bank's U.S. Capital Markets Group, I am responsible for foreign exchange, securities, and risk management products.

Given the current controversy over derivatives, our subject could not be more timely. And, as often happens when the popular press sets its sights

on financial markets, there is a good deal of misinformation in this area. Derivatives, of course, have been blamed for large losses at municipalities, college pension funds, and even a number of large, highly respected corporations. Critics of corporate and market behavior, true to form, are viewing such losses as the tip of the iceberg, the first signs of some expected revelation about the extent of derivatives speculation in corporate America.

But, as most of you in this room are well aware, derivatives, when used properly, are highly effective tools for managing corporate exposures to financial variables such as interest rates, foreign exchange rates, and commodity prices. And if we want to understand why the corporate use of derivatives has exploded in the last 15 years or so, we need only look at the dramatic changes in the volatility of financial markets during the past two decades. Today's extraordinary levels of interest rate volatility, for example, got their start at the end of the 1970s, when Fed chairman Paul Volcker first attempted to target monetary aggregates rather than interest rates—and that is when financial futures, forward rate agreements, and, a couple years later, interest rate swaps began to emerge. And beginning with the oil spike in the early 1970s, commodity prices of all kinds—particularly of petroleum-related products and metals—have continued to experience periodic surges in volatility over the past 20 years. And foreign exchange markets, of course, have not been immune to the financial markets roller coaster. In the past year alone, the dollar has lost 20% of its value against the yen and DM.

But let me stop here and make a confession. I like volatility, I like chaos, I like markets that move. Volatility—whether it's volatility in $/DM, in $/yen, in Mexican pesos, or in

Brady bonds—creates demand for derivative products both by corporates and by large investors. It makes all of you here need to do something to manage your exposures—and that, frankly, is how I make my living.

As a kind of nighttime job, I have had the honor of speaking for the securities industry several times this year. I have testified before Congress three times since January on the fallout from derivatives episodes like Credit Lyonnais, Orange County, bank portfolios and money market mutual funds, Gibson Greeting, P & G, and so forth. Let me comment briefly on the lessons to be drawn from that experience before we plunge into our subject of corporate risk management.

In recent years, our financial markets have become quite adept at creating derivative instruments with very specific payoffs. When used properly, these instruments can be used to provide highly efficient, cost-effective hedges of financial risks associated with either an investor's portfolio or a corporation's businesses. In addition, if an investor wants to structure a portfolio that performs well under certain interest rate environments, financial instruments can be tailored to carry out the desired strategy. If interest rates behave the way the investor anticipated, those instruments will perform well. Nevertheless, the investor—and this goes for corporate risk managers, too—should understand that if interest rates do not behave as anticipated, the instruments will produce losses. It should also be understood that if the investor or corporation loses money on a financial instrument, the instruments themselves are not the culprits; they will behave as expected.

Take the much-publicized case of Orange County. The losses suffered by Orange County's cash management fund can be attributed to three principal factors.

First, Orange County invested in medium-term notes which, like all fixed-income securities, are subject to market risk as interest rates change. Throughout much of 1994, such securities fell substantially in price because of sharp increases in interest rates.

Second, Orange County used short-term borrowings to leverage its investment portfolio to several times its original holdings. By borrowing against its portfolio, the County was able to raise additional funds to buy even more securities, thus amplifying the effects of the price fluctuations just described.

Third, the County invested in certain interest-rate-sensitive structured securities, instruments that typically combine an "embedded" derivative such as an interest rate option within an ordinary straight-debt instrument. Because such structured securities are so highly customized—often for a single investor that purchases the entire issue—such securities are hard to value and therefore less liquid, a factor that almost certainly contributed to problems suffered by the County.

In sum, the County appears to have structured a portfolio that would perform very well if rates either fell or stayed the same, but that would sustain large losses if rates increased significantly. And, of course, interest rates went up dramatically. Yields on five-year notes rose over 200 basis points in 1994, producing an overall return of negative 5.01%, the worst one-year performance of that security ever. Twenty-year Treasuries had their second worst year ever. And Orange County's portfolio, with its use of leverage and special structured securities, produced losses on the order of 20%.

The lesson from Orange County, then, is the importance of distinguishing between the County's investment strategy and the instruments used to execute the strategy. The instruments behaved pretty much as expected; the strategy was radically flawed. Instead of protecting the value of its fixed-income portfolio against rate increases, Orange County doubled up, indeed probably *quadrupled*, its exposure to interest rates.

When abused, derivatives can enlarge existing exposures and create new financial risks. But, when used properly (and this part of the story seems to have eluded the popular press), derivatives have enabled corporations to isolate and manage financial exposures far more efficiently and cheaply than ever before.

Robert McKnew
Bank of America

And the same lesson, of course, applies to the current controversy over derivatives and corporate risk management. Used properly, derivatives have enabled corporations to isolate and manage financial exposures far more efficiently and cheaply than ever before. (And this part of the story, as I suggested, seems to have eluded the popular press.) But when abused, as we have seen in cases like P&G and Gibson Greeting Cards, they can actually enlarge existing exposures and create new financial risks.

So, with these ramblings as prelude, let me introduce the panelists in this discussion of corporate risk management. In alphabetical order, they are:

TOM JONES, who is Vice President and Treasurer of Union Carbide. Tom, as you will hear, is a veteran in the practice of corporate risk management and a long-time user of derivatives.

LYNN LANE is Vice President and Treasurer of R.J. Reynolds Tobacco Company. As head of the company's worldwide Tobacco Treasury function, Lynn is responsible for RJR's extensive program for managing its foreign exchange risk.

JONELLE ST. JOHN is Vice President and Treasurer of MCI. Under Jonelle's supervision, the treasury group at MCI recently developed a proposal for an expanded derivatives program designed to manage the currency and other cross-border risks associated with the firm's overseas expansion plans.

JOHN VAN RODEN is Vice President and Treasurer of Lukens, Inc. Among his many other responsibilities, John is chairman of Lukens' newly-formed risk management team.

And I will now ask John to start things off by telling us about the new risk management program at Lukens.

The Case of Lukens

JOHN VAN RODEN: Let me begin by giving you a brief overview of the history of risk management at Lukens—and this should be very brief, since we really didn't begin to take a systematic approach to managing risk until 1993. Lukens is a producer of carbon, alloy, and stainless steel. Our operating earnings are affected by fluctuations in the prices of nickel and natural gas (among other commodities), and we attempt to limit these price exposures through our risk management process. Prior to 1993,

we did some hedging of nickel and natural gas prices—and, occasionally, of interest rates as well—but this was all done on an ad hoc, unstructured basis. Each business entity made its hedging decisions independently, there were no established limits on trading positions or counterparty credit exposures, and there was no reporting of derivatives positions and the associated risks to management and the board.

Then, in 1993, we developed a more formal approach to risk management, and we put together a team to develop and carry out our risk management policy and strategies. In December of '93, our original risk management team executed its first trade—a purchase of nickel futures on the London Metals Exchange. In 1994, we drafted a formal Risk Management Policy, which was approved by the Finance Committee of our Board near the end of that year. And, in early 1995, we had our risk management process and policies reviewed by an outside consultant, Arthur Andersen. The consultant's most important recommendation—one which we acted upon and which I will discuss later in more detail—was that we strengthen the reporting and communications that take place between the risk management function and top management and the board.

One of the distinctive—and, in my view, most valuable—features of our risk management program is that it takes a *team* approach; it involves participation by people from several disciplines within the company. The team includes the VP-Purchasing of our Carbon & Alloy Group, the Director of Materials Management–Stainless Steel, our Manager of Corporate Accounting, our Corporate Risk Manager, and the VP & Treasurer (that is, me). This risk management team meets regularly to discuss our markets, exposures, and hedging strategies.

We have drafted a mission statement that reads as follows: "*The team will identify noncontrollable costs and risks that affect Lukens' operations. Alternative strategies will be analyzed, including existing and innovative financial products, in order to determine the most effective way to address these costs and risks. The team will be responsible for executing the optimal risk management strategy that will add value to the business.*"

Our risk management *policy* addresses issues of implementation, such as: Who is to be on the risk management team? Who is responsible for executing trading activities? What are the limits of their decision-making authority, expressed in terms both of hedge size and duration? What approvals are required for decision-making that goes beyond these limits? And how are positions to be reported to management and the board?

In formulating our risk management *strategy*, we began by examining in a more systematic way the various financial exposures of our businesses. Besides fluctuations in nickel and natural gas prices, we also looked at other potential sources of financial risk—for example, changes in foreign currencies and interest rates, and in the price of aluminum and carbon scrap. We collected data on the historical volatility of each of these financial variables; and then, with the help of outside advisers and feedback from our suppliers, we attempted to determine how such volatility affected our bottom line and overall competitive position.

Having identified our major exposures, we then looked at the array of financial vehicles that could be used to hedge these exposures. In reviewing hedging vehicles, we had two major requirements: (1) the instrument must trade in a well-established, highly liquid market; and (2) there must be a strong correlation between the price of the traded instrument and the price exposure being hedged. For each of the different hedging vehicles we considered, moreover, we attempted to evaluate the associated costs and risks—including the counterparty credit risk in OTC derivatives and the basis risk from lack of a perfect correlation between the financial hedge and the underlying exposure.

The conclusion we came to was basically this: We will hedge only significant exposures, principally nickel and natural gas. Moreover, we will pursue a strategy of *active* risk management—that is, we will hedge only a fraction of our exposures and the percentage we choose to hedge will be subject to continuous review. We decided on "active" management for two reasons. First, the cyclical swings in the steel products business mean that there is a lot of uncertainty about the actual size of our exposures; that is, because we don't know at the beginning of any year how much steel we will end up selling that year, we don't know how much to hedge. The second reason for our active management approach is our belief that, by operating with a cross-functional team approach, we can add some value by changing our hedging position when we have a view about future developments in our markets. We will act on our views only in "familiar" markets like nickel and natural—not in interest rates or foreign exchange—and we will act only with the unanimous consent of the team.

After developing the outlines of a hedging strategy for each exposure, we then considered issues of decision-making authority, execution, and control. The result of this process was a risk management policy containing explicit limits, controls, and provisions for centralized recordkeeping and settlements. Finally, there are extensive regular reporting requirements, along with the stipulation that the entire policy be subjected to further review at the end of each year.

As I mentioned earlier, after formulating our entire risk management policy, we then had our policy and procedures audited by Arthur Andersen. Andersen gave us their "AA" rating, citing as strengths our cross-functional approach in developing hedging strategies and our recordkeeping & settlements and other controls. Our policy audit did suggest, however, that we had not done such a good job in communicating to management and the board our strategy for managing each of our various risks. And we're trying to do better there. In fact, we have designed a new format for reporting on our derivatives positions to our board.

> *Our risk management policy is to hedge only our significant exposures, principally nickel and natural gas. Moreover, we pursue a strategy of* **active** *risk management.... We obviously have views on certain markets, and we sometimes take financial risks in the sense that we choose to leave part of our exposures unhedged. But we make such decisions through a team, one that includes operating people with bottom-line responsibility.*
>
> *John van Roden*
> *Lukens, Inc.*

John
van Roden

To give you an idea of the kind of information we now report to our board, take the case of nickel. As I mentioned earlier, half of Lukens' business is stainless steel, and 50% of the cost of stainless steel is in nickel. And so we often hedge against nickel price increases.

Here is a chart that shows the path of nickel prices between January of 1985 and October of 1994. There's a good deal of volatility in this picture. As you can see, there was a big spike up to over $8 a pound in '88 and '89. But, by the beginning of 1993, nickel prices had fallen to $2.80 a pound; and, at that price, the cost to Lukens for buying nickel based at then current levels of steel production was $110 million. Today, our nickel costs are running about $230 million, reflecting both a sharp increase in nickel prices since the end of '92 and the increase in the volume of our business.

How has our hedging helped us? Between December of 1992 through August of 1994, there was a 33% increase in the price of nickel. But, by buying nickel futures on the LME representing about half of the nickel we used in our business during that period, we were able to hold the increase in our overall cost of nickel to 19%.

Now, there is one potential source of basis risk in our hedging program. We buy our nickel in scrap most of the time, which does not trade completely in sync with nickel prices on the LME. But the correlation is very strong; when we back-tested the relationship, we found out that the correlation coefficient was about 95% between the scrap and futures prices.

So, this is the kind of information that we provide both our board and the operating people who are concerned about managing their own costs. We share with them the data used in our decision-making process, and our operating people provide us with valuable added perspective on market conditions—perspective that we draw on in making our hedging decisions.

The Case of MCI

McKNEW: Thanks, John. Now, we will hear from Jonelle St. John, who is Vice President and Treasurer of MCI.
JONELLE ST. JOHN: Let me start off by saying a little bit about MCI's risk management policy. Our management is fairly conservative, and our corporate policy has for the most part been to avoid use of derivatives. Our treasury group has made some use of derivatives on a highly selective, case-by-case basis. But these require prior approval by the CFO, and, depending on the size of the transactions, by the board.

Nevertheless, the continued growth of our business—particularly, in the form of overseas investments contemplated in the next few years—is forcing us to rethink this policy. We have developed and submitted to our board a proposal that would allow us to make greater use of derivatives in managing financial exposures. The guidelines that have been proposed reflect the recommendations of the "Group of 30" report on derivatives as well as input from a variety of functional areas within MCI—accounting, internal audit, tax, and so forth. Without getting into specifics, let me just say here that our proposal has counterparty credit limits, exposure limits stated in mark-to-market terms, and a list of permitted and prohibited transactions.

As with all our other financial management policies, our proposed risk management and derivatives policy would be monitored at the top management level, but decision-making would rest with treasury people operating within explicit guidelines and risk tolerance limits set by management. The policy is designed to keep executive management and the board well-informed about treasury activities, but at the same time to give us enough flexibility to do the things we need to do without going to management for approval.

Now, why do we want to make greater use of derivatives at MCI? The answer, as I've already suggested, is that our exposure to foreign exchange risks is expected to grow significantly in the next few years.

We are already managing some very specific, transaction-based foreign exchange risks. For example, we have annual settlements with foreign "PTTs" that require us to make payments in dollars based on the SDR exchange rate. Because the exchange rate of the SDR is a combination of the U.S. dollar (about 40%) and foreign currencies such as the pound sterling, German mark, French francs, and Japanese yen, a weakening of the dollar relative to these currencies would increase the dollar value of these payments.

To manage this currency exposure, we use FX forwards, options, and collars on the individual currencies comprising the SDR that allow us to hedge against fluctuations in the SDR. At the beginning of each year, we hedge 100% of the plan of our expected foreign settlements based on the contracts we have in place with our customers. Now, because we tend to bring in new business during the year and beat our plan, we generally end up hedging less than 100% of our payments to the PTTs at the end of the year. But that's basically a conservative hedging policy; that is, we can't justify hedging more than our expected outflows without effectively speculating on the SDR.

In the future, we will be making direct equity investments in various foreign countries. Mexico is the one that we're going to be moving on fairly quickly. We've announced a joint venture in Mexico with Banamex. We're going to construct a long-distance network in Mexico that has a number of risks associated with it that we have not encountered in the past. In addition to standard transaction and translation types of foreign exchange risk, we've also got to consider the sovereign and political risks associated with our investments. We also have to think about dealing with restrictions on repatriating and converting our overseas funds back into dollars. Our current plan calls for reinvesting earnings from Mexico for a long period of time; but, at some point, we need an effective means of converting the investment back into dollars.

Fortunately, we did not commit any of our funds to Mexico *before* the recent devaluation of the peso. So that's the good news. But there have also been negative consequences from the current uncertainty in Mexico. Given our intention to invest in Mexico, we now face a very limited market for both financing and hedging facilities. If such facilities were available, financing in pesos would have provided a natural hedge for our investment, since our net revenue stream will be primarily in pesos. But combining revenues in pesos with financing costs in dollars means considerable currency risk for our Mexican P & L, and we need to take that into consideration in the business plan.

Besides Mexico, we are also considering the possibility of expanding into several other countries in Latin America. Indeed, Latin America is one of our strategic expansion areas. For this reason, we are looking at the extent of the correlation among the various Latin American currencies—and, in particular, for the existence of domino effects. We are also exploring the possibility of moving currencies around within the various countries

instead of pulling them all back into U.S. dollars.

In sum, our plans to invest in Mexico and Latin America mean that we're going to have to plan for a host of risks that we would typically not face in more mature markets. The way we

*W*by do we want to make greater use of derivatives at MCI?

The answer is that our exposure to foreign exchange risks is expected to grow significantly in the next few years. In addition to some very specific, transaction-based exposures that we are already managing, we are also looking at large direct equity investments in a number of foreign countries—investments that will present sovereign and political risks as well as the standard transaction and translation types of risk to which we are now accustomed.

Jonelle St. John
MCI Communications

are going to approach these risks is by developing cross-functional teams within MCI. The tax function will have to be involved in the planning pro-

cess. And so will accounting, especially since the FASB is moving forward on changes in how you report hedging facilities—that is, whether changes in the value of derivatives are going to be on the balance sheet or the P&L. Tax and accounting consid-

erations, along with the company's general conservatism, may force us to restrict our hedging products to those that do not affect the P&L.

The Case of Union Carbide

McKNEW: Thanks, Jonelle. Now let's turn to Tom Jones, Vice President and Treasurer of Union Carbide

TOM JONES: Risk management at Union Carbide is nothing new. All corporations face business, physical, and financial risks. But we have been actively managing these risks for many years. The risk management part of the Treasurer's Group works with business management to identify physical and financial risks, to assess the potential impact on the business of these risks, and to determine what needs to be done to control the risks.

Managing physical risk typically involves the purchase of insurance products. But in the financial risk area—interest rates, foreign exchange, commodity price movements, and equity price movements—risk management sometimes means the use of derivative products. Although derivatives are not the only tool for managing financial risks, they have become increasingly popular because they are typically more available, more flexible, and less costly than the alternatives. My focus will be on the use of derivatives in managing these financial risks.

One of the most difficult tasks in financial risk management is to determine your exposure. It's fairly easy to determine interest rate exposure, but foreign exchange is more challenging. We spend a good deal of time trying to determine our exposure on the foreign exchange side. We sell a lot of products in many different currencies. We talk to our business people about their gross margin risk. In cases where they are able to adjust their selling price when a currency moves, they don't have currency risk. But, in many of our businesses, the managers can't adjust their selling price, and so they have currency risk.

But let me start by taking a brief look at interest rate risk. Our debt over the past years has been as much as $3 billion, but today it is running at about $1.2 billion. Our annual interest expense over that period has ranged from about $270 million to $70 million in 1993. Our interest cost for 1994 was about $80 million.

Now, these numbers are a little misleading because we are involved in quite a few joint ventures, and there will be more in the future. We are a partner in a $2 billion joint venture in Kuwait that will start in 1997 and will have $1.2 billion of debt in it. We are also in a $1 billion Italian joint venture with $500 or $600 million of debt. In all of our joint ventures, we will probably have $3 to $4 billion in debt, and thus the interest cost that we try to manage is significantly more than what we have in our corporation.

In the early 1990s, we did a study to try to determine the optimal duration for our debt. After looking at how the performance of our businesses and their competitors were affected by changes in inflation and interest rates, we concluded that a target rate of four years was right for us. And let me explain briefly how we arrived at this target.

Some of our businesses are commodity businesses that do very well when inflation and interest rates are high; but when interest rates and inflation are low, these businesses tend to be at the bottom of their cycle. Because such businesses have no interest rate exposure—or perhaps even a slightly negative exposure to increases in rates—they should be funded with short-term, or floating-rate, money. But we have other businesses that are adversely affected by inflation and high interest rates. And so, by taking a weighted average of the interest rate exposures of all our different businesses, we arrived at a targeted duration of four years.

Now, the target doesn't necessarily mean that the duration of our debt is always going to be precisely at four years. When interest rates are going up, we will generally aim to be somewhat longer than the target to give us partial protection against further rate increases. Conversely, when rates are coming down, we want to be somewhat shorter than the target to benefit from further declines. Given the recent downward trend in rates, the duration of our debt today is probably about three and a half years.

Let me also point out that our duration target would not stop us from going out longer than four years if we thought we saw a financing bargain. We believe interest rates are very attractive today; and, if there was a need for funds, we would do a 30-year bond issue at 8% or lower without any hesitation. But, at the same time, we could swap the issue right back to maintain our three- or four-year duration. And, as this example is meant to illustrate, the use of derivatives is key to our management of interest rate risk. We use interest rate derivatives—mainly swaps—to manage the duration of our debt, to adjust the fixed vs. floating mix of our debt, and to control interest costs.

Now let's talk about foreign exchange, which is where much of our risk management efforts are centered. We have a natural net inflow of European currencies and Japanese yen— about $10 to $15 million a month— that comes from export sales, sales of technology, and dividends from affiliates. But we do not always hedge these currency exposures. We will hedge as much 100% in some cases or we will hedge zero or somewhere in between, depending upon what we feel is the trend in the U.S. dollar. If the U.S. dollar is weakening relative to the DM and yen and we expect that trend to continue, then we will just let the foreign currency come in and convert it when we receive it. But if the dollar is strengthening, then we will hedge up to 100% of the expected inflows by selling all or part of our receivables in advance. Although we generally look out over the next 12 months at our expected inflow of currencies, our hedges typically don't go beyond about six months.

We have the opposite situation in Canadian dollars, in that we pay Canadian dollars rather than receiving a net inflow. And so we use the reverse strategy—that is, the more we expect the Canadian dollar to strengthen, the larger the percentage of our payments we hedge.

We operate in a lot of developing countries where there are not many hedging alternatives. We use natural hedges any place we can—for example, funding in currencies where we produce and sell; or, when possible, locating manufacturing or sourcing in countries where we sell. But there is still considerable room for financial solutions to risk management after the natural hedges are in place. Our primary role in such cases is to act as financial advisers to the subsidiaries and operating units.

In our joint ventures, we strongly recommend the establishment of finance committees to develop and oversee risk management for the joint venture. Such committees will typically have someone from the partner's financial organization, someone from Carbide, and, of course, some financial managers from the joint venture itself. If we are aware of any practice that is contrary to our risk management philosophy, we will see that it is reported to our senior management.

Now, the fact that there are partners in joint ventures and that they may have different views of risk management adds a degree of difficulty in carrying out our policy. It can be especially challenging when you're working with partners who have never

used hedges or derivatives. But there are normally some major currency risks that must be addressed in managing overseas ventures. Take our Kuwait joint venture. It will sell in all different currencies, while funding itself primarily with dollar debt. Our

currencies. Financial management of these overseas ventures requires that you really take a good look at your currency cash flow and understand your exposures. And, as I mentioned, management of these exposures is supervised by finance committees that

> *We all have friends in the financial community that say they wouldn't hedge because derivatives are bad things to use. The irony, of course, is that by making that statement, they've effectively made a decision that they're going to accept the risk. But this hypocrisy, or at least confusion, persists in part because the two kinds of losses don't get accounted for in the same way. Unhedged losses don't show up anywhere. But hedging losses are reported separately— typically independently of the position they're being used to hedge—and they are now being held up for very strong scrutiny.*

Thomas Jones
Union Carbide

Italian joint venture is another good example. It's about a $1 billion venture. Fifty percent of it is in lira, but the other 50% is in all the other European

meet at least three or four times each year—and with a very full agenda.

Let me just quickly mention two other areas: commodity risk and equity price risk. We have very strong management in our business areas— people who feel very comfortable living with commodity risk and managing it primarily with non-financial means. They feel comfortable with the cycles in the commodity business, and with their own ability to increase prices to offset increases in their own cost of raw materials.

In the equity market, we have a stock buy-back program that has now been increased to 30 million shares. We sell puts from time to time to help with these stock purchases. Because of the fairly steady appreciation of our stock in the past few years, we have had an almost unblemished record in selling these puts. That is, in most cases, after we have sold the put our stock has continued to move up, and so the put has gone unexercised. And the net effect of these put sales has been a reduction in the cost of our share-repurchase program.

Let me just say something about the management of corporate derivatives programs, which of course has gotten a tremendous amount of attention in the past year or so. At Union Carbide, we have clear and firm rules governing the use of derivatives:

1. We do not allow leveraged derivatives, the kind that have caused problems at other companies. Our derivatives have to move in direct proportional relationship to the exposure that they are covering; they cannot move twice as fast or three times as fast as the underlying exposure being hedged.

2. When we are hedging a financial exposure faced by a specific business, we have to get the manager running that operation to approve the hedge. Even if we think something should be done, if he doesn't approve it, we don't do it.

3. We have a risk management committee that meets weekly, and that includes the principal financial officer, the treasurer, and assistant treasurer. We have clear exposure and loss limits for all of our derivatives positions, and we report these positions on a regular basis to senior management.

4. One of our most important risk management rules is that we can hedge only specific transactions that have been clearly identified. Now, there is some flexibility in defining "transactions." Export and import transactions in a foreign currency qualify, of course; and so do net inflows and outflows of various currencies expected over the next 12 months—at least in those cases where gross margins are at risk because of pricing constraints. We will also hedge non-dollar dividends or royalties expected over the next 12 months, and non-dollar acquisitions or divestitures with a signed letter of intent. This past January, for example, we signed a letter of intent on our Italian joint venture. Our capital contribution was to be 320 million denominated in DMs, or roughly $200 million. Because the dollar was weakening at this time, we chose to buy the DMs then. By the time the deal closed two months later, we ended up saving about $15 million.

Now, did this decision to hedge involve some risks? Yes, it did; in fact, it was almost controversial. If this joint venture had fallen apart after the letter of intent, we would have had a $200 million uncovered position in DM. And if the dollar had instead strengthened by the same amount that it depreciated, we could have had up to $20 million in losses to explain.

Let me just close with a brief list of the kinds of controls that we have found valuable at Carbide.

Derivatives should be easily priced; you have to know the value of the instrument at any time and be able to unwind the position. We had an ex-perience years ago in which we had a number of swaps that we wanted to get out of. And when the market turned out to be less liquid than we thought, we lost some money. So market liquidity is essential for us.

In response to the Group of 30 study, we are also doing sensitivity studies designed to show us the range of likely and possible losses on our derivatives positions. We look at what a couple of standard deviations in these positions would do to our profitability and financial condition. And, based in part on these sensitivity studies, Carbide's Board of Directors has set limits on the company's derivatives market risk by setting a cap on losses from the uses of derivatives in managing interest rate, foreign exchange, and commodity price risks.

We are also very sensitive to counterparty credit risks. Counterparties must have a credit rating not lower than A by Standard & Poor's and BAA by Moody's. And we not only do careful credit analysis when entering into a transaction, but we really work to monitor our credit exposures on an ongoing basis.

We do extensive reporting of our positions; in fact, we mark our derivatives positions to market on a daily basis within the Treasurer's group. Reports to management are weekly. And, if any of our contracts has a loss of 5% or more, continuation of the position has to be approved by senior management. Carbide's risk management activities are also reviewed annually by both the internal audit department and our external auditors.

Well, let me conclude by just telling you that we all have a tough job today. While we all know that derivative products are essential to managing financial risks in today's volatile markets, it has also become clear that derivatives can be abused in ways that end up imposing risk on the corporation. Our job is both to demonstrate to our management and our boards the benefits of derivatives in managing risks, and to reassure them that our risk management program isn't *creating more risk*. I believe that such a comprehensive review of risk management procedures and controls is now going on in every major corporation in America.

The Case of RJR Nabisco

McKNEW: Thank you, Tom. Now, we'll hear from Lynn Lane, Vice President and Treasurer of R.J. Reynolds Tobacco.

LYNN LANE: I want to talk to you today about how we manage our foreign exchange risk at RJR. As a multinational company, our international entities produce significant net revenues, which creates foreign exchange exposure for us. Complicating matters, these overseas entities do business not only in their country of domicile, but often in several other countries as well, thus creating significant cross-border flows.

We address foreign exchange risk management through a multi-stage process. The stages can be summarized as follows: (1) formulation and statement of hedging objective; (2) senior management planning and policy formulation; (3) identification of significant exposures; (4) development of hedging strategy (including decisions whether to hedge various risks); (5) policy implementation; and (6) safeguards and controls. I should also point out that this process does not proceed in just a one-way, linear fashion; it should rather be viewed as one with lots of feedback, and subject to continous monitoring and revision. For example, the evaluations and audits at the back end of the process can in turn provide the basis for adjustments to our policy and even of the objective itself. I will now spend a few minutes

discussing each of these aspects of the process.

First, let's talk about the objective of our foreign exchange program. Our objective is to maintain strong and predictable cash flow and earnings through the management of the company's consolidated foreign exchange exposures, including those arising from specific transactions. Treasury is not a profit center; we aim to minimize risk, not to create risk. And, as I suggested, we also constantly review our objective to ensure that it is providing the proper guidance for our risk management activities.

The second step is to develop a policy. Our policy is best described as one of "selective" hedging. In managing our various currency exposures, we can be hedged anywhere from zero to 100%. Normally, it's not on either end of this spectrum but somewhere in the middle. In our view, hedging either 0% or 100% of an exposure amounts to taking a very strong view on the market. Making a decision to do nothing—that is, hedging 0%—is a decision to take the currency risk. But hedging 100% could mean forgoing a positive movement in prices that one of your competitors may choose not to hedge.

At RJR, both the identification of exposures and the decisions to hedge involve the operating units working together with the treasury department. Treasury provides the expertise in the foreign exchange markets and hedging tools, but the operating managers are the people with direct responsibility for foreign exchange since it hits their bottom line. So, it's very much a team effort, a partnership. We work with the operating units to identify currency exposures and, based on their input, we suggest hedging strategies. But the operating people, as I said, make the final decisions about whether and how much of the exposure to hedge on the local entities'

books. Treasury does, however, have veto power if we feel strongly one way or the other.

The operating units report their exposures to us every two months on a rolling 12-month basis. And although we have the tools to manage our exposures as far out as 24 months, our hedging focus tends to be confined to just the current year.

As I also mentioned earlier, we consider hedging all transaction exposures. As most of you know, transaction exposures result from specific business decisions—say, a large payable or receivable, or a royalty payment or dividend to the parent—involving an actual exchange of funds in two or more currencies.

But we take a somewhat different approach with translation exposures. Translation exposures result from the translation of the earnings of foreign operating units into U.S. dollars for reporting purposes. At present, we do not actively hedge translation in the foreign exchange market, but we may use other mechanisms for so doing.

Before describing our policy, let me give you a couple of examples that affect us on the *transaction* side. We have a company that manufactures product and sells within Germany. But it sources product in dollars, and it also sells in France, Italy, and the U.K. So the company has significant $/DM transaction exposures, as well as several transactional cross-currency exposures. We evaluate each of these exposures as candidates for hedging.

Another example of a transactional exposure is our finance company that was set up in the early '80's in Geneva, Switzerland. The company is used primarily for liquidity netting; that is, our European and Far East entities both borrow from and lend to this center. And because this finance company is a dollar-based company, it has very large transactional exposures that we manage using the swap market.

A good example of *translation* exposure is our subsidiary in Mexico. Before the devaluation of the peso, we spent a lot of time thinking about what we should do to control the currency risk facing the net earnings of that subsidiary. And we decided to

earnings. And, as I said, we were fortunate enough to make this adjustment before the devaluation, thus protecting our consolidated P&L.

Our approach to transaction and translation exposures has varied somewhat over time, depending on

and ignored translation effects. At other times, we have hedged both transactions and translation. Today, as I mentioned, we actively hedge transaction exposures but not translation effects.

Having identified our exposures, we next develop a strategy—again, in partnership with our operating units—for dealing with them. In some cases, we decide to hedge such exposures, and in others we choose to do nothing.

But, again, our foreign exchange strategy is dynamic and subject to continuous review. And, before even considering financial hedges, we try to use natural hedges whenever possible, either within specific subsidiaries or even across subsidiaries. Setting up cross-subsidiary natural hedges can be a challenge because what's good for one unit is not necessarily good for another. But while the operating units are focused on their own results, it's our job at treasury to evaluate the entire hedging program on a consolidated economic basis to ensure the hedging activities of the units are not working at cross purposes.

Once we have developed the strategy, we're ready for implementation. All of the execution of financial hedging is done by treasury. We use a variety of products: spot swaps, forwards, and over-the-counter options—all pretty much plain vanilla. We also try to manage the balance sheets of our foreign entities—say, by borrowing in the local currency instead of dollars—to offset their asset or revenue exposures.

And, last, let me briefly mention some of our safeguards and controls, because these are an essential part of any well-run risk management program. First and foremost, senior management must be involved not only in setting up the program and policies, but in continuous monitoring. This is the only way to ensure that there will

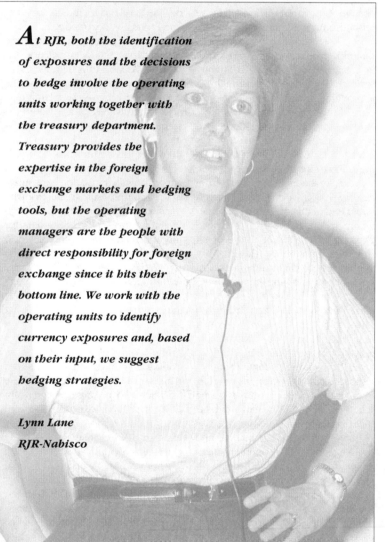

*A*t RJR, both the identification of exposures and the decisions to hedge involve the operating units working together with the treasury department. Treasury provides the expertise in the foreign exchange markets and hedging tools, but the operating managers are the people with direct responsibility for foreign exchange since it hits their bottom line. We work with the operating units to identify currency exposures and, based on their input, we suggest hedging strategies.

Lynn Lane
RJR-Nabisco

make adjustments to the capital structure—specifically, injecting equity and paying off U.S. debt—to reduce the translation exposure of our Mexican

management's objectives and on how the performance of our operating units are measured. At times we have hedged only transaction exposures

be no surprises. Top management must understand both the policy and the basic strategy, and they must be informed on a regular basis as to how it is being carried out.

As part of our formal policy, we have also established operational controls similar to those used by commercial banks. We set limits for our counterparties, and we review the credit ratings of our counterparties on an ongoing basis. We also ensure there is separation of duties between the front-office traders and the back-office operation personnel. We feel this is extremely important, and we've had our internal auditors examine the process to make sure they're comfortable with it. And we have continuous reporting to top management to make sure everyone is on board and knows where we stand.

Risk Management: Hedging or Speculation?

McKNEW: Thanks, Lynn. Now, I'd like to open up the discussion to the panelists and to everyone in the room. But let me start things off by asking each of the panelists a very basic question.

Tom, when you're hedging, do you trade? Do you make money hedging?
JONES: We do not trade, but we may report gains or losses on a derivative position from time to time. We are not a profit center. Our use of derivatives is consistent with Carbide's overall risk management program—a strategy that reduces, but never increases, the financial risk of the company.
McKNEW: Lynn, I assume you would say that RJR doesn't trade either.
LANE: That's essentially right.
McKNEW: But you earlier said that you typically hedged less than 100% of your currency exposures. Why would hedging anything less than 100% hedge of an exposure not be a trade, a kind of speculation?

LANE: It is our philosophy that if you're 50% hedged, that's kind of the neutral position. You have no view. What we try to do is to analyze the market and determine, based in part on our judgment about the likely size and direction of future price movements, what's the best position for our company. We don't say we *know* where the market or rates are going. But based on the particular conditions, and based on what our competitors are doing and what we're trying to accomplish, we end up hedging somewhere between zero and 100% of each individual exposure.
McKNEW: So, you're *managing* risk as opposed to eliminating it totally. John, what do you think about this? Are you always hedged?
VAN RODEN: No, we aren't always hedged. The steel business is a very cyclical business. And we will not hedge more than 50% of our nickel supplies precisely for that reason. That is, we could plan one year that we're going to sell X tons of steel, but sales may well end up being only half of X. And if in that case we hedged the entire amount that we planned to sell, then we would be significantly overhedging—we would end up with a very large uncovered long position in nickel futures.

So, in this sense, yes, we do trade. In fact, our team will get together every week to evaluate our position. And if we were 50% hedged at a given time, but we felt there was going to be a big move up or down in the price of nickel, then we might increase or decrease our hedge to reflect our view.
McKNEW: Okay, so it sounds as if all of you sometimes trade, at least in the sense that you allow your view of the market to influence your hedging position. But, do any of you ever consciously *create* risk? That is, do you ever hedge less than 0%—say, like Orange County, by doubling up

an already existing exposure—or more than 100% of your exposure?
LANE: We do not. Our stated mission, as I mentioned earlier, is to minimize risk. So, even if we felt interest rates or currencies were about to move in a given direction, we would never use foreign exchange products or interest rate products to create a new risk, or to add to an already existing exposure.
McKNEW: How about the rest of you? Does risk management mean totally eliminating risk as best you can do it, taking into consideration operating variables and, therefore, measured exposures? Or does it mean sometimes managing risk down and then managing it back up based on some view of a market rate or price?
VAN RODEN: We try to manage risk, but not to eliminate it.
McKNEW: So you would increase risk if you felt that a certain currency or commodity price was going to move in a certain way?
VAN RODEN: That's right. For example, if we had a strong conviction that nickel prices were not going to rise and might even fall sharply, we might well choose to increase our exposure to nickel by reducing our hedge.
McKNEW: Okay. So, does anyone think there is anything particularly wrong with that?
JONES: Well, it sort of depends on what you mean by increasing risk. If you say, "I've got 5 million DMs coming in, but because I think the dollar is going to strengthen, I'm going to hedge 10 million," I would say, "No, we don't do that." We manage only the risk associated with our operating cash flows. We don't volunteer to take trading risks independent of those cash flows. And we don't double up existing exposures or get into leveraged derivatives.

But, having said that, there are financial risks associated with almost any hedging position you choose to take. We don't choose to create risk, but you have risk one way or the other. If we do a derivative, we've taken a risk. If the position produces losses—even if it's a well-designed hedge—you may have difficulty explaining them to management. Life is full of risk. But we don't try to create any additional risk.

You Can Hedge, But Don't Lose Any Money Doing It

McKNEW: In identifying your financial exposures, do any of you take into account the expected effect of price changes on your competitors? That is, in setting your own hedging policies, do you consider your competitors' exposures and how they will react to the price changes?

LANE: I think this kind of analysis is potentially very useful. In setting a risk management strategy, you ought to know how your competitors are positioning themselves to handle their exposures. In fact, that is one of the reasons we think that a 100% hedge amounts to taking a very strong view of the market. If you hedge 100% of your exposure in the forward market, but prices end up moving against your hedge and in favor of your natural position, you are giving up the upside. And if your competitors are not hedging in this case, then your competitive position could suffer.

JONES: I agree, at least in theory, but I am not sure that this kind of analysis ends up producing any basis for hedging policy. We have done some studies as to where our competitors source their raw materials and what currencies they're paying in. But such studies have never really caused us to change our strategy.

McKNEW: Well, the problem I've always had with trying to sell that approach to corporations is that if you're right, nobody ever knows about

it. Even if a hedging strategy ends up improving your competitive position relative to other companies, nobody will ever credit risk management for that—the credit will go instead to marketing or strategic planning. But, if you're wrong—say, the hedge loses money and your competitors react differently than expected—then everybody will know about it. Explaining to people that you made a fundamentally sound decision that didn't work out is a very difficult message to get across.

LANE: That's right. Unfortunately, in today's market, people focus on the tools instead of the underlying exposure. People in risk management are often judged according to how the tools perform, and independently of what happens to the underlying exposure.

ANIRUDDHA ROY: Yes, that's very true. Even when companies are supposed to be hedging, in practice the success of the risk management function often seems to be judged by how much money they make on their derivatives positions. But, in a properly run corporate risk management operation, the treasury cannot operate as a profit center. If you are really hedging, and not just taking positions, you ought to be expected to show losses from time to time. And that ought to be clearly understood by management and the board from the outset.

JONES: I agree with you that that's how things should work, but it's also clear why companies don't want to report derivative losses of any kind, legitimate or otherwise. Take the case of Carbide. As a company, we're doing very, very well today. And nobody wants something to sidetrack us by having a derivative loss that gets a lot of publicity in the current environment. And I don't think Carbide is unusual in this. Managements and boards everywhere are very concerned about derivative losses, even those

that are incurred in legitimate hedging operations.

ROY: What you're saying, then, Tom, is that losses on derivatives are subjected to much closer scrutiny than losses resulting from leaving an exposure unhedged. For example, let's say you were receiving an inflow of DMs, and that because you expected the dollar to weaken, you chose not to hedge the exposure. In such circumstances, you would receive much less criticism if you turned out to be wrong by failing to hedge than if you had instead hedged the DM with, say, futures, and those futures ended up producing a loss—even when those futures were hedging an expected cash inflow.

So unhedged, or "natural," losses that increase volatility are preferred to "artificial" or derivatives losses that actually serve to reduce overall volatility. Do I have this right?

JONES: Yes, that's right. We all have friends in the financial community that say they wouldn't hedge because derivatives are bad things to use. The irony, of course, is that by making that statement, they've effectively made a decision that they're going to accept the risk.

But this hypocrisy, or at least confusion, persists in part because the two kinds of losses don't get accounted for in the same way. Unhedged losses don't show up anywhere, they aren't broken out into a separate account; and so the board never sees it, and the media never report it. But hedging losses are reported separately—typically independently of the position they're being used to hedge—and they are now being held up for very strong scrutiny.

LANE: You're both absolutely right. This kind of double standard goes on all the time, and I have yet to see much attention—certainly not in the popular accounts of derivatives—being devoted to this problem.

Can You Hedge Without Speculating?

STEPHEN PAGE: I'm a little confused about what I've heard so far in this discussion. Everyone says they are trying to avoid speculation. But, at the same time, everyone also seems to say that they are willing to let their hedging decisions be influenced by their views on interest rates or currencies. In my view, if you have a DM transaction exposure and you leave it up to a local treasurer to decide whether to hedge or not to hedge the exposure, then you are effectively encouraging a form of speculation.

Now, if we surveyed the people in this room today, we would probably hear ten different views of the dollar/DM. So, this tells me that it depends only on who your treasurer is at the time as to whether or not you can speculate. It seems to me that if you hedge anything less than 100% of your exposure, you are choosing to take an open position, you are taking a speculative position.

McKNEW: I understand your point. I've always had problems with the imprecision, or even confusion, that surrounds the terms in this business of risk management. "Hedging," "speculation," "trading," "risk-taking," risk avoidance"—we all seem to be using these words somewhat differently.

So, when someone begins by saying that their treasury is not a profit center, but they add value by taking views on a selective basis, that statement raises questions about the objective of the risk management program. And, because this kind of confusion is so widespread, I would argue that unquestionably the most important step in risk management is figuring out exactly what you're trying to accomplish. And your corporate objective should be expressed in very specific terms, if possible even with quantitative indicators of success.

For example, you might say that your policy is always to hedge at least 30% but never more than 100% of a certain kind of exposure (and the kind of exposure ought to be identified as clearly as possible). Or, using Tom's policy at Carbide as a model, you might say that you will never deviate more than, say, one year from your targeted interest rate duration of four years.

JONES: Well, Bob, I'm not sure you can ever formulate policy with that degree of precision. When you get into project financing or a joint venture, it may be easier to provide very clear objectives. For example, let's say the success of a project is based on obtaining an all-in financing cost of no more than 9%. In that case, if the project financing was based upon a 9% interest rate and you succeed in locking it in at 8-1/2%, then even if rates end up going to 5%, you've done the right thing. Now, it's true your venture partner may say to you after the fact, "Well, why didn't we get the advantage of the downside, why didn't we get 5%?" But, as long as your objective of beating 9% was clearly stated from the outset, and your partner was part of that understanding, then this is an effective risk management program.

But things are different in a large corporation, with multiple exposures and where everything is changing daily. It is much tougher in such cases to formulate objectives that are not subject to change.

And, by the way, I agree completely with Steve's distinction between hedging and speculation, and we have lots of discussions of these terms at Carbide. If we believe the dollar is strengthening or weakening, then we should either be zero or 100%. If you're in the middle, it's not clear what you are doing: Are you hedging or speculating?

VAN RODEN: I'd just like to add to that. We at Lukens obviously do have views on certain markets and we do take financial risks. But we do it through a team and so you get the opinion of a lot of people. And you get the opinion of the operating people, as opposed to those of us who don't have responsibility for bottom line.

I would also mention the importance of regular communication and reporting. As of next week, we will begin sending monthly updates to management outlining our positions and strategies for all the various commodities we consider hedging. Now, this won't prevent us from making bad decisions. But, if we turn out to be wrong, at least we will all know why it happened.

LANE: I earlier mentioned the importance of considering your competitors' exposures in developing your own risk management strategy. But let me elaborate on this point a little, because I think this point bears on how you distinguish between hedging and speculation. If you hedge 100% of a currency exposure and the dollar goes against you, but your competitor has chosen to leave the same exposure unhedged, then your ability to maintain market share—that is, your competitive position—could end up being reduced by your hedging decision. So that's why I say that hedging either zero or 100% of an exposure may involve taking a strong view.

ST. JOHN: I tend to agree that the distinction between hedging and trading is not clearcut. I too am not sure that you can hedge without taking a view. That is, whether you choose to hedge 0% or 100% of an exposure, your position will never be completely insulated from changes in financial markets. And so I think the objectives of corporate risk management programs will inevitably have to leave some room for taking speculative positions or trading, if you will.

PAGE: Well, I would like to disagree. I think corporaations can practice risk management without taking a view. For example, you can say that you are going to cover 100% of all transaction exposures. And, at the same time, you can say that you will attempt to hedge all your expected cross-border translation exposures based on current forecasts—for example, much as MCI hedges its expected overseas payment to its PTTs.

Now, although this approach doesn't completely eliminate currency exposure (because your actual exposure may turn out to be somewhat different from what you projected), it neutralizes the effect of currency changes on your *expected* operating performance. And that may be the best you can do. In this kind of risk management system, you will have effectively eliminated any role for subjective judgments about future currency moves; you will not be taking a view.

Moreover, if you do lock in a given currency value by hedging 100% of expected exposure, then the resulting increase in your level of certainty about translated year-end results can help you in setting your pricing structure and in establishing targets for managers of foreign operating units at the beginning of the year.

Mark-to-Market Reporting of Derivatives

McKNEW: As a market-maker and trader in derivative instruments, I actually *can* be in a position of taking no risk simply by choosing to do nothing. In overseeing trading accounts, I can say—at least in theory—that I will take no risk; I will just not write any tickets myself, and completely offset everything that my customers bring to me. In that sense, my job's a lot more straightforward than all of yours, because virtually all of the

risks that we take in trading accounts are explicitly quantifiable and usually explicitly offsettable, more or less simultaneously.

JONES: Bob, why do you want to be paid for it if you don't take any risk?

McKNEW: I fully realize that the Lord don't owe me a living, and if I don't take any risk I won't get paid. But, in fact, we get paid in part for making markets for our customers, and in part based on the outcome of those positions we choose to take in the process of serving our customers.

But that brings me to another point. I live in a mark-to-market world. Everything I do is marked to market on almost a real-time basis. I know when I go home every night how much all of the activities in my department have made or lost, plus or minus a few thousand dollars. And this is real, hit-the-income-statement-of-the-bank kind of money.

But these obvious differences notwithstanding, I'm essentially in the same business that all of you are in. And, for this reason, I'm curious as to how many of you mark to market, in any sense, the risk management activities you engage in. Put another way, if you are not always 100% hedged, how are your decisions not to hedge 100% being reported to management? And when I say "reported," I mean expressed in such a way that somebody in senior management can look at your decisions and evaluate them against an explicit, unambiguous standard. I'm talking about meaningful internal or management accounting systems, not just adhering to external reporting conventions.

JONES: We mark to market daily all of our derivatives positions, but we don't do the same for the underlying exposures. Is that the direction you're going in?

McKNEW: Yes, but that only serves to support my point. My question is: How does marking to market the

hedges but not the positions being hedged give you a reliable guide to the performance of the risk management function?

VAN RODEN: We actually do something like what you're suggesting, Bob. For instance, in the case of nickel, we mark our hedges to market every day. At the same time, on a weekly basis, we update our forecast of total nickel costs for the rest of the year based on current nickel prices. And combining these two measures—that is, actual costs based on current prices plus hedging gains or losses—allows us to project our total nickel costs and their effect on bottom-line earnings.

McKNEW: So, using current price levels, you would estimate both your expected nickel costs and your expected hedging results? And this would in turn give you some basis for judging the effectiveness of your hedging program relative to either doing nothing or, say, hedging 100%?

VAN RODEN: Yes, that's basically right.

McKNEW: That's interesting. Does anybody else do anything similar to that? . . . No response. I wonder why. Is it because the accountants don't require you to do it? Or is it because you cannot develop the systems capable of doing it?

ROBERT BUTLER: We do something like this on a once-a-year basis. But I think the main problem here is that setting up such systems is a costly undertaking. It's not something that goes into the financial statements. It involves calculating all the various exposures, and, perhaps even more difficult and time-consuming, getting agreement on the calculations. If performance evaluations and treasury group bonuses are going to be affected by how you estimate the exposures, then reaching agreement could be difficult.

McKNEW: Yes, I see.

Derivatives and Pension Fund Management

BUTLER: I'd like to bring up one other area in the use of derivatives that has come up in our company—one that is particularly sensitive today. What kind of restrictions or policies do you impose on your investment managers in your pension fund? I think this question is particularly important because you've got to use derivatives in a pension fund, you've got to allow the managers to use them.

McKNEW: Do you need derivatives to manage duration?

BUTLER: Well, yes, duration is one concern. But we're also worried about the currency risk faced by our equity managers. Derivatives have made these financial markets ten times more efficient, no 100 times more efficient, than they were in the past. And by preventing our managers from using derivatives, we are really tying their hands—forcing them to accept exposures that could easily be hedged with derivatives.

Derivatives have gotten a bad name primarily because of people who were trying to make a profit center out of the treasury function. They were trying, for example, to report zero interest cost for the year when they should have taken $200 million of interest cost; and, when rates turned against them, they ended up getting $800 million worth of interest cost. And that's the problem in a nutshell.

For this reason, I think the current crackdown on derivatives is going to end up imposing large and costly constraints on our pension funds. And, I'm interested in hearing what others in this room are experiencing in this regard.

McKNEW: Well, at Bank of America, it is my area—trading—that now gets the most attention in terms of compliance and risk management controls. And we have lots of infrastructure

built up to ensure that we're doing what we're supposed to be doing. As I said, we mark our positions to market every day and our results hit the bottom line directly.

The next most closely scrutinized part of the bank is corporate trea-

sury, which, in our institution, is very similar to yours. Some of their activity is mark-to-market, some of it isn't. Their decision-making is not as immediate as ours, but its still quite current—and they get a lot of attention. And the third area of derivatives concern is the activities in which we act as a fiduciary—activities such as mutual fund and trust departments in which we manage other people's money.

Now, although the money management area doesn't get as much attention at B of A, I agree with your statement. More and more of the investment that's going to take place in this country, if only because we baby-boomers are getting older, is going to take place in pensions—that is, in fiduciaries, investment companies, investment managers, trust departments, pension funds, all of that stuff. And this means that the potential benefits of using derivatives—and the costs of not using them—are also going to grow.

But, at the same time, it's seems clear to me that the money management industry is going to have to become a lot more transparent in terms of what it's doing. It's going to have to do a much better job explaining to us what they're doing with our money, and what the associated risks are.

JONES: As you know, Bob, there's a lot of education about derivatives that needs to be done in this country. I sit on a committee that looks after employee savings plans and things of that nature. And everyone on that committee was scared to death that any of the funds we were overseeing might be using derivatives. The best answer for a fund manager facing boards like ours was a firm, "No, sir, we do not use derivatives." That was the only response our committee was comfortable with. And, I'm afraid we're not going to make much progress on this issue as long as we keep having episodes like Orange County and Baring Brothers.

McKNEW: Well, let me offer the following suggestion in closing. I wonder if, in a perverse way, the Orange Counties and Barings and P&Gs might not actually be serving to strengthen the long-term outlook for the risk

management and derivatives industry. At Bank of America, we currently have somewhere between $250 billion and $750 billion (if you include futures, foreign exchange forwards and options, and all of the other stuff) of derivatives on the books. Yet, I believe it was only a little more than a year ago that our department made its first explicit presentation in an educational sort of way to our board on this activity. And I suggest that this is probably also the case with most of the corporations represented in this room.

And, as a participant in the marketplace, I am frankly grateful for Orange County—not that Orange County happened, but that something like Orange County is causing us to have conferences like this one. Orange County is causing everybody from Congressmen and regulators to accountants to learn more about derivatives and risk management. At the same time, people inside corporations are starting to take documentation seriously. And they're worrying about credit risk, which they maybe

never did before. Over the longer term, these developments are all positive in that they are going to allow us to use these instruments—which I think we would all say are pretty basic tools to our trade—a lot more freely and in a much more transparent way going forward.

One last point I'd like to make in closing: We're all more or less front-office people; we worry about measuring risk and taking care of it. An awful lot of what affects our market, however, takes place in the back office—documentation, operations, accounting, and so on. And we don't talk enough about these back-office functions. I know that we at B of A are spending an awful lot of time making sure that we operate and account for our derivatives activities appropriately. And I'd encourage all of you to do the same thing with your back offices—again, just for the betterment of our markets going forward.

I would like to thank our panelists for taking some time to prepare and share their thoughts with all of us. I think it's been a great discussion.

EVALUATING AND FINANCING FOREIGN DIRECT INVESTMENT

In April 1996, The Bank of America convened a group of about 50 senior corporate finance executives from major American corporations to discuss the management and monitoring of foreign direct investments. Four executives were chosen as panelists to present the experiences of their companies, and the lessons learned from those experiences. The discussion was moderated by Professor Roy C. Smith of the Stern School of Business, New York University. Smith is a professor of finance and international business, and a former partner of Goldman, Sachs & Co. responsible for international business.

ROY SMITH: Good morning, and welcome to this discussion of corporate overseas investment. Since the collapse of the Bretton Woods Agreement 25 years ago, the intensity of international activity in American business has grown steadily. Today, about a quarter of the country's GNP is represented by international trade, about double what it was in 1970; and foreign direct investment by U.S. companies has reached about $1 trillion. About a quarter of the total manufacturing capacity of U.S. companies is now located abroad, and this has turned many of our corporate managers into global allocators, motivators, and risk controllers. Meanwhile, another half a trillion dollars has been invested in the U.S. by foreign direct investors, and cross-border mergers and other investments have swollen to record levels, even in emerging market countries.

Today about 25% of the global trading transactions in stocks and bonds are international transactions, which means that money is now more free than ever to go wherever it wants. And such global capital flows can, of course, have large effects on the prices of securities and currencies everywhere. Markets are more globally integrated today than ever before. And, as such, they discipline each other, exerting pressure on government everywhere to adopt beneficial regulation—or at least to avoid inappropriate regulation.

So, today's financial managers can truly say they have come a long way down the path of internationalization, and survived many exciting—and instructive—adventures along the way. Much of what our panelists, and those in our audience today, have learned during their careers comes out of these adventures.

But they ain't seen nothin' yet. As fast as things have changed in the past 25 years, they are changing faster now and perhaps more profoundly. And let me just mention some of the most important changes now taking place.

■ The European Union has been formed, and in a much different image from its predecessor, the old socialist-protectionist EEC. The EU now bases its economic policies on the premise that unless Europe can compete with America, Japan, and the most competitive of the emerging market economies, its relative prosperity will be seriously endangered. Ironically, these ideas have led the old world to reform itself into a reflection of the new— a confederation of states linked mainly through economic intercourse, investment, and private sector activity.

First to go was the idea that principal economic assets should belong to the state. Vast privatization efforts have begun and are continuing all over Europe. Second was the idea of intra-European economic sovereignty. Much will have to be given up to allow a truly free and single market to develop in Europe, a region capable of integrating 400 million people and becoming, once again, the center of the world's economic activity and wealth. It hasn't happened yet, but the Europeans are trying to make it do so—but not, of course, without certain amounts of backsliding. But there are plenty of opportunities for U.S. and non-European companies while things get sorted out.

■ The Asian tigers continue to provide the role model for other serious-minded emerging market countries. Growth and development, and increasing democracy, are all associated with the amazing economic results in recent years in countries like Indonesia, Thailand, and Malaysia. And other nations like Vietnam and the Philippines now seem to be getting with the program.

■ The Banana Republics are shaping up. For most of the last 25 years, the principal countries of South America have been economic basket cases. Each has been a land of much promise, but none seemed to be able to make anything work for very long. Now, suddenly, things are different.

Despite its peso crisis in 1995, Mexico has effected enormous reforms, joined NAFTA, and released the private sector from the death-grip of the government. And now Chile, Brazil, Argentina, Colombia, and Peru have begun to march down the same road. As a consequence, explosive inflation rates and negative real growth are becoming things of memory.

■ But most dramatically, about half of the world's population during the past ten years has peacefully changed the system of economic governance under which they lived. This is the change from Communism and strict Socialism (as practiced in India) towards market economies and capitalism. This half of the world is perhaps one fifth as well off as the other half, in terms of GNP and invested capital per capita. Surely, having made these shifts, the countries involved are going to try to make the most of it—not perhaps through enlightened government policies, but rather through incremental shifts toward freer markets that are allowed to direct ever more of the allocation of capital.

If Southeast Asia and Latin America can do so well, why not the others? China has been growing at 10% or more for a decade, and India has been doing nearly as well for the past five years. Soon India may displace the United States as the country with the largest middle class, over 200 million people. This has not been the general experience in Eastern Europe as yet, though respectable progress has been made in East Germany, Poland, Hungary, and the Czech Republic. Some other countries—notably Rumania, Bulgaria, Latvia, and Lithuania—are making headway. Russia, of course, is a disappointment, but the people are managing somehow, while the pri-

Roy Smith

vate sector grows steadily through privatization and the "underground" market continues to grow.

Where this will lead in a few years is not clear. What is clear, however, is that, without direct investment from the private sector, not much will happen—the resources of government and institutional aid are too limited. There will be a huge demand for capital and investment in these countries, and rates of return will have to reflect the risks.

This brings me back to the main subject of our panel, foreign direct investment. Our corporate executives must choose among all the different countries now seeking investments, try to determine how to measure the risks of those countries and investments, and then look for returns that are sufficiently high to justify the risks. They will have to learn new skills for operating in hazardous economies, find ways to manage currency exposures of fledgling economies, and devise new systems for getting paid and collecting on old debts. In short, they will have to learn to do differently everything they now know how to do in order to respond effectively to these new challenges.

With that as introduction, I will now introduce our four panelists in the order they will be speaking:

DAN COHRS is Vice President and Treasurer of GTE Corporation. Dan is going to tell us about GTE's investment in the privatization of Venezuela's national telephone company.

ALAN GAUTHIER is Executive Vice President and Chief Financial Officer of the Exide Corporation in Reading, Pennsylvania. Alan is going to talk about some of Exide's recent efforts to expand in Europe.

PAUL BULL is Vice President of International Borrowings and Global Banking at General Motors Acceptance Corporation. Paul will discuss a number of operating and financial issues relating to GMAC's operations in overseas markets.

DENNIS LING is Vice President and Treasurer of Avon Products, and he will discuss some of Avon's investments in Latin America. Avon, as you will hear, has had some remarkable successes in these markets.

So, let me turn the panel over to Dan Cohrs. Dan told me last night that he began life in a career path that was the reverse of mine. He started out as a professor at the Harvard Business School, then became a consultant, next moved on to Marriott and Northwest Airlines, and is now with GTE.

Investing in Venezuela: The Case of GTE

DAN COHRS: Thanks, Roy. In late 1991 GTE wrote a check to the Venezuelan government for almost $1 billion to buy what amounted to a 20% interest in a company called CANTV, which is the national phone company of Venezuela. After this privatizing transaction, the ownership structure of the company was as follows: 40% of the equity was controlled by a consortium led by GTE (and, since we represented 51% of that consortium, we had just over 20%); 11% was owned by the employees of CANTV (people who had functioned essentially as government bureaucrats up until that time); and the remaining 49% continued to be owned by the government of Venezuela. To give you an idea of the company's size, it had about $700 million in revenues at today's exchange rate, and annual capital spending at the time was $50 to 70 million.

So, in 1992 we found ourselves with effective operating control of a partially privatized government bureaucracy that was running the national phone company of Venezuela. And, as one might expect from a bureaucratic organization, the business was losing money, there were massive inefficiencies, and service was awful. As one illustration of how bad things were, it was then a common practice of Venezuelan businesses to hire people just to pick the telephone up off the hook and then wait for a dial tone. It was also common to hire people to dial the telephone repeatedly until they could get an international line to make an overseas phone call.

Given these conditions, why did we choose to invest at this time? In the early 1990s, the Venezuelan government began to implement market-oriented reforms of the type Roy has just described. During the administration of Carlos Andres Perez (which became known as the "CAP regime"), economic reforms started to take hold and the economy began to open up. The Venezuelan Administration was doing some of the sensible things that Salinas was doing in Mexico, and that had already been done in Chile with considerable success. Inflation was pretty much under control, and the currency was floating in a sensibly managed way. The central bank was acting very responsibly. And all the best political and financial advice we were receiving about the evolution of the economy in Venezuela seemed to point to the continuation of these favorable trends.

But, as things turned out, this analysis failed to anticipate some major problems. With hindsight, it looks as if the CAP regime opened up the Venezuelan banking system a little too quickly, and so made it vulnerable to insiders. Soon after the reforms were enacted, a lot of money disappeared overseas—much of it spent on corporate jets for the bankers—and we ended up with a banking collapse. But I will come back to that part of the story later.

A more fundamental question, I suppose, is why are we getting involved in *emerging* markets at all? That question puts me in mind of Willy Sutton's famous reply to the question of why he robbed banks. He said, "Because that's where the money is." In our case, by far the greatest need for new telephone service is in the emerging markets. And so we started looking for business in places like Venezuela, Argentina, China, and Brazil.

But, having made this commitment to explore emerging markets, we then had to formulate a strategy for picking our spots. And I will describe our strategy below.

Number one, we look for markets that have fundamentally good economic policies, acceptable business practices, and demographics that indicate that people can afford a lot more telephones than they now have. We place heavy weight on a factor that we call "teledensity"—that's the number of telephones per 100 people. In emerging markets, there tends to be 6 to 8 telephones per 100 people. (In the U.S. it's more like 60 telephones per 100 people.) Then we perform a regression analysis of teledensity against GDP per capita. Countries that fall below the regression line in this analysis are the places where we will consider investing because the residents appear to be able to afford a higher level of teledensity.

So, we look for countries where there's a pent-up demand for telecommunication services because the economy is starting to develop. We also look for places where GTE has considerable operating experience. We have a long history in Latin America. We have operated in the Dominican Republic for many years. We also used to own and operate Sylvania, which had big operations in Latin America, including Venezuela.

In addition to our focus on Latin America, we have also decided to target Asia. Asian markets are simply too big to ignore; the need for more telephone service is so great that we have to be there. Given the size of our company, and the size of our industry, we need to go into relatively large markets in order to have an impact on our results. Fairly large opportunities are also necessary to justify the investment of time and effort necessary to do one of these privatizations.

Along with the above considerations is the need to act quickly and decisively when opportunities do emerge. In our business, we have to take a very opportunistic view of our overseas investment opportunities. We can do all the strategizing and all the country selections and demographic analysis we want. But the fact is, we simply can't go into a country unless there's a privatization type of opportunity. In theory, we have three basic choices: we can buy an interest in a privatizing telephone company; we can obtain rights to radio spectrum so that we can start a cellular telephone business; or we can try to persuade the local government to allow us to start a new telephone business of some kind. But the most common opportunity has been some sort of privatization.

So, our overseas investment opportunity set is restricted by the governmental and regulatory structures common in our business. We can target a certain country for investment, but then wait years to have an opportunity come up. When the Venezuelan privatization came up, it was seen as a very juicy opportunity. TelMex in Mexico had just been partially privatized (and, even after the "Tequila effect," that still looks like a good investment for Southwestern Bell). And, so, when the opportunity to privatize the Venezuelan phone company came up, it appeared to have all the characteristics that we were looking for.

Given that the investment made a lot of sense strategically, the next step was to evaluate this investment from a financial standpoint. We went through all of the due diligence nec-

Dan Cohrs

essary to create a cash flow forecast well into the future (and we used both exit multiples and assumptions of perpetual growth in performing this analysis). In coming up with a discount rate for these cash flows, we examined the yields on Brady bonds and sovereign debt, as well as country risk ratings to provide measures of the risk premium we would want for investing outside the U.S. In Venezuela, we are looking for rates of return that are at least in the high

teens—returns that are considerably higher than the returns on our domestic investments.

One of the distinctive features of overseas investments is that we are generally forced to enter these markets through an auction process. Unlike the case of many domestic investments, we don't have the option of a "green field" development—the kind of investment where you go in and buy some land, invest in capital equipment, and then start selling products. And because we usually have to participate in some sort of an auction to invest overseas, that means that we have to be especially careful in pricing our deals. Investing through an auction process is, in a sense, like buying real estate. In both cases, the markets are not as efficient as the stock or bond markets, partly because you can't sell short. Auctions are systematically designed to find the highest bidder: there is nothing to drive the price down, only forces pushing the price up. It's not like the stock market, in which the intersection of the supply and demand curves for the bidders and the sellers produces a market-clearing price.

This tendency of the auction process to push prices up makes it very challenging for us to find overseas opportunities where we can still generate acceptable returns after paying the entry price. But, in the case of CANTV, after going through the quantitative investment evaluation process I've just described, we decided that the promised long-run payoff was large enough to justify our investment of close to a billion dollars.

When evaluating our foreign investments, we also need to think about management and control in these different operating environments. Basically, our objective is to apply our management skills in operating telecommunication services. That is what we think we're good at, and we want to create value by applying our skills to network design and management. We're not really that focused on owning these assets; it's just that some degree of ownership is usually necessary to get operating control of the assets and to reap the rewards from applying our management skills.

Our challenge in structuring this kind of investment thus becomes how to achieve management control through a minority equity stake. We really don't care about having 51% ownership. In fact, in this business the government generally will not allow foreigners to have majority ownership. But, even without majority ownership, we are able to achieve the amount of operating control we want through the contracts we set up. By "contracts" I mean things like corporate governance provisions and rules about the way the board operates, voting rights (including minority blocking rights), and management contracts.

Our financial goal is to make a large enough one-time equity investment to gain operating control and properly capitalize the company, and then have the overseas operation become a self-financing, non-recourse entity after the initial investment. To make these investments self-financing, however, requires that a number of issues be addressed up front. In most of these markets, telecommunications requires a lot of capital at the beginning. Building or improving these systems generally requires hundreds of millions, if not billions, of dollars. And, because the local capital markets are totally inadequate, off-shore capital is critical.

We have huge capital budgets that are paid for in dollars, and huge financing requirements that are generally also denominated in dollars. But because the business generates mainly local revenues, we have a very large currency mismatch. In most of these markets, moreover, there are no financial instruments you can use to hedge your exposure. There are no currency derivatives—no forwards, futures, or swaps—for a place like Venezuela because those markets have not yet developed. And you can't even borrow very much locally to offset that risk.

In such circumstances, we face a large *maturity* mismatch as well. Telephone companies are accustomed to issuing 30-year bonds—a maturity that reflects both the fact that the payoff from capital investment in this industry is longer-term, and the relatively low risk associated with such investments. But, in funding higher-risk, overseas investments, you're lucky if you can issue two- or three-year debt in the Euro markets, although you might find a bank willing to lend you five-year money.

In the case of Venezuela, these currency and maturity mismatches were compounded by the fact that, within two years of taking over, we raised enough debt to take capital spending from $70 million to $700 million to improve and expand that network. We found ourselves with a debt portfolio of a billion dollars, of which about $600 million had a maturity of less than one year.

Then, about two years into the deal, and facing the need to roll over this short-term debt, our worst fears were suddenly realized. As I mentioned earlier, there was a collapse of the banking system that was blamed on the CAP regime. Then there was a coup attempt, the president was thrown in jail, and a 78-year old socialist was eventually elected—one who promptly instituted economic policies from the 1950s such as currency controls and price controls. At this point, the economy started to go downhill, inflation went to 60%, and there was a huge devaluation. The new government responded by fixing the exchange rate and rationing currency, and so making a bad situation worse from the point of view of foreign currency lenders and investors.

In this environment, none of our lenders was eager to roll over its short-term debt, so we were forced to come up with a financial restructuring plan. (Bank of America, by the way, was included in our group of 36 banks.) We entered into a full year of negotiations with this group of banks to lengthen the maturity of the debt. And how we eventually succeeded in this is a long story I won't trouble you with today.

Suffice it to say that these kinds of financing and liquidity problems can come up in emerging markets. And, to the extent that it's possible, you need to anticipate how you will respond when the liquidity crisis hits. What tends to happen when these problems arise is that the finance people are brought in to tighten up controls over cash flow and to negotiate a restructuring with the creditors, and perhaps with the partners. This creates some very heavy staffing demands. It's not easy to free up the people required to go and deal with these problems, and it's not easy to find people who are capable of parachuting into a different environment and dealing with a financial crisis of this kind.

Let me conclude with a brief overview of some of the problems that come up with emerging market investments. The investments are large, and we have both currency and maturity mismatches. Hedging is impossible. And, when things go wrong, they really go wrong—that's why we have these high risk premiums in our discount rates when we evaluate the investments at the beginning. Although having a high risk premium doesn't protect us against things going wrong, it certainly discourages us from overpaying. Sensitivity analysis helps us to do some "contingency" planning—that is, what do we do if problems materialize?

Moreover, in the case of direct foreign investment—and this is especially true of emerging markets—we have learned that we really have to be patient and take the long view. Fifteen years ago, we wrote off our entire investment in the Dominican Republic. Today we're making a very good profit in that country.

From the financing point of view, it pays to explore the possibility of obtaining funding or credit from suppliers and governments. Start by getting the EXIMs and OPICs of the world to help as much as possible. We have to try to create some kind of a liquidity cushion, although that's very difficult because it is almost impossible to arrange revolving lines of credit for ventures like this. We have to be prepared to make some strategic financing choices: Should the parent provide guarantees? And, even if the debt is not backed by the parent, should the parent make additional infusions of capital if the venture gets into problems? That becomes a new investment decision all over again.

I don't need to tell the people in this group that you need good local partners who can help you at the front end and also if things go wrong. But perhaps the most important ingredient in overseas investing is not a matter of financing at all; it's making sure that you have the right people. If these are good investments, the capital markets are fairly efficient, and funding should be available. But the market for people who can operate in these countries, whether it's expatriates or locals, is something else—and you really need to find people you

can trust. Getting the right people to move their families and suceed in these environments is the biggest challenge we face. We're not talking London, Paris and Tokyo here. We're talking about Caracas and Beijing and places like that.

And this issue of finding the right people applies to finance very directly. I could raise $2 billion in capital for GTE almost without leaving my office. But one of these deals for Argentina or Venezuela requires people full time for periods of 12 to 18 months just to arrange the initial financing. And if things go wrong, it could be another 12 to 18 months to clean up the mess.

SMITH: Dan, you mentioned that you used a required rate of return in the high teens in this case. Could you tell us a bit more about how you quantify your discount rates for these kinds of investments?

COHRS: First of all, we calculate different discount rates for different countries. And, because we tend to be in bidding situations, I'd prefer not to tell you the exact numbers we use. Conceptually, we begin with our own weighted average cost of capital for domestic telephone investments. Because telephone investments tend to be highly leverageable, and because interest on debt is tax deductible, our domestic telephone investments tend to have relatively low costs of capital. But, in coming up with an overseas discount rate, we add a country risk premium to that domestic cost of capital that reflects various country risk ratings as well as the yields on stripped Brady bonds and sovereign debt. We typically try to take some sort of moving average for these market variables to avoid the possibility that spikes in such rates will distort our analysis.

And, as I suggested earlier, the net result is that for most of these countries we end up using discount rates in the high teens or low twenties.

Let me also say that there are a lot of specific adjustments that sometimes need to be made in order to capture tax effects. For example, in Mexico interest payments on local debt are not fully deductible. And so if you did the same calculations in Mexico, you might come up with a higher cost of capital because of the tax impact.

SMITH: Are those hurdle rates used for discounting cash flows that can be repatriated back to the U.S.?

COHRS: Yes, absolutely. We start by doing the cash flow analysis in the local currency first. You need to compute the cash flows in local currency in order to do the taxes properly. Then, after subtracting all taxes from the local currency cash flows, we pretend that we remit the available cash back to the parent in the U.S. and take into account any further taxes. We translate those after-tax remitted cash flows back into dollars at a forecast exchange rate that is usually fairly close to purchasing power parity (based on projected relative rates of inflation). Finally, we discount those translated projected dollar cash flows at the hurdle rate I mentioned above—one that is essentially a dollar hurdle rate for dollar flows, but that is adjusted upward for the risk of investing in that country.

SMITH: How do you evaluate your ability to repatriate cash flows? Or do you just assume you will eventually find a way to accomplish that?

COHRS: Well, that's something that we always look at very carefully. When we made the investment in Venezuela, it was not very hard to get money out. Today,* if you want to get

---

*Editor's Note: This statement was true at the time of the conference. Since then, the currency regulations have been eliminated and it is once again possible to obtain and remit foreign currency from Venezuela.

money out of Venezuela, you have to go to the foreign exchange bureaucracy and get permission. Every single dime that comes out is ruled on by a set of bureaucrats.

SMITH: Did you consider purchasing insurance against political risk?

COHRS: No, we did not take out insurance for ourselves on the original investment. Our assessment was that, given what's available and how much it costs, it was not worth purchasing protection of our equity investment; it was better for us to self-insure. When I was talking about EXIM and OPIC earlier, I was talking more about on the debt side, where it can be extremely valuable to have the export credit agencies supporting the equipment purchases.

SMITH: Thank you, Dan. Now let's turn to Alan Gauthier, who is Executive Vice President and Chief Financial Officer of Exide.

European Consolidation: The Case of Exide

ALAN GAUTHIER: As Roy mentioned, I'm going to talk about Exide's recent European expansion. But, before I do that, let me first tell you a little bit about the company because, unlike GTE and Avon and General Motors, many of you may not know much about Exide. In fact, when I first came to work for Exide, my mother thought I was working for Exxon. We are the battery company, not the oil company. We make automotive batteries, which includes virtually any kind of lead acid battery as well as nickel cadmium batteries and some other exotic types.

There is sort of an interesting history to the company that I will just mention in passing. Thomas Edison founded the company in 1888. During one period Exide actually had 100% worldwide market share. But, in 1954, the U.S. government in its infi-

nite wisdom forced the company to divest all of its foreign operations.

Our next notable milestone was in 1973 when Exide became the subject of the first hostile takeover and was taken over by INCO, the producer of nickel and other metals. The current management acquired the company from INCO in 1983 by means of a leveraged buyout.

Today, Exide is the world's leading battery company. We have 23% of worldwide market share in lead acid batteries. Number two is the Japanese company Yuasa, which has a 15% share, and number three is the German firm, Varta, which has about 10%. Yuasa, I should mention, is our joint venture partner in a couple of ventures in the United States. The only other U.S. producer with a significant share is Delco, which accounts for about 6% of the market.

In a category called Starting Lighting Ignition batteries—or SLI for short—we have 40% market share in both North America and Western Europe. Our European *automotive* battery business can be divided into two large pieces: original equipment, where we have about 40% of the market, and the after market, where our share is 37%. We also have a roughly 40% market share of the European *industrial* battery market. And this market can also be further divided into two components: the "traction" business, which is basically batteries for electric lift-trucks; and the standby market, which is standby power supplies and the like. In Western Europe, we have 43% of the traction market, and 33% of the standby market.

We are vertically integrated. We manufacture our own lead, our own plastic, and our own separators. And, although vertical integration does not work for all companies, it has worked very well for us. We are the technological leader and the low-cost producer in the world.

To give you some idea of the growth we have experienced in recent years, consider that in 1986 Exide had sales of less than $200 million. In 1992, sales were about $570 million. In 1996, we project that our sales will run about $2.5 billion. In 1986, Exide had a mere 4% market share in North America, and that share was actually dropping. Today, we have 17 of North America's top 20 customers and market share that, as I mentioned, runs about 40%.

Moreover, in the past 18 months or so, we have experienced dramatic growth in Western Europe. We focused on Europe for a couple of reasons. First was size; Europe is the only market that is comparable to North America. Although it has roughly the same number of units as the North American market, the European market looks much like the North American market did 20 years ago. That is to say, it's a highly fragmented market. There are 143 battery manufacturers in Western Europe. Twenty years ago there were 150 battery manufacturers in the U.S.; today there are less than 15.

So, the industry consolidation that has occurred in North America over the past 20 years is beginning to take place in Europe. And it's our company, Exide, that is causing this to happen.

The other thing that attracted us to the market in Europe was that product pricing was generally higher than it is in North America—in some cases, two or even three times higher. In addition, the European manufacturers were high-cost producers, in part because they generally lack advanced product and process technologies.

Our strategy has been to establish market share leadership in Europe. We want to dominate the European market just as we have the North American market. We are aiming to achieve broad geographic coverage, to build a widely recognized brand name, and to establish ourselves as the low-cost producer in these markets. We have also been intent on extending our established distribution and customer relationships into these new markets.

We started fairly small. We bought a company in the U.K. that had less than 4% market share. Within six months of that first European acquisition, we acquired the third largest battery manufacturer in Europe—the Tudor group in Spain. Soon after that we acquired the largest battery manufacturer in Europe, CEAC, which gave us the dominant market share in Europe. Through this series of acquisitions, we have achieved the geographic coverage we were seeking. We have also acquired the brand names that are so important to doing business in Europe.

We were also interested in acquiring management talent. We are a very leveraged company, we operate lean and mean, and so we don't have a great deal of depth in management. For this reason, it was important to us that we acquire good managers. And we did that with some of the acquisitions we made in Europe. The people were very good.

Another aim of our acquisition strategy was to enhance the low-cost production ability of the plants we acquired. As a result of our recent series of acquisitions, we now have 30 battery manufacturing plants in Europe, as compared to only five plants in the United States. There are some very large differences in the operating efficiency of our plants. Take the case of our plant in Salina, Kansas, which is both the largest and the lowest-cost battery plant in the world. We manufacture a battery in Salina for about $13, and we produce about 9 million

THE EUROPEAN MARKET LOOKS MUCH LIKE THE *North American market did 20 years ago. That is to say, it's a highly fragmented market. There are 143 battery manufacturers in Western Europe. Twenty years ago there were 150 battery manufacturers in the U.S.; today there are less than 15. The industry consolidation that has occurred in North America over the past 20 years is beginning to take place in Europe. And it's our company, Exide, that is causing this to happen.*

Alan Gauthier

batteries at that plant a year. Our low-cost European producer, which is located in Manzanares, Spain, produces about 4 million batteries a year at an average cost of about $18. At the other extreme is our plant in Kassel, Germany, where it costs $38 to manufacture the same battery. They manufacture a million a year.

Given both the large differences in operating efficiency and the scale economies in this business, we are closing plants at a very significant

rate. For example, the million batteries that we manufacture in Kassel are being moved to Manzanares in Spain, where as I mentioned we produce the same battery for $18. That's a $20 difference in per unit cost; and, since they make a million batteries, that means a savings of $20 million. So, we are pursuing a simple strategy of consolidation, going from the high-cost plants to the low-cost plants, and reducing overhead in the process. By the turn of the century, we expect to have gone from 30 battery plants down to 12 battery plants.

Now, that brings me to the question of how we financed our acquisitions in Europe. As I mentioned, there were three deals that were all closed within a 14-month period: B.I.G. in the U.K., which had a purchase price of $35 million and closed in March of 1994; Tudor in Spain for $235 million, in October of 1994; and CEAC in France for $425 million, in May of 1995. The total purchase price for the three transactions was thus about $700 million. We financed the three deals (and refinanced part of the acquired debt) with a combination of bank debt (a U.S. credit facility of $550 million), public debt ($300 million of senior 10% notes), and a public equity issue (raising about $250 million).

Since we were now operating in every country in Europe, and our acquisition funding was in U.S. dollars, we had exposures to a variety of exchange rates that we wanted to reduce. We came up with a unique *multi-currency, multi-borrower* working capital facility (equivalent to $525 million) that was designed in large part to hedge our different FX exposures. This financing arrangement allows 33 borrowers in nine different countries to borrow in various local currencies.

We also make it a policy to net our exchange exposure between companies. Now that all of these companies are in the Exide group, we don't want people in France paying people in Germany in real currency. We want to net the exposure among the group, and we accomplish that through a central treasury operation that we have set up in Paris.

SMITH: How much resistance do you face in attempting to close plants?

GAUTHIER: Some, but not a lot. Before coming to Exide, I spent most of my career with General Electric. General Electric has several multinational companies and many plants in Europe. When I was still working at GE, we had a plastics plant in the Netherlands, and that was the only plastics plant we had in Europe. We also had an electrical apparatus plant outside of Milan, and that too was the only such operation in Europe. If we got into financial trouble in this situation, it was very difficult to get concessions from the unions. If you tried to reduce wages, or just hold the line on increases, the workers went on strike. If they struck the electrical apparatus plant in Milan, we were out of luck; that was the only plant that could produce transformers and switchgear. If they struck the polycarbonate plant in the Netherlands, we were out of luck for polycarbonate.

Exide is in a much different situation. We have 30 battery plants in Europe, all of which are capable of producing our full range of products. So we don't care if the workers at one of our plants go on strike; we will close the plant and walk away from it. Also, the fact that we have such large cost disparities among our different operations—you might recall that our Spanish plant had a $20 cost advantage over our German plant—and the size of these savings means that we can afford fairly generous severance packages when clos-

ing plants. Most European countries have a month's salary for every year of service. But, although it's quite expensive, we're willing to pay the price. We can afford to be quite civilized in these circumstances.

SMITH: Can you tell us a little more about how you went about establishing a brand name?

GAUTHIER: Before we were forced to divest our overseas operations in 1954, Exide had a brand name that was established throughout the world. But we didn't have that when we launched our European program in 1994. When we acquired the Tudor Group that year, we were effectively acquiring the number one brand name in Spain and Scandinavia. And, when we acquired CEAC in 1995, we were also buying the number one brand name in France, which was Fulman. So, we needed to build our brand presence. Buying just the manufacturing facilities would not have accomplished this. We needed the brand names to go along with the plants, and we wanted the distribution. Batteries are not exactly easy to transport, and distribution is very important.

SMITH: Thanks, Alan. Now let's turn to Paul Bull, who heads GMAC's International Borrowing and Global Banking functions.

Financing Overseas Operations: The Case of GMAC

PAUL BULL: I am going to address five issues that we at GMAC look at when we are going into new countries.

■ First, how do we select these countries?

■ Second, what are our minimum required returns on investment in such cases?

■ Third, how do we structure our investments? Does it generally take the form of a wholly owned subsidiary or a joint venture operation?

■ Fourth, how do we handle the management and control issues?

■ Fifth and last, how do we fund our operations?

A short time after we went through the peso crisis in Mexico, I ran across a quote in *Euromoney* that I think serves as a useful introduction to investing in these markets. "*Emerging markets,*" it warns, "*are not for sissies. You have to be willing to live though the agony as well as the ecstasy.*" When Mexico erupted, we felt the impact through a variety of our operations around the globe. And, as I will suggest later in my presentation, your ability to weather a crisis like this depends a lot on your management team and on your organizational structure.

Before I start, I would like to give you a little bit of background on GMAC's overseas operations. We operate in 28 countries outside the U.S. Each country in which we operate mirrors in many respects what we do in the United States. Obviously the size of our operations varies by country, and it is determined in large part by the level of GM sales. But the size of our operation is also affected by the interest rate, competitive, and legal environments, and by the willingness of consumers to borrow money. And, finally, our volume of financing also depends on our ability to finance other manufacturers' products.

In each country—and this is a critical point—*we are financing in the local currency.* We won't try to finance a Mexican buyer in dollars and take exchange risks. We will enter into some cross-border funding but we avoid significant currency risks.

Our primary focus is to finance the dealer inventories and the retail purchasers—that is, small fleets and individuals. Wholesale financing, by its nature, is very short term—30 to 60 days. Retail is longer-term—two to three years. Our retail portfolio can be funded with short-term debt, or with a combination of short-term and medium-term (and the latter can be either fixed or floating). Each country has a manager on site, and that manager's responsibility is the bottom line for that country. We give our local managers a good deal of autonomy in order to allow timely decision-making and increased responsiveness to the market.

As I mentioned, we operate in 28 countries. We think of these countries as constituting three major regions plus Canada. In Europe, we operate in 16 countries with $9 billion in debt. This is by far our largest region and, as you might expect, our largest concentrations of assets are in the most established European countries. Germany and the U.K. represent approximately 75% of our European activity. We recently entered Hungary and anticipate starting an operation in Poland in the first quarter of this year. From a GMAC perspective, however, Europe in general is a mature market, and the outlook there is for moderate growth.

In the region that includes Australia as well as Asia, we are operating in four countries with $2.1 billion in debt. This is a high-growth, high-focus area for GM and GMAC. We recently started an operation in Indonesia, and are very close to opening up in Thailand. In addition, we are looking at China, India, Korea, and the Philippines. As a result, we are spending a lot more time and effort in this part of the world.

In Latin America, we operate in seven countries, and have approximately $600 million in debt. This is also a high-growth, high-focus area. We recently opened up operations in Argentina and Ecuador.

■■■■■■■■■■■■■■■■■■■

THE MAJORITY OF OUR INTERNATIONAL OPERATIONS, *those in 18 out of 28 countries, are set up as wholly-owned finance subsidiaries. The other ten cases are about evenly divided between banks and joint ventures. Which of these three different structures we choose is driven primarily by the operations or asset side of the business. We ask ourselves: Which structure, wholly-owned subsidiary or bank or joint venture, gives us the most latitude to offer the broadest range of products?*

Paul Bull

Concerning the question of operating structure, GMAC uses various frameworks based on the local regulations and market practice. We may operate as a bank, as a partner in a joint venture with a commercial company, or as a non-bank bank or finance company. The majority of our international operations—those in 18 out of 28 countries—are set up as wholly-owned finance subsidiaries. The other ten cases are about evenly divided between banks and joint ventures.

Which of these three different structures we choose is driven primarily by the operations or asset side of the business. We clearly look to achieve as much operating flexibility as we can. We ask ourselves: Which structure, wholly-owned subsidiary or bank or joint venture, gives us the most latitude to offer the broadest range of products? Some of these structures permit us to engage in some activities— say, retail lending or leasing— but not others.

We found in the case of Argentina, for example, that by having a joint venture partner we were able to create a structure that allowed us to maximize our product offerings. When GM made the decision to go into Argentina, we clearly did not have the critical mass in terms of product and volume to penetrate that market and make our presence meaningful. But, by entering into a joint venture with CIADEA, we were able to generate volume by financing Renaults pending the build up of GM sales. In so doing, we eventually established a presence with a meaningful operation in a very short period of time.

As we expand farther into what we perceive to be riskier operations, we are using the joint venture structure as opposed to a stand-alone entity much more frequently. The first joint venture that we entered into was in Austria in the early 1980s—and our choice of a joint venture with a local partner was a requirement of the Austrian government. Our partner is a bank, and the venture has worked out extremely well. But operating in Austria was not high risk. We have complete operating and management control, make all the decisions, and share the profit with the joint venture partner.

We've also started joint ventures in Indonesia, Mexico, and Poland in the past 12 months. Although we had a presence in Mexico for about 30 years, we operated from a single location: Mexico City. Mexico covers a large geographic area, which makes it difficult to service out of just one office.

In response to these problems, we set up a joint venture with a local entity called Abaco Grupo Financiero and used their branch structure. We moved the operation from Mexico City to Monterey, which has meant a better quality of life for our employees and improved service covering the entire country.

In the case of Indonesia, we formed a joint venture in large part to address a regulatory issue. Our joint venture partner is Lippo Bank, and we're in the first year of operation. In the case of Poland, we actually bought a local bank. It was a small operation with a clean balance sheet. And, although it is too early to know the outcome, we are very comfortable with the level of our investment.

So, as you can see, we're already well established in the developed countries and we're now making our way into what are clearly the more difficult or emerging markets. But, before I go any farther on this subject, let me step back for a moment and comment on the role of GMAC within GM. GMAC's mission, in brief, is to support GM sales. But, in the process of accomplishing this goal, we are also clearly charged with the responsibility of achieving a standard of profitability.

In the past we would take a somewhat passive approach to entering new overseas markets. We would wait until there were sufficient GM volumes to justify the investment and generate the returns that we were looking for. But today we take a more active approach. When we go into a country, we meet with the local GM management and the dealers to determine exactly what their needs are, and assess the competitive environment. We find out what kind of auto financing, if any, is being conducted and by what institutions. We ask ourselves: Does it make sense to work with local banks, or are there finance companies that have been set up to operate in these markets? We determine whether it makes sense to have a joint venture partner—and, if so, we identify potential candidates.

We also consider the available operating structures, what rights we can attach to each of the alternative entities, and how the local tax code would affect them. As part of this process we meet with legal counsel, accounting firms, and government authorities to develop an understanding of what our legal rights would be under various scenarios.

At the same time we probe these issues—there are a number of basic issues in emerging markets that we take for granted in the U.S.—members of our treasury centers will meet with many of the same people. But, in addition to the local managers and the lawyers and accountants, our finance people will also meet with local banks and, if possible, try to arrange funding from multi-national banks. Bank of America, I might add, is an obvious choice for us, both as a source of information and as a potential source of funding.

We review our funding alternatives and consider the issues of risk, liquidity, and interest rate volatility that will help determine the structure of our financing. For example, we will determine if there is a term market that we can use to match-fund our retail lending operation. Is there a developing capital market? What cross-border funding capability exists, and what are the risks associated with it? Are there cost-effective ways of managing these risks? What, if any, savings are available from this type of borrowing?

We also review cash management issues. How do we collect money from dealers? How quickly can we get value for our money? These are clearly critical issues in emerging markets, particularly in places like Indonesia, where dealers and retail customers are potentially based in remote locations.

You also need to determine how you will service the retail customer in these markets. In Argentina, for example, the majority of people do not have bank accounts. They line up and make cash payments on the date that their payment is due. In addition, how will you make credit decisions? In Argentina, there are no credit bureaus.

These are some of the funding and operating issues that we need to evaluate carefully before entering a new market. After we've visited the country several times, we'll put together a business plan and make a recommendation. The major criteria for us are: Will our presence in any way help GM to increase its penetration of that market? Can we fund adequately on shore? Based on the answers to the first two questions, will the operation be profitable?

If we are satisfied with the above, we obtain the necessary approval from our executive committee. Once we have obtained this approval, then the real work begins. We identify a country manager—and, in fact, that choice may be made well in advance, as that person may participate actively in the country visits. We normally staff a new operation with one or two International Service Personnel and hire local people and train them by sending them to other operations in the region. This way, when we do open our doors for business, our people understand how our processes work.

In addition to lining up the manager and staff, we develop more detailed plans, contracts that conform to local law, accounting systems for retail and wholesale lending, and banks for credit facilities. GMAC's general funding strategy is to enter these countries with a relatively small amount of capital (we may put in less than $5 million in equity). One thing that enables us to go in with such low capitalization is that, in most cases, GMAC provides a parent guaranty for the debt of these operations (although the guaranty is for commercial risk only).

We focus primarily on the banking system for funding. GMAC may be a single A in the United States, but with a parent guaranty we're a triple A in most of these countries when compared to other credits in the local market. Besides translating into competitive funding, the parent guaranty also assures us, for the most part, of liquidity in difficult environments. When things tightened up in Argentina in early '95 and access to credit was restricted, our Argentine operation's access to liquidity remained relatively unaffected, in part due to the parent guaranty and our close relationships with our banks.

In dealing with banks, we standardize our documentation to the degree possible from country to country and bank to bank. No bank gets special covenants because they negotiate or drive a harder bargain. This is a very important issue for us. By treating all lenders the same, we ensure that, in the event of difficulty, all loans are effectively treated equally.

Besides the banks, we will also evaluate any capital market instruments that might exist. Can they be used to supplement our bank funding? Are they cost-effective? What are the risks involved in using them? Offshore funding possibilities are something that we are cognizant of, but rarely use in emerging markets. In developed countries like Germany, Canada, and Australia, we make very aggressive use of capital market in-

struments. But, in the higher-risk areas, we are much more conservative.

I trust this provides some insight into GMAC's approach to emerging markets. I would be pleased to answer any questions you may have.

SMITH: Paul, can you tell us a little about the role of the local partner in terms of removing regulatory barriers?

BULL: Having a well-connected local partner is one of the great attractions of joint ventures. It gives you some comfort that you have somebody with local influence. In most of our ventures, we are the majority holder of the investment and have most of the say in operating matters. But joint venture partners are good sources of information and are capable of adding tremendous value. Five years ago, we were very skeptical of the benefits of joint ventures. But, as we penetrate deeper into emerging markets, I think we will continue to make more and more use of this structure.

SMITH: How do you evaluate the risk-reward tradeoffs for these overseas operations, and how do they compare to domestic returns?

BULL: Well, for starters, we have a fairly extensive database provided by those 28 countries in which we now operate. And this data gives us some basis for evaluating the risk of entering a new market. Moreover, the returns that we have achieved to date on our four or five start-up operations have been impressive.

Let me also say, however, that we do not rely solely, or even primarily, on quantitative methods for evaluating these trade-offs. There are too many soft issues that must be factored into the decision-making and, if we can help GM sell an additional 3,000 vehicles, we would accept a slightly lower return on our investment.

SMITH: Thanks, Paul. Now, Dennis Ling is going to tell us about some Avon's successes in South America and, more recently, in Asia.

Making it Big Abroad: The Case of Avon

DENNIS LING: Good morning. Avon has a great success story and I am very happy to be here to share it with you. But, before I begin, let me provide a little background on the company.

Avon is 110 years old. It is one of the oldest public companies in America, and one of the largest direct selling companies in the world. We have 32,000 employees worldwide. We recorded $4.5 billion in sales last year, and our business is all done through two million independent sales Representatives around the world. Our products are now sold in 125 countries, and more new markets are planned. We are the largest cosmetics and fragrance brand in the world, and we're also one of the largest fashion jewelry manufacturers in the world. We now have direct investment subsidiaries in 41 countries, which includes 18 manufacturing sites. Our sales are about one third in the United States and one third in Latin America, with the remaining one third split fairly evenly between Europe and the Pacific.

Every two to three weeks, we conduct sales campaigns in different countries. Each campaign has its own sales brochure, with the result that we produce nearly 700 million sales brochures a year that are written in 15 different languages. This also makes us one of the largest publishers in the world.

Our sales are predominantly in cosmetics, fragrances, and toiletries; these three categories make up about 62% of the total. We also have a very large business in gift and decorative items, which accounts for another 18%. Our apparel business accounts for 11%; and jewelry and accessories is another 9%. With the exception of a relatively small direct mail catalogue business, all of our products are sold via the direct selling format. As I said, we have two million independent Representatives around the world—and they collectively earn about two billion dollars annually in sales commissions.

Over the past eight years, Avon has achieved a compound annual growth rate in sales of 7% and in earnings per share from continuing operations of 16%. During that period we've also reduced our debt from over $1 billion to $160 million at the end of 1995. Since 1989, when the present management team took over, we have increased the market value of the company from a little over $1 billion to nearly $6 billion. Our total annual (compounded) shareholder return of 26% during that time has been 10% above the average return for the S&P 500 over the same period.

We have achieved these results with a simple three-pronged growth strategy. The first strategy is expansion into new geographic markets. Our second strategy is to achieve growth in developed or established markets like the U.S. or Europe by improving access to Avon and giving customers more choice in how they can buy from Avon. Most customers buy from an Avon Representative, but there are others who don't but who would be willing to buy our products in other ways that are convenient for them. Customers now can order through catalogs, phone, fax, and even retail shops in some countries. Just a few weeks ago, we launched our own home page on the Internet as well. We're also growing in developed countries through new products and product innovations, especially in the United States, and through a major advertising program to improve the image of Avon.

The third leg of our growth strategy is to leverage the strength of our

PURELY QUANTITATIVE ANALYSIS IS NOT OUR SOLE basis for decision-making. We would certainly not reject a promising market entry just because our analysis indicated a low IRR. But such an analysis might cause us to change our approach, to find another way to structure our investment—say, by reducing our initial cash commitment—to make the returns more attractive.

Dennis Ling

unique distribution channel by introducing new product categories into the channel. One example of this is our move into lingerie and apparel, which is now a $500 million business for us globally. That business generated $160 million in sales in the U.S. in its first full year. We also sell about $50 million worth of vitamins and other nutritional products in six countries. And we are now one of the largest home video marketers in the U.S., with sales of over $100 million.

But, let me return to our first strategy, which is to enter new geographic markets. We view expansion into new markets as a key strategy for the company because of the unique features of our direct selling business format. We think we have a major opportunity to expand our independent sales force in emerging countries. These markets have lower per capita incomes, so the earnings opportunity for an Avon representative there is particularly attractive. In such countries, women are in the labor force to a lesser extent and have fewer opportunities to generate income for themselves.

These are also countries that lack a well-established retail infrastructure. In most developing economies, people don't have access to a broad range of consumer products, and we can bring these products to them very quickly. And the fact that there is generally a high demand for international-quality cosmetics at mass-market prices also works in our favor, because we are a mass-market brand.

Another advantage for us in emerging markets is that our new market investment requirements are not necessarily capital-intensive. We have entered some new markets by setting up manufacturing operations, but we also have the choice of importing the products from other locations.

Today, developing countries contribute about 38% of Avon's sales, and over 52% of our profits. And our growth rates in the developing countries are much higher than in developed countries. Our new market focus has been on China, India, South Africa, and a number of countries in Central Europe, Russia, and southeast Asia. In China, for example, we will have about 74,000 sales Representatives by year end, and our business there is growing very fast. Again, this is a country that does not have a well-developed retail infrastructure, and women are not heavily in the work force. You may have read about the Avon Representative in China who makes more money than a medical doctor. We now have 45 sales branches throughout China, and expect to have about 70 by the end of the year.

In addition to China, since 1990 we have entered 14 new markets, including Russia, Ecuador, Bolivia, Poland, Hungary, the Czech Republic, and Slovakia. In each of these countries we have grown from a sales base of essentially zero in 1990 to $100 million in 1995, and we expect sales in all these countries to be substantially higher this year. We are just getting started in India, and have recently acquired a small company in South Africa. We are also now looking at countries like Ukraine, Romania, and Vietnam.

So, that's a brief introduction to Avon and what we are doing in new markets. Now let me say just a little about the procedure we go through in selecting new markets, and how we finance these investments. We perform investment, discounted cash flow, and financial analysis that is similar to what the other panelists have already described. We also have hurdle rates that incorporate risk premiums for foreign investments. As just one example, we typically assess an additional 3% risk premium for investment projects with paybacks longer than three years. We have additional risk premiums related to project risk and to country or sovereign risk.

But that kind of purely quantitative analysis is not the sole basis for decision-making. We would certainly not reject a promising market entry just because our initial financial analysis indicated a low IRR. Such an analysis

might cause us to change our approach, to find another way to structure our investment—say, by reducing our initial cash commitment—to make the returns more attractive.

In financing an operation, we aim to achieve the lowest after-tax cost of capital for the company, after adjusting for factors like currency risk and country risk as well as consolidated taxes. We continuously monitor our currency and investment exposures in all markets around the world. We are active hedgers in the foreign currency markets. Financial hedging is an important part of our risk management program, provided the cost of hedging is reasonable and the hedge is consistent with our outlook for the currency. Depending on our view, our policy is to hedge up to 100% of the currency exposures that are created in the normal course of our business. We don't go out and create new exposures for the company, though in some cases we will choose to take no action on an exposure that the business naturally creates if the cost of hedging is excessive. Our hedging positions go out as far as 24 months. Moreover, we have hedged in emerging-market currencies that include Mexican pesos, Brazilian reals, and Argentine pesos.

SMITH: Dennis, do you have different time horizons for evaluating new investments in developing countries as opposed to established countries?

LING: We look at most of our investments as long-term investments for the company. We also do not base a new market entry decision on projected financial returns alone. For example, when Avon made its initial investment in Brazil over 40 years ago, we did not envision it would become the huge business it is today. So, we try to take the long view. We view ourselves as planting the seeds in these markets that will become in 10 to 20 years what Brazil is today.

SMITH: Can you tell us a little more about the payback method you just mentioned?

LING: We calculate net present values and investment returns based on cash flow projections. We also use a very simple cash payback calculation. For example, many years ago, when the company had much more debt to service, capital was very scarce for us. And because we felt we really didn't have the luxury of having long paybacks on projects at that time, we emphasized investments with shorter cash paybacks.

SMITH: Do you find that you're able to use your distribution channels differently in overseas markets?

LING: Yes, as I mentioned earlier, our second major growth strategy is to leverage our sales channel to sell other product categories. In some countries, particularly in Latin America where our direct selling business is very strong, we have had the ability to sell different categories of products. In Latin America, we have distributed Disney licensed products, Duracell batteries, and a variety of household goods that we do not sell in the U.S. and other developed countries.

Postscript

SMITH: Thanks, Dennis. Well, that brings to an end our series of presentations by the panelists. They have done a good job so far, but I'd like to get a little more work out of them before we quit.

I think we have to give the first prize to Avon for producing a 26% compounded return on shareholder investment in a company that has 49% of its profits from investments in emerging markets. As Dennis mentioned, these areas of the world are growing faster and thus provide a potential for profit growth that may not exist elsewhere.

Paul Bull gets the prize for the nifty slogan of the day with his comment that emerging markets are not for sissies. I think we all have come to recognize the truth of that remark, and the fact the net stock market returns from emerging markets as a group over the past five years have been essentially zero bears this out.

Alan gets the prize for the most opportunistic foreign strategy—that sort of Viking-like, smash-and-grab kind of approach to Europe. The idea of acquiring a dominant position in a whole market territory and then introducing American technology and management techniques to achieve cost reduction is certainly a compelling one. And it's conceivable that you may be able to take this strategy into some emerging markets as well.

Finally, I think we have to give a prize to Dan for telling us something that I for one had a hard time believing. After saying that GTE invested a billion dollars for a 20% stake in a company, he said that GTE would really prefer just to manage these operations rather than own them. I think he raises an interesting issue of comparative advantage here—or perhaps it's an issue of risk management, of minimizing one's exposure to political risk. That is, had GTE been able to reduce its initial investment and instead take its returns in the form of a management contract, the reduction in risk exposure may well have justified giving up larger potential equity returns. Staying away from parent guarantees of local borrowings might also be a cost-effective device for limiting risk. The one chink in GMAC's armor, as I see it, is its agreement to make good on all its local borrowings.

Before we adjourn, I'd like to ask the panel members to comment on two basic issues. One, do you find that you take a portfolio approach when evaluating the performance of your investments in developing countries? Given the long payoff periods

and the volatility of the individual investments, it would seem to be difficult to assess your global investment strategy by evaluating each country's performance on a stand-alone basis. My second question is, How much *financial* re-engineering do you typically have to do to make some of your investments in emerging markets work. That is, let's say that the numbers don't work, but you are convinced you want to be there. It's like the Avon decision to go into Brazil 40 years ago; the company knew it was a good strategic move, but it was hard to prove your case with the numbers. What do you do in such cases? Do you broaden your financial perspective to take account of strategic factors? Or do you change your financial strategy in ways that improve your expected returns?

LING: I'd like to respond to both of those questions. Do we take a portfolio approach to our new market investments? Absolutely. We have found that there's always going to be a problem market in any given year. In a diversified portfolio there will always be overachievers and underachievers. It always seems to be the case for us. I think it's only recently that Wall Street has understood that Avon is large enough, and diversified enough in its portfolio of markets, to withstand a shortfall in one or two of them—say, a major devaluation of a currency. Mexico, for example, is one of our largest profit contributors. And although we suffered a 40% drop in Mexican profits last year because of the devaluation of the peso, we still managed to deliver on the financial targets for the company as a whole.

Now let me turn to the second question: What sort of financial re-engineering can be done if the projected returns don't meet the hurdle rates? One approach we take is go back and change the business format to reduce initial investments or in-

crease returns. For example, our normal direct selling system is to ship an order directly to a Representative's home. But, in places like China, Indonesia and the Philippines, it's actually less capital-intensive for us to set up sales branches where the orders can be sent in bulk and the Representatives then pick them up using their own transportation. We also have the flexibility to manufacture locally from the outset or to import finished goods from other markets. In Russia, we took a different approach. Instead of direct selling, we started off with just a wholesale business; we just shipped bulk quantities of cosmetics to wholesalers in Russia. This approach significantly reduced our investment requirements and therefore our risk exposure.

SMITH: Paul, do you have any thoughts on these two issues?

BULL: I'm not sure how useful the portfolio approach is for evaluating GMAC's overseas operations. We really try to make sure that each entity is profitable in its own right. And as I mentioned, we structure them in a manner that tries to create all the benefits of our operations anywhere else in the world. Now, if there is a problem in a particular country, we're clearly prepared for one or two of these operations to have difficulties now and again; and, in that sense, our businesses can be viewed as a portfolio. But, again, we look for each one of these entities to be profitable in its own right.

With respect to re-engineering our investments, we are fairly active in exploring different organizational structures and financing arrangements. If the returns are not what we think they should be, we'll try and figure out whether there is a better way to do things. As I mentioned earlier, in Mexico we decided to change our operating structure into that of a joint venture and relocated the operation—and that has worked quite well. And we've done something similar in Sweden.

SMITH: Paul, how does GTE think about its investments?

COHRS: I can't describe GTE as taking a portfolio approach because we really have only three investments in emerging markets that have amounted to anything. As I said earlier, we are certainly willing to take the long view of these investments—and we thus expect to experience some volatility. In that sense, we take a portfolio view. But our main focus in emerging markets is to manage these things as best we can, to respond efficiently to problems as they arise, and to generate the profits over time necessary to justify the investment.

Financial re-engineering is going on all the time, and in all phases of these operations. As we look at these projects, we are constantly figuring out the best way to finance them and to minimize taxes. In Mexico, for example, we are looking at setting up a finance subsidiary because it has certain tax benefits. So, this kind of re-engineering is not only part of designing the initial investment; it also comes up if you run into problems like the one we ran into in Venezuela. That was essentially a massive financial engineering exercise that was undertaken to restructure the balance sheet and allow that entity to get back on it's feet again.

SMITH: What you've just described, Dan, may be the crux of the value added that managers really bring. Good managers ought to be good at re-engineering these projects, at operating their way out of a hole. In fact, I can't think of a better experience for a 20-something career finance guy in the company than to help clean up a couple of Latin American blood baths. These are enormously valuable learning experiences—experiences that will prepare these people to respond to the next crisis. And managing your way through crisis is an important part of what investing in emerging markets is all about.

So, on that cheerful note, let me bring this to an end by thanking all our panelists for doing such a great job.

ROUNDTABLE ON U.S. RISK CAPITAL AND INNOVATION (WITH A LOOK AT EASTERN EUROPE)

Sponsored by the

Financial Management Association

and

Baylor University

Chicago ■ October 9, 1991

DON CHEW: Good afternoon, and welcome to the First Annual Roundtable on Risk Capital and Innovation. (It may also be the last, of course, but I'm hoping it will have a successor.) My name is Don Chew, and I will serve as co-moderator of this discussion along with Bill Petty and John Martin, the principal organizers of this session. I am Editor of the Continental Bank's *Journal of Applied Corporate Finance.* The aim of the *Journal* is to "translate" outstanding research in corporate finance—conducted primarily by academics at our business schools and published in academic journals—into reasonably plain English for corporate executives. It attempts to provide a meeting ground for theorist and practitioner by stressing the practical import of the research.

With this aim in mind, I would like to use this discussion to give people in the business world a look at the thinking and research now going on at our universities and business schools on the subject of venture capital—or, to use the more inclusive term, *risk* capital. Stated as broadly as possible, the main issues are these: What is happening today in U.S. venture and other risk capital markets? What do we know about how the functioning of these markets affects the economy at large? And, can we use some of the practices of our own risk capital markets to help in the ongoing transformation of Eastern European economies?

Another promising line of inquiry is to ask what lessons from venture capital can be applied to the financial management of our large public corporations. For example (and I'm betraying my own biases here), some corporate finance scholars, notably Michael Jensen, have argued that the LBO phenomenon represents an on-the-whole successful application of some of the principles of venture capital—especially concentration of ownership and intensive monitoring by a financially interested board—to the management of mature public companies. More recently, Jensen has also argued that the "overshooting" and boom-bust cycle experienced by the LBO market were likely caused by a "contracting failure"—that is, by a rather gross misalignment of incentives between the LBO sponsors and the limited partners who provided the funds. And, as Jensen himself suggested, this kind of "contracting" problem may well explain the recent boom-bust cycle and thus part of the currently depressed state of the venture capital market.

The practices and conventions of our venture markets may also contain at least partial solutions to the problems faced by our largest companies in raising capital—especially the credibility gap with investors that academics have called "informational asymmetry," but also the so-called "agency cost" problem, the separation of ownership from control that reduces the value of many of our largest companies. Large public companies may also be able to learn from venture capitalists in funding and structuring their own R&D and other growth investments. For example, before the changes in tax law brought about by the Tax Reform Act of 1986, R&D limited partnerships appeared to be providing a tax-efficient vehicle for importing the entrepreneurial spirit into the corporate R&D effort.

This discussion has been set up to fall into two distinct parts. In the first—and by far the longer of the two—we will talk about current developments in U.S. risk capital markets. Where is the money coming from for new ventures? How is that changing, and why? How much does the capital cost, and how are the deals structured? In the second part, we will try to extend some of the insights from U.S. venture capital practice to current developments in Eastern Europe.

Venture capital alone clearly is not the answer to the problems of Eastern European economies. Perhaps the major information "asymmetry" now discouraging foreign investors is one that only government policymakers can correct—that is, the absence of well-defined property rights. But, on the basis of what we know about U.S. ventures, is there much in the private sector alone that can be done to stimulate new business development in the Eastern bloc countries? The privatization of state enterprise is also expected to play a major role in transforming these economies. So, to what extent can the conventions of our own venture markets be exported both to create new businesses and to bring about stronger incentives for improved efficiency within state-owned businesses?

To discuss these issues, we've assembled a group of people that represent a variety of perspectives and experience. And I'll now introduce them.

■ GORDON BATY

is the Managing Partner of Zero Stage Capital Company, a well-known venture capital firm based in Cambridge. He has over 20 years of experience in the formation, financing, and operation of new high-technology firms. Gordon was the founder and CEO of two early-stage, high-technology companies that he later sold to Fortune 500 corporations. He holds a Ph.D. in Finance from MIT and his latest book is *Entrepreneurship for the Nineties* (Prentice-Hall, 1990).

■ WILLIAM BYGRAVE

is the Frederic C. Hamilton Professor of Free Enterprise and academic coordinator of entrepreneurial studies at Babson College. Bill's current research interests center on high-potential start-ups, and he is the co-author of a book on venture capital that will be published by the Harvard Business School Press in 1992. Like Gordon, Bill also has considerable experience in the formation of high-tech ventures; and he served on the investment committee of the Massachusetts Capital Resource Company, a state-supervised venture capital fund. Bill, by the way, has led a double academic life, earning a Ph.D first in physics from Oxford and much later a doctorate in Business Administration from Boston University.

■ PATRICK FINEGAN

is a Partner of Stern Stewart & Co., a corporate finance advisory firm specializing in corporate planning, valuation, restructuring, and value-based incentive compensation. Pat leads Stern Stewart's industrial consulting practice for smaller and private companies.

■ KENNETH FROOT

is the Thomas Henry Carroll-Ford Visiting Professor at the Harvard Business School, where he teaches finance. Ken has been a consultant to many international companies and official institutions, including the International Monetary Fund, the World Bank, and the Board of Governors of the Federal Reserve; and he is currently serving as adviser to the Prime Minister of the Yugoslav Republic of Slovenia.

■ THOMAS GRAY

is currently Chief Economist of the Small Business Administration, where he has worked since 1978. His major duties include the development of a small business economic data base, and the supervision of research on the following areas: structural changes in small businesses in response to changing demographics; small business adoption of new technologies; and the relationship between small business development and the efficiency of the American economy.

■ JOHN KENSINGER

is Associate Professor of Finance at the University of North Texas. John has published widely on corporate restructuring and innovations in corporate organizational forms such as R&D limited partnerships, project finance, and network organizations. John is also co-author of *Innovations in Dequity Financing*.

■ GARY LOVEMAN

is Assistant Professor at the Harvard Business School. His research focuses on changes in both the demand and supply side of labor markets, and the human resource management issues posed by these changes. Gary is also currently involved in a field study of private small business development in Poland.

■ STEPHEN MAGEE

is the Fred H. Moore Professor of Finance and Economics at the University of Texas at Austin. He has served on the Economic Advisory Board to the U.S. Secretary of Commerce and the National Science Foundation Advisory Committee for Economics. Steve's primary research interest is the effect of law and regulation on economic efficiency and growth. He is currently a visiting professor at the University of Chicago.

■ JOHN MARTIN

one of my co-moderators in this discussion, is the Margaret and Eugene McDermott Centennial Professor of Banking and Finance at the University of Texas at Austin. John has written four books, as well as a number of articles on financial planning, corporate restructuring, and the impact of legal and organizational issues on financial management.

■ BRUCE PETERSEN

is Associate Professor of Economics at Washington University, and was formerly a senior economist at the Federal Reserve Bank of Chicago. His areas of research include industrial organization, public finance, and the microfoundations of macroeconomics. Bruce is especially interested in the question of how the choice of internal versus external financing affects corporate spending on capital investment and R&D.

■ WILLIAM PETTY

my other co-moderator, is Professor of Finance and the W.W. Caruth Chairholder in Entrepreneurship at Baylor University. Bill's research publications have been focused in the area of corporate finance, with a developing interest in entrepreneurial finance.

■ WILLIAM WETZEL

is the Forbes Professor of Management at the University of New Hampshire's Whittemore School of Business, and also serves as Director of the School's Center for Venture Research. His professional and research interests include the role of the entrepreneur in economic development, the financial management of high-growth private companies, and the functioning of informal venture capital markets. Bill also founded and serves as president of Venture Capital Network, Inc., a not-for-profit corporation designed to assist entrepreneurs in finding venture capitalists.

PART I: DEVELOPMENTS IN THE U.S. VENTURE CAPITAL MARKETS

CHEW: Let me start by asking Bill Wetzel to give us a working definition of "risk capital." How is that different from the venture capital market most of us are familiar with? And can you tell us a little about who you think are the major players in this market, how much money they have to contribute to entrepreneurs, and what sorts of activities they like to fund?

In Search of Angels

WETZEL: I'd like to start off by confessing, as Don did earlier, that my own biases are going to be reflected in my statement of the issues. The area I know most about in venture capital is the so-called "angel" marketplace (which I will get to in a minute), although I'm not unacquainted with the other aspects of the venture capital business.

But first let me say that the set of issues surrounding innovation in business and technology—and the role of venture and other forms of risk capital in stimulating the *process* of innovation—is just absolutely critical to the economic future of this country. In the most recent President's Economic Report to the Nation, it was pointed out that innovation and its diffusion accounted for over half of the increase in our standard of living over the last couple of generations.

It should also be pretty obvious by now that our large established corporations are no longer the primary engine of economic growth. During the 1980s—and this was well before the current recession set in—our Fortune 500 companies lost something on the order of four million jobs. Over roughly the same period, our smaller companies created something like 17 million net new jobs. On the

> I would suggest there are a quarter of a million active angels in this country—that is, self-made high-net-worth individuals who, to some degree, will help fund the next generation of entrepreneurs in the U.S. I would guess that they invest annually somewhere between $20 and $30 billion, which is at least 10 times the amount invested by institutional venture funds... As the institutional funds continue to reduce their already small commitment to early-stage seed financing, we ought to do everything we can to avail ourselves of the knowhow and the capital that are in the minds and the pocketbooks of the angels.
>
> —BILL WETZEL—

basis of these two numbers alone, I would submit that this country's entrepreneurs and its high-risk investors—and our success in strengthening the connection between these two groups—constitute one of our vital competitive edges in world markets. It's an edge we need to maintain in the face of global changes that could very quickly erode that competitive position.

Now, in thinking about what, if anything, we ought to be doing from a public policy standpoint to encourage the formation of risk capital, it's useful to begin by identifying both the principal innovators or entrepreneurs—that is, the potential users of

the risk capital—and the investors, or the suppliers of that capital. There are several distinct groups of both innovators and investors, and I'd like to attempt to set up some categories for classifying members of each of these two groups.

The innovators—the ventures that are creating the jobs, the new technology, the products, while also paying taxes and increasing exports—can usefully be divided into four categories: (1) unaffiliated, individual inventors; (2) start-up ventures; (3) large, established technology-based companies; and (4) non-profit organizations such as universities and teaching hospitals.

By far the most productive among these four groups, I would argue, are the firms that fall within the second category—that is, the start-up ventures. Now, I suggest we can usefully talk about three classes of start-ups: First is what I call "lifestyle ventures"— these are firms whose sales potential is limited to, say, $10 million. Second are what I call "middle market ventures"—those that have the potential to be a $50 million company in a relatively short period of time, but that are likely to remain privately owned rather than going public or being acquired by a larger company. Although these companies are relatively invisible, they in many ways constitute the backbone of the economy. They are the real workhorses in the job-generating process. And, third and finally, we come to the "high potential ventures"—firms whose growth potential is likely to go well beyond $50 or even $100 million within five years of starting out. These are the more visible companies, and they are the ones institutional venture capital funds tend to focus upon.

Now, to give you some idea of the relative contributions of these various classes of innovators, let me cite some numbers I've appropriated from the work of David Birch. Birch has concluded that there are on the order of 50,000 new start-ups in this country every year. And about 5% of these total start-ups would fall into one of these two larger start-up categories that I've called "middle market" and "high potential" ventures.

With respect to existing companies, Birch has pointed out that, of the roughly 10 million "small businesses" in the country, over 500,000 are growing faster than 50% per year. And some recent surveys lend support to Birch's estimates. For example, the median annual growth rate of *Inc.* magazine's list of the 500 fastest-growing private companies in America is something like 95% per year; the 500th firm on the list is growing at 65%. So those companies are out there, and they're doing some remarkable things. But they tend not to make the headlines.

Birch has attempted to translate these kinds of numbers into an annual venture capital requirement—or at least into an annual *equity* capital requirement—that is, the amount necessary to fund all of these innovators. His estimate comes out in the range of $50 to $100 billion a year. And, that, I think, sums up the importance of the question we're dealing with here today. That is, where is the capital coming from to finance this potentially very large group of innovative ventures?

Let me now turn from the users to the sources, the providers, of risk capital. Here I'm going to talk just about two sources: (1) the formal institutional venture capital funds and (2) the informal or angel market I mentioned earlier.

As you all know, there have been some disturbing trends in the institutional venture capital market. Last year, for example, there was only about $2 billion invested by the institutional venture funds—which

amounts to about half a day's trading volume on the New York Stock Exchange. And that money was invested in only about 1,000 companies. (Remember, Birch is talking about half a million companies that could use something on the order of $50 billion.) Also disturbing to me is the fact that, of the 1,000 companies receiving venture capital funding, only 250 were getting venture backing for the first time. The rest were follow-on fundings of companies already in venture capitalists' portfolios. And, perhaps even more troublesome, only $60 million dollars, or 3%, of the venture capital invested last year went into seed and start-up deals.

The professional venture funds, to be sure, never really have gotten much involved in financing genuine start-ups, but they're even less into it now. So, the issues I would raise are these: What are the causes of the current trend in venture capital? And can that trend be reversed, perhaps by enlarging the pool of funds currently available for venture capitalists? And if the answer is no, then who's going to bankroll our next generation of entrepreneurs?

The second source of innovative risk capital that I'd like to talk about is the "angel" marketplace, or the invisible providers of risk capital. I define angels as primarily self-made, high-net-worth individuals who are unaffiliated either in a family or managerial sense with the ventures they back.

To give you some sense of the importance of angels to new business growth, I will just quote very briefly from last Sunday's *Boston Globe Magazine.* In an article entitled, "Baby Boomers to Inherit Vast but Uneven Wealth," the author says, "By far the biggest financial gains from inheritances are likely to come not from the stock market but from parents who owned or started their own firms."

One of my favorite pastimes is looking at *Forbes'* portraits of the 400 richest people in the U.S., the annual ridiculous edition that comes out every October. I'm interested in it because I'm curious as to where the wealth comes from in these megabuck families. At the top of this year's list you'll find Henry Kluge, the German immigrant who founded Metromedia. Number two is Bill Gates, the 35-year-old founder of Microsoft, with a net worth of something like $4.8 billion. And third is Samuel Walton, an entrepreneur in the middle of Arkansas, who has also accumulated a fortune of incredible dimensions. The average net worth of the people on that list is $720 million; the bottom one is $275 million. Now, if you add up all this wealth, the people listed in the *Forbes 400* alone represent a pool of capital of $288 billion dollars!

Now, with respect to the entire angel marketplace, which of course extends well beyond the *Forbes 400*, I will cite the following data—and I can say this with some confidence, because nobody can prove me wrong; there just aren't any sources of really good data, which is one of the troubles with research in this area.

On the basis of this admittedly preliminary data, I would suggest that there are a quarter of a million active angels in this country—that is, self-made high-net-worth individuals who, to some degree, will help fund the next generation of entrepreneurs in the U.S. I would guess that they invest annually somewhere between $20 and $30 billion, which is at least 10 times the amount invested by institutional venture funds. To be sure, the angels put that money out in much smaller chunks than do conventional venture capital firms. I would also estimate that the number of companies receiving backing from angels is probably on the order of 80,000 to 100,000.

Using data we collected at our Center for Venture Research, we looked at sources of funding for new technology-based firms that were founded in New England between 1975 and 1986—that is, during the heydays of the venture capital industry. And we found that over 80% of the angel deals involved the commitment of less than half a million dollars. In the same period, only 13% of the venture fund deals were in that size range. Whereas the median angel deal was $150,000, the median venture capital deal was in excess of a million. Equally important, whereas 60% of the angel deals were seed or start-up deals, only 28% of the institutional venture deals were start-ups.

So, let me summarize this phenomenon by proposing that the angel marketplace is really not a competitive or alternative marketplace to the institutional marketplace, but rather a complementary one. I would also argue that, as the institutional funds continue to reduce their already small commitment to early-stage seed financing, we ought to do everything we can to avail ourselves of the knowhow and the capital that are in the minds and the pocketbooks of the angels. Because it's this group of individuals, not the institutional venture funds, that really are the farmers of American industry. They are plowing and seeding the ground for the next generation of entrepreneurs.

So the issues I would raise here with respect to angels—and, again, I consider them absolutely critical to the future of our entrepreneurial economy—are as follows: How many active angels are really out there? Are their investment decision models different from those of the venture funds? And let me tip my hand by saying I think that they are quite different. I think the angels respond to some personal "hot buttons," if you will. I'm convinced they get "psychic

income" that prompts them to behave in ways that are significantly different from venture fund managers who are trustees for other people's money. I suspect they have greater tolerance for risk and perhaps longer time horizons than conventional venture capital fund managers.

And I will bring this peroration to a close by suggesting that the active angels in this country are probably outnumbered by what I call "virgin angels"—that is, potential venture investors—by about five to one. And thus a very pressing issue for me is: How do we convert these virgin angels into streetwalkers?

CHEW: Bill, we know that the institutional venture capital market is down from a high of about $4 billion in 1987 to less than a billion this year. What, if anything, do we know about current trends in the angel market?

WETZEL: We don't have the data yet to be able to say. We are now in the middle of collecting it. But my sense is that the angels have become more active as the venture market has gone down.

CHEW: But doesn't that suggest that the two groups of investors are not just complementary markets, as you said? They may also function in part as "substitutes." The angels may be picking up the slack, funding some of the opportunities now being passed over by the institutional venture capitalists.

WETZEL: Yes, I agree. I think that's happening to some degree.

CHEW: Also, Bill, what you are calling the angels' hot buttons or psychic income may also be reflections of what economists call lower "information costs." Having angels instead of venture fund managers provide capital for start-ups may well be a highly efficient way of overcoming the large information costs that confront anybody trying to raise outside capital for risky ventures. In many cases, I would

guess that the angels either know the entrepreneurs personally, or they understand the business of running start-ups because they've done it themselves.

WETZEL: That's right. Angels typically fund people they know working in fields they know.

The SBA Looks at Angels

TOM GRAY: We at the Small Business Administration were fortunate enough to work with Bill when he first started measuring the angel market. We have done a number of follow-up studies since then, and I would like to use these studies as a basis for expanding on several points that Bill made.

In particular, I think this information issue that Bill and Don have raised is absolutely critical to how these risk capital markets work. And it's not so much information *costs* I have in mind, but what I would call the positive, or synergistic, information *benefits* that often arise from the union of investor and entrepreneur. In the angel venture market, investors often provide not only capital, but also their own expertise. From our studies, it appears that investors' willingness to commit their capital seems to depend on their own industry-specific knowledge, or on their familiarity with the particular marketplace that the venture is aimed at. The investors are bringing much more than their wealth, they're also bringing knowledge.

WETZEL: That's right, they're value-adding investors.

GRAY: I would also agree with Bill's statement that there appears to be growth of activity in this angel marketplace, even as the institutional market continues to decline. The Federal Reserve does a survey on an irregular basis of the wealth status of American individuals. They survey what they call "well-to-do" families, those with annual incomes of over $100,000. And one of the findings that's truly startling to me is that over half of those families own at least a partial interest in a business. These people either have a family or personal business, or they are angel investors in other people's businesses—or both. In fact, a lot of these people fall into the "both" category.

CHEW: That must include a lot of physicians and dentists?

GRAY: Sure. But, the evidence also suggests that 80% of angel investors are themselves entrepreneurs. They're not just wealthy people, they're people who have launched their own businesses. And that's what I mean when I say the angels are bringing knowledge to the market. By and large, the angel market is a matter of entrepreneurial people funding other entrepreneurs. To use Don's terminology, this has got to reduce information costs.

WETZEL: Let me add that there's evidence that 80% of the millionaires in the U.S. are self-made entrepreneurs. And this supports my contention that there's a large stock of untapped angel capital in this country.

Hurdle Rates in Venture Capital

BILL PETTY: Bill, there was a recent article in the *Wall Street Journal*, which cited your work, where the author presented a pretty compelling case for the relationship between the capital gains tax and the level of entrepreneurial investments. As part of the article, the writer described the four basic risk capital markets: (1) professional venture capitalists, (2) initial public offerings, (3) angels, and (4) mom-and-pop operations. Drawing on Commerce Department and Federal Reserve figures, he claimed that in 1986 these four markets produced about $180 billion in new entrepreneurial investments. He further esti-

> From our studies, it appears that investors' willingness to commit their capital seems to depend on their own industry-specific knowledge. Our evidence also suggests that 80% of angel investors are themselves entrepreneurs. They're not just wealthy people, they're people who have launched their own businesses. And that's what I mean when I say the angels are contributing much more than just their wealth, they're bringing their knowledge. By and large, the angel market is a matter of entrepreneurial people funding other entrepreneurs. And, to use economists' terminology, this has got to reduce information costs.
>
> **—TOM GRAY—**

mated that the make-up of these markets were two percent from professional venture capitalists (after removing leveraged buy outs and acquisitions), 13 percent IPOs, 23 percent from angels, and 62 percent from the moms and pops of the world. However, by 1990, the $180 billion market was thought to be about $90 billion—half of its former size of only four years earlier, with no apparent change in the make-up of the market.

BRUCE PETERSEN: These numbers just confirm my suspicion that the great preponderance of risk capital in this country is internally generated; it doesn't come from outside sources.

In fact, internal finance has probably always been the dominant form of finance for high-risk start-ups, with institutional venture capital accounting for a fairly minor share of that market.

And I don't believe that's about to change much either. If we can believe Bill Sahlman's recent article on venture capital in the *Journal of Financial Economics*, venture capitalists are using discount rates in the range of 40-60% in evaluating new projects. Such high discount rates probably reflect not only the great uncertainty and risk of such ventures, but also major information asymmetry and moral hazard problems. Remember that if entrepreneurs know a lot more about their chances of success than the people they're asking to fund them, this can lead to an adverse selection problem in which venture capital investors get stuck with a disproportionately large proportion of losers. For this reason, venture capitalists may rationally require 40% rates of return on individual projects.

Such high hurdle rates would in turn explain why venture capital plays such a limited role in start-up ventures. It just doesn't seem to me that many projects can pass that kind of a test. It doesn't appear that many venture capital deals are going to get done if those are the kind of discount rates they need to break even.

CHEW: What are the discount rates for angels, Bill? Is there a survey that tells us they will accept expected rates of return as low as, say, 25% because they personally know the people and the process they're working with?

WETZEL: I'm going to go out on a limb here. I think angels are very much like venture capitalists in that they don't want to lose money. They're just as diligent in investigating the downside risks. But I believe they attach more weight to the upside potential; this is what I mean by the "psychic income" I mentioned earlier. I think that if an entrepreneur can strike a deal with an angel, whether it's a woman looking for financing for an inner-city venture, or a new technology that the investor knows something about, the cost of that capital will be significantly lower than if you had to go to a venture capitalist.

So, I will go out on a limb and say angel money is cheaper as long as there's a good match between the hot-button or psychic dimensions of the deal.

GRAY: Our evidence suggests that most angels are satisfied to earn 20 to 25% per annum on their entire portfolio—and that's based on the assumption that they're going to lose half their investment in three out of every ten cases.

CHEW: But that's not much different from our historical experience with institutional venture capital, is it? Haven't venture capitalists earned averaged returns of between 20% and 25% over long periods time?

WETZEL: Actually, many probably only wish they had earned 25%.

PETERSEN: Yes, but you're getting away from my point here. My understanding is that that 25% is an *ex post* rate of return. That's what they earned in fact on the entire portfolio. My question is about what they *expect* to earn on successful projects in order to get that 25% return on their total portfolio.

GRAY: We asked the angel investors this *ex ante* question. What kind of returns are you looking for when you go into these deals, and their answer was 20% to 25%, which we thought was amazingly low.

WETZEL: Was that independent of the stage of the deal?

GRAY: Well, these people were mainly making first-stage investments. About 60% of the investments were first stage.

■

Bill Sahlman's study suggests that venture capitalists are applying *ex ante* discount rates of 40% to 60% to individual deals, partly out of fear that they may be getting more than their share of lemons. Venture capitalists may need this kind of "lemons premium," if you will, to ensure they will earn a high enough rate of return on their winners to make up for their losses. Such high hurdle rates would also explain why venture capital plays such a limited role in start-up ventures. I've got to believe these kind of discount rates are denying funding for a lot of otherwise viable projects.

—BRUCE PETERSEN—

PETERSEN: But if what you're saying is true about these lower angel discount rates, then that leads me to question even more the efficiency of the institutional venture capital markets. Bill Sahlman's study suggests venture capitalists are applying *ex ante* discount rates of 40% to 60% to individual deals, partly out of fear they may be getting more than their share of lemons. Venture capitalists may need this "lemons premium," if you will, to ensure they will earn a high enough rate of return on their winners to make up for their losses. And I've got to believe these kind of discount rates are denying funding for a lot of otherwise viable projects.

KEN FROOT: Well, it's not clear to me what these information asymmetries are in the case of new ventures, and whether there really is a potential adverse selection problem. Now, I agree that a medium-size company with a choice between the debt or equity markets might have adverse selection properties associated with it. That is, if the company's management thinks the stock is overvalued based on it's view of the future, then it will come to the equity market instead of raising debt. And the market is well aware of that incentive. In fact, that's probably the main reason why stock prices fall—by about 3%, on average—when new equity offerings are announced.

But, in the case of venture capital, you can only get that kind of adverse selection if the entrepreneur with the idea has somewhere else to go for capital. So, it doesn't seem likely that venture capitalists are getting more than their share of the lemons. They're probably getting all of them, good and bad alike—except perhaps for the ones who happen to have an angel, or happen to be pretty rich themselves.

So this brings us back to the question: Why are venture capitalists asking for 50% returns? I don't know the answer to that. But there may be some confusion here about whether that 50% is really an *expected* return. My suspicion is that Sahlman is really reporting expected returns *conditional* on succeeding. In other words, venture capitalists are probably saying to entrepreneurs, "Show me a business plan that, if it succeeds, is likely to deliver 50% per annum. Because I have all this downside risk, I need 50% returns on my winners to get my total portfolio return of 25%."

PETERSEN: Well, I'm not convinced that venture capitalists really are getting *all* the entrepreneurs, good and bad alike. A 1990 study by Barry, Muscarella et al. in the *Journal of Financial Economics* reported that only a minority of all firms that went public in recent years made any use of venture capital. So, I don't think you can so easily dismiss the possibility of a serious adverse selection problem here, especially given the functioning of this alternative angel market Bill's described.

Measuring Rates of Return in Venture Capital

BILL BYGRAVE: I've done a good deal of research in this area, and let me warn that you've got to be careful with these surveys and especially with self-reported rates of return. I was sitting in a room at Harvard one day in 1988 with people that represented about one third of venture capital in America. And Bill Sahlman had these people fill out a questionnaire in which they were asked to project over the next five years both their own portfolio's rate of return and the average rate of return of the entire industry. The most interesting finding to me was that these fund managers thought that, although their own realized rates of return would be about 25%, the industry rate of return would be 15% or less.

Another case in point: In the summer of 1983, Congress did a survey of some 250 venture capital firms. In that survey, the fund managers said they expected to earn between 30% and 40% per annum over the next five years. The actual returns reported by those same firms over the next five years turned out to be in the range of 12% to 14%.

So, self-reported numbers are extremely unreliable. It's a bit like bragging rights. Fund managers need to project high rates of return in order to go out and raise their next fund. You want to be able to say that you're expecting to earn 30% on your fund because 15% is not enough to impress the pension fund managers.

CHEW: Do all the studies of venture capital suffer from this self-reporting bias?

BYGRAVE: No, they don't. Thanks to *Venture Economics*, we've got the actual numbers now; we've got rates of return with high statistical reliability. I helped *Venture Economics* set up its returns database, the numbers were checked carefully, and we went to great lengths to make the sample of firms representative.

PETTY: And what do the numbers indicate?

BYGRAVE: Well, if you throw all the venture capital firms together, then the median annual return since 1986 is actually below 10%. But this broad average is not very meaningful. The year a given deal got its start seems to have been critical in determining its success, and thus it's more instructive to break out the returns by what venture capitalists call "vintage," or what economists call "cohort."

What we've found, for example, is that many of the funds started in 1978 earned better than 40% rates of return. 1978 was a wonderful year to start. There was a shortage of venture capital then, and there were a lot of new technologies just becoming commercial. Microprocessing was one. Biotechnology, although not commercial, was beginning to excite people. So there were a lot of entrepreneurs ready, as it were, to be invested in. And we also had this wonderfully hot over-the counter market in the early 1980s, which peaked in the first half of 1983. This enabled many of the deals in the late '70s to make their exit by going public and thus earn their 40%.

But each generation of funds since then has earned progressively lower rates of return. And, frankly, most of the post-1985 funds are down in the single digits, some are negative, and some are even going to fail. If they do fail, I believe they will be the first failures in the 45-year history of this industry.

Venture Capital Contracts and The Boom-Bust Cycle

CHEW: Is this a normal competitive cycle, the kind where you seem inevitably to get too many players chasing too few good deals?

GORDON BATY: I don't think we've been around long enough as an industry to say what's normal. I think we're looking at a bunch of first-time phenomena.

CHEW: But, given that everybody expects the other guy to earn 15% or less, isn't it the general perception of the industry that there are too many players?

BATY: I'm not so sure that's the case now. That was certainly the perception about three years ago. But because of the recession and a number of other sort of exogenous factors, the industry has changed a lot. You certainly don't have as many deals now, and you have a lot fewer players. Even those funds with significant amounts of liquidity are sitting on it because they know they're going to have great difficulty in raising the next pool.

CHEW: But, I thought the peak for venture capital deals came back in 1987, well before the recession?

BATY: That's right, and that was the interval when you in fact had too many dollars chasing too few deals.

CHEW: Gordon, my understanding is that venture capitalists like yourself that serve as general partner and put the deals together typically put up only about one percent of the equity—and the limited partners supply the rest. It thus seems to me that the dealmakers don't really bear much downside risk; it's all been put off onto the limited partners. Is it conceivable that this problem of too many deals could be corrected by making the venture capitalists put up more of the equity—say, as much as 5 or 10% of the deal?

BATY: I very much doubt that you could get the general partners to put up 10% of these huge pools. I think that it's a problem that would be more directly addressed by showing some decent returns so that we could attract more professionals into the industry.

CHEW: But wouldn't this possibly help reassure investors—some of whom may have already been burned once—if the general partners went to them and said, "Look, I'm putting 5% of my own capital on the line to show you that my interests are closely aligned with yours"?

BATY: I don't think it would have much of an effect. Although there are some wealthy venture capitalists who could do that, they don't represent a large fraction of the population.

But, as I said, I think there are probably other ways that you could achieve that same effect if that were a major concern. For example, the limited partner investors are increasingly insisting on a minimum rate of return—at least a Treasury rate of return—before the general partner is allowed to share in any upside. That's one mechanism that the big pension fund managers are increasingly insisting on.

CHEW: But the general partners still get their management fee every year, don't they? And that's not based on performance, it's just a fixed percentage of the amount invested.

BATY: Yes, but even that is under a lot of pressure.

CHEW: Really? That's interesting.

BATY: It's happening.

BYGRAVE: The gatekeepers are changing the industry.

BATY: That's exactly right.

BYGRAVE: By "gatekeepers" I mean people like Stan Pratt, who take one

---

> **If you're an entrepreneur today, it's literally harder now than it would have been in 1981 to raise your first million dollars to get a company off the ground. On an inflation-adjusted basis, there's probably 20% fewer dollars under management for seed and early-stage ventures....**
>
> **If there were some new kind of liquidity mechanism—something akin to what Salomon did in the early '80s to securitize house mortgages, some way to securitize a bundle of venture capital partnerships—this would help reduce this large illiquidity premium that's restricting venture capital investment today.**
>
> **—GORDON BATY—**

---

percent for taking money from limited partners and then choosing a fund like Gordon's to invest that money in. This trend has brought some standardization of the management fee and compensation structure. Today, for example, the capital gains residuals are almost always split 80/20 between the limited and the general partner.

But, Don, to come back to your point, I don't understand why you need this extra equity from the general partner. I would have thought the 20% participation in the upside would have been more than enough motivation for Gordon to go and do a great job for me.

CHEW: Well, it gives him an upside option, but it doesn't force him to bear any downside risk. And, as I think we saw from our experience in the LBO markets, this gives some dealmakers—the marginal players, if you will—financial incentives just to do deals, even when the payoffs are not likely to be there.

BYGRAVE: I don't agree with that. I think the downside risk is that he's going to want to raise another fund, and his ability to raise that fund will depend on the rates of return he provides his limited partners. So, there *is* a real downside here: Who wants to employ another unsuccessful venture capitalist these days? They're a dime a dozen.

BATY: Yes, we would have to go out and get a real job then. And that's a nasty business.

CHEW: Okay, but this reputation effect, if you will, doesn't seem to have prevented some dealmakers in the LBO and HLT markets from overpaying, from doing a lot of uneconomic deals. Only a few firms in the LBO market today seem to be working hard to salvage their reputations.

Gordon, would you agree that the venture market could conceivably have produced some players with short horizons—people who had already raised some money and were willing to do deals just to break into the business and get some of their limited partners' money invested?

BATY: I doubt it.

CHEW: I asked the wrong person.

GARY LOVEMAN: Don, you might be interested to know that one of the largest U.S. venture capital operations today invests 10% of the capital in any venture capital pool they manage for pension funds. And if you ask them why they use their own capital, they say it's essentially for the reasons you've just mentioned.

CHEW: I would assume that kind of statement is very helpful in raising money from the limited partners, especially in the current environment.

LOVEMAN: That's right, they are saying that they're in the deal *financially* as well as emotionally with their limited partners; that's very clear from the terms of the contract.

CHEW: Is there any sign that they are having more success in raising money than the average venture capitalist?

LOVEMAN: I'm not an expert on this, but my sense is that they've done very well. They certainly haven't had any problem raising money. And we're talking about several billion dollars under management.

Angels and Capital Gains Taxes

BATY: There's a whole raft of interesting things that Bill Wetzel raised in his opening remarks that I think are worth returning to. One I'm acutely conscious of is this fact that the amount of institutional money committed to seed and start-up deals has actually gone down in the last decade. So you have this enormous paradox: If you're an entrepreneur today, it's literally harder now than it would have been in 1981 to raise your first million dollars to get a company off the ground. On an inflation-adjusted basis, there's probably 20% fewer dollars under management for seed and early-stage ventures.

Many of the people with the skills and experience of putting together and financing early-stage technology start-ups have gone out of the business entirely. They've discovered it's a lot easier to make a living running a $400 million fund than running a $40 million venture capital fund. And there's just no way on earth you could possibly make 400 individual investments in million-dollar start-ups—which is about the average initial investment in this business.

So it is a source of concern. The angels do have to take up the slack.

Bill, you said you thought you perceived more angel activity now than perhaps in earlier years. And that puzzles me a little, especially given that we now have no capital gains tax differential. It's been pretty well proven that capital gains doesn't affect anything in the institutional world. But, in the world of angels, I would think that capital gains taxes are very important. What tax impact do you see, if any, on the proclivity of angels to invest today?

WETZEL: Well, the tax impact is a question not of direction, but of degree. Clearly angels respond negatively to increased capital gains taxes. But the work I've done, or am familiar with, seems to indicate that the effect of taxes is relatively marginal in the context of the entire investment decision. But, that does not mean that capital gains taxes are not hurting investment. One of the most insidious effects of the capital gains tax—and this will not show up in the statistics—is that it effectively locks up a significant part of the capital that might otherwise have been liquidated and then moved into other kinds of investment, including start-up ventures.

PAT FINEGAN: I disagree. The capital gains tax is more likely to affect the *structure* of angel-financed deals than the availability of financing. Most "angels" are themselves successful entrepreneurs with their own private companies. By adopting a holding company structure, they often plow otherwise taxable distributions from their core business into promising angel-like ventures.

The point is, unlike a large publicly-held company, where a purely diversifying investment adds no value if it can be replicated individually by its shareholders, many private companies avoid double taxation by managing individual portfolio decisions at the corporate level. Also, by entrusting a series of otherwise independent investment decisions by

passive family members to one steward, the CEO, fear of double taxation and of recognizing capital gains may actually *extend* the group's investment horizon, inclining it toward more venturesome angel-like investments.

Of course, not all such ventures will make Bill's census of angel deals, since many are structured as unincorporated business units, product extensions, or divisions. And those that do make the list may have poorer odds of success than ventures funded directly by individuals if (1) they hold out less equity participation for the venture's managers or (2) they exercise less than arm's-length restraint when advancing additional funds to the venture.

Where I see problems with the capital gains tax is in its second order effect—perpetuating holding periods. Because cashing out is so expensive, many of the private companies I work with have evolved into mini-conglomerates containing lots of what were once angel ventures—many of which have foundered for want of discipline or incentives, or been sustained only by repeated uneconomic cross-subsidies. In many private companies, diversification becomes so expansive, so ingrained, that it gives rise to significant "agency" problems. The tensions can become so fierce in second and third generations that active and passive family members literally tear the company apart.

WETZEL: Let me make one other comment on this issue of capital gains taxes. Economists have estimated that the public or social rate of return on investment in technological innovation is at least twice the private rate of return. So there's a compelling reason for public policymakers to stimulate this kind of investment. And, with minimal impact on the federal revenues, I believe we could target a capital gains tax differential to encourage direct equity investment in seed-capital or in smaller venture type deals. I'd offer as a model Senator Bumpers' proposed bill, which says that if an investment is held five years or longer, the gains tax drops to half the current rate; and if you hang onto it for ten years, it drops to zero. So, if we really believe that this is the engine that drives our economy, we ought to establish a capital gains tax differential for investment in start-up and early-stage companies that is designed to unlock more of this pent-up angel capital.

The Social Returns from Innovation

PETERSEN: Bill, what is the evidence that social returns from technological innovation are twice private returns?
WETZEL: Well, a secondary source is the President's Economic Report to the nation back in 1989. The primary source I have in mind was a study by Edwin Mansfield, an economist at Penn, who looked at some 18 innovations. And, although I don't recall either the nature of the innovations or the time period, Mansfield reported that the "social ROI," if you will—and, not being an economist, I'm not sure how he measured this—was over 50%, while the private ROI was in the 25% range.
PETERSEN: I have seen several other studies. Zvi Griliches has written a whole book on this, published by the National Bureau of Economic Research, that also finds very high rates of return from innovation. This large "wedge" between the social and private returns from private investment is thought to be the result of a diffusion or spillover effect. The innovating companies can't appropriate all the gains from their own innovations. And I think this inability to appropriate gains confronts all types of technology investments, not just those funded by venture capital.

> ■
>
> **Unlike a public company, where a purely diversifying investment adds no value, many private companies avoid double taxation by managing individual portfolio decisions at the corporate level.... Where I see problems with the capital gains tax is its effect of perpetuating holding periods. Because cashing out is so expensive, many private companies I work with have evolved into "mini-conglomerates" containing lots of what were once angel ventures—many of which have foundered for want of discipline or incentives. Diversification becomes so expansive, so ingrained, that it gives rise to significant "agency" problems.**
>
> **—PAT FINEGAN—**

FINEGAN: I would guess that the principal beneficiaries of innovations are the customers of the innovating companies. Take the case of the computer industry, where the prices of these high technology products coming out of Boston have fallen very rapidly.
CHEW: Can someone tell us a little bit about how economists measure these gains?
FROOT: It's actually a matter of looking at chunks of areas under demand curves where technologies lead to price reductions and quantity increases. Some of the gains fall into private hands, but the rest is assumed to be increases in consumer surplus.

GRAY: We've sponsored some of the follow-up studies to the original Mansfield work. And one study in particular, by Romeo & Rappaport, compares the effects of innovations by small firms to innovations by large companies. The study finds that the gap between the social and private rates of return is even larger for innovations by smaller companies. And this is what you would expect: A smaller company simply doesn't have the market power to capitalize on its innovation. Competitors typically come in and appropriate much of the gains.
PETERSEN: It's also interesting to note that the private rates of return on investment in technology and R&D tend to be much higher than the private rates of return on physical investment. This supports my contention that companies face much greater difficulty in raising capital for R&D than for physical investment. And higher *actual* returns typically imply higher *required* rates of return.

Accounting for R&D

WETZEL: That last statement reminds me that I really have a bitch with the accounting profession.
CHEW: I don't think you're alone in that, Bill.
WETZEL: But I don't know quite what to do about it. My problem is with the GAAP requirement that says that corporations must expense their corporate R&D immediately even though they can capitalize their investment in tangible assets. For companies that invest heavily in R&D, this reduces current earnings per share and thus presumably also reduces stock prices and managerial bonuses—and I use the word "presumably" by design.
CHEW: I'm sure some of us will question your assumption. But don't let me stop you.

WETZEL: Now, one possible solution to this accounting deficiency would be for companies to talk about their R&D in, say, the cash flow section of the corporate annual report. I think there's room there for management to make adjustments of their GAAP numbers and to explain to investors what sort of returns they expect to earn on that R&D. The accounting profession effectively assumes that R&D is going to have no return. It's all just money down the drain.

FINEGAN: Most R&D-intensive corporations do mention and, indeed, they highlight their R&D spending. In fact, it's a 10K requirement.

CHEW: John Kensinger has recently published a study of the stock market reactions to corporate R&D announcements. John, could you tell us what you found?

JOHN KENSINGER: John Martin, Su Chan, and I recently published a study in the *Journal of Financial Economics* that looked at the stock market's responses to 95 corporate announcements of increased R&D expenditures. We found that the average market response was significantly positive, on average—and this was the case even for a smaller sample of firms in which the announcements came in the face of an earnings decline. We also found the market responded very positively to announced R&D increases by high-tech firms, but negatively to similar announcements by low-tech companies.

R&D Limited Partnerships

CHEW: So, the stock market, as short-sighted as its critics have made it out to be, does seem capable of anticipating future benefits from R&D, even if the accounting conventions assume they are zero. And, John, isn't it also fair to say that the market seems to attempt to discriminate between promising and not-so-promising R&D?

KENSINGER: Yes, that's what our research suggests. But there's also been another trend in corporate R&D that may have been motivated, at least in small part, by accounting considerations. Many public companies in the '80s began to fund some of their R&D "off balance sheet" through a vehicle called the R&D limited partnership, or RDLP. Since the first RDLP was formed in 1978, almost $4 billion has been raised through roughly 250 individual RDLPs. While it's true that a change in the tax law in 1987 reduced the attractiveness of some of these deals, close to a billion dollars in RDLPs has been raised since then.

To list some of the deals done this year, Gensia raised $26 million through an RDLP this summer; Genetics Institute did one for $37 million in July; Synergen did one for $50 million in February; and PaineWebber Development raised a $50 million RDLP pool to fund corporate R&D projects.

CHEW: Are the limited partners basically the same institutional investors that might otherwise invest in venture capital funds?

KENSINGER: That's right. These are all private placements with institutional investors.

CHEW: And why would a company choose that vehicle instead of funding the project internally?

KENSINGER: Well, as I said, there were probably some tax and accounting considerations at work here. But I think there's something more fundamental as well. During the corporate restructuring movement of the '80s, investors rewarded companies for transactions that loosened management's control over assets. Such transactions in effect gave the decision to reinvest corporate profits back to the investors who originally supplied the capital. RDLPs, for example, are finite-lived entities that require that all profits from the venture be returned to the investors. By so doing, they

eliminate the temptation of corporate management to redirect corporate profits into unprofitable areas they want to subsidize. The high debt financing in LBOs and HLTs, especially those involving restructurings of conglomerates, accomplished much the same end. And investors have volunteered to pay significantly higher prices for projects where they have this kind of control. They'd rather finance specific projects than entire companies because companies last forever; once the capital's gone in, it's tough to get it out again. But if you invest in a discrete project—say, a drug development project—then your capital has a well-defined repayment schedule and the project has a finite life, usually ten years or less.

FINEGAN: But, in the case of a new drug project, wouldn't the parent company sponsoring the RDLP also serve as the distribution arm for the product? If so, it seems to me that at least some of these RDLPs represent a kind of strategic alliance. For example, a drug company whose special strengths are sales, distribution, and marketing may want to keep its R&D outside the corporate structure in order to provide an entrepreneurial environment and incentives for the key engineers that are going to take it into the next century.

KENSINGER: Yes, I agree that specialization and incentives are important motives behind these RDLPs. And, to add to your point about strategic alliances, PaineWebber Development puts together pools of R&D projects for institutional investors; and since there is no corporate general partner to market the products resulting from these projects, PaineWebber will often find or create marketing partners for these technology ventures. As the general partner, PaineWebber will build alliances between the technology and marketing ventures.

FINEGAN: Right, but it seems to me you could get the same specialization and incentive benefits by spinning off the corporate R&D effort into a partially-owned subsidiary, and then giving the key engineers significant ownership of the subsidiary. For this reason, I think one of the main motives for RDLPs was to allow companies to shift the sharing of income and losses for tax purposes over time.

BATY: I think the real reason for RDLPs runs deeper than that. Actually, there are a lot of benefits for investors, but one is the fact that their returns are a function not of profits, but revenues. They get their money back based on the top line, not the bottom line. They don't care if the product is sold unprofitably, they care only that it gets sold. And, unfortunately, revenues arrive a great deal more reliably than profits, particularly in start-up and early-stage technology deals.

CHEW: John, I thought there were also some major conflicts of interest between the sponsoring corporation that served as general partner and the limited partners supplying the capital. Wasn't it partly this problem that gave rise to the demand for R&D pools set up and managed by third-party investment bankers?

KENSINGER: That's right, but besides the third-party pools, there's been another major change in the structure of the deals that helps overcome this conflict-of-interest problem. Most of the more recent deals by single corporate sponsors—including one that was done by Genentech in 1989 and all the deals done this past year—now include substantial stock warrants in the sponsoring company along with the standard partnership units. Besides mitigating the conflict of interest, these warrants have also effectively allowed companies to place equity without going through a public underwriting.

■

During the corporate restructuring movement of the '80s, investors rewarded companies for transactions that loosened management's control over assets. Such transactions in effect gave the decision to reinvest corporate profits back to the investors who originally supplied the capital. RDLPs, for example, are finite-lived projects that require that all profits from the venture be returned to the investors. By so doing, they eliminate the temptation of corporate management to redirect corporate profits from profitable areas into other areas they want to subsidize. The heavy debt in LBOs and HLTs accomplished much the same end.

—JOHN KENSINGER—

LOVEMAN: In some cases, RDLPs are also being used as a vehicle to finance joint projects involving more than one company. And there's also an interesting "managerial" twist to these joint venture RDLPs. This idea came to me when I was listening to Scott McNealy of Sun Microsystems talk about their deal with AT&T. He said that there is an important difference between undertaking a joint *venture* and a joint *project* like an RDLP. The important diffence is that a project, as John said, has a contractually defined end. This means that if you have two companies with conflicting cultures and incentives, they have an incentive to get the thing done—basically,

just because they don't like having to deal with each other. The contractual structure *forces* them to do the unpleasant rather than let the arrangement die through sheer neglect. In the case of joint ventures or strategic alliances, by contrast, there seems to be a strong feeling among a lot of corporate CEOs that indefinite partnerships between two companies like IBM and Microsoft are almost certain to fail. It turns into an endless struggle until one side finally agrees to sell out its investment to the other.

CHEW: So, is this all we can expect from our much vaunted joint ventures and strategic alliances?

LOVEMAN: Well, that seems to be the case when the companies are very different.

A New Breed of Venture Capitalists

LOVEMAN: A number of the big venture capital funds have recently made huge investments in old-line companies that are now virtually bankrupt. These venture capital funds—which include one bank that you would all recognize immediately—come in and buy up a controlling interest. So some venture capitalists have wandered far afield from funding path-breaking technologies. They're in the business of *financial* restructuring.

BATY: You're making a point I think is worth amplifying here. When the general lament starts about how the flow of money into the venture capital industry has fallen way off from its former peak, I would suggest you go back and look at the composition of that peak. Of the $4 billion that went into the industry in 1987, $2 billion really went into just two funds that were doing financial restructuring. They don't represent *venture* capital, they're what Bill Bygrave and Jeff Timmons call *merchant* capitalists.

They're opportunists operating diversified equity pools whose aim is to stab whatever bleeds. They're not starting high-tech or innovative firms; they're not funding the Federal Expresses or the Intels of the future. They're white-gloves people who have no interest in getting dirt under their fingernails.

So, if you ignore that $2 billion of merchant capital, the real peak for venture capital in '87 was only around $2 billion. Now, I don't think we're going to reach $2 billion this year; in fact I think we'll probably end up at about a billion. But, while that's not that great, it's also not the disaster that is sometimes portrayed by people who write for the *Wall Street Journal*.

BYGRAVE: To evaluate the current level of venture capital, you really have to use a little historical perspective. As recently as 1974, there was only about $20 or $30 million a year in new money. On an inflation-adjusted basis, I think we're still on a much higher level than we were in, say, 1968, which was the last peak of the venture capital cycle.

BATY: Oh, easily.

CHEW: So, if you remove these LBOs and financial restructurings from the totals, then there is no trend, or just a slightly upward trend?

BATY: No, the trend is definitely down from the peak, or what I would call the period of "excess," of the mid-'80s. No question about that.

But, you see, that's the mechanism by which the returns are going to start coming back to some kind of historical average level. And there are two effects at work here. First, the investment decisions will become more conservative and the ROIs at harvest are going to be higher. And second—and although this has largely escaped the scrutiny of academia, I think it's going to turn out to be important—there's a tremendous secondary market developing in partnership

interests. When a bank goes defunct and they have on their balance sheet a $20 million investment in venture capital partnerships, there are venture capital funds set up to go bottom fishing and buy up those outfits at anywhere from 25% to 75% of the original cost basis—that is, at very low valuations. And that activity alone is going to give a significant uplift to the ultimate returns to the industry. So, even as we sit around and lament and hang crepe, I think the returns are on their way back up.

Now, the returns are almost certainly not going to rise to the 40% levels that Bill was attributing to 1982-83—and I think that will turn out to have been an anomalous era. What I think we will find is a return to something more equivalent, say, to the average of the last 12 or 15 years.

PETERSEN: Well, let me point out that in the case of this bottom fishing in the secondary market, the increase in investor returns does not represent an increase in the *social* return. It's just taking an asset off of one balance sheet and replacing it on another; one party's loss is another party's gain. And from a social point of view, it's thus a zero-sum transaction.

CHEW: But I think Gordon's also suggesting that this kind of *financial* investing performs a social function just by helping to revive the market. Strengthening the secondary market may be what's necessary to get the primary market back on its feet.

BATY: Yes, that secondary market activity will increase the propensity of some of the people who have pulled away from venture investment to move back into it once they see the returns coming back.

Illiquidity and High Expected Returns

BYGRAVE: Let me just say something about returns. Given our present knowl-

edge that historical returns have run on the order of 15% to 20%, this should help educate investors and help manage their expectations: 15-20% is really not at all bad for a pension fund that invests in, say, 60 different venture capital funds. Except for the last ten years, when the S&P has performed extraordinarily well, I think a normal rate of return on the S&P would run in the range of 7-10%. So, placed in this historical perspective, 15-20% for venture capital is probably quite acceptable.

FINEGAN: But it seems to me you have to adjust all these return calculations for interest rates. Have you attempted any of these adjustments?

BYGRAVE: I agree that we should. But, let's say that the expected rate of return on venture capital is 15%, and that the expected rate on the S&P 500 is half of that (as the actual return frequently turned out to be in the years between 1946 and 1981). In that case, I would say that 15% is not a bad return for pension fund managers absolutely swamped with money flowing in every day—and terrified about where they're going to invest it before the day is out. And I think once fund managers come to accept that 15-20%, not 30-40%, is the realistic range of expectations, they will actually find that historical yield attractive.

CHEW: Based on current long Treasury yields of about 8%, I would guess that the expected return on the S&P 500 would be at least around 14-16% today. If that's true, then a 15-20% expected return on venture capital seems like a pretty meager premium above the S&P 500 when you consider the illiquidity along with the level of risk.

BATY: Well, one man's illiquidity is another man's stability. The pension fund manager has a number of problems besides illiquidity. He needs the ability to plan liquidity; and venture capital can play a role in that planning. A whole portfolio of venture capital partnerships would not be a great pension fund. But one that includes a few funds makes all kinds of sense from a liquidity planning point of view.

BYGRAVE: I believe the entire pool of U.S. pension fund money is about $3 trillion. And let's say there is about $30 or $40 billion tied up today in venture capital. Now, if that amount could come from pension funds, then we'd still only be talking about one percent of all pension monies going into venture capital. So, when you say you're concerned about the illiquidity of venture capital, I think you ought to keep in mind that pension funds can certainly afford to have such small amounts in a relatively non-liquid form.

CHEW: But the question I'm asking is about the *marginal* effect of venture capital investment on the risk and liquidity of a portfolio. Investors' required rates of return, at least as I understand the theory, are supposed to be determined by the effects at the margin.

FINEGAN: This may be another reason why the market for angel financing seems to be going strong while institutional venture capital financing is down. I think it has less to do with individual risk preferences and people's willingness to put money on the line than with turnover expectations—with how frequently investors expect to want to enter and exit a security. As long as the time horizon between transaction costs is longer for a so-called angel than for a passive venture fund investor—as I think it inevitably will be—then the angel can afford to pay a higher entry price because the exit costs will be less; the exit costs will be lower not only for that particular investor, but for all subsequent investors.

To illustrate how illiquidity raises expected returns and lowers prices,

> The practices and conventions of our venture markets may contain at least partial solutions to the problems faced by our largest companies in raising capital—especially the credibility gap with investors that academics have called "informational asymmetry," but also the so-called "agency cost" problem, the separation of ownership from control that reduces the value of many of our largest companies. For example, large public companies could probably learn much from venture capitalists about how to fund and structure their own R&D and other growth investments.
>
> **—DON CHEW—**

look at the current condition of the junk bond market. I've been involved in some recent work valuing a number of junk bond portfolios owned by bankrupt institutions. Because of the lack of liquidity in the current environment, to sell a junk bond portfolio you essentially have to perform an IPO. You essentially have to re-market the portfolio to the investment community.

For a thinly traded junk bond, the costs of such a re-offering often run as high as 400 to 500 basis points. And if you consider that the average turnover of junk bonds in institutional portfolios is still, even in today's distressed marketplace, about 18 months,

and if you assume we will have an illiquid market in most junk bonds for at least another three or four more years, then you're talking about taking off 10 or 15% of the portfolio's value in transaction costs. This is the sheer cost of illiquidity.

So, I think the average expected turnover is a critical pricing variable in a highly illiquid market that, like venture capital, has high search costs associated with valuing the assets. And given this kind of illiquidity premium today, if you were a small private company seeking access to capital, you would do everything within your power to resist the temptation to use the debt markets currently. Small companies can't afford to give up that much money upfront. And, to a similar degree, I think the liquidity crunch is probably troubling the institutional venture capital markets. So, to the extent angels really do have longer horizons, they can be expected to fund more start-up ventures than the institutional venture firms.

BYGRAVE: Another potential problem with venture capital investment is that pension funds are forced to undergo quarterly performance evaluations. When we were surveying pension funds and banks on their propensity to invest in venture capital, one pension fund manager complained that he was being evaluated not on a quarterly, but on a *monthly* basis—just like the people on the trading floor. Now, it's obvious you can't judge venture capital monthly. Almost all the value is in the residual, which is just not liquid.

FROOT: I agree with Bill that this kind of periodic evaluation process could certainly skew investment decisions away from highly illiquid investments. And this is not a problem of short-sighted investors or market myopia; it really reflects a kind of principal/agent problem between the pension beneficiaries and the pension fund manager. If you're a pension fund manager managing money for others who don't share your confidence in your own ability, it's easier for you to demonstrate your confidence by volunteering to subject yourself to a review 12 times a year instead of only once or twice. And if you know you're going to be reviewed 12 times a year, then you're going to want to concentrate your holdings in relatively liquid investments with values that can be readily confirmed.

Increasing Liquidity

BATY: You know, if this group of august thinkers had a valuable contribution to make today, it would be to come up with some workable proposals for adding liquidity to the venture capital pool. Illiquidity is one of the main reasons why a lot of investors such as small pension funds and small insurers stay away from it.

CHEW: Do you mean an exit route?

BATY: Yes, an exit route, or possibly some other kind of liquidity mechanism—something akin to what Salomon did in the early '80s to securitize house mortgages. If there were a way that could be proposed by somebody a lot smarter than I to securitize a bundle of venture capital partnerships, that would eliminate one of the main reasons why this enormous risk premium is expected. As you point out, it's not a risk premium so much as it's a liquidity premium.

CHEW: Well, how efficient is this market for rescuing distressed venture funds that you were talking about?

BATY: It's not efficient at all. It's as inefficient as anything could be.

WETZEL: I have an idea that's been stewing around in my head that I've never really explored thoroughly. The managers of pension funds are assumed to be skilled at managing portfolios of listed securities and in evaluating the track record of estab-

lished companies. And they are also permitted by ERISA law to invest some fraction of their portfolio in the venture capital business.

Why wouldn't it make some sense to amend the ERISA law to permit pension fund managers to put a fraction of their assets into established *private* companies, where they really do have the technical ability to evaluate the merits of the investment? Pension funds could thereby provide an exit mechanism for seasoned companies that don't want to go public or be acquired. This would add an element of liquidity to the system—one that would also end up allowing money to be recycled back into the early-stage developments that Gordon manages. It strikes me that there's a real opportunity here to add an element of liquidity; and this liquidity would permit professionally-managed venture money to circulate much more rapidly than it currently can because of the limitations of the acquisition and the IPO market.

BATY: It's an interesting thought. It certainly addresses one of the principal problems of the venture capital process. It's real easy getting into deals, but it's very hard to get out of them. And it's particularly hard to get out of deals in the intervals when the NASDAQ is in the toilet. It's particularly difficult to get out during a recession when the companies that you would normally sell your deals to are themselves struggling. I think any alternate mechanism that would provide liquidity to the investors in venture capital pools is going to do a lot to recycle the pool itself.

BYGRAVE: Gordon, do you mean it will help us unload the losers?

WETZEL: Well, presumably the pension fund managers will be able to separate the lemons from the winners in these more established companies. That's why I think there's some reason to believe this would work.

PETTY: The American Stock Exchange recently announced that it's going to begin to list emerging companies. Will this have any significant impact in this situation?

BATY: Could be. Any time people reduce the standards for listing, we all cheer.

More on Angels

LOVEMAN: Let me just add one thing there. As a consequence of spending a lot of time in Warsaw recently, I've gotten into a number of discussions with venture capitalists—the kind of people who these days are getting invitations to Poland all the time. And from these talks I've reached the conclusion—and this is admittedly a very unscientific discovery process—that the art of venture capital is not running numbers or surveying the industry (although venture capitalists do employ lots of Ken's and my Harvard MBA students to do these things). The real art of venture capital seems to be in deciding whether the guy or the gal who runs the company is the right person to back. And if the answer is yes, then it's largely a matter of building the right incentive structure for that person.

Now, when I heard this concept of angels—one which I hadn't heard before today—that got me thinking that these wealthy self-made entrepreneurs are probably the people who are best qualified to make these kinds of judgments about who to back. They may well understand the world in which they've gained their own wealth far better than the average venture capitalist. Bill Gates, for example, could personally finance a pretty big venture capital fund if he wanted to; he meets the minimum capital requirements quite comfortably. The alternative, though, is that he becomes an angel and does it on his own. And if he does it on his own, it's presumably because he believes he has better information about the individuals who run these operations than the venture fund managers.

BYGRAVE: Gates does fund some ventures, by the way. For example, he and a number of other wealthy individuals funded ICOS, a bio-pharmaceutical start-up. He invested $5 million in June 1990. His investment was worth almost $14 million one year later when ICOS went public.

WETZEL: So do Ross Perot and Steve Jobs.

BYGRAVE: And so did Robert Noyce of Intel. And the d'Arbeloff brothers used to do the same thing in the Boston area. One reason these people are encouraged to participate is the kind of certification effect their participation has. If Noyce is willing to put his own money into it, this puts a seal of approval on the deal.

CHEW: And they can then raise capital from others on the strength of that participation?

WETZEL: That's right. It's a form of signalling.

Changes in Deal Structure

PETTY: Gordon, given the declining rates of return in venture capital, have there been any pronounced changes in the structure of the contracts between the general partners running funds such as yourself and your limited partners? And a related question: Have there been changes in the contracts between you and the entrepreneurs that you provide funding for?

BATY: Well, I guess the most obvious change since the peak period of 1987-88 is probably the fact that so many of the people who used to fund early stage and start-up ventures don't do it any more. That means those of us who still do it—and we're one of a handful of companies left—have really almost no competition in funding early stage deals. So there's no restraint on our avarice other than our own self-interest in making sure we leave the entrepreneur with enough equity to motivate him to get him out of bed in the morning.

PETERSEN: So, you're leaving the entrepreneur with a *Malthusian* rate of return?

BATY: Thank you for giving me a label.

CHEW: Gordon, how do you sort out the good deals from the bad? Do you use the contracting or negotiating process to in some sense flush out the entrepreneur you're considering funding? Do you offer him a menu of deals and then ask him to choose one?

BATY: Yes, we do in fact.

CHEW: Can you tell us a little bit about that?

BATY: Well, the price is only one dimension of a really complex, multidimensional negotiation. You look at one of these investment agreements for a preferred stock placement, for example, and there must be 15 variables. There's a question of whether it's participating preferred or straight preferred, and there's a question of the conversion rights and when they first come into effect. It's sometimes a question of whether there's a dividend due, under what circumstances it's payable, and whether it accumulates or not.

So, the poor guy across the table has to have a Ph.D. in finance to figure out where his self-interest lies. If you push down on one variable, another one invariably pops up. It's like pushing the bubble around in an air mattress.

But, at the end of the day, the deals are tougher now than they were two or three years ago. That's the principal distinction. We expect our entrepreneurs to do more with fewer dollars. I think that, as an industry, we venture capital people are inclined to undercapitalize things. And there's a strange conspiracy at work between the entrepreneurs and the investors that almost guarantees things are always undercapitalized and starving: We don't want to put more money at risk than we have to, and the entrepreneur doesn't want to put more equity on the table than he has to. So everyone kind of joins hands and jumps off the cliff without the money that we should have—and we all pretend that we believe the business plan.

CHEW: But, Gordon, that partly makes sense, doesn't it? The entrepreneur gets a review, in effect, when he runs out of cash. And it seems to me the earlier he's willing to submit to that review, the more confidence he's expressing in the deal. And this in turn gives you more flexibility as to whether or not you want to fund future development. It gives you a valuable option.

And the more willing the entrepreneur is to undercapitalize himself, as I said earlier, the stronger signal he's sending to you about his own level of confidence in his plan. So, in this sense, it may make a lot of sense to undercapitalize entrepreneurs at the start; it may be an effective signalling mechanism.

BATY: Well, you've just sort of epitomized the Yankee type of venture capital deal as opposed to the California deal. In fact, if we could, we would have a closing every week. That's the way we Yankees tend to think. And it may in fact turn out to be a bit penny-wise and pound-foolish, given the enormous success of the California venture capital community relative to the depressed condition of the Northeast in recent years.

CHEW: Is that a well-established view, that the California style works better?

BATY: Well, if you look at the enormous growth of Silicon Valley in recent years, it's easier to accept this argument than to disprove it.

BYGRAVE: That would be a good area to research, to see if in fact rates of return have been systematically higher in the California ventures than in the Northeast. But there may be some contaminating factors at work. For example, we've got a huge recession in Massachusetts. We're in the third year of what is at least a five-year recession, in my opinion. We have not had a billion-dollar start-up since Prime Computer in 1972. Since then, California's had Apple, Sun Microsystems, Tandem, Seagate, and Conner. So, it may just be that California happens to be geographically situated at the right point. That's where the chip manufacturers are, and since everything's based on the chip these days, location may be the critical factor in the California successes.

But, maybe you're right, Gordon. Maybe it *is* a matter of too much parsimony among our venture capitalists in Massachusetts.

Higher Investment Stakes and Strategic Alliances

STEVE MAGEE: Well, what's happening to the rate of innovation in the U.S. today? You've got to keep in mind that we're always going to pass up some good deals. There's type one and type two errors, and we're going take some dogs and we're going to let some great ones get away.

BYGRAVE: Well, there was a big fuss among the federal policymakers that a lot of promising high-tech people, the next Ken Olsen and the next Bill Gates, weren't getting funded. But I don't think there was really any evidence for that.

Gordon, do you have a strong sense that today there are really deserving entrepreneurs and deserving technologies that aren't being commercialized, either not at all or not as fast as they could be through lack of venture capital?

■

John Kensinger and I have been studying cases where a corporation makes a minority equity investment in a key supplier or customer. In the past ten years, for example, IBM has made 13 such investments and Hewlett Packard has made six. Most of these represent sums far in excess of the typical venture capital investment. This is evidence that large integrated corporations are increasingly serving as a source of risk capital. Further, as the size of the investments required to enter high-tech industries escalates, I think we will see new start-ups become increasingly dependent on financing sources other traditional venture capital.

—JOHN MARTIN—

BATY: I don't have any real sense of that, Bill. And it's a *lack* of evidence, not evidence to the contrary. I just have no way of knowing. We have a constant parade of people through our office. Every morning I've got a foot of business plans on my desk. And the question I ask myself every day is, Which *one* is going to get read that day? Because one a day is about all I can handle.

But, even with the tight conditions today, I suspect that there are probably more or less the same number of underfunded geniuses going without today as there were a decade ago.

BYGRAVE: Al Bruno and Tyzoon Tyebjee did some work for the Na-

---

tional Science Foundation that attempted to identify the opportunities that got away—the ones that never got funded. The premise underlying this work was that deserving entrepreneurs weren't getting funded and that, somewhat like the unemployed, they got discouraged and dropped out of the entrepreneurial pool. But their work didn't come to that conclusion. It suggested instead that entrepreneurs don't disappear, but rather they sort of hover around, and then come back and try again—and sometimes they succeed in getting venture capital.

GRAY: We haven't really addressed the size issue in this discussion. We've been talking about the very bottom end of the market, with the angels, and then we've moved up a little bit to relatively small corporate projects. We also mentioned that back in the late '70s there were a lot of technologies ripe for the picking. A lot of those technologies have matured. And the reality today is that, where we once needed relatively small investments to develop, we now need large investments to play in the game.

I'm thinking in particular of a case like the relationship between Compaq and Conner Peripherals. Conner had an innovation that had to be marketed quickly if they were going to grab the market. If they went in slowly and fought to raise the capital, their ideas would have been appropriated before they could have captured a market share big enough to warrant their investment. So Compaq came to them and said, "Not only will we buy the product, but here's $100 million to help make it."

That has raised the investment ante in the game tremendously, and it strikes me that's what's happened to a lot of this market. We're now talking about biotechnology and about computer-related innovations. These are areas where the price of entry is much higher than the venture capital market was ever equipped to deal with. And there's a demand for speed as well as capital: If you're going to capture the gain from your investment, the competition is such that you have to be able to move quickly, and move quickly with large dollars.

FINEGAN: Do you expect to see this reflected in the number of strategic alliances forged each year in high-tech land? They seem to be growing at a rapid rate.

GRAY: I think they're growing tremendously. In fact, I suspect that simply because of the increase in the size of the investments required, U.S. corporations are now taking the place of venture capital firms in a great many instances.

JOHN MARTIN: I think you're right, Tom. John Kensinger and I have been studying cases where a corporation makes a minority equity investment in a key supplier or customer. In the past ten years, for example, IBM has made 13 such investments and Hewlett Packard has made six. I don't know the dollar amounts involved in most of these cases, but I can tell you that most represent sums far in excess of the typical venture capital investment. For example, Ford, Kubota, and Tenneco together invested some $250 million in Cummins Engine. Now, it's true that Cummins and other recipients of this kind of financing are certainly not the typical start-ups served by venture capital firms; but I think this is evidence nonetheless that large integrated corporations are increasingly serving as an important source of risk capital.

Let me conclude with the example of Hal Business Systems. Hal is a new start-up enterprise that has offices in Austin and is a member of the Austin Technology Incubator. The company was founded by a former IBM employee, Andrew Heller, with the financial backing of Fujitsu Corpora-

tion. The interesting thing about this start-up is the magnitude of the start-up financing. Hal obtained a commitment for over $40 million from Fujitsu before the firm was to have a sellable product.

So, I think that corporations may well be playing a venture capital role in these high-dollar start-ups. Further, as the size of the investments required to enter high tech industries escalates, I think we will see new start-ups become increasingly more dependent on financing sources other than traditional venture capital.

BYGRAVE: I don't believe that start-ups are turning to corporations simply because of the amount of money they need. Rather, it's because corporations are willing to offer the entrepreneur cheap capital, relatively speaking, in the hope of receiving benefits from a strategic alliance with a dynamic young company. That is why some "high-profile" entrepreneurs such as Finis Conner, the founder of Conner Peripherals, prefer to get their funding from corporations instead of venture capital firms.

Look, for instance, at how Steve Jobs financed NeXT. He raised about $20 million from Ross Perot for about 16% of NeXT's equity, and then, a couple of years later, raised another $100 million from Canon for another 16%. Remarkably, even after Canon's investment, Jobs still owned more than 50% of NeXT, with a paper worth of $300 million plus. And NeXT was then a company that had not shipped product. If Jobs had instead financed NeXT with venture capital, he would not have owned even 10% at that point—maybe much less. Canon was more generous than a venture capital syndicate would have been with its financing terms because it was entering into a strategic partnership with NeXT. Besides getting a share of NeXT's equity, it also got marketing rights to NeXT's products.

Now when it comes to harvesting mechanisms, it may be that corporations are playing an increasing role. We know that, since around 1985, proportionately more venture-capital-backed companies have been acquired by corporations than have gone public, which is a significant break with the past. Certainly, there have been some spectacular acquisitions of venture-capital-backed biotech companies by multinational pharmaceutical corporations. In some of those cases, the amount of money was probably more than could have been raised through a public offering, let alone a private venture capital placement. For instance, the Swiss pharmaceutical giant, Roche Holdings, bought 60% of Genentech for $2.1 billion. I think it worked out to be a P/E of about 80. But we are not talking about a start-up here. Genentech is a 15-year-old public company with revenues of about $500 million. Again, as with Canon's investment in NeXT, those kind of valuations are justified only by the investing company's perception of substantial strategic synergies from the deal.

Let me also mention that I know someone who is starting a venture capital fund, and right in his prospectus it says that the harvest mechanism for his portfolio companies will be selling them to strategic partners. In fact, it's partly because of the unreliability of the market for public offerings that strategic partnerships have become so popular in the biotech industry.

The Next Wave

BYGRAVE: I think we're all waiting for another technology wave. There's only so many technologies that come along. We had a miraculous wave of technologies in the '70s and I don't see anything as spectacular as the personal computer on the horizon.

The PC business went from zero to a $100 billion business worldwide in 15 years. The biotech sector, by contrast, has got only four billion dollars of total revenue right now. Communications also have a lot of promise. But I really don't see any miraculous wave of electronics technology that's going to generate a $100 billion market in ten years.

Cold fusion could have been something very big. It promised an abundant—indeed, a limitless—source of cheap electricity. Unfortunately, it turned out to be a mirage. If it had been real, it would have solved the problem of generating electricity, which is one half of the electricity equation. But we may now be close to a solution to the other half of that equation, which is minimizing electricity losses. High-temperature superconductors show great promise for transmitting electricity with little or no losses. They have the potential to trigger a revolution bigger than anything since electricity was first used commercially a century of so ago. But we're not there yet.

So development in the biotech sector and these other areas isn't going to replace the jobs being lost in the PC market anytime soon. Maybe they will eventually, but it will take a while. According to one estimate, biotech won't be a $50 billion market for another decade or so.

BATY: I'm not smart enough to say what's going to be the key technology in a decade. When I was working for Burroughs back in 1979, I bought one of those crafty little Apple II computers because they ran a spreadsheet. In those days, a computer to me was something that would have filled this room—that was a computer! So I wouldn't have invested any money in Apple, or Kaypro, or any of those people.

BYGRAVE: That's right. The technology field is just full of gurus who have

> Since around 1985, proportionately more venture-capital-backed companies have been acquired by corporations than have gone public, which is a significant break with the past. In some of those cases, the amount of money was probably more than could have been raised through a public offering, let alone a private venture capital placement. For instance, the Swiss pharmaceutical giant, Roche Holdings, bought 60% of Genentech for $2.1 billion. Those kind of valuations are justified only by the investing company's perception of substantial strategic synergies from the deal.
>
> **—BILL BYGRAVE—**

made wrong forecasts. In 1943, Tom Watson predicted that the total world market would be ten very large computers. Ken Olsen said he couldn't imagine why anyone would ever want a computer at home—and that, by the way, was after committing to make the Rainbow personal computer.

A Network for Angels

GRAY: When we did our surveys of the angel market in '87-'88, one of the questions we asked was: If there were additional ventures available with characteristics similar to those ventures you've already invested in, would you have been willing to make addi-

tional investments? From the responses, we estimated there was over 50% excess capital available at that point in the angel market. And I've argued ever since then that we have an opportunity-constrained situation here. Capital is clearly not the scarce resource.

CHEW: But, again, there may be very high search or information costs in linking angels to entrepreneurs. As you yourself suggested, Bill, angels are likely to fund only people they know in businesses they know. And that's a very real constraint.

FROOT: Well, from Gordon's story, it also sounds like human capital may be constrained as well. There may be a real shortage of people like Gordon with the experience and knowhow to read these business plans and turn them into productive businesses.

BATY: I can manage about ten companies in my portfolio at any given time, but I can't manage twenty. So if you handed me twice as much money as I'm currently managing, I could either decline it, or I could go out and hire some bright MBA to run part of the portfolio. But the average quality of the management is going to go down.

BYGRAVE: Maybe it will go up, Gordon. Who knows?

BATY: Right, maybe it will go up—or sideways. I withdraw the foregoing.

BYGRAVE: When I started my first company back in 1970 with venture capital, it was a tremendously secretive industry. There were no directories then and you didn't have any idea whom to contact or how to go about doing it. Today, there's almost an overabundance of people like myself and Bill Wetzel who will freely supply information about the venture capital industry—about how to negotiate with Gordon, and how to raise capital. And that must surely have helped to increase the efficiency of the marketplace.

WETZEL: But there has not been a great deal of this kind of activity in the *angel* marketplace.

BYGRAVE: No, you're right. You're virtually alone, Bill, in providing a means for people to find angels. Sometimes would-be entrepreneurs come to see me, and I tell them, "Oh, that's not a venture capital deal, that's an angel deal." And they say, "What's an angel? And you then explain to them that an angel is this thing with feathers and wings.

Then they say, "Well, do you know of any?" And of course you do, but you don't want to risk a friendship. So you instead tell them to call Bill Wetzel because Bill's got this venture capital network, which has just been moved to MIT. And before Bill tells you more about it, let me say just that I think the formation of this network is a very positive step. It should really improve the efficiency with which we connect promising entrepreneurs with other entrepreneurs with capital.

WETZEL: Well, this angel network is still an experimental undertaking. It was started at the University of New Hampshire, where I teach. And it's just been moved down to MIT as part of the MIT Enterprise Forum. I hate to use the analogy, but I can capture the sense of it fairly easily by calling it a "dating bureau." It gives an individual investor who will never be listed in the Pratt's Guide to Venture Capital Sources (they keep very low profiles for obvious reasons) a chance to remain anonymous, but still have an opportunity to look at a partially screened deal flow.

Our entrepreneur database is also confidential. It requires an entrepreneur to submit a two-page executive summary of the business plan (that appears in our database without the name of the entrepreneur or any proprietary information). If there seems to be a match between the entrepreneur's proposal and an angel's

---

■

Stewart Myers and Nicholas Majluf demonstrated that information asymmetry leads to underinvestment by "outsiders." Nowhere is this problem more acute than in the case of risk capital, particularly when it comes to bank financing. While venture capitalists can structure deals to reduce the problem significantly, U.S. banks are prevented from doing so by regulation. In Western Europe, for example, where banks have far greater freedom in contracting than in the U.S., they have provided at least 40 percent of venture funding, as compared to only 5 percent in the U.S. (mostly through SBICs, which are themselves a dying breed).

—BILL PETTY—

---

expressed area of interest, those pieces of data change hands. And if there's further interest, the two are introduced to one other, and it goes on from there. We have not yet proven that this network is going to be a significant factor in the angel marketplace, but we have high hopes for it.

MARTIN: Bill, I would like to add briefly that we have started a similar *dating* service in Austin. It is called the Texas Capital Network and it is a non-profit corporation that operates as a member firm in the Austin Technology Incubator. Although the Network is less than two years old, it has already succeeded in matching up a number of small firms with investors.

PART II: EASTERN EUROPE

PETTY: Well, let's turn now to the role of venture capitalists in funding growth in Eastern Europe. Is there a role for institutional venture capital? If not, then where is the new money going to come from?

An Alliance between Public Capital and Private Management

BYGRAVE: The largest venture capital fund in the world is in fact an English institution called "3i." Quite interestingly, it was started in 1945 by a socialist government in those dark days when the socialists were busily nationalizing all of the strategic industries—coal, steel, railroads, transportation. And yet, in spite of these unlikely beginnings, that company has an extraordinary record. It has invested in some 10,000 companies. And, as of year-end 1991, the company had over $5 billion under management that was invested in about 4,000 active companies in its various portfolios. It invests as little as $100,000, and as much as $10 million, in any single venture. It also provides funding for companies in all stages of development. In 1989, for example, it did over 200 start-ups, and about 800 deals in total. Its return on equity in the late 1980s was about 25% (although, unlike most venture capital firms, it has considerable debt as well as equity on the right-hand side of its balance sheet).

What is especially interesting to me is the difference between how this British venture fund operates and the way most of our funds operate in the U.S. In 1989, for example, 3i paid out only $20 million in dividends while reporting $464 million in capital gains. The fund manager's policy is to plow most of their current returns back into new investment; and the company's been doing that ever since its beginnings. U.S. venture funds, by contrast, operate very much on a project-by-project basis, returning most of their profits to the limited partners as they are earned.

Now, let me also say that although the initial capital for 3i came from the Bank of England together with the five major English banks, the fund itself is run completely privately, with no outside interference from government. And it seems to me that this kind of alliance between public funding and private management might be applied to Eastern Europe. This might provide a superior alternative to the "impatient" model of venture capital in the U.S. It's true that most U.S. funds will give ventures as long as ten years to develop, but that may not be long enough, especially in a case like Eastern Europe.

BATY: That's right. You don't want a lot of limited partners who are sitting around looking at quarterly IRRs.

BYGRAVE: Exactly. And so the important thing here, I think, is to get the central banks involved. At the same time you want to give the investors strong incentives to keep the money in the venture capital partnership as long as possible. So, if it were European banks that were involved, for example, you might want to offer some special tax benefits for keeping the money invested.

3i, incidentally, has also cloned their model in India, with Grindley's Bank, and in Australia with Westpak. And, to my knowledge, the fund with Westpak is one of the only two viable venture capital funds remaining in Australia. The other Australian funds were started mainly in Victoria using a lot of government subsidies and initiatives. And the outcome has been an enormous waste of capital in terrible deals that have been ruined by the combination of inexperienced venture capitalists and too much government interference. Almost all the Australian venture capital funds have failed miserably. But it seems to me that some modification of the 3i model that unites public money with private management might have a shot at working in Eastern Europe.

GRAY: The World Bank has funded a number of small, venture-type groups in Eastern European countries, which is a departure from their typical role of funding large infrastructure projects. But, as far as I know, they have lost every penny they've ever put into Eastern Europe.

BYGRAVE: In Massachusetts, we've got a similar fund, Mass Capital Resources, that attempts in a small way to do what 3i has done in Britain. I served on the investment committee for a while. It was started at the initiative of Dukakis back in the late '70s, but all the money was put up by Massachusetts insurance companies and pension funds. The insurance companies hired the people to run the fund, so it was run entirely by the private sector. And that fund has been quite successful in terms of the dividends it's paid to its investors and the number of ventures it's financed.

But there was another fund started at state initiative, Mass Technology, which is staffed by people I would describe as "quasi-government appointees." And that fund's not been nearly as successful. It's arguably been successful in the sense that it's funded lots of technologies without losing very much money. But the truth of the matter is that it couldn't pay back its initial capital to the state when the state wanted it back last year to help cut the state's deficit. The fund managers told the state, "Well, if you want the money back, then we will have to shut down." Mass Capital, by contrast, could easily pay back its investment if it chose to do so, and then raise new money in the private sector.

So, my point is that you probably need some government initiative and funding to get large venture projects off the ground. But once you've done that, then you've got to have the fund run by the private sector with no government interference whatsoever.

GRAY: There are a number of state venture capital funds that are run like your successful Mass Capital fund—that is, they combine government money with private management. We don't yet know whether they are performing well. The definitive studies haven't been done. But my feeling is that, if the states have enough patience to leave the funds there, they will eventually be profitable.

The Irrelevance of Venture Capital to Eastern Europe

LOVEMAN: I don't want to bury this discussion, but I would argue that the venture capital industry is almost entirely irrelevant to the current predicament of Eastern Europe. Think about Gordon sitting in his office with 20 business plans on his desk. Now, although many of these plans are probably moonshine, at least they're written in English and Gordon can understand how the numbers were calculated and so on.

In Poland, however, consider that the Prime Minister Bielecki—who is also the country's most famous management consultant—will be the first to admit that, if you asked for the financial statements of a particular company, you would get a document that would be almost incomprehensible. He would also warn you that, if you talked to the top management of such companies, you would likely be dealing with people who have risen to prominence largely on the basis of their capacity to mislead anyone who wants to know anything about what they do. And because the Information Age has not arrived in Poland, the capacity of bureaucrats to mislead is enormous.

For example, when the World Bank did a survey of Polish industry, they looked at the tax registries to determine what people are in what industry. And what they found, quite simply, is that most people lie about what industry they're in. In fact, in a study they've done recently, they found that only about 25% of the addresses listed in the tax registry physically exist anywhere in Poland. So, there are some really basic problems that exist in trying to find anyone that you would want to do business with.

Now, this is not to say that there aren't remarkable opportunities in Poland. We run across entrepreneurs there all the time who are able to exploit these niches in the market that have been created by 40 years of gross mismanagement. There are people who, after the liberalization, imported bananas because you could never get a perishable good to market under the old system.

CHEW: Are these natives or foreigners you're talking about?

LOVEMAN: This guy was a native, and his incredible insight was that you could book bananas on Lufthansa and get them to market before they spoiled. And the guy's made a fortune. There are lots of these kinds of very basic opportunities.

For outsiders, however, the problem is that such opportunities come and go in an instant. Competition sets in very quickly. But when you start looking for business opportunities that are sustainable, then you really run into complications. And, as a consequence, the Poles have had great difficulty in raising capital for new investment.

The first people the Poles looked to for capital were the *Polonia*, people of Polish origin living in the United States. The most famous one was a Mrs. Johnson (née Piasecka), heir to the Johnson & Johnson fortune, who expressed interest in buying the Lenin

■

Here is the situation the Polish government is faced with. There are currently seven or eight thousand state enterprises in Poland not yet privatized. The value of these companies is falling virtually every day, because the workers are literally walking off with the assets. The best workers and managers are going to the private sector, and the state budget is an unmitigated disaster. So, not only do they have to act quickly, but they have to do it en masse. They have got to find a way to transfer ownership of a very large number of companies to the private sector in a single transaction, or through a single legislative act.

—GARY LOVEMAN—

shipyards. She almost promised to buy the company before she bothered to find out what the assets might be worth and whether the workers would be willing to give up their right to strike. That deal fell through.

So, what you need, at a minimum, are people who have remarkable motivation and the resources to slug it out in an environment where things are changing just constantly. Property rights, in many instances, are poorly defined. There is no bankruptcy law in Poland. It's completely unclear what it means to go bankrupt. There's no incentive for banks to push creditors into bankruptcy so that they can recover collateralized assets.

WETZEL: To go back to your original point, Gary, what about the bigger ventures? Are there many of these going on?

LOVEMAN: There have not been a large number of big ventures in Poland. I know of one venture capitalist from a very well-known fund who has made about 20 investments in Czechoslovakia. And he's already devoted about two and a half years to this effort. But let me also point that these investments don't take a great deal of money since relative prices are very low in these environments. And, in the case I just mentioned, the money is coming from the same sources that the fund is using to fund its more traditional investments in the U.S. and in Western Europe.

GRAY: Are these forms of what you might call bootstrap financing?

LOVEMAN: Well, in his case, it's big pension fund money, just some small portion of which is beginning to find its way into these places.

But, again, the Poles have been very frustrated by their inability to raise money from just about anywhere. The Minister of Privatization is just this month beginning a dog-and-pony show all around the United States, trying to appeal to Polish Americans in particular. But such efforts, as I mentioned, are running up against these kinds of information problems, the ambiguity surrounding property rights and legal structures, and the complete ineffectiveness of the banking institutions in Poland. All of these things are fundamental to foreign investment of any size.

GRAY: Yes, but my impression is that there's an American on every street corner saying, "You've got to privatize, you've got to establish property rights, you've got to put a bankruptcy law into place." So, it's clear what needs to be done. My question is, What's holding up the process on the Polish end?

LOVEMAN: Well, it's mainly political. The first fully free parliamentary election in Poland will be held the 27th of this month. Sixty-five parties have registered candidates for that election, and until that process is complete, no one is going to really do anything. The privatization issues have so many constituencies around them that it's difficult to get any movement forward.

But let me make one other point here. As Bielecki would be the first one to admit, the truly scarce resource in Poland is competent managers. I've been contacted by a number of American companies who want to do something in Poland. They will ask me, "Can't you simply find me a Polish manager who can prepare a budget, hire some other people, and do some fairly basic things? We'll do everything else. We'll give them money, we'll buy the land if we can do it." So I've sensed that a good number of these deals are not happening in large part because you can't find well-trained Polish managers.

Vertical Integration Gone Haywire

GRAY: In Moscow McDonald's put in a very large operation. But before they did that, they spent about five years building an infrastructure that would support their market. They went out and actually taught the farmers what they meant by a head of lettuce. They literally took every aspect of their production function and said, "We've got to vertically integrate this all the way up and down. And until we get that infrastructure built, we aren't going to put a hamburger patty out on the stand."

CHEW: What's the expected rate of return on that investment?

GRAY: Well, I don't know. I think McDonald's makes good money in this country doing the same thing.

CHEW: Yes, but they presumably don't have to build infrastructure here.

FROOT: Well, I think the justification for this investment is this: If and when the Soviet Union turns around, then McDonald's will be there first.

But let me also say there's not much evidence that this kind of vertical integration is effective. In fact, there is already a degree of vertical integration in the large state-owned enterprises in Eastern Europe that most of us, I suspect, would find astonishing. For example, Polish LOT Airways tends its own pigs in order to be able to feed their employees pork for lunch. There has been this huge—I would call it "cancerous"—growth in the size and scope of firms that has created just massive inefficiency. And it has also bred a large bureaucracy that will resist any attempt at change.

So, if you want to privatize these huge state enterprises, it will involve far more than just finding investors willing to put up capital. In most cases, it will require a complete restructuring, a complete rethinking of the activities in which these firms participate.

CHEW: You mean you will first have to break these huge companies into their separable parts?

FROOT: That's probably right, in most cases. And, as Gary mentioned, there's a real scarcity of managerial talent and experience. Part of this shortage arises from the fact that the key managers within these firms have not been given product or line responsibilities, as in U.S. firms; instead they have been assigned to deal with specific government agencies. It's as if a U.S. firm told its CEO and top managers to spend most of their time lobbying in Washington. In Polish firms, for example, one high-level position is responsible for dealing with the Finance Ministry, another with the Planning Ministry, and yet another with the Pricing Ministry.

These people are essentially the equivalent of an American CFO, director of corporate planning, or director of marketing. Given that Polish managers have effectively been rewarded according to their ability to manipulate the political system, it's understandable that managerial expertise in marketing, finance, or operations has not developed at all.

On top of that, as I mentioned, there are all these vested interest groups resisting change. In every country, there are powerful people who have a substantial amount of control. And, as Gary said, the problem is political. They stand to benefit from blocking change. You can see this clearly in the Soviet Union and in every Eastern European country.

Starting Over with Small Firms?

CHEW: Well, given these massive inefficiencies and resistance to change in state enterprises, wouldn't it make more sense for outsiders to build their own businesses from the ground up? Perhaps you could build your own organizations just by pulling employees out of existing organizations?

LOVEMAN: This is what's happening. This is the good news in Poland. In the past, the Communists have been very effective at driving small businesses out of existence; so, to the extent the small business sector exists, it has been underground. And because this economy is virtually invisible, everyone's attention in Poland has been focused on the restructuring of the large state sector firms.

But what's happened since 1990 is that the state sector has begun to disintegrate very rapidly, and the private sector has really begun to grow rather dramatically. We are seeing the most enterprising people seeking the highest returns in the private sector.

CHEW: In very small firms?

LOVEMAN: Yes, in firms that might have, say, 50 people or, under the most remarkable circumstances, 500 people. These firms have found products or services the market wants; and they have discovered ways of building alliances with suppliers that allow them to provide these products at prices that people can afford. But, for would-be investors, the problem is that these entrepreneurial firms are hard to find. Such firms may be reluctant to take venture capital money even when it's offered because they risk losing control.

PETTY: But don't these companies represent a very small percentage of the GDP *vis-a-vis* large state-run manufacturing firms?

LOVEMAN: Oh yes, it's tiny.

PETTY: So they're really not contributing that much to a general recovery.

LOVEMAN: That's right. On the other hand, every little bit helps, and it's got to start somewhere.

MARTIN: An article in *The Economist* said that although there are something like 1.2 million small or privatized firms, they accounted for only 2.7 million employees. That's only about two employees per firm.

BYGRAVE: Well, then, do these companies really need more capital? If they had more capital, could they then grow faster, and is that the best hope for the economy? What I'm hearing from you is that it is in this small private sector that the real entrepreneurial talent lies.

FROOT: In Poland, when you walk down the street today, you just see a million street vendors selling all kinds of goods that are hawked from the streets of West Germany. The whole business of retailing has been stimulated and undergone this dramatic transformation. But these are very small-scale operations.

But if you look at the Polish successes on a meaningful economic

---

The key managers within Polish firms have not been given product or line responsibilities; instead they have been assigned to deal with specific government agencies. For example, one high-level position is responsible for dealing with the Finance Ministry, another with the Planning Ministry, and another with the Pricing Ministry. These people are the equivalents of the American CFO and directors of planning and marketing. Since Polish managers have been rewarded according to their ability to manipulate the political system, it's understandable that expertise in marketing, finance, or operations has not developed at all.

—KEN FROOT—

---

scale—the products they have been able to export to the world market—then you would think about light manufacturing of things like golf carts. These products are made by medium-sized or larger firms with substantial capitalization, and these firms today have significant capital needs.

BYGRAVE: Have any of those firms been privatized?

FROOT: No, most of them are still not privatized. Very little progress has been made in privatizing companies.

BYGRAVE: So presumably the opportunities for what we would call MBOs are very great. Are any MBOs going forward, at least in the planning stages?

LOVEMAN: Mainly in smaller firms.

BYGRAVE: If there were capital available, though, would that make a significant difference?

LOVEMAN: No, I don't think so. Again, the problem here is primarily political. If you allow the current management to buy the companies they run, guess who the current management tends to be? Communists. In fact, anyone in a position of power or authority today is widely believed to hold that position arbitrarily; the current endowments, if you will, are all perceived to be unfair. For example, if you work for reasonably successful companies like LOT or the Polish Merchant Marine, you are viewed as having either been lucky, or the recipient of political favor. Those companies will probably survive. But if you happen to work at the steel plant, your probability of success is zero.

So, if you allow people access to state-owned assets on the basis of where they happen to work or manage, that's a political nonstarter.

FROOT: To even think about a solution here, you have to separate the questions of deciding on the ownership rights to existing assets and the kinds of financing mechanisms you're going to put into place to grow those assets that are productive. The changes in ownership of state assets that I believe will eventually be made will involve some amount of widely distributed citizen share ownership, some amount of worker control—albeit not a huge amount—and some amount of foreign participation.

But the most important question here is not how you divide up the existing claims—although that obviously is a very politically sensitive issue—but whether or not you're going to have the kind of political and economic stability that's going to encourage large infusions of capital and thus provide the basis for future growth. If you look at the history of developing countries' ability to attract capital inflows from abroad, the preponderance of that investment has almost never come in the form of private foreign direct investment. During the 1970s, it came primarily in the form of commercial bank loans from developed countries.

So, I would argue that foreign direct investment tends to follow rather than to ignite the growth of developing countries. And this presents a problem for Eastern Europe: Given that the international financial institutions and creditor governments in developed countries are not particularly rich at this time, where is money going to come from to start growth off in the first place? Where is the combustion going to take place to start things moving?

Learning from Maquiladora?

WETZEL: Ken, both you and Gary have spent a good deal of time in these countries and observed these changes firsthand. Is there something akin to the Maquiladora concept that could provide a workable transitional model to get the wheels of industry turning? What I have in mind here is sort of a partnership between a Western European firm that builds a plant on the border to make use of low-cost Eastern European labor. Would that overcome some of the major objections and obstacles we're hearing about here?

LOVEMAN: I think it might work. I've discussed this possibility with people from The Limited. They have places all around the world that make undyed cloth that they can then turn into dresses or shirts or whatever. So, could they do it in Poland? Yes. But is it better to do it in Poland than in Sri Lanka? Maybe not.

So, the issue is not simply can you make it possible for this to happen in Poland, but rather can you attract money into Poland that would otherwise be going to Mexico, Latin America, or any other developing country. One of the great headaches for a guy like Bielecki is that every day there's a new country, every one of which is going to compete with him for the little money and markets that are available.

FROOT: Yes, but the Maquiladora example is one that's predicated on geographical proximity. The idea is that you can integrate a depressed economy into a more vital one and spread the prosperity through trade.

GRAY: But in Poland it's actually the other way right now. It's a "reverse Maquiladora." They're building warehouses not in Poland, but in Germany right on the Polish border. This way they can sneak goods across the border. And there's a large and flourishing industry that does that every day of the week.

FROOT: Well, there's also a political obstacle to this in the Western European countries. Countries like Poland, Czechoslovakia, and the Baltics all actually do produce a lot of agricultural goods. And they do so efficiently enough to wreak havoc with Western Europe's common agricultural policy.

So there's not a lot of enthusiasm in Western Europe for the idea of finding employment for some 30 million workers within a thousand kilometers of Berlin who will work for less than 50 cents an hour. These people are not going to be received with open arms by either East Germans or Western Europeans. That's a real barrier and a problem.

In fact, from the surveys I've seen of firms that actually have gone into Eastern Europe, those firms have identified their principal motive not as gaining access to cheap labor. Instead their response is, "We want to get there first." So it's very much an orientation not of producing there with the intent of selling elsewhere, but instead of getting there to secure rights to local consumer markets.

And those are going to be slow-growing markets. Those countries are not going to get rich rapidly. So these experiments of McDonald's are going to be banner kinds of investments. They're way out-of-the-money strategic options, if you will. McDonald's bet here is that the Republic of Russia is going to turn into the next Korea.

PETERSEN: Other than in agriculture, do you have any sense of what Poland's comparative advantage might be five or ten years down the road?

LOVEMAN: Well, Poland has a huge number of people, some 40 million, and a labor force of about 20 million. It has, by European standards, a massive agricultural sector; and, as Ken suggested, they have a certain comparative advantage in agriculture. They also have this old textile sector in Lodz, which has done reasonably well—and they do export textiles. As I also mentioned, the Polish merchant marine is very effectively internationally, and has been for a long time. There is also a strong skilled craft sector in Poland, and the Poles have been successful in assembling construction crews and exporting them to build things in other countries. They build bridges in Germany, for example. But there aren't a lot of manufactured durable products.

GRAY: There is another political problem, and that is the very large inflow of people into Western Europe from all of the countries in Central Europe. It's a flow of illegal immigrants, and the Western Europeans are suddenly becoming unusually sympathetic to some of the immigration problems we've experienced for decades—because they're now experiencing them in spades.

FROOT: The most popular T-shirt in Berlin this summer had written on the front of it, "I Want My Wall Back."

GRAY: Unfortunately for Eastern Europe, the folks who are leaving are the ones endowed with the energy and risk-taking capability that characterize most emigrants. And these people are exercising their powers, as immigrants do, by crossing the border into Western Europe.

LOVEMAN: At the same time, let me add that Poland is actually receiving a large and continuous stream of immigrants from various parts of the Soviet Union. If you go to the Polish-Russian border, you'll see many Russian cars where people sit and sleep for days and days, because the guards only allow a few in each day. They come in with their trunkfuls of babushka dolls and other things they will sell in Warsaw. And then, once their permit expires, they go back out and fill their trunk again and get back in the queue.

Angels in Eastern Europe

PETTY: What I'm hearing you all say is relatively pessimistic. Is there any good news?

LOVEMAN: It seems to me—and this is a very tentative argument—that you really have to start betting on individuals rather than companies, because companies come and go very quickly. You have to find people who have a demonstrated record of success and you have to be willing to invest only relatively minor sums of money. You don't need massive amounts of money. But you need to be very patient.

Now, to proceed in this way would chew up a lot of Gordon Baty's time. There has to be some reason why he'd be willing to go at it in this way. But I don't see any other way.

WETZEL: Sounds like an angel deal to me.

CHEW: What is the potential role for angels in Eastern Europe? I've been told, for example, that taxi cab drivers have mattresses stuffed full of "hard" currency, and that they are a prime source of capital for new ventures? Or what about other informal lenders like loan sharks—they have low bankruptcy costs, or at least very efficient enforcement mechanisms?

LOVEMAN: Well, some of this is happening. There is a car dealership in Warsaw that sells only the top model Mercedes and BMWs. There aren't many people who can afford to buy them, but there are some; and these people are potentially very important in the process of investment and intermediation in the country.

The problem is, there just aren't enough of them. Remember, in Poland you have a hyperinflation with annual rates of inflation of more than a thousand percent. This means that anyone who held their wealth in domestic currency is penniless today. So it's only people who've saved in hard currencies who were able to accumulate any wealth.

CHEW: But, today these people could conceivably invest in these smaller ventures with an informal set of property rights. They could perhaps devise their own enforcement mechanisms to make sure their claims are upheld.

LOVEMAN: Today, if you were to start a joint stock company, the property rights are clear. For the most part, that's no problem. Where things get very messy is when you get into the existing state sector. That's where all the risk and uncertainty is.

FROOT: Poland has passed a joint venture law and various laws on foreign investment, so that some of the laws are in place. But, as you mentioned, the bankruptcy side is very underdeveloped.

CHEW: So there won't be any debt financing?

FROOT: Who's going to arbitrate the claims you have when you go into some kind of restructuring? The courts don't really understand the difference between liquidation and financial restructuring.

Now, from the legislative point of view, property rights are in a sense defined. But that doesn't mean investors will feel confident that their claims will be upheld. Investors in U.S. companies today have considerable uncertainty about how their claims will be upheld under the U.S. bankruptcy system, but in Eastern Europe the uncertainty is much, much greater.

So things are still very much up for grabs at every level; and that's why the kind of activity you're seeing right now is at the very, very small end. For these small operations, the legal and bankruptcy issues don't really matter.

CHEW: But is it conceivable you could build up a large, privately-owned family business, like a Cargill for example, which today has something like $40 billion in assets?

WETZEL: That may well be the only thing that is conceivable.

GRAY: Yes, but take a look at the Hungarian experience. They've argued that for 20 years they've had entrepreneurial successes. And although that's partly true, such entrepreneurism has not been permitted to grow into anything larger than single-family ownership. In 20 years, Hungary has produced some 5,000 viable, entrepreneurial businesses. But most of them are relatively small storefront operations: delicatessens or restaurants or retail.

FROOT: I think the whole experiment of Eastern Europe rises and falls not on whether these private company empires are possible, but on whether large-scale industry can be made efficient and profitable. Large industry, after all, accounts for a substantial fraction of employment; and, as I said earlier, the average firm size is many times larger in Eastern Europe than in the U.S. If the state-owned sector founders completely, and unemployment across Eastern Europe turns out to be very, very high, then you're going to have real political problems—and, then, who knows what?

Privatization Schemes

CHEW: Gary, can you tell us about the Polish privatization plan, since that seems to be one way of attempting to reform large state enterprises?

LOVEMAN: The privatization plan you're referring to is actually only one aspect of a larger scheme to sell off state assets in a variety of ways. Part of the scheme includes IPOs for some companies; there have been management buyouts or MBOs for companies at the small end; and then there have been proposals for sales of those companies that are attractive and large enough to support the cost of having outside analysts come in and determine the value of the company. In a few cases, however, companies have found that the consulting fees for all this analysis have exceeded the sale price of the firm.

But here is the situation the Polish government is faced with. There are currently seven or eight thousand state enterprises in Poland not yet privatized. The value of these companies is falling virtually every day, because the workers are literally walking off with the assets. The best workers and managers are going to the private sector, and the state budget is an unmitigated disaster. So waiting any longer is not feasible. And not only do they have to act quickly, but they have to do it en masse. They have got to find a way to transfer ownership of a very large number of companies to the private sector in a single transaction, or through a single legislative act.

So what they have proposed is a very complicated scheme in which they will package together about 500 companies that have positive net cash flow and meet certain financial health considerations. To invest in this group of 500 companies they propose to create 20 intermediary funds called National Wealth Funds. Each of these 20 funds will own a 33% stake in 1/20 of the 500 companies, as well as small percentage stakes (about 3.5%) in the remaining 95% of the companies.

CHEW: Is this designed to ensure that each company has at least one large owner who will serve as a monitor for the other minority interests?

LOVEMAN: That's right. And that brings me to the ownership and management of the funds. According to the proposal, every Polish citizen over the age of 18 will receive a share in each of those 20 funds. These shares will not be sellable for two years. And the expectation is that, in the intervening two years, the fund managers are going to be out there busting their tails to restructure these companies that are in their portfolios.

The problem, however, is that during the six months that have elapsed since this plan was proposed, instead of their being 500 companies with positive net cash flows there are now only about 300. That's how fast the economy is deteriorating. The kind of reorganization and restructuring that this will require is enormous. And the Polish people will have to be educated about what a share is, and what it entitles them to—because there are not yet any tradeable shares in the constituent companies. And then there are other difficult issues: How do you evaluate and monitor the performance of a fund manager when there are no market valuations of the firms he or she oversees? And how do you find the people to run the funds? Their idea was that they could hire people like Gordon to come in and run these funds. They would find Westerners because only Westerners know how to do this stuff.

CHEW: Are Westerners lining up for these projects? They're going to have to supply the expertise, and a lot of it's going to be free labor if the plan doesn't work. And how much capital, if any, are these firms willing to put in upfront?

LOVEMAN: Some firms have expressed a willingness to think more about it. The problem is this: Imagine, based on the political reaction in the U.S. to corporate restructuring, what would happen if Gordon walked into Lodz and said that he wanted to close five textile plants? It would not take long for that to become a political issue and Gordon would quickly be sent on his way back to Cambridge.

So I don't think Westerners will be running these funds. A more likely alternative is that the funds will be run by Poles, with Western venture capitalists and management consultants being hired on an advisory basis. And those Poles running the funds will have a significant financial interest in the performance of the firms.

FROOT: These fund managers will have to be a kind of hybrid between a venture capitalist and a portfolio manager; they will have very active roles in some individual companies, but they will probably not end up pumping a lot of money into the Polish economy. Their real job will be to revitalize the economy by moving labor out of hopeless industries, closing down outmoded plants, and finding productive uses for their existing resources.

CHEW: So there's no proposal for new money in this scheme?

LOVEMAN: That's right. But the proposal would give these people the power to raise money from outside sources. To the extent that such money exists, they could certainly go out and raise debt financing. The question of equity financing is tricky, however, because as soon as you raise the issue of outside equity, you disturb the ownership structure that they've worked so hard to try to gain acceptance for among the Poles. But the bigger question is whether anyone will provide new equity for these firms under *any* circumstances.

WETZEL: Aren't there a couple of big Eastern bloc pools that have been put together by Salomon and people like that? What are they doing with that money?

LOVEMAN: I don't know, I'm not familiar with what Salomon's doing there. A lot of the money that people have put together in places like the World Bank and the European Bank for Reconstruction and Redevelopment has gone largely for "technical assistance," which means paying consultants to come in and help out with what ought to be done.

But the odds that even this privatization proposal—and you can imagine what it would be like to try to explain this to your average Polish farm worker—the odds that this will fly politically are fairly small. And if it doesn't, there's really nothing around to replace it. So I'm very pessimistic.

CHEW: But why wouldn't this proposal fly if there were going to be a generous representation of Poles on the boards of all these mutual funds?

LOVEMAN: The problem is, if you've just spent the last 15 years of your life trying to get out from under authoritarian rule, you're very unlikely to let other people come in and take that job again. They're going to insist on some system of checks and balances. There have been several scandals already among financial institutions in Poland. There was what amounted to a kiting scheme in Poland that they had no capacity to detect until it became clear that someone had managed to expropriate a sum that was something like 2% of the GDP. As a consequence of things like this, there's tremendous skepticism about giving people real power, the power

that will be necessary to restore efficiency in these companies.

The Ultimate Free Market Solution

MAGEE: Given that these old party members are still running the show in most of these countries, it seems clear that until they're out of the way that not much is going to happen. These people have a vested interest neither in leading the way for change nor even in just getting out of the way. And if the whole free market experiment collapses, then they're right back in business. Is there any sign that the bureaucrats are being dislodged?

LOVEMAN: They're certainly not out of the way. In Poland they occupy the majority of the seats of the Parliament until the 27th of this month. And they continue to have most of the management positions in the major firms in the state sector. They have a tremendous amount of power.

BATY: It sounds like Poland doesn't have any problems that the U.S. capital industry can do much about. Is there any other country in Eastern Europe with better prospects?

LOVEMAN: Poland is actually better off in the sense that it doesn't have these ethnic rivalries that are tearing some countries apart.

FROOT: I would have guessed that Hungary and Slovenia are probably among the top places where there really is an existing stock of human resources, people who really understand what it means to produce for and sell to a market.

BYGRAVE: I think Slovenia would be a huge success if it wasn't for this damn civil war. They have considerable entrepreneurial experience, in terms of world markets, in terms of raising money, in terms of management. And in fact the civil war's really being fought over that issue: Croatia and Slovenia are much wealthier per capita than the rest of the country.

FROOT: Yes, that's right. Slovenia has ten times the per capita wealth of the rest of Yugoslavia. One reason why at least parts of Yugoslavia function well is that the country has been on a market-based system for some time. And so, assets weren't crazily allocated for long periods of time, the way they were in Poland and the other Eastern European economies. But, in Yugoslavia you do have exactly the same problem as far as the Bolsheviks being in control of the major banks, the major companies, and in appropriating capital as they liked, before these legal questions of ownership are fully resolved.

PETTY: What about the Baltics?

FROOT: The Baltics are just in real disarray. The thing about the Hungarians and the Slovenes is that they understand well their capacity, at least in principle, to export to Western Europe—and they are doing it. But it's hard to imagine a rapid turnaround in the Baltics because so much of the infrastructure has been dedicated for so long to trade with the Soviet Union.

LOVEMAN: There was a recent study by George Akerlof and his colleagues at the Brookings Institute that suggested that, given current prices and the one-to-one parity of the West German and East German currencies, less than 10% of East German firms have any chance at competing in the newly unified Germany. And you've got to remember that East Germany was widely thought to be the best off of all of these countries, as well as having the benefit of close ethnic ties to West Germany.

FROOT: One major problem at this point, though, is that so many policymakers across Eastern Europe are looking at the East German example and are concluding that it's a reason not to plunge ahead with drastic change, but rather to take a gradual approach to change. But, meanwhile, as we've observed, the assets are being stolen and conditions are rapidly deteriorating.

And I think the interpretation that's being put on the East German experience is incorrect. The problems in integrating East Germany are really being driven almost exclusively, in my view, by the insistence on wage parity between East and West German workers. The socio-economic problems associated with bringing back some part of what was formerly the nation, and having garbage workers demand that they get paid the same in the east as they do in the west, simply wouldn't exist in Poland, Czechoslovakia, or any of these other countries. And so the likelihood of large-scale unemployment resulting from a rapid, decisive transition to a free market economy is a lot lower. On the other hand, there's only so low wages can go and they're now pretty close to that level in many of these countries.

WETZEL: Well, when everything is stolen, privatization will be complete.

LOVEMAN: It's true. One proposal that people typically make in jest is that the best thing the Poles might actually do is to just let it happen—just let the state sector be dismantled piecemeal by the workers, and then let free enterprise rise up in the vacuum. This way, you can just start over with what's left and avoid all the political pain of this privatization.

MARTIN: It seems to me that the whole problem may stem from this paradox that the Poles are trying too hard to *manage* their move to an *unmanaged* economy. Maybe the best solution is to quit managing the move. Maybe they should just let it alone, let it burn down, and something better will rise up in its place.

GRAY: Well, these huge bureaucracies that have managed things totally for years are seeing the disappearance of their reason for existence. They'll fight it tooth and nail.

MARTIN: That's why I say this may be the only way; it may be the only way to get rid of the bureaucrats. Let the employees take it home.